PRAISE FOR

# ROMANTIC OUTLAWS

"An innovative dual biography that foregrounds the writing of two women who disregarded the moral codes of their eras and shaped their own destinies. [Charlotte] Gordon's parallel mapping of their lives reveals fascinating similarities in the ways writing sustained, and sometimes saved, them both."

—*Financial Times*

"[An] exhilarating dual biography . . . explored with remarkable insight and perspicacity."

—*Publishers Weekly* (starred review)

"An excellent and poignant book whose heroines breathe in its pages."

—*The Times* (London)

"[A] rewarding read . . . Gordon's style is warm and engaging and she has produced a fascinating and detailed analysis of two extraordinary women and how they lived their lives in a patriarchy as writers and reformers."

—*The Independent* (London)

"Charlotte Gordon's *Romantic Outlaws*, a portrait of Mary Wollstone-craft and her daughter Mary Shelley, explores what it cost women to live with integrity in the 18th and 19th centuries, what it gained them, and how they reckoned with the ledger's final balance."

—*The Washington Post*

"The lives of both Marys, intertwined here, were ringed with trag-edy: illness, the death of young children, heartbreak, depression. But the book, written with the galloping pace of a skilled novel peopled with fascinating characters, is ultimately uplifting; you close it relieved that these women live on in its pages."

—*The Seattle Times*

"[A] thoughtful, intelligent and deeply felt book."

—*The Sunday Times* (London)

"Gordon infuses literary history with electrifying discoveries in this symbiotic portrait of radical mother-daughter writers who indeli-bly changed society and the arts. . . . The first to fully investigate the life-determining influence Wollstonecraft's feminist writings had on Mary Shelley, Gordon chronicles their harsh, tragic, and courageous lives in alternating chapters that are as emotionally incisive as they are finely particularized in their astute renderings of tumultuous settings and dire predicaments. . . . She delivers overdue justice to two . . . thinkers and writers who risked everything to protest in word and deed crimes and discrimination against women."

—*Booklist* (starred review)

"Gordon's prose is compelling and her scholarship meticulous; her contention that both women led 'lives as memorable as the words they left behind' is brilliantly supported."

—*Library Journal*

"Gordon salutes her subjects because they 'asserted their right to de-termine their own destinies, starting a revolution that has yet to end.' "

—*The New York Times Book Review*

"Charlotte Gordon reunites a mother and daughter tragically separated at birth in this rousing and surpassingly readable epic spanning the Romantic era. Wordsworth and Byron must step aside to make room for two brilliant women, Mary Wollstonecraft and her daughter Mary Shelley, early and late Romantics whose remarkable contributions to their time and ours lend Gordon's artfully twined tale special significance."

—MEGAN MARSHALL, Pulitzer Prize–winning author of *Margaret Fuller* and *The Peabody Sisters*

"*Romantic Outlaws* is a gripping account of the heartbreaks and triumphs of two of history's most formidable female intellectuals, Mary Wollstonecraft and Mary Shelley. Gordon has reunited mother and daughter through biography, beautifully weaving their narratives for the first time."

—AMANDA FOREMAN, author of *A World on Fire*

"A fascinating, thoughtful, and continuously absorbing book, one to which I know I shall return on many future occasions."

—MIRANDA SEYMOUR, author of *Mary Shelley*

"Mary Wollstonecraft and her daughter Mary Shelley stand out as daring, unconventional, and courageous women—in their times and ours. Appreciate the 'heroic exertions' of their lives and savor the skill with which Charlotte Gordon tells their intersecting stories."

—SUSAN WARE, general editor, *American National Biography*

"Ingeniously constructed . . . Charlotte Gordon has managed to produce that rare thing, a work of genuinely popular history. Her weaving together of the two lives . . . works beautifully."

—*New Statesman*

"An exceptional achievement."

—*The Daily Telegraph* (London)

## BY CHARLOTTE GORDON

*Mistress Bradstreet: The Untold Life of*
*America's First Poet*

*The Woman Who Named God:*
*Abraham's Dilemma and the Birth of Three Faiths*

*Romantic Outlaws: The Extraordinary Lives of*
*Mary Wollstonecraft & Mary Shelley*

# ROMANTIC OUTLAWS

WOLLSTONECRAFT       SHELLEY

RANDOM HOUSE

NEW YORK

# ROMANTIC OUTLAWS

*The*

EXTRAORDINARY LIVES OF
**MARY WOLLSTONECRAFT
& MARY SHELLEY**

**CHARLOTTE GORDON**

2016 Random House Trade Paperback Edition

Copyright © 2015 by Charlotte Gordon

Published in the United States by Random House,
an imprint and division of
Penguin Random House LLC, New York.

RANDOM HOUSE and the HOUSE colophon are
registered trademarks of Penguin Random House LLC.

Originally published in hardcover in the United States
by Random House, an imprint and division of
Penguin Random House LLC, in 2015.

Published in the United Kingdom by Hutchinson,
a member of The Random House Group, London.

LIBRARY OF CONGRESS CATALOGING-IN-PUBLICATION DATA
Gordon, Charlotte.
Romantic outlaws : the extraordinary lives of
Mary Wollstonecraft & Mary Shelley /
by Charlotte Gordon.
pages    cm
Includes bibliographical references and index.
ISBN 978-0-8129-8047-9
eBook ISBN 978-0-8129-9651-7
1. Wollstonecraft, Mary, 1759–1797.
2. Shelley, Mary Wollstonecraft, 1797–1851. I. Title.
PR5841.W8Z716 2015 828'.609—dc23
[B] 2014014841

Printed in the United States of America on acid-free paper

randomhousebooks.com

2 4 6 8 9 7 5 3

Book design by Barbara M. Bachman

*To my mother,*
*Emily Conover Evarts Gordon*

The memory of my mother
has always been the pride
and delight of my life.

—MARY SHELLEY

# CONTENTS

———

# INTRODUCTION

———

*I*N LONDON, ENGLAND, ON AUGUST 30, 1797, A NEWBORN BABY FOUGHT for her life. Small and weak, she was not expected to survive. Her mother struggled to deliver the afterbirth, but she was so exhausted a doctor was called in to help. He cut away the placenta but had not washed his hands, unwittingly introducing the germs of one of the most dangerous diseases of the era—childbed or puerperal fever. Ten days later, the mother died, and, to the surprise of everyone, the baby lived. For the rest of her life, she would mourn her mother's loss, dedicating herself to the preservation of her mother's legacy and blaming herself for her death.

This is one of the most famous birth stories in literary history. The dead woman's name was Mary Wollstonecraft. Five years earlier, Wollstonecraft had scandalized the public by publishing *A Vindication of the Rights of Woman*—a denunciation of the unfair laws and prejudices that restricted eighteenth-century women's lives. The daughter she left behind would become the legendary Mary Shelley, the nineteen-year-old author of *Frankenstein,* a novel so famous it needs no introduction.

Yet even those who are familiar with Wollstonecraft and Shelley are still sometimes startled to learn they were mother and daughter. For generations, Wollstonecraft's premature death led many scholars to overlook her impact on Shelley; they viewed mother and daughter as unrelated figures representing different philosophical stances and literary movements. Shelley appears in the epilogues of biographies of Wollstonecraft, and Wollstonecraft in the introductory pages of lives of Shelley.

*Romantic Outlaws* is the first full-length exploration of both women's lives. But long overdue though it is, this book is deeply indebted to the work of earlier scholars. Without their efforts, it would have been impossible to explore Wollstonecraft's contributions to Shelley's life and work, or Shelley's obsession with her mother.

This might sound like an odd proposition. How could a mother who died ten days after she gave birth have had such an inordinate impact on her daughter? But strange though it may seem, Wollstonecraft's influence on her daughter was profound. Her radical philosophy shaped Shelley, sparking her determination to be someone and to create a masterpiece in her own right. Throughout her life, Shelley read and reread her mother's books, often learning their words by heart. A large portrait of Wollstonecraft hung on the wall of Mary Shelley's childhood home. The girl studied it, comparing herself to her mother and hoping to find similarities. Mary Shelley's father and his friends held up Wollstonecraft as a paragon of virtue and love, praising her genius, bravery, intelligence, and originality.

Steeped as she was in her mother's ideas, and raised by a father who never got over his loss, Mary Shelley yearned to live according to her mother's principles, to fulfill her mother's aspirations, and to reclaim Wollstonecraft from the shadows of history, becoming, if not Wollstonecraft herself, then her ideal daughter. Over and over again, she reimagined the past and recast the future in a doomed effort to resurrect the dead, gazing back at what she could never regain but sought to duplicate in very different times.

As for Wollstonecraft, though she shared only ten days with her child, she was profoundly influenced by the *idea* of children. She had directed most of her life's work toward the next generation, dreaming of what life might be like for them and how she could help them inherit a more just world. Wollstonecraft's earliest works, written before her famous *Vindication,* were education manuals, books about how to teach children, and *what* to teach children, especially daughters. Condemned by her own era, she turned to those who would come after, drawing inspiration from those who might read her books once she was dead, never once dreaming that one of her most important readers would turn out to be the daughter she left behind.

*Romantic Outlaws* alternates between the lives of Wollstonecraft and Shelley, allowing readers to hear the echo of Wollstonecraft in Shelley's letters, journals, and novels, and demonstrating how often Wollstonecraft addressed herself to the future, to the daughter she planned to raise. There are many comprehensive biographies of both women, written by some of the most distinguished literary scholars of the preceding generations, but *Romantic Outlaws* sheds new light on both Wollstonecraft and Shelley by exploring the intersections between their lives. And the intersections are many.

Both mother and daughter attempted to free themselves from the stranglehold of polite society, and both struggled to balance their need for love and companionship with their need for independence. They braved the criticism of their peers to write works that took on the most volatile issues of the day. Brave, passionate, and visionary, they broke almost every rule there was to break. Both had children out of wedlock. Both fought against the injustices women faced and both wrote books that revolutionized history.

Their achievements are all the more remarkable because they lived during a time when women were considered incapable of directing their own lives. Although it was a revolutionary era—Wollstonecraft was alive during both the American and French Revolutions, and Shelley came of age at the height of Romanticism—most of their contemporaries considered the concept of women's rights to be as absurd as the rights of chimpanzees. In fact, chimpanzees (and other animals) would gain legal protection in 1824, twenty years before the first law was passed that limited, but did not prohibit, violence against women. Experts preached that women were irrational and weak. Girls were taught to submit to their brothers, fathers, and husbands. Wives could not own property. Except in very rare circumstances, they could not initiate divorce. Children were the father's property. Not only was it legal for a husband to beat his wife, but men were encouraged to keep women in check, punishing any behavior they regarded as unruly. If a man failed in these duties, he was considered the subject of petticoat government, his manhood called into question. If a woman tried to escape from a cruel or violent husband, she was considered an outlaw, and her husband had the legal right to imprison her.

Not surprisingly, in such a climate, critics derided the work of both mother and daughter. Their contemporaries ridiculed and abused them, calling them whores and worse. Even their own families rejected them. To their enemies, they were like bolts of lightning, destructive and unpredictable. Given the hostility they faced, their story is one of courage and inspiration. Wollstonecraft and Shelley weathered poverty, hatred, loneliness, and exile, as well as the slights of everyday life—the insults and gossip, the silences and turned backs—in order to write words they were not supposed to write and live lives they were not supposed to live. They sustained themselves by dreaming of the day, long after they were dead, when readers would agree with their ideas: that women are equal to men; that all people deserve the same rights; that human reason and the capacity for love can reform the world; that the great enemies of happiness are ignorance, poverty, cruelty, and tyranny; and that every person is entitled to justice and freedom. Particularly the last. To both mother and daughter, freedom was what mattered most, the key that would unlock the gates of change.

ROMANTIC OUTLAWS

"*The epitaph on my mother's tomb being my
primer and my spelling book. I learned to read.*"
*From* Mrs. Leicester's School, *published
by William Godwin.*

# CHAPTER I

# A DEATH AND A BIRTH

———

[ 1797–1801 ]

ON A SUNNY AFTERNOON IN LATE AUGUST 1801, A FEW MILES NORTH of London, three-year-old Mary Godwin held her father's hand as they walked through the gates of St. Pancras churchyard. They were on their way to visit her mother's grave in a cemetery as familiar to Mary as her own home. She and her father, William, came here almost every day. The churchyard was more like a pasture than a burial ground. The grass grew in uneven clumps; old gravestones lay toppled on the ground, and a low rail separated the grounds from the open countryside.

William Godwin did not think it was odd to teach his small daughter to read from her mother's tombstone. And Mary was eager to learn anything her father had to teach. In her eyes, he was "greater, and wiser, and better . . . than any other being." He was also all she had left.

She began by tracing each letter with her fingers: "Mary Wollstonecraft Godwin." Except for the "Wollstonecraft," this name was the same as hers: MARY GODWIN. One dead. One alive. This gravestone could be her own. She yearned to be reunited with her mother, Mary Wollstonecraft, the woman she had never known, but whom she loved all the same.

Mary Godwin had been born on August 30, 1797, at the end of a month when a comet had burned through the London skies. People all over England had speculated about its meaning. A happy omen, her parents had thought. They could not know that Wollstonecraft would die of childbed fever ten days later, leaving behind a daughter so small and weak it seemed likely she would soon join her mother. But under the care of Wollstonecraft's dear friend Maria Reveley, Mary gradually grew stronger, and by the time she was a month old, though still undersized, she howled at all hours of the day and night. Her sweet-tempered half sister, three-year-old Fanny, Wollstonecraft's illegitimate child by another man, tried to calm her tears, but there was nothing anyone could do. Mary would not be soothed.

Godwin asked his friend William Nicholson, an expert in physiognomy, to measure Mary's cranium and facial features, but the baby shrieked through the entire examination, leading an exasperated Nicholson to report, "The mouth was too much employed to be well observed." However, he told Godwin he saw evidence of "considerable memory and intelligence" as well as a "quick sensibility." The only potential negative, Nicholson said, noting her screams, was that she could be "petulant in resistance."

*The Polygon, Somers Town, in 1850.*

Godwin, Fanny, and Mary lived at No. 29 the Polygon, a semicircular block of tall Georgian homes in Somers Town, about two miles north of St. Paul's.

The Polygon has long since been torn down, and though a plaque on Werrington Street says that the Godwins once lived here, it is an act of the imagination to picture them behind St. Pancras today. Hospitals, new developments, and council estates have replaced the shops, rose gardens, and cow sheds of Mary's childhood. In the early 1800s, her home was deep in the country. A dirt path led through a white turnstile into Clarendon Square, where thirty-two terraced buildings had been constructed as an early experiment in suburban living. No. 29 had a large parlor with a marble mantelpiece where Godwin received guests and where Mary and Fanny learned to be quiet during grown-up conversations. The family ate their suppers upstairs in the dining room and could stand outside on a wrought iron balcony to gaze out over the wild heaths, Hampstead and Highgate. From her bedroom window on the top floor, Mary could see the River Fleet and the narrow lane that led to her mother's grave.

Spacious and elegant, these homes were affordable because they were far from the fashionable West End, but for the Godwins and many like them, Somers Town was the ideal compromise, a modern realtor's truism: the tranquillity of a small town within walking distance of the city, an "outleap" of London, as one contemporary called such developments. When Mary was old enough, she and Fanny toured the square with their nurse, gazing in the plate glass windows of the apothecary, the toymaker, the mercer, the haberdasher, the saddler, and the milliner. Sometimes, they were allowed to pick out a ribbon, or drink a frothy syllabub, a delicious whipped cream confection, at the tea shop. A muffin seller whose nickname was the Mayor of Garratt circled the square, pushing his cart and ringing a handbell. Watchmakers and goldsmiths hunched over worktables, hammering precious metals or examining pocket watches with a magnifying glass. These men were refugees from the French Revolution, and if the girls were lucky, one might look up and salute them with a little bow, or say *bonjour* through the open door, an exotic experience.

Godwin adhered to a routine that to his daughters seemed carved in stone, as unwavering as the steady tick of the clock. A renowned political philosopher and novelist, Godwin did not allow any interruptions when he was writing; ideas came first in the Godwin household. He worked until one, lunched, and then read to the girls.

Together they enjoyed Perrault's *Mother Goose* and La Fontaine's *Fables*. On special days, Godwin chose the book their mother had written for Fanny before she died. Wollstonecraft's warm, chatty style made it seem as though she were actually in the room: "When you were hungry, you began to cry," she said, addressing Fanny directly. "You were seven months without teeth, always sucking. But after you got one, you began to gnaw a crust of bread. It was not long before another came pop. At ten months you had four pretty white teeth, and you used to bite me. Poor mamma!"

Reminders of this loving mother were everywhere, from the portrait that hung in Godwin's study to the books that lined the shelves. Godwin did his best to honor his dead wife, but he was not well suited for the education of small children. He had been a bachelor for most of his life, marrying Mary Wollstonecraft when he was forty-one. Raised by stern Calvinists, he could be excruciatingly reserved and was stingy with both time and money, carefully parceling out his hours to avoid losing any work time.

In the late afternoons, distinguished men and women flocked to pay him tribute. Many of Godwin's visitors were eager to meet Wollstonecraft's children, particularly Mary, who, as the daughter of two such intellectual heavyweights, seemed destined for fame. She had grown used to hearing a hush when she entered the room, an intake of breath, as though she were a great dignitary; they pointed to her fine reddish hair, her large light eyes—how like her mother, they said—how wonderful the first Mary had been, how wise and brave, how loving; a genius and a beautiful woman, too. Surely, her daughter would follow in her footsteps.

Brown-haired and scarred by a bout with chicken pox, Fanny receded into the background during these events. She knew that she came second to Mary. When Godwin married Wollstonecraft, he had adopted Fanny, who was the daughter of Gilbert Imlay, Wollstonecraft's previous lover. Godwin loved Fanny, but he adored his "own"

*Mary Wollstonecraft, pregnant with Mary Godwin,*
*portrait by John Opie, 1797.*

daughter, describing Mary as "quick," "pretty," and "considerably superior" to Fanny, who was "slow" and "prone to indolence." If anyone had pointed this out to him—his obvious favoritism—he would have said he was simply stating the truth; all evidence pointed to little Mary's superiority, an observation that had the added benefit of demonstrating his own superiority over Imlay. To his credit, Godwin had never judged Wollstonecraft for her affair, but he was not above being jealous of the passion she had felt for Imlay.

Godwin's infatuation notwithstanding, young Mary did strike others as an unusual child. Delicate, with pale, almost unearthly skin, coppery curls, enormous eyes, and a tiny mouth, she had entered the world in such a tragic fashion that sorrow trailed behind her like the train of a wedding dress. When visitors talked to her, they were impressed by what seemed to be her preternatural intelligence. George Taylor, one of Godwin's fans, called on the widower twice during the first year of Mary's life. On the first visit, although he enjoyed playing with baby Mary, he did not notice anything out of the ordinary. It was on his second visit that he was startled when it seemed the nine-month-old "knew me instantly and stretched out her arms." How could she have remembered him?

One of Mary's particular devotees was the poet Samuel Taylor Coleridge, who first visited the Polygon in the winter of 1799 when he was twenty-seven years old and Mary was two. An admirer of Godwin, but even more so of Wollstonecraft, the young poet was lonely, estranged from his wife and living apart from his own family. When he came to dinner, he stayed long past the girls' bedtime, keeping the Godwins up late with his stories.

To the girls, he was like a magical creature from *Mother Goose*. With

*Engraving of Samuel Taylor Coleridge by William Say (1840), based on James Northcote's portrait of the poet as a young man in 1804, around the time that Mary first knew him.*

a dimpled chin, a pudgy face, long messy hair, bushy eyebrows, and astonishingly red lips, Coleridge was a spellbinding storyteller. Even the pedantic Godwin was content to sit and listen to him.

Coleridge, though, was startled by the stillness of his audience. Godwin had trained his daughters to be perfectly behaved in company—too well behaved, Coleridge thought. Even Mary, who was far more free-spirited than her sister, could be silent for hours in the presence of guests, hardly even fidgeting. Later, Mary would say that though her father loved her, he was a stern taskmaster and rarely affectionate. In one of her fictional portraits of a father and daughter based on her own relationship with Godwin, she wrote:

> [My father] never caressed me; if ever he stroked my head or drew me on his knee, I felt a mingled alarm and delight difficult to describe. Yet, strange to say, my father loved me almost to idolatry; and I knew this and repaid his affection with enthusiastic fondness, notwithstanding his reserve and my awe.

Godwin's coldness was harming his daughters, Coleridge thought. Fanny and Mary should be more like his own little boy, three-year-old Hartley, who was rarely quiet and never still. He rode the wind like a bird, Coleridge said, "using the air of the breezes as skipping-ropes." Initially, Godwin was impressed by the proud father's description of this young free spirit, but he changed his mind when he actually met Hartley, who, as Coleridge remembered it, "gave the philosopher such a rap on the shins with a ninepin that Gobwin [as Hartley called him] in huge pain lectured [Coleridge's wife] on his boisterousness."

However, Godwin had enough respect for the poet to allow his friend to try to enliven his daughters. Although Coleridge was the author of somber poems such as *Dejection: An Ode* and *The Ancient Mariner*, he liked jokes of all kinds and had a vast repertoire of tricks. He loved ghost stories and knew quantities of nursery rhymes. "I pun, conundrumize, listen and dance," he once said to a friend. He made his fingers gallop like horses or "fly like stags pursued by the staghounds"—a trick he immortalized in a letter to Wordsworth in which he tells his fellow poet how to make his hands do "the hop, trot and gallop" of hexameter lines.

Few could resist Coleridge's charm, and Fanny and Mary were no exception. The poet was a thrilling departure from anyone they had ever met. When he sat in their front parlor, anything might happen: a witch might tumble down the chimney; a specter might float by. When he spilled wine on the carpet, instead of frowning as he did when the girls made such mistakes, Godwin actually laughed. Although some physical ailment always troubled the poet—his head ached, his throat was sore, his eye was infected, his stomach churned— these ailments did not stop him from devoting himself to the Godwin girls.

Tapping into his enormous capacity to be fascinated, Coleridge bestowed on the girls—even Mary, who could barely remember her first visit with the great poet—the feeling that they were delightful and their ideas worth listening to. He called them forward, and although Fanny resisted, Mary loved the sensation of coming out from behind a curtain, of being pushed onstage in a house where her father ruled supreme. For her, and all the Godwins, it was a sad day when Coleridge left to rejoin his family in the Lake Country in 1802. But within a few weeks, Mary and Fanny settled back into the comforts of the nursery and their quiet routine, and it was only Godwin who continued to suffer. Restless and lonely, he wanted to remarry, to find a wife to share his life, his bed, and the burden of raising children. Coleridge had made it clear to him that his daughters needed more than he could provide. They needed a mother's touch.

# CHAPTER 2

# MARY WOLLSTONECRAFT:
## THE EARLY YEARS

———

[ 1759–1774 ]

MARY WOLLSTONECRAFT'S CHILDHOOD COULD NOT HAVE BEEN more different from her daughter's. Far from being the favorite, Wollstonecraft was the invisible second child in a family of seven. While Godwin was controlled and predictable, Wollstonecraft's father was hot-blooded and capricious. An alcoholic who squandered his family's money, Edward Wollstonecraft brutalized his wife and children. Mary's mother, Elizabeth, was so browbeaten that she did little to defend her sons and daughters. The only child she had much use for was her firstborn, Ned. When she gave birth to Mary on April 27, 1759, Elizabeth packed her new daughter off to a wet nurse instead of breast-feeding as she had with her son. This meant missing all of Mary's firsts—tooth, smile, step—but such was the custom of the era, and breast-feeding Ned had been the exception, not the norm. Later in life Mary would criticize this practice, writing, "[A mother's] parental affection . . . scarcely deserves the name, when it does not lead her to suckle her children."

When one-year-old Mary rejoined her family after she was weaned, it soon became clear that, in one of those ironic twists of genetics and family legacy, Mary, who hated her father's brutality, was more like him than like her weak-willed mother. She shared Edward's ferocious temper and his hatred of restrictions. She fought with her big brother when he tried to bully her, resisted her mother's rules, and began a lifelong insurgency against her father, using the very tools he had passed on to her: rage, stubbornness, and a deeply rooted sense of being entitled to a better life.

The first four years of Mary's life were spent in an undistinguished house on Primrose Street, near modern-day Liverpool Street Station. Primrose Street has long since vanished, but during Mary's childhood it twisted through the center of the ancient market town of Spitalfields. Huddled to the east of the city walls on the site of an ancient Roman cemetery, this village was polluted by the stench that emanated from the enormous vats of urine used in the nearby tanning factories, and it was one of the most violent, class-riven neighborhoods in eighteenth-century London. Although some Spitalfields residents, including Mary's grandfather, had amassed substantial fortunes and lived in fine homes on Fournier Street or the newly built Spital Square, the majority of its inhabitants made their living from trade or manufacture: merchants, tanners, salesmen, weavers, wig and mantua makers, porters and street vendors, and those who preyed on them: thieves, beggars, and prostitutes. Crowded, noisy, and filthy, this East End outpost was not the sort of place for a person with genteel aspirations such as Mary's father.

Four years is not long enough to make much of an impression, especially at the outset of life, but it was the Spitalfields way of looking at things, the Spitalfields jaundice, passed down by way of her father, that would sensitize young Mary to the base injustices the poor suffered at the hands of the wealthy. The Wollstonecrafts had more money than most Spitalfields residents, but this did not ease their resentment of the upper classes. Like many people lower down on the social ladder, Edward Wollstonecraft was an expert on the rungs above, where he believed he deserved to be, unlike the lucky devils who were already there, lapping up all the cream. This unfair existence, these laws of class and economics, were the source of an abiding Wollstonecraft grudge against the world, an attitude Mary absorbed before she could even speak.

Edward's father, Edward Senior, had started out as a silk weaver, working his way up to become the owner of a profitable silk business. He resented the aristocrats who bought his gloves, gowns, and cravats even though they had made him rich, and he was not alone. Spital-fields silk weavers were famous for their hatred of the upper classes. Radicals preached on the street corners, stirring up tempers already unsettled by long hours, tedious labor, not enough to eat, and too much gin: The poor were downtrodden. Cheap foreign silk came straight from the devil. Free trade would ruin the world. If someone were foolish enough to walk down Primrose Street wearing French silk, the weavers would slash it to shreds; they rioted and staged so many protests that protesting became a way of life, a badge of iden-tity. In 1765, when Mary was six years old, the weavers, in an attempt to stop the importation of silk from France, forced the House of Lords to adjourn with their threats of violence. They also attacked the Duke of Bedford's house and tried to pull down the walls, accus-ing the duke of accepting bribes to promote trade with the French. The Spitalfields message was clear: Upper classes beware! Aristocrats toe the line! No one was safe from the weavers' wrath, no matter how highly born.

Although Edward Senior and his son were by no means radicals, they shared the grievances of the rioting weavers: How was it fair that the gentry resided in grand houses near Westminster while they, the Wollstonecrafts, lived near the tanneries? Furthermore, why did nobles get to drink brandies, flirt with ladies, gamble fortunes away, enjoy elegant parties, race fine horses, and feast on oysters while Wollstonecrafts worked long hours cutting silk gloves and setting up their looms?

But whereas the weavers wanted to force the government to change trade policies, the Wollstonecraft men simply wanted to get rich. Soured by Spitalfields and endowed with more than his share of grandiosity, Mary's grandfather spent his final years trying to join the ranks of the enemy, styling himself a gentleman and pushing his son to shake off the grime of the silk trade. Indeed, if the Wollstonecraft men held any potentially revolutionary belief it was this: social classes were mutable; you could change your place in society if you made a lot of money, married the right person, or moved to the right neigh-borhood, opportunities unheard of a hundred years earlier but that had come into being thanks to the burgeoning industrial revolution.

Motivated by his belief that he was just as good as anyone else, Mary's grandfather looked for a new home for his son's family that would place them squarely in middle-class circles, and in 1763, he found it, "an old mansion, with a court-yard before it" in Epping, on the edge of Epping Forest, about fifteen miles northeast of London, more than a day's journey from Spitalfields. Here, there would be no more stitching handkerchiefs, no more waiting on customers. Edward Junior could present himself as a gentleman farmer instead of a weaver's son. His grandchildren would be able to mingle with the better sort.

Epping was like paradise after the squalor of London. There were woods, ponds, swamps, and fields to play in, and Mary spent as much time outside as she could, daydreaming and exploring. Out of sight of both parents, Mary, who "despised dolls," climbed the ancient beech trees and stared up at the clouds for hours, finding inspiration and exhilaration in the natural world—a discovery that would stand her in good stead in years to come. Always, she was careful to avoid seven-year-old Ned—the "deputy tyrant of the house," as Mary called him. Almost everything Ned did was objectionable. He tortured insects and small animals, as well as his younger, weaker siblings; not only four-year-old Mary, but also two-year-old Henry, who had joined them while they were in Spitalfields, and even the new baby, Eliza, who arrived shortly after the move to Epping. This was his birthright, their mother felt, and so she never reprimanded him, giving him free rein to punish anyone who crossed him.

After a year in Epping, Edward moved the family into the village to be near a pub, the Sun and Whalebone, where he could more readily indulge his drinking habit. Already a volatile man, Edward became frighteningly unpredictable under the influence of alcohol. Sometimes he was loving—extravagantly so, Mary said—but he had a "quick and impetuous temper." He would hug his wife and kiss his children, then overturn the table or hit the nearest child, perhaps because the cat had knocked something over, or rain had blown in an open window. One awful day, for no apparent reason, he hanged the family dog. The irrational nature of this act made it all the more horrific. For the rest of her life, Mary would hate the sound of a dog crying, as it brought back what she called the "agony" of her child-hood. At night, he terrorized Elizabeth, raping her and beating her so painfully she could not stifle her screams. Her terrible wordless out-cries swept through the thin walls of their house straight into Mary's room, where she lay chafing against her mother's helplessness as well as her own. Finally, when she was a teenager, she rebelled, setting up camp outside her mother's door, waiting for her father to come home so she could stop him from crossing the threshold. But her efforts to save Elizabeth only made matters worse. Edward pushed her out of the way and Elizabeth accused Mary of inflaming her father's rage, but Mary did not stop trying. Night after night, she took up her post.

In 1765, when Mary was six years old, Edward Senior died, leav-ing his son £10,000. This was Edward Junior's opportunity to im-prove the family's fortunes and provide his daughters with a dowry, but instead of investing in a business he knew something about, or at the very least saving for the future, Edward moved his family to an expensive estate near Barking, a market town eight miles east of Lon-don. This new home, far grander than he could afford, suited his in-flated sense of what the world owed him. In Barking, he and Elizabeth whiled away their time dining with other wealthy families and mak-ing occasional visits to the city, where Elizabeth could shop and Ed-ward could join the gentlemen who tip-tapped down Primrose Street with their white-knobbed canes.

For a little girl, the Barking countryside was even more welcom-ing than Epping's. The meadows were dotted with sheep and cattle. The hills were gentle. The Roding River had many moods, quiet and stormy but never menacing. Mary would wander alone for hours, easing her loneliness by peopling the countryside with invisible friends. To the south lay the Marshes, where she would "gaze on the moon, and ramble through the gloomy path, observing the various shapes the clouds assumed, and listen to the sea that was not far dis-tant."

In 1768, when Mary was nine, Edward's money finally gave out. To avoid paying the landlord, he fled north with his family to Walk-ington, a tiny village more than three miles from the closest town, Beverley, in the East Riding. The rents were much lower here than in the south. Few families wanted to live in such a remote area, as the land was unforgiving and the people notoriously insular.

The Wollstonecraft brood now included three-year-old Everina, as well as a new baby, James, to whom Elizabeth paid little attention. As always, Ned remained her favorite, but Mary, desperate for her mother's affection, strove to be helpful. She looked after James, Henry, Eliza, and Everina while her mother rested. However, instead of being grateful, Elizabeth devised severe punishments for Mary, as though she were trying to convince herself and her eldest daughter that she had some measure of power. For minor infractions, she forced Mary to sit by the fireside for three or four hours "without daring to utter a word." In later life, Mary wrote that if she had been disciplined for doing something wrong, she would have accepted it. What she hated was her mother's injustice; Elizabeth's punishments were inconsistent and contradictory. She enforced restraint in the most trivial matters and unconditional submission to orders from all her children, except Ned. Mary did not stop hoping for tenderness, though. Sometimes she would try to tell her mother little secrets, hoping for a soft reply, but her mother only pushed her away.

For the next two and a half years, Edward Wollstonecraft attempted to farm in the North Country, but it was difficult for anyone to eke out a living in this inhospitable part of the world, let alone Edward, who lacked both the will and the expertise. When the crops failed and the sheep sickened, Edward drank to cope with his despair. Trapped in the family's small cottage, it was difficult for the children to escape from their father's moods. Mary said, "the whole house was expected to fly, at the word of command." As the family's fortunes shrank, Edward's behavior worsened. Finally, in the summer of 1770—immediately after Elizabeth had her last child, Charles—Edward gave up the Walkington farm and moved the family to nearby Beverley.

In the 1770s, this market town boasted about five thousand inhabitants, positively metropolitan after the small farming communities Mary had lived in since she was four. Everything seemed strange and sophisticated. It was a shock for her to discover, years later, how much less there was to the town than she had imagined. But at age eleven she felt she had landed in some deliciously foreign place, as exotic as Rome or Paris. There were stores for everything: hats, shoes, linens, saddles, woven goods, wallpaper, gold jewelry, cheese, gloves, glassware, umbrellas. She was used to eating country fare— rough brown bread, eggs, apples, and occasionally beef, lamb, or pork, when Edward slaughtered a pig or bought meat from a neighbor. In Beverley, the shops sold foods that Mary had never tasted— cinnamon, oranges, saffron, cumin, chocolate, and spun sugar cakes. The London newspapers arrived by coach. There was a circulating library and fancy dress balls. Plays were put on in the local theater.

Convinced that he would soon earn back the wealth he had lost, Edward managed to persuade a naïve landlord to rent him a two-story brick house with handsome doors, sash windows, and classical moldings located in one of the most expensive parts of town, Wednesday Market. Perhaps if the landlord had realized that Edward's moneymaking schemes consisted largely of betting on horses at the nearby racetrack, he might have hesitated, but Edward's bluster convinced him, and the Wollstonecrafts were soon installed in elegant lodgings. On market day, Mary could smell oysters frying, taste a cup of cider, admire the bookshops, and compare the prices of ribbons. Farmers, flower girls, pie men, milkmaids, and traders peddled their wares. Cows lowed. Horses got loose. Drovers penned lambs and geese. Merchants hammered up booths. Gypsies swallowed fire, silhouettists sketched profiles, silk awnings fluttered like medieval banners. Over everything, chilling and inspiring, rose the limestone towers of the ancient Beverley Minster, not quite a cathedral. Inside, when the sun shone through the clerestory windows, she could admire the carvings, which had been paid for by the donations of a musicians' guild: miniature men and women playing perfectly carved little instruments, a cat fiddling for some admiring mice, a puffing dragon, and a blacksmith putting horseshoes on a goose, or trying to.

At home, Elizabeth retired to the sick chamber, brooding over her disappointments, cataloging Edward's sins, and complaining about her household burdens. Ned had left home for a law apprenticeship in London. But Henry, Eliza, Everina, James, and baby Charles depended on Mary to darn their socks, butter their toast, hug them, and defend them against Edward. In their eyes, she seemed like a grown-up, even though, at eleven, she was only a few years older.

To Mary, the most exciting part of the move was the opportunity to go to school. They had all learned to read at home, but she was hungry for more education. On the first morning of school, Henry and James trotted off to the Beverley Grammar School to learn history, mathematics, and Latin. But when Mary, Eliza, and Everina arrived at the local girls' school, they found that their curriculum would be limited to needlework and simple addition.

Mary fumed. The list of what they were *not* learning went on forever: Latin, Greek, French, German, history, philosophy, rhetoric, logic, mathematics. Then there were her schoolmates. With indignation she later recalled how the girls played "jokes and hoyden tricks" on her. Local dialect sailed right over her head: if it was raining out, the Yorkshire children would say it was "siling down"; a "buffit" was a small stool; a drunk person was "Cat Hawed." They called their lunches "lowances." To their Beverley classmates, the Wollstonecrafts—gawky, earnest Mary and her odd little sisters—were easy targets. The two younger girls barely spoke, and the older one spoke too much. Clearly, this Mary Wollstonecraft did not care about being a proper young lady. Didn't she know that too much education could hurt your chances to make a good marriage? Her schoolmates' taunts echoed the opinions of the time: "If you happen to have any learning, keep it a profound secret," said one father, instructing his daughters not to frighten away their suitors. The noted intellectual Lady Mary Wortley Montagu advised her talented granddaughter to hide her mathematical prowess "with as much solicitude as she would hide crookedness or lameness."

Fortunately, there was one girl who did not laugh at the Wollstonecrafts and even seemed to respect Mary's eccentricity. Jane Arden was a year older than Mary. She was serious and well read, and Mary set her sights on winning Jane's affection. At Beverley Minster, Mary plumped herself down in the pew next to Jane. She went to the Ardens' house for meals, tagged behind Jane in the afternoons after school, and before long had extracted confessions of friendship from her beloved. One can almost feel sorry for Jane. How could she have realized what this relationship would entail? There were spats, arguments, jealous negotiations, apologies, love declarations, and long tear-streaked missives. Mary did not want to share Jane with other girls. Jane should love her most. If Jane sat next to someone else in church, Mary's heart cracked. "If I did not love you I should not write so," she exclaimed:

> I have formed romantic notions of friendship. . . . I am a little singular in my thoughts of love and friendship; I must have the first placc or none.—I own your behaviour is more according to the opinion of the world, but I would break such narrow bounds.—I will give you reasons for what I say;—since Miss C—— has been here you have behaved in the coolest manner.—I once hoped our friendship was built on a permanent foundation:—.

In letter after letter, Mary laid out her requirements: Jane must single her out. Jane must not favor other girls, even out-of-town guests. "Love and jealousy are twins," Mary declared when the two girls debated the rules of their friendship. She fought with Jane's friend Miss R. and would not say she was sorry. When Jane did not try to soothe her ruffled feelings, she refused to go to the theater with the other girls, choosing to stay home and sulk. She resolved to end things with Jane but could not stand the thought of losing her friend, confessing, "I spent part of the night in tears. . . . I cannot bear a slight from those I love."

Mary also adored Jane's father. A self-appointed ambassador of the Enlightenment, John Arden, a Catholic apostate, spread the gospel of science, earning a substantial living by lecturing on electricity, gravitation, magnetism, and optics. It had become fashionable to have at least a smattering of knowledge about science and philosophy. But in this era, when there were no strict rules about what constituted scientific or philosophical investigations, scientists and showmen were interchangeable. Eager crowds, untroubled by the mix of the alchemical and chemical, the astrological and astronomical, the philosophic and the superstitious, paid high prices to see demonstrations and experiments.

Jane's father was a more rigorous scientist than the charlatans who dominated the lecture circuit, and he took an interest in his daughter's earnest friend, including her in the lessons he gave his children, teaching her to peer into microscopes and point a telescope up into the sky. Mary did not discover any planets, but she did find her own capacious curiosity. Astronomy was teaching her to view the quest for knowledge differently. If three hundred years earlier everyone thought the sun revolved around the earth, what other misconceptions might there be? What might be discovered today?

Already, Mary's restlessness was taking a different form from that of her father and grandfather. Like them, she was ambitious and discontented, but she understood something they did not: that education was the key to her future. Schooling would be her way out of the degradation and violence that characterized her family. And so, when the Ardens suggested she read thick, difficult volumes such as Dryden's restoration era stage play *The Conquest of Granada* and Goldsmith's satirical account of English manners *Letters from a Citizen of the World* (1760–61), she leapt at the opportunity. With each book she read, she could create more distance between herself and her parents.

For all of the trials Mary put her through, Jane remained loyal to her prickly friend. On clear afternoons, the girls strolled on the Westwood, common land on which cows grazed at the edge of the town. They went to dances and concerts at the assembly rooms and whispered about the flirtations they saw. "The oddest mortal that ever existed has become one of Miss C——'s suitors," Jane wrote Mary, who delighted in this kind of gossipy information and wrote Jane back to say, "Her over-giddiness, and his over-graveness must be superlatively ridiculous;—in short you must allow me to laugh." Mary was making up for lost time. After years of living in the country, with only her family for company, she threw herself enthusiastically into the social whirl. With Jane at her side, she attended many parties, delighting in the novelty of meeting so many new people. She was also discovering her own social abilities. People were drawn to her warmth, and she was adept at the quick banter and witty exchanges that were the currency of such gatherings.

In 1774, Mary's father announced he had found a fresh business opportunity in Hoxton, a depressing village north of London, notorious for its three lunatic asylums. Fifteen-year-old Mary would have to leave Jane behind—a rude shock, as after so many moves she had been lulled into thinking that Beverley would be her home forever. However, her father had lost so much money at the track he could no longer even pretend to afford Wednesday Market. To Mary's shame, the neighbors had predicted her family's ruin. She complained to Jane that they "did not scruple to prognosticate the ruin of the whole family, and the way he [her father] went on, justified them."

The Wollstonecrafts moved in the winter, when Hoxton was at its least appealing. London's lunatics were housed in the crumbling remains of the village's Tudor estates, and there were also several workhouses for the poor. On bleak afternoons, Mary walked the rutted streets, appalled at what she saw. Beggars were bad enough, but to watch the insane, she said, was to contemplate "the most terrific of ruins—that of a human soul." Decay, insanity, imprisonment: Mary would set her last book, *Maria,* in an asylum. "Melancholy and imbecility marked the features of the poor wretches who strayed along the walks," she said later, remembering her years there.

Not all of Mary's neighbors were lunatics, however. Dissenters from the Church of England, barred from attending other universities, flocked here, founding their own college, Hoxton Academy, now part of New College London. Hoxton students were taught the radical principle that human beings were naturally good and had the right to be free. This was the opposite teaching from that of the Church of England, which held that human beings were sinners and needed strict rules and authoritarian governments to contain their evil impulses. One Hoxton student drank in these ideas so eagerly that when he left the Academy, he would devote the rest of his life to the fight for freedom. His name was William Godwin, and twenty years later, he would marry Mary Wollstonecraft.

But while her future husband was immersed in the ideas that would shape his life's work, Mary was consumed by domestic duties.

Indeed, few circumstances better illustrate the divide between middle-class men and women in the eighteenth century than the Hoxton days of William Godwin and Mary Wollstonecraft. They lived only a few hundred yards apart, but their lives could not have been more different: she, tending to her siblings and preoccupied with the running of the household; he, bent over his books, studying political philosophy and conjugating Latin verbs. Both wanted to march into the ring, fists raised against injustice, but while Godwin would have many opportunities as a well-educated young man, Mary was supposed to serve her family. Women could not participate in the era's debates even as minor contributors, let alone as serious combatants.

Even the reform-minded men at Hoxton Academy agreed with the principle that women belonged in the home. They promoted revolution, corresponded with angry colonials in America and radicals in France, fought against slavery and religious intolerance, debunked tyranny, argued against despotism, and prayed for the dispersal of irrational beliefs, but not once did they advocate for women's independence or promote the idea that women should be allowed to argue for their beliefs in public. For all that they had been trained to protest injustice, they failed to notice the chains that bound their mothers, daughters, and wives.

While Hoxton was Godwin's launching pad, it could never be Mary's. Even as his horizons were expanding, hers were shrinking. Once again, her only companions were her sisters and brothers, although the boys would leave soon enough. The world was theirs to conquer.

# CHAPTER 3

# MARY GODWIN: CHILDHOOD
# AND A NEW FAMILY

———

## [ 1801–1812 ]

F MARY GODWIN'S FIRST TRAGEDY WAS THE DEATH OF HER MOTHER, the second was the marriage of her father to a plump thirty-five-year-old named Mary-Jane Clairmont who had moved next door in 1801. The mother of two small children, Mary-Jane was eager to find a husband. To preserve her respectability, she claimed to be a widow, but in reality she had never been married, and her children each had a different father. She had run away from England as a teenager to live with her French cousins and had spent most of her adult life abroad. Now that she was home again, she wanted the security of marriage and was elated to find an eligible widower conveniently nearby. Undeterred by trivialities such as Godwin's unappealing appearance—he was short, with a long sloping nose—she planned her approach carefully, reading as much of his great work, *Political Justice,* as she could stand and learning his habits. This last step was not hard. Godwin, averse to spontaneity in all its various forms, adhered to routine with the devotion of a medieval monk.

Their first meeting occurred on a May evening, shortly after she moved in. As was his custom, Godwin emerged onto the second-floor balcony to enjoy the spring air. Mary-Jane bustled into her garden and called up to her neighbor: "Is it possible that I behold the immortal Godwin?" Godwin, who was famously susceptible to flattery, smiled gracefully and acknowledged that yes, he was indeed

*Engraving of William Godwin, based on the painting by James*
*Northcote (1802). Godwin sat for this portrait in July 1801, two*
*months after he met Mary-Jane and right before Mary turned four.*
*He felt it captured his essence better than any other portrait and*
*had it hung in his home, where it remained until his death.*

William Godwin. Mary-Jane clasped her hands and breathed, "You great Being, how I adore you!"

For Godwin, this was a pleasant change from the hostility he had faced ever since he had fallen into disrepute for his radical political views in 1798. Once renowned as the intellectual leader of the reform movement with the publication of *Political Justice* in 1791, Godwin argued that all government should be abolished, since by its very nature, government infringed on mankind's natural rights. This bold attack on civil authority inspired reformers to push for dramatic political change. Liberals praised Godwin's daring philosophy. However, by the end of the decade, the political winds had shifted. To most English people, the chaos and bloodshed of the French Revolution made security, safety, and order seem far more important than liberty. Godwin, along with other radicals, now seemed like troublemakers, and, even worse, "French"—one of the worst insults one could levy at a politician or intellectual. In 1798, Godwin had made matters worse by publishing a memoir of Wollstonecraft after her death, exposing her sexual escapades to the public. Roundly condemned, Godwin lost many of his fans. Now only old radicals and young Romantics like Coleridge came to visit him.

To his credit, Godwin refused to renounce his views, holding to them in defiance of the times. But he was lonely. Three long years had passed since Mary Wollstonecraft's death, and his search for a new wife was not going well. A stickler for the truth, he insisted on announcing not only to his friends but to the women he was courting that no one could match Mary Wollstonecraft's perfections. As a result, he had faced many rejections, and Mary-Jane's warmth and persistence were a welcome new development. When he retired inside that first evening, he noted their meeting in his diary, writing "Meet Mrs. Clairmont," an expansive phrase for a man who summed up enormous life events with lines drawn horizontally across the page (Mary Wollstonecraft's death), a four-letter abbreviation ("Panc") for their marriage at old St. Pancras church, and a series of dots and dashes, as well as French phrases, to denote sexual intimacy.

During the next few weeks, whenever Godwin stepped outside, Mary-Jane would appear, ready for a walk or a chat on the doorstep. She introduced her own children, Charles, age five, and Jane, age three, to Mary and Fanny. Before long, the families were seeing each other almost every evening. By the beginning of July, they went on outings together: *Puss in Boots* at Astley's Theater in Lambeth and picnics in the countryside. In the second week of July, she and Godwin consummated their relationship, an occasion commemorated by Godwin with an X in his diary. It was his first sexual encounter since Wollstonecraft had died.

Despite the growing intensity of this new relationship, Godwin kept Mary-Jane a secret. He knew that any potential replacement for

Wollstonecraft would face hostility from his friends. And Mary-Jane was no paragon. Although she was clever and well read and had a wry sense of humor, she had an ugly temper and made scenes in public whenever she felt slighted, which was often. "Manage and econo- mize your temper," Godwin admonished her. Do not let yourself be "soured and spoiled." But Mary-Jane felt that people deserved what she dished out and never attempted to restrain herself.

In September, she discovered she was pregnant. Godwin had been through this once before with Wollstonecraft, whose pregnancy with Mary had occurred unexpectedly, forcing them into marriage, an in- stitution they had both opposed. In *Political Justice,* Godwin had ar- gued that a husband's legalized "possession of a woman" in marriage is "odious selfishness." The radical Wollstonecraft agreed, but she had discovered how cruel the world could be to an unwed mother when she had Fanny. She did not want her second child to suffer the igno- miny she feared lay in Fanny's future. And so, even though it was against their principles, they decided to conform to convention.

After Wollstonecraft died, Godwin, the sole protector of two daughters, became more conservative. He revised *Political Justice* to restate his views, backing off his earlier claim that marriage should be abolished and conceding that it was a necessary evil in a flawed soci- ety such as nineteenth-century England. If one of his girls became pregnant outside wedlock, he would want the father of her child to marry her to save her from social exile. It followed, then, that the right thing to do was to give Mary-Jane and the new child the protec- tion of his name. Besides, he liked the idea of gaining a companion, and, as Coleridge had pointed out, his girls needed more than he could provide; they needed a mother. The early signs of trouble— Mary-Jane's temper, jealousy, pushiness, and overall abrasiveness— did not deter him. "Do not . . . get rid of all your faults," he told her. "I love some of them. I love what is human, what gives softness, and an agreeable air of frailty and pliability to the whole."

Godwin was the first man Mary-Jane had encountered who em- braced his responsibilities as a father. Letting her guard down, she confessed her romantic history, including the fact that she had never been married. Her first love, a French soldier, had died tragically, she said, leaving her with an infant, Charles. Her second suitor, a scoundrel, left her with a second baby, Jane, and a pile of bills, which she could not pay. Far braver and more resourceful than her stepdaughter Mary would ever acknowledge, she survived many misfortunes, including a three-month stint in debtors' prison with two babies. When she got out, she used her fluency in French to get work as a translator; her translation of *The Swiss Family Robinson* (1814) would be the standard English version for more than a century.

After these hardships, Mary-Jane wanted stability. Unlike Godwin and Wollstonecraft, she was a pragmatist, not a dreamer, and it was money—making it, spending it, saving it, and appearing to have it—that was her primary concern. Godwin did not like Mary-Jane's materialistic leanings, but for him, it was a relief to be with a woman who did not challenge his ideas the way Wollstonecraft sometimes had.

Late that December the couple slipped off to church without telling the children. To save Mary-Jane from being exposed, they had come up with a daring plan, staging an illegal ceremony for their friends in which Mary-Jane maintained her false identity as the widow Clairmont. When it was over, they took a coach to a different church. Here, they had the legal ceremony performed: the marriage of William Godwin to the spinster Mary-Jane Vial on December 21, 1801.

They spent their wedding night in a country inn and returned home the next day. Godwin told Fanny and Mary that he had given them a new mother, a "second mamma." But neither Mary nor Fanny wanted a second mamma, particularly not Mary-Jane, whom they regarded as an interloper. For four-year-old Mary, who had, as she later said, an "excessive and romantic" attachment to her father, Mary-Jane's arrival spelled disaster. Her once undemonstrative father now embraced Mary-Jane with enthusiasm, kissing her in the hallway and indulging in a kind of lovers' patter that embarrassed onlookers. Did he no longer care about his favorite daughter? And what about her own mother? Had Godwin forgotten her entirely?

Within two weeks, the Clairmonts had moved into No. 29, shattering the quiet order of the Godwin household. Mary-Jane slammed doors, tore up letters, shouted at the servants, slapped her children, then begged forgiveness. She thought Godwin had spoiled Mary, and to compensate she treated the little girl with unmerited severity. Fanny she largely ignored.

Mary-Jane's own daughter, three-year-old Jane, was far from being a model of good behavior. Prone to tantrums, she pouted and wept stormily when reprimanded, a new spectacle in the Godwin household, since Fanny and Mary were rarely disobedient. Charles played outdoors and tried to avoid the dramatic scenes that took place inside. Poor Jane did not know what to make of her new stepsisters; they were not the kind of playmates she was used to. In fact, they were not like other girls at all. They did not giggle, play dress-up, or sing, nor did they shriek if their wills were crossed. Fanny seemed dull. The brilliant Mary could already read and write. Jane wished she could be more like her; maybe then her new stepfather would notice her. She was jealous of the attention he paid to his own daughter. Although he tried to be kind, he rarely spoke to the Clairmont children. Charles did not seem to mind; outnumbered by the girls, he ran up and down the stairs and galloped outside in the fields near the Polygon. But Jane was her mother's daughter. She fought for Godwin's love, striving to triumph over Mary.

Over time, Godwin made matters worse by reading books to Mary but not Jane, discussing philosophy and politics with his own daughter while ignoring his stepdaughter, driving a wedge between the girls that grew deeper as the years passed. For the rest of her life, Jane would struggle with feeling second best to her stepsister. Mary, for her part, quickly came to regard her stepsister as a competitor, someone who wanted to see her fail so she could steal her place in Godwin's affections. There was loyalty and affection between the two girls as well, but thanks to the Godwins' notable faults as parents, a famously complicated relationship had begun.

The differences between the two families soon calcified into fixed points of hatred. The Clairmonts resented Godwinian condescension; the Godwins despised Clairmont histrionics. When she was older, Mary would use "Clairmont" as an adjective that meant selfish, self-dramatizing, and coarse. Mary-Jane, in turn, would accuse Mary of being a liar, and she made matters worse by going out of her way to enforce her authority. She felt it was up to her to break Mary's will. She banned any mention of her predecessor, insisted on being called "Mamma," and was furious when Mary resisted. She fired Fanny and Mary's beloved nurse, Marguerite, as well as Godwin's maids and the cook—all the women who had cared for the Godwin girls since their mother died. In their place, she hired strangers, including a governess and a tutor. Overnight, the Godwin girls were evicted from the comfort of their nursery and plunged into the rigors of the schoolroom. Godwin did not intervene, having decided to relegate all child-rearing matters to his new wife.

It was not that Mary-Jane was always cruel. She applied her formidable organizational skills to feeding and clothing four children on very little money and made sure their sheets were clean and their mattresses aired and hard (for the rest of her life, Mary could not bear sleeping on soft beds). She took them for romps on Hampstead Heath, and to plays, exhibitions, and spectacles; she nursed them when they were sick, taught the girls to sew and embroider, tucked them into bed, and worried about their manners. But she could never bring herself to truly love the Godwin girls. Even if her eviction of the old staff had been her only unkind act, which it was not, it exemplified her lack of empathy for her stepdaughters. Fanny, especially, mourned the drastic break from her old nurse, her last tie to her mother.

In June, Mary-Jane gave birth to a little boy who died a few minutes after delivery. Angry and grieving, Mary-Jane was more short-tempered than ever. Eighteen months later, she had a baby who lived, William Junior, delighting Godwin, who had always wanted a son, but shocking Mary into outright rebellion. Now that she had to share her father with baby William, she outraged Godwin by fighting Mary-Jane like a partisan; anything was fair game—chores, what dress to wear, how to brush her hair. Despite her envy of her stepsister, Jane usually sided with Mary, further enraging Mary-Jane. Fanny, on the other hand, kept her head down. She did not like Mary-Jane, but she was far too insecure to rebel.

When Mary was eight years old, Coleridge paid a visit to London. Mary and Fanny had not seen the poet since Mary-Jane had married their father, but Godwin had kept his memory alive by reading aloud his letters and poetry. Mary-Jane did her best to stop Coleridge from seeing them. She was suspicious of Godwin's old friends, fully aware that they made insidious comparisons between her and Wollstonecraft. But in Coleridge's case, she could not prevail. Godwin loved the younger man too much to turn him away.

On the evening of Coleridge's visit, in a petulant show of power, Mary-Jane sent all four children to bed instead of allowing them to stay up to listen to the poet's stories. Nothing could have been better calculated to alienate her younger stepdaughter, who stole back downstairs, followed by the admiring Jane. The girls crept into Godwin's study and hid behind the couch, just as Coleridge began to recite *The Rime of the Ancient Mariner.* For Mary, Coleridge's rounded, rolling voice created wild imaginary scenes she would never forget. For the rest of her days, she would be able to recall each word, reciting it to the poets she would later come to know, ensuring Coleridge's influence on the next generation of Romantic writers.

The story was at once terrifying and familiar to Mary: the mariner had killed an albatross and caused the death of his shipmates, just as she had caused her mother's death by being born. How much of this Mary understood at the time is another matter, but when Coleridge intoned the famous stanza

> *Ah! Well a-day! What evil looks*
> *Had I from old and young!*
> *Instead of the cross, the Albatross*
> *About my neck was hung,*

Mary could sympathize with the mariner; she, too, suffered under the weight of a heavy guilt. She could not yet articulate why, but this burden would one day spur her to create her own work of art, one in which she would explore and lay bare the oppressive feelings of self-blame that had plagued her all her life.

At the same time, she was absorbing another, even more disturbing story: the poet's helpless struggle with his own invention. Coleridge's Mariner cannot rid himself of his tale—he must retell it endlessly as punishment for his "crime." As an adult, Mary would understand that *The Rime of the Ancient Mariner* is essentially a report from the deep, an exploration of the dark grottoes of Coleridge's mind. But as a little girl, she experienced this viscerally, felt firsthand how creations can control their creators.

To both Godwin and Coleridge, the poet's recitation was more important than Mary-Jane's rules, and if they did see the two small girls, as seems likely, they would not have sent them away. However, Mary-Jane had no such reverence for poetry. When she discovered their empty beds, she flounced into Godwin's study, pulled the culprits out from behind the couch, and marched them back up to the nursery. She had won this skirmish, but at a cost. Her stepdaughter would not forget this humiliation. A wiser parent might have tried to assuage Mary's rage, but Mary-Jane was not wise; she lacked the steadiness and agreeable calm that would have helped her make peace with her furious small opponent.

Godwin did nothing to ease the conflict between Mary and Mary-Jane. Consumed by financial worries, he did not bother himself with domestic disputes. His income, always unsteady, was stretched beyond its limits by his new family. Before long, Mary-Jane was reduced to buying groceries on credit, negotiating with angry merchants, and lying to the landlord about the rent. Haunted by memories of debtors' prison, she urged her new husband to change his ways and earn some income. He needed to stop dabbling in philosophy and write books that sold. Or, if he insisted on pursuing unpopular subjects, he needed to write faster so he could bring in more cash.

But Godwin could not, or would not—she was not sure which— write different books or write more quickly; he hated intellectual sloppiness and imprecision, and so his advances ran out long before he finished. Even more frightening, Godwin had begun to experience blackouts, losing consciousness for extended periods of time. These fits of what he termed "deliquium" worried his already anxious wife and further delayed his writing projects. His doctor accounted for these episodes with a diagnosis of mental stress. But the stress showed no sign of letting up. His book sales continued to drop.

After three years of enduring the threats of local merchants and the landlord, Mary-Jane, a canny businesswoman, took matters into her own hands, declaring that it was time to open their own book-shop. Aware of the growing market for children's literature, she de-cided that juvenile literature should be their specialty, making their store one of the first of its kind. This was an excellent plan, as it would remove them from competing against other more established booksellers. Also, they could supply their own material: Godwin had some tales he had written for his daughters, including a version of *Aesop's Fables* in which he emphasized the evils of tyranny and the importance of freedom.

But Godwin was reluctant to enter the commercial world, and it was not until their financial situation took an even more dramatic turn for the worse that he relented. In the summer of 1807, just before Mary turned ten, the family moved into London, skulking out of the Polygon to escape paying the back rent.

41 SKINNER STREET, THE GODWINS' new home, was five ramshackle stories tall. It was unpainted and ugly. Newgate Prison was a block away, and on execution days, the bells of the neighborhood church, St. Sepulcher, rang the condemned to death and crowds rushed by on their way to watch the hangings. From the schoolroom windows on the top floor of their house where they had lessons each day, Mary, Fanny, and Jane could witness the prisoners making their final jour-ney from Newgate to the gallows at Tyburn.

They could also see the River Fleet, dark and poisonous looking. How could this be the same river that meandered past St. Pancras churchyard? Here it was like a black snake, coiled at the base of Hol-born Hill. Closer to home, the carcasses of cattle, sheep, and pigs hung on racks outside the butcher shops of the Newgate Market, making it difficult to walk without stepping in puddles of blood. On hot summer days, the cries of the animals from the nearby Smithfield slaughterhouses drifted through the open windows.

The noise, poverty, and stench of Skinner Street were overpower-ing. Merchants vied for customers, loudly peddling their wares. Once Mary-Jane opened the shop on the ground floor, the girls' free time

*View of Newgate Market in Paternoster Square,
London, c. 1850, showing "carcasses hanging on
hooks and a crush of figures."*

evaporated. They packed, unpacked, and shelved the volumes. When they were older, they helped Mary-Jane wait on customers. Charles, away at boarding school, escaped these obligations, and William was considered too young to help.

Mary chafed at these restrictions, adding them to her long list of complaints against Mary-Jane. To her, Skinner Street represented the evils of life with "second mamma," whereas the tranquillity of the meadows near the Polygon symbolized Mary Wollstonecraft's virtues. In Somers Town, the girls had been allowed to roam at will, but here it was unsafe to go outside alone. The old St. Pancras churchyard took on a special nostalgic glow. After all, not only was it the place where her mother was buried, this was also where Mary had spent hours alone with her father.

There were some bright spots. The Godwins had moved into the heart of the publishing world. Authors stopped in to visit. Books were everywhere, stacked on chairs and on the floor. Godwin steered Mary in the direction of the social theorists he and her mother had admired, Rousseau and Locke. Family dinners were often spent discussing these authors. Godwin subscribed to Rousseau's idea that society corrupted human nature, and so from her earliest years Mary absorbed the Romantic idea that the chains of convention should be broken. Her father demanded that she try to answer the questions of all reformers: What were the best ways to change the world? What role should the government play in the lives of the people? Should there even be a government? While Fanny and Jane looked on in awed silence, Mary delivered her opinions, skillfully citing examples from the books her father had given her to read.

Skinner Street's central location also made Godwin more accessible to his admirers. Even though he was still considered a notorious radical by many conservatives, political reformers continued to seek Godwin out. Among the most notable was America's third vice president, Aaron Burr. In 1808, Burr had been driven out of the United States by his enemies, only three years after serving as second in command to Thomas Jefferson. During his last year as vice president, Burr had fought a duel and fatally wounded his political rival Alexander Hamilton. Now the fifty-two-year-old was at the low point of his career, and Godwin was one of the few brave enough to befriend him.

A lifelong devotee of Mary Wollstonecraft, Burr believed in the equality of men and women and had encouraged his beloved daughter, Theodosia, to learn Latin, logic, and higher mathematics. But in 1811, tragedy struck: twenty-nine-year-old Theodosia was drowned in a shipwreck off the South Carolina coast. The heartbroken Burr comforted himself by taking a particular interest in the three Godwin girls, nicknaming them "les goddesses." The girls in turn loved Burr. He did not stand on ceremony with them, allowing the girls to call him "Gamp." Sometimes he could be induced to visit them upstairs in the nursery. On one such occasion, they persuaded him to listen to eight-year-old William deliver a speech that Mary had written, entitled "The Influence of Government on the Character of the People." Fanny served tea while Burr admired a singing performance by Jane, who was, as usual, determined not to be outdone by Mary.

Burr praised the tea and the song, but he reserved his greatest praise for the speech and the speechwriter. Even at thirteen, Mary knew that she was the one who had taken the laurels. She had won Burr's attention with her pen. Her father had taught her that writing was her legacy, that she was the daughter of Wollstonecraft and Godwin, the child of philosophers. When she felt alone and wished she had a mother who loved her, she tried to comfort herself by thinking that fate had raised her above ordinary people. She had a pedigree that the Clairmonts could never take away. But these consolations did little to dispel her loneliness. Her father was no longer hers—he had been taken over by Mary-Jane. Fanny was too timid to be any solace. And Jane, a far better companion than Fanny, was a dangerous competitor, only too ready to take Mary's place if she fell.

# CHAPTER 4

# MARY WOLLSTONECRAFT:
# HOXTON AND BATH

———

## [ 1774–1782 ]

ITH EACH PASSING WEEK IN HER FAMILY'S NEW HOME IN HOX-ton, the fifteen-year-old Mary Wollstonecraft grew increasingly gloomy. Home with her mother while her younger siblings were in school, she tried to shore herself up, writing to her friend Jane Arden, "My philosophy, as well as my religion will ever teach me to look on misfortunes as blessings." Despite her best efforts, her darkness deepened. Her father's drunken rages were becoming more frequent and her mother grew steadily weaker both physically and emotionally. Frustrated and angry, Mary lost her temper and then tortured herself for it, worrying that she was becoming like her father. She turned to prayer and "began to consider the Great First Cause, formed just notions of his attributes, and in particular dwelt on his wisdom and goodness."

Her mother, meanwhile, spent hours draped on the daybed, complaining about her ailments, reading romances, and napping. Although Mary felt contempt for Elizabeth's helplessness, she could not help continuing to yearn for her attention. Not much had changed since Mary was younger. Although Ned had left home, he was still his mother's favorite, still the only child she ever thought about. Mary tried to confide in her mother, as she had when she was younger, but Elizabeth laughed at her. Without the Ardens and without the opportunity to read and study, Mary could not shake her melancholy. Unless she got married, an idea she was strongly opposed to after witnessing her father's abuse, she would have to live with her mother for the rest of her life. In a classic case of eighteenth-century injustice, Ned, now eighteen, worked at a London law firm, and Henry, age thirteen, was serving as an apprentice to a surgeon back in Beverley. They were both independent from their family and earning their own way, while she, who yearned to be in the world, was forced to remain within the confines of their home.

By the turn of the year, Mary was on the brink of a breakdown: she had stopped eating and washing her hair, and she suffered headaches, fevers, and nervous fits. She stayed up most of the night brooding, and during the day she was exhausted. Fortunately, Mrs. Clare, one of the Wollstonecrafts' neighbors, had taken note of the morose teenager and invited her for tea. This initial visit went so well that others ensued, and before long Mrs. Clare and her husband, the Reverend Henry Clare, asked Mary to stay with them for weeks at a time. Mary's mother, who would have preferred her daughter to be at home running the household, did not have the backbone to say no. Nor did she have the capacity to envision where these visits might lead. If she had, she might have put up a stronger fight, or brought Mary's father, Edward, into the fray.

Henry Clare was a strange man. Even in Hoxton, a village of lunatics, he stood out as odd. He had worn the same pair of shoes for fourteen years, because he almost never went outdoors. Alarmingly thin, stooped, and the color of paper, he had long ago devoted himself exclusively to the study of poetry and philosophy and was incapable of small talk. His cheerful, hardworking wife kept up relationships with their friends and neighbors and conducted the household business, allowing him to stay up at night writing, wrestling with sentences few people would ever read. Purposeless though the clergyman's activities may have seemed to someone like Elizabeth, it was his apostolic intensity, his high-minded dismissal of pedestrian concerns, that drew the fifteen-year-old Mary Wollstonecraft. In fact, Reverend Clare was precisely what she needed.

To the Clares, it was immediately clear that Mary was not like other girls her age, concerned with fashion and marriage. Frustrated at how the move to Hoxton had interrupted her education, she asked Mr. Clare for advice about what books to read and what philosophers to study. Clare allowed her into his study, which was an honor, as he rarely let anyone into his inner sanctum. Here, she attached herself to him with a devotion that would have pleased a saint, and that the otherworldly Clare treated as a sacred responsibility. He introduced Mary to the ideas of John Locke, whose writing had been banned by Oxford University in 1701, spurring dissenting liberals like Clare to study him with the kind of analytic fervor they had hitherto reserved for scripture.

The great political philosopher's principles—"creatures of the same species and rank . . . should . . . be equal," and a husband should have "no more power over [his wife's life] than she has over his life"—revitalized Mary. She had always felt that her father had no right to tyrannize her family and that the preferential treatment he and her mother bestowed on Ned was unjust. Now, after reading Locke, she had an ethical foundation for her feelings. Not only was it her right to shape her own future; it was everyone's right. In fact, Locke's social contract made protest seem the only rational response to injustice; it was humanity's obligation to overthrow tyranny; a government that does not protect the people's freedom is illegitimate. A father who abuses his wife and children forfeits his power.

Seventeen seventy-five was a revolutionary year. The firebrands of the era—Thomas Paine, Patrick Henry, and John and Samuel Adams, to name just a few—were all racing toward the same conclusions. While the teenage Mary Wollstonecraft was reading Locke, Adam Smith was writing *The Wealth of Nations* and Edward Gibbon was finishing the first volume of *The History of the Decline and Fall of the Roman Empire,* radical for its critique of Christianity and its praise of pagan Rome. In March, the statesman Edmund Burke, arguing on behalf of the American colonists, told Parliament that the United States should be a "sanctuary of liberty." Dr. Richard Price, a Unitarian minister, also advocated for American liberty in his wildly successful *Observations on the Nature of Civil Liberty,* a pamphlet that sold sixty thousand copies. The week before Mary's sixteenth birthday, Paul Revere made his famous ride, the musket shot fired on Lexington Green was heard round the world, and a thirty-one-year-old Virginian named Thomas Jefferson scoured Locke's *Second Treatise on Government* for the ideas that would, a year later, inform his claims for American independence.

One day that spring, Mrs. Clare took Mary to visit the Bloods, friends who lived in the village of Newington Butts, south of the Thames. It was an unimpressive town; the houses were small, the gardens simple. But when Mary and Mrs. Clare arrived at the Bloods' cottage and were welcomed inside by the eighteen-year-old Fanny Blood, Mary was overcome by admiration. The eldest daughter of the family had a gentle grace that thrilled Mary. While Mrs. Clare chatted with Mrs. Blood, Mary watched the delicate Fanny, busily employed in feeding and managing her younger siblings. When Fanny and Mary had the chance to talk, Mary was enchanted by the older girl's intelligence, tact, and patience. By the time the visit was over, she had promised herself that she and Fanny would be friends.

Like Mary, Fanny Blood was the oldest sister of a large brood of children. Also like Mary, her father was an alcoholic and a gambler, and although he was not violent, he could not earn a living. Mrs. Blood took in small sewing jobs, but it was really Fanny's income that supported the family. A talented artist, she had been hired by William Curtis, a botanist, to draw wildflower specimens for his two-volume series *Flora Londinensis,* or *The Flowers of London.* Fanny's employment was Mary's first true example of the power of female resourcefulness. Fanny, with the help of her mother, put food on the table and enabled the family to maintain a genteel lifestyle without the assistance of any man.

Since the girls lived too far apart to see each other frequently, Mary asked Fanny's permission to begin a correspondence. None of these missives survive, but Mary regarded her friend's writing as far superior to her own. Fanny's intelligence was "masculine," Mary said, an adjective she reserved for women of "sound judgment." When Mary confessed she wanted to learn to write as well as Fanny, Fanny agreed to teach her. Mary declared that she had never loved anyone as much as she loved Fanny. "I could dwell for ever on [Fanny's] praises," she wrote Jane Arden, with no apparent contrition that she was treating Jane precisely as she had accused Jane of treating her, abandoning her for a new friend. Fortunately, the generous Jane expressed no hurt over her friend's mercurial loyalties.

Before long, Mary began to dream of a new future, one that would allow her to break away from her family without getting married: she and Fanny would set up a household together, where they would be able to read and study without interruption and live as equals. She wrote Jane that she would rather share life with her new friend than marry any man, declaring, "I know this resolution may appear a little extraordinary, but in forming it I follow the dictates of reason as well as the bent of my inclination."

In the eighteenth century, it was fashionable for women to write extravagant letters to their friends, hold hands, dance together, and express feverish longing for one another without thinking of themselves as lovers. Even Mary, who was often caught up in passions for other women, thought it was important for close female friends to observe "decent personal reserve." She considered moving in together "the most rational" next step in her friendship with Fanny, because Fanny's erudition and sophistication would help Mary improve herself, and Mary's strength and bravery would protect them from the harshness of the world. Together, they could free themselves from the tyranny of the men in their families.

But Mary had chosen to overlook an important fact: Fanny was engaged. Her suitor was a portly self-satisfied man named Hugh Skeys, who had courted her for more than a year, then handed her a small portrait of himself and sailed off to supervise his business concerns in Portugal, promising to return and marry her once he was certain of his financial future. To Mary, his leaving was evidence that Hugh did not truly love Fanny. Fanny, though, clung to the idea that he would return. She had affection for Hugh, and marriage to him would provide her and her family with financial stability. Mary could not offer Fanny this kind of economic support. The only employment possibilities for middle-class women who did not have a talent like Fanny's were low-paying positions as teachers, governesses, or lady's companions. But unpleasant as these options were, Mary was determined to start a life with her friend—and so she decided to secure a job. This was a difficult proposition, as it was considered unseemly for a properly brought up young woman to approach strangers for employment. Fortunately, probably through Mr. Clare, Mary learned of an opportunity to become the paid companion of an older widow who lived in Bath. She would have preferred to be a teacher, or even a governess, but what really mattered was earning money. Certainly there would be no financial assistance from her family. Although Ned had recently come of age and received a generous inheritance from their grandfather—one third of the estate, or approximately £5,000—he was not about to offer any help. Even when he got married—a time when brothers traditionally gave their unwed sisters a small dowry or invited them to live with them—he kept the Wollstonecraft fortune, such as it was, for himself. The injustice of this infuriated Mary. Without a dowry, it would be difficult for her younger sisters to find husbands, and although Mary herself did not want to get married, she felt Eliza and Everina deserved the opportunity. As for herself, just a small nest egg, a fraction of her brother's wealth, would have helped her start a new life and freed her from the necessity of working.

In the spring of 1778, nineteen-year-old Mary took the public coach to the home of her new employer, the ill-tempered and arrogant Sarah Dawson, who had already driven away a succession of companions. But Mary was made of stronger stuff than her predecessors. She disliked Mrs. Dawson but saw this job as a necessary evil, pouring out her sufferings to Jane Arden in a long letter: "Pain and disappointment have constantly attended me. . . . I am among Strangers, far from all my former connexions. . . . I am quite a piece of still life. . . . [I] have not spirit sufficient to bustle about."

To the rest of the world, however, Bath, at the height of its popularity, was the place to be. The rich and famous came to take the spa waters, which were supposed to heal most ills, and strolled through the assembly rooms to see and be seen.

Thrown into fashionable society for the first time, Mary complained about the insincerity of people's manners and sneered at "the unmeaning civilities that I see every day." She accompanied Mrs. Dawson wherever she went but was forced to remain on the sidelines,

The South Parade, Bath *by James Gandon (1784),*
*after a painting by Thomas Malton the Younger.*

watching, not speaking unless spoken to, an enforced marginaliza-
tion that infuriated her; it was all too reminiscent of her mother's
punishments.

Some of her scorn for high society may have been rooted in Mary's
relative poverty. She could not afford to dress fashionably even if she
had wanted to. Young women bought luxurious striped taffeta for
underskirts and fainted from lacing their expensive corsets too
tightly. They wore stiff silk panniers around their hips that cost a
fortune and were at least five feet wide, making it difficult to navigate
the dance floor, pass through narrow doorways, or even curtsy without tipping over.

Society ladies coated themselves in a costly white powder made of
lead, although everyone knew that "white" had caused the death of
fashionable women, most notably the Gunning sisters. Maids painted
rounds of rouge on their mistresses' cheeks and sometimes penciled
a dark "birthmark" near their lips. Hair was worn in steep towers
at least two feet tall, a costly engineering feat that required highly
trained servants to attach a wire cone to the top of the head, comb the

hair into vertical swatches to cover the structure beneath, and then "teaze" it so that it appeared "frizzled." If a woman did not have enough hair to accommodate the style, she could buy artificial curls made of horses' tails or hair from a wig shop to supplement her own. The entire structure was often topped with rare (and pricey) ostrich feathers or ribbons, and then powdered with flour.

The key to eighteenth-century beauty was demonstrating how rich one was. Like the formal gardens of this period, with their emphasis on the gardener's ability to control and shape Nature—the evergreens pruned into tight conical shapes, the tidily shaped geo-

The Lady's Maid or Toilet Head Dress,
*caricature of eighteenth-century hair fashions.*

metrical paths, the perfectly symmetric Greek temple—a woman's appearance was meant to demonstrate how many maids she could afford and how many jewels she owned. Every lady worked diligently to disguise or augment her natural attributes—no dress was too grand, no skirt too wide, no hairstyle too outrageous. Artificiality was a virtue—evidence of exquisite craftsmanship and distinguished taste. To commemorate a victory at sea, one woman topped her head with an outrageously expensive model ship. Others sported miniature trees, birds, and fruit. People bought and studied books that taught refinement and manners. Complicated dance steps were the rage. Marie Antoinette, who had become the queen of France only four years earlier, was held up as an ideal, her dresses copied by dressmakers, her taste celebrated. That she would one day become one of the most hated symbols of aristocratic wealth was unthinkable, as was the idea that anyone would want to appear spontaneous rather than elegant, natural rather than refined.

Mired in the extravagances of aristocratic Bath society, Mary felt decidedly out of her element. True to form, she made a virtue out of her alienation, writing Jane Arden, "I wish to retire as much from [the world] as possible. I am particularly sick of genteel life. I am only a spectator." But this was an inaccurate description if ever there was one. Even as a hired companion, Mary attracted attention. She had loops of reddish-gold hair that she only reluctantly powdered at Mrs. Dawson's insistence. She had a perfectly shaped mouth and a womanly figure; her skin was creamy and her cheeks pink. When she laughed or smiled, her face glowed with warmth. She loved to talk, as long as the topic was philosophy or literature, and she struck people as dramatic and acutely intelligent. Men were drawn to her, and she seems to have enjoyed a flirtation during her tenure with Mrs. Dawson, as some of her letters were found in the possession of a distinguished older clergyman, Joshua Waterhouse, after he died. For a single man and woman to correspond during this time period was unusual enough to mark the relationship as at least potentially romantic.

Mary would have known, however, that a man like Waterhouse was out of her league. Her family was too poor and he too highly placed in society. Instead of being cast down by this, she wore her poverty like a badge, declaring herself superior, a woman of principle, capable of self-discipline, unlike those with whom she lived. She owned only simple dresses and used no makeup. She did not yearn for a life of luxury. Instead she went to church, worried about the poor and the sick, and wished she could alleviate their suffering. She read Milton's *Paradise Lost* and James Thompson's long contemplative poem *The Seasons*. Whenever she could, she took long walks, seeking comfort in "the various dispositions of light and shade" and "the beautiful tints the gleams of sunshine gave to the distant hills." While Mrs. Dawson and her friends devoured pastries and succulent roasts and poured cream into their hot chocolate, Mary adhered to a monkish diet. "I am just going to sup *solus* on a bunch of grapes, and a bread crust," she wrote Jane. "I'll drink your health in pure water."

Unlike previous companions who had fawned over her, complimenting her beauty, elegance, refinement, and wit, Mrs. Dawson soon found that this new young woman seemed to have contempt for everyone and everything; even royalty was not exempt from Mary's sharp tongue. In fact, when she heard that the king had driven his horses until the poor creatures dropped dead, she expressed righteous outrage: "I think it murder to put an end to any living thing unless it be necessary for food or hurtful to us."

During this time, Mary wrote home as little as possible to avoid the recriminations she knew she would face. Her mother had been angry when she left for Bath, accusing her of not having enough "regard" for her family. Her younger sisters felt abandoned. Mary had always managed the household, taking care of all of them and fending off the threats of their drunken father. Now, left to fill Mary's shoes, they felt resentful and inadequate. How were they supposed to tend to their younger siblings and their ailing mother? Mary was the eldest daughter; running the home was her job, not theirs. Why had she left them behind? Did she think she was better than they were? How dare she try to strike out on her own? Her loyalty should have been to her family. The letters they exchanged were angry, with Mary defending herself against the worst accusation a woman of her time period could face: selfishness.

But Mary drew courage from Locke's theories, and from the works of Rousseau, who took Locke's ideas one step further, arguing that freedom was what mattered most and that obedience and subordination were symptoms of societal oppression. Mankind must relish the inborn right to independence, Rousseau argued. And so must womankind, Mary reasoned, which meant she had the right to resist her family's demands. She knew she was breaking convention; she felt sorry for her sisters and disliked her mother's judgment of her; but she remembered how hopeless she had felt in Hoxton, how imprisoned and claustrophobic, and knew it would be dangerous to return. She might never have the strength to make another bid for freedom. It was better to be ordered around by Mrs. Dawson, ignored by Mrs. Dawson's guests, despised by the rest of the staff, and forced to endure the frivolities of Bath society than to be trapped at home. At least Mrs. Dawson paid her, and with that came the promise of future independence, however distant. With her sisters and her mother, the future would seem blank, the days rolling monotonously past.

In the fall of 1781, Elizabeth Wollstonecraft developed an illness so grave that Mary could no longer withstand her sisters' calls for help and reluctantly returned home. Her mother was painfully swollen from an unspecified disorder. Mary termed it dropsy. Today, it is known as edema, the bodywide retention of fluid, probably caused by a liver or kidney dysfunction. With each month, Elizabeth's skin tightened further from the pressure, making it more and more difficult for her to move her limbs. By the spring, she was no longer able to feed herself. Her daughters had to clothe her, bathe her, and try to soothe her pain. Ironically, it was Mary she leaned on the most, complaining bitterly if her eldest daughter left her bedside.

Not surprisingly, the Wollstonecraft men felt no obligation to help. Edward had largely disappeared at the onset of his wife's illness, although he did continue to help cover the family's expenses, dropping in from time to time to pay the most pressing bills. Mary used her earnings to help cover the rest. Ned remained almost entirely out of the picture; Henry had vanished so completely that it was impossible to trace his whereabouts. James had been sent to sea, and Charles was still only twelve years old. However, if Mary had refused to go home, her family would never have forgiven her, and she might never have forgiven herself, so firmly implanted was the societal value of daughterly self-sacrifice.

For the next two years, until she was almost twenty-three, Mary devoted her energy to caring for her mother. While Mary had lived with Mrs. Dawson, the family had moved several times, ending up in Enfield, about ten miles north of Charing Cross. Unable to afford one of the elegant houses in the fashionable part of town, they lived in cheap housing on the outskirts of the village, where Mary felt marooned, far away from her friend Fanny Blood and imprisoned with her sisters. On April 19, 1782, Elizabeth slipped into a final coma, but first she murmured words that Mary would remember for the rest of her life, in part because they were not at all what she wanted to hear: "A little patience and all will be over." This passive acceptance of suffering was not the deathbed rapprochement Mary yearned for. In *Mary,* the novel she would write a few years later, the dying mother says, "Alas my daughter, I have not always treated you well." But Elizabeth never apologized to her eldest daughter. She had never stopped favoring her eldest son, and had never overcome her dislike of Mary's passionate nature and her disregard of proper feminine behavior.

After her mother's death, Mary wrote Jane Arden that she was "fatigued," contrasting her misery to Jane's cheerfulness: "You are a laugher still, but I am a stupid creature, and you would be tired to death of me, if you were to be with me a week." Mary's father arrived home with a new wife, Lydia, a few days after Elizabeth died. He had begun this affair while Elizabeth was alive, but no one knew how long they had been together. Taking Charles, they moved to Wales, leaving Mary to pack up and distribute her mother's few possessions, find living quarters for herself and her sisters, and scrape money together for food and clothing. Mary tracked down Ned and talked him into hosting the two younger girls in his large house on St. Katherine Street, near the Tower, and then, at Fanny's urging, she herself moved in with the Bloods in Walham Green, a pleasant village a few miles west of Chelsea, near Putney Bridge on the Thames. Here she did her best to shoulder some of the economic burden by helping Mrs. Blood with her sewing. Fanny's health, never strong, declined during Mary's year with the Bloods. She coughed up blood and was diagnosed with tuberculosis. Although Fanny's case was comparatively mild, Mary felt fiercely protective of her friend. She urged her to cut back her work hours, even though the dip in Fanny's income meant their dream of a life together would grow more remote. But, to Mary, Fanny's recovery was what mattered most.

Despite these worries, Mary was living with a family she loved and who loved her. Eliza and Everina, on the other hand, were unwanted indigent sisters in the household of a domineering brother and grudging sister-in-law. They could have pursued positions as governesses or paid companions, but they lacked their eldest sister's initiative. Instead, having watched Mary's desperate struggle to build a life for herself without a husband, nineteen-year-old Eliza, who was vivacious and attractive, fell into the arms of a respectable bachelor, Meredith Bishop, a shipbuilder. She married him on October 20, only six months after Elizabeth died. Mary wrote Jane Arden that her sister had "done well, and married a worthy man, whose situation in life is truly eligible." She did not condemn Eliza for taking this route to security and in fact felt some relief. Eliza was Bishop's responsibility now; he could take care of her, leaving Mary with one less person to worry about and more time to focus on creating a life with Fanny.

# CHAPTER 5

# MARY GODWIN: SCOTLAND,
# AN "EYRY OF FREEDOM"

———

[ 1810–1814 ]

*Y*OUNG MARY GODWIN WAS CONVINCED THAT IF HER MOTHER HAD lived she would have been much happier. For one thing, she would not have had to contend with her stepmother, a competitive stepsister, or a little brother who stole her father's attention away from her. Most important, she would have had a mother who adored her, of this she was certain. She only had to read the books Wollstonecraft had written for Fanny to see how loving her mother had been.

Although to outsiders Mary and her stepsiblings seemed to enjoy a happy family life, the enmity between Mary and her stepmother had only worsened over time. When Mary was thirteen, the tension manifested itself in an excruciating bout of eczema on her hands and arms. Mary-Jane did what she could to help, shuttling the girl back and forth to doctors and taking her on a trip to the seaside. But Mary continued to resist Mary-Jane's authority. She did not throw tantrums like Jane, but instead resorted to stony silence and sly, sarcastic remarks, making it clear that she did not respect her stepmother.

When the eczema failed to improve, the Godwins sent Mary to a boarding school in the popular seaside resort of Ramsgate, about eighty miles from central London, hoping that a prolonged stay in the fresh air would help her heal. But Mary was miserable among the holidaymakers and tourists who flocked there to take the waters, and after six months she left the school, her eczema uncured. When she returned home, she found that Mary-Jane had scraped together enough money for Jane—and only Jane—to study French and have singing lessons. Mary-Jane urged her daughter to perform for guests, and although Jane enjoyed the attention and Fanny applauded her stepsister's talent, Mary seethed at the fact that she and Fanny had been so intentionally overlooked.

If Fanny shared Mary's outrage, she never showed it. Worried that she was a burden to her stepparents, Fanny strove not to cause any trouble. She did not like to assert herself and was plagued by depression, a "torpor" that she could not shake. Although Mary felt sorry for Fanny, Jane was impatient with her, as was Godwin, who misread Fanny's depression as "indolence." Fanny never seemed to expect anything more than this. She preferred being invisible—a troubling tendency, although neither of the Godwins expressed any real concern about it. Her silence was far easier to cope with than Jane's histrionics or what Godwin called Mary's "bold" ways.

But though he considered her "imperious," as Mary grew older, Godwin expected more of her, taking time out of his busy work day to supervise her intellectual development. Later, Mary recalled what these sessions were like:

> Godwin . . . extended his utmost care to the task of education; but many things rendered him unfit for it. His severity was confined to words, but they were pointed and humiliating. His strictness was undeviating. . . . He was too minute in his censures, too grave and severe in his instruction.

Even Godwin admitted that he had a tendency to be too critical, but he could not help himself. He wanted Mary to exert herself more vigorously. She had such potential; why would she not apply herself? Faced with such pressure, it was difficult for Mary not to feel rebellious, although she was always deferential to Godwin. He made no allowances for her age: Mary had to be superior to other children. Worse, he always supported Mary-Jane when conflict arose. To Mary, this was a betrayal. He put his wife first—his *second* wife—while she, his own daughter, was somehow always in the wrong.

Mary's loneliness and rage mounted until at last, when she was fourteen, Godwin decided to send his unhappy daughter to Scotland. This unusual decision was prompted by an invitation from William Baxter, a radical Scotsman who had read *Political Justice* years earlier and struck up a correspondence with Godwin, touting the glories of life in his remote Scottish village. When Baxter, a recent widower, heard about Mary's troubles, he told Godwin to send her to him. Unlike Godwin and Mary-Jane, Mr. Baxter, the father of four daughters, was used to a household of girls. She would fit right in, he declared, and the fresh air of Scotland would cure her ills.

Although he had never actually met Baxter, Godwin agreed to the plan. To prepare his friend for Mary's arrival, Godwin wrote a rather schoolmasterly description of his daughter: "I believe she has nothing of what is commonly called vices, and that she has considerable talent. I am anxious that she should be brought up . . . like a philosopher. . . . I do not desire that she should be treated with extraordinary attention. I wish, too, that she should be excited to industry. She has occasionally great perseverance, but occasionally, too she shows great need to be roused." He wanted the Baxters to take her seriously as a young intellectual, but he did not want them to coddle her.

On June 7, 1812, Mary boarded the *Osnaburgh,* bound for Scotland. Godwin and her two sisters, Fanny and Jane, came to see her off; Mary-Jane made no pretense of being sad and stayed home, relishing her victory. Mary was prone to seasickness, and in an unguarded moment Godwin admitted to Baxter that he felt "a thousand anxieties" about sending his fourteen-year-old on a weeklong voyage by herself. He searched the decks for a trustworthy older woman to look after his daughter, but the woman he found abandoned Mary the instant the ship set sail. Inexperienced Mary, who was miserably ill for the entire voyage, had her money stolen while on board and arrived in Dundee penniless and weak from seasickness.

But she did not complain. This difficult journey marked the start of a new chapter in her life. At last she would be free from her stepmother. She would miss her father, but it was a relief to be away from his scrutiny and harsh reprimands. Boarding school had given her a taste of what it felt like to live away from home. But there she had been hemmed in by rules, and Mary-Jane and her father had been close enough to keep their eye on her. Ultimately, it had been the worst of both worlds: none of the comforts of London and even more restrictions than Mary-Jane had enforced in their home on Skinner Street.

Besides, Scotland was no Ramsgate. One of the most civilized cities in Europe lay in the southeast: Edinburgh, home to a great university as well as the Enlightenment philosophers David Hume and Adam Smith. The Highlands, on the other hand, were among the wildest, most dangerous places in the world, the stage for countless rebellions against English rule.

To the nineteenth-century English tourist, Scotland was an extraordinary place. Mary was following the footsteps of earlier Romantic travelers who had gone there to escape civilization and written ecstatic accounts of their experiences. William and Dorothy Wordsworth had hiked through the open countryside with Coleridge in 1803 and been delighted with its empty reaches and solitary cottages, its green hills and wide stretches of heath. The streams in Scotland did not need bridges, Dorothy Wordsworth said, because, unlike the English, who wore shoes, the Scots did not mind getting their bare feet wet. The inns were dirty, but Romantics like the Wordsworths did not mind suffering a little discomfort to travel this land of rugged countryside and old stone churches, tranquil lanes and military garrisons. After their visit, Dorothy declared what Mary would soon discover for herself: "Scotland is the country above all others that I have seen, in which a man of imagination may carve out his own pleasures."

By the time Mary Godwin arrived in June 1812, the Highlanders had surrendered to the Crown, but they were still brandishing their swords, waiting for a chance to overthrow King George III. Rebels staged guerrilla attacks, sabotaging English troops if they ventured too deep into clan territory; the English commanders responded by torturing, jailing, and executing anyone suspected of fomenting revolt. Owning a bagpipe or even playing one could land a Highlander in prison. Tartans had been illegal for most of the century; only recently had the ban been lifted. For a teenage girl, these dangers seemed thrillingly romantic. Sir Walter Scott had published his dramatic poem *The Lady of the Lake* in 1810, and throngs of English tourists rushed to the Highlands, reciting Scott's words as they hiked down gorges and gazed at plunging waterfalls. To Mary, Scott's noble heroine Ellen Douglas embodied all she hoped to become: beloved, brave, and tragic.

The Baxter family lived a few miles east of Dundee, in the village of Broughty Ferry on the north bank of the Firth of Tay, not far from the North Sea and the southern Highlands. If Mary had not been a nature lover before, she became one now. In Broughty Ferry, the wind seemed to blow all the time. Clouds sailed across a sky that renewed itself continually, so much cleaner and wider than the grimy haze that hung over London's city streets. At sunset and sunrise, canopies of orange and pink stretched overhead, with shocking explosions of red, like the Turner paintings Mary's father had taken her to see in the artist's gallery on Harley Street. Behind the city, the hills sloped up to the Highlands, and to the south, the firth rippled moodily, shining and darkening with the wind.

Mr. Baxter was honored to welcome Godwin's daughter to his grand old house, "The Cottage," and Mary was delighted by the warmth of his reception. Old radical that he was, Baxter still embraced the tenets of the French Revolution, and he gave his daughters far more independence than Mary had dreamed possible. Later, she would say that while other people might experience this part of Scotland as "blank and dreary," she had found Dundee an "eyry of freedom."

Sixteen-year-old Isabella, the Baxter daughter closest to Mary in age, had spirals of black curls, dark eyes, and a sensitive, intelligent face. Vivacious and warm, she was everything Mary wanted to be; she chattered and laughed and was generally at the center of things, while Mary tended to remain silent, an observer rather than a leading lady. To Isabella, Mary's heritage made her seem glamorous; she was the daughter of Mary Wollstonecraft, one of Isabella's heroines, and her quiet manner rendered her mysterious, as though she had secrets she would not share unless you earned her favor. It did not cross Isabella's mind that she might simply be shy.

Isabella shared her father's enthusiasm for the French Revolution. She studied its events, large and small, and read biographies of its leaders. She revered Charlotte Corday and Madame Roland, two famed revolutionaries, and talked about them as though she had known them personally. Madame Roland's words before she died on the guillotine—"O Liberty! What crimes are committed in thy name!"—seemed almost unbearably poignant, and Charlotte Corday's brave assassination of Jean-Paul Marat was the sort of self-sacrifice Isabella yearned to make for her country. This passionate relationship with history was a revelation for Mary. Her father had always praised historical scholarship, but Isabella scoured the past for clues about the present, for ideas about how to live a Romantic life, a far more appealing prospect than scholarship for scholarship's sake.

Although Broughty Ferry was on the edge of the wilderness, no one worried when Isabella and Mary disappeared for hours, sometimes even entire days. Occasionally, Mary left Isabella behind and spent long hours by herself in the fields along the sea. It was here, she said later, that she first began to dream about writing "fantastic" stories, relying on her imagination to "people the hours with creations."

Near the Baxters' house, a fifteenth-century fortress guarded the mouth of the Tay, its sides bare and straight. From the top of its tower one could look across the river to the village of Newburgh, where Isabella's eldest sister, Margaret, lived with her eccentric husband, David Booth. When the weather was clear, the two girls crossed the firth to stay with the couple in their gray-shingled cottage clinging to the hillside overlooking the water. Margaret was an invalid and could not entertain the girls. While she napped and rocked in her chair, her forty-seven-year-old husband, who was called "the devil" by his neighbors because of his radical politics and his prodigious store of arcane knowledge, discussed the evils of tyranny and the glories of liberty with Mary and Isabella. Mary was thrilled to be treated like an adult by this man, who Godwin said was the only radical he knew who was smarter than himself. Booth was eager to exchange ideas with the daughter of Godwin and Wollstonecraft, talking to Mary as though she were extraordinary, a genius just like her parents.

At the Baxters' house, Isabella and Mary shared a room, often staying up late exchanging secrets and stories, many of which featured David, whom both girls admired. Isabella even dreamed of trading places with her sister. On one of their visits, they scratched their initials into a windowpane with a diamond ring, never dreaming that one day Mary would have fans who would travel thousands of miles to see her wobbly *MWG;* the cottage became a pilgrimage site until the window was stolen from the house in the 1970s.

Occasionally, the Baxters visited Dundee. Isabella had memorized reams of poetry and loved Dundee's legends and ghost stories. At the end of Guthrie Street, there was a small hill where hundreds of women had been burned as witches and where the locals said their spirits still walked. Behind the town rose a bald basalt hill called the Law. According to local folklore, if a virgin climbed to the top and made a wish, it would come true. Whether or not Mary and Isabella actually did this, both girls had plenty of wishes. Neither wanted to be ordinary; they dreamed of huge operatic lives with tragedies and sacrifices, glory and fame. It helped that they looked like heroines: Mary with her startlingly white skin and halo of reddish-gold hair, Isabella with her vivid dark eyes and unruly curls. In the only surviving portrait of Isabella she is dressed in costume as Lady Jane Grey, the tragic young queen famed for her scholarship and her beauty, who ruled England for only nine days before she was executed.

With each passing week, Mary grew healthier and stronger, and the eczema disappeared. But Godwin and the Baxters had agreed on only a short visit—five months—and even though Mary wanted to stay longer, she returned to England in November. Back at Skinner Street, it was as though she had never left. Old quarrels flared, new ones arose. Mary-Jane was as intransigent as ever. Godwin shut himself into his study, complaining about the noise. Fanny retreated even further into the shadows. Jane trailed after Mary like a puppy. Mary herself was resentful and quarrelsome. Fortunately, the Baxters wrote to invite her for another stay, and as soon as the weather broke in June 1813, Godwin packed Mary back to Scotland.

She arrived near the end of a mild spring, her heart rising as she traveled north to Dundee. The air was damp, the land was green. The chestnut forests bloomed and the blue hills promised mystery and romance. But when she reached The Cottage, she found its inhabitants in mourning. Margaret, Isabella's sister and David Booth's wife, had died. Although this was painful for the family, it did raise an interesting quandary. David Booth was now free to remarry. At first, he flirted with Mary, but although she was flattered, Mary wanted to be swept off her feet by someone impossibly romantic. Booth had just turned forty-eight years old; he was short and barrel-chested. Doctrinaire and stern, he was hardly the ideal suitor.

When David Booth realized that Mary was not interested in him, he quickly changed course. A few weeks later, he declared himself in love with Isabella—a thoroughly sinful choice as far as the local church was concerned, since it was against ecclesiastical law for a man to marry his wife's sister.

But the shocking nature of Booth's proposal was exactly what Isabella had always wanted: a rule to break, a taboo to embrace. Besides, she had always been slightly jealous of her older sister. Mary encouraged Isabella from the sidelines. To her, the uproar made the relationship seem all the more exciting. If the couple loved each other, which she was sure they did, then the more than thirty-year age difference should not be a stumbling block, nor should the church's disapproval.

Like Mary, Isabella's father believed that love should triumph over all. He knew that there would be an outcry, but he remained loyal to his daughter, even when the entire family was excommunicated after the couple announced their engagement that fall. To Mary, this was a satisfying conclusion to the story. The Baxter family had championed love and freedom over old-fashioned rules and restrictions.

In March 1814, it was time for Mary to sail back to England. She said goodbye to the Baxters with sorrow, dreaming of a time when she and Isabella would be reunited to cut a swath through the world together, twin heroines united in their dedication to romance.

When Mary arrived back home, clutching the tartan she had bought to remind herself of Scotland, she was ready for her own grand love affair, preferably with the same ingredients as Isabella's:

rebellion, exile, and scandal. She was sure her father would support her in her choice of partner even if the entire world disapproved. Isabella's father, after all, was a Godwin disciple, and he had blessed his daughter's unorthodox union.

But in actuality, her father was as remote as ever, desperately trying to avert the financial ruin always hovering on the horizon. Their best hope for solvency, he said, was a young nobleman he had met while she was in Scotland. With curly brown hair and huge blue eyes, Percy Shelley was rich, wild, and charming. He had a wicked sense of humor, radical political views, and a propensity for shocking people. Shelley had been expelled from Oxford, along with his best friend, Thomas Hogg, for publishing a diatribe against religion; his renegade behavior recommended him to the Godwin household. He had read *Political Justice,* and now, at age twenty-one, inspired by Godwin's philosophy of freedom, had rushed off to Ireland to help organize the protests against British rule. In return for Godwin's advice, he promised to help him financially. Shelley had visited the family frequently while Mary was away, where he talked so gently and quietly to Fanny and laughed so uproariously at Jane's giddiness that both girls fell a little in love with him, or so said the Godwins many years later. Unfortunately, he already had a wife. Nineteen-year-old Harriet Westbrook impressed both Fanny and Jane with her fashionable dresses and her beauty.

It was important for Mary to join the family in trying to please this young man, Godwin said. When Shelley came to visit, she should be on her best behavior. If he would give them a loan, then Godwin would be able to right the ship. If not, all could be lost.

What Godwin did not realize was that Shelley's ability to raise funds rested entirely on a precarious future inheritance controlled by Shelley's father, Sir Timothy, who had stopped speaking to his son when he was expelled from Oxford. Each penny the younger Shelley wrested from his family's estate was the result of long, bitter legal proceedings, or from an archaic borrowing system known as post-obit loans. These "post-death" payments stipulated that when Shelley became Sir Percy, he would have to pay as much as four times the amount of the loan in interest. Shelley, who viewed his family estate as a funding source for his favorite revolutionary projects, had promised Godwin that he was next on his list of beneficiaries.

Godwin was also unaware that Shelley, who had always been at the mercy of fluctuating moods, was in a particularly volatile state that spring. He had left Harriet six months earlier, and though he did not want to live with his wife, he was lonely without her. Originally, Shelley had viewed his marriage as a glorious rescue mission; he had freed sixteen-year-old Harriet Westbrook from her stifling and conventional home, or so Shelley believed—Harriet gave no sign of feeling trapped until she met Shelley—and they had run away to the north, getting married only because she insisted on it. Shelley himself was against marriage, having read Mary Wollstonecraft's condemnation of the institution in *A Vindication of the Rights of Woman* as well as Godwin's early thoughts on the subject. In the unrevised first edition of Political Justice, Godwin had declared:

> Marriage, as now understood, is a monopoly, and the worst of monopolies. So long as two human beings are forbidden, by positive institution, to follow the dictates of their own mind, prejudice will be alive and vigorous.

Godwin had long since reversed his opinion on the matter, but Shelley, unaware of his mentor's change of heart, believed that Godwin still supported the idea of free love.

Enraptured as she was with Shelley, Harriet had underestimated his resistance to their vows. She followed him to Ireland and then to Wales, where Shelley dreamed up new ideas for inciting protests, including throwing bottles with incendiary messages into the sea. But everything changed in 1813, when Harriet gave birth to a daughter, Ianthe, and overnight (or so it seemed to Shelley) began nagging him about money and their frequent moves. He was disillusioned. What about philosophy? The Irish rebellion? Did she no longer care about the grand ideal of freedom? Now he regretted their elopement, viewing it as a calamity and "a rash and heartless union." Most troubling of all, if Harriet was not who he thought she was, then their union was predicated on falsehood, poisoning his dream of dedicating himself to the truth at all costs, of living a philosopher's life. He was haunted by a guilty sense of his own hypocrisy. A few months later, he would describe this sensation to his friend Hogg: "I felt as if a dead & living body had been linked together in loathsome and horrible communion."

Soon after Shelley left Harriet, she discovered she was pregnant again and begged him to come back, but he shuddered at the idea; living with Harriet once more would feel like a step backward. He wanted to be liberated from his old life and was on the lookout for an omen—a hawk, an eclipse, a dream—anything to show him what path to take next.

Mary, too, was watching for a sign of transformation that spring. The quiet blue-green landscape of the Scottish countryside seemed a lost dream amid the noise and dirt of the city. Gone were the silent hours alone in the fields. Gone, too, were the long tramps in the hills. Instead, there were enforced tea times with Mary-Jane, Fanny, Jane, and her half brother, William. In the crowded rooms of the house on Skinner Street, privacy was impossible. Mary was lonely. She missed her soul mate, Isabella.

As her mother had observed, there were few choices for young women in Mary's position. Godwin's debts and notoriety made her future unpromising: no suitor would want a bride without a dowry; and if she did not want to be a teacher, governess, or lady's companion, Mary would have to wait on customers in the bookshop and perhaps write children's books to boost the family's income. The life she dreamed of, filled with love and passion, seemed impossible, a glorious adventure that happened to other people, not to her.

# CHAPTER 6

# MARY WOLLSTONECRAFT:
# INDEPENDENCE

———

[ 1783–1785 ]

*I*N AUGUST 1783, THE TWENTY-FOUR-YEAR-OLD MARY WOLLSTONECRAFT became an aunt. Less than a year after nineteen-year-old Eliza married Meredith Bishop, she gave birth to a little girl whom she named Elizabeth Mary Frances Bishop, in homage to her mother, her eldest sister, and Fanny Blood. At first, Mary reveled in the happy news. A healthy baby. A little girl. A namesake. But that November, a few months after little Mary (as they called her) was baptized, an urgent letter came from Eliza's husband. Eliza had gone mad, he wrote; he begged Mary to come help.

When Mary arrived at her sister and brother-in-law's large house in Bermondsey, a middle-class enclave south of the Thames, Eliza was having what Mary called "fits of phrensy." Her eyes rolled back in her head; she shook as though she had a fever. She muttered to herself and did not recognize her sister. The rest of the household was in chaos, but Eliza did not seem to notice anything or anyone; she had retreated far inside herself and could not be reached. As Mary put it, she did not have "the least tincture of reason."

Mary had intended to stay in Bermondsey for only a day or two, but her sister's plight was so extreme that Mary felt she could not leave her. She did her best to reach Eliza, sitting with her for hours every day, cradling her in her arms, reading to her, praying with her, and taking her for drives in a coach. After a few weeks, Mary wrote

Everina that the fits had stopped but that Eliza was not any more rational. "Her ideas are all disjointed and a number of wild whims float on her imagination and uncorrected fall from her."

To Mary, it seemed likely that Eliza's delusions stemmed from the trauma of childbirth, and that with careful nursing she would recover. The term "postpartum depression" had not yet been invented, and yet the time after birth was still widely known as a dangerous one for women, both physically and emotionally. In a famous case a few decades later, the writer William Thackeray's wife grew so despondent after her second child that she had to be institutionalized. At first this theory seemed correct, as after a month or so under Mary's watchful eye Eliza slowly grew more coherent. Then came a new development. Mary noted that her sister shuddered whenever Bishop approached, crying and accusing him of cruelty. Was this evidence of further derangement, or was it the root cause of Eliza's breakdown? Mary was not sure. Had the affable-seeming Bishop been harsh to her sister? He seemed heartbroken by her illness. During the first days of the crisis, Mary had listened sympathetically to Bishop's feelings, but after noticing Eliza's fear in his presence, she became increasingly suspicious. Having witnessed her father's dangerous fluctuations in mood, she knew that good humor in public did not preclude violent tirades at home, and she felt even more worried when one of Bishop's friends told her that Bishop could be either a "lion or a spannial"—it was a phrase that could easily have described Edward Wollstonecraft.

During these weeks of indecision, Mary wrote many letters, trying to sort through her feelings, reflecting on her own state of mind as well as her sister's. In one revealing letter to Everina she describes how confused she felt: "I don't know what to do—Poor Eliza's situation almost turns my brain—I can't stay and see this continual misery—and to leave her to bear it by herself without any one to comfort her is still more distressing—I would do anything to rescue her from her present situation."

There was an added urgency, since whether or not Bishop was right and Eliza had lost her mind, he had the legal authority to send her to an asylum. Institutionalization was a common enough solution for wives who were troublesome, as English law granted husbands absolute power in marriage. A wife was not allowed to own anything. She had no legal rights of any kind. Later, Mary would say "a wife being as much a man's property as his horse, or his ass, she has nothing she can call her own." Without legal protection, women were vulnerable to all sorts of abuse. Husbands could beat their wives and declare them insane. If a woman tried to flee, her husband had the right to bring her back by force. A man could starve his wife and keep her locked indoors. He could also prevent her from seeking medical care, or from having visitors who might help ease her suffering. For most women, death and desertion were the only ways to escape a miserable marriage. To get a divorce, one had to go through the lengthy and prohibitively expensive process of petitioning Parliament; only 132 such cases were granted before 1800, and the plaintiffs were all men. In the eighteenth century, only four women managed to win a legal separation. Not until the 1857 Matrimonial Causes Act could both sexes initiate divorce proceedings.

The injustice of this legal system stayed with Mary, shaping the arguments in her most famous work, *A Vindication of the Rights of Woman,* and it was still with her, many years later, in her final novel, *Maria,* in which she would depict the suffering that occurs when an evil husband imprisons his virtuous (and perfectly sane) wife in a mental asylum with the full sanction of the law.

In December, Eliza began to have moments of lucidity, but she was still unable to describe what Bishop had done to her other than repeating that she had been "ill-used." The best that Mary could surmise was that Bishop could not refrain from "gratification," Mary's word for nonconsensual sex, since there was no term for marital rape. In fact, rape within marriage was not recognized as a crime in Great Britain until 1991. Whether Bishop had acted out of insensitivity or outright aggression was not important. What mattered to Mary was that Eliza was terrified. Bishop, too, was beginning to expose his true colors. He angrily denied Eliza's accusations, and Mary was struck by how unsympathetic he was. If just once Bishop had expressed any empathy for his frightened young wife, Mary might not have sided against him, but now that Eliza was saner, he resorted to what Mary called despotism, trying to force Eliza back into the marriage. He was so impatient that Mary worried about what might happen if she was not there to protect her sister. To Everina, Mary wrote, "I can't help pitying B but misery must be his portion at any rate till he alters himself—and that would be a miracle."

To Mary, it was now clear that Eliza's suffering had not come solely from the difficult experience of childbirth. She tried repeatedly to talk to Bishop, asking him to try to understand Eliza's fears. But Bishop refused to listen, insisting that there was nothing wrong, Mary wrote Everina, "even tho' the contrary is as clear as the noon day." By early January, Mary had made up her mind. She was not going to let Eliza continue to live with Bishop. She asked Ned if Eliza could seek refuge with him, but Ned refused, undoubtedly hoping to avoid a scandal, since it was illegal for wives to leave their husbands. This was an unfortunate turn of events, since if Eliza could have lived with their brother, she could have brought her baby along on what could have been called an extended family visit. Otherwise, she would have to leave little Mary behind, as eighteenth-century English mothers had no rights to their children. The baby was now five months old and could smile, nestle into loving arms, and even lift her head, but she was technically Bishop's property.

Despite the dangers she knew they would face, Mary began hatching plans for Eliza's escape, reassuring herself that they would rescue the baby as soon as Eliza was safe. Unlike Ned, she could not allow her sister to decline into madness, and she believed that if Eliza stayed with her husband, she would never fully recover. The universal principles of justice and morality decreed action, Mary felt. Locke had given her the theoretical premise she needed to justify her position: Bishop had abrogated his rights as a husband by infringing on Eliza's natural liberty. Indeed, Eliza's "situation" had ceased being only about Eliza. Freeing her from Bishop, whatever his "crimes" had been, was about freedom in all its forms: personal, sexual, financial, spiritual, legal, and political. Here at last was Mary's chance to redress the injustice she had railed against all her life. "Those who would save Bess [Eliza] must act and not talk," she wrote to Everina. The only questions left, as far as she was concerned, were where to go and when.

The proficiency with which Mary laid out her strategy made it seem as though she had been preparing for this emergency all her life. And in many ways, she had. Having failed at protecting their mother, Mary was determined to keep her sister from living life as a victim. She reserved a room in a lodging house in Hackney, a village about five miles north of central London, stashed supplies with Everina, who was still living in Ned's house on the other side of the river, and gathered up what little cash she could. When she whispered the plan to Eliza, her sister welcomed the idea, though she wept about not being able to take the baby.

On an overcast January day, they were ready. When Bishop left the house after lunch, Mary rushed to hail a coach, but just as Eliza was about to shut the front door, she frightened her sister by hesitating. She could not bring herself to separate from her child and refused to climb into the coach. Finally, Mary pulled her aboard. At first, it was a relief to drive away from the house, but on a busy afternoon it was impossible to avoid traffic, and with each stop, Eliza grew increasingly agitated. To Mary's horror, she got a wild look in her eyes and began gnawing her wedding ring. Mary tried to calm her, but Eliza would not stop until she had bitten the ring into pieces.

They changed coaches to throw Bishop off the trail, and after more than an hour of tense travel, they arrived at their quiet Hackney lodging house, where they registered using the somewhat unimaginative aliases "the Misses Johnson." Luckily, the proprietress, Mrs. Dodd, did not challenge their right to be there. "I hope Bishop will not discover us," Mary wrote to Everina when they were safely in their room, confessing that she "could sooner face a Lion" and that "my heart beats time with every carriage that rolls by and a knocking at the door almost throws me into a fit." Eliza, meanwhile, had become quite calm, sleeping peacefully while Mary kept anxious watch.

To Mary's relief, Bishop did not follow them. Instead, he sent a message through Ned that if Eliza would return he would "endeavor to make Mrs. B. happy." But Eliza, supported by Mary, refused to soften. Living with Bishop was out of the question, she told Ned, who, despite his initial refusal, had become the mediator between his sister and her husband. Bishop, furious at being rejected, refused to let Eliza see her daughter and cut her off without a penny.

Punishing errant wives by separating them from their children was almost as common as interring them in asylums, and was often more effective. After all, wives might hate their husbands, but they loved their babies. And no woman was immune from this treatment. The famous Georgiana, Duchess of Devonshire, put up with her husband's affairs, even accommodating his mistress in their home and raising his illegitimate children, because he had threatened to take her own daughters away if she did not submit to his wishes.

Even when there was evidence of cruel treatment, sympathy for a runaway wife was hard to come by. Mary heard rumors, probably spread by Bishop, that she was to blame for being "the shameful incendiary in this shocking affair" and for acting "contrary to all rules of conduct." Fortunately for the Wollstonecrafts, their close friends remained loyal. Mrs. Clare, the clergyman's wife, traveled up to Hackney with food and wine and offered to lend them money. The Bloods invited them to stay in their home. However, despite this support, the Wollstonecraft name had been sullied. Remarriage for Eliza was out of the question without a divorce, and, given the scandal, it was unlikely that Everina would attract any suitors. To survive, the sisters would have to find jobs, but that was a possibility only if prospective employers had not heard about Eliza's flight.

Mary's solution was something she had been dreaming of for a few years: they would start a school. Her friend Jane Arden had founded one with her sister a few years earlier, and in an enthusiastic letter, Mary had declared her support: "Let not some small difficulties intimidate you, I beseech you;—struggle with any obstacles rather than go into a state of dependence—I speak feelingly.—I have felt the weight, and would have you by all means avoid it."

Before Eliza's crisis, she had drummed up a few interested students. Now she turned her attention back to the many problems she faced. She needed funding and she needed students. But daunting though these were, she took heart from her success in freeing her sister from Bishop. After years of trying to save her mother from her father, she had rescued her sister from harm. Newly galvanized, she was confident that she could overcome the challenges that lay ahead.

She had also come to a new conclusion. After her immersion in the Bishop household, she realized Eliza's weakness was as much a problem as Bishop's anger and insensitivity. Frightened wives would never be able to stand up to their husbands, and cowering only made matters worse. If Eliza had been able to advocate for herself, she and Bishop might still be living together, and little Mary would be raised by a strong, self-respecting mother.

To Mary, this realization gave even more urgency to the idea of starting a school. Teaching girls to cultivate their minds and bodies so they could become independent would help create a society in which wives could defend themselves and single women could exist on their own terms. In this utopia, there would be no more need to rescue women like Eliza. They would be able to rescue themselves.

But even Mary Wollstonecraft could not start a school on the strength of her own zeal. She needed money, backers, and a building, all of which seemed impossible to obtain—until she met a Mrs. Burgh, the wealthy widow of the educator and author James Burgh, a well-known activist for educational reform. None of Mary's biographers know how the two women met, though it is possible that it was through the Clares. But all agree that Hannah Burgh offered Mary precisely what she needed at this crucial juncture in her life: funding, advice, and practical support.

Hannah Burgh's mission in life—bestowed on her by God, she believed—was to educate young women to be good Christians and useful citizens. Girls needed to learn how to be independent women so they could contribute to society. She did not agree with her contemporaries who held that all young middle-class women needed was to acquire a little polish by learning some French, knowing the latest dance steps, and playing a few light pieces on the piano. When she clapped eyes on Mary, a young woman who radiated intelligence, conviction, and confidence, Mrs. Burgh realized she had found just the right schoolmistress. Together, they could create an environment where girls would learn to live more meaningful and more virtuous lives. With admirable efficiency, the two women came to an agreement. Mrs. Burgh would supply Mary with a house and twenty students, and Mary would be free to run the school as she wished.

Mrs. Burgh did have one requirement, however: that they build the school in her own village, Newington Green, a center for Nonconformists since the Restoration. Two miles north of London, this pleasant rural hamlet did not look like a hotbed of dissent. It had all the attributes of a staid English village: a shady green in the center of the village populated by grazing sheep, stately Georgian houses, steepled churches, and flower gardens. A pretty river, which supplied London with fresh drinking water, wound past the outskirts of the town.

Yet Newington Green's residents were among the most radical in eighteenth-century England, drawn there by the town's revolutionary tradition and by the current minister of the Newington Green Unitarian Church, Dr. Richard Price, a famous insurrectionary preacher. Mary was about to enter a political and religious community unlike any she had known before and unlike any other in England.

Early in the spring of 1784, Mary left London to begin her new venture. She brought Everina and Eliza with her to serve as teachers. Together for the first time since their mother had died, the Wollstonecraft sisters settled into the huge empty house Mrs. Burgh had obtained for the school. Mary bought furniture, books, and needles for sewing; she hired a cook and maids with the tuition money that parents had sent in advance (half a pound each quarter). Two families decided to board their children, paying extra fees that helped cover expenses. Mary had written a series of letters to Fanny trying to persuade her to join them, and finally, to Mary's delight, she decided to come, arriving before the summer. Her lackluster fiancé, Hugh, was still in Portugal, showing no interest in marriage, and Fanny wanted to be with her dear friend. Although she was still weak from tuberculosis, she could contribute by teaching a few classes in botany and painting. Mary's world was now complete. She was with the woman she loved most in the world. She was living according to her most deeply held beliefs. She had achieved independence, although it was difficult to feel entirely independent when plagued by the worries of such an enterprise. How many students did she need to keep the school viable? Would parents protest if she implemented some of her revolutionary ideas? If even one of the families defaulted on tuition, she might have to close the doors.

But despite these fears, Mary resolved not to compromise. She wanted to teach her students to think for themselves. She had a few boys, but most of her students were girls, ranging from seven or eight years old to fifteen or sixteen, and she pushed them to go further than memorizing the literary truisms of the day: "I am sick of hearing of the sublimity of Milton, the elegance and harmony of Pope, and the original, untaught genius of Shakespeare," she declared. If her students learned to value their own minds, they might be less likely to succumb to the pitfalls of the fashionable world and better able to contribute to society. She believed that each of her pupils was unique and therefore required "a different mode of treatment"—a tenet of today's progressive schools, but an almost entirely original approach in 1784. Treat students as individuals! Require girls to use their reason! If conservatives got wind of what she was up to, she would be sharply criticized. Mary's fellow reformers, on the other hand, found her ideas so congenial that they invited her to join their weekly discussion group.

Dr. Richard Price, their leader, was sixty-two when Mary first met him. Short and thin with thick black eyebrows, a plain black coat, and a tightly ordered white wig, he had a stern appearance that belied his gentleness. He used his pulpit to preach Enlightenment ideals, speaking so quietly that it was difficult to hear him unless one sat in the front rows. That spring, he declared that the world was progressing, pointing to the American victory over the British as evidence—the Treaty of Paris that officially ended the American Revolution had been signed just months earlier. His list of supporters was a roll call of revolutionaries—Ben Franklin, John and Abigail Adams, Thomas Jefferson and Thomas Paine. Mary relished Price's optimism. Liberation from tyranny: this was his theme, and hers as well.

Like Jane's father and the Reverend Clare before him, Dr. Price immediately recognized Mary's originality and her eagerness to learn. But he was also interested in her passion for reform, and he shared her ambition for schooling future radicals. To Dr. Price, education was the pathway to a more perfect future. He pointed to America as an example; without an enlightened citizenry, he said, the American experiment would surely fail, which would in turn be a tragedy for all humankind. To Mary, this hit home. After all, education had changed her life. If she had not read Locke and found the words to express her feelings of injustice and rage, she might not now be fighting for freedom for herself and others. She might not have had the courage to save her sister. Starting a school was truly an elevated endeavor. It was not just a personal bid for independence but an avenue to reform. She would inspire her students to forge their own lives.

From the moment they arrived, Mary treated the children the way she wished she had been treated as a girl: with respect and tenderness. She championed healthy eating habits and vigorous exercise to help them become strong and capable. Instead of shaming them or doling out punishments, Mary won her students over with kindness and sympathy. She could not offer them French or music lessons, but there were plenty of students whose families could not afford to pay for a fancy education but who still needed to learn the basics. Instead of assigning readings from primers, Mary encouraged the children to compose their own stories. "Let there be no disguise for the genuine emotions of the heart," she would later write. She dismissed rote learning and encouraged her charges to think for themselves, to explore what lay off "the beaten track." Above all, she prized integrity, creativity, and self-discipline. In an era when other schools punished trifling mistakes with beatings and economized by restricting food and heat, when a young Jane Austen almost died from neglect at the Abbey School (a few generations later, the two eldest Brontë girls actually did die of tuberculosis at Cowan Bridge School), Mary's insistence on the physical, spiritual, and moral welfare of her students was a beacon of Enlightenment values.

Mary hoped that her sisters would follow her example and devote themselves to their teaching duties. But both Eliza and Everina disliked the long days and hard work and did their best to shirk their duties. They were supposed to teach reading, writing, and sewing. Everina also helped Fanny teach sketching. Unlike Mary, they did not want to change the world, student by recalcitrant student. They wanted a pleasant life with few demands. Eliza, who was still recovering from her harrowing escape, was fragile, and, in August, a month before her baby's first birthday, she received the terrible news that her daughter had died. Left in the care of maids and wet nurses, the child had weakened and caught a disease. To Mary, this was further evidence of Bishop's villainy; he had probably neglected his daughter to punish his renegade wife. Eliza never voiced regret for her decision, but she was left with a depression she could not shake. Her freedom had been purchased at the cost of her child's life.

Nineteen-year-old Everina was also struggling. Hardly older than her charges, she was finding it difficult to hold herself and the students to Mary's educational standards. She resented Mary's advice about how to manage a classroom and teamed up with Eliza, both of them complaining about their eldest sister behind her back. As a result, the three Wollstonecraft women were continuously on edge; there were flare-ups and countless spats. Her sisters' lassitude infuriated Mary. Didn't they realize how important this project was? Not only was their independence at stake, but they had the opportunity to improve women's lives and reform society.

But neither sister shared Mary's idealism. Nor did they have her drive to become independent. They did not have Mary's dreadful memories of working for the grumpy Mrs. Dawson. Instead, they expected Mary to take care of them, which was as it should be, they felt. She was their older sister; their mother had died; their father was useless; who else would look after them? They had no interest in joining Newington Green's intellectual community. They did not like being left to mind the students when Mary went to lectures and discussion groups. They were even more annoyed when a new friend of Mary's, the Reverend John Hewlett, an aspiring writer with literary connections, took her to meet the ailing Samuel Johnson without inviting them. Johnson was the most celebrated writer of the time; their sister was stealing the limelight, they said, while they, the drudges of the school, were overlooked and undervalued.

Mary's closeness to Fanny made matters still more difficult. She had never shared a house with her sisters and her friend at the same time, and the combination was disastrous. Mary herself was partially to blame; she refused to confide in her sisters or consult them on important decisions, leaving them feeling shut out, as though she discounted their opinions. They were irritated that she did not respect them as adults and treated them like the students. Fortunately, Fanny was a gentler soul than Mary and was adept at smoothing feathers. She stayed home when Mary went out and insisted on including the younger Wollstonecrafts in decisions concerning the school, despite Mary's resistance. By keeping the tension between Mary and her sisters from turning into full-blown fights, Fanny helped keep the school alive, but it was at the cost of her own health. She suffered from coughing fits and grew gradually weaker. Toward the end of the school's first year, just as the cold weather arrived in earnest, Fanny's tuberculosis worsened, and by the fall of 1784, it seemed clear that if she stayed in damp, chilly England, she was going to die. Terrified, Mary urged Fanny to contact the hesitant Hugh.

After having backpedaled for years, Hugh had recently written to tell Fanny he was ready for marriage; his business in Lisbon had become successful enough to support a family. But now that it was time to make this leap, Fanny was not so sure. Hugh had humiliated her by making her wait so long. In addition, she hadn't seen him in years. Their correspondence had been infrequent at best, as Hugh was not an inspired letter writer and the mail delivery between Portugal and England was unreliable. Above all, she would miss her beloved Mary. However, it was Mary who persuaded her to accept Hugh's proposal; in her mind it was better to lose Fanny to marriage than to death. Perhaps in hot, dry Lisbon her friend would get better. So, in January 1785, Fanny voyaged to Portugal to marry Hugh, who, it turned out, had aged considerably. "He is much fatter, and looks at least ten years older," Fanny wrote in February, also disclosing that she was pregnant after just one month of marriage.

When she heard this news, Mary was deeply concerned. Childbirth was a risky enough business for healthy women, but for those who were already weakened by chronic illness, it was a very dangerous and potentially fatal undertaking. She wanted to go straight to Fanny but was reluctant to leave the school in her sisters' hands. During the long summer break, she was torn, haunted by the possibility of losing her dearest friend but unwilling to jeopardize the school's future. Eliza and Everina were impossible to rely on and difficult to love: "I could as soon fly as open my heart to them," Mary wrote to Fanny's brother, George.

In June, Newington Green played host to two celebrities from across the ocean, John and Abigail Adams. At age fifty, Adams had come to London in 1785 as the first American ambassador. Rather than attend an elegant West End congregation, he and Abigail had chosen Dr. Price's church. Londoners sneered at them for preferring the old dissenter's sermons to the preaching of a more fashionable minister. However, to the Adamses, there was no question about which parish would be theirs. Price had been, and still was, one of the most notable advocates for the American cause. Price's ideas, said Adams, represented "the whole scope of my life." Besides, the Adamses fit in there. To the radicals of Newington Green, Abigail's homemade bonnets and John's awkward manners, both of which occasioned hilarity among fashionable West Enders, were reassuring evidence that this couple cared more about the principles of liberty than the latest London trends. Law was essential, Adams wrote, to protect the weak from the strong and to safeguard the liberty of each citizen. Not only did Abigail agree, she also championed legal protections for women as well, having written to her husband when he and his fellow colonials were on the brink of declaring independence,

> in the new code of laws which I suppose it will be necessary for you to make, I desire you would remember the ladies and be more generous and favorable to them than your ancestors. Do not put such unlimited power into the hands of the husbands. Remember all men would be tyrants if they could. If particular care and attention is not paid to the Ladies, we are determined to foment a Rebellion and will not hold ourselves bound by any Laws in which we have no voice, or Representation.

Although there is no record of Mary and the Adamses actually meeting that summer, it seems likely that in this small community their paths would have crossed. Certainly, Mary knew who the Adamses were, even if they were not yet aware of her. And soon enough the tables would turn—only a few years later, Abigail would become such a fan of Mary's work that John would call her a "disciple of Wollstonecraft." He himself would read Wollstonecraft's book on the French Revolution, writing in the margin when she praised the American Revolution, "I thank you Miss W. May we long enjoy your esteem."

By the fall of 1785, Mary could no longer assuage her worries about Fanny's health. She persuaded Mrs. Burgh to lend her money to book her passage to Lisbon. Though parents threatened to withdraw their children from the school if Mary was no longer at the helm, she brushed their concerns aside and set sail, arriving, after a thirteen-day voyage, just as Fanny's labor began. Four hours after Mary walked in the door, Fanny gave birth to a baby boy. But neither Hugh nor Mary could rejoice, because Fanny was severely weakened by the travail. Over the next few days, she slowly faded away, brightening only when she held her child or saw Mary. By the end of the week, both she and the baby had died.

For Mary, the loss was devastating. She tried to turn to faith, but she wrote to Fanny's brother that "life seems a burden almost too heavy to be endured. . . . My head is stupid, and my heart sick and exhausted. . . . I can only anticipate misery. . . . I hope I shan't live long."

# CHAPTER 7

# MARY GODWIN: "THE SUBLIME AND RAPTUROUS MOMENT"

[ 1814 ]

IN APRIL 1814, SHORTLY AFTER SIXTEEN-YEAR-OLD MARY returned from Scotland, Godwin warned his family to brace for the worst. His savings were all but depleted and he could be facing debtors' prison, humiliation, and ruin. As a last hope, he invited Shelley to dinner to urge the young man to make good on his promises of a loan.

When the fateful evening arrived, everyone was on edge, including Shelley. Thrown off course by his failed marriage, he felt demoralized and purposeless. But when he entered the drawing room at 41 Skinner Street, he knew instantly that something was about to change. A few nights earlier, on a long evening walk, he had seen "manifestations" that told him he would soon meet "the female who was destined to be mine," as he later wrote his college friend, Thomas Hogg. He had even begun to "compose a letter to Harriet on the subject of my passion for another." When the door of the drawing room opened and a pale girl with a blaze of red hair appeared, Shelley knew that his vision had just come true; this was the young woman of his dreams. She was Wollstonecraft's daughter, the one Godwin daughter he had yet to meet. Transfixed, he stared, while she, newly aware of her power over men after David Booth's attentions, allowed herself a flirtatious sidelong glance.

Shelley seemed the very essence of a Romantic poet, with his disheveled hair, muddy boots, and passionate eyes. He had a general air of disarray and bewilderment, as though the world were too extraordinary for him to fathom. He wore his shirt open, exposing a pale chest. A few months before, Hogg had described him as "wild, intellectual, unearthly; like a spirit that has just descended from the sky; like a demon risen at that moment out of the ground." For Godwin and Mary-Jane, Hogg's portrait would prove to be eerily predictive. At first, Shelley seemed angelic, but before long he would harm every one of the Godwin girls, whether he meant to or not.

*Portrait of Percy Bysshe Shelley by Amelia Curran, 1819.*

When they took their places at the table, Jane was her usual talkative self, while Mary remained silent. Their sister Fanny was absent. Earlier that spring, she had become so depressed that Mary-Jane had packed her off to visit her Wollstonecraft aunts; later, Mary-Jane would claim that Fanny's troubles were a result of her unrequited love for Shelley.

To Shelley, Mary seemed remote, as pale and distant as the moon—the image he would come to use for her in his poetry. She had "thoughtful" greenish-gray eyes, an oval face, a small mouth, and a "gentle" voice. Her most notable attribute, though, was her hair. According to Jane, it was "of sunny and burnished brightness like the autumnal foliage when played upon by the rays of the setting sun; it sets in round her face and falls upon her shoulders in gauzy wavings and is so fine it looks as if the wind had tangled it together into a golden network . . . it was so fine one feared to disturb the beauty." Though she was mostly silent, when she did talk, her frequent allusions and quotations revealed her erudition. Shelley was confounded. He had never met anyone like Mary Godwin. This is what her mother must have been like: an intellectual woman, a beautiful philosopher. His excitement grew as the dinner progressed. Here was the answer he had been seeking. Mary Godwin would spark his genius.

In many ways it seems inevitable that Percy Shelley would fall in love with Mary Godwin. He was already half in love before they met, fascinated by the idea that Godwin and Wollstonecraft, the two standard-bearers of political liberty whom he admired with an almost religious fervor, had a daughter. With such parents, Mary had to be exceptional. Even when he was still happily married to Harriet and had first met Godwin, he had gazed appreciatively at the large portrait of Mary Wollstonecraft in Godwin's study, intrigued to hear that young Mary was "very much like her mother." Two years later, he would immortalize her heritage:

> *They say that thou wert lovely from thy birth,*
> *Of glorious parents, thou aspiring Child.*
> *I wonder not—for One then left this earth*
> *Whose life was like a setting planet mild,*
> *Which clothed thee in the radiance undefiled*
> *Of its departing glory; still her fame*
> *Shines on thee, through the tempests dark and wild*
> *Which shake these latter days; and thou canst claim*
> *The shelter, from thy Sire, of an immortal name.*

As for Mary, she was watching Percy as carefully as he was watching her. Like him, she was already half in love. From time to time that first night, he looked at her as though he were drinking her in, staring straight into her eyes as no one else ever had. Later he would say that he could see her soul glowing like "a lamp of vestal fire."

By the end of dinner it seemed to Mary that Shelley was the most fascinating man on earth. She also suspected that there was no better way to win her father's heart than to befriend the young man. Godwin nodded after every word Shelley spoke, sending a signal to the family to defer to the young man's opinions. Mary was happy to oblige, though disappointed that Shelley was already married. She consoled herself that Harriet was nowhere to be seen and that Shelley had already hinted at tragedies unseen in their marriage, misunderstandings cruel and heartbreaking. In fact, to her, he seemed lost and uncertain, a child who needed love.

In the days that followed, Shelley and Mary saw each other when he came to dinner or when she worked behind the counter in the family's store. The more time they spent together, the more attracted they became. To Mary, Shelley seemed both glamorous and profound, the most appealing man she had ever met. However, she was well aware that if they had a love affair, she, like Isabella, would have to brave a hostile world; there were few greater taboos at the time than a liaison with a married man. But Mary felt certain her father would support her just as Isabella's father had given his blessing to his daughter. She knew her mother's story, that Wollstonecraft had had Fanny out of wedlock, and that Godwin had still married her. He was the great philosopher of freedom. He had loved Mary Wollstonecraft, who had scorned the rules of society. Surely he would endorse a love affair with Shelley, especially since he had recommended the young man so enthusiastically.

By June, Mary and Shelley wanted to meet privately, although still as "friends," and they enlisted Jane to help them steal away. Jane agreed, though she was jealous that Shelley had chosen Mary and not her. Little had changed between the sisters; Jane both envied and admired Mary and still followed her brilliant half sister's lead. Now Jane threw herself into helping the two young people arrange meetings and exchange messages, playing the role that Mary had with Isabella, enjoying the secrecy and the drama, but secretly hoping that Shelley might change his mind and pick her instead.

In the afternoon, the girls set out together from Skinner Street. Fanny had returned from her visit to the Wollstonecraft aunts, but Mary and Jane left her behind, not trusting her to keep Mary's secret. Once they were a safe distance from the house, Shelley appeared and Jane discreetly dropped back.

The London streets were lovely at this time of year. Shop owners planted tubs of geraniums; ladies strolled past in their colorful muslin frocks; the mercers flung their doors open, hoping to tempt shoppers with their silks and satins. There were gardens scattered throughout the city if you knew where to find them, which Shelley did. Later, a nosy gardener told Mrs. Godwin that Jane had walked alone up and down the paths of Charterhouse Square "while the fair young lady and the young gentleman always retired to sit in the arbour."

As their relationship intensified, it became increasingly difficult to hide their feelings from inquiring eyes. Thomas Hogg came to visit Shelley and accompanied him on the brief walk from Shelley's lodgings in Hatton Garden to Godwin's bookshop, where Hogg thought they were going to meet the famous philosopher. But when they got there, "the door was partially and softly opened," not by Godwin, Hogg recalled, but by a small figure who was "fair-haired, pale indeed, and with a piercing look." She was wearing a tartan, he remembered, and in "a thrilling voice called, 'Shelley!' A thrilling voice answered, 'Mary!'" She beckoned to Shelley and the young couple darted out of the room, leaving Hogg alone in the shop.

Matters grew more serious when Mary took Shelley to her sacred spot, her mother's grave in St. Pancras churchyard, and this soon became their favorite place to be alone. Here, they read aloud from books they carried with them, often Mary's mother's volumes, and discussed their favorite topics: Mary-Jane's boorishness, Harriet's lack of compassion, the sins of Shelley's father, freedom, literature, the imagination, and the potential for a true and equal love between a man and a woman. They were both intrigued by dreams, visions, and the question of what happened after death. Was there rebirth? Was there an afterlife? Did Mary's mother linger somewhere as a spirit, invisible to them, but alive all the same? Mary was sure she did; often, she could feel her "pale ghost" nearby. Difficult though it must

The Lovers' Seat *(1877): Victorian image of Shelley and Mary Godwin in old St. Pancras churchyard, painted long after both were dead.*

have been for her, Jane maintained a discreet distance, giving them the opportunity to talk without being overheard.

For the first six weeks of their relationship, they maintained a strict physical distance during these meetings. For them, language was a passionate medium, and conversation an essential component of an intimate union. Later, Shelley would explain to Hogg that he fell in love with Mary not because of her beauty or the delicacy of her manners, which were self-evident and which any man might admire, but because of her originality, which he felt surpassed his own "in genuine elevation and magnificence." He was also drawn to the "wildness and sublimity of her feelings" and her capacity for "ardent indignation and hatred" toward society's injustices. Mary was moved when Shelley, a man whose friendship her father valued and needed, who had boldly published his own ideas though he was persecuted for his beliefs, told her how miserable he had been before he met her, how his marriage to Harriet was a sham, and how, during the past winter, he had "resigned all prospects of utility or happiness," exhausted, trapped in a union that was "a gross & despicable superstition."

In mid-June, Shelley dined at the Godwins' ten nights in a row. Oddly, Mary-Jane and Godwin did not appear to notice the growing attraction between the two young lovers, even though each evening they disappeared from the house for hours, ostensibly to take long walks. Perhaps this is because they always left with Jane in tow, or maybe it was because the Godwins were preoccupied with their money troubles. At any rate, without Fanny to act as informer, they remained entirely in the dark.

Finally, on June 27, Mary took matters into her own hands. She stood in front of her mother's gravestone, looked straight into Shelley's eyes, and did what no young woman was supposed to do: she declared she loved him and threw herself into his arms. As Shelley remembered it, Mary was inspired "by a spirit that sees into the truth of things. . . . The sublime and rapturous moment when she confessed herself mine, who had so long been hers in secret cannot be painted to mortal imaginations."

They lay on the grass and touched each other with the "full ardour of love," as Mary later reported. What exactly she meant by these words is not clear. It seems unlikely that they fully consummated their relationship on Wollstonecraft's grave, given all the difficulties involved—Mary's inexperience and the public setting, not to mention the complicated undergarments worn by Englishwomen. Nevertheless, both of them marked this day as the start of their sexual relationship.

Both Mary and Shelley would have been startled to know that this intensely private moment would become famous, that their kisses would be discussed in literary conferences and college classrooms, their affair the subject of speculation and a focal point for literary critics. But the union of Shelley and Mary is a literary moment like no other. Their love would beget some of the greatest works of the entire Romantic movement. Shelley would immortalize his feelings for Mary in the dedication of his poem *The Revolt of Islam*:

> *How beautiful and calm and free thou wert*
> *In thy young wisdom, when the mortal chain*
> *Of Custom thou didst burst and rend in twain.*

For Mary, this was her first moment of unrestrained self-expression, her chance to assert her own radical ideas about relationships. It was also a way to leave Skinner Street, a way to break free from Mary-Jane. Always her mother's daughter, she believed she and Percy could make their own rules. Later, Shelley would capture her words in his poem *Rosalind and Helen,* in which Mary's alter ego, Helen, tells her lover, "But our church shall be the starry night, / Our altar the grassy earth outspread, / And our priest the muttering wind."

Afterward, they referred to this date as Shelley's birthday, the day he was truly born, but it would have been more accurately described as Mary's birthday, since it was her life that would take the more decisive turn. Shelley was already a social outcast; he had been expelled from college for atheism, broken ties with his father, and eloped with Harriet. An affair with Mary could not do his reputation much more harm. But by kissing Shelley, Mary had committed a far graver offense than Shelley ever could; the conventions that governed women's behavior were far stricter than those that governed men's. In Jane Austen's novel *Mansfield Park*—which was being readied for publication even as Mary was lying down in the grass with Shelley—the doom that came to young women who stray was laid out with the exactitude of a Greek tragedy. Pretty Maria, who runs away with a handsome scoundrel, is ruined, condemned to spend the rest of her life in exile.

These were the rules and Mary knew them—all genteel young women did—and yet, although she suspected there would be trouble, she did not dread the future. Just the opposite. This is what she had been dreaming of, a grand romance! She felt as though she had been led into a sacred precinct where few had traveled, and she listened raptly to Shelley's stories of suffering, never suspecting that many of them were false. Shelley claimed untruly that his father had once banished him to a mental asylum. He also hinted that his wife Harriet had been unfaithful and that he was not sure if the baby she was expecting was really his—another fabrication.

Confronted with such a tangle of truth and deception, it would be easy to regard Shelley as a libertine who wanted to take advantage of Mary's naïveté. But that was not what Mary ever believed, even when she was older and could see Shelley, and the details of their situation, with more perspective. In fact, she never faulted Shelley for his tales, understanding that he usually believed the stories he wove. Certainly, Shelley *felt* his stories were true. Harriet may not have been unfaithful to him with a lover, but she had betrayed him by changing after she had a baby. In his mind, philosophical infidelity was a far graver offense than any sexual dalliance could ever be. His father may not have literally put him in an asylum, but to the young Shelley it felt as though he had. After Shelley's atheistic declarations at Oxford, Sir Timothy had prevented the young man from having any contact with his beloved mother and younger sisters, telling the family that Percy was insane. Cruel and punitive, Sir Timothy had tried to stop his son's allowance, even when it meant that Percy might go to debtors' prison. For Percy, it was an easy next step to believe his father wanted to see him imprisoned.

At any rate, Mary was not suspicious by nature, and did not waste time trying to sift through Shelley's tales for the truth. Driven by her own agenda, she yearned to live up to her mother's legacy and get out from under her stepmother's thumb. Later, Harriet, who had an understandably bitter take on what happened, wrote, "Mary was determined to seduce him. She is to blame. She heated his imagination by talking of her mother and going to her grave with him every day, till at last she told him she was dying of love for him." In truth, Mary would never have denied the role she played in initiating her relationship with Shelley. She was proud of it. Having assumed her father would give his blessing to their affair, she was shocked to discover the opposite was true. When she and Shelley announced their love to the Godwins in early July, her horrified father ordered Mary to the schoolroom and banished Shelley from the house. Godwin, however, had underestimated the lovers. Incipient writers that they were, they immediately applied themselves to composing long epistles that Jane delivered, delighted at being an insurrectionary go-between.

As the days passed, the drama escalated. Harriet, alerted by rumors, had set up residence in her father's London house, and on July 14, Shelley called a formal meeting with her, telling her their marriage was over. He reported this event to Godwin, thinking it would win the older man's approval. But Godwin, appalled at Shelley's behavior, rushed to Harriet the next day reassuring her he would argue her case with Shelley and Mary. That afternoon, he lectured his daughter on the dire consequences of her actions, until Mary reluctantly promised she would stop encouraging Shelley's affections.

But Godwin's efforts to put a stop to the affair were undercut by his own financial desperation. Even as he was trying to separate the two young lovers, he was still seeking to finalize a loan from Shelley; during the third week of July, he met with Shelley each afternoon to discuss financial affairs. But if Godwin could carry on these conversations as though nothing were amiss, Shelley could not, and finally the young man snapped. In the last week of July, he hammered on the door at Skinner Street, rushed past the maid, shoved Mrs. Godwin out of the way, and charged up the stairs to Mary. By the time Mary-Jane caught up with him, he had a pistol out and was waving it around with a wild look on his face, shouting that he could not live without Mary. He pulled out a bottle of laudanum and shook it, declaring that if Mary swallowed the drugs, he would shoot himself and they would be together in death like Romeo and Juliet, or Tristan and Isolde. Mary-Jane screamed in horror. Godwin might have been able to soothe Shelley's frayed sensibilities, but he was not there, and so Mary, with tears streaming down her cheeks, pleaded with her lover to calm down and go back home. She swore she would never love another man, and declared that he must not kill himself.

Shelley left, but later that week his landlord banged on the God-

wins' door, shouting that Shelley had swallowed a large dose of laudanum. By the time Godwin and Mary-Jane reached Shelley's rooms,
a doctor was already there tending to the overwrought patient. Mrs.
Godwin stayed with Shelley the next day, nursing him until he felt
better.

While Shelley was recovering, Mary brooded upstairs in the
schoolroom, rereading his letters and studying his long poem *Queen
Mab*. In a note at the end of the poem he declared that any law that
required husband and wife to live together "after the decay of their
affection, would be a most intolerable tyranny." Here was Shelley's
rationale for ending his relationship with Harriet and beginning
his affair with Mary. To say that a person was forever bound by his
marital vows was an infringement of that person's natural rights, he
declared. Mary agreed, of course. These were the same ideas her parents had espoused—that is, before Godwin's retraction. To Mary, it
seemed clear that marriage was an absurd institution. Who could
control the heart? One should not stay with someone simply because
of society's rules. One must always be true to one's passions. As her
lover declared, "Love is free," and "to promise for ever to love the
same woman is not less absurd than to promise to believe the same
creed."

She scrawled her own note in the back of the precious volume:

> This book is sacred to me and as no other creature shall ever
> look into it I may write in it what I please—yet what shall I
> write that I love the author beyond all powers of expression
> and that I am parted from him.
>
> Dearest and only love by that love we have promised to
> each other although I may not be your[s] I can never be an-
> other's
>
> But I am thine exclusively thine—by the kiss of love

Mary may have thought Shelley would never read these words.
Forced to remain at home, it seemed possible she would not see him
again; so she wrote down his last words to her, as reverentially as
though he had uttered them on his deathbed:

*I remember your words, you are now*
*Mary going to mix with many and for a*
*Moment I shall depart but in the solitude of*
*Your chamber I shall be with you—yes you*
*Are ever with me sacred vision.*

But if self-abnegation came easily to Mary, it did not to Shelley. While she read and reread his poetry, locked away on the top floor like Rapunzel, Shelley raged at his helplessness. Nothing raised his ire more than being prevented from doing what he wanted; his goal in life was to free himself (and others, to be sure) from oppression. His delight in carrying off Harriet had largely stemmed from his triumph over Mr. Westbrook and his own father rather than from any deep romantic feelings. He had even dreamed of kidnapping his own sisters and taking them along to further undermine his father's authority. Thus Godwin's attempts to block his access to Mary, rather than thwarting his desire, stirred Shelley further, inspiring him to take drastic action.

Of course, Shelley's definition of *oppression* was somewhat idiosyncratic. As a little boy, he had shrugged off the limits his father tried to place on him, reasonable though they may have been (no snakes in the house; no playing with fire). He ran away when he was disciplined, chopped down his father's precious fir trees, poked holes in the ceiling to find fairies, used gunpowder to blow up the playground fence and his schoolroom desk, accidentally set the butler on fire, and terrorized his sisters with ghost stories and experiments. His younger sister Hellen remembered how he would "collect" his little sisters and "plac[e]" them "hand-in-hand around the nursery table to be electrified." One night, while tinkering with electricity, he ignited his parents' baronial estate. The flames were put out, but the young Shelley, rather than being chastened, was disappointed he had not destroyed the house.

By the time Shelley met Mary, his enthusiasm for his "experiments" had grown, not lessened with age as his father had hoped. Like most intellectuals of the era, Shelley regarded science as a branch of philosophy, or sometimes as an offshoot of the occult. He searched for spirits as avidly as he stared through his solar microscope, studied chemistry even as he sought to summon the devil. One night, he sneaked into a church to spend the night in the burial vault, hoping to see ghosts. Shelley's scientific explorations were of great interest to Mary, since she, too, was intrigued by the idea that electricity, or electrical fire, could spark birth, animate the inanimate, and bring the dead back from the grave. Not that she truly believed such things were possible, but it was a compelling idea: the power of natural forces over human life.

For Shelley, such "explorations" remained linked to his father. In his mind, scientific inquiry, apparitions, explosions, fire balloons, ghouls, individual freedom, justice, love, and rebellion were all jumbled together. And so, while Mary sat quietly in her garret, reading and writing, Shelley applied his powers of invention to coming up with a plan of escape that would free his love from her prison, and better yet, would assert his will over Godwin's. It would be a grand adventure, a thrilling new innovation, to run away with Mary Godwin. The world needed to be stirred up, enlivened, and turned upside down, and he was the one to do it.

# CHAPTER 8

# MARY WOLLSTONECRAFT:
## *ON THE EDUCATION*
## *OF DAUGHTERS*

———

[ 1785–1787 ]

A HEARTBROKEN MARY WOLLSTONECRAFT SAILED TO ENGLAND from Portugal in December 1785. Fanny Blood's death made it seem impossible to go forward. When she arrived in Newington Green, the days were dark; the water had frozen in the washbasins; her sisters acted aggrieved and put upon. The school was limping along, but only barely; many students had dropped out and more were planning to leave. But without Fanny, Mary no longer cared. And so when Mrs. Burgh decided they should close at the end of the academic year, Mary didn't protest. "I can scarcely find a name for the apathy that has seized on me—I am sick of everything under the sun," she wrote Fanny's brother George. She blamed herself for Fanny's loss. If only she had not encouraged her friend to marry Hugh, then Fanny would still be with her; the students would be flourishing, and she would not have to worry about what would become of her younger sisters, or herself. "My hopes of happiness are extinct," she said.

By spring, the last student was gone. Although Mrs. Burgh had provided much of the financial backing for the school, Mary had borrowed money to cover her own expenses and those of her sisters. Now creditors were demanding payment, chasing her like "furies." One night she had a dream that Fanny beckoned to her, telling Mary to come join her in heaven. Her friends saw her despair and were worried. What had happened to Mary's grand ideas and conviction? Where was the energetic young woman who had arrived two years earlier? In her place was a bleak and dispirited twenty-six-year-old, as lost as she had once been sure.

Fortunately, John Hewlett, the friend who had taken her to meet Samuel Johnson, had an inspiration. Five years younger than Mary, Hewlett had admired Mary's fiery idealism when they first met at the Newington dinners. An intellectual and a mathematician, he agreed with her ideas about education and, more to the point, felt confident he could help her overcome her grief. Mary should write a book, he said. The world needed to hear her ideas.

A devout Christian, Hewlett told Mary that she had lessons to learn from Fanny's loss: if she could remember the transience of human life, that the pleasures of this world are fleeting, then she could devote herself to the true path of virtue, which was "the diligent improvement" of her "intellectual powers." Indeed, according to Hewlett, this is what God was: pure intellect, a perfect brain without human weaknesses. Grief-stricken though Mary was, she liked the idea that it was her God-given duty to devote herself to her studies. When Hewlett suggested that it was her Christian obligation to go back to work and that Fanny herself would want Mary to continue her mission to reform education, she listened.

And so, once the last student had gone, Mary began writing. She wanted to show the world how difficult it was for single women to support themselves. In her heart, she linked this problem to Fanny. If Fanny had been able to make more money, if she could have supported her family financially, she might not have felt the need to marry, and if she had not married, she would still be alive.

Fueled by her sense of injustice, Mary felt her energy return. It was not fair that unmarried women like herself and her sisters had so few choices. She asked herself why women's options were so restricted. Not only was this bad for women, it was bad for the world. Within a few weeks, she had produced forty-nine pages, *Thoughts on the Education of Daughters: With Reflections on Female Conduct, in the More Important Duties of Life*. As the length of this title indicates, Mary wanted to be taken seriously. Not only was she writing to give advice, she was writing to assert her rights as a rational being. With Fanny, her sisters, and herself in mind, she composed a chapter called "[The] Unfortunate Situation of Females, fashionably educated, and left without a fortune." The chapter begins:

> Few are the modes of earning a subsistence [for the single woman], and those very humiliating. . . . Painfully sensible of unkindness, she is alive to every thing, and many sarcasms reach her. . . . She is alone, shut out . . . dependent on the caprice of a fellow creature.

For the time, Mary's ideas were highly original, as was her voice. In 1786, no one else had detailed the suffering of young women seeking independence, except to warn against the dangers of prostitution. Unlike other writers, who relied on formal pronouncements to convey their authority, Mary used a colloquial voice to express her sense of outrage. She wrote to survive, emotionally and financially—her debts were mounting—and she was able to write quickly because over the course of the previous two years, she had discussed her ideas on childrearing, schools, women, education, and marriage with her friends and at the Newington supper meetings until they were fully developed, ready to pour onto the page. Who was the ideal woman? Mary asked. Was she a fainting maiden, easily fatigued and naïve? No! She was a resourceful intelligent human being.

Mary, as usual, was alone with her ideas, a single candle in the darkness. Despite the popularity of advice manuals on the "education" of women, written by comparatively enlightened authors, the tone of these purported experts was absurdly patronizing, even though many were women themselves. The poet Anna Barbauld, herself an accomplished writer and schoolmistress, declared girls too "delicate" to be independent from men, even as she took care of her mentally ill husband and was her family's sole provider. For Barbauld, females were created "for pleasure and delight alone," and, therefore, teachers should focus on teaching girls how to please. The bluestocking Hannah More believed that parents and teachers should drive the "bold, independent, enterprising spirit" out of girls while nurturing it in boys—a philosophy based on the principle that women should be subordinate to men and learn to obey, not lead. Mary found these ideas intolerable. Although she reserved judgment about just how strong the female mind would prove to be when educated—she argued that until women's talents were cultivated, no one would know their true capabilities—she was certain that training girls to be simpering society misses was not only bad for the girls, but bad for everyone. It created a generation of silly young women, unable to support their husbands in times of crisis, raise their children, or contribute to their communities.

Hewlett raced the finished manuscript to a friend, Joseph Johnson. One of the most famous publishers in London, Johnson was committed to the cause of reform. His authors were among the most radical of the era—Benjamin Franklin, William Blake, Erasmus Darwin (the grandfather of the famous Charles), Joseph Priestley, and William Cowper. Bringing such writers before the public eye was a dangerous business in the late eighteenth century. Publishers could face charges of treason if their writers criticized the government, which almost all of Johnson's authors did. But Johnson felt a personal and ethical obligation to his authors. In 1799, he would land in prison for bringing out a pamphlet that lambasted Parliament.

Johnson instantly understood that Mary's book had commercial potential and invited her to come to the city to discuss the possibility of publication. In the late eighteenth century, reformers and their opponents had become increasingly preoccupied with the question of women's education. The experts agreed with Mary that a mother who had been educated improperly could wreak havoc on society by raising selfish, spoiled children. But debate raged about what the proper curriculum for young women should be. If women were weaker than men, as the medical professionals decreed, then one had to be careful not to overly tax a female's brain. Mary's cogent arguments for improving women's education and expanding opportunities for women to earn a living spoke directly to these concerns. Moreover, her writing style was uniquely accessible. She wrote the way she spoke, directly and without any unnecessary flourishes, a conscious decision on Mary's part, as she hated the flowery style of other authors, both female and male. Eager to meet such a distinguished personage, Mary promptly took the coach to Johnson's offices near St. Paul's.

At age forty-eight, Johnson was short and plainly dressed with simple manners that put Mary at ease. When he offered her ten pounds for her manuscript, Mary was astonished. Although she was a literary novice, she knew enough to realize that Johnson's endorsement was extraordinary, and she was even more taken aback when Johnson upped the ante, making an unusual offer: if she sent him any new work, he would consider publishing it. By the time she left his offices, Mary had glimpsed a new and different path, one out of the reach of most people, let alone a twenty-seven-year-old spinster— the path to a real literary career.

With this new dream, the future suddenly seemed more appealing, though there was still the money problem. Ten pounds was a significant amount—the equivalent of £1,500 today—but it would not cover what she owed. In addition, she had her sisters to provide for, and she wanted to help the Bloods, who were also suffering financially. She needed a job, one that would support her until she could earn a living from her writing. Her friends put the word out,

*Joseph Johnson, one of the most famous publishers in London.*

and early that summer an offer came through Dr. Price. Robert and Caroline King, Lord and Lady Kingsborough of Mitchelstown, Ireland, needed a governess. They liked the sound of Mary; she was the correct age and she was an experienced schoolmistress. They were willing to pay £40 for a year's service, a far more generous salary than Mary had anticipated. She estimated (inaccurately, as it would turn out) that £20 would pay off her debts, and the other £20 could help her and her sisters start a new life.

As Lady Kingsborough wanted her to begin right away, Mary arrived in Mitchelstown in October 1786. Most people were impressed by the splendor of the Kingsborough estate, but Mary felt she had entered a prison. Her loyalties lay with the tenant farmers, whose hovels she had passed on the approach to her new home. Circumstances had forced her—she, who hated oppression in all its forms—to live with those she despised, English overlords who had stolen Irish land. And Lord and Lady Kingsborough were not just any overlords; they were the largest landowners in Ireland. They had received their seat in County Cork as a reward for their enthusiastic participation in the wars against the Irish. In return, they helped enforce British rule—an unjust system in Mary's eyes, which effectively established two different codes, one for Irish Catholics and another for English Protestants. Catholics could not hold office, vote, carry a gun, become lawyers, go to school, or even own an expensive horse. The English, on the other hand, felt entitled to enjoy their freedoms at the expense of their Irish neighbors.

Mitchelstown was a large, castle-like house, renovated in the latest style. A long yew-lined avenue led toward the pillared mansion and its outbuildings—stables, laundry, kitchens, bakery, blacksmith, and offices, all connected by open colonnades. This was precisely the kind of excess Mary disliked—why should the employers have so much and their tenants so little? Even the glorious location chilled her soul. Originally a fortress, the estate was as isolated and difficult to leave as an island, deepening Mary's feeling of imprisonment. To improve his view, Lord Kingsborough had razed the original village and had it moved to another nearby location out of his sight.

When Mary was shown into the front hall, she saw that the rape of Proserpina was painted on the ceiling, the young maiden's arms flung back in helplessness as she was ravaged. Rape was an occupational hazard of being a governess. Although Charlotte Brontë would romanticize the relationship between a young governess and her employer a generation later in *Jane Eyre,* there was nothing consensual about what happened to those governesses who fell victim to their employers' sexual advances. Mary had heard whispers that Lord Kingsborough, a famous philanderer, had taken advantage of the last governess and that Lady Kingsborough had dismissed her out of spite. In the large receiving room, Mary met a battery of well-trained servants and "a host of females—my Lady—her step mother, and three sisters—and Mrse's [*sic*] and Misses without number." To her dismay, the ladies examined her with the most minute attention. Faced with these stiff women in their jewel-encrusted gowns, their towers of hair making them seem much taller than they were, her confidence began to slip. "I am sure much more is expected from me than I am equal to," she confessed to Everina.

At first Lady Kingsborough was gracious to the new member of her household. Married at age fifteen, her ladyship was barely thirty when she hired Mary, and she prided herself on being a good employer. She gave Mary presents and paid her small flattering attentions, inviting her to dine with the family and attend balls and concerts with them. Highly placed servants like governesses were usually grateful for such gestures, but Mary, filled with both pride and shame, brushed off her ladyship's attempts, prickling at her gifts and refusing her invitations. Even if she had wanted to go to the Kingsboroughs' parties, she did not have the money to buy a new dress or to pay a maid to style her hair.

Mary's refusals mystified her ladyship. She had wanted a conventional governess—someone who was deferential and modest and would rush to do her bidding. But Mary was more radical than ever, having spent the previous summer studying political philosophy, as though she were preparing to lead a revolution rather than educate the scions of an aristocratic family. Of course, she had also worked on improving her skills in the subjects she was expected to teach—French, music, and art—but only cursorily, as she had resented her new job before she even got there.

Mary included her charges in her general condemnation of Mitchelstown. "Wild," she thought contemptuously when she first laid eyes upon stocky, spotted Margaret, age fourteen, and her two prettier sisters, Caroline, age twelve, and seven-year-old Mary. The girls were united in their desire to drive this new governess away, and Mary wrote them off as "not very pleasing."

However, before long Mary began to pity her students. Lady Kingsborough had little use for her children, having, as Mary said, "no softness in her manners." Her ladyship liked parties and enjoyed flirting and gossiping about her friends and their love affairs. No one, it seemed, was faithful to anyone else. At home, she turned to her yappy dogs for entertainment, cradling them in her arms during tea, laughing as they ran through her chambers, chewed up pillows, or nipped at Mary's heels, and ignoring them when they relieved themselves in the middle of the room. She spoke to them in baby talk, a mode of address that Mary disapproved of with children, let alone animals.

About a month into Mary's stay, the three girls fell ill. Instead of caring for her daughters, Lady Kingsborough avoided their sickbeds. Mary, appalled at her ladyship's cold heart, immediately stepped in, taking over their care. Mary's kindness was a new experience for the Kingsborough daughters, and their rebelliousness evaporated. Margaret, who, as the eldest, had taken the brunt of Lady Kingsborough's ill humors and was "very much afraid of her mother," grew the most attached. Mary understood what it felt like to have a cold and distant mother and reached out to the girl, discovering before long that Margaret was intelligent and had a loving disposition.

In the schoolroom, Mary did not hide her contempt for Lady Kingsborough or her disdain for the shallow life of society women. To the astonishment of her charges, she called the accomplishments their mother deemed so important—fancy needlework and French pleasantries—a "heap of rubbish."

Every morning she took the children for walks outside—an innovation for the sisters, who were used to being cooped up in the schoolroom—and created lessons based on their questions and observations. Concerned about their lack of compassion for the poor, she took them to visit the tenant farmers. In the schoolroom, she not only talked to them about their ideas, she comforted them when they were worried or sad. Having never met a person like Mary, someone who took them seriously and actually cared about their feelings, by Christmas, all three girls were devoted to their governess.

But the affection of her students was not enough to disperse the cloud that hung over Mary's head. Even the news that *Thoughts on the Education of Daughters* had appeared in the London bookstalls did not cheer her up. At night, she closed the door to her room at the back of the enormous house and wept over the loss of Fanny, as well as the sacrifice of her independence. She penned unhappy letters to her sisters. Only gradually, as the winter deepened, did she act on her dream of being a full-time author, sketching out an idea for a book in which she could express her outrage at her situation in life and reveal the ideas and opinions she had to keep hidden while working at Mitchelstown.

By January, Mary no longer hid her criticism of Lady Kingsborough's "haughti[ness]" and "condescension." Although she was pleased that she was treated as a gentlewoman, her position remained a lonely one. More than eighty servants worked for Lord and Lady Kingsborough, but she had as little in common with them as she did with the aristocrats. She was trapped in a strange netherworld between classes—"betwixt and between," as she said.

On those occasions when she did join Lady Kingsborough's elegant soirees, Mary sought out what she called "rational" company, particularly if the rational individual was a handsome man. But her ladyship disapproved. To her way of thinking, Mary did not act as a servant should; instead of retiring into the shadows where she belonged, she thrust herself into the center of animated conversations, stealing attention from her mistress. Toward the end of March, Mary wrote Everina about a friend of Lord Kingsborough, George Ogle, who was "between forty and fifty—a genius and unhappy. Such a man, you may suppose would catch your sister's eye." However, Lady

Kingsborough also liked Ogle, and she competed with Mary for his attention, increasing the friction between them. Mary took pleasure in triumphing over her ladyship, telling Everina, "Lady K. has chosen him for her flirt—don't mistake me—her flirtations are very harmless and she can neither understand nor relish his conversation."

As the spring turned slowly into summer, tensions were compounded by Margaret's rebellious behavior. Inspired by Mary, Margaret protested against her mother's teas and resisted making a society marriage. She wanted an education, not a husband, and having absorbed her governess's contempt for fashion, shocked her mother with her "disgust to the follies of dress, equipage & the other usual objects of female vanity." Lady Kingsborough may have been willing to overlook the oddities of her governess, but she had plans for her daughter—potential suitors had already been picked out—and it was Mary's job to help bring these plans to fruition.

But Mary's restlessness had become impossible to hide. In the privacy of her room, after the girls were asleep, she read Rousseau's *Émile,* relishing the author's glorification of his hero's sensitivity. Perhaps her own moods were symptoms not of weakness but of greatness. She filled her letters with descriptions of her aches and inner torments, wearing them like badges. She told her sisters that one day at church her nerves were so disordered, "I fell into . . . a violent fit of trembling . . . and it continued in a lesser degree all day—I very frequently am very near fainting and have almost always a rising in my throat, which I know to be a nervous affection."

However, although she admired Rousseau's writing and was inspired by the importance he attached to emotions and political freedom, she did not like his depiction of women. She grumbled that Sophie, Rousseau's heroine in *Émile,* existed solely for the benefit of the hero and that her only role was to desire and be desired, to attract and charm. Where was Sophie's inner life? "Rousseau declares that a woman should never, for a moment, feel herself independent," Mary wrote, "that she should be governed by fear . . . and made a coquettish slave in order to render her a more alluring object of desire, a *sweeter* companion to man." It was time, she declared, to show readers "the mind of a woman."

That June, Mary devoted her time to what was fast becoming a novel. On the opening page, in the novel's "advertisement," she announced that her heroine would not be a "Sophie," but would be a woman with "thinking powers," a character different from those generally portrayed by male novelists. With an autobiographical flourish, she named her heroine Mary and structured most of the plot using elements from her own life: an oppressive father named Edward and a best friend who dies of consumption while living in Lisbon. In the second half, Mary is forced to marry a villain and collapses on her deathbed before the marriage can be consummated, rejoicing that she will soon enter "that world where there is neither marrying nor giving in marriage." Throughout, Mary emphasized the interior life of her heroine, determined to demonstrate that women do not simply exist for the benefit of men. She also took revenge on her enemies, particularly Lady Kingsborough, who is the basis for the heroine's mother:

> She had . . . two most beautiful dogs, who shared her bed, and reclined on cushions near her all the day. These she watched with the most assiduous care, and bestowed on them the warmest caresses. This fondness for animals was not the kind of *attendrissement* which makes a person take pleasure in providing for the subsistence and comfort of a living creature; but it proceeded from vanity, it gave her an opportunity of lisping out the prettiest French expressions of ecstatic fondness, in accents that had never been attuned by tenderness.

Although *Mary* shares many of the characteristics of other novels of the period—a sighing, weeping heroine, a gothic plot—Mary's dark vision of marriage is antithetical to the eighteenth-century principle that a happy wedding should reward a well-behaved heroine. Having witnessed the suffering of both her mother and her sister, Mary hoped to galvanize her readers, to stir them to fight for a world where women were allowed to develop freely without being fettered by, or abused by, men.

Mary finished the first draft late in the summer of 1787. By the time it was completed, she was consumed with impatience at her own lowly position. Even Margaret's loyalty did not assuage her despair. She was tired of swallowing annoyances, enduring trivial conversations, and pretending she did not have opinions. In July she and Lady Kingsborough had several full-blown quarrels, and by the end of August her ladyship finally dismissed Mary, casting her out into the world without a job or a place to stay.

This was just the dramatic break Mary needed. She packed her bags with relief, angry but not afraid. Although they would never meet again, Mary would rail against Lady Kingsborough for the rest of her life, using her ladyship as the basis for many critical portraits of the aristocracy in her future work. Lady Kingsborough, on the other hand, was convinced that Mary had ruined her daughters. Only Margaret viewed her governess's tenure with satisfaction. Later in life, long after Mary was dead, she declared that Mary had "freed her mind from all superstitions." She made an unhappy marriage, but instead of resigning herself to a life of suffering, Margaret rebelled, disguising herself as a man to train as a doctor in Germany, then moving with her lover to Italy. Mary's grown daughter, the motherless Mary Shelley, would one day seek out Margaret, giving Margaret the opportunity to befriend her beloved governess's daughter, just as Wollstonecraft had once befriended her.

# CHAPTER 9

# MARY GODWIN:
# THE BREAK

—

## [ 1814 ]

*I*N THE DAYS IMMEDIATELY FOLLOWING HIS DRAMATIC INVASION OF Skinner Street, Shelley swung into action, sending notes with detailed plans to Mary via a bribed servant after Jane was caught delivering their letters. Having eloped three years earlier, he knew exactly how to proceed, and he was happy to discover that, unlike Harriet, Mary was not dismayed by the prospect of living with a man out of wedlock. This was precisely the kind of excitement she had dreamed of in Scotland. She had no use for custom; what did marriage matter when two hearts were one? Her only hesitation was leaving her father.

For all the complexity that marked Jane and Mary's relationship—the competition, the jealousy, the one-upmanship—Jane was still Mary's only true confidante. Fanny would have felt duty bound to report all to Godwin. Jane, on the other hand, enjoyed being in on the secret. Her only caveat was that she did not want to be left behind. Not only did she dread the prospect of facing Godwin and Mary-Jane after the lovers had fled, she hated that Mary was always the special one. First Godwin, and now Shelley.

Well aware of Jane's envy, Mary was not eager to have her stepsister join them, but Shelley liked the idea of releasing two young women from domestic imprisonment. It had been his dream for his own younger sisters. Besides, Jane would be a fine addition to their trip. She was a vivacious, ringleted sixteen-year-old, and she spoke French, which would be helpful since they hoped to reach Paris. He would even have liked to bring Fanny, but he agreed with Mary that the poor pliant nineteen-year-old could not be counted on to keep quiet about their plans.

Shelley sent word to the two girls to meet him on July 28 at four in the morning. On the night before, Mary and Jane tried to act normally. They joined the family for dinner and retired to bed at the usual time. If Mary-Jane and Godwin had been more attentive, perhaps they would have noticed that Mary was a little more pale and Jane less talkative than usual. But instead, they said good night to their daughters and settled down to sleep, never suspecting the drama that was about to unfold. The girls lay awake, their nerves stretched taut. Jane was excited for their adventure to begin, but Mary was anxious. She wanted to be with Shelley, but once she left Skinner Street, she knew that her life would never be the same. When at last it was time to go, in the predawn darkness, with the stars still out, they stole down the stairs and ran toward the waiting vehicle on the corner of Hatton Garden, Jane bursting with anticipation, Mary still unsure. When they reached Shelley, Jane climbed right into the carriage, but Mary froze. She could picture her father's disappointment, his hurt and rage, and it was too much to bear. She turned on her heel and fled back home to scrawl a last-minute note begging him to understand. She propped the note on her father's dressing table and tiptoed down the stairs, running back to her lover, who held her tightly in his arms as they rattled over the cobblestones.

They had chosen France as their destination, because Mary's mother had lived there during the Revolution, but first they had to cover the seventy-five miles to Dover, where they would cross the Channel. The road was deeply rutted and Mary, always a poor traveler, could do little more than sink against the cushions. The sturdier Jane gazed out the window, exhilarated but afraid of being caught. Shelley, too, was worried about pursuers and did not allow his beloved's suffering to slow them down, stopping only a few times to rest. At Dartford he hired four fresh horses, and at four in the afternoon, after twelve hours of traveling, they arrived in Dover. Mary was so ill that she was close to losing consciousness. Still Shelley did not stop. Certain that they were being followed and anxious to depart, he hired a fishing boat to ferry them to France immediately. Mary lay in Shelley's arms, seasick, cold, and frightened. After midnight, the wind picked up and the waves towered over the bow, and before sunrise, a thunderstorm struck, drenching them and swamping the small vessel. Mary cowered in the bottom, gripping Shelley's knees. Shelley was ecstatic; this was just the sort of danger he loved. Jane feared for their lives but prided herself on not being seasick.

In the morning, the sky cleared and a strong wind blew them straight into the harbor at Calais. The day was bright and fresh as though there had been no storm just a few hours earlier. "Mary, look; the sun rises over France," Shelley exclaimed. Mary was delighted. The beautiful day was a glorious omen, she believed, just like the comet that had marked her birth.

In Calais, Shelley checked them into the most expensive rooms at Dessin's, the hotel of choice for wealthy English tourists, where they napped, exhausted from their adventure. That evening, a servant knocked on the door and told them "a fat lady" was there, demanding her daughter. Somehow, Mary-Jane had found them. She seized Jane, carried her off to her own room, and tried to persuade her daughter to come home. Having suffered from her own youthful indiscretions, Mary-Jane knew only too well the difficulties Jane would face as an unmarried woman with a dubious reputation. Jane wavered, but Shelley took her for a walk and talked her into staying, reminding her of their ideals: freedom from slavery; the rejection of bourgeois values; a life of passion. If she wanted to be a true radical, then she must follow in Wollstonecraft's footsteps and persevere against Mary-Jane and the conventional forces of society. The starstruck Jane fended off her mother's entreaties until Mary-Jane conceded defeat. She blamed Shelley, but she reserved most of her anger for her implacable opponent of the last twelve years, her stepdaughter. Mary had triumphed at last. There was no better way to hurt a mother than to harm her daughter.

But Mary-Jane was a dangerous enemy. An effective writer in her own right, she knew how to exact revenge with a pen. In long letters to her friends, Mary-Jane raged against Mary Godwin, maintaining that the girl had corrupted Jane. Shelley's abandoned wife, Harriet, also launched a letter-writing campaign, against not just Mary but the whole Godwin family. Shelley had already told her that he had fallen in love with Mary Godwin, but she had hoped his infatuation would pass and that he would return to her before the birth of their new baby. Now that the situation seemed hopeless, she told her friends that Godwin had sold his two daughters to Shelley for £1,500. There was a grain of truth in the accusation, as right before he fled Shelley had at last lent Godwin the money he had promised, saving the philosopher from financial ruin.

Without any defenders, the trio were berated by London society. The scandal would burn for years. Shelley, the heir to a distinguished title, had run away with two teenage girls, one of them the daughter of the scandalous Mary Wollstonecraft. Wasn't one girl enough? Did he plan to sleep with them both? Had Godwin really auctioned off his daughters into sexual slavery? Sir Timothy, Shelley's father, was profoundly humiliated and never forgave his son for this second elopement, writing off the Godwin/Wollstonecraft girl as a whore.

Still, as Shelley watched Mary-Jane's ship disappear against the horizon, he was elated. He had won. The parents had been defeated; the children were in charge. This was a triumph for the oppressed everywhere. The Irish. The peasant. The slave. Mary, too, was thrilled to see Mary-Jane retreat, but her feelings were more complicated than her lover's. She hated her stepmother, but she had never wanted to be free of her father. Ever since she could remember, she had wanted him to love her more than Mary-Jane. She would even write a novel a few years later in which a father would confess his incestuous love for his daughter. Unlike her lover, she had never regarded Godwin as a tyrant and had not wanted to hurt him. She yearned for his praise and worried that she had lost him forever. But it was impossible to be too downcast when she was with Shelley, and the three young people left for Paris full of anticipation, despite the fact that the weather was hot, the horses glistened with sweat, and the girls suffered in their black high-necked traveling dresses.

But when they arrived in the capital on August 2, 1814, dusty and tired, *fraternité* and *liberté* were nowhere to be found. They checked into the unprepossessing Hôtel de Vienne on the edge of the Marais and roamed through the city streets, disappointed to find most Parisians war-weary and cynical. Napoleon's defeat earlier that year, a relief to many as it meant the end of the war, was also a blow to French honor. No one was preaching revolution anymore. Many of the people they met were royalists, eager to restore French *gloire*. Justice and freedom were passé. The martyred revolutionaries Madame Roland and Charlotte Corday, so inspirational to Mary when her friend Isabella had talked about them in Scotland, were long dead. And so, for that matter, was Mary Wollstonecraft.

On pilgrimages of this sort it was tempting to think the dead might materialize, that a visit to an old home or a walk through old haunts might bring them back. When the trio read Wollstonecraft's work out loud, which they did frequently, she felt close by. Perhaps if they looked hard enough they might catch a glimpse of her striding down one of the narrow streets, the long skirts of her muslin dress trailing behind her. Instead they saw nattily dressed men sipping coffee, young men and women flirting and gossiping as though no revolution had ever taken place. Fashionable ladies minced by in high-heeled, sharp-toed slippers, holding up the skirts of their light clingy gowns. Buttoned up to the chin in their conservative dresses, Mary and Jane knew they looked irrevocably English. They wore black bonnets and brushed their hair behind their ears like schoolgirls, while the French women lacquered their hair into elaborately sculptured masterpieces.

And yet, despite these disappointments, on the first night in Paris, when they closed their door on the city, Mary and Shelley were "too happy to sleep." It was what Shelley would later call their "bridal night." For the first time, they were alone, free from their pursuers and free from Jane, who was safely installed in her own room. Mary had been yearning for this moment ever since she declared her love for Shelley on her mother's grave. Shelley, too, had been dreaming of the time that he and Mary could be together without worry or guilt. For him, sex was an almost mystical experience, a passage into spiritual "ecstasies." But although he desperately desired her—commemorated in a poem in which he celebrated "her eager lips, like roses," "her white arms lifted through the shadowy stream / Of her loose hair"— he did not rush them to bed.

First they talked, sharing their dreams about writing and their literary future. Mary told Shelley about her years in Scotland and showed him some of the letters Isabella had written her. They read Byron's poetry aloud, and only then did they make love. Shelley later wrote:

> *I felt the blood that burn'd*
> *Within her frame, mingle with mine, and fall*
> *Around my heart like fire.*

Afterward, they fell into what Shelley called a "speechless swoon of joy." He was calm, finally at peace after the frantic anxiety of the last few months. Mary told Shelley that she never wanted to leave the circle of his arms.

The next morning, however, they had to face their responsibilities. There was Jane to worry about, as well as the need to eat— though Mary said she could do without eating, she was so happy. Most worrisome of all, they were almost penniless. Having left England in such a rush, Shelley had not thought to bring along spare funds, and they were out of cash. After a long search, they found one brave banker willing to advance them sixty pounds on the strength of Shelley's noble name. This seemed a large sum to Mary and Jane, but it would not last long, given the extended pilgrimage they had planned. Shelley was aware of this but waved all concerns aside. He was sure they would find funds and make do somehow.

With each passing day, Paris grew less glamorous. Notre Dame was not as splendid as they had hoped. The Tuileries gardens were ugly. The hotel was dark, cramped, and unbearably hot. On August 8, after almost a week there, they gave up on finding the Revolution in the city and headed into the countryside. In an effort to economize, Shelley, ignoring the warnings of their hotelier, decided it would be more "delightful" to walk than to hire a carriage. He and

Jane went to buy a donkey to carry their possessions while Mary rested at the hotel, feeling weak and anxious. But neither Shelley nor Jane knew much about choosing donkeys. Although the poor creature was friendly and willing enough, it collapsed in the heat not long after they began their journey, leaving them stranded with their books, clothing, and boxes. At the next town, they traded the donkey for a mule, but after four days of this new arrangement, Shelley, displaying a distressing propensity for accidents, twisted his ankle and could not walk. They had to unpack the mule and let Shelley climb aboard while Jane and Mary trudged along behind, laden with their belongings and hoping for a refreshing stop at a country inn or a friendly peasant's thatched cottage.

But there were neither friendly peasants nor refreshing country inns—a rude shock for three young people who had prepared themselves for their journey by gazing at eighteenth-century prints of the bucolic French countryside, complete with pink-cheeked milkmaids, handsome shepherds, and dutiful farmers tilling the dark earth. The land they found had barely survived the final years of the Napoleonic wars. Just a few months earlier, in retaliation for Napoleon's invasion of Russia, the Cossacks, along with the Austrian and Prussian armies, had galloped into France. They stole livestock and trampled fields, burned villages, killed children, and raped women. Napoleon's troops were little better, pillaging the countryside for food and treasure. Finally, on April 11, Napoleon had surrendered, but the country remained in crisis. Dusty dirt tracks, ruined crops, and barren hillsides had replaced prosperous farms and pastures dotted with fat cows. The people were starving. "Filth, misery, and famine [are] everywhere," Shelley declared. The French themselves were, according to Shelley, "the most unamiable, inhospitable, and unaccommodating of the human race." Stray English visitors like the bedraggled trio were easy prey for famished peasants who charged exorbitant rates for everything, even a glass of sour milk. Sometimes all they could find to eat was dry bread that had to be soaked in water to make it palatable. At night, they slept in haylofts and cots in farmhouses. In Troyes, about a hundred miles east of Paris, they did find an inn, but rats ran across

Jane's face in the middle of the night and she fled into Mary and Shelley's room, screaming so loudly they had to take her into their bed.

Disheartened, Shelley suggested they change course and head for Switzerland. This was the true land of freedom and joy, he declared, basing this claim on Godwin's novel *Fleetwood,* a celebration of William Tell and "the glorious founders" of Swiss liberty. According to Godwin, the Swiss were a noble people, above the petty restrictions of bourgeois life.

But they should have known better. Godwin had never been to Switzerland, and although he was a careful researcher, his goal had been to write a good novel, not provide an accurate travelogue. Mary understood this, but missing her father as she did, she hoped that if they retraced his novelistic journey, he might come to approve of her actions, or at least see how much she admired and loved him. The August heat made the journey miserable, and their pace slowed, especially since Shelley was still limping. Finally, despite their rapidly dwindling funds, they hired a coach and driver to take them to Neuchâtel.

Mary and Shelley had been keeping a joint journal since the beginning of their adventure in which Shelley raved about Mary's brilliance, the nature of true love, and the novel he wanted to write, while Mary composed passages about the view and their travails. Both had grown impatient with Jane, who recorded her squabbles with both Shelley and Mary in her own diary. Secretly, Jane considered herself in love with Shelley, but Shelley was too smitten with Mary to pay her much attention, although he did remember Harriet with affection, even writing her a letter declaring himself a "firm and constant friend" and inviting her to join them as a comrade in the utopian society he wanted to create. Harriet, quite understandably, did not reply.

"Their immensity staggers the imagination," Shelley remarked in their journal when they finally saw the snow-capped peaks of the Alps. But the journey had taken its toll, as had the frantic search for money. Mary missed her father and was finding Shelley not quite the romantic hero she had imagined him to be. In Paris, sharing a bed with her new lover had more than made up for her disappointment in the city. But after enduring ten hot days of walking in the bleak French countryside, it was difficult to feel those same stirrings of passion. They were hungry, sweaty, and exhausted. Besides, it was nearly impossible to find privacy in a hayloft or a peasant's kitchen. Even the magnificent peaks did little to cheer her up; she grew silent and withdrawn, and one afternoon she reflected gloomily that nothing ever turned out the way people thought it would. A person might act with good intentions, but there could still be painful results. Although she spoke in broad philosophical terms, Shelley understood her meaning and accused her of regretting her decision to run away with him. Mary quickly retrenched, but Jane noted in her journal that Mary had lied. Shelley was right. Mary was unhappy with her lover and the whole escapade. They were not living in the free Eden he had promised, but had been on the brink of disaster ever since they left London.

One afternoon, the heat was so smothering Shelley suggested that Mary take a dip in one of the woodland pools they saw from the road. He would screen her from any passersby and dry her off with grass and leaves. Instead of being enchanted by this idea, as Shelley thought she should have been, Mary was annoyed. What an indelicate proposition! There was the driver to consider, not to mention any strangers who might happen by. She did not want to strip in the middle of the woods for Shelley's viewing pleasure or, for that matter, anyone else's. Jane thought Mary was being ridiculously puritanical. If Shelley had invited her to bathe naked, she would have jumped at the offer, she noted grumpily.

When at last they crossed the border, it was raining. They had been on the road for almost three weeks and were prepared to be delighted with the Swiss. But the hardworking businessmen, clean streets, tidy front steps, well-fed children, and cheerful wives that usually delighted English tourists were deeply disappointing to this trio. Jane spoke for all of them when she wrote that the Swiss "are rich, contented & happy and uninteresting for they are most immoderately stupid & ugly almost to deformity." The respectable townspeople must have wondered about this odd travel-stained threesome—or at least the three young renegades hoped so, as they liked the idea of appearing different, "conjectur[ing] the astonishment" of those they met, as Mary said.

The rain had broken the August heat, and although that was a welcome change, they could hardly glimpse Lake Lucerne through the fog. Nor could they find Godwin's forests of beech and pine or the wild and romantic countryside of Fleetwood's adventures. In Brunnen, nearly halfway through the sixty pounds Shelley had borrowed in Paris, they rented a house on the lake for six months. But after the first day they were bored. Switzerland was not for them after all. Returning to France was out of the question. After discussing the matter, it turned out that all three were ready to head home. In fact, they wanted to leave right away. However, they had to wait for the laundress to return their clothing, and when she did, their clothes were still wet, which meant their departure was delayed to the next day—an annoyance that Shelley noted in their journal. Mary and Shelley tried to console themselves by reading Tacitus to each other, but Jane sulked. She did not like it when they ignored her.

To avoid any further encounters with French peasants, they decided to book passage on a barge up the Rhine and cross the Channel from Holland. This route had the added advantage of being cheaper than the overland journey back through France. As it was, they would have to be very careful in order to have enough money to make it home.

Floating downriver was certainly more pleasant than hiking through the devastated French countryside, but although Mary was inspired by the dramatic sweep of the Rhine Valley, she was appalled at the vulgarity of their fellow travelers, who drank all day long, getting louder and more crude as the hours passed. She and Jane tried to avoid them, but on such a small craft, it was impossible. After the first day, Mary snapped in her diary, "Our only wish was to annihilate such uncleansable animals. Twere easier for god to make entirely new men than attempt to purify such monsters as these . . . loathsome creepers."

One day, early in September, when the barge had paused at Gerns-heim, a few miles north of Mannheim, she and Shelley stole away from Jane and strolled past the gabled cottages, along the cobbled streets, and out into the surrounding countryside. In the distance against the sky, they could make out the towers of a picturesque cas-tle named Frankenstein.

There was a disturbing legend associated with this castle, and in exchange for a few coins, a villager told them the story. A notorious alchemist named Konrad Dippel had been born there in 1673. Dippel was obsessed with finding a "cure" for death and conducted macabre experiments, digging up graves to steal body parts and grinding the bones into dust that he mixed with blood and administered to corpses in an attempt to bring them back to life. He died a failure, leaving the question unresolved: Is it possible to bring the dead back to life?

Afterward, Mary and Shelley spent their time on the barge talking about this story and the books they had read and the books they wanted to write. Jane immersed herself in one of Wollstonecraft's favorite books, Rousseau's *Émile*. Like Wollstonecraft, Jane found that she admired the French philosopher's ideas but loathed his por-trayal of women, which was not surprising, since she tended to agree with most of Wollstonecraft's views.

In the last few days of their journey, they took turns reading aloud from Wollstonecraft's writings. All three felt heartened to have Mary's mother as their fellow traveler. But for Jane, this renewed exposure to Wollstonecraft's radicalism deepened her resolve to forge a new identity, distinct from her own mother. Like Mary and Shelley, she believed that they were all disciples of Wollstonecraft, but she was starting to think that she, Jane, was actually her truest heir. Shelley was a man, so he was in a different category, and though Mary was brilliant, she was sometimes weak—too weak, Jane thought, to be Wollstonecraft's standard-bearer. After all, Mary had made many false steps (as Jane had noted in her diary): she had refused to bathe naked; she was frequently unwell; she had harbored doubts about their grand adventure. Jane, on the other hand, had remained loyal to their enter-prise, priding herself on her strength and her determination.

Bad weather trapped them in Holland's port city of Maasluis, where Mary began writing a story with the angry title "Hate"; unfortunately, no drafts of this early work remain, but its title suggests Mary's frame of mind. She had felt increasingly ill over the last few weeks, and before they boarded the boat to England, she discovered why. She was pregnant.

# CHAPTER 10

# MARY WOLLSTONECRAFT:
# LONDON

—

[ 1786–1787 ]

*I*F LADY KINGSBOROUGH HAD HOPED TO VANQUISH HER GOVERNESS by firing her, she had sadly underestimated Mary Wollstonecraft. Mary's departure from Mitchelstown that August marked the start of a new era for the twenty-eight-year-old. Never again would she allow herself to work in such a degrading situation. She had resolved to earn her living with her pen.

She boarded the Bristol coach to London, her bags packed with her books as well as her completed manuscript. She did not let Eliza and Everina know where she was going—a secrecy that may seem trivial to the modern reader but was actually an assertion of her right to shape her own life. She had done her best to fulfill her responsibility as an eldest sister before she left for Ireland, finding a position for Eliza as a teacher in a school near Newington and persuading Ned to allow Everina to return to his house. Instead of being grateful, however, her sisters complained, and the exhausted Mary had little sympathy left for them. Most unmarried middle-class women, herself included, had to take what they could get: either demeaning wage labor or dependency on relatives and friends. Her sisters should be thankful they were not on the streets, and if they were unhappy, she felt they should exert themselves rather than depending exclusively on her.

After a sixteen-hour coach ride Mary arrived in hot, crowded

London, a dramatic contrast to the seclusion of the Kingsborough country estate. But the jostling strangers, the unfamiliar storefronts, even the foul smell of the sewers represented hope. In the anonymity of the city she could break free of the entanglements that had held her back. With this goal in mind, she headed directly to Joseph Johnson's bookshop to hand him her novel.

Dressed in a homespun shift and thick-soled, sensible walking shoes, with her hair hanging down her back under a dark beaver cap that sat flat on her head, she knew she looked dowdy compared to the stylish young ladies in their light summer muslins, petticoats, wide-brimmed hats, and dainty slippers. But to Mary, this disregard for fashion was part of her newfound liberty. She no longer had to fit into a world she loathed. Indeed, she would not have been at all distressed to hear that some of her new acquaintances would refer to her as "a philosophical sloven" behind her back. Having removed herself from the marriage market as well as the drawing rooms of the rich and well-connected, she no longer needed to waste time making herself attractive for the benefit of others.

Johnson's office was at 72 St. Paul's Churchyard, the tallest house in the courtyard of St. Paul's Cathedral. A swarm of interesting-looking people milled about on the cobblestones outside; after being the odd one out in a household of aristocrats and servants, it was a relief for Mary to mix with "the middling sort." Very few lords and ladies came to this part of London, the heart of the book trade. Forty other publishers crowded nearby on Leadenhall Street, Paternoster Row, and Ave Maria Lane. Paper sellers, publicists, book buyers, authors, and auctioneers were joined by lawyers, jurists, and curious onlookers on their way to see the hangings at the nearby gallows, since the notorious Fleet and Newgate prisons were just a few streets away. Other women might have feared for their safety; the romantic heroines in the popular novels of the era would certainly have fainted at the squalor. But Mary was thrilled by it. This was exactly where she wanted to be.

When Mary knocked on Johnson's door, she expected him to greet her kindly, but she was surprised by the extent of his generosity. He invited her upstairs into his cluttered chambers, away from the bustle of the shop. They settled themselves in his dining room with its view of the cathedral to discuss Mary's future. She showed him *Mary,* her novel, and mentioned another idea, a collection of educational tales based on her experience as a teacher and governess. Johnson agreed to publish the novel and the educational book as soon as it was written, and assured her that if she worked diligently she could earn enough to live on.

In the meantime, Johnson offered to find her new lodgings, inviting her to stay with him until he found a suitable accommodation. Mary agreed, though it was an unusual and improper arrangement: a single woman and a single man sleeping in the same house without supervision. But Mary trusted him to be a safe roommate. They had not spent much time together, but they had corresponded while she was in Ireland; he had never evinced any romantic interest in her, or any woman, for that matter, and Mary was intent on carving out a literary career, not initiating a love affair.

Johnson's quarters were far from elegant. The floors were uneven, the walls rough. Every available surface was covered with books and dusty papers. Even the bedchambers and dining room were lined with volumes. From outside, the shouts of street vendors and the calls of the crowd could be heard late into the night. Yet Mary was overjoyed. Each day she felt more rejuvenated, freed from the stifling quiet of the Irish countryside. After breakfast, Johnson spent most of his day downstairs in the shop and she tagged along, the only woman in what was essentially a man's world. Although Johnson did publish a few other female authors, they were the exception and were rarely seen in public.

Many of Johnson's writers stopped in to discuss politics or to ask for advances on their work. Often, they stayed for dinner. As the days passed, Mary found that she and her publisher had similar opinions on politics and literature. She already knew that Johnson had made a name for himself by publishing the works of famous radicals. What she found out now was how deeply he shared her hatred of injustice in all its forms, and how dedicated he was to promoting the rights of women, Jews, and slaves; he had also campaigned against the abuse of child labor. Like her, he hated convention and hypocrisy. Also like her, he believed that ideas could change the world, that the written word could reform humanity.

But Johnson was not simply an otherworldly idealist. Canny and a shrewd negotiator, he would become one of the most successful publishers of his time. In order to keep his books affordable, he skimped on production costs. Thus the volumes he produced were not particularly elegant, but he supported his writers, bailing the fiery Thomas Paine out of jail, supplying William Blake with engraving jobs, lending William Cowper money during the poet's early years, and sharing the profits liberally once an author's work began to make money. Mary had found exactly the right man to help her launch a literary career. During the three weeks they spent together that summer, the two laid the foundations for what would come to be one of the most important friendships of Mary's life.

Toward the end of her stay, Mary confessed to Johnson that she was deeply troubled by "despair and vexations." She was concerned that she'd be unable to take care of her sisters as well as herself and feared she might have to return to the grim life of a governess in order to do so. Johnson expressed empathy and told his protégée to be brave. Her talent would overcome the hurdles that blocked her path. He also made another offer, promising to supply Mary with steady writing assignments, enough to earn a regular income. But there was one caveat. She would have to believe in herself. In fact, Mary's confidence was the linchpin of their whole enterprise. She would have to guard against her tendency toward self-doubt. Otherwise, her gloomy outlook would destroy her chances.

Early that fall, Johnson found Mary a small yellow brick house at 49 George Street (now Dolben Street), about a ten-minute walk from St. Paul's, on the other side of the river, near the newly constructed Blackfriars Bridge. The south side of the Thames was an unfashionable neighborhood, but Mary didn't care; she was delighted to have a home of her own. She did not bother to decorate her rooms. A bed, a table, and a chair—that was all she needed, though Johnson supplied her with a servant to help with the daily chores of cooking, marketing, and cleaning. From the window of the top floor where she worked she could survey the rooftops of the grimy city she was coming to love.

In 1787, London was bursting at the seams. Between 1750 and 1801, it mushroomed from 675,000 to 900,000 souls, almost double the size of eighteenth-century Paris. As the novelist Henry Fielding wrote, "Here you have the Advantage of solitude without its Disadvantage, since you may be alone and in Company at the same time, and while you sit or walk unobserved, Noise, Hurry, and a constant Succession of Objects entertain the Mind."

London's growth was all the more remarkable given that the mortality rate worsened with each decade. The Scottish physician George Cheyne attributed this high death rate to the city's overcrowding and poor sanitation, noting that

> the clouds of Stinking Breathes and Perspirations, not to mention the ordure of so many diseas'd, both intelligent and unintelligent animals, the crowded Churches, Church Yards and Burying Places, with the putrefying Bodies, the Sinks, Butcher Houses, Stables, Dunghills etc . . . putrefy, poison and infect the Air for Twenty Miles around it, and which in Time must alter, weaken and destroy the healthiest of Constitutions.

The poet William Cowper described the city as "a common and most noisome sewer," and even Mary, despite her affection for her new surroundings, would have admitted that Cowper had a point. Twice as many people died as were born. Gin was the most popular drink of the poor. Violence and crime dominated the streets, from prostitution to murder. Dirt, trash, and even dead bodies littered the cobblestones. Privacy was nonexistent. The enclosed "water closet" had yet to be invented. People emptied their chamber pots out the windows, leaving puddles of waste for pedestrians to slosh through. The lack of clean water, the close quarters, and the pressures of poverty led to the rapid spread of seasonal epidemics, smallpox in the winter and dysentery in the summer. Since so many of its inhabitants died prematurely—the average age of death was around thirty-seven—London's growth depended on the influx of newcomers rushing to the city, a number that increased steadily despite the many dangers of urban living. Not only were wages higher, London also offered relief from the constraints of provincial living, where family and friends enforced social conventions and restrictions. Besides, it was exhilarating. There was always something new to see or do. As Samuel Johnson famously claimed, "when a man is tired of London, he is tired of life."

In Mary's area, the hubbub of the city was compounded by the busy waterfront nearby. Captains crowded their ships so closely together that the river "was almost hidden by merchant vessels from every country." The poet James Thompson compared the long lines of ships to "a long wintry forest" with "groves of masts."

For Mary, the virtue of all this was that she could easily blend in. There were far greater oddities in this part of London than a professional writing woman. No one commented on her appearance or her habits. During the day, she worked on the revisions to *Mary* that Johnson had suggested and studied foreign languages, as he had told her that her first assignments would probably be translations from the French and German. She also began her new project of educational tales that she had decided to call *Original Stories*. At five o'clock, she would walk across the bridge to Johnson's house for dinner, where she would meet men such as Henry Fuseli, a German-Swiss artist who bragged about his sexual exploits and scorned conventional morality; John Bonnycastle, a mathematician who wrote books that attempted to make math and science accessible to the common reader; and Erasmus Darwin, whose sexualized depiction of flowers in his bestselling book-length poem *The Loves of the Plants* had recently been deemed too explicit for unmarried female readers. Despite the diversity of their interests, what these men—with the exception of Fuseli—shared with Mary was a belief that educating everyone, including women, could improve society. Like Voltaire, they viewed themselves as popularizers of knowledge rather than inventors, believing that if they wrote clearly enough, their readers would learn from their ideas and be inspired to push for reform.

The food at these dinners was simple: fish, vegetables, and occasionally a pudding for dessert. Fuseli's semipornographic painting *The Nightmare* hung over Johnson's dinner table: its depiction of a beautiful young woman flinging her head back in painful ecstasy while a devil sits suggestively on her loins shocked ordinary onlookers, but Johnson's guests were not ordinary.

*Fuseli's famous painting* The Nightmare.

You could not be a prude and dine with Johnson. And Mary, despite her sexual inexperience, was no prude. Johnson's guests enjoyed discussing topics usually deemed improper for female ears, anything from adultery to bisexuality. These issues were of great interest to Mary as they pertained directly to the lives of women, and so, although at first she was a quiet onlooker, it did not take her long to become passionately involved, eager to offer her own opinions and ideas. Like the Newington radicals before them, this group of intellectuals appreciated Mary's originality and forthrightness. Before long she was a vital member of Johnson's supper club.

By November, Mary had finished revising her novel. She knew that her decision to be a writer was unorthodox, but she felt confident enough now to send a letter to her sisters to explain her new undertaking. To hide her fears, she used grandiose terms: "I am then going to be the first of a new genus. . . . I must be independent. . . . This project has long floated in my mind. You know I was not born to tread in the beaten track—the peculiar bent of my nature pushes me on." She begged them not to say anything to their friends and family, as she did not want anyone to try to dissuade her: "You cannot conceive how disagreeable pity and advice would be at this juncture."

There were other women who earned a living with their pen, Anna Barbauld and Fanny Burney among the most famous. But Mary was the first female writer who would receive a reliable stream of work from her publisher on a retainer basis. Johnson could afford to be generous because of the boom in the publishing industry in the 1780s. Earlier in the century, most readers were aristocrats, men of wealth and family. But by the time Mary arrived in London, the middle class had entered the market, demanding books that would improve their minds and their manners, equipping them to move in the best circles. Lending libraries and book clubs had sprung up all over the country. Travel books, advice books, sermons, romances, poetry, and children's books—the list of popular categories went on and on.

As soon as Mary's sisters received the news that she was in London, they clamored to come live with her. But Mary did not want to share her home. Alone, she could do as she pleased, eat and sleep when she wanted, write and study without interruption, and attend Johnson's dinner parties. She wrote to Fanny's brother George, "I have determined on one thing, never to have my Sisters to live with me, my solitary manner of living would not suit them, nor could I pursue my studies if forced to conform." However, she considered the girls, as she still called them, her responsibility, and by Christmas she had made plans on their behalf, though she did not consult them about what they might desire for themselves. Eliza would stay in her current teaching position. Everina would go to Paris to learn French, which would enable her to get more desirable teaching jobs in the future. Mary's independence was safe, but her sisters were indignant. Their eldest sister had always been high-handed, but this time she had gone too far. Everina did not want to go to Paris, and Eliza was jealous that she had to stay behind.

But Mary kept moving forward with her plans. In her quest for her sisters' welfare, it did not cross her mind that she should take their wishes into consideration. By January, she had supplemented her own earnings by borrowing from Johnson and gathered together enough money to house Everina with a Mademoiselle Henry in an elegant apartment on the Rue de Tournon, the center of the Faubourg Saint-Germain, a neighborhood that even then was crowded with intellectuals and artists. It would have been a perfect spot for Mary to live, but not Everina, who, from the moment she arrived, wrote to Mary complaining about trivial "disasters and difficulties" and begging her older sister to visit because she was lonely. Mary, who had consigned herself to living in straitened circumstances for Everina's sake, was annoyed: "If I have ever any money to spare to gratify myself, I will certainly visit France," she wrote her younger sister sternly; "it has long been a desire floating in my brain." Even the self-absorbed Everina could not miss her older sister's point: Mary could not come because she had already spent all her money on Everina's unasked-for sojourn in Paris.

In the spring of 1788, only nine months after Mary had arrived in London, Johnson published two new books by Mary Wollstonecraft: *Mary* and *Original Stories from Real Life. Mary,* the novel, did not receive much notice from critics, but *Original Stories* would become a staple of the advice literature on the moral development of children for almost fifty years. In this, her second book on education, Mary returned to the themes she had emphasized in *Thoughts on the Education of Daughters,* but this time she went further, highlighting the need for ethical training for young girls by depicting a series of lessons taught by a governess she named Mrs. Mason. Through Mrs. Mason,

Mary demonstrated how easily girls can be educated, countering Rousseau's belief that women's minds were too weak to grasp moral truths and logical problems. She also included an aggressive assault on social and economic injustice. Mrs. Mason tells stories about the sufferings of the poor, made even more graphic by the genius Johnson hired to do the illustrations, William Blake. Blake's six woodcuts for Mary's book depict desperate haunted beggars and starving hollow-cheeked orphans. Mrs. Mason not only teaches the importance of caring for the indigent but also points an accusing finger at the callousness of the upper classes, which Mary had witnessed while living on the Kingsborough estate.

Œconomy & Self-Denial Are Necessary, *one of William Blake's six woodcuts for Mary Wollstonecraft's* Original Stories from Real Life.

In fact, poverty was a nagging concern for Mary, despite the steady wage she was now earning from Johnson. The financial insecurity of her childhood haunted her, as did the precariousness of her writing life. The threat of running out of money drove her to write, study, and publish at a feverish pace. That summer, despite her shaky language skills, she tackled two translations: a treatise by the French finance minister, Jacques Necker, *The Significance of Religious Theories,* and a German educational book, Christian Salzmann's *Elements of Morality, for the Use of Children.* Both books stretched Mary's capacities to the breaking point, but she managed to complete them.

For the modern reader, these volumes are noteworthy because Mary made many dramatic departures from the original texts, not because of her poor grasp of the languages but for purely philosophical reasons. This was particularly true of the Salzmann work. When she disagreed with his theories or felt he was neglecting an important point, she felt no compunction about altering his words. For instance, she loathed his celebration of aristocrats and his sentimental effusions about family life, especially his belief that the wife must be completely subordinate to the husband. Sometimes she even omitted entire passages, inserting in their place her own treatises on the evils of female fashion and the importance of a good education for girls— insertions that anticipate some of the most important themes in her future work. She changed the name of Salzmann's heroine to Mary and invented a scene in which Mary begs her mother to let her get dressed up for a wedding the family has been invited to attend. Her mother cautions against this, but Mary persists, and on the morning of the wedding, she puts on stays for the first time and discovers they are like "fetters." Things get even worse when the hairdresser arrives:

> [He] put her hair in papers, which used to flow in natural locks on her neck and shoulders; he twisted them very hard, and pinched them with hot irons. Poor Mary trembled, because she expected every moment that the hot irons would touch her forehead or cheeks, and asked every moment if he would not soon be done. But he begged her to have patience, and, after curling and frizzling her hair above half an hour, he bid her

look in the glass, where she saw a little face peeping out of a curled wig. She had then a silk slip laced tight to her body, and over it a long gauze dress so stuck out with trimmings and artificial flowers, that she could scarcely move, being so incumbered with finery.

Mary eventually pleads with her mother to leave the wedding early and go home. When her mother asks, "Why do you wish to go, when you see such good company and amusement here?" Mary replies:

Of what use are they to me . . . when I cannot enjoy any thing? If I had on my cotton jacket and straw hat, then I should be merry, and run and skip; but in this dress I am bound like a prisoner. Sometimes my hair tickles me, my feathers and flowers keep my head stiff, my stays hurt me, and when I begin to play, my flounces, flowers, or frock, catch every tree. Nay, the boys tread on my train on purpose to see me look silly.

Of course, "Mary's" lament is the translator's, not the author's, but because Wollstonecraft's name was not attached to *Elements of Morality,* the reader was led to believe that this vivid description of the restrictive nature of women's clothing was composed by the German scholar, a brilliant strategic maneuver on Wollstonecraft's part; she could air a controversial view and save herself from public castigation. What better way to enter the debate over the limitations placed on women than under the cover of a foreign male author's identity? Salzmann himself never found out. The irony is that her disguise proved so effective that for more than two hundred years her ideas on this subject remained buried in this little-read tome and were only recently unearthed by literary scholars.

In 1787, however, Mary was encouraged by the fact that no one greeted the Salzmann translation with outrage. She felt increasingly confident about her abilities to express her opinions in print. And so when Johnson and his friend Thomas Christie asked Mary to serve as one of the primary book reviewers for a new literary magazine that would feature the writing of their intellectual circle and defend the cause of reform against conservatives, Mary was elated to accept their offer. This new challenge would allow her to develop her ideas and sharpen her skills as a member of a stable of writers, rather than have to forge a literary career entirely on her own.

# CHAPTER II

# MARY GODWIN: LONDON
# AND BISHOPSGATE

———

[ 1814–1815 ]

ARY, JANE, AND SHELLEY SAILED BACK TO ENGLAND IN THE MID-
dle of a September storm. Mary "was sick as death & was obliged to
go to bed," Jane wrote, happily recording that this left her alone with
Shelley on the deck while "the waves which had become terribly
high broke over us." They did not have enough money to pay the
captain for their passage, but Shelley reassured the worried girls that
he would find the funds once they docked. However, when they arrived ashore and went straight to Shelley's London bank for the cash,
they discovered that Harriet had emptied his account. Shelley wanted
to go to her and demand his money back, but Mary urged him to
avoid a confrontation. She suggested that they approach her childhood friends, the Voyseys, a family with two daughters around the
same age as Jane and Mary, for a loan and a place to stay. But when
they arrived at the Voyseys' house, Mrs. Voysey refused to see them.

This was their first taste of the rejections, rebuffs, and snubs that
lay ahead. Despite its rapid growth, middle-class London was still a
small town. Everyone had heard about the girls' escapade and few
people wanted to befriend them. Scandal was contagious, particularly sexual peccadilloes. If any young woman admitted that she even
knew Mary Godwin, she endangered not only her reputation, but
that of her entire family. Social survival depended on shunning those

who had gone beyond the pale; few had the imagination or the courage to break this code.

Left with no other option, Shelley hired a hackney to take them to the Westbrooks' stately home on quiet Chapel Street near Grosvenor Square where Harriet, in her last trimester of pregnancy, was living with her parents. This well-to-do neighborhood was very different from any Mary and Jane had ever inhabited, and the squalid inns they had endured in Europe had reinforced the girls' sense of their own poverty. They had tried to view their privations as the price of freedom, but rats, dirt, and dry crusts of bread are not the stuff of romance, and it seemed unfair that stolid, bourgeois Harriet had Shelley's money and they did not.

The captain had not trusted Shelley to return and so had sent one of his boatmen to travel with them until they came up with the payment. When Shelley disappeared into the Westbrooks' house, the sailor and the girls were forced to wait outside for more than two hours, an awkward arrangement that no amount of banter or good cheer could rescue. The girls worried that Shelley would change his mind, that Harriet would talk him into giving their marriage another try, or, worse, that she would decide to join their trio. Neither Mary nor Jane was at all keen on this last idea, but Shelley still nursed the notion of creating a commune of free-minded, loving young people.

At last Shelley emerged, smiling, with the funds they needed, and after a night in an inn on Oxford Street, he found them a simple house on Margaret Street, near Chapel Street so he could continue his negotiations with Harriet. Mary, meanwhile, tried to think of any friends or acquaintances who might sympathize with her. She made overtures to an old governess, Maria Smith, but the Godwins had already turned Smith against her. One afternoon, Mary-Jane and Fanny paid an awkward visit to Margaret Street, ringing the bell but refusing to come inside when Shelley invited them. They only wanted to see Jane, they said, leaving Mary to watch from the window while they talked to her stepsister on the front steps. Furious at the pain they had caused Mary, Shelley wrote Godwin a letter that afternoon demanding a reason for their cruel treatment. He and Mary had done nothing wrong, he said; they had only attempted to abide by Godwin's own philosophy of freedom and free love. A week later Godwin's reply came: He wanted nothing more to do with Mary and had ordered his family and friends to shut her out of their lives.

Shelley was all Mary had left. In tears, she told him that he would have to be everything to her now: father, lover, and friend. Jane was there, too, of course, but her presence had become increasingly troubling. In the early stages of pregnancy, Mary went to sleep early, and instead of keeping her company in bed, Shelley stayed up late talking to her stepsister. Mary had no illusions about the situation, knowing that Jane was relishing her time alone with Shelley. As the fall wore on, the two of them drew closer, and instead of regarding Jane as a charming nuisance, as he had in France, Shelley now sought her out, confiding in her and taking her on jaunts around the city while Mary rested.

One night early in October, Shelley, who liked frightening people—particularly young girls, a habit left over from the days when he had terrorized his little sisters—regaled Jane with a lurid description of how disobedient soldiers were punished by having strips of skin peeled from their backs with a sharp knife. Jane squirmed in delicious horror. When the candles had burned low, Shelley could not resist topping off the night by saying it was now "the witching hour," the time when evil spirits roamed the earth and ghosts took possession of human bodies. Jane screamed and fled upstairs to her room. Happy with his night's work, Shelley repaired to the bedroom he shared with Mary, only to be interrupted by an excited Jane. Shelley recorded what happened next:

> Just as the dawn was struggling with moon light Jane remarked in me that unutterable expression which had affected her with so much horror before. She described it as expressing a mixture of deep sadness & conscious power over her . . . her horror & agony increased even to the most dreadful convulsions. She shr[i]eked & writhed on the floor.

Shelley relished the effect he had on Jane, whose volatility was so different from the silence of his self-contained lover. Theatrical and imaginative, Jane was the perfect audience. She gasped at his tales. She wanted him to comfort her afterward. True, Jane was far less mature than Mary: she could not talk to him about his artistic soul, reassure him of his own genius, steady him by discussing Tacitus, or help him understand Byron's poetry as Mary did, but Jane was exhilarating precisely because she loved surprises. If there was nothing exciting happening, she was instantly bored.

One might think that there was enough real-life excitement in their lives to satisfy Jane's cravings. However, Jane was finding social ostracism more tedious than she had expected. Instead of being lionized as disciples of Mary Wollstonecraft, they were completely ignored. No one came to call. No one seemed to admire them. She and Mary napped, sewed, and read while Shelley drummed the streets of London looking for money. With his customary flourish, Shelley assured them he could take care of things. But when it became clear to Harriet that her erstwhile husband was not going to return she refused to hand over the rest of the funds she had taken from his bank. After all, she, too, was pregnant, and her baby was due soon. Shelley's father was no help either. Shocked at his son's behavior, Sir Timothy would not advance any money, and so, unable to pay their bills, Shelley became an expert at avoiding creditors, sleeping away from the house and spending time in remote spots to avoid being thrown into a debtors' prison.

This level of deprivation was new to both girls. Although they had grown up in a house perennially short on cash, they had always had new dresses, wholesome meals—Mary-Jane was a good cook— and vacations away from the city in the summer. They had not known how difficult it was to be poor, truly poor, nor how lonely life in a big city could be. To help Shelley, they spent hours in the offices of banks, appeasing and avoiding creditors, writing pleading letters to acquaintances who might help them, and, worst of all, packing their things and moving, constantly moving. They changed lodgings four times that first year to escape from angry merchants and to avoid paying rents they could not afford. It was neither fun nor dramatic to live in small apartments in unsafe parts of town and scrimp on everything, even food. The pregnant Mary was unable to do much, and so most of the heavy work fell to Jane and one hired servant. It is no wonder, then, that Jane and Shelley relished their nights of excitement. Under cover of darkness, Jane could be a beautiful damsel, helpless and passionate, desirable and interestingly vulnerable. For the first time, she could also feel superior to Mary. As for Shelley, with Jane, he could escape his growing sensation of helplessness by being both knave and rescuer, torturer and comforter—all of which were better than being a debt-ridden, cast-off son, an irresponsible husband to Harriet, and a disappointing lover to Mary.

The weather was beautiful that fall, and in the afternoons, when they were not fending off creditors, the trio would stroll to a pond near Parliament Hill, where Shelley would launch small paper boats he had spent hours creating in their drawing room. Sometimes they would return to the pond in the evening, light the boats on fire, and watch them flash and sizzle out on the water, the charred skeletons floating for a moment before they sank. Many years later, Mary would remember the eagerness with which he sailed his tiny craft, remarking that this was how he "sheltered himself from the storms and disappointments, the pain and sorrow, that beset his life."

MARY-JANE HAD NOT GIVEN up hope that her daughter might return home to Skinner Street. She argued that the family could repair the damage done to Jane's reputation by blaming the entire situation on the two lovers and that Jane could settle back into her old life without too much difficulty.

Jane, however, did not relish the idea of being an ordinary girl again. She liked being out from under her mother's thumb and decided to act on her feeling that she was one of Mary Wollstonecraft's "true" daughters by adopting Wollstonecraft's birthday (April 27) as her own. What better way to demonstrate her rebirth and assert her independence from Mary-Jane? In this spirit, she also decided to change her name. No longer would she be known as Jane, with its echo of her mother, but by the more romantic-sounding name of Claire. Mary did not record her feelings about Jane's metamorphosis, but her irritation at her sister was steadily mounting. Not only did Jane/Claire want to steal Shelley, she wanted Mary's legacy, too. The sisters squabbled and fought. But Jane persisted, undeterred by Mary's disapproval.

For Jane, one of the most appealing parts of her name change was its symbolism. In French, *claire* means clear or transparent, as Jane well knew, but during the Revolution it had also come to mean authentic, sincere, and truthful. Even better, Clara (the anglicized version of Claire) was the name of a famous literary character in the English translation of Rousseau's bestseller *La Nouvelle Héloïse*. In this romantic love triangle, Julie, the heroine, and Clara, her best friend and cousin, are both in love with St. Preux, their tutor. St. Preux loves Julie but confides in Clara, paradoxically drawing closer and closer to Clara, until, one day, Julie tragically dies. With Julie out of the picture, St. Preux realizes that he loved Clara all along. He pursues her, but Clara rejects him.

This was a gratifying plot from the newly minted Claire's point of view. Rousseau glorified the position she found herself in with Mary and Shelley. Instead of simply being the third wheel, she could see herself as a heroine in her own right, the closest confidante of both the hero and his beloved. The best part for Claire, of course, was how Clara eventually wins the day, taking center stage at the end of the story. In his *Confessions,* Rousseau said that he had designed two heroines with "analogous characters":

I made one dark, the other fair; one lively, the other gentle; one prudent, the other weak, but with so touching a weakness, that virtue seemed to gain by it. I gave to one a lover, whose tender friend the other was, and even something more; but I admitted no rivalry, no quarrelling, no jealousy, because it is difficult for me to imagine painful feelings.

These parallels were not lost on Claire, having steeped herself in Rousseau at the end of the summer. She was dark, like Clara. Mary was fair, like Julie. She was lively; Mary was gentle. She was not particularly prudent, but Mary was most certainly weak. In fact, Mary, like Julie, might well die prematurely—a sad thought, but an enticing one for Claire, since then the way would be clear.

*Portrait of Claire Clairmont by Amelia Curran, 1819.*

Imagining herself as a literary heroine elevated the ordinary moments of Claire's day, adding glamour to the many privations of her life. Inspired by Shelley, she even began talking about forming a "community of women." She dreamed of writing a novel whose heroine would bravely flout anything that stood in the way of her desires; the most important thing, she believed, was to live authentically. Shelley had urged her to read one of his favorite books, James Lawrence's *Empire of the Nairs; or, The Rights of Women*. Mary had read it, too, but had not been enthusiastic about Lawrence's unorthodox pronouncements on love. "Let every female," he declared, "live perfectly uncontrolled by any man and enjoying every freedom, which the males only have hitherto enjoyed; let her choose and change her lover as she please." Although Mary appreciated the idea of independence for women—after all, this was the central tenet of her mother's work—she was less keen on the idea of having many different lovers.

To Mary, an ideal relationship was a permanent connection. To please Shelley, she said she supported Lawrence's vision, but in her heart she clung to her belief in commitment. But Claire, like Shelley, was inspired by Lawrence's philosophy. In the years to come, she would hold to these principles, refusing all offers of marriage.

One day Mary saw her father on the street and he turned away. Another afternoon, she knocked on the door of Skinner Street, and he would not allow the maid to let her inside. When Fanny dared to make a visit, she told the girls Godwin had forbidden her to talk to Mary. Initiating a pattern she would follow for the rest of her life, Mary turned to a disciplined program of study for comfort and began to learn ancient Greek. Shelley gave her lessons, and she practiced copying down verbs and declining nouns. All three continued to rely on the example of Wollstonecraft to sustain them, reading and rereading her books. That winter, they took lodgings near the girls' old home in Somers Town to be near Wollstonecraft's grave.

Although Shelley did not like to see Mary suffer, he had never really enjoyed having a pregnant wife. During Harriet's first pregnancy he had begun an affair with another woman, a rural schoolteacher whose life was ruined as a result. He had left Harriet for Mary during Harriet's second pregnancy. Now, deprived of the attention he craved from the weak and exhausted Mary, he increasingly devoted himself to Claire. While in hiding from the bailiffs, he wrote her long letters, but only jotted short notes to Mary, for whom it was increasingly excruciating to watch Shelley turn toward her stepsister. She knew that Shelley wanted to live a life that was free of societal conventions, which meant that if they fell in love with other people, they were free to act on their feelings, but she had never dreamed that he might choose Claire over her. Instead of blaming him, however, she directed her anger at Claire, just as she had chosen to blame Mary-Jane for "stealing" her father's affection.

That November, Harriet had a son; Shelley was proud to have an heir, and his enthusiasm about the new baby annoyed Mary. She retreated into silence, always her default position, and wrote sardonic entries in their journal, muttering that this event "ought to be ushered in with ringing of bells &c. for it is the son of his *wife*." At this point in her life, consumed with her own melancholy, Mary had no room for sympathy for Harriet. Instead, she hoped that when she had her baby, Shelley would show her tenderness once again. If he remained distant, she consoled herself by imagining a child whom she could love and who would love her in return. But later, when Mary too had suffered terrible losses, she grieved over the pain she had helped Shelley inflict on Harriet, whose plight as an abandoned wife in a judgmental age was a desperate one.

As Mary's pregnancy progressed, she felt worse rather than better. Shelley continued to disappear for hours with Claire, and most biographers assume that they became lovers, but neither Shelley nor Claire left a record of their feelings for each other during that winter. In fact, pages from both Claire's and Mary's journals during this crucial period have been torn out, indicating that they, or one of their Victorian descendants, tried to cover up what happened.

Whether or not Shelley and Claire were actually romantically entangled, for Mary the result was the same: she felt desolate. In an attempt to fix matters, Shelley took the unconventional step of encouraging his friend Thomas Hogg, who had arrived in London that winter, to win Mary's heart. He hoped an affair would distract Mary from her jealousy of Claire, as well as further his plans for a community based on free love. Hogg, who was familiar with his friend's ideas, agreed to the plan; but though Mary tried to smile on Hogg's suit, she was too in love with Shelley to want anyone else. She suffered acutely when Shelley and Claire went off on one of their adventures or giggled together in another room, but she did her best to please Shelley by getting to know his friend, discussing philosophical topics such as "the love of Wisdom and free Will"—the closest she could come to flirtation. But even as an intellectual companion, Hogg was inferior to Shelley. When they debated the principles of liberty, she thought his arguments were weak and confused. He was dull, his manners abrasive. Ultimately, she could not help confessing how much she loved Shelley to her new suitor. "I . . . love him so tenderly & entirely. . . . [My] life hangs on the beam of his eye and [my] whole soul is entirely wrapt up in him," she declared.

Prodded by Shelley, Hogg stepped up his campaign, setting up camp in their lodgings and spending the night on a regular basis, until finally in January Mary backpedaled, promising him (and Shelley) that she would consider a sexual relationship once the baby was born in April. This delay only served to heighten Hogg's ardor. But events took a tragic turn. On February 22, Mary gave birth to a premature little girl. Born eight weeks too early, the baby survived for only thirteen days. On March 6, Mary wrote a tear-stained letter to Hogg describing what had happened:

> My baby is dead—will you come to me as soon as you can—
> I wish to see you—It was perfectly well when I went to bed—I
> awoke in the night to give it suck it appeared to be sleeping so
> quietly that I could not awake it—it was dead then but we did
> not find that out till morning—from its appearance it evidently died of convulsions—
>
> Will you come—you are so calm a creature & Shelley is
> afraid of a fever from the milk—

Whether Shelley was afraid for Mary or for himself is unclear, but another limitation of their relationship was becoming clear. Although Shelley turned to Mary for comfort and wisdom, she could not rely on him for reciprocal support. Plagued by his own phobias, he seemed unable to empathize with Mary. If she wanted solace, she would have to look elsewhere.

Hogg did come, but he was little help. Never a quick-witted conversationalist at the best of times, he was at a complete loss when faced with his weeping friend. And so Mary mourned the loss of her baby alone. Night after night, she dreamed the baby lived, writing in her journal, "Dream that my little baby came to life again—that it had only been cold & that we rubbed it by the fire & it lived—I awake & find no baby—I think about the little thing all day."

Finally, in April, Shelley shook off his self-absorption and took Mary on a pleasure jaunt to Salt Hill, near Slough, about twenty miles west of London. They spent a few nights in a pretty country inn. The fruit trees were in bloom; bluebells carpeted the fields; the village gardens were alight with sweet peas, larkspur, and foxgloves.

Without Claire, their romance reignited, and Mary felt herself coming back to life. Still, she was haunted by guilt. If she had done things differently, would the baby still be alive? Should she have fed the infant more frequently, or been more careful of her own health? But it was hard to be too miserable during this time alone with Shelley, their first since they had fled London ten months earlier. She wrote witty little notes to Hogg, who understood his cause was over and retreated sullenly to his own quarters. Shelley was feeling more optimistic himself, as his grandfather had died a few months earlier and, after much wrangling, he and his father had agreed he would receive an annual income of £1,000, as well as some additional sums to settle outstanding debts.

All signs pointed toward a happier future, but when Mary and Shelley returned to London, Claire was furious at having been abandoned, believing that Shelley had only used her while Mary was pregnant. Which of them did he love more? She forgot about playing Rousseau's Clara to Mary's Julie. Now the jealousy that had always been between them flared into outright battles. There were screaming matches, and ever after, both Claire and Mary would look back on this period as one of the darkest in their lives. Still, it was a wonder that the tension had taken so long to come to a head. The girls had been bred to be rivals: Godwin favored Mary; Mary-Jane favored Claire; the parents competed, the girls competed, and Fanny stood on the sidelines, the only one not in the contest.

By May, Mary was no longer even able to utter Claire's name, an awkward situation since they were living together. She referred to her stepsister as Shelley's "friend" and, terrified that she was going to become a "deserted thing no one cares for," in her journal she kept obsessive track of the time the two of them spent together: Shelley walked with "his friend" or talked with "the lady." Unable to pacify the two rivals, Shelley sought tranquillity in the Stoics, reading Seneca, until finally Claire made a sudden departure on May 13, traveling south to a little cottage Shelley rented for her in a small Devon village, as far off the beaten track as possible. Both sisters were relieved by the distance between them. Claire wrote to Fanny that she was glad to have some peace after living through "so much discontent, such violent scenes, such a turmoil of passion & hatred. . . ."

This decision—to send Claire to a place where she knew no one— hints at the reality of a sexual relationship between Claire and Shelley. It also accounts for the sudden intensity of Mary and Claire's battles. In general, young girls like Claire made rural retreats like this only when pregnant. If Claire had discovered she was going to have Shelley's baby and announced this when Mary and Shelley returned from their weekend away, this would certainly help explain the ferocity of their struggle. It also suggests that Mary made an ultimatum to Shelley: He could be with either Claire or her, not both. Unfortunately, it is impossible to know exactly what happened, since these pages from Mary's journal have disappeared. However, this attempt to conceal the course of events, combined with the young people's endorsement of free love, makes it seem likely that Shelley and Claire had been lovers.

Mary's journal entries do not resume until after Claire's departure, when she began a new diary. In an undated entry, Mary celebrated her "regeneration" with Shelley. She had won the battle for his love, at least for now. However, she had also discovered how tenuous their relationship actually was. She knew that Shelley missed her stepsister, and she kept a watchful eye on his moods in case he was secretly planning to leave her.

A few weeks after Claire left, Mary began to feel tired and ill, and discovered she was pregnant again. Shelley, too, felt weak and listless, perhaps as a result of the vegetarian diet he had decided was the only ethical way to live. A visit to the doctor had turned up a diagnosis of consumption, and although this later proved false, it deeply worried Mary. Here was another threat to their happiness, more dangerous than Claire. She could lose him forever if he did not take care of his health. They could not stay in the city a moment longer, she decided. Shelley needed country air for his lungs.

In June, with the money he had inherited from his grandfather, Shelley purchased a lease on a two-story red brick mansion with extensive gardens in Bishopsgate, near Eton, a mile from the town of

Windsor and just a few steps from the eastern entrance to Windsor Great Park. Shelley loved this part of England. He had blissful memories of roaming the countryside as a schoolboy here and wanted to introduce Mary to its beauties.

In their new home, Mary hired her first cook and a small cadre of servants so that instead of spending her mornings on domestic chores, she had time to read, write, and study Greek. Having inherited Godwin's belief in routine, she adhered to the schedule she had learned from him—work in the morning, dine, then walk in the afternoon—structured behavior that helped steady the erratic Shelley, who flitted in and out of the house longing for inspiration. He had no awareness of mealtimes and ate only when hungry, which was not very often. When he did eat, he devoured loaves of bread and had a schoolboyish habit of rolling the bread up into pellets and shooting them at people. "Mary, have I dined?" he would sometimes ask. Mary did not mind his forgetfulness, attributing it to genius. She told the cook to make them the vegetarian meals he insisted on and to omit sugar from their puddings, so as not to support the slave plantations. Doing without sweets was a significant sacrifice for Shelley, who loved sugar. According to Hogg, one of his favorite dishes was one he made himself. He would tear several loaves of bread into a bowl, pour boiling water on top, let it steep for a while, then squeeze out the water, chop it up with a spoon, and sprinkle it with huge amounts of sugar and nutmeg. Hogg teased him that he gorged himself on this "pap" so voraciously that he was like a Valkyrie "lapping up the blood of the slain!"

" 'Aye!' [Shelley] shouted out, with grim delight, 'I lap up the blood of the slain!' "

Thereafter, to the astonishment of guests, whenever he was eating this sugary mixture, he would cry, "I am going to lap up the blood of the slain! To sup up the gore of murdered kings!"

He also loved gingerbread and puddings of all kinds. But for now he had decided to give up all such treats. As long as there were slaves in the world, he refused to indulge in sugary delights.

Gradually, their health improved. Shelley felt stronger after spending hours outside, and now that Mary had endured the initial months of pregnancy, her sickness passed. After breakfast, she worked and Shelley roamed about outside with his little notebook or a volume of poetry. In the early afternoon, he would usually reappear and they would ramble through Windsor Great Park or climb nearby Cooper's Hill and explore the ruined abbeys, the ancient royal castle, Bishopsgate Heath, Chapel Wood, and the meadows of Windsor. Mary shared her mother's belief in exercise as a curative for most ills, and now that she felt stronger, she insisted on hikes that lasted all afternoon. On particularly fine days, she and Shelley took their books into the park and read under the ancient oak trees. Sometimes deer would wander past or rabbits would rustle the dark green undergrowth while the two of them discussed art, philosophy, and their aspirations. Shelley respected what he called Mary's "hereditary aristocracy," her calm, quiet ways, and her intellectual acuity. He also relished her contempt for hypocrisy. Mary once again believed that they were living out her mother's dream, establishing a union between equals in which both the man and the woman had important work to do—an idea that Shelley fully endorsed. But the question was, what was this work to be?

When Shelley met Mary he was torn between pursuing philosophy and poetry. His first published poem, *Queen Mab,* was a strange amalgamation of both, as Shelley had added extensive notes to the poem, arguing the merits of vegetarianism, sexual liberation, and freedom. Mary had been trained by Godwin to think logically and did not hesitate when Shelley asked her what she thought he should do with his life. She urged him to embrace poetry as his true calling, citing her mother's belief that poetry, not philosophy, was the apex of human achievement. Shelley believed that Mary must be right, not only because she was wise and learned, but because he felt she understood him more fully than anyone else. Poetry would be his life's work, he declared, and once he had made that decision, he felt great relief, writing Hogg, "I never before felt the integrity of my nature." To Mary, he wrote, "You alone reconcile me to myself & to my beloved hopes."

Having decided on a goal, Shelley set right to work. With another school friend, the writer Thomas Peacock, who lived nearby, and Hogg, who often came up from London to visit, he embarked on a rigorous study of the Greek and Italian poets. With Mary, he steeped himself in English poetry. They read Spenser's *The Faerie Queene,* which inspired Mary to call Shelley her "elfin Knight." Although they were thrilled by Spenser's romance, with its thickets of epithets and glorious stanzas, neither Mary nor Shelley liked his preachy tone. Chastity, temperance, obedience—these were not the values they espoused. What about liberty? What about the imagination? That fall they read *Paradise Lost* and were awestruck by Milton's vivid depiction of a rebellious Satan. Here was a poet unshackled by petty moralizing. Here was a poem worthy of emulation.

The eventual impact of these discussions both on Mary's and Shelley's work and on that of future writers is incalculable. Shelley would give voice to the ideas they developed in his *Defense of Poetry,* praising Milton for allowing his imagination free rein and criticizing Spenser for his philosophical limitations. Most early-nineteenth-century readers admired Milton, but to place him above Spenser, who was considered the greatest of the English poets, was scandalous. Centuries later, however, Shelley and Mary's ideas continue to exert their hold. Shelley's *Defense* has been read by generations of college students and is still a staple in the classroom, shaping the perspective of countless scholars and writers. Now, Shelley and Mary's belief that the imagination should be preeminent in literary endeavors, that the artist should not preach but should rely on vision and inspiration, is a literary commonplace; young writers are taught to show, not tell, to convey their ideas through imagery and plot rather than lecturing or sermonizing. And though these tenets may no longer hold sway as much as they once did, Shelley's *Defense* is undoubtedly one of the great Romantic manifestos, famous for overturning some of the most dearly held principles of English literature, as well as upending the Christian emphasis on literature as a tool of conversion.

Yet Mary's role in shaping Shelley's revolutionary theories is rarely acknowledged. Rather, critical debate has centered on Shelley's influence on Mary. In part, this is Mary's own doing. In her version of events, Shelley was the great man and she the diminutive follower. But her representation of their relationship has more to do with her own complexities than with the actual partnership they formed in Bishopsgate. The proof of this lies in the dramatic shift Shelley's work took that summer and fall. On the strength of the ideas they had developed together, Shelley began to compose *Alastor*, the first poem of significant length he had written since he had met Mary and generally considered his first mature literary endeavor. Instead of relying on long endnotes to express his ideas, as he had in *Queen Mab*, Shelley would employ simile, metaphor, allusions, and fresh imagery to infuse his thoughts with life. Even more important, for the first time, Shelley allowed himself to explore his own consciousness, to reveal what Mary called "a poet's heart in solitude," giving *Alastor* a psychological sophistication that is lacking in *Queen Mab*.

While Shelley was coming to terms with his identity as a poet, Mary, too, was immersed in a literary apprenticeship, although she was not yet quite sure what she would write. She worked on her Greek and read assiduously, keeping a detailed list of the books, including the works of her parents as well as philosophy, science, classical literature, political theory, travel writing, history, and even a gothic novel or two. During the final months of her pregnancy, the issue that most gripped her was slavery. Although the Abolition Act of 1807 had outlawed trafficking on English soil, slavery was still thriving in the West Indies, Brazil, and Cuba as well as in North America. Deeply disturbed by the conditions of the slaves and the ill treatment they faced, Mary read firsthand accounts of the slave trade and researched its history until her first labor pains forced her to put aside her books. On January 24, 1816, she gave birth to a boy. She named him William after her father, hoping that this gesture might help bridge the gap between them. But Godwin did not soften. He still refused any contact with his daughter, although he continued to pester Shelley about a loan. Finally, Shelley lost his temper:

My astonishment, and I will confess when I have been treated with most harshness and cruelty by you, my indignation has been extreme, that, knowing as you do my nature, any considerations should have prevailed on you to be thus harsh and cruel.

Mary, meanwhile, sought to ease the pain of her father's rejection by immersing herself in caring for her healthy new son. She did not resume her reading on slavery. Instead, she memorized Greek verbs, read her mother's books, and wrote in her journal. The only hardship she experienced that spring was Shelley's frequent absence; a year after his grandfather's death, he was still battling his father's lawyers about the status of his inheritance and had to go to London too frequently for Mary's liking. Fortunately, the fight ended well for Shelley. Sir Timothy agreed to pay some of his debts and to continue his allowance of £1,000 a year. From his annual income, he gave £200 to Harriet—a stingy allotment for the mother of his two children, but Shelley had written her off as a traitor, telling himself that she would be able to live independently if she exercised restraint.

Although the remaining £800 a year did not make Shelley a wealthy man, it did enable him to live comfortably. At a time when the annual income of skilled laborers ranged from only £50 to £90 and lawyers earned at most £450, members of the gentry could live on less than £500 a year if they were careful. On the other end of the spectrum, Jane Austen's Mr. Darcy had an annual income of £10,000, which made him an enormously wealthy man, the rough equivalent of a millionaire today.

In March, Claire returned from exile to visit Mary. If she had given birth to a child, there was no evidence of this now. Perhaps she had given her baby away for adoption, had a miscarriage, or consulted a midwife to abort her pregnancy. But perhaps she had not been pregnant at all. Whatever the case, Claire and Mary soon fell back into their old uneasy camaraderie. There were no more outright battles. Mary could afford to be forgiving now that she had Shelley's son, but she could still sense her stepsister's jealousy, tempered though it was by rekindled affection and admiration.

To Claire, once again, Mary appeared to have everything—a lover, a child, and a home. However, Mary's life also seemed intolerably dull. Sitting by the fire with a baby, jiggling him up and down, or pushing him in his pram were entirely unsatisfactory activities for a lively eighteen-year-old like Claire. But if she had indeed just given up her own child, they would also have been heartbreaking. Before long, Claire was traveling back and forth to London, upsetting Mary by staying with Shelley in his temporary lodgings. Sometimes she visited her mother and Godwin at Skinner Street. Shelley and Mary hoped she could talk the Godwins into accepting them as a couple. But Claire had little interest in making her stepsister's life easier. She was intent on another scheme, one inspired by her desire for the spotlight and her hunger for adventure, and yet destined to cause her so much pain that in later years she would wish she had paused and considered before plunging ahead.

# CHAPTER 12

# MARY WOLLSTONECRAFT:
# THE FIRST VINDICATION

----

[ 1787–1791 ]

MAGAZINES WERE COMPARATIVELY NEW INVENTIONS WHEN twenty-nine-year-old Mary Wollstonecraft began reviewing books for Johnson's newly minted *Analytical Review*. Unlike the daily "rags," where writers gossiped, preached, raged, and snarled about everything from what boots to buy to what members of Parliament to endorse, the *Analytical Review* was a high-minded affair that came out once a month and was over one hundred pages long, more like a book than a pamphlet. Johnson and Christie had serious philosophical and political aims. They called their reviewers "the HISTORIANS of the Republic of Letters," and their mission was to create a well-informed public by highlighting important publications that would "add to the stock of human knowledge." Conservatives viewed the new magazine as a dangerous mouthpiece for radicals, arguing that Johnson and Christie wanted to bring down the government. But the *Analytical Review* prided itself on its moderate and rational stands, advocating for the gradual reform of Parliament and opposing violence and factionalism in all their forms.

Women were not meant to take part in serious debate of the kind endorsed by the *Analytical Review*. If a woman wanted to write, she was supposed to stick to gentle religious reflections, books of calming advice, brief homilies, or fanciful romances. Certainly she should not try to compose highly informed, intricate dissections of contemporary literature and politics. Nor should she form opinions that ran counter to the accepted truths of the day. True to form, Mary ignored these assumptions and jumped right into the literary fray, wielding her pen like a knife, skewering the books she did not like as ferociously as any of her male peers. The sentimental novels Johnson assigned her to review were "trash," she wrote. They reinforced the pernicious ideas that women needed to be rescued by men and that women needed men to tell them what to do. This was destructive drivel, declared Mary. The "unnatural characters, improbable incidents, sad tales of woe rehearsed in an affected half-prose, half-poetical style, exquisite double-refined sensibility, dazzling beauty, and elegant drapery" were not only absurd, they were harmful to their female readers.

It was not that she disliked novels—she, of course, had written one—it was the formulas employed by so many "scribbling women" that disturbed her. Fainting maidens, handsome suitors, fluttering ball gowns, forbidding castles, and black-cloaked villains "poison the minds of our young females," she said. "Why is virtue to be always rewarded with a coach and six?" In her own novel, "Mary's" mother, already a weak woman, is further enfeebled by reading such romances. This does not mean that Mary was against sentiment, having learned to pride herself on her highly refined feelings after reading Rousseau, but she rejected the idea that her feelings clouded her ability to make logical decisions. She believed that she was as capable of rational thought as any man and wanted to read and write books that were worthy of her intellect.

As the months passed, Johnson's prediction came true. Mary was earning more money than she could have dreamed of a year earlier. Rather than saving for her own future, however, she sent money to Paris for Everina's upkeep, pushing her sister to extend her stay in France indefinitely. She found a better situation for Eliza at a school in Putney, where she could be a "parlour boarder"—a position in which one earned one's board through teaching. Everything else— aside from the bare minimum—she gave to Fanny's grieving family.

Although these obligations depleted her purse, Mary still enjoyed a fast-paced literary life and entertained men in her apartment without a chaperone, unconventional though this was. Even more unconventional was her style as a hostess. She shocked acquaintances when she served wine to the visiting French politician Prince Talleyrand "indiscriminately from tea cups." Mary, however, was loosening the knots that had bound her since she was a girl. No more frivolity or artificiality: one's natural impulses mattered more than good manners; genius lay in the core of one's being, not in the clink of fine crystal.

During Mary's first years in London, the topic on everyone's mind was France. The country was in financial and political crisis. King Louis XVI had resisted the advice of his counselors for too long. The government was in dire need of funds, but if he raised taxes one more time, it seemed possible there might be a revolt. Already there were outbreaks of violence in Paris. French intellectuals published one furious pamphlet after another: the government was corrupt; the rich were too rich; the poor, too poor. From her work translating Louis XVI's finance minister, Jacques Necker, Mary had become knowledgeable about the financial situation in France, and she was a significant contributor to the discussions about the unrest in Paris with Johnson and his friends. All of these men were progressive and agreed on basic tenets—the rights of the individual versus the state, the importance of freedom, and the inherent corruption of inherited position and property—but arguments still swept around the table: What was the best way to reform society? Should there be new laws? Were violent uprisings necessary? How effective were protest marches and petitions? What were the rights of kings? Should France institute a parliamentary system? What about England? Should there even be a monarchy?

To Mary's delight, despite his failing health, Dr. Price, her hero from Newington Green, traveled into the city to lead some of these debates, praising the radicals and lambasting the French king. Citizens had the right to choose their rulers, he argued, citing Locke. Mary agreed with her old mentor and listened carefully to his points. Johnson was beginning to give her more important reviewing assignments, political works and histories rather than just romance novels, which allowed her to develop the revolutionary ideas she had been formulating at his table while also teaching her crucial lessons as a writer: how to create a public voice that lay outside the purview of "femininity"—how to offend, alienate, and strenuously disagree.

Her task was made easier by the protections built into eighteenth-century journalism. Most writers signed their articles with their initials, and so, under the genderless guise of M.W., she could take leaps, assert views she knew would be unpopular, inveigh against writers she thought were fools, and preach on behalf of her favorite issues—the education of women, the virtues of freedom, and the evils of wealth—without fearing any personal assaults. Those who did oppose M.W. did so on an ideological basis, not because M.W. was female. Before long, she was lobbing insults with the best of them, calling her opponents at *The Critical Review* "timid, mean" and assessing one book as "an heterogeneous mass of folly, affectation and improbability."

In 1789, during Mary's third summer in London, the news from France took a dramatic turn. The citizens of Paris had marched on the Bastille prison, overcome the king's guards, and released the prisoners who had been rotting there for decades. To Mary, who had compared her sojourn with Lord and Lady Kingsborough to life in the Bastille, this triumph had a strangely personal feel. She was free; the French prisoners were free. Liberty had triumphed over aristocratic tyranny. Her friend the poet William Cowper, who often attended Johnson's dinner parties, immediately penned an *Address to the Bastille:*

> *Ye dungeons, and ye Cages of Despair!—*
> *There's not an English heart that would not leap,*
> *To hear that ye were fall'n at last.*

In the *New Annual Register,* a young journalist named William Godwin rejoiced: "Advice is received from Paris, of a great revolution in France." Conservatives, on the other hand, were alarmed. Revolutions were contagious and the ripples of the French Revolution could soon reach England. Already, the poor were restless. Between 1740 and 1779, the Enclosure Acts had taken thousands of acres of common land and placed them in the hands of wealthy landowners,

increasing the gap between rich and poor. There had been many violent demonstrations in London; workers had taken to the streets,
burning effigies of the king and rioting against the high price of
bread. In fact, riots had become part of the fabric of English culture.
As Ben Franklin put it, when he visited in 1769, "I have seen, within
a year, riots in the country, about corn; riots about elections; riots
about workhouses; riots of colliers, riots of weavers, riots of coal-
heavers; riots of sawyers." The implications of this unrest were not
lost on English aristocrats. Tensions had reached dangerous, potentially explosive levels.

For Mary, the revolutionaries in France proclaimed the ideals she
held most dear—the renunciation of tyranny and the redemption of
the poor and oppressed; the new National Assembly had even sworn
to uphold a "Declaration of the Rights of Man" inspired directly by
Rousseau. The destruction of the Bastille was an event that "hailed
the dawn of a new day," she wrote, "and freedom, like a lion roused
from his lair, rose with dignity, and calmly shook herself."

In her private life, Mary was also undergoing a transformation.
That September, she had fallen into the habit of talking late into the
night with one of Johnson's closest friends, the forty-nine-year-old
Swiss artist Henry Fuseli.

Fuseli's favorite topic was sex. His paintings featured imps nuzzling the bare pink breasts of fairies, naked Greek gods flexing their
muscles, and lascivious witches. At first, it was difficult for Mary to
accept the idea that sexuality could be a positive force. In *Original
Stories,* she had warned young girls against giving way to their desires, preaching against sexual infatuation.

But Fuseli was dedicated to the principle that no sex act should be
taboo. He explained pleasures that were entirely new to her and told
her about his liaisons with men and women, most notoriously with
the niece of his erstwhile male lover, a Protestant priest. He thought
women should be allowed to discover and express their sensuality.
He said masturbation was important; human sexuality needed to be
lifted out of the sewers and honored as the life force it was. He owned
a large collection of explicit drawings that could never be shown in
public, the most unusual of which were his sketches of women with

*Self-portrait of the Swiss artist Henry Fuseli.*

"phallic coiffures." Recent scholars have even suggested that he was having a secret affair with Johnson.

By that summer, Fuseli had persuaded Mary to believe that sexual impulses should be acknowledged, even celebrated. However, learning about desire from a master had its drawbacks; it was becoming difficult to manage her feelings. Although Fuseli was not particularly handsome—he was short and bowlegged—his powers of seduction were legendary. Mary yearned to be closer to him, but after their late-night discussions, Fuseli always returned home to the bed of his wife, an ex-model who was extremely pretty, though far inferior to Mary intellectually. Mary struggled to accept the limitations of her relationship with this compelling man, telling herself that even if he was not in love with her, their explicit conversations were evidence that she had been accepted into an exclusive club of male intellectuals. But this was not much comfort when she yearned for more.

Mary's acknowledgment of her own sexuality was itself a courageous act. "Experts" of the time held that females who felt desire were trespassing into dangerously masculine territory. Women were believed to be so weak that they could easily be overwhelmed by passion and lose all capacity for reason. Mary was cautious, keeping her feelings to herself. She realized that if anyone from her previous life—her sisters or old friends—knew of the attraction she felt, she would be condemned. Merely being alone with a man went against the strict moral code; talking about sex with him, even if you never acted on it, was considered immoral and scandalous.

Mary's flirtation with Fuseli was just one of her many departures from the traditional road she had long ago forgone. She had strong opinions—"truths," she would have said—that she wanted to express in what she called a "masculine" style: bold, honest, and eminently rational rather than trivial, weak, and flowery, the unfortunate list of adjectives attributed to "feminine" writing by most in the eighteenth century. She had a history now of reviewing books that would ordinarily have been the province of men—a book on boxing, an encyclopedia of music—and she was ready to take on new challenges, whatever they might be.

At the same time, Mary, who had already been inspired by Rousseau, was now ready to embrace the new ideals of what would come to be called Romanticism, a literary movement that she would be one of the first to promote in England: the elevation of emotion over reason, passion over logic, spontaneity over restraint, and originality over tradition. Although she protested against those who said that women were too easily ruled by their feelings and had little capacity for logical thought, she also agreed with Fuseli and her new friends at Johnson's table that emotions had been stigmatized by previous generations. Passion could be a driving force for reform in the world and should be revered. This departure from Enlightenment beliefs represented an important evolution in her thinking and now she wondered if it was possible to employ a direct, rational "male" style and yet still champion these new ideals.

In her columns in the *Analytical Review,* Mary grappled with this contradiction, praising a new novel, *Julia,* by Helen Maria Williams, precisely because of its "artless energy of feeling." Unlike the romances she had railed against, Williams's fiction seemed to Mary to promote honesty rather than artificiality, Nature rather than society.

If one viewed women's capacity for passion as a strength rather than a weakness, then one could combat the assumptions of those critics who ridiculed women's writing as overly emotional and irrational. In other words, far from being "merely" the province of women, there was nothing trivial about feelings. The Bastille had been won because the people had been ignited by their passions, and Mary could feel this truth in her own life; she felt alive, aware of her own capabilities. By connecting the freedom to express one's passions with the freedom to protest against the state, the freedom of women with the freedom of the artist and intellectual, Mary was learning a significant lesson. No political issue was free of personal implications. No reasonable cause was free of emotions. Logical discourse was important, but passion was even more so. If dishonest sentimentality made for poor writing, so did dry reason. Reason and sentiment. Passion and logic. The two had to be combined.

Having tackled this contradiction in her writing life, she wanted to liberate herself from the restrictions that governed sexuality—a more dangerous enterprise than any she had embarked on before. Although the details are missing from the historical record, by early fall her relationship with Fuseli was sufficiently charged to make Fuseli's wife uneasy. The two translated revolutionary pamphlets together and talked of taking a trip to France. Mary relished her life and their relationship. She wrote Everina, "My die is cast!—I could not now resign intellectual pursuits for domestic comforts."

Although to the modern ear, the phrase "intellectual pursuits" might sound rather tame, it was code for a remarkable proclamation. Mary was declaring her right to live the kind of public life most people believed was impossible for women. Granted, she had been living as an intellectual for the last three years and had already declared that she was the first of "a new genus," but she had never before stated her position with such force to herself or to her sisters. Now she was fiercely asserting her right to break the rules that governed women, even though she knew that a truly public life devoted to politics and ideas, rather than a private life of domesticity, would expose her to bitter criticism.

The first test of her mettle came that November, when the sixty-year-old Edmund Burke, the greatest Whig orator and writer of the era, condemned the French Revolution, publishing an angry response to Dr. Price's book of the previous year, *Reflections on the Revolution in France,* which Mary had praised in a review for Johnson. Mary read Burke's attack with outrage. Tradition should be respected, Burke intoned, government revered. Above all, change should be regarded with suspicion and liberty treated with caution.

To Mary, this was anathema. Just twenty years earlier, Burke had supported the American Revolution, staking his reputation on the just cause of liberty for the United States. She was indignant that this champion of freedom was now arguing *against* the greatest revolution of all time. But Burke had actually always been far more conservative than his supporters realized. He represented the interests of the landed gentry and only viewed American independence as the proper course because the colonies were costing the British government more than they were worth. In addition, he felt they had displayed a talent for self-government since the seventeenth century. When it came to the French, Burke deplored what he viewed as the Revolution's irrational and apocalyptic leap into a future that dispensed with the traditions he believed were crucial to preserving civilization.

Burke's call to arms was an instant success. He had tapped into the age-old English distrust of their French neighbors, stirring up fear that revolutionary fever might spread across the Channel, launching a wave of conservatism that swept across London, crushing liberal politics and politicians with its force. Mary hated how readers swallowed Burke's propaganda. He attacked all that she valued, placing "precedent, authority, and example" ahead of the claims of liberty. In addition, he had insulted her mentor, Dr. Price.

It was time to act, Mary decided: she would write a rebuttal to Burke's *Reflections*. When she proposed this idea to Johnson, he immediately saw its merits, ethically and financially. He promised to print her response to Burke as fast as she could write it, but would do so without revealing her identity.

Mary set to work. Her refutation would be direct and truthful, she decided, as though she were at Johnson's dinner table, bringing up topics as they occurred to her instead of preaching from a pulpit. She would also allow herself to make use of emotion to charge the piece with Romantic fervor. She wanted to differentiate herself from Burke's carefully constructed imagery and "turgid bombast," criticizing his "flowers of rhetoric," which, ironically, she characterized as feminine. A veteran columnist, Mary knew that her best strategy would be to reveal him as the self-aggrandizing politician she believed him to be.

Her well-reasoned, often witty rebuttals show how carefully she crafted the paragraphs she claimed were spontaneous. When Burke wrote, "[The poor] must respect that property of which they cannot partake. . . . They must be taught their consolation in the final proportions of eternal justice," Mary returned, "It is, Sir, possible to render the poor happier in this world, without depriving them of the consolation which you gratuitously grant them in the next." Her opponent's reverence for tradition, she said, led him to endorse all sorts of evils simply because they existed in the past. Slavery was a case in point. Should we cling to this hideous trade simply because it is "old"?

She also took issue with Burke's praise of the English aristocracy for its paternalistic attitude toward the poor. "Charity is not a condescending distribution of alms but an intercourse of good offices and mutual benefits, founded on respect for humanity," she wrote. No aristocrat had ever taken care of her debts, or supported her endeavors, whereas Johnson, her dear middle-class friend, had supported her and paid her generously for her work. She responded to Burke's gilded overview of English history by accusing the statesman of being a "champion of property" rather than a "friend of liberty." It is the future, she said, that holds promise. Reformation, not nostalgia, will save humanity. If men like Burke would step aside and make room for the new era, the utopian visions of the revolutionaries had a chance of becoming reality.

Halfway through writing, Mary broke down. It hit her, quite suddenly, that she was going head to head with one of the most powerful men in England, debating principles the majority of Englishmen regarded as cornerstones: the sanctity of property, the preservation of inheritance, and the essential value of the aristocracy. In despair, she trailed over to Johnson's house, tail down, and told him she was going to quit. Johnson, who by now knew how to handle her moods, let her make her excuses—her ill health, her poor endurance, her lack of a formal education—and then said he would destroy the pages she had already sent him and that she did not need to finish, especially if she did not think she was up to it. No approach could have been more effective. She later admitted he had "piqued her pride."

Reignited, she went back to work, finishing so quickly that only twenty-eight days after Burke's *Reflections* was published, *A Vindication of the Rights of Men* appeared in the bookstores, the first response to Burke in what would soon become a frenzied debate. Despite her hesitation, Mary had written faster than any of Burke's other opponents, and within three weeks *Rights of Men* had sold out. As her readers well knew, Mary's title was a direct reference to the French revolutionaries' *Déclaration des droits de l'Homme et du Citoyen* of the previous year, and was a trumpet call, announcing her support of the French revolutionaries.

At 150 pages, or about 45,000 words, *Rights of Men* was a substantial piece of work, and it received positive reviews. Even opponents acknowledged that the anonymous author had written a strong argument infused with passion. After such a warm reception, Johnson and Mary decided to reveal her name in the second edition, a radical step. But their optimism proved to be misplaced. With the revelation of Mary's identity, reviewers condemned her as a female upstart rather than addressing the ideas she had put forth. Critics who had originally praised the work now complained about its faults. The book was suddenly incoherent and absurd. Horace Walpole, the archconservative writer and art historian, called Mary a "hyena in petticoats." Other critics contented themselves with ridicule:

> The *rights of men* asserted by a fair lady! The age of chivalry cannot be over, or the sexes have changed their ground. . . . We should be sorry to raise a horse-laugh against a fair lady; but we were always taught to suppose that the *rights of women* were the proper theme of the female sex.

Mary was prepared for these attacks. She knew that she was venturing into taboo territory. But after the positive response to the first anonymous edition, her courage had grown. She was ready to stand behind her ideas. Eliza's example had shown her the crippling consequences of the basic precepts of English common law—that wives could not own their own property, enter into business contracts, or control their own money. In 1782, there had been an attempt to reform the misogynistic legal code, but the best that lawmakers could do was to declare it illegal to beat one's wife with a stick that was thicker than a thumb. In the intellectual world, these beliefs translated into the assumption that women were incapable of independent thought. To Mary, the best way to fight back was to prove what a woman could do, and that meant acknowledging her role as the author of *Rights of Men*.

Fortunately, her fellow radicals gave her enthusiastic support. Thomas Paine, deep into the composition of his own *Rights of Man,* told Mary that he regarded her as a comrade in arms, and when Mary sent her *Vindication* to the frail Dr. Price, he said he was "happy in having such an advocate." Many new supporters also came flooding in, liberals who believed that the author of *Rights of Men* had taken on a tyrant—Burke—and come out the victor. They clamored to meet Mary, buying her book in droves. As a result, the book sold about three thousand copies, a significant number for the time.

Flush with her earnings, the most she had ever made, Mary bought new furniture, adopted a cat, and moved to a house on Store Street in Bloomsbury, which was larger and far more gracious than her rooms in Southwark. Visitors flocked to her doorstep, wanting to meet this outspoken woman. When she was not working or receiving admirers, she strolled with friends through the nearby gardens that stretched behind the British Museum, now the site of University College London.

One of Mary's admirers, William Roscoe, commissioned her portrait, and the famous artist John Opie also asked to paint her. Sitting for these portraits forced Mary to think more carefully about how she appeared in public. She still refused to twist her hair into ringlets, paint her cheeks with rouge, or wear a frilly gown. But she did pin up her hair and buy expensive new dresses made of rich fabrics. For the Roscoe portrait, she wore black (no lace, no pink) with a plain white fichu tucked into her bodice, which made her look more like a prime minister than a young female radical.

*Engraving by Ridley, based on a painting by Opie.*

M^{RS}. WOLLSTONECRAFT.

In the Opie portrait, she looks slightly more approachable, but she still wore a dark dress and again refused any of the standard feminine props of the era.

The overall impression created by both pictures is one of gravitas. She does not smile. She does not try to charm her audience. Her stern, steady gaze says she is a woman capable of reasoned and essential argument, a philosopher as well as a person of deep feeling, possessing both passion and conviction, idealism and empathy. The portraits capture her right at the moment when she was on the brink of becoming the Mary Wollstonecraft readers recognize today, author of one of the most important works in the history of political philosophy.

# CHAPTER 13

# MARY GODWIN:
# "MAD, BAD AND DANGEROUS
# TO KNOW"

———

## [ 1816 ]

*I*N THE WINTER OF 1816, LONDON WAS TRANSFIXED BY THE SCAN-dalous doings of the twenty-eight-year-old Lord Byron, one of the most famous men in Europe. His poems had brought him fame, and his shocking love affairs had given him notorious superstardom. Having left Mary behind in Bishopsgate, her stepsister Claire had decided to stay in the city, sometimes with Shelley, sometimes with the Godwins, and before long she, too, was gripped by Byron fever.

To Claire, as to many young ladies of the era, Byron's name served as both cautionary tale and aphrodisiac. She had read many of his poems, which were famous for their frank descriptions of illicit love affairs and their exotic settings. In 1814, he had published *The Corsair*, set in a Turkish harem, which sold ten thousand copies on the day of publication—a feat no other author had ever accomplished. Proper English ladies warned their daughters to beware of his wiles, but how could they resist? Byron was wickedly handsome and his poems too thrilling to ignore. He was "mad, bad and dangerous to know," said Lady Caroline Lamb, one of his spurned lovers. A world traveler, a man pursued by legions of women, a radical who spoke on behalf of the working people, and a bestselling poet: in Claire's eyes, he was just what she needed.

Claire was excited to hear that Byron had recently returned to

London and had been spotted attending plays at Drury Lane, the city's premier theater. If she could get him to take an interest in her, in her singing or perhaps her acting, then she could begin to make inroads in her competition with Mary. If she could do more—get him to befriend her, or, best (and most impossible) of all, fall in love with her—she would for once have the upper hand. No one had yet heard of Shelley, but everyone had heard of Byron. With him at her side, Claire would at last be the victor in her struggle with her stepsister.

She began her campaign by peppering Byron with letters, introducing herself as a sophisticated radical who believed that marriage was one of the great evils of modern society: "I can never resist the temptation of throwing a pebble at it as I pass by," she declared. She also made sure to reveal her connection to Godwin, as well as to Shel-

*Portrait of Lord Byron by Thomas Phillips, 1814: "Mad, bad and dangerous to know."*

ley and Mary, telling Byron the story of their escapades in France and Switzerland and the ostracism Shelley and Mary now faced. Byron was already interested in the younger poet, who had sent him a copy of *Queen Mab,* a work Byron deemed promising. A veteran of scandals and gossip, he felt sympathy for Shelley's situation. In addition, he was intrigued by his liaison with Mary. He admired Wollstonecraft as well as Godwin. Like most radicals, he was fascinated by the thought of their daughter and was curious to meet her.

At another time in his life, Byron might have ignored Claire, but that winter he was in a miserable state of self-doubt and loneliness. He was not writing any poetry. The public had gone from worshipping him to viewing his escapades with fascinated horror. His yearlong marriage to Anne Isabella Milbanke, which he had imagined would give him stability, respectability, and companionship, had erupted into recrimination, slander, and threats of prosecution. Anne had fled back to her parents and told everyone that her husband had abused her and was having an affair with his half sister Augusta—claims that were mostly true. Augusta, who was pregnant (the paternity of this baby is still uncertain), had lived with Byron in his stately home at 13 Piccadilly Terrace, opposite Green Park, but had moved out that spring in a vain attempt to quiet the gossip. Although Byron supported this decision, her departure had left him feeling abandoned. He was not invited anywhere. Old friends turned their backs on him. Yet crowds of curious fans still flocked to Piccadilly Terrace trying to peer in his windows or climb over the garden walls. When he was not drinking, or riding his Flemish mare, he was immersed in legal negotiations with Anne's family for the couple's separation. Claire's letters, with their rushes of compliments and airy references to literature and philosophy, were a welcome balm. Here was a young woman who still admired him despite, or maybe even because of, the scandals he had caused.

He wrote back to her and proposed an assignation. Claire, delighted at her success and hoping to lure him closer, revealed that she had no guardian, parent, or brother to cause any difficulties. This suited Byron very well; he was tired of fending off the angry husbands and fathers of his lovers. He told her to meet him in his private box at the theater and then again, secretly, at Piccadilly Terrace, where they made love almost immediately. Claire was exhilarated: she had only dared to hope for a few conversations; now, she was the great man's lover. Maybe she would even become his permanent mistress. After all, if Mary could live with Shelley, she could live with Byron. It would be good for Shelley's career; Byron would help him. And good for hers as well, although what her career was going to be was as yet unclear. All she knew was that she was a freethinker and that she intended to carry the lamp of Enlightenment forward in the spirit of Mary Wollstonecraft.

For a few weeks, Byron was intrigued. He read Claire's story "The Idiot" and praised it; unfortunately, no copy of this story still exists. When he heard her sing, which was Claire's special talent, her voice became the inspiration for one of his most beautiful love poems:

> *There be none of Beauty's daughters*
> *With a magic like thee;*
> *And like music on the waters*
> *Is thy sweet voice to me.*

But his enthusiasm soon ebbed. When Byron told her that he did not want a mistress and was not in love with her, Claire, desperate to retain her hold, upped the ante. Mary had come up to London that spring to join Shelley while he fought his legal battles. Realizing that Byron would be intrigued, Claire offered Mary to Byron as a kind of prize, telling him her stepsister admired his work and would like to meet him. It was true that Mary did love Byron's poetry. Long before she had met Shelley, Byron had been her image of the ideal poet. She and her sisters had read accounts of his adventures in the newspapers and, like other girls their age, had hoped to catch sight of him at society functions. She had memorized long passages from *Childe Harold; To Thyrza,* which she also knew by heart, had buoyed her during the terrible weeks before she ran away with Shelley. She had inscribed four of its most famous lines in the copy of *Queen Mab* that Shelley had given her, starting off with her own solemn vow of love—"But I am exclusively thine—by the kiss of love"—and then adding Byron's words:

*The glance that none saw beside*
*The smile none else might understand*
*The whispered thought of hearts allied*
*The pressure of the thrilling hand*

After which she concluded with her own dramatic flourish: "I have pledged myself to thee and sacred is the gift," words that sound strikingly similar to a marriage vow, a substitute for the ceremony they had not yet undertaken.

But despite all this, Mary had expressed no desire to meet the great poet. To persuade her sister, Claire told Mary that Byron was interested in offering Shelley his assistance; she did not mention that she had wooed the poet into bed, and she made Byron promise not to mention their affair. For Mary, it must have been surprising to hear that Claire was on friendly terms with his lordship, but since Mary's journal pages are missing from this period, it is impossible to know how Claire explained the situation. In later years, Claire would say that she and Byron had met through a mutual acquaintance, never revealing that she had been the one to make the first overture.

Once the two principals had agreed, Claire set the time. She had some trepidation about Byron's dependability, as he had a history of keeping her waiting, and urged him to be on time. However, Byron treated his appointment with Mary with far more respect than his assignations with Claire. He was interested in meeting this young woman, the daughter of such a famous mother and father. A few years earlier, Byron, an admirer of *Political Justice,* had donated some of his own earnings to the perpetually cash-strapped Godwin. He had long revered Wollstonecraft. Mary and Byron both counted Coleridge as a friend and both admired his poetry. Byron had urged Coleridge to publish *Christabel,* a supernatural poem Byron loved so much that he memorized it when he read it in manuscript version. Both Mary and Byron valued scholarship, beautiful language, and flights of the imagination, no matter how disturbing.

At their first meeting, Mary was quiet, respectful, and serious. Byron was polite and expansive. Despite his wild life and the scandals he created, underneath it all, he had a deeply conventional streak.

Mary's good manners and composure pleased him. He did not try to flirt with her, nor she with him. From her earliest days, Mary had conversed with famous men, the great poets and intellectuals who came to the Godwin house. She was able to talk to Byron as though he were a friend or comrade, an unusual experience for the poet, who was used to young women either shrinking from him or attempting to seduce him. For Mary, Byron was fascinating not for his looks or his reputation as a lover, but solely because he was a brilliant writer and a rebel.

Nevertheless, much as he had enjoyed meeting Mary, Byron's interest in Claire continued to wane. She was not easily put off, however. When she discovered that Byron planned to spend part of his summer in Geneva, she begged to be taken along; when he refused, she used Mary once again, telling him that her stepsister yearned to write to him and wanted his address in Geneva: "Mary is delighted with you as I knew she would be. . . . She perpetually exclaims, 'How mild he is! How gentle! So different from what I expected.'"

Byron saw right through this. Having spent a long afternoon with the dignified Mary, Byron knew that Claire's description of her stepsister's feelings was a ploy. Such fulsome terms seemed unlikely to have come from such a reserved young lady. He was perfectly happy to sleep with Claire while he was still in London, but had no intention of taking her with him on his travels. As a last resort, Claire turned to Mary and Shelley, suggesting that they all take a trip to Geneva to be near Byron. Mary liked the idea of escaping the hostility of London and felt that three-month-old William would benefit from the clean air of Switzerland. For Shelley, Claire's proposal came at just the right moment, since it dovetailed with a plan he had been brooding over for months, instigated by an unpleasant rejection from Godwin.

In February, Shelley had attempted to make amends with Mary's father, ringing the bell at Skinner Street hoping to see the philosopher. When Godwin sent the servants to turn him away, Shelley refused to leave and kept on ringing the bell. But Godwin remained adamant and Shelley was forced to leave, hurt and angry. The older man had won that round, but at great expense to his own future happiness. After the incident, Shelley sounded the first warning, writing Godwin that he was tempted to "desert my native country." He was tired of suffering "the perpetual experience of neglect or enmity from almost everyone."

The impetus to leave was further compounded by the critics' hostile reception of *Alastor,* which Shelley had published that winter. They ignored it so entirely that Shelley felt humiliated, confessing that he was "morbidly sensitive to . . . the injustice of neglect." Until Claire's suggestion, Shelley was not sure where he wanted to go. All he knew was that he wanted to spurn everyone who had rejected him. Geneva seemed as good a location as any, particularly since he was eager to meet the famous poet. And so, once the weather warmed, Shelley decided to make good on his threat of departure, taking Mary and baby William with him. It would be a temporary exile—but then again, maybe not. Perhaps they would never return.

When Claire wrote to Byron of their plans, he was interested enough not to veto it out of hand. He did not want to encourage her, but he liked the idea of setting up camp with the younger poet and the daughter of Godwin and Wollstonecraft. At the end of April, when the legal proceedings faced by both men drew to a close, each household set forth for Switzerland.

Claire attempted to mask her true intentions in a letter to her reluctant lover, telling him she expected him to have an affair with Mary that summer, not her:

> You will I dare say fall in love with her; she is very handsome & very amiable & you will no doubt be blest in your attachment; nothing can afforde me such pleasure as to see you happy in any of your attachments. If it should be so I will redouble my attentions to please her. I will do everything she tells me whether it be good or bad for I would not stand low in the affections of the person so beyond blest as to be beloved of you.

An older Claire would never have written such a letter. But barely eighteen and used to men choosing Mary over herself, she did what she had always done—she diminished herself, in this case promising to be Mary's slave—in order to curry favor with the man she wanted. The scars of the Godwin/Clairmont union had not faded; Shelley, Byron, and Godwin were largely interchangeable in the drama between the stepsisters. For Claire, it did not matter how unworthy Byron was of her adoration. He was an essential component in her struggle to win love and attention.

MARY, SHELLEY, CLAIRE, AND baby William arrived in France in early May. They anticipated a pleasant journey through the mountains now that Shelley had the money for a private coach, but the expedition proved far more difficult than expected. Nicknamed "the year without a summer," 1816 is a famous anomaly in climate history. A volcano had erupted in Indonesia the preceding April, the world's largest explosion in over fifteen hundred years, spewing thick ash into the atmosphere and disrupting the normal weather patterns in Europe, Asia, and even North America. The Yangtze overflowed. Red snow fell in Italy. Famine swept from Moscow to New York. Grain froze and corn withered. Food prices soared and death rates doubled.

Switzerland was hit particularly hard by the erratic weather patterns, and snow was still falling heavily when they arrived in the foothills of the Alps. The unseasonably cold weather had already hindered their progress through France, and they were impatient to begin their vacation on the lake. Foolish as always when it came to travel, Shelley insisted on starting the climb in early May, on an evening when a blizzard was causing a virtual whiteout. Fortunately, the locals intervened, urging him to hire ten strong men to accompany them in case they got stuck and needed to be shoveled out.

Despite having a fussy infant on her lap, Mary recorded her impressions of their ascent in her journal, writing passages that she would later use to describe the wintry landscape in her novel *Frankenstein:*

> Never was a scene more awefully desolate. The trees in these regions are incredibly large, and stand in scattered clumps over

the white wilderness; the vast expanse of snow was chequered only by those gigantic pines, and the poles that marked our road: no river or rock-encircled lawn relieved the eye. . . .

It took them all night to achieve the summit, but as they began the descent, the snow melted slowly away, until at last they reached the green fields and well-tended orchards of the valley of Geneva. When they drove into town, the bad weather finally broke and the sun came out, allowing them to see the quiet beauty of the lake that lay before them. The streets were empty, the parks deserted, as the season had yet to officially begin. They were staying at the imposing Hôtel d'Angleterre in the heart of the city, on the Quai du Mont Blanc, the conventional choice for well-to-do English tourists, where unmarried guests would not have been welcome. By now an expert in subterfuge, Shelley told the proprietor, Monsieur Dejean, that Mary was his wife and booked them a suite of rooms on the top floor with views over the lake, which Mary described as "blue as the heavens" and "sparkling with golden beams." On clear afternoons, they could see the triumphant steeple of Mont Blanc rising majestically in the distance.

Mary's pleasure was diminished by her worry over William, who had suffered on the journey. Fortunately, once they settled into a regular schedule, he began to regain his strength, nursing at predictable intervals and napping in the morning and the afternoon, giving his mother a chance to rest—that is, when she could get away from Claire, who talked excitedly and continuously about what they—and she in particular—would do once Byron arrived. Yet, as the days passed, Claire grew increasingly apprehensive. Each afternoon, she paced the shores of the lake, restless with anticipation, while Mary and Shelley enjoyed the tranquillity of their new surroundings.

The weather remained pleasant after they arrived and the sun shone almost every day.

One of the first orders of practical business for the family was to find a reliable nurse for William, as this would allow Mary to spend time with Shelley and attend to her studies. When they met Elise Duvillard, a young Swiss woman, who also had a baby and no apparent husband, they knew they had found the right person. Elise was cheerful and bright-cheeked, and she loved small children. Mary gladly surrendered William to her arms, a tribute to Elise, as, after the loss of her first baby, Mary did not like being apart from her son.

Delighted with their surroundings, Mary and Shelley happily embraced their new routine. Mary wrote:

> We do not enter society here, yet our time passes swiftly and delightfully. We read Italian and Latin during the heats of noon, and when the sun declines we walk in the garden of the hotel. . . . I feel as happy as a new-fledged bird, and hardly care what twig I fly to, so that I may try my new-found wings.

In the evening they sailed across the lake—sometimes accompanied by Claire—and often did not return until the moon rose. Mary reveled in "the delightful scent of flowers and new mown grass, and the chirp of the grasshoppers, and the song of the evening birds." They could see all the way to the bottom; now and then clouds of minnows floated by. These details stayed with Mary, and a few months later she would use them in her description of Frankenstein's one afternoon of happiness, drifting on a lake with his new bride, who exclaims, "Look . . . at the innumerable fish that are swimming in the clear waters, where we can distinguish every pebble that lies at the bottom. What a divine day! How happy and serene all nature appears."

On May 25, two weeks after they arrived, a huge carriage came thundering down the alpine road in the middle of the night. Military blue with flashy red and gold stripes, this extraordinary conveyance was an exact replica of Napoleon's imposing war carriage. From the imperial arms on the doors to the four iron candleholders screwed onto each corner, the resemblance was so close that if onlookers did not know better they might think the fallen conqueror had escaped from captivity on St. Helena and was now rolling into Geneva.

Byron, who had this vehicle built at great expense, would have been delighted to cause a mix-up of this sort, as he was convinced that he and the emperor were almost the same person, or, at the very least, shared similar destinies. Both had risen to great heights and then fallen. Byron collected Napoleon memorabilia and owned an engraving of the emperor under which he sat to write his poems. He was fresh from a visit to Waterloo, where the grand pathos of Napoleon's final surrender had moved him to tears. The extinction of greatness, the enormity of his hero's ruin, tormented Byron. He and the emperor had "soar[ed]"; they had stood gigantic and singular; they "dazzled and dismay[ed]." They had both fought for the same cause—Liberty—although Byron had used art, not arms, to show the people that they deserved to be free. Now, like Napoleon, Byron was exiled. Or at least he felt as if he had been exiled. His fight to liberate his readers from the shackles of convention had inspired hatred, a fate shared by the heroes of his poetry—a point not lost on his contemporaries. When the novelist Walter Scott heard that Byron had left England, presumably for good, he declared the poet had "Childe Harolded himself, and outlawed himself, into too great a resemblance with the pictures of his imagination." Byron had even adopted his defeated hero's voice in a poem he had completed right before his arrival in Switzerland, *Napoleon's Farewell,* in which Byron's emperor says,

> *Farewell to the Land where the gloom of my Glory*
> *Arose and o'ershadow'd the earth with her name—*

For all of his conviction that he was different from everyone else, Byron headed straight to the Hôtel d'Angleterre. Just like all the other Englishmen, he would not have dreamed of staying anywhere else. The racket of his entrance awoke the sleeping residents. Byron never traveled without his menagerie of "eight enormous dogs, three monkeys, five cats, an eagle, a crow, and a falcon." Other times he traveled with peacocks, an Egyptian crane, geese, a heron, and a goat with a broken leg, all of which lived indoors with him. He did not care whom he inconvenienced. In college, he had even adopted a tame bear, installing the animal in his rooms to protest the college's rule that he could not live with his dog, a huge Newfoundland named Boatswain.

Claire went down to greet him, but Byron was exhausted, signing his age as 100 in the hotel register and sweeping off to his room before she could find him. The next day passed without Byron's making any effort to contact Claire or Shelley. Having stayed up all night waiting for a message, Claire felt deeply injured, writing Byron a hurt, touchingly childish note the next morning: "I have been in this weary hotel this fortnight," she scrawled angrily, "and it seems so unkind, so cruel of you to treat me with such marked indifference. Will you go straight up to the top of the house this evening at ½ past seven & I will infallibly be on the landing place and show you the room."

A little later that morning when Claire looked out her window, she saw Byron and his twenty-one-year-old personal physician, John Polidori, rowing on the lake. Dragging Mary and Shelley with her, Claire made them walk back and forth along the beach until Byron spotted the little party and came ashore. Shelley was stiff and silent, suddenly overtaken by a mix of admiration and jealousy. Mary was quietly polite, while Claire chattered and laughed. Polidori kept careful track of events. Fortunately for posterity—if not for Byron—Polidori was in the secret pay of John Murray, the publisher; his job was to provide the details of Byron's personal life for the gossip columns.

To the young doctor, Shelley appeared "bashful, shy, consumptive," but he was also struck by the poet's modern scientific outlook; Shelley asked Polidori to vaccinate baby William almost upon first meeting, and Polidori did so at once. Shelley thanked him with a gold chain and seal for his efforts. Mary, meanwhile, remained very much in the background until a few days later, when Shelley urged her to recite Coleridge's *A War Eclogue* by heart, a rather savage poem for a properly brought-up young lady to have memorized. But Mary performed it with relish, particularly the section in which Fire, Famine, and Slaughter condemn Prime Minister Pitt to hell—and Polidori was instantly infatuated. An aspiring writer himself, he regarded Mary as beautiful and sophisticated, and over the next few months, instead of keeping as meticulous a record of Byron's escapades as Murray would have liked, he listed his activities with Mary, which were plentiful: "Read Italian with Mrs. S"; "went into a boat with Mrs. S, and rowed all night till nine; tea'd together, chatted, etc."

The day after they met, Shelley and Byron dined together and discovered they shared similar obsessions: liberty, poetry, Napoleon, the Greek poets, the hypocrisy of London, and, of course, themselves—their struggles with melancholy, the criticism they had endured, and their commitment to art. Together, they took a day trip to Plainpalais to pay homage to Rousseau, whose bust sat squarely in the middle of the park. Claire, frustrated that she did not have more time alone with Byron, volunteered to copy his most recent poems. But all this did was turn her into a secretary; she toiled, alone with his manuscripts, struggling with his handwriting, while Byron sailed, rowed, swam, and visited with the others. His fascination with the rise and fall of heroes, or, to be more precise, with his own rise and fall, may well have fired his poetic compositions with passion and originality, but it made him much too self-absorbed to be a good candidate for a love affair.

The season was by now in full swing, giving a festive air to the evenings. When it was not raining, lanterns were hung from posts for outdoor suppers; dances were organized; English ladies and gentlemen spooned sorbet out of cut glass bowls, criticized each other's dress and manners, compared the views from their rooms, and chatted about mutual acquaintances and London. Naturally, the Shelley entourage and Byron were not welcome at any of these soirees, although they did provide an engrossing topic of conversation.

For the ordinary English tourist, staying in a hotel with his lordship was like living in close quarters with an ill-behaved rock star. In their letters home, people took pleasure in noting Byron's shocking behavior. One Englishman who did not know the names of the Shelley trio referred to Claire as an actress, the nineteenth-century euphemism for a woman of ill repute. He wrote, "Our late great Arrival is Lord Byron, with the Actress and another family of very suspicious appearance. How many he has at his disposal out of the whole set I know not. . . ."

In London, the newspapers began to refer to the friends as a "league of incest." When either Mary or Claire entered the public rooms, they were greeted with silence and hostile stares. When they fled, they could hear whispering, like a wind at their back. Impatient with this ill treatment, Shelley rented a chalet called Maison Chapuis on the opposite side of the lake from the hotel. They arrived there on the first of June, and before long Byron and Polidori followed, moving to the beautiful Villa Diodati about fifty yards up the hillside. This grand stucco house with three stories, pillars, and a capacious front porch had plenty of room for Byron's menagerie and extra guests. The entire party was delighted to learn that Milton had once stayed there, an astonishingly good omen for this group of young people who by now saw themselves as fallen angels, like Milton's Satan: rebellious and misunderstood.

Even here, across the water, they were not safe from prying eyes. Monsieur Dejean set up a telescope so his guests could scrutinize the little party. Byron later said, "There was no story so absurd that they did not invent at my cost. I believe they looked on me as a man monster." When Byron's servants draped white cloths out to dry on the Diodati's porch, the hotel guests assumed that these were petticoats and debated whether they belonged to Mary or Claire. They would, perhaps, have been titillated to learn that the white drapes were actually Byron's bedsheets.

From Shelley's chalet, a hillside path ran up to the Villa Diodati, an easy climb even when one was encumbered by long skirts. Byron and Shelley, it turned out, shared a passion for sailing and split the cost of leasing a small sailboat, which they moored in the little harbor below Shelley's house. Whenever they could, they went onto the lake, though this was not as often as they would have liked, as the weather was becoming increasingly stormy. Ash-colored clouds poured over the mountains from Chamonix. The lake churned; lightning shot across the sky. Everything on the opposite shore—the cottages with their red roofs and the terraced vineyards, the Hôtel d'Angleterre with its scandalized guests—disappeared behind a curtain of gray sleet, leaving the little party with what initially was a delicious sense of being cut off from the rest of the world but gradually turned worrisome to those who tended to worry and tedious to those who were prone to boredom, trapped as they were indoors, day after day.

Of the group, it was only Mary who was contented. She devoted herself to William and her studies, thriving on the opportunity to

*The Villa Diodati in Geneva.*

work. Shelley, on the other hand, grew increasingly restless; he wanted to take their boat onto the lake and go for long walks; he hated being cooped up. Byron, too, felt impatient. Without being able to exercise his broad-backed mare, go shooting, or sail, he quickly became agitated—dangerously so, since he was famous for stirring up trouble when he had nothing to do. Claire interrupted him when he was writing and annoyed him by gazing at him during the long evenings the two households spent together. Polidori was no better off; he yearned for Mary, a condition made more miserable by Byron, who teased him mercilessly about his "lady love." It was clear that problems were brewing. Tempers were short. It was difficult to dream up activities. They desperately needed something to break the dullness, the stultifying deadness of each day.

# CHAPTER 14

# MARY WOLLSTONECRAFT: "A REVOLUTION IN FEMALE MANNERS"

———

[ 1791–1792 ]

AVING SURVIVED THE OUTCRY OVER HER IDENTITY AS THE FEMALE author of *A Vindication of the Rights of Men,* Mary Wollstonecraft was ready to write a new book. She had been under time constraints with *Rights of Men,* and now she wanted to develop her ideas more fully. This fresh project would be a book where "I myself . . . shall certainly appear." It would explore the theme most calculated to infuriate her critics: the rights of women. And so, in October 1791, Mary shut the door of her study and put her pen to paper again. This time she did not break down halfway. Nor did she need Johnson's encouragement. Although sometimes the writing process was a struggle, mostly she was gloriously happy, reveling in "the glowing colours" of her imagination as well as "the gleams of sunshine" and "tranquility" that she experienced while at her desk. She was so certain of where she was heading that she produced over four hundred pages in just six weeks. By January 1792 *A Vindication of the Rights of Woman* was delivered to bookshops and lending libraries.

When one opens *Rights of Woman,* Mary strides right on the stage, her voice clear and sharp. She is funny, quick, and irritable—as she must have been in person—but also rigorously logical, giving *Rights of Woman* the virtuoso flair of a Socratic dialogue.

Mary still appealed to readers' emotions as she had in her first *Vin-*

*dication,* but she also intentionally wrote "as a philosopher." She declared that her book was essential for the future of humanity because it outlined the evils of the present state of society, and introduced solutions that would redeem men as well as women.

Yes, men.

From first page to last, Mary emphasized that women's liberty should matter to everyone. In fact, she wrote *Rights of Woman* for readers who were learned and well versed in political theory—and in 1791 that usually meant men, not women. Using what she called "strength of mind," supposedly only a masculine attribute, Mary promised to reveal the "axioms on which reasoning is built by going back to first principles"—precisely what Locke, Rousseau, and Adam Smith had tried to do. Who are human beings without the trappings of civilization, she asked? What laws do we need to govern ourselves? Are men and women intrinsically different?

To this last question, every male thinker (with the exception of Locke, who believed that the minds of both men and women were blank slates at birth, which is why his writings had so thrilled sixteen-year-old Mary) gave a resounding yes: women were inferior in all areas of human development. Whereas men were capable of self-discipline, possessing the capacity for ethical rectitude and formidable reasoning powers, women were luxury-loving, fickle, selfish, lacking in passion—or sometimes, depending on the critic, too full of passion—gullible, susceptible to seduction, coquettish, sly, untrustworthy, and childish.

To all this, Mary declared, "What nonsense." But hers was a lone voice. Feminine deficiency was an assumption most people did not think to question: fire was hot, water was wet, and women were foolish and weak. Even more pernicious, as Mary saw it, women bragged about such frailty, regarding weakness as an asset. If a female fainted easily, could not abide spiders, feared thunderstorms, ghosts, and highwaymen, ate only tiny portions, collapsed after a brief walk, and wept when she had to add a column of numbers, she was considered the feminine ideal.

Mary scorned the idea that being "delicate" made a woman more attractive. Women had been trained to be empty-headed, she declared; they were not intrinsically less reasonable than men, nor were they lacking in moral fiber. After all, if a woman is told over and over again that she does not have the ability to reason her way through a philosophical problem, that she does not have the strength to climb a hill, that she is incapable of making the right choices, of course she will doubt her own abilities. If she is deprived of all "reasonable" education and instead taught to tinkle a few songs on the pianoforte, dance a minuet, and say *enchantée*—if her sole occupations are to study fashion plates, read silly novels, and gossip—then of course she will lack discernment and depth. The real problem, said Mary, was not women, but how men wanted women to be. Here, she cited Rousseau, whose theories on natural law and the importance of emotions she still admired, but whose ideas about women continued to annoy her. His teaching methods struck her as particularly noxious:

> The education of the women [Rousseau says] should be always relative to men. To please, to be useful to us, to make us love and esteem them, to educate us when young, and take care of us when grown up, to advise, to console us, to render our lives easy and agreeable: these are the duties of women at all times, and what they should be taught in their infancy.

That the great champion of liberty refused to endorse freedom for women was an irony not lost on Mary, and she was determined to prove him wrong, just as she had tried to do in her novel. Why should women have to please men? Are men gods? The degradation of women that he held up as ideal, she argued, had negative consequences for men, too. When husbands, fathers, and brothers are granted absolute power, their morality vanishes; they become tyrants. If men are allowed to act on their impulses without any checks on their behavior, they will be no better than animals. If women are trained to measure their worth solely by their ability to be attractive to men, then being loved will be the extent of their ambition. For a society to flourish, both men and women must have higher aspirations than these; they must also be governed by reason.

In addition, it was sacrilegious to teach females that their only responsibility was to be useful to men—that notion directly contradicted scripture. God did not create women "to be the toy of man, his rattle." Besides, souls do not have gender, and so men *and* women must both strive to be virtuous. This was a favorite point of Mary's, and she often noted alongside it that the word "virtue" came from the Latin word for "strength."

Women must learn to imagine themselves as more than the heroines of grand love affairs, Mary argued:

Love, in [women's] bosoms, taking place of every nobler passion, their sole ambition is to be fair [pretty], to raise emotion instead of inspiring respect; and this ignoble desire, like the servility in absolute monarchies, destroys all strength of character. Liberty is the mother of virtue, and if women be, by their very constitution, slaves, and not allowed to breathe the sharp invigorating air of freedom, they must ever languish like exotics, and be reckoned beautiful flaws in nature.

To Mary, the greatest tragedy of all was that neither men nor women saw anything wrong with their culture's assumptions about femininity. Progress required a dramatic change in how both sexes imagined themselves and their relationships. Liberty, true liberty, blew down walls, tore open gates, and destroyed the fences of enclosure. Women needed to learn there was more to life than romance and men needed to aspire to more than sexual conquest, not just for their own sakes, but for the sake of a more just world. And in the same way that women should not surrender their rights to men, humankind should not sacrifice their rights to tyrants. "A revolution in female manners," cried Mary, gathering steam, "[would] reform the world."

Mary knew that the link she made between the tyranny of governments and the tyranny of men over women would enrage many of her readers, but she did not care. "I here throw down my gauntlet," she declared. Like her male contemporaries, Mary had dedicated herself to creating a new political vision. Both jeremiad and prophecy, *Rights of Woman* reveals her as a teacher, a hellfire preacher, a satirist, and a utopian dreamer. Some write of what *was;* others of what *is,* she said, but I write of what *will be.*

*A Vindication of the Rights of Woman* was just as successful as her *Rights of Men,* selling approximately the same number of copies. Mary had succeeded in making a name for herself not only as a liberal opponent of Burke, but as an original philosopher in her own right, at least to her admirers. To her detractors, she had confirmed her identity as a dangerous radical, trespassing in realms that properly belonged to men. Of course the irony is that Mary's "trespass"—her insistence that women's rights be included in a society founded on the basis of personal liberties—was one of her most important contributions to political philosophy and what would come to be known as feminism. Ultimately, her work would reshape the contours of the discipline and extend the boundaries of political discourse. She argued that the distribution of wealth and the genesis of tyranny, as well as issues relating to sex, including contraception, marital law, rape, sexually transmitted diseases, and prostitution—topics considered outside the precincts of eighteenth-century femininity—were linked directly to the oppression of women and vice versa. In other words, the "woman question" was a linchpin, a crucial touchstone in the overall battle for social justice.

At the time, however, not everyone understood the far-reaching consequences of Mary's arguments. Those who did thought they seemed dangerous—even her admirers did not fully support how she had enlarged the discussion. Indeed, by daring to connect the condition of women to the distribution of wealth and power, she became the target of brutal attacks. Thomas Taylor, one of her family's former landlords, wrote a vicious pamphlet called *A Vindication of the Rights of Brutes.* If women were equal in nature to men, he sneered, then so were beasts. Other critics claimed that she had violated all standards of decency and propriety, and that her blunt style was a poor substitute for the "pleasing qualities" of the truly feminine writer. A reviewer for the stodgy *Critical Review* laughed at "the absurdity of many of her conclusions" and leered at Mary's unwed status:

As this is the first female combatant in the new field of the Rights of Woman, if we smile only, we shall be accused of wishing to decline the contest. . . . We must contend with this new Atalanta; and who knows whether, in this modern instance, we may not gain two victories by the contest? There is more than one batchelor in our corps; and if we should succeed, [M]iss Wollstonecraft may take her choice.

One critic, unaware that his remarks would prove ironic, harped on the weakness of Mary's logic, declaring that she had wholly failed as a writer and ending his review by saying, "We . . . shall leave [M]iss Wollstonecraft . . . to oblivion: her best friends can never wish that her work should be remembered."

Mary had touched a nerve. By daring to challenge Rousseau, she had lost the support of many liberals who might otherwise have listened to her. For conservatives, she was already a lost cause: "a whore" and a wild woman out to dethrone the king, dismantle the family, and ruin England. She had waved a red cape at John Bull. But having toiled for many years against the prejudices she faced as a single woman, she had reached the limits of her patience. In *Thoughts on the Education of Daughters,* she had addressed her concerns in a more tepid fashion; her collection of children's stories was also intended to promote her educational ideals—gently. Now she had taken a different, more ferocious tack. She knew that in many ways, her critics were not so far off the mark. She did want to overturn the world: shake the rich out of their golden chairs, bring down bullies, and raise up the poor. The people needed to have a voice, she believed, and she would be their mouthpiece.

The criticisms that did nettle her were the comments directed at her writing style—her work was sprawling, disorganized, and uneven, hostile reviewers said, criticisms that are still repeated today. It took her five years to respond to these critiques, but at last, in 1797, she defended her aesthetic choices, in an essay she called "On Taste." A good piece of writing should be spontaneous and honest, she said. The mind and heart should appear on the page. Writers should not try to seduce their readers with a "mist of words." The point of a good book was to provoke both ideas and emotion in the reader, not to engage in a battle of wits with a straw opponent. But these were Romantic ideals in an era still governed by the Enlightenment values of reason, order, and formality, despite the inroads of Rousseau and the French Revolution.

On November 13, just as Mary was finishing *Rights of Woman,* Johnson hosted a dinner party to honor the fifty-four-year-old Thomas Paine. Fresh from America, Paine had published his own *Rights of Man* earlier that year and had already sold fifty thousand copies. He was in the midst of putting the last touches on his *Rights of Man, Part the Second,* in which he would make his most decisive statement on behalf of liberty. Johnson invited Mary because Paine had expressed admiration for her work. He also invited William Godwin, then a journalist without any books to his name, largely because he had pestered Johnson for an invitation.

Like Mary, Godwin was in the middle of writing the work that would make him famous. Both arrived at the party fresh from their desks: Mary had been composing moody phrases such as "the most melancholy emotions of sorrowful indignation have depressed my spirits," while Godwin, proud of his formal paragraphs, had been steadfastly penning sentences in which he referred to himself in the third person: "Another argument in favour of the utility of such a work was frequently in the author's mind, and therefore ought to be mentioned. He conceived politics to be the proper vehicle of a liberal morality."

Two more opposite approaches and two more opposite people can scarcely be imagined; Mary's "melancholy emotions" had no place in Godwin's philosophical constructions, because he did not usually express emotion, either on the page or in person. He was certainly capable of strong feelings, however, and he fervently wanted to meet Paine, although he had no interest in meeting Mary, whose *Rights of Man* he had found messy and poorly written.

Mary, too, was focused exclusively on Paine. Born in England, this son of a Quaker corset maker had devoted his life to the fight for liberty. He had immigrated to America at Benjamin Franklin's suggestion and served in the Continental army, bringing his notebook with him to the battlefield and writing dispatches by the light of the campfire. In December 1776, when Washington's war-weary troops ground to a halt on the wrong side of the frozen Delaware, the general ordered his officers to read Paine's words aloud to the exhausted soldiers:

> These are the times that try men's souls. The summer soldier and the sunshine patriot will, in this crisis, shrink from the service of their country; but he that stands it *now,* deserves the love and thanks of man and woman. Tyranny, like hell, is not easily conquered; yet we have this consolation with us, that the harder the conflict, the more glorious the triumph.

After they heard this stirring call to arms, the troops rallied and made their famous crossing, despite the fact that it was almost midnight and the snow was driving down. In the early morning light, they stormed Trenton, catching the British by surprise, and claimed the victory that would turn the tide of the war. To Benjamin Franklin, who had famously said, "Where liberty is, there is my country," Paine replied, "Where liberty is not, there is my country."

Now, on the night of Johnson's dinner party, this famous revolutionary sat quietly swallowing his potatoes. Both Godwin and Mary were on tenterhooks: What inspirational words might Paine utter? But Paine seemed content simply to eat and listen. And the person he listened to most was Mary, not Godwin. This was not just because Mary was a passionate talker; it was also because at dinner parties such as this one, Godwin tended to observe from the sidelines, although occasionally startling others with barks of laughter.

This is not to say that Godwin did not have opinions; in fact, he had intransigent opinions about most things, and when he had a chance, he expressed these opinions with the sharp-edged righteousness of a trained evangelical minister. But dressed in a decidedly unfashionable black coat, due at that time to parsimoniousness, not poverty, laboring under a set of self-imposed rules—five hours of writing every day, two hours of reading, and a one-hour walk—with a downturned mouth, a receding hairline, and a stiff back, he looked as uncomfortable as he usually felt. Later in life, he described his feelings of social awkwardness:

> I can scarcely begin a conversation where I have no preconceived subject to talk of; in these cases I have recourse to topics the most trite and barren, and my memory often refuses to furnish even these. I have met a man in the street who was liable to the same infirmity; we have stood looking at each other for the space of a minute each listening for what the other would say, and have parted without either uttering a word.

He did not want to offend people, but he was all too well aware that people often found him abrasive:

> I have a singular want of foresight on some occasions as to the effect what I shall say will have on the person to whom it is addressed. I therefore often appear rude, though no man can be freer from rudeness of intention and often get a character for harshness that my heart disowns.

Mary, on the other hand, having been told to be silent all her life, had no patience with the sidelines. On this evening, she was eager to tell Paine her views on liberty, education, justice, and just about anything else that occurred to her. Paine listened meekly, while the other guests swallowed their ale (and their own thoughts) and spooned down Johnson's cod stew. The more she talked, the more resentful Godwin grew. When he attempted to interject, praising Voltaire's atheism, Mary cut him off: Godwin's words, she sniffed, "could do no credit either to the commended or the commender." She did not hold with the policies of the Church of England, but she was still a believer and was "provoked" by Godwin's radical dismissal of religion.

Humiliated, Godwin was at a disadvantage. He could not keep up with Mary's rapid zigzagging, and in fact disapproved of her conversational style altogether. He preferred to set his ideas in order before he spoke (or wrote), and he felt dinner parties should proceed the same way he organized his books.

Nothing could have been more antithetical to Mary's approach. She believed sudden inspiration was more valuable than adherence to any one system of ideas: "It is wandering from my present subject, perhaps, to make a political remark; but as it was produced naturally by the train of my reflections, I shall not pass it silently over," she declared in *Rights of Woman*. In person and on the page, she sailed from idea to idea as quickly as they appeared on the horizon. On this particular night, vanquished by Mary's speed and forcefulness, Godwin subsided, but he noted somewhat grumpily that no matter the topic—art, politics, France, America, or King George—Mary found the "gloomy side" and only seemed content when "bestowing censure." No doubt Mary would have given a different account, but since she did not record her thoughts, we have only Godwin's; and to a man who had not yet given up his belief that the ideal female had "the delicate frame of the bird that warbles unmolested in its native groves," Mary seemed brash and markedly "unfeminine."

Although some modern critics have assumed that the differences between Mary and Godwin are the differences between a woman and a man, a female writer and a male writer, Mary would have dismissed such a view, and she would have been right. The differences between Mary and Godwin cannot be reduced to gender stereotypes. They were both committed to thinking, speaking, and writing about social justice; both considered themselves philosophers. The contrast in their styles lies in their attitudes about accessibility and audience. Mary, by now an experienced journalist, had trained herself to catch and engage her readers, just as she liked to rally opinions back and forth across a table. She let cracks appear in her authorial armor on purpose, inviting readers to engage with her, just as she welcomed a good sparring match at a party. Godwin, on the other hand, did not view himself as a journalist trying to interest a general audience, but exclusively as a dispenser of ideas to learned readers, a pure intellectual. It followed, then, that Godwin, who preferred conversations to proceed by logical steps, would rather speak *about* sincerity while Mary prided herself on speaking *with* sincerity. By the end of the evening, he felt annoyed and tired. Never could he have imagined that one day he would fall in love with this opinionated, dominating woman—passionately so.

THE MONTHS THAT FOLLOWED the publication of *Rights of Woman* seemed empty to Mary. For the first time since Fanny died, she did not have a specific book to work on. By April, she felt adrift. She had spent the last few years driving herself to finish two books, both of which had been greeted with mockery and cruel jabs at her intellectual abilities, her appearance, and her marital status. Of course, she had earned acclaim as well, but now that the excitement had subsided, she was left with the haunting sense that *Rights of Woman* was not quite what she had wanted to write. "Had I allowed myself more time I could have written a better book," she confessed to a friend.

In May, after Paine published the second part of his *Rights of Man,* King George declared him a criminal, charging him with sedition and banning his work. Hate mobs chased Paine out of the country to France, where he was instantly hailed as a hero. Angry at this treatment of her friend and inspired by his example, Mary longed to join him there. By the end of June she had talked Johnson and Fuseli into crossing the Channel with her. Fuseli, always interested in diversion and fascinated by the unfolding drama in Paris, was happy to indulge Mary, although he brought his wife along.

The strangely mismatched quartet set out for Dover in early August, but just as they were to embark, frightening news arrived: the Tuileries Palace had been attacked, the French royal family thrown into the Temple prison, the Legislative Assembly dissolved, and Lafayette, the moderate leader of the National Guard, driven out of the country by radicals who had seized control of the Revolution. Mary wanted to continue, but she was outvoted. They turned back to London, and though Mary spent a few weeks in the country with Johnson, her spirits were low. There seemed nothing to look forward to. She longed to be in Paris; how could she be a true reformer if she did not witness the Revolution?

Without a project to occupy her mind, Mary's focus on Fuseli intensified. She assured him her passion was platonic, since he was married and adultery was against her principles. Had she not just written an entire book about the dangers women faced when they indulged in illicit affairs? "If I thought my passion criminal, I would conquer it, or die in the attempt," she declared. All she wanted, she wrote, was "to unite [myself] to [your] mind." He had helped her learn to enjoy herself. Before their relationship, she had consigned herself to an ascetic life:

> [I] read no book for mere amusement, not even poetry, but studied those works only which are addressed to the understanding; [I] scarcely tasted animal food, or allowed [myself] the necessaries of life, that [I] might be able to pursue some romantic schemes of benevolence; seldom went to any amusements . . . and [my] clothes were scarcely decent.

These words are pieced together from the few fragments that remain of Mary's letters to Fuseli, but Mary's point is still clear: Fuseli had introduced her to new pleasures. After she encountered his "grandeur of soul" and "lively sympathy," he had become essential to her happiness. It was not about sex, she protested. "For immodesty in my eyes is ugliness; my soul turns with disgust from pleasure tricked out in charms which shun the light of heaven."

The harder she pushed, the more Fuseli withdrew. By October, she was writing Johnson that she "was in an agony. My nerves [are] in such a painful state of irritation—I suff[er] more than I can express. . . . I am a strange compound of weakness and resolution. . . . There is certainly a great defect in my mind—my wayward heart creates its own misery—Why I am made thus I cannot tell; and, till I can form some idea of the whole of my existence, I must be content to weep and dance like a child—." What happened next is unclear. According to Fuseli, Mary decided to take matters into her own hands. She arrived at his house, banged on the front door, and when his wife, Sophia, appeared, announced, "I find that I cannot live without the satisfaction of seeing and conversing with [your husband] daily." Before the startled Mrs. Fuseli could stop her, she explained that she would like to move in with the Fuselis. There would be no threat to the Fuselis' marriage, as her "passion" was spiritual; she did not want to share their marital bed; she simply wanted Fuseli as her constant companion. Alarmed, Mrs. Fuseli banished Mary from the house, forbidding her husband to see Mary again. Fuseli did nothing to challenge his wife's edict, he said later, because Mary's attachment had become something of an embarrassment. In fact, he would never speak to her again.

But in 1883, Godwin's biographer, C. Kegan Paul, questioned the story of Fuseli's wife throwing Mary out, arguing that Mary's enemies had spread this rumor as part of a campaign to discredit her as a desperate, love-starved spinster. Paul was one of the last to see the remaining correspondence between Fuseli and Mary before it was destroyed by Mary's descendants, giving his words an authority lacking in the Fuseli account. Furthermore, Fuseli was notorious for spreading malicious gossip about both friends and enemies. After Mary died, he declared that she had been relentless in her pursuit of him, regaling his friends with the story in large part to taunt Godwin about Mary's attachment to him.

At any rate, since Mary's version of events is missing, it is impossible to know what really happened in this stage of their relationship. What is clear is that if she was heartbroken, she managed to recover quickly. By November she was able to write to her friend William Roscoe, who had commissioned her portrait the previous year, that she was through with Fuseli: "I intend no longer to struggle with a rational desire. . . . I am still a Spinster on the wing." With Johnson, she came up with a new plan for her future: she would go to France, where she would write up her observations and send them home for publication in the *Analytical Review*. The proceeds from these articles would fund her trip. She would be, for all intents and purposes, a foreign correspondent.

It was a dangerous undertaking. If consulted, most of her friends would have advised Mary to stay home. The violence in Paris had escalated that autumn. Twelve thousand political prisoners had been murdered in their cells; women were being raped and men tortured in full view of an applauding mob. One of the most horrifying events occurred when Marie Antoinette's close friend and reputed lesbian lover, the Princesse de Lamballe, was stripped naked and dragged through the city streets, "her breasts and vulva cut off—the latter worn as a moustache." She was beheaded and her head mounted on a pike outside the queen's window. English visitors fled, alarmed by these atrocities and afraid of meeting the fate of those tourists who had already been murdered in their beds. But if anything, these reports whetted Mary's appetite. She packed her bags and gave away her cat, even as the rumors flew: "I shall not now halt at Dover, I promise you," she wrote Roscoe, "for as I go alone, neck or nothing is the word."

# CHAPTER 15

# MARY GODWIN:
# FITS OF FANTASY

———

## [ 1816 ]

AFTER A WEEK OF BEING SHUT INDOORS BY THE STEADY RAIN, BYRON amused himself by suggesting that the lovesick Polidori demonstrate his chivalry by jumping off the porch—an eight-foot drop—to offer Mary assistance as she made her way up the wet, slippery path. Polidori was too naïve to know what Byron knew instinctively, that a man who took such extraordinary measures would appear foolish. Sure enough, when the smitten Polidori took his lordship's advice and leapt, Mary was startled but certainly not impressed. Even more embarrassing, Polidori sprained his ankle upon landing, with the result that when he and Mary made their way to the house, the young knight had to lean on his lady's shoulder rather than the other way around. Wincing, irritable, and out of sorts, he retired indoors, fully aware that he had been ridiculous.

Confined to the couch for the rest of the week, Polidori brooded over Mary's perfections—her slanting sidelong looks, her air of hidden secrets—until he could bear it no longer.

He confessed his love, hoping Mary would welcome his advances; after all, she had scorned the social code by living openly with Shelley and bearing his children. Perhaps she would welcome a new suitor. But he was quickly disabused of this notion when Mary told him she thought of him as a little brother and that she was in love exclusively with Shelley. This was a humbling moment for the ambitious young

*This portrait of a young woman is traditionally identified as
Mary Shelley at age nineteen.*

man who, although he was a physician, wanted to be a writer and believed his literary talents rivaled those of Byron.

If June 15, the day of his infamous jump, loomed large as one of the most humiliating episodes in Polidori's short and troubled life—he would commit suicide only five years later—it has also become notable in literary history for the chain of events that began later that evening. To cheer up the injured young doctor, the group agreed to hear him read the first draft of his new play. Although no one thought highly of this work—they said it was "worth nothing," he recorded dolefully in his journal—it did spark a conversation that would have important ramifications for all assembled, so important that literary scholars are still trying to piece together exactly what happened that night.

Creation and human nature—these were the topics on the table. They were themes that had long preoccupied Byron, Shelley, and Mary. Polidori volunteered to read his notes from a series of lectures he had attended in London given by the renowned anatomist William Lawrence. Both Mary and Shelley knew Lawrence, as Shelley had selected him as his physician precisely because of the doctor's avant-garde theories that the origins of life were based in Nature, not divine will. Lawrence argued there was no such thing as a "super-added" force like the soul, and that human beings were made of bone, muscle, blood, and nothing more. The public's response to these lectures had been hostile:

> [W]hat is it that Mr. Lawrence . . . requires us all to believe? That there is no difference between a man and an oyster. . . . Mr. Lawrence considers that man . . . is nothing more than an orang-outang or an ape, with "more ample cerebral hemispheres"! Mr. Lawrence strives with all his powers to prove that men have no souls!

But, not surprisingly, the residents of the Villa Diodati had the opposite response. Lawrence's ideas fascinated them. If the doctor was right and God was not the creator of life, then this restored power to human beings—a Promethean theme that had long obsessed Shelley and would inspire him to write *Prometheus Unbound* a few years later. In fact, argued Shelley, if God did not create human beings, was there not a good chance that human beings created God and that Christianity was a sham? Byron, too, explored this theme in a poem about the powers of human creation, *Manfred*. He did not go as far as Shelley—he had more inherent respect for religion than the younger man—but he embraced the principle that Nature was the generative force of the universe.

Before long the conversation turned to electricity and "the experiments of Dr. Darwin," Charles Darwin's grandfather, who had dined with Mary's mother long ago at Joseph Johnson's table. Byron and Shelley particularly liked the story about how Darwin had applied an electrical charge to "a piece of vermicelli in a glass case, till by some extraordinary means it began to move with voluntary motion." But though Shelley rejoiced in the idea of human beings creating life, Mary would later say, in a preface to her revised edition of *Frankenstein,* that she found the principle "supremely frightful," confessing that she worried about "the effect of any human endeavor to mock the stupendous mechanism of the Creator of the world."

Mary's doubts stemmed from her deep reservations about the ability of human beings to improve themselves or the world. Evil, she felt, was lodged too deeply inside the human heart. Even those men who appeared to have the highest possible aims—truth, knowledge, liberty—seemed to her to be motivated by the desire for power and recognition, an insight gained, perhaps, from her life with Godwin and now Shelley.

The next night, June 16, was even wilder. As lightning flashed and the rain poured down, the little party huddled by the fire at the Villa Diodati. To while away the hours, Byron read aloud from an old volume of ghost stories that he had found in the villa. Although everyone else was agreeably frightened by these tales, Byron grew frustrated. At last he threw the book down. They needed something new, something more terrible, he declared: everyone should write a ghost story, and then they would select a winner. He was confident that he could easily triumph over Shelley; he never considered the talents of Polidori or the two women.

That night everyone slept at the Villa Diodati; it was too stormy for the Shelley party to venture back down the path. When they returned home the next day, Mary tried to focus on writing her story while Elise watched William, but whether she had immediate success is not clear, as there is so much mythology about what happened next.

In later years, Mary said that it took her a long time to come up with an idea, and that when the idea did arrive, it came in the form of a nightmare:

> I saw—with shut eyes, but acute mental vision—I saw the pale student of unhallowed arts kneeling beside the thing he had put together. I saw the hideous phantasm of a man stretched

out, and then, on the working of some powerful engine, show
signs of life, and stir with an uneasy, half vital motion.

This dream synopsis does indeed encapsulate the plot of what
would soon become Mary's most famous work, her novel *Frankenstein*. These are her own words, and so on the face of it there seems
little reason to question her account of her story's genesis—except
that both Shelley and Polidori had a different version of what happened and both men were writing closer to the time. In the preface to
the first edition, Shelley makes no mention of Mary's struggling to
come up with an idea. Nor does he mention her dream. All he says is
that the group of friends "agreed to write each a story, founded on
some supernatural occurrence." Polidori's diary supports Shelley's
account. Even though he was often unreliable, with Mary he was
usually spot-on, and in his journal, he records that everyone except
himself got right down to work. He makes no mention of any difficulties on Mary's part, casting doubt on her version, since if she were
having trouble, it seems likely he would have noticed, given his obsessive surveillance of her daily activities. Besides, it would have been
a point of connection between them, one he would have been delighted to share.

Accordingly, Mary's story about the composition of *Frankenstein*
is probably just that, a story, a fiction tacked onto her larger fiction,
another layer in a many-layered book. She made this claim in 1831, in
the preface to a new edition of the novel. More than fifteen years had
passed since Geneva and she faced enormous financial and social pressures. The knowledge that a woman had written *Frankenstein* was so
shocking in many circles that it hurt the book's sales and Mary herself
was ostracized, albeit in part because of her scandalous romantic history. In the early nineteenth century, women artists were by definition monstrous. Despite the best efforts of Wollstonecraft and her
fellow radicals, society still believed that women were supposed to
create babies, not art. If Mary could improve her sales and her reputation by being self-effacing, then it made sense to distance herself from
the novel's inception and say that she had not consciously created the
story, that she was neither a genius nor particularly talented:

When I placed my head on my pillow, I did not sleep, nor could I be said to think. My imagination, unbidden, possessed and guided me, gifting the successive images that arose in my mind with a vividness far beyond the usual bounds of reverie.

However, buried within this self-deprecation was another, prouder claim. Like Coleridge, who had given a vivid account of the hallucination that led to *Kubla Khan,* his famous fragment of a poem published in the fall of 1816, Mary was asserting her qualifications as a true artist. A dream vision could only reinforce one's Romantic credentials. Dreams were unbidden; you could not force them into existence. But dreams were not particularly democratic, either. They did not come to just anyone, at least not the kind of extraordinary dream Mary was describing. Artists. Poets. These were the true prophets, the ones with the most profound vision. Thus at the same time that she was downplaying her initiative, trying as a female writer to have her work accepted, she was also asserting her identity as an artist. No self-respecting Romantic writer (with the exception of Edgar Allan Poe) would ever have admitted (as Poe did with *The Raven*) that his work was the result of a careful intellectual process, a cold and pedestrian endeavor of plotting and outlining. Sudden bursts of inspiration, visitations from spirits in the night—these were the true sources of art to Mary and her friends.

With everyone hard at work, Claire grew irritable. She wasn't trying to write a story. She was hurt that Byron continued to avoid her and that when he did pay her attention, it was usually destructive. He teased and ridiculed her. This treatment was painful in and of itself, but it was made even more so by the fact that he treated Mary so differently. He listened admiringly when she spoke and respected her intelligence and her scholarship. He had not stopped sleeping with Claire, because, as he later told a friend, she threw herself at him and he was not about to say no to her advances, even though he had no real affection for her.

This was typical Byron: he rarely thought about Claire or her feelings, being more drawn to Shelley than to anyone else, including Mary. His earliest love affairs had been with his male schoolmates

("Thyrza," the subject of the poem Mary had inscribed in her copy of *Queen Mab*, was actually a boy), and throughout the course of his life he had many male lovers. One of his motivations for leaving England was to have homosexual affairs without facing the dangers of prosecution; such relationships were still illegal in England, punishable by death. Shelley's poetic sensibility, fits of hysteria, and brilliant ideas intrigued him; he respected his erudition and commitment to poetry; and he was entertained by the younger poet's spouting of atheistic principles.

For Shelley, the relationship was more complicated. The more time he spent with Byron, the less he seemed able to write. It was Mary who had the simplest relationship with the older poet: they shared a pessimistic streak, both regarding human beings as inherently selfish. His lordship had discovered he trusted Mary's literary judgment and liked to read his work to her, often asking for suggestions. Sometimes, Mary complied, honored to be asked, but she had her own work and a baby to look after, not to mention the constant task of fending off Polidori, who continued to pursue her.

On the night of the eighteenth, the group reconvened at the Villa Diodati. It was still stormy and the drawing room was even darker than usual. Toward midnight, they "really began to talk ghostly"—of spirits, ghouls, and hauntings. They wondered aloud whether the dead could come back to life, and why Mary's dead baby continued to appear in her dreams.

Byron recited his favorite poem of Coleridge's, *Christabel,* which was a favorite of Mary's, too. In *Christabel,* an innocent young maiden—the Christabel of the title—meets a beautiful lady in the forest. She takes this mysterious lady home, watches her undress, and is entranced with her beauty. But just as it seems that a sexual encounter might ensue, she discovers the woman is horribly disfigured and is actually a witch.

The room was silent as Byron spoke, but when he came to the climactic stanza:

> *Beneath the lamp the lady bowed,*
> *And slowly rolled her eyes around;*

> *Then drawing in her breath aloud*
> *Like one that shuddered, she unbound*
> *The cincture from beneath her breast;*
> *Her silken robe, and inner vest*
> *Dropt to her feet, and in full view,*
> *Behold! Her bosom and half her side—*
> *Hideous, deformed, and pale of hue—*

Shelley terrified everyone by suddenly "shrieking and putting his hands to his head." Polidori described the scene that ensued with a doctor's eye for detail:

> [Shelley] ran out of the room with a candle. Threw water in his face and after gave him ether. He was looking at Mrs S, & suddenly thought of a woman he had heard of who had eyes instead of nipples, which taking hold of his mind, horrified him.

Eyes instead of nipples. Breasts that could see. This strange image did not come from Coleridge's poem—at least not directly.

On the one hand, it seems clear that this was an almost entirely unconscious event as Shelley was overwhelmed, rendered helpless by the power of his vision. Yet it is also possible to trace the origin of Shelley's vision to a story that Mary had once told him: Coleridge's initial plan was to place eyes on the lady's breasts, but at the last moment he had retreated, deciding that this was too horrific an image. Thus Shelley's grotesque vision *of* Mary actually came *from* Mary, though he was probably unaware of this.

Polidori, who was unaware of Mary's role in Shelley's nightmare vision, was so struck by the poet's "fit of fantasy," as Byron called it, that he used a version of it for his own story, *The Vampyre,* which he published in 1819. This immensely popular work would inspire many others, most famously Bram Stoker's *Dracula.* The rest of the party, however, was less inspired than shaken. No one thought that Shelley's terror was insignificant because it had stemmed from his imagination. To believe so would have been a slur against the powers of the mind;

nothing could be more real or more terrible than what the self had created. Shelley had seen what he had seen. The group had seen him see it.

Four days after his *Christabel* vision, the weather broke, and Shelley urged Byron to accompany him on an adventure to see more of Rousseau's old haunts. Despite Rousseau's shortsighted view of women and their education, both men still felt that the dead philosopher was one of the great spokesmen for freedom. With Shelley away, Mary began to write her story in earnest, "so possessed" by her mad creator, Victor Frankenstein, that she felt "a thrill of fear." The first sentence she wrote—"It was on a dreary night of November that I beheld my man compleated [*sic*]"—seemed to unleash all that would come next, as though the story were waiting to spill onto the page. Outside the shuttered windows she could hear the wind driving across the lake while she imagined a pale young scholar manufacturing a man out of body parts stolen from graveyards and butcher shops, drawing on her memories of the slaughterhouses and meat markets near Skinner Street to build her story, as well as the legend of Konrad Dippel from their visit to Castle Frankenstein.

After eight days of touring the lake, Shelley came back from his trip and told Mary that he and Byron had barely survived a sudden squall that had blown down from the mountains. They had taken down the sails of their little boat and gripped the sides, waiting to capsize. Fortunately, the wind had eventually subsided and they continued on their way without mishap. Shelley could not swim and his fear was that Byron, a superb swimmer, would risk his life trying to save him, which would have been a true embarrassment. Stories like this make one wonder why the sailing-obsessed Shelley never learned to swim and why his friends did not insist he learn. A summer on the shores of Lake Geneva would appear to have been a perfect opportunity.

Having almost lost the man she loved, Mary found the themes of *Frankenstein* even more compelling. When she showed Shelley the pages she had written, he urged her to develop them into a longer story. Encouraged, Mary allowed herself to imagine Frankenstein more fully, tapping into her own experiences as a child whose mother

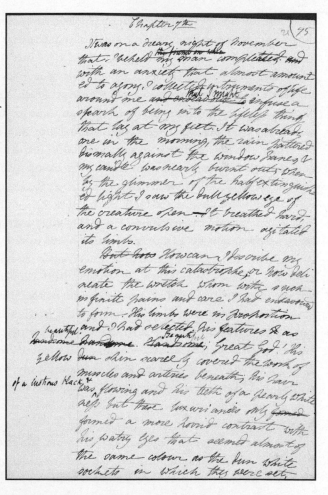

*The original beginning of Frankenstein in Mary Shelley's hand. "It was on a dreary night of November that I beheld my man compleated."*

had died after giving birth, whose father had rejected her, and whose society had condemned her for living with the man she loved. She explored her interior life—her rage, her hurt, her pride—and at length added the brilliant plot twist, the surprise that would set her story apart from others and would make her one of the most famous authors in English literary history: instead of regarding his handiwork with pride, she had her young inventor be repelled by his creation, abandoning his "compleated man" in horror. If Shelley or Byron had written this story, it seems unlikely that either would have—or could have—imagined such a scenario. In fact, in the works they began that summer, Byron's *Manfred* and Shelley's *Mont Blanc* and *Prometheus Unbound,* both poets invented creator protagonists whose abilities made them seem heroic. But Mary was ambivalent about the prospect of men creating life. She had given birth to a toddler she loved, but she had also lost a baby, and lost her own mother as a result of childbirth. If men could control life (and death), then she would not have suffered these tragedies. On the other hand, she wondered what would happen to the special role of women if it was possible to create life via artificial methods. She was also concerned about what would happen to God, or the idea of God, the mysterious, even mystical power behind Nature. Haunted by these worries, Mary stopped writing from the point of view of the creator and switched her vantage point to that of the created, sending Dr. Frankenstein's creature in search of his father. But when the creature finds Frankenstein, instead of a happy reunion, the young scientist pushes him away, just as Godwin had pushed Mary away. Enraged and hurt, the creature murders all the people Frankenstein loves, from his best friend to his bride. Mary's story had evolved from a tale of the supernatural to a complicated psychological study with multiple perspectives. She had moved from exploring the creative power of humankind—a favorite theme of Shelley and Byron—to plumbing the depths of human nature.

Everyone in the small group sensed that Mary had struck gold. In the grip of imaginative composition, she devoted herself to her manuscript as much as she was able. Far from being intimidated by her accomplished male companions, she took heart from the idea that in becoming an author she was living up to her literary heritage. Shelley had given up entirely on the ghost story idea and returned to his own work. Byron, too, had turned to other projects. But Mary's story had influenced them more than they realized or would ever acknowledge. The poems both men worked on that summer also explore the power of human invention for good or evil, freedom versus enslavement, and the majesty of Nature. This shared focus was a tribute to the importance of their literary friendship. For the rest of their lives, all three would turn to each other for inspiration and confirmation, competition and revelation.

THE TRIP AROUND THE lake had not eased Shelley's restlessness, and within a few weeks of his return, he made plans for a journey with Mary and Claire to the then-remote Alpine village of Chamonix, with its famous glacier, the Mer de Glace, at the foot of Mont Blanc. Mary, knowing it would be unwise to bring her child on this expedition and that Shelley would not be eager to have William as a traveling companion, regretfully kissed her "pretty babe" goodbye, leaving him with Elise. On July 21, they traveled up into the high country, shivering in their cloaks and marveling at the rivers of ice and fields of snow. The journey was dangerous, with floods and avalanches, but the trio made it safely across the Alps. Although she longed for her little boy, Mary was stimulated by the strangeness of the setting.

In general, the other English visitors to Chamonix were a pious crew, eager to bear witness to God's glory as evidenced by the glacier and Mont Blanc. Fifty years later, the poet Algernon Swinburne would observe how the entries in the hotel register were "fervid with ghostly grease and rancid religion." Annoyed at the many Christian testimonials in the hotel's guest book, Shelley wrote in Greek that he was a "Democrat, Philanthropist and Atheist." Under "Destination," he wrote, "L'enfer." He relished shocking his fellow tourists and would make similar declarations in hotel registers throughout the Alps.

These entries quickly became notorious. The Greek was no barrier for other British travelers of the day, who shared Shelley's classical education and could easily decipher his firmly printed letters. Certainly he could not have come up with more incendiary terms. His declaration of atheism was perhaps the worst offense, but a "democrat" was synonymous with a revolutionary, while a "philanthropist" (a lover of men) seemed like a reference to Shelley's irregular love affairs—proof at last to his enemies that Shelley was truly immoral. Even Byron was shocked at his young friend's indiscretion, and when he visited the region a few months later, he crossed out all such entries he could find. Fortunately for history, if not for Shelley's reputation among his contemporaries, Byron missed the Chamonix register, and so these three words would haunt the poet for the rest of his life.

The travelers hiked the glacier and were astonished at the immensity of the mountain that shadowed their hotel. One day it rained so hard they were forced to stay inside, and Mary pored over her notebook, deciding that one of the climactic scenes between Dr. Frankenstein and his creature would take place on the Mer de Glace. "[The view of the glacier] filled me with a sublime ecstasy," Frankenstein says, his sentence sounding remarkably as if it was lifted straight from his creator's journal.

When they returned to Geneva on July 27, Mary worked on extending her story even further: she had Frankenstein swear revenge and chase the creature, the hunted becoming the hunter, the hunter becoming the quarry. She also played with baby William, walked with Polidori, studied Greek with Shelley, and occasionally commented on early drafts of Byron's new poems. The world seemed to be opening up for her, just as she had always hoped it would.

For Claire, the opposite was true; she had discovered she was pregnant by Byron, and though at first she hoped this would bind the reluctant poet to her, Byron—who was heartily sick of Claire—saw no reason to step forward with either financial or emotional assistance. She had enjoyed the privilege of having sex with him. What else did she want? Shelley tried to persuade Byron to help Claire, but he was recalcitrant, unsure the child was his. He had heard the rumor that Shelley had also slept with Claire, and, rebel though he was, Byron regarded Shelley's relationship with both sisters—no matter how ambiguous—as unorthodox and foolish.

Realizing that Claire's situation was desperate, Shelley settled an allowance on her and the unborn child, an act that Byron regarded as further evidence of the baby's true paternity. Things might have stalled here, but Shelley persisted, and at length he managed to convince Byron to acknowledge the baby as his. Ironically, this was a concession that made the famous poet even less supportive of Claire; although he had never evinced any interest in the other illegitimate children he must have fathered over the years, Shelley's interference made Byron suddenly proprietary. He did not want his progeny raised by bohemians, he declared, and announced his intention of placing the child in the aristocratic care of his half sister—and putative lover—Augusta. Claire was appalled at this proposal (a reaction that made sense, especially if she had in fact been forced to give up her first child or had lost it). She protested so vigorously that Shelley persuaded Byron to let her care for the infant herself, posing as the baby's aunt to protect herself (and Byron) from further scandal. Byron agreed, with the caveat that he could send for the child whenever he wanted.

Shelley, Mary, William, Elise, and Claire arrived back in England in the beginning of September, right after Mary's nineteenth birthday. They could not return to Bishopsgate—despite his allowance from his grandfather's estate, Shelley had neglected to pay their bills before they left England, and creditors were once again looking for him, having already confiscated the valuables they had left behind. London, too, was out of the question, as it was already obvious that Claire was pregnant and this would have placed them at the center of a new wave of gossip.

After some debate, they decided to find a house in Bath; the season had ended there and the town would be empty of gossiping Londoners. Mary disliked this plan, as Shelley had to stay in London to see the lawyers about his finances and she did not want them to be separated. But she had little choice, and Shelley thought Mary should stay with Claire during her pregnancy. Mary, however, did not want to take care of the stepsister who had tried to sabotage her relationship with the man she loved. She was sure the unborn baby was not Shelley's, but she also knew that the rest of the world would think it could be. She dreaded the months to come: the loneliness, the quarreling with her stepsister, the worry that Shelley might abandon her, the drabness and small-town feel of Bath. She missed the Alps, the lake, and above all the communal life where she had felt insulated from the judgmental eyes of the world and inspired to envision what was supposed to be unthinkable: a human being playing God. Now, without Byron, without the reassuring presence of Shelley, and without the exhilarating feeling of being far from stuffy England, she would have to go forward alone, rewriting and expanding her manuscript during the long, gray autumn that stretched miserably ahead.

# MARY WOLLSTONECRAFT:
## PARIS

———

[ 1792–1793 ]

ARY WOLLSTONECRAFT COULD DISCERN LITTLE THAT WAS BEAUTIFUL as her coach rolled through the city gates into the French capital and onto the Boulevard Saint-Martin. It was mid-December 1792, and the horses splattered through the dirty streets, splashing mud on the hapless pedestrians who were trying to avoid the deep sinkholes between the paving stones. She had caught a cold on the long uncomfortable journey from London, and after so many days of traveling, she was looking forward to meeting her sisters' friend Aline Filliettaz, the daughter of Mrs. Bregantz, the headmistress of a school in Putney where Eliza and Everina had both taught. She knew no one else in Paris, as Eliza had come home in 1788 before the Revolution gathered steam. Both of Mary's sisters now had teaching positions, Eliza in Wales and Everina in Ireland, and both wrote frequently detailing their miseries and asking for money. They had no one else to complain to and blamed Mary for their unhappiness. To them, she seemed to be leading a glamorous life, while they were still essentially servants. These laments were difficult to hear, as it was clear that they thought Mary should be working harder to make their lives happier: she should find them new employment or send them enough money so that they did not have to work. Mary empathized with how degrading and unpleasant their jobs were. But she had already spent considerable time finding them employment, and she had already sent them much more money than she could afford. Now that she was in France, she had plans of her own that she wanted to fulfill.

When she arrived at 22 Rue Meslée (now Meslay), a side street deep in the Marais, Mary discovered that Aline and her husband had been unexpectedly called away. She was left in the hands of servants who spoke a colloquial French that was very different from the scholarly language she had studied. Try as she might, she could not make herself understood. "You will easily imagine how awkwardly I behaved unable to utter a word," Mary wrote Everina.

A young maid led Mary through "one folding door opening after another," leaving her marooned in a room far from the servants' quarters. Aline's house was a grand residence six stories high with wrought iron balconies and long windows that opened onto the street. The last time Mary had lived in such splendor was when she was a governess for the Kingsboroughs. The elegant red brick Place des Vosges, one of the most prestigious addresses in Paris, was a short walk away. Nearby was the Temple, a turreted medieval fortress where King Louis and Marie Antoinette were imprisoned.

For the next week or so, Mary was forced to stay indoors and try to recover from her cold. But her isolation grew more difficult with each passing day. The silence of the house was suffocating. She wrote Johnson, "Not the distant sound of a footstep can I hear. . . . I wish I had even kept the cat with me!" Although the maids tried to help, Mary could not find the words to explain herself: "I apply so closely to the language, and labour so continually to understand what I hear that I never go to bed without a head ache—and my spirits are fatigued with endeavouring to form a just opinion of public affairs."

When at last she was able to explore, she was disappointed in what she found. The city looked scarred: statues of the French monarchs had been pulled down or defaced, leaving empty pedestals and piles of marble; iron railings had been ripped off windows to make pikes for the workers to carry as weapons. Signs were posted on the street corners warning people not to cheer for the king. The sansculottes, the revolutionary workers, wearing their trademark striped trousers and liberty cockades, shook their standards—"an old pair of

breeches . . . on the top of a pike"—at anyone who looked too aristocratic; Mary had been told not to speak English on the streets, as people believed English visitors were either nobles in disguise or spies.
Even the names of shops, streets, bridges, and towns had been changed
to eradicate any royal allegiances. Although Mary approved of this
attempt to start anew, there were few updated maps available, making it "very difficult," according to one English traveler, "for a stranger
to know anything about the geography of the kingdom."

Eventually, Mary learned to thread her way through the rabbit
warren that was eighteenth-century Paris, the streets so narrow they
were like passageways. Although she rejoiced in the architecture of
the Marais, the buildings were taller than in London and set more
closely together, shutting out the sky. A seventeen-foot stone wall
surrounded the city. If you did not have the right paperwork, you
were not permitted to leave, a precaution that allowed the authorities
to block the fifty-four tollgates at will. Not that Mary wanted to escape, but the city was claustrophobic. Walking was unpleasant; she
hated the dirty streets. Like Londoners, Parisians dumped waste out
the windows, but in Paris, unlike London, there were no sidewalks
and few parks. When traffic backed up and carriages crowded past,
the only choice was to press against the buildings to avoid being
trampled; pedestrians frequently lost their lives in traffic accidents.
All in all, Mary was shocked by "the striking contrast of riches and
poverty, elegance and slovenliness, urbanity and deceit."

If navigating the city was difficult, calculating the time and date
was even more challenging. The revolutionary leaders had changed
the clock and the calendar to reflect the new society they wanted to
create. This meant the French names for the days of the week that
Mary had learned (*lundi, mardi, mercredi,* etc.) were now meaningless.
Instead, weeks were now ten days long, beginning with *primidi* and
ending with *décadi.* There were still twelve months, but each month
was divided into three revolutionary weeks. At the end of the year,
which began on the first day of the autumnal equinox (Mary had arrived in the third month of Year I of the French Republic), extra days
would be added to approximate the solar year. Even more confusing

was the concept of decimal time. Days were no longer twelve hours; instead, they lasted ten very long hours. Each hour was 100 decimal minutes and each minute was 100 decimal seconds, which meant a revolutionary hour consisted of 144 conventional minutes. There were even new decimal clocks, which no one could read. Newspapers, pamphlets, official documents, even Mary's passport followed this system, reinforcing France's isolation from neighboring countries.

To top all this off, Paris was a veritable nest of gossip. Confused and still struggling with her French, Mary found it hard to distinguish between the swirl of false reports and reality. The week before Christmas (in English time), the city buzzed with stories: the king had escaped; the Austrians were invading the city; radical factions were planning a coup. Frustrated by her lack of information, Mary took a cab to the home of a literary Englishwoman, Helen Maria Williams, whose book she had reviewed favorably the previous spring. Williams had since moved to Paris, where she published glowing reports of the Revolution that enthralled British liberals like Mary. At Helen's, Mary was able to hear the news in a language she could understand. The king had not escaped. He was going to face the National Convention on the day after Christmas. Helen and her circle of friends had mixed opinions on what Louis XVI's fate should be: The guillotine? A constitutional monarchy? A republic? Mary was against execution. Although she abhorred the traditions of aristocracy and monarchy, she felt empathy for the king and hated the mounting bloodshed. Other liberals agreed. Thomas Paine argued that Louis should be exiled to America rather than beheaded.

And so, when December 26 came, it was with divided feelings that Mary climbed the stairs to the attic of 22 Rue Meslée to watch Louis pass by on his way to the National Convention. Around nine in the morning, she heard "a few strokes on the drum" and then the wheels of the king's cart. A throng of National Guards, dressed in their dark blue coats with red collars and white lapels, marched alongside Louis's coach, keeping any would-be rescuers at bay. The air was still and Mary was struck by the silence that greeted the procession. She wrote Johnson:

The inhabitants flocked to their windows, but the casements were all shut, not a voice was heard, nor did I see any thing like an insulting gesture.

. . . I can scarcely tell you why, but an association of ideas made the tears flow insensibly from my eyes, when I saw Louis sitting, with more dignity than I expected from his character.

That night Mary could not sleep. "I cannot dismiss the lively images that have filled my imagination all the day," she confided in Johnson. "Nay, do not smile, but pity me; for once or twice, lifting my eyes from the paper, I have seen eyes glare through a glass-door opposite my chair, and bloody hands shook at me. . . . I want to see something alive; death in so many frightful shapes has taken hold of my fancy.—I am going to bed—and for the first time in my life, I cannot put out the candle."

Mary's reference to "bloody hands" was an allusion to one of her favorite plays, Shakespeare's *Macbeth*. To Mary, Louis's doom now seemed as inevitable as the Scottish king's, and she felt implicated in what was to come, unsure whether she should be protesting what she had just seen. Like Macbeth, she and the French people were soon going to be guilty of regicide and could soon find themselves haunted by the king's death. All she was certain of was that she had just watched an extraordinary event—a king going to trial, as though he were an ordinary citizen. The world would never—could never—be the same. This was a solemn thought, but also an inspiring one. With renewed energy, Mary took notes, planning to use them for an eye-witness account of the Revolution.

Unable to attend the trial proceedings herself, Mary had to rely on the newspapers' detailed coverage of the trial. President Barère, the president of the Convention, spent the morning preaching to the 749 delegates: "Europe observes you; history records your thoughts and actions; incorruptible posterity will judge you with inflexible severity. . . . The dignity of your sitting ought to be responsible to the majesty of the French Nation; she is ready by your organ to give a great lesson to Kings, and to set an useful example for the emancipation of nations."

These words resonated with Mary. She, too, could feel "incorruptible posterity" judging her actions, and when, after several weeks of debate, the Convention voted for the death penalty, she steeled herself to record all that she observed. Disillusioned by the revolutionary government's tyranny, she wrote, "I am grieved—sorely grieved—when I think of the blood that has stained the cause of freedom at Paris." Earlier that year, the guillotine had been set up in the Place de la Révolution, today's Place de la Concorde, near the Louvre. Mary had already gone to see it, and although the killing device was horrifying to behold, she knew it was meant to be more humane than the old-fashioned stake burnings and hangings of the ancien régime. Its inventors boasted of its efficiency, and it was widely praised as a symbol of the Revolution's egalitarian philosophy, since in the past, commoners had had to endure long, excruciating deaths on the wheel, while aristocrats received a comparatively merciful sharp blade. Now everyone, including the king, would suffer the same death. But democratic though it might be, Mary was still disturbed by the guillotine's prominence. The authorities had placed it in front of the Hôtel Crillon, where Marie Antoinette used to take piano lessons and sip tea in the afternoons, asserting the Convention's triumph over the royal family. Mary did not miss this symbolism, noting that the new government had as much lust for power as the old. It was beginning to seem that the only true difference between the regimes was a change in name.

On January 21, the day of the execution, the city was eerily silent. Citizens were ordered to keep their windows shut under pain of death. The sky was overcast and guards marched the streets ready to suppress any protests on behalf of the king. Mary stayed locked behind the tall shuttered doors and iron-grilled windows of 22 Rue Meslée. Fortunately, Aline had returned to Paris, and Mary was not alone as tensions were running high in the city. It was dangerous on the streets, particularly for an Englishwoman. No one knew what would happen next, whether the people would rise up and seize control after the king was killed, whether civil war might be on the horizon. Outside Paris, royalists staged violent protests.

At 10:00 a.m., thirty-nine-year-old Citizen Louis Capet, as the revolutionaries called the deposed king, climbed the steps to the guillotine. Shut indoors as she was, Mary did not get to be an eyewitness to what followed, but when she heard the reports, she was moved once again to tears. Showing more strength in the final moments of his life than during the years of his indecisive reign, Louis proclaimed his innocence, publicly forgave his people, and urged them to put a stop to the killings. There was a respectful silence while everyone waited for the blade to fall, but afterward, when the executioner held up Louis's head, people rushed forward to plunge their hands in his blood, shouting, *"Vive la République!"* It was the beginning of a new life, a new epoch, the newspapers crowed. Without the king, everyone would become rich and free. But Mary did not agree. She believed that Louis's death marked the Revolution's turn toward disaster.

Mary's assessment was shared by most English and European leaders. Enraged and saddened, George III, the English king, joined the Austrians and Prussians already fighting the revolutionary troops led by an ambitious young general named Napoléon Bonaparte. Even in France, the celebrations would soon die down and Mary's Shakespearean premonition would come true: Louis's death would come to haunt future generations. For Camus, the king's execution marked the end of meaning, the disappearance of God from history. Another twentieth-century philosopher, Jean-François Lyotard, would maintain that modern France owed its birth to a murder and was therefore doomed to corruption.

Sensing the darkened mood of the country that spring, many expatriates fled back to British shores. Mary herself was tempted to leave Paris, since there might come a time when it would no longer be possible for her to return home. But she resisted the impulse, deciding to brave it out for the sake of history, spending February and March practicing her French and recording more impressions of the city. As a celebrated author, she was invited to many of the most important salons and political gatherings. Although she reported that one gentleman teased her about her habit of saying *"oui, oui"* in response to everything because in actual conversations her "fine French phrases . . . fly away the Lord knows where," she gradually was able to speak more fluently. People liked her in this new world and she liked them; it was refreshing to live in a society that valued women and their ideas. In London she had been a rarity, often the only woman at Johnson's dinner parties, but in Paris, the social climate was entirely different. The Revolution had played a positive role in women's lives, granting them significant legal privileges. Divorce had been legalized the preceding August, and in April 1791 the government had decreed that daughters could inherit property. Now the marquis de Condorcet, one of Mary's new friends and an influential deputy in the Convention, was arguing on behalf of women's right to vote: "Women should have absolutely the same rights [as men]," he declared; "either no individual member of the human race has any real rights, or else all have the same."

Her friendship with Helen Maria Williams was also deepening that spring. Helen Maria's *Letters from France* had won the pretty, idealistic author the attention of a young English poet, William Wordsworth, who traveled to France to meet her and witness the miracles she had described. In later years, he remembered this time as glorious, exclaiming:

> *Bliss was it in that dawn to be alive,*
> *But to be young was very heaven!*

He also painted a picture of the sentimental Helen in a sonnet titled "Upon Seeing Miss Helen Maria Williams Weep at a Tale of Distress": "She wept. Life's purple tide began to flow / In languid streams through every thrilling vein / Dim were my swimming eyes."

Before long, Mary felt comfortable enough to confide in Helen about Fuseli, and she relied on "the simple goodness of [Helen's] heart" to help her navigate Parisian social politics. Like the salon hostesses of the ancien régime—the handful of privileged women who had led the cultural life of the city by hosting receptions for the rich and powerful, the intellectuals and politicians—Helen Maria prided herself on knowing everything about everyone: who hated whom, who had a secret lover, who supported the moderates and who the radicals, who was to be trusted and who not. This was valuable knowledge in a time when everything was changing so rapidly. The plunge from power to prison could take place in a matter of hours.

Sexual mores were also undergoing a revolution. By 1793, so many traditions had been thrown out the window that it seemed nothing was now taboo. Helen Maria, for example, lived with a married Englishman, John Hurford Stone, and yet visitors still crowded into her drawing room for her Sunday evening parties. Madame de Staël, another important hostess, was pregnant with her lover's child. Joseph Johnson's good friend Thomas Christie, cofounder of the *Analytical Review* (the journal that still employed Mary as a staff writer), had moved to Paris and was now embroiled in ongoing conflicts between his wife, Rebecca, and an aggrieved mistress who had borne his child. Most Parisians, having watched their world turn upside down, found it hard to take marital vows seriously. Of course, adultery had been common enough before the Revolution, but affairs had generally been conducted with discretion. Now the old morality was seen as evidence of the corruption of the old regime; people rushed in and out of love affairs, explaining their behavior as an expression of the new freedom. Political and sexual liberty appeared to travel hand in hand, just as Mary had always hoped they would. This was what she had envisioned in her *Rights of Woman*: if the will of the people could overcome the tyranny of kings, the bonds of unequal marriages could be broken. Men could learn to view women as worthy partners. And women could find their own moral strength and philosophical capacities. Most of all, people would be free to follow their hearts.

Mary's embrace of revolutionary morals squared with her analysis of marriage in *Rights of Woman*. When she had criticized the relationship between men and women, Mary had not intended to argue against sex, nor had she intended to argue against love. Rather, she had meant to expose the dangers for women in a society in which the balance of power was skewed in favor of husbands, fathers, and brothers, in which men had the legal sanction and economic power to victimize women. There could only be true love, she believed, if the partners were equal, and so the Revolution gave her new hope, not only for the relations between men and women in general, but for herself. Perhaps in this new world she could have a meaningful relationship with a man. Perhaps she would no longer have to content herself with the sort of "spiritual" union she had attempted to achieve with Fuseli.

Certainly, men seemed to find Mary far more attractive in Paris than they had in London. They flocked to her, flattering her and inviting her to theatrical events, parties, and private dinners in their lodgings. One of her suitors, Count Gustav von Schlabrendorf, a wealthy Silesian, remembered Mary's "charming grace. Her face, so full of expression, presented a style of beauty beyond that of merely regular features. There was fascination in her look, her voice, and her movement." He called her simply "the noblest purest and most intelligent woman I have ever met." These flirtations helped her set aside thoughts of Fuseli, but they also demonstrated how far she had traveled from England, where her unconventional manners and attitudes had frightened most men away. Here, it was precisely her originality that attracted everyone, men and women alike, even though she was far from being the most radical woman in Paris.

The notorious Olympe de Gouges, for example, had just published her *Déclaration des Droits de la Femme et de la Citoyenne (Declaration of the Rights of Woman and the Female Citizen),* which made far more outrageous claims than Mary's *Rights of Woman.* "Woman is born free and lives equal to man in her rights," de Gouges proclaimed.

The forward thrust of the Revolution had allowed the thirty-seven-year-old de Gouges to dream of an equity between the sexes that had seemed impossible to Mary only a few years earlier. De Gouges called on "mothers, daughters, and sisters" to create their own national assembly; promoted the education of girls, divorce rights for women, and homes for unwed mothers; and proposed reforms that included "legal sexual equality, admission for women to all occupations, and the suppression of the dowry system through a state-provided alternative." Having been forced to marry a man she did not love when she was only seventeen, de Gouges declared, "the only limits on the exercise of the natural rights of woman are perpetual male tyranny." On a darker note, she added that if "a woman has the right to mount the scaffold, she must possess equally the right to mount the speaker's platform."

Mary never met de Gouges, but was well aware of her calls for reform, since, in the spring of 1793, many of de Gouges's radical ideas seemed on the verge of being adopted, at least in Paris. The marquis de Condorcet, a moderate leader, even recruited Mary to help the National Convention devise a plan for the education of women.

Even more notorious was the thirty-year-old Théroigne de Méricourt, whom Mary had met while having dinner with Thomas Paine at his elegant hotel at 63 Faubourg Saint-Denis. Theatrical and impulsive, de Méricourt had swaggered in with dueling pistols attached to her belt and a sword at her waist. Famous for her outlandish behavior, she did not want to *discuss* the rights of women, she wanted to *act* on them, preferably with her sword. A courtesan and opera singer before the Revolution, de Méricourt had discarded the trappings of the coquette—the frilly low-cut dresses and lacy bonnets—and wore instead a severe white riding habit and a round-brimmed hat, the closest she could come to dressing like a man without wearing trousers. She refused to bathe, regarding personal hygiene as a reminder of the days when she had to please men in order to survive. Every day she attended the meetings of the National Convention, eager to "play the role of a man," she said, "because I had always been extremely humiliated by the servitude and prejudices under which the pride of men holds my oppressed sex." More extreme than either Mary or Olympe, Théroigne was thrilled with the death of the king, urging women to revolt against the tyranny of all men. "Let us raise ourselves to the height of our destinies," she declared; "let us break our chains!"

In April, Mary attended a party at the Christies' house. She was grateful to Thomas Christie for his support of her work at the *Analytical Review* and knew that Johnson thought highly of him. She did not condemn him for his adultery, but she did feel sorry for his wife, Rebecca. The two women had become close friends. Rebecca, a gentle and empathetic listener, valued Mary's intelligence and warmth. On this particular evening, Mary was soon at the center of the throng, laughing, interrupting, and arguing fervently about the future of the

Revolution with the flashes of insight and wit that everyone always remarked upon, entirely unaware of a handsome young American named Gilbert Imlay eyeing her from across the room.

With her chestnut hair falling out of its pins, her flush of energy, and her voluptuous figure, Mary seemed to Imlay to be eminently desirable. It would be his mission, he decided, to get her to notice him. She was different from any female he had ever met, and that was no small feat, since he had known many. Too many, he sometimes thought. Women seemed to thrive on suffocating him, smothering him. But this independent woman appeared to value her freedom as much as he valued his, which meant that a liaison with her would be an unmitigated delight with no guilt involved. For the time being, though, he contented himself with watching her in action: beautiful, intelligent, and full of life.

*Mary Wollstonecraft, in an etching and aquatint after physionotrace, early nineteenth century.*

# CHAPTER 17

# MARY SHELLEY:
# RETRIBUTION

—

[ 1816–1817 ]

*S*HELLEY FOUND A HOUSE FOR HIMSELF, MARY, AND CLAIRE NEAR the center of Bath, at 5 Abbey Churchyard. From the front window, Mary could see bonneted ladies tripping up and down the street, visiting shops, paying calls on neighbors—and pointedly ignoring their household. Claire was too heartbroken to care; she sat at their writing desk scrawling letter after letter to Byron, pleading with him to return, writing him, "I shall love you to the end of my life & nobody else."

It was a rainy autumn, but the gloomy weather did not deter Shelley and Mary from going for long walks in the drizzle. They also enjoyed cozy afternoons, which Shelley immortalized in a letter to Byron: "Mary is reading over the fire; our cat and kitten are sleeping under the sofa; and little Willy is just gone to sleep." But when Shelley was in London battling his father over his inheritance, Mary felt bereft. To distract herself, she attended lectures at Bath's Literary and Philosophical Society Rooms, took drawing lessons, studied Greek verbs, and worked on finishing *Frankenstein*.

She had decided to make the narrative longer by adding a new character, Robert Walton, an arctic explorer, who is searching for the North Pole. Walton befriends Dr. Frankenstein and recounts Frankenstein's story in a series of letters to his sister, Margaret Walton Saville, providing the reader with another version of the young scientist's tale. Like Frankenstein, Walton is obsessed with proving his own genius, but Frankenstein cautions the young explorer: "Seek happiness in tranquillity, and avoid ambition, even if it be only the apparently innocent one of distinguishing yourself in science and discoveries." His sister also warns Walton against giving in to his ambition, and at last Walton chooses to listen, saving his own life and that of his men by turning back from his hunt for the North Pole.

Walton's decision offers a hopeful alternative to the disastrous choices made by Frankenstein and the creature. Although Walton sees himself as a failure for surrendering his quest, he is actually depicted as a hero by Mary for freeing his sailors and listening to his sister. Unlike Frankenstein, Walton proves himself able to protect those who are close to him. In part this is because Walton has learned from Frankenstein's story—but his change of heart also stems from his relationship with Margaret, who has cautioned him against his voyage from the beginning. Interestingly, despite the importance of her viewpoint, Margaret appears in the story only indirectly, through the letters of her brother—a structural echo of the role most women were forced to play in the lives of men, one step removed, distanced from the action. But invisible though Margaret is, her cautionary words are crucial for creating a counterpoint to the unchecked ambition of the male characters. And Walton's letters to Margaret add an invaluable commentary on the central drama: what matters most, Mary implies through Margaret, is not the quest, not the search for knowledge or justice, but the relationships we have with those we love. The importance of Margaret's character is underscored by the fact that Mary gave Margaret the initials she would have if she were married to Shelley: MWS.

Mary's three-pronged narrative, her Russian doll technique of nesting one story inside another, provides the reader with three different versions of the same set of events. This was a daring departure from the didactic novelists of the preceding generation (such as Samuel Richardson and her own father) and it gave Mary the opportunity to create a complex narrative that asked far more of her readers than if she had written a simple parable against the dangers of invention. Careful not to weight the story in favor of either the creator or the created, Mary conjured a sense of moral suspension in which the conventional questions—Who's the hero? Who's the villain? Who's right? Who's wrong?—no longer applied. The creature and Walton undermine Frankenstein's version of events, allowing us to see what he never acknowledges: that he was at fault because he did not provide his creation with love or an education. Monsters, says Mary, are of our own making.

Mary dedicated *Frankenstein* to her father in yet another effort to win back his affection. But the book was also an expression of longing for her mother, a longing that had been intensified by Godwin's harsh treatment. Mary was sure that if Wollstonecraft had lived, she would never have severed their relationship as Godwin had, and as Frankenstein had with his creature. Now that she was a mother herself, she could not imagine cutting herself off from a child.

Fathers, though, seemed able to reject their children without even a backward glance. Or so it seemed to Mary in the fall of 1816 as day after day, Godwin maintained his flinty silence. She poured her sorrow and outrage into her novel by spelling out the consequences of Frankenstein's rejection of his son. Like Mary, the creature has only a father, and his father fails him, leading the creature to seek murderous revenge. In a world without mothers, she suggests, havoc reigns and evil triumphs.

For Mary, there was only so much solace to be had from writing a book and attending public lectures. She continued to miss Shelley. Claire's situation was a terrible reminder of the vulnerable position all unmarried mothers faced. Always, she worried that Shelley would abandon her and never return. The only contact she had with Skinner Street was through Fanny. Never a particularly cheerful correspondent, Fanny had been penning increasingly melancholy letters. On September 26, she wrote to tell them the Wollstonecraft aunts, Everina and Eliza, had rejected her request to join them in Ireland. These prim ladies thought Fanny's connection to Mary and Shelley would damage their reputation. A week later, Fanny wrote again, delivering an angry message from Godwin: Mary should push Shelley to help him financially. How could Godwin write books if he had to keep doing menial jobs to earn money?

Unfortunately, Mary's responses to Fanny have been lost, but that she was exasperated by her sister and Godwin's requests is clear from her journal. On October 4, she noted that she had received a "stupid letter from F." But poor Fanny was through with belonging nowhere, of being wanted by no one. Each household castigated her for her relationship with the other; each used her as a weapon and a go-between. The Godwins, particularly "Mamma," wanted Fanny to deliver hurtful messages to Mary, and Mary retorted in kind. In a last desperate appeal, Fanny seems to have tried to switch camps. On one of his trips to London, Shelley saw Fanny, and it appears she asked if she might come live with them in Bath. But if that was the case, Shelley refused. He did not want the Godwins to find out about Claire's pregnancy, and neither Mary nor Claire trusted Fanny to keep the secret. A few months later he would write a poignant poem of regret:

> *Her voice did quiver as we parted,*
> *Yet knew I not that heart was broken*
> *From which it came, and I departed*
> *Heeding not the word then spoken.*

On October 8, Fanny slipped out of the Skinner Street house in her Sunday best and headed out of London. She mailed two farewells from Bristol, a "very alarming" letter to Mary that has since been lost or destroyed, and one to Godwin in which she told her stepfather that she wanted to "depart immediately to the spot from which I hope never to remove." Godwin, fearing the worst, traveled to Bristol and then Bath, hunting for her. Shelley, too, immediately set off. But Fanny had covered her tracks and was long gone by the time the men came looking.

Shelley did not give up, however. He raced to Bristol, where he discovered that Fanny had traveled to Swansea, a coastal resort in Wales. When he arrived there on October 11, he found that "the worst" had happened. The local newspaper, the *Cambrian,* reported that a young woman's body had been discovered in the Mackworth Arms. She had been wearing stays with the initials MW—her mother's.

After interviewing the people at the inn, Shelley pieced together what had happened. Fanny had told the chambermaid not to bother her and locked herself in her room. Here she wrote a brief suicide note, took an overdose of laudanum, and lay down on the bed to die. Her intention, she said, was to end the life "of a being whose birth was unfortunate and whose life has only been a series of pain to those persons who have hurt their health in endeavoring to promote her welfare." Her use of the word "unfortunate" is a sad echo of her mother, who had referred to Fanny as "unfortunate" in a note she wrote when she, too, had been in the grips of despair.

Hoping to disguise Fanny's identity, Shelley destroyed her signature on the suicide note. In a tragic gesture, Godwin wrote his first message to Mary since Mary had run away: "Go not to Swansea, disturb not the silent dead; do nothing to destroy the obscurity she so much desired." Both Shelley and Godwin were motivated by the desire to protect Fanny from societal condemnation. In 1816, suicide was considered a crime. No one wanted her to be buried at a crossroads, the usual fate of suicides, and no one wanted more scandal associated with the family. When people asked about her, the Godwins said she had died of a severe cold on her way to visit her aunts.

If Fanny wanted to punish her family, she had succeeded. But instead of accepting responsibility for their mistakes, Godwin and Mary-Jane declared that Fanny had died because of her hopeless love for Shelley, and Shelley and Mary blamed Mary-Jane for her focus on her own daughter and her neglect of Fanny. Only Claire was not guilt-ridden; nor was she particularly heartbroken. She and Fanny had not been close. If the girl wanted to end her life, that was her business. Claire knew that Wollstonecraft, like many Enlightenment figures, had believed that suicide was an honorable option, and this gave Fanny's actions legitimacy in Claire's eyes. If you were tired of being dependent on those who regarded you as a burden, why not kill yourself?

But Mary could not share Claire's equanimity. She was plagued with regrets: if only she had reached out to her sister, if only she had not left her behind, if only she had paid more attention to her. She should not have been impatient with Fanny's passivity; she should have empathized more with her position as an unwanted daughter in the Godwin household. Mary herself was vulnerable, and she knew it. Their mother had struggled with depression. Godwin had acknowledged this legacy by teaching the two girls that they should guard against their dark moods and stamp out the tendency to brood. Fanny had lost a battle that Mary continued to fight.

In December, Mary was still shaken, writing Shelley that she was "much agitated" and felt guilty for not offering Fanny "a proper asylum [*sic*]." Yet she continued to work on *Frankenstein*. When Shelley was there, she gave him the manuscript so he could read it at night. Shelley made comments in the margins, corrected Mary's grammar, and, with her permission, rewrote some phrases, making her sentences more formal. In Mary's original version, Walton observes that Frankenstein's story is "peculiarly interesting," but at Shelley's suggestion, Mary changed Walton's words to "almost as imposing and interesting as truth." They also tinkered with the original first sentence, changing "I beheld my man compleated" to "I beheld the accomplishments of my toils." Mary allowed Shelley to insert philosophical and political observations in a few key chapters. In chapter 8 (volume 1), he tacked in a brief passage explaining how the Swiss democratic tradition was superior to the governments of France and England, and in chapter 4 (volume 1), he wrote a paragraph on the influence of Agrippa and Paracelsus on modern science.

Shelley's active role in editing the book has since led to accusations that Mary was not the real author of *Frankenstein*. However, scholars who have studied the final draft that the couple worked on together estimate that Shelley contributed, at most, about four thousand original words to Mary's 72,000-word novel—a contribution that demonstrates the substantial role he played in shaping the book but which also illustrates that it was mostly written by Mary. Furthermore, fifteen years later, long after Shelley had died, Mary would make extensive revisions, producing the version read by most students today.

But unfortunately, there are still those who claim that *Frankenstein* was essentially Shelley's creation, despite all the evidence to the contrary. Great male authors have rarely faced such attacks, even though other works of literature, such as *The Waste Land* and *The*

*Great Gatsby,* were edited far more extensively than *Frankenstein.* There is a particular irony to these accusations since Shelley's emendations did not always improve Mary's story. In fact, sometimes his suggestions made passages wordier and more difficult to understand. Moreover, both Mary and Shelley prized their ability to collaborate. Their shared passion for literature was one of the reasons they had fallen in love in the first place. Indeed, Frankenstein is doomed because he seals himself off from others—his family and friends as well as his creature.

At any rate, for Mary, there was no reason to steal from Shelley's trove of ideas when she had so many of her own. The creature's suffering was meant to reflect her situation, not Shelley's. Unmarried mothers and illegitimate children were hated by society, just like Frankenstein's creature. Wollstonecraft became an outcast the moment she had Fanny. Fanny became an outcast the moment she was born. This was profoundly unfair, Mary believed, the result of blind prejudice. Fanny was an innocent child. Her mother had done nothing wrong. She should not have been ostracized. Neither, for that matter, should she. Her crime was nothing more than loving Shelley. Claire, too, was about to give birth to an illegitimate child. For all that Claire and Mary competed with one another, Mary did not think that Claire deserved condemnation for loving Byron, and neither did her unborn baby.

Ten days before Christmas, more bad news arrived in a letter from Shelley's friend and bookseller Thomas Hookham. The abandoned Harriet, who had been silent that autumn, neither responding to Shelley's letters nor initiating any contact herself, had jumped off a bridge into the Serpentine. According to the newspaper report, she was "far advanced in pregnancy." Harriet had joined the pantheon of those who, hated by the world, chose death over the pain of rejection. But in Harriet's case, Mary had participated in the ruin by running away with Shelley. She knew that Harriet had blamed her for stealing her husband, and she wept over her complicity in Harriet's suffering. If Shelley were ever to abandon her, Mary worried that she would follow in the footsteps of Harriet and her sister. She wrote to Shelley that winter, "Ah! My best love to you do I owe every joy every perfection that I may enjoy or boast of—Love me, sweet, for ever—"

These two tragic deaths marked a turning point in Mary and Shelley's life together. Mary was plagued with depression and guilt, and Harriet's death spurred Shelley into a burst of frenetic activity. Having evinced little interest in three-year-old Ianthe or two-year-old Charles while their mother was alive, he raced up to London to demand sole custody from Harriet's grieving parents, the Westbrooks, who were horrified. How could this wild-eyed lunatic who had ruined their daughter's life think he had any right to children he hardly knew? But opposition such as theirs generally inspired Shelley to rise to new antagonistic heights. And so when it was clear the Westbrooks were going to refuse his demands, Shelley launched a campaign, just as he had when he had tried to foment revolution in Ireland or when he had persuaded Mary to run away with him. He wrote letter after letter to influential friends and members of Harriet's family and plotted various plans of action, many of which included kidnapping.

To build his case, Shelley decided that he and Mary should get married immediately, and so Mary left William behind with Claire, traveled to London, and vowed to love and honor Shelley in St. Mildred's Church on Bread Street. Afterward, Shelley wrote to Byron, "I need not inform you that this is simply with us a measure of convenience, and that our opinions as to the importance of this pretended sanction, and all the prejudices connected with it, remain the same." Worried that Claire would feel betrayed, Shelley wrote her a consoling note, revealing his tangled loyalties; he commiserated with her about her loneliness and reassured her that the marriage was only to keep "them" quiet, though whether he meant the Godwins or Harriet's family is unclear: "Dearest Claire . . . Thank you too, my kind girl, for not expressing much of what you must feel—the loneliness and the low spirits which arise from being entirely left."

Mary's casual attitude toward the event is reflected in the fact that she recorded the wrong date, December 29, in her journal. The union had taken place on December 30. Certainly, a less romantic wedding for this pair of young Romantics can hardly be imagined. But Mary would have seen it as a betrayal of her mother to harbor dreams of herself as a conventional bride. In her experience, marriage was a double-edged sword: it provided women with the stamp of societal approval, but it also took away the few rights they possessed.

And yet while she did not embrace the idea, Mary understood that she needed to take this next step if she wanted to be able to move more freely in the world. She also suspected that a wedding would regain her father's approval, and sure enough, once he heard that his daughter was to be married, Godwin consented to see her, visiting her two days before the event, and eagerly attending the wedding.

As Shelley complained to Claire, "Mrs G. and G. were both present, and appeared to feel no little satisfaction." Shelley's observation was all too apt. Godwin was proud of Mary's union, bragging to his relatives that his daughter had made a "good marriage" to the eldest son of a baronet.

IN THE TWO AND a half years since father and daughter had seen each other, the sixty-year-old Godwin had grown grayer and more stooped. Money troubles, scandal, and health problems had taken their toll. Mary, too, had changed; no longer the rebellious teenager Godwin remembered from the summer of 1814, she had become a mother, had adventures he could not imagine, and been to countries he had never seen. Godwin did not marvel at her growth, though, nor did he ask her about little William or her travels. Not once did he apologize for his silence. Instead, he brought up his financial situation. Now that his daughter was actually marrying Shelley, he demanded a transfusion of funds from his soon-to-be son-in-law. Over the last two years, he had never stopped asking for money from Shelley, but now he wanted an even larger sum that they could not possibly afford. Mary tried to overlook her father's behavior, but it was difficult to avoid acknowledging his hypocrisy. The philosopher of truth and freedom, the man who had once argued against marriage, was finally willing to talk to her again because she was getting married. And all that he seemed to want was money.

She poured her disillusionment into the last pages of *Frankenstein*. When she had run away with Shelley, everyone, even her own father, had acted as though associating with her was dangerous. No one had taken her true character into account, just as everyone failed to see past the monster's appearance to his inner nature. Mary had learned a painful lesson about the cruelty of human nature. She could not retaliate by going on a murderous rampage, like her creature, but she could imagine such a rampage and describe it in vivid, visceral detail. The creature would take revenge on her behalf.

After they were married, Shelley redoubled his efforts to claim his children, spending the spring in London for the court proceedings, battling charges leveled by Harriet's family that he was immoral and an atheist to boot—difficult accusations to fight, since in the eyes of English society he was both. As for Mary, although some women might have winced at the prospect of adopting another woman's children, for her, a lifelong motherless child, it never occurred to her to reject them. "Those darling treasures," she called them. She admitted that she worried about William, who would turn one year old that January, losing his status as the eldest son—his aunt Claire had teased him about how he would "lose his pre-eminence and be helped third at table"—but she remained eager to take in both children.

Mary spent January in Bath and was present for the birth of Claire's baby, Clara Allegra Byron, on January 12. Afterward, when she was not helping Claire or taking care of William, or Wilmouse, as they now called him, Mary worked on *Frankenstein* and continued her rigorous course of literary self-education, studying Latin and reading Milton's *Comus,* Smollett's *Roderick Ransom,* Sidney's *Arcadia,* and Robert Southey's translation of *Amadis of Gaul.* But knowing her husband as she did, she also took the time to write to Marianne Hunt, the wife of Leigh Hunt, Shelley's host in London, to ask small favors, such as to send his dirty clothing to the laundry, all while apologizing for Shelley's thoughtlessness in such matters.

After a few weeks of being apart from Shelley, Mary, who had been feeling tired and depressed, discovered she was pregnant once again. She wrote Shelley anxious letters, reminding him that he was all that kept her from Fanny's fate (and, implicitly, Harriet's, though she never mentioned her). Most of all, she was tired of living with her stepsister. She had not fled Skinner Street simply to end up housemates with Claire. Alarmed at how low she sounded, Shelley told her to come to London, and on January 25, Mary joined him at the Hunts' rented cottage in Hampstead.

Leigh Hunt was a glamorous figure, a writer, editor, and political activist eight years older than Shelley. The two men had met the preceding fall, when Shelley, who admired Hunt's radical politics, sent him some poems to publish in Hunt's new journal, *The Indicator,* as well as some money to keep the cash-strapped publication on its feet. Although the disorganized Hunt had lost Shelley's work, he had read the poems and been impressed by them. He was also interested in courting a young man who apparently had cash to spare. And so, when Shelley arrived in London, Hunt gave the poet a warm welcome.

The son of a wealthy West Indian plantation owner, Hunt was considered something of an outsider by conventional society. His

*Leigh Hunt, one of the founding editors of* The Examiner.

skin was dark, his lips full. He looked exotic—a polite way of saying that he did not look entirely British or entirely white. A founding editor of the liberal newspaper *The Examiner,* Hunt had become the darling of radicals—most famously Byron—for an attack on the Prince Regent. The prince's outrageous lifestyle and exorbitant spending made him an easy and frequent target of liberals, but Hunt's editorial was so vehement that it earned him a two-year prison sentence. He endured his time in jail with equanimity, decorating his rooms with floral wall hangings, planting a perennial garden outside his window, playing games with visiting friends, and continuing to excoriate the government in masterful articles.

After prison, Hunt developed a reputation for eccentricity, wearing silk dressing gowns all day long and putting on clothes only if he went out, which he rarely did since he had become agoraphobic after his two years' imprisonment. If his friends wanted to hear about his most current ideas, they had to go see him—a significant undertaking as his cottage was not easy to reach. Hampstead was a rural village in those days, and Hunt's home was a ten-minute walk from its center.

However, for those visitors who did make the trek, the rewards were immediate. Hunt would whisk them off to his study for private tête-à-têtes. This tiny room was the hub of his universe, and therefore of the literary universe—or at least the liberal literary universe—as he was the acknowledged leader of the reform movement. Here he made and broke careers, discovering new writers and eviscerating old ones. Yet his office had none of the trappings of power; if anything, the decorations were oddly effeminate. There was no huge desk. No dark colors. No solemn wood paneling. Instead, the walls were painted green and dotted with white flowers. The furniture was green and white to match. The chamber was so small that it could contain only two chairs, which forced Hunt and his visitors to huddle together, an intimacy that some did not like but that Shelley enjoyed.

When Mary and Shelley stayed with Hunt and his family that winter, Hunt was intent on advancing the career of a young, previously undiscovered poet, John Keats. No other critic was ready to take up Keats's cause. *The Quarterly Review* had recently called him "unintelligible," "tiresome," and "absurd." Other critics, who disliked him for his association with Hunt's liberal politics, ridiculed his "Cockney" background and his humble beginnings as an apothecary's apprentice.

But Keats was precisely the sort of writer who would become Hunt's trademark. When it came to literary talent, Hunt was like a bloodhound. That fall, he had written an essay called "The Young Poets," in which he named Shelley and Keats as two stars on the rise. Always short of money, he was happy to accept donations from Shelley, and he was sometimes accused of using his charm to fleece people. But the more Hunt came to know Shelley, the more he was struck by the younger man's talent, and just as with Keats, he decided to promote his career. He introduced the two poets, and though Shelley was interested in the younger man, Keats was suspicious of Shelley's aristocratic background. He thought Shelley was being patronizing when he advised him to wait to publish, although in actuality Shelley was trying to protect Keats from the cruel treatment he had received from critics with his own *Queen Mab* and *Alastor*.

More worldly-wise than Hunt's other protégés, Shelley did not need Hunt to guide him through society's treacherous waters, whereas the younger, poorer Keats was in frequent need of advice and money. Despite their age difference, Shelley was more of an equal to Hunt, who found him tremendously amusing. In fact, it is thanks to Hunt's reminiscences that Shelley's eccentric sense of humor has been preserved for history—a pleasant surprise, given the humorless, saintlike image Mary would help promulgate after her husband died. In Hunt's version of the man, Shelley is a young mischief maker who enjoyed shocking people and had a predilection for shouting out literary quotes if he thought it might make a stir. One day, the two men were riding in a stagecoach with another passenger, an elderly lady, when, according to Hunt, Shelley, who "had been moved . . . by something objectionable which he thought he saw in the face of our companion," burst out with a favorite passage from Shakespeare's *Richard II* in which the king says mournfully:

> *For Heaven's sake! Let us sit upon the ground,*
> *And tell sad stories of the death of kings.*

The poor old lady was "startled into a look of the most ludicrous astonishment and looked on the coach-floor, as if expecting to see us take our seats accordingly."

In the years to come, this friendship would become a touchstone for both men. Hunt's opinions mattered to Shelley; he was inspired by Hunt's political engagement and took confidence from Hunt's belief in his work, especially when it seemed no one cared if he wrote another word. As for Hunt, who was also a poet, Shelley's commitment to his art represented the sort of writing life he had once imagined for himself. Hunt would do his best to bring his friend's poetry to the attention of the public, and after Shelley's death, Hunt would become one of the most important promoters of Shelley's literary legacy.

For Mary, the Hunts' busy home was a refreshing change after her isolated life in Bath. The Hunt children clattered up and down the stairs, made faces at Wilmouse, and begged Shelley to play with them, which he did, chasing them down the hallways and tramping with them through the countryside. The Hunts' eldest son, Thornton, remembered a game Shelley invented called "frightful creatures," in which Shelley would terrify Thornton by " 'do[ing] the horn,' which was a way that Shelley had of screwing up his hair in front, to imitate a weapon of that sort." When the wind was high, Shelley sailed his paper boats on Hampstead's ponds, often accompanied by one or two Hunt children.

Hunt's shelves were crowded with books and figures of Greek and Roman gods made by his artist wife, Marianne. Mary and Marianne spent much of their time together, taking long walks, organizing the meals and activities for the children, and working—Mary on her book and Marianne on her art. A sculptor and painter—her silhouette of Keats is one of the few images of the poet—Marianne shared many of Mary's challenges: a complicated marriage to an exceptionally talented husband, the difficulties of having her own artistic career, motherhood, tight finances, and, strangely enough, the problem of having an attractive unmarried sister in love with her husband.

Elizabeth Kent, or Bess, was five years younger than Marianne. Like Hunt, Bess was a writer and an intellectual; over the course of her life she wrote books on natural history as well as a children's book. She had met Leigh Hunt when he was courting her older sister and had been devoted to him ever since, listening eagerly to his rants about the government's treachery, contributing her own opinions to many of his articles, and even transacting many of his business deals with publishers and bankers while Marianne was busy with the children or her own work. When Hunt was in his two-room cell, although it was the custom for wives to join their husbands in prison, Marianne asked Bess to take her place. She was worried that the jail was too damp and unhealthy for their new son, Thornton. Bess jumped at this opportunity, making Hunt's meals, proofreading his work, helping him entertain visitors and colleagues, and generally serving as a kind of auxiliary wife while Marianne was home with the baby.

Rumors of an affair swept periodically through literary and political circles, and these were exacerbated when Hunt published a poem, *The Tale of Rimini,* that retold, and appeared to celebrate, the story of Paulo and Francesca, the incestuous lovers from Dante's *Inferno*—confirmation, according to critics, of his immoral relationship with his wife's sister. Although it is unlikely that Bess and Hunt ever consummated their relationship, it is true that, as with Shelley and Claire, there was a strong attraction and an intimacy that often trumped that of husband and wife.

This situation was all too familiar to Mary, so she was not surprised to find that Bess and Marianne fought almost all the time. But it was shocking to wake up one morning and hear that while everyone was asleep, Bess had thrown herself in the pond behind the house, where she would have drowned had she not been discovered in time by the servants. Mary empathized as she watched Marianne struggle to manage the guilt, remorse, and anger that Bess's act had evoked.

To Mary, Bess's suicide attempt was a warning bell. For all of her conflicts with her stepsister, Mary did not want Claire to kill herself, nor did she want their relationship to become as embittered as that of the Kent sisters. She knew that Bess had turned to opium and Marianne was already well on her way to alcoholism, and this was not the future she wanted for her sister or herself. However, she felt trapped.

Their lives were too entangled, especially now that Claire was a single mother and even more dependent on Mary and Shelley. There was also the additional question of what to do with Allegra. If the baby remained with Claire, people would begin to suspect that Claire was her mother, not her aunt, which would shut the door on any future opportunity to appear in polite society. This was something Claire said she did not care about, but Mary did. She wanted her sister to become independent from her and Shelley, and societal acceptance was a necessary first step in making an advantageous marriage, or securing a job as a governess or teacher—the best options for Claire's future. And so, after many weeks of discussion, Mary, Shelley, and the Hunts came up with a scheme: the Hunts would take Claire's baby into their family for a few months and pretend she was theirs— they had four children; who would notice one more? Then the Shelleys and Claire would "adopt" Allegra back into their own household, letting the world think the baby was a little Hunt. It was an imperfect solution, far-fetched even, but Mary fully supported it, hoping that it might hasten the day when she would finally be free of Claire.

# CHAPTER 18

# MARY WOLLSTONECRAFT:
# IN LOVE

———

[ 1792 ]

A LADIES' MAN, A VETERAN OF THE AMERICAN REVOLUTION, A LAND speculator on the lookout for fast money, an amateur philosopher, an author, and, some say, a spy, Gilbert Imlay is still something of a mystery today. Before he arrived in revolutionary France, he had spent a few years undercover, running from creditors. Now that he was in Paris, he hoped to sell land on the American frontier to those who were disenchanted with the Revolution or who had run afoul of the authorities.

Imlay had been invited to the Christies' party on the strength of his friendship with Joel Barlow, another American and an acquaintance of Mary, who adored Barlow's wife, Ruth. In the weeks following the party, Imlay began to pursue Mary, and although she had not noticed him at first, her other suitors soon paled beside the exotic American. Imlay had a frontiersman's quiet dignity; when he had an opinion, he got straight to the point, not waiting to hear what others thought. His manners were forthright, his American accent distinctive. Before long Mary discovered that their political views were almost identical. They both believed in liberty, equality, and women's rights. Both supported the Revolution; both were worried about the escalating violence.

He was also an excellent conversationalist—witty, flirtatious, and charming. Mary was entranced by the picture he drew of America: a republic with rippling green cornfields, small farms dotting the hill-sides, strong men, pioneer women, and red, white, and blue flags of freedom waving from the liberty trees. During the next two weeks, as they sipped English tea at Helen Maria's or chatted in the Barlows' elegant drawing room at 22 Rue Jacob, Imlay inspired Mary by tell-ing her that America was a place where utopian dreams could become reality, where men and women could learn to live together as equals, where slaves could be freed, where tyranny could, at last, be entirely eradicated from the earth. He had written two books that proved his credentials as a bona fide idealist. The first was a paean to the frontier. *A Topographical Description of the Western Territory of North America* not only provided the most accurate description of the trans-Allegheny region in print, it was a celebration of life in the wilderness. America, Imlay declared, was a country where "freedom is enthroned in the heart of every citizen." His novel, *The Emigrants,* attacked the slave trade, inherited wealth, monarchies, strict divorce laws, and all impo-sitions on freedom, including marriage, which he called a "state of degradation and misery" for women.

Even before meeting Imlay, Mary had been interested in America; back in England, she had helped her brother Charles emigrate there and it had been a frequent topic of conversation at Johnson's dinner parties. One of Johnson's regulars, the scientist Joseph Priestley, had intrigued Mary by declaring his intention to move to America and breathe the air of freedom.

The more Imlay talked, the more fascinated Mary became. Her dreams of America became entwined with her dreams of Imlay. The man, the country—both seemed to promise liberty and a new life. She and Imlay went for long walks around Paris and now, under these romantic circumstances, Mary saw the city differently. Paris was a "fairy scene" that "touch[ed] the heart." She delighted in the "charm-ing boulevards" and the city's "simple, playful elegance." The heav-ens seemed to "smile." Even the air was "sweet" with the fragrance of the "clustering flowers." Eventually, she confided in Imlay about Fuseli, and in return he told her about a "cunning" woman who had broken his heart. On April 19, Joel Barlow wrote his wife, Ruth, in London that he suspected Mary and Imlay were beginning an affair.

"Between you and me—you must not hint it to her or to J[ohnson] or to anyone else—I believe [Mary] has got a sweetheart, and that she [will] finish by going with him to A[merica] a wife. He is of Kentucky and a very sensible man."

As the days grew warmer, the political situation became increasingly unsettled. The death of the king had not solved the people's problems. Bread was still expensive and they were still poor. Angry outbursts erupted on street corners, and more and more "enemies of the people" were denounced. Gilbert and Mary watched as their French friends, the moderate Girondists, battled for their lives against the radical Jacobins. Even Théroigne de Méricourt, radical though she was, was attacked while giving an outdoor speech on the rights of women. A crowd of red-pantalooned working women pelted her with stones, knocked her off the podium, tore off her clothes, and smashed her skull open. Though de Méricourt did not die, she never fully recovered; imprisoned by the Jacobin police, she sat in a dark cell, injured and terrified, refusing to speak to any of her old friends.

Mary was well aware that if the Jacobins came into power, Madame Roland, Olympe de Gouges, and many others who had opposed the execution of the king faced grave danger, as did their English sympathizers, including herself, Thomas Paine, and Helen Maria Williams. In addition, when England declared war on France, British citizens had immediately become enemies of the state. Only Imlay and Barlow were safe, because the French considered Americans comrades in arms. Everyone knew the situation was truly dire when the brave Madame Roland stopped holding her salons that spring; thereafter, Mary and her friends grew cautious about where they went in the city and what they said in public.

To Mary, alarmed by these terrible accounts of violence, Imlay's tales of America sounded more and more attractive. In the middle of May, about six weeks after they met, he declared his love and asked her to move back there with him, far from the excesses of the Revolution and the corruption of Europe. Mary was filled with rapture at the thought. Together they walked to his apartment in Saint-Germain-des-Prés and they made love—she for the very first time. Later she remembered how Imlay's eyes "glistened with sympathy," how his kisses were "softer than soft." At a party, a Frenchwoman seeking to win Mary's approval said that she thought love affairs were unnecessary and that she herself was above them. *"Tant pis pour vous"* ("Tough luck for you"), Mary replied, filled with the rosy glow of passion. She had finally discovered what she had long suspected was true: sexual ardor was an essential component of loving a man, even if marriage was not. What mattered was the union of two hearts. True chastity lay not in virginity, but in fidelity to one's beloved. There was no need for a legal document. If two people truly loved each other, then they would remain together forever. She could not imagine being with anyone but Imlay and she was sure he felt the same way. They were part of the revolution, pioneering a new kind of relationship between a man and a woman—a love affair between equals—something she had thought impossible, at least in her own lifetime.

It was an extraordinary time to fall in love. On May 31, eighty thousand Parisians took to the streets, protesting the price of bread and calling for the ouster of the Girondists. The radical Jacobins capitalized on the riots, arresting many prominent leaders of the moderates, including Madame Roland. On June 1, it was announced that all resident aliens had to chalk their names on their doors. On June 2, the Girondists were forced from the Convention. The city had become a prison, and Mary worried that the paranoid authorities would accuse her hosts, Aline and her husband, of harboring a British spy. She decided to move to a cottage owned by the Filliettazes' gardener in Neuilly, about four miles northwest of the city walls.

Safety concerns aside, this cottage was a stroke of luck. Mary savored the idea of having a place of her own. Spending the night with Gilbert had been an awkward and almost impossible proposition while she was living with the Filliettazes. Open-minded though they were, her hosts were more conservative than Mary's new revolutionary friends and would have been scandalized if she had hosted a male visitor. If she had disappeared to Gilbert's house and not come back until morning, they would have been alarmed for her safety. But now Gilbert could come and stay with her. They could sleep in the same bed, share meals, and have long quiet evenings, just the two of them.

Her first night in the cottage was strangely silent after Paris. Here there were no inquisitive neighbors or shopkeepers, no mobs patrolling the streets, no provocateurs shouting in the squares, no parties to attend, no host and hostess. She had not lived in the country for many years and reveled in the beauty around her, although it seemed odd to be in such a bucolic setting when only a few miles away the city was in turmoil. She spent hours reading and writing. The Filliettazes' gardener liked her, as most servants did. He left her baskets of grapes and peaches and expressed concern about her habit of taking long walks alone when vagabonds and brigands hid in the woods. Undeterred, Mary roamed through the nearby fields, even trekking eleven miles to Versailles. She would be one of the last to see the deserted palace before the royal furniture was auctioned off later that summer. It was still very much as it had been when the king and queen lived there, though the halls echoed with emptiness. The "air is chill," she wrote, "seeming to clog the breath; and the wasting dampness of destruction appears to be stealing into the vast pile on every side." It was an eerie experience, walking alone through the Hall of Mirrors, the War Salon, the Hercules Room, the queen's chambers. She felt surrounded by ghosts: the "gigantic" portraits of kings "seem to be sinking into the embraces of death." Outside, all of the famous grottoes and statues were still there, including Marie Antoinette's "Temple of Love" and her infamous "farm," the *petit hameau,* where she and her ladies had dressed as shepherdesses and milked the prettiest, most gentle cows the servants could find. But now the grass was overgrown and the flowerbeds unweeded. Mary was both shocked and saddened by what she saw, writing, "I weep, O France, over the vestiges of thy former oppression." Yet while she disapproved of the opulence of Versailles, its glorification of kings and their armies, she was also appalled at the reports she heard about the Jacobins' abuse of power, killing people "whose only crime is their name." Hope lay in freedom, she believed, not in tyranny, whether the tyrants were republican leaders or monarchs.

When Gilbert came to visit her, she met him at the gates of the city. He smiled and embraced her, calling her "dear girl." She told him how much she loved him, spilling out her plans and her hopes, which continued to evolve as the summer passed. Financial independence and literary fame were no longer enough. Now she wanted a snug domestic life with Gilbert, a simple cottage, a flower garden, and "cheerful poultry." They could own a small plot of land and a cow. Maybe they could settle on the banks of the Ohio River, which Gilbert had assured her was one of the most captivating places on earth. There they could write and read and study, working to bring freedom to the rest of the world.

However, there was a darker side to falling in love, she discovered. When Gilbert could not visit her, she despaired. If he had to cancel their meetings or did not appear, she was hurt and angry. Her notes to Gilbert reflect the complexity of her feelings, as well as the anxiety she felt that her ardor might drive him away. She did not want to frighten him, but she wanted him to know how much she loved him, expressing the same sort of passion she had once felt for Jane, Fanny, and Fuseli:

> You can scarcely imagine with what pleasure I anticipate the day, when we are to begin almost to live together; and you would smile to hear how many plans of employment I have in my head, now that I am confident my heart has found peace in your bosom.—Cherish me with that dignified tenderness, which I have only found in you; and your own dear girl will try to keep under a quickness of feeling, that has sometimes given you pain—Yes, I will be good, that I may deserve to be happy; and whilst you love me, I cannot again fall into the miserable state, which rendered life a burthen almost too heavy to be borne.

For all her protestations of "confidence," Mary was worried. She knew her happiness was contingent on Gilbert's love and if he went away she would be lost. She tried not to press him too hard, looking forward to the day when they would "almost" live together, letting the prospect of sharing a house seem tentative. She knew that he did not like her melancholy or her rage when she sensed him distancing himself. She tried to control her feelings the way he asked her to, but she could not help herself. It was terrifying to need a man this much.

As the summer faded into fall, the Jacobins tightened their grip on the city. Each week, Mary heard of new imprisonments: Olympe de Gouges, the Christies, Thomas Paine. Just how tense things had become was made clear one day when Mary paid a visit to the city and stepped in blood, running like rainwater down the street from the nearby guillotine. When she gasped, a passerby hushed her, warning her to keep quiet. It was crucial to express joy over the daily murders or one might be charged as a collaborator, a traitor to the Revolution. Even if she behaved with uncharacteristic circumspection, Mary knew it was not long before she, too, would be imprisoned.

Faced with these mounting dangers, she began to worry that she would have to leave France, but she resisted making any plans for departure. She was not through witnessing this "revolution in the minds of men," and she did not want to separate from Gilbert, who was now deeply enmeshed in his moneymaking schemes. England had placed an embargo on trade with the French, and Imlay, always on the lookout for new ventures, had stepped into the breach, masterminding French trade with America for soap, wheat, and other essentials.

In August, they decided the best plan would be to have Gilbert register Mary as his wife at the American embassy. As "Mary Imlay," she would be safe from the French authorities. In the eyes of the world, the couple would become man and wife without Mary's having to forgo any of her legal rights and without Imlay's having to swear to take care of her until the day he died.

At the end of the summer, Mary returned to Paris to live with Gilbert in the Faubourg Saint-Germain. Imlay's apartment was in a neighborhood that was quieter and less dangerous than the Marais, where she had lived before. The houses here were newly built out of white stone. They had high ceilings and tall windows and were set farther apart than in the older quarters. A few decades earlier, Saint-Germain-des-Prés had been more like a village than a part of Paris—bucolic and off the beaten track—and it still retained a rural flavor, with trees lining the streets and flower gardens. Many foreigners had moved there in an effort to avoid prison or death. When Mary walked down the street, she could hear a polyglot of languages: English, German, Italian, and Russian as well as French.

After she had unpacked her boxes of books, Mary settled down to writing. Events were occurring so quickly it was hard to stay abreast of the latest news. She busied herself, taking notes and visiting friends she had not seen since her summer retreat, and at first all went smoothly, despite the tension that ruled the city. Her days with Imlay were blissful. They ate their meals together and had long conversations in the evening about the future, their own and that of France. She felt cherished, idealized, and charmed by his humor and warmth. Best of all, she was living in accordance with her philosophy. She had not surrendered her independence and yet was living with the man she loved. But this idyll was quickly cut short. Soon after Mary moved in, Imlay left for business, traveling 120 miles northwest to Le Havre to oversee his trading company, which had expanded beyond America to focus largely on Sweden and Norway.

This was a tricky enterprise, since overseas trade meant skirting the British blockade against France. Clever and ambitious, Imlay came up with a plan in which his French customers would pay for the commodities he imported in Bourbon silver—an illegal currency in Britain, Austria, and Prussia, with whom France was at war, but perfectly legal in out-of-the-way Scandinavia, where Imlay established a contact: a merchant named Elias Backman, who was based in Gothenburg. Backman was happy to take French silver in exchange for the goods he had to sell, such as wheat, soap, and iron, or to convert the silver into currency that Imlay could use in Britain and America. As the middleman, Imlay hoped to become rich, very rich. If this happened, he told Mary, they could go to America.

But Mary was disappointed that he had gone away and annoyed by his mercantile ambition. She did not like that he was so eager to advance himself in business. Where was his idealism? Why did he need to make so much money if they were going to become American farmers? Living alone in Saint-Germain-des-Prés was not what she had dreamed of during the summer. Also, she often felt "inclined to faint," and that September, when she missed her period, she began to wonder if she was pregnant.

Mary's concerns about her own future were dwarfed, however, by the drama playing out in Paris. On October 1, the British army won an important victory at the French port of Toulon and declared the young Louis XVII king of France, which enraged the radical leader of the Jacobins, the stern, unbending Robespierre, who regarded the monarchy as one of the most pernicious evils of the ancien régime. A controversial figure even today—bloodthirsty dictator or an idealistic leader?—Robespierre urged his followers to stamp out counter-revolutionary forces, using violence if necessary, in order to protect liberty and the sovereignty of the people. At his instigation, revolutionary authorities searched the city for remaining British citizens and, between October 10 and 14, locked 250 of them into the Luxembourg, a palace that had been converted into a jail, not far from where Mary was living. Remaining Girondist leaders were also rounded up, and Condorcet, who had asked Mary to work on the plan for the education of women, was condemned to death. Mary witnessed the secret police moving through the city, kicking in doors and arresting people in public squares. At Robespierre's insistence, workers removed all religious symbols (crucifixes, paintings, crosses) from Notre Dame Cathedral and converted it into a "Temple of Reason." The French people no longer needed the corrupt Catholic Church, Robespierre declared; they needed to be weaned from their superstitious beliefs. The ancient medieval chapel not far from Mary's house, Saint-Germain-des-Prés, was looted by an anti-Catholic mob. Mary's imprisoned French friends were preparing to face the guillotine. Madame Roland spent her time in prison studying Plutarch to ready herself for martyrdom.

Danger drew even nearer when Helen Maria Williams was thrown into prison. The odds were against the execution of a well-connected Englishwoman, and Helen Maria, who shared Mary's belief that they were living through historic times of enormous import, was sanguine enough about her prospects to record her experiences in letters, which she would ultimately publish in England. And yet she was still terri-fied. At night she wept, feeling the blade of the guillotine trembling over her head and yearning "for the wings of a dove, that I might flee away and be at rest!" Fortunately, she and her family were rescued by wealthy friends and escaped to Switzerland in the spring of 1794. But the impact of Helen's imprisonment left its mark on Mary, who would commemorate her friend's ordeal in her next novel, naming her imprisoned heroine Maria.

Back in England, people were horrified by the violence in France. Liberals lost their enthusiasm for the Revolution and conservatives nodded their heads sagely; the radicals had spun out of control, just as they had predicted. To many, even her erstwhile friends, Helen Maria was no longer a sympathetic figure, a Romantic heroine. Rather, her imprisonment seemed a just punishment, not only because of her support of the Revolution, but because she was a *woman* who had dared to involve herself in politics. In a review of volumes 3 and 4 of Helen Maria's *Letters from France,* published while she was still in prison, a writer for the *British Critic* declared, "If this young lady now suffers captivity in France . . . her own fate is the best commentary on the wild doctrines she has vindicated." Another critic condemned Helen Maria's involvement in public life altogether: "politics are a study inapplicable to female powers by nature, and withheld from us by education." Englishwomen were not the sole victims of these attacks. "Madame Roland," one London critic intoned, "received a severe lesson of the dangers in which ambitious women involve themselves by undutifully aspiring to notoriety in troublesome times, and by interfering with what does not regard their sex." None of this boded well for Mary, since she, like Madame Roland and Helen Maria Williams, felt a personal obligation to involve herself in poli-tics, to speak out on behalf of reform.

But soon there would be no place left to go, as the French attitude toward women was about to take a dramatic turn for the worse. On October 16, Robespierre executed Marie Antoinette, and with the death of the queen, a storm swept the country. The revolutionary leaders said that the queen had been governed by "uterine furies."

They wanted the new France to be like ancient Rome, where "each sex was in its place . . . men made the laws . . . and women, without allowing themselves to question it, agreed in everything." One of Robespierre's deputies, Jean-Baptiste Amar, speaking for the Committee on General Security, issued a definitive condemnation: "In general, women are not capable of elevated thoughts and serious meditations, and if, among ancient peoples, their natural timidity and modesty did not allow them to appear outside their families, then in the French Republic do you want them to be seen coming to the bar, to the tribune, and to political assemblies as men do?"

Jacobin leaders, inspired by Rousseau's vision of the ideal woman—the very same vision that Mary had protested in both of her *Vindications*—declared that women should be at home raising children. On October 30, they rescinded the rights women had won in the early days of the Revolution—divorce, inheritance, and legal representation—and barred women from joining revolutionary clubs and taking part in political demonstrations. Even the iconography of the Revolution underwent a change: the female figure of Liberty, the initial symbol of the new regime, was replaced with a heroic male figure, Justice. Only images of chaste young virgins were allowed to remain in the public sphere, representing virtuous republican domesticity rather than impassioned female leadership. Helen Maria said it best when she declared that force had defeated sensibility and the lust for power had triumphed over reason. She could easily have added that male ambition had utterly vanquished the women's movement in France.

Mary did not comment on the growing backlash against women; she knew it was too dangerous. On October 31, the Girondists who remained alive were put to death. When Mary heard the news, she fainted. On November 3, Robespierre's minions guillotined Olympe de Gouges after first stripping her naked and examining her genitals, ostensibly to check her gender. This insult only further inflamed de Gouges; she went to her death refusing to recant, proclaiming, "My sentiments have not changed." The authorities warned others against following her example and even called her sexuality into question. "Recall that virago," they warned, "that man-woman, the impudent Olympe de Gouges, who was first to institute women's societies, who abandoned the care of her household, who wished to play politics and committed crimes. [She has] been annihilated under the avenging sword of the laws." Finally, on November 8, Madame Roland was executed; her final words—"O Liberty! What crimes are committed in thy name!"—would ring through the decades. In Scotland, twenty years later, the young Isabella Baxter would recite them for the benefit of her new friend who was visiting from England, fifteen-year-old Mary Godwin.

Even as she mourned the loss of these courageous women, Mary discovered that her missed period was neither a fluke nor a response to the tensions of the day; her stays had become tight and she felt little flutters inside her abdomen. In early November, around the time of Madame Roland's execution, Mary wrote Gilbert:

> I have felt some gentle twitches, which make me begin to think, that I am nourishing a creature who will soon be sensible of my care—This thought has not only produced an overflowing of tenderness to you, but made me very attentive to calm my mind and take exercise, lest I should destroy an object, in whom we are to have a mutual interest, you know. Yesterday—do not smile!—finding that I had hurt myself by lifting precipitously a large log of wood I sat down in an agony, till I felt those said twitches again.

One might think that Mary would feel trepidation at this new development—having a baby in a war-torn land, away from home and family—but she relished the prospect of motherhood. She had met with more adventures in the last eleven months than she could have dreamed of when Fuseli's wife had pushed her out the door. Even though she was watching the rights of women disintegrate all around her, even as she heard the critics rising up against Helen Maria and knew that this was the antagonism she, too, would face when she published her history of the Revolution, Mary felt excited and proud. Her baby would be a testimony to the relationship she and Gilbert had forged, a product of true revolutionary values—trust, loyalty, and equality—rather than tyranny and slavish dependence. She would be putting her ideals into action, creating an equal partnership with a man, joining the ranks of mothers, and staking her life and her child's life on the principles she believed in with all of her heart.

# CHAPTER 19

# MARY SHELLEY:
# MARLOW AND LONDON

———

[ 1817–1818 ]

THE DEBATES ABOUT WHAT TO DO WITH ALLEGRA HAD EXACERBATED Shelley's anxiety about his children with Harriet. That spring, the trial for their custody was reaching a dispiriting end. In a final, desperate attempt to win his children, Shelley went on the offensive. He was not the only sinner on trial, he said. Harriet might be dead, but she was not blameless: she had been pregnant when she killed herself. This fact prompted an unsavory debate about the unborn child's paternity, a debate that Shelley capitalized on. Although there is a remote possibility that Shelley was the father—he had visited London without Mary a few months before they left for Geneva—what seems more likely is the story accepted by Harriet's family and friends: she had become lovers with a soldier, and when he abandoned her she had tried to return to her family's house, only to be rejected by her father. About six weeks before her death, she had disappeared. Some whispered that she had been living as a whore, the story Shelley presented to the court, declaring that Harriet had "descended the steps of prostitution until she lived with a groom of the name of Smith, who deserting her, she killed herself."

However, the court ignored Shelley's accusations. In its final decision, the judges admonished him and refused his claim, an extremely unusual ruling in the nineteenth century, when a father's rights were rarely questioned. There was no appeal process, no fighting the decision. Shelley's friends managed to appoint a clergyman to talk him out of his wild kidnapping plans. The Westbrooks would keep Ianthe and Charles because of Shelley's "immorality," and neither child would ever see their father again.

To Shelley, the court's refusal to give him his children was evidence of how much London hated him, and so, in the spring of 1817, he moved Mary, William, Claire, and Allegra to a handsome property in Marlow, near the home of his old school friend Thomas Peacock. On the strength of the allowance he had begun receiving after his grandfather's death, Shelley purchased a twenty-one-year lease on Albion House, an even more elegant residence than Bishopsgate, about thirty miles west of London. This rambling five-bedroom mansion with stables and a huge garden that pleased Mary with its flowers and stately trees had, as its best and most important feature, a cavernous library. When they moved in, they found two chipped statues of Apollo and Venus discarded by the previous tenants; to Shelley and Mary, it was as though the fates had left a calling card. Here were the god and goddess of Poetry and Love, Creation and Desire—their guiding principles. Shelley was delighted that they were just a short walk from the Thames. He bought a small rowboat and left it tied to the dock, ready for expeditions.

Mary wrote to the Hunts, urging them to visit. She wanted to see them and she was eager to implement their plan for Allegra. If the Hunts came that summer, the children would blend together and no one would notice that Allegra actually belonged to Claire. Hunt, who was, as usual, strapped for money, instantly saw the economic advantages of living with the Shelleys. Emerging from his agoraphobia, he rented out his house and brought Bess, Marianne, and their four children to Marlow, arriving on April 6 and staying until June 25. Despite the length of this visit, the two families managed to preserve their enthusiasm for one another. Hunt enjoyed nineteen-year-old Mary, calling her "yon nymph of the sideways looks," and introduced her to the opera, taking her to see Mozart's *Marriage of Figaro* in London. For the rest of her life, Mary would delight in music and would never miss an opportunity to attend a concert. But, reserved as always, she kept her excitement to herself; even Hunt had no idea how enthusiastic she was, seeing only "a sedate-faced young lady . . . with her great tablet of a forehead, and her white shoulders unconscious of a crimson gown."

The weather was mild that spring. The Hunt children played with William in the back garden or slid down dusty hills with Shelley, while little Allegra, or Alba, as they called her, looked on from her mother's lap. Wilmouse "jumps about like a little squirrel—and stares at the baby with his great eyes," Mary reported to Shelley when he was up in London, attending to the aftermath of the failed custody suit. They told everyone that Allegra was the Hunts' newest child, but anyone who visited would have been able to see that Claire was the baby's mother. Allegra clung to her, reaching out her arms whenever she left her sight.

In this house full of guests, with six small children underfoot and a husband whose unpredictability was now fairly predictable, Mary finished what she called a "fair copy" of *Frankenstein*. It had taken her nine months to complete this final draft, from late June 1816 to March 1817, and then about six weeks to copy it into a document suitable for publishers. While she wrote the final paragraphs in March, she had been troubled by nightmares "of the dead being alive." Her baby girl. Fanny. Her mother. And the most terrifying: Harriet, her hair streaming, floating up from the Serpentine, staring at the woman who had stolen her husband.

The significance of the novel's gestation was not lost on Mary, who was pregnant while writing the final draft, having conceived in December 1816. She frequently referred to the book as her "offspring" or "progeny." In the 1831 introduction, she would describe the act of writing *Frankenstein* as a "dilat[ion]." She even linked the story to her own birth. The tale begins December 11, 17—, and ends in September 17—. (Although Mary did not provide the exact year, Walton sights the creature on Monday, July 31, and July 31 falls on a Monday in 1797.) Mary Wollstonecraft conceived in early December 1796, gave birth to Mary on August 30, 1797, and died on September 10, 1797.

By connecting *Frankenstein* to her own genesis, Mary hints at the many ties she felt to her story. Like the creature, she felt abandoned by her creator. Like Frankenstein, she felt compelled to create. Her own birth had caused the death of her mother, but it had also brought life to her characters. Since the novel is framed by Walton's letters to Margaret, whose initials were the same as Mary's now that she had married Shelley (MWS), it is as though she wrote the tale for herself, becoming both author and audience, creator and created, mother and daughter, inventor and destroyer. For Frankenstein, however, Mary makes it clear that his attempt to manufacture a human being by artificial methods is doomed. No matter how hard he tries to appropriate the role of mothers and Nature, his story is still embedded in the nine-month gestational period of the human being.

Although Shelley encouraged his wife's work and made time to read the drafts she presented to him in the evening before bed, not once did he offer to help with domestic obligations. As the resident genius, he wandered in and out of the house at any time of day or night. If he missed dinner, he sat at the kitchen table munching bread and raisins. He carved Greek poetry into the trees, made an altar to Pan with Peacock and Hogg, who came up from London on the weekends, and floated down the river in his boat, lying on the bottom reading, as Bess later recalled, "his face upwards to the sunshine." He was aghast at the poverty he saw and gave away anything that was in his pockets, and, once, his own shoes. He talked Mary into taking in a village girl, Polly Rose, whose family was too poor to provide for her. Years later, Polly would remember that Shelley used to play games with her and all the children. Her favorite was when he lifted her onto a table with wheels and rolled her up and down the corridor. She also kept a small flowered plate that Mary had given her as a memento and recalled that Mary was "fair and very young" and would tuck her in at night, telling her about the discussions they had downstairs, "always winding up with, 'And now, Polly, what do you think of this?'"

The villagers adored Shelley, although they thought he was mad, but the country squires were appalled by his eccentricities and wanted nothing to do with either Shelley or Mary. To them, Albion House was incomprehensible—some kind of commune, with an uneven number of gentlemen and ladies, which made it impossible to tell who was married to whom. Shelley was frequently seen in the company of an attractive dark-haired woman (Claire) who was not, by any stretch of the imagination, Mary Godwin. And when the Hunts returned to their own home, leaving Claire and Allegra behind as the sole houseguests, the gossip became more pointed. Shelley was living in a harem; he had two wives. Even Godwin, once he and Mary-Jane had been told that Allegra was actually Claire's child, believed that Shelley was the father.

Shelley and Mary went up to London briefly that spring to find a publisher for the almost finished *Frankenstein*. To their disappointment, two passed on it, and it was not until August that Lackington's, an undistinguished house with a list of hack writers, agreed to do a small print run of five hundred copies, using the cheapest materials available. Everyone agreed that it would be best if Mary remained anonymous. However, she would keep the copyright and a third of the profit, a potentially beneficial arrangement as Lackington's had a circulating library and a popular shop so huge that on opening day a coach and four drove around its counters as a publicity stunt.

Once she had finished *Frankenstein,* Mary did not remain idle, although she was now in the last trimester of pregnancy. She had discovered that she was happiest when she had tasks to accomplish. Also, haunted by the memory of the bailiffs seizing their possessions from Bishopsgate, she desperately wanted to contribute to their income. Like her mother and father, she was endlessly worried about money. Shelley, on the other hand, was remarkably untroubled by their bills. He kept giving loans to needy friends and had spent far more than his allowance on a piano for Claire, books for their library, and trips back and forth to London.

Accordingly, Mary began and almost finished a new writing project, all the while continuing to run the household—an extraordinary demonstration of her organizational capabilities. Her new book, *A History of a Six Weeks' Tour,* was modeled on her mother's book *Letters Written During a Short Residence in Sweden, Norway, and Denmark,* and was a travelogue of her trips to France and Switzerland. This was a less strenuous task than plotting out the fate of a mad scientist and his creature; all she had to do was revise her travel journal and recopy the long letters she had written to Fanny in 1816. Shelley contributed to the project as well, adding two letters he had written to Peacock while they were abroad and his poem *Mont Blanc*. Hunt's friend Charles Ollier agreed to publish *A History of a Six Weeks' Tour,* but before Mary could ready the manuscript for publication, she went into labor, giving birth to a little girl on September 2. Mary named the baby Clara after her stepsister, signaling a change in the relationship that had occurred over the last year. Although Mary still wanted Claire to establish an independent life for herself, and had never stopped being annoyed by Claire's dramatic moods, the loss of Fanny had sobered Mary. Claire was the only sister she had left. In addition, Claire's obsession with Byron, despite his obdurate refusal to respond to her letters, had lifted her out of the competition for Shelley's attention. After Alba was born, she had turned the force of her passion onto her daughter, which had made her much easier for Mary to love. They could commiserate over the difficulties, the joys, and the worries of babies.

Exhausted from the birth and from nursing Clara, who cried relentlessly because Mary was not producing enough milk, Mary pushed herself to finish *A History*. By the end of September, she had completed the editing process, and in October she transcribed a fair copy of the manuscript for Ollier. In November, *A History* appeared in the bookstalls. It was Mary's first published book, preceding the publication of *Frankenstein* by two months.

Although Mary had done all the work of editing, compiling, and rewriting, once again they decided that only Shelley's name would appear on the cover. Mary did not resent this arrangement, as she knew that the book would have a better reception if the public thought a man had written it. But unfortunately, the ploy did not work. *A History* did not receive much notice, and few copies sold. Mary had made no money. Still, those critics who did read the book gave it good reviews, heartening the author. Years later, Mary would

tell a new publisher that *A History* had garnered her "many complements [*sic*]." The reviewer at *Blackwood's* was the most enthusiastic,
writing "the perusal of it rather produces the same effect as a smart
walk before breakfast, in company with a lively friend who hates
long stories."

Shelley, too, had a productive summer. Since Mary managed the
household, he could vanish—worry-free—for the day, notebook in
hand, to write in the woods or on his boat. Hunt's support of his
work inspired Shelley to try his hand at a long poem, but this time
one with the great theme of liberty. Throughout the year, there had
been food shortages and bread riots; workers protested the working
conditions in the northern factories. In London, the Prince Regent's
coach was attacked on its way back from Parliament. The government cracked down severely on protesters, suspending habeas corpus
and instituting a gag law to silence all opponents. Was this the true
spirit of England? Shelley asked. What had happened to the principles of freedom? Having written to Byron that the French Revolution was the "master theme of the epoch," he was determined to
describe both the heady optimism of the revolutionaries and their
despair when the Revolution gave way to tyranny.

By setting the poem in the Far East, Shelley managed to escape
censorship, although his readers would easily have recognized the
basic outline of events in France. The central characters, Laon and
Cyntha, a brother and sister team, fight oppression, stir up revolution, lead workers, pronounce long philosophical speeches on behalf
of liberty, and fall in love; they also supplied the title of the poem
until Shelley's publisher convinced him to drop the incest theme and
change the name of the poem from *Laon and Cyntha* to *The Revolt of
Islam*. Shelley was disappointed, as he had wanted "to startle the reader
from the trance of ordinary life. It was my object to break through
the crust of those outworn opinions on which established institutions
depend." However, even without the incest plot, the poem remained
startling enough to shock nineteenth-century readers, particularly its
insistence on sexual as well as political reform. Cyntha makes many
Wollstonecraft-like speeches on behalf of women's rights:

> *Can man be free if woman be a slave?*
> *Chain one who lives, and breathes this boundless air,*
> *To the corruption of a closed grave!*
> *Can they whose mates are beasts, condemned to bear*
> *Scorn, heavier far than toil or anguish, dare*
> *To trample their oppressors?*

She also starts the revolution in her city without waiting for Laon to take the lead, which is fine by Laon as he regards Cyntha as his equal. The two assail slavery, protest religious hypocrisy and false morality, and in the end are burned at the stake.

With its demands for change—Men should not be allowed to dominate women! The government should not exploit the individual! Freedom is a natural right!—the poem introduces many of the themes that would drive Shelley's political work for the rest of his writing life. And while *The Revolt of Islam* is not one of his greatest poems, the 4,818-line ode to freedom demonstrates Shelley's mastery of imagery, as well as a hard-won metrical sophistication.

Shelley finished the poem on September 20, just three weeks after Clara was born, and he wrote a dedication to Mary that summed up the happiness they had enjoyed that summer while acknowledging how distant he had been while he worked:

> *So now my summer task is ended, Mary,*
> *And I return to thee, mine own heart's home;*
> *As to his queen some victor Knight of Faery,*
> *Earning bright spoils for her enchanted dome.*

Yet in October, the weather and their moods both took a dark turn, ending the long string of sunny days they had enjoyed in August and September. The rain battered the house and the rooms were damp. Mary worried about Wilmouse and his tendency to catch colds. Their books began to wrinkle with mold. Her newfound tranquillity with Claire was wearing thin. At ten months, Alba was thriving and no longer occupied all of Claire's time. She was beginning to accept that Byron meant what he said and was turning back to Shelley for comfort. Shelley was happy to respond, since after Clara's birth Mary no longer had the time or strength to be Shelley's "queen." Once again, Claire became Shelley's primary confidante, and Mary was jealous. The competition between the sisters was renewed. Everything and everyone grated on Mary's nerves, even the Hunts when they came to pay a visit. Shelley, who never had much patience with newborns, let alone impatient and irritable wives, left Marlow to set up a base in London, taking Claire and Alba with him.

Before he left, Mary urged Shelley to tell Byron to adopt Alba. She knew that without the child, Claire would need less support and would be better able to strike out on her own. Claire did not want to part with Alba, but she nursed a secret hope that when Byron met his new daughter and saw how beautiful she was, he would fall back in love with her. Shelley obliged his wife by painting a pretty domestic scene in a letter to Byron to try to persuade him to assume responsibility for Alba: "Mary has presented me with a little girl. We call it Clara. Little Alba and William, who are fast friends, and amuse themselves with talking a most unintelligible language together, are dreadfully puzzled by the stranger, whom they consider very stupid for not coming to play with them on the floor." This was propaganda on Shelley's part, and Byron was no fool. He could see that though Shelley clearly enjoyed Alba, now that Mary had a second child, Byron's daughter was in the way.

But immersed in a new life in Italy, Byron ignored Shelley. He was still interested in the younger poet, but after he arrived in Venice he had exhausted himself, bedding countless women, drinking excessive amounts of alcohol, and, in the midst of all this, writing stanza after stanza of poetry. The last thing he wanted was to be saddled with Claire and her baby.

Mary, on the other hand, continued to worry about the growing intimacy between Shelley and Claire. She wrote Shelley many letters that fall lamenting their separation. Alone on the anniversary of Fanny's death, she begged him to return to Marlow, but he responded by explaining that he was in financial crisis. The creditors were searching for him and it was too dangerous for him to come home.

Even more worrying, he added that his tuberculosis seemed to have worsened and that Dr. Lawrence was too concerned about his health to allow him to travel—perhaps he would die before the year was out. Though Mary was concerned about her husband's health, she could not forgive him for deserting her despite his explanations.

Finally, in November, just as *A History* entered the bookstores, Shelley brought Mary to London to be with him. He was still dodging creditors, as he had not bothered to pay off his debts, but he did not allow his financial situation to distract him from his political work. He was busy writing an essay that Mary helped him revise, challenging the government's suspension of civil liberties: "Mourn then, People of England," he declared, "LIBERTY is dead." Mary met with *Frankenstein*'s publisher to go over some emendations, and she asked her father for permission to dedicate the book to him. By now, Godwin had read the fair copy and agreed with pride; *Frankenstein* was a remarkable book, he felt, and would reflect well on him; his daughter should feel confident in her skills as a writer.

The critics did not agree. *Frankenstein* debuted after Christmas and received immediate and angry reviews. Mary was not surprised; she knew she had tackled a controversial subject. She, or rather the anonymous author, was condemned as an atheist. *The Quarterly Review* called the book "a tissue of horrible and disgusting absurdity." *The Monthly Review* disparaged it as "uncouth" and entirely amoral. The reviewer in *La Belle Assemblée* was kinder, admiring the writing and creativity but condemning the story as unrealistic. One of the few positive notices came from Sir Walter Scott, an old friend of her father's and a hero of Mary's. Thrilled that he liked the book, Mary dropped her disguise, writing to tell him she was the author. She had not wanted anyone to know her identity, she explained, out of "respect to those persons from whom I bear it." But he was an exception, as there were few authors she admired more.

Mary's book may have disgusted the reviewers, but that did not stop people from reading it or speculating about the identity of its author. Most people assumed Shelley had written the story, not only because of the atheistic ideas, the shocking narrative, and the Godwinian philosophy, but because he had written the preface and the dedication was to his father-in-law. No one considered that the author might actually be Godwin's daughter. A woman could never have written such a daring book.

Although the negative critical response to *Frankenstein* was dispiriting, Mary still hoped that the book might bring them some money. By the end of the month, however, despite the gossip on London streets, it was clear that the novel's sales were going to be weak. In one of the great ironies of publishing history, *Frankenstein* would earn no royalties for its author. Instead, Mary and Shelley set their hopes on *The Revolt of Islam,* which was also due out soon; they were convinced that this work, at least, would bring them some much-needed income and make Shelley famous.

But when *Revolt* did come out, nothing happened. It was the worst kind of anticlimax; there was complete silence from the reviewers—the kind of horrifying silence that devastates writers, as it means no one thinks the book is worth reading. Shelley had dreamed that *Revolt* would be his *Childe Harold.* He yearned to assume the mantle of a great poet, to have his position in society redeemed. To Mary and Shelley, the silence seemed like a terrible mistake—how could people not admire *Revolt*? It must be because no one knew about it yet, they decided; Shelley pushed his publisher to promote the book while Hunt helped as best he could from his Hampstead office, printing selections from the poem and praising Shelley's work as brilliant. But as the days passed, it became clear that Shelley was being snubbed, and both he and Mary felt it deeply.

Finally, a few grudging reviews did appear, but the reviewers focused solely on Shelley's "vile" political views and scandalous behavior: he was not a Christian; he had been kicked out of Oxford; he had broken Harriet's heart and caused her suicide; he promoted anarchy and the death of kings. Their columns read like exposés, cheap and gossipy, designed to sell papers. For Mary and Shelley, these attacks on Shelley's character were worrying. If Shelley became too notorious, the courts might take William and Clara away, a threat the prosecution had made during the custody trial for Ianthe and Charles. And what would happen if people found out who really wrote *Frankenstein*?

For the past two years, Shelley had suspected that he and his family could no longer live in England, that here, on "their home isle," they were misunderstood and reviled, their work rejected. Plagued by ailments, including a new intestinal complaint brought about at least in part by his odd eating habits—he lived on a lump or two of bread for days at a time—Shelley lay for hours on the drawing room couch, medicating himself with laudanum. His only delight was watching Wilmouse and Alba play. Shelley was proud of his son for sharing his treats with the little girl, toddling over and placing half in her mouth. Alba, Shelley wrote to Byron, had become "affectionate and mild."

After a few weeks of this malaise, at Mary's urging he consulted Dr. Lawrence, who revised his opinion on the dangers of travel for Shelley's health and suggested Italy as a curative. Maybe in the warm Mediterranean air Shelley would be released from his mysterious pains. Italy had the added benefit of offering safety from bailiffs and courts, cruelty and slights.

Mary liked the idea of "pure air & burning sun," not to mention the possibility of leaving Alba with Byron in Venice and then getting rid of Claire, since Claire would then be free to do as she wished. Claire did not protest. Not only did she cling to her hope that Byron would change his mind and they could live together as a family, she was well aware that she could not provide for Alba or protect her as Byron could. She also knew that Mary's motives were not entirely selfish. Fanny's suicide continued to be a cautionary example. Both sisters were fully attuned to the dangers that illegitimate daughters faced. Allegra's famous, rich father could help her live the life of independence and dignity that had been denied Fanny.

By the end of January, they had made the decision to go. They sold the lease on Albion House and spent February and March in a whirlwind, winding up their affairs. In the evenings they went to the opera, the theater, and supper parties with the other radicals daring enough to acknowledge them. The Hunts were so heartbroken over their friends' departure that they could not bring themselves to leave on their final evening together, falling asleep in the Shelleys' rooms and only tiptoeing out at dawn.

During these last weeks in England, when Mary was preoccupied with the pragmatic details of their decampment, Shelley fled the packing crates to spend hours with his friends in the newly established British Museum. Here he observed the marble ruins that Lord Elgin had recently brought back from Greece and Italy; to Shelley, each column, each statue of a pagan god, hinted at the riches he would soon discover in the land of antiquity. There were also some new Egyptian finds in the museum, dating from as far back as 2000 B.C.E., including a seven-ton statue of Pharaoh Ramses II carved from a single block of blue and tan granite. Ramses' eyes appeared to look down at visitors, giving one a strange feeling of being watched. Shelley was so moved by the statue, so grand that Napoleon had once lusted after it, that he proposed to his friend Horace Smith, a financier who would represent the Shelleys' affairs once they were out of the country, that they each write a poem in its honor. Smith agreed, composing some entirely forgettable lines. But Shelley, fueled by anger at his neglect by the literary establishment, his disillusionment with the repressive English government, and his rancor at how he had been treated by the world in general, composed *Ozymandias*—the most famous sonnet he ever wrote, and among the most evocative:

> *I met a traveller from an antique land*
> *Who said: "Two vast and trunkless legs of stone*
> *Stand in the desert. Near them, on the sand,*
> *Half sunk, a shattered visage lies, whose frown,*
> *And wrinkled lip, and sneer of cold command,*
> *Tell that its sculptor well those passions read*
> *Which yet survive, stamped on these lifeless things,*
> *The hand that mocked them and the heart that fed.*
> *And on the pedestal these words appear—*
> *'My name is Ozymandias, king of kings:*
> *Look on my works, ye Mighty, and despair!'*
> *Nothing beside remains. Round the decay*
> *Of that colossal wreck, boundless and bare*
> *The lone and level sands stretch far away."*

These were the last words that a slighted Shelley would write on English soil. His meaning was clear: all tyrants die; all empires crumble. England herself would one day be forgotten. Only the work of the true artist would endure.

Early in the morning of March 11, they rolled out of London, a party of eight, with Claire, Alba, William, Clara, and their two nursemaids, Elise and Milly Shields, a young girl they had hired in Marlow. It was time to break free, to live in the land of the Romans and the Roman gods. No one could know that of this group only Mary, Claire, and Milly would return to England. Shelley would never see his native land again, and neither would his children.

# CHAPTER 20

# MARY WOLLSTONECRAFT:
# "MOTHERHOOD"

———

[ 1793–1794 ]

*N*OT ALL OF MARY WOLLSTONECRAFT'S ACQUAINTANCES IN PARIS shared her excitement over her pregnancy. Some contented themselves with whispering behind her back, but others turned away from her in public, expressing shock when her stomach began to protrude. After one such encounter, she exclaimed in a letter to Imlay: "I told them simply that I was with child: and let them stare! . . . all the world, may know it for aught I care!"

Fortunately for Mary, her friend Ruth Barlow was happy to hear her news. Often, the two women met for breakfast to "chat as long as we please." Usually, they went to Ruth's favorite place, the Chinese Baths, a new restaurant and spa that was popular with Americans. Mary never tired of hearing Ruth's stories about the United States and was curious about what it would be like to live there with Imlay. Ruth assured Mary that America was every bit as beautiful as Gilbert said and that they could reside in peace with other freedom lovers on the frontier.

But November came and went and Imlay still had not returned home, leaving Mary anxious and angry. She tried to reassure herself with visions of him sitting by the fire, reading aloud to her while she snuggled their baby, but when the autumn rain beat against the windows, flooding the roads and making it difficult to go outside and see friends, she felt increasingly melancholy. To console herself she wrote

Gilbert long letters. Sometimes she lamented his departure: "I have been following you all along the road [in] this comfortless weather; for when I am absent from those I love, my imagination is as lively, as if my senses had never been gratified by their presence—I was going to say caresses—and why should I not?" Other times she complained: "Of late we are always separating—Crack!—crack!—and away you go." She tried "to write cheerfully" but then would start to weep. She worried that Gilbert would stray; he was too susceptible to other women's charms. She was not tempted by anyone else; why could he not be more like her? "I can find food for love in the same object, much longer than you can," she declared; "the way to my senses is through my heart; but, forgive me! I think there is sometimes a shorter cut to yours."

As the weeks drew on, she began to blame his absence on his pre-occupation with money and told him she did not like his "money-getting face." His time away was making her sick: "My head aches, and my heart is heavy." She was depressed—" 'I am fallen,' as Milton said, 'on evil days' "—and it was all because of his neglect. During the summer, she had thought she lived in paradise, but now, "The world appears an 'unweeded garden' where 'things rank and vile' flourish best."

Imlay tried to keep up with Mary's steady flow of letters but often fell short. He reassured Mary that he "loved [her] like a goddess," but instead of being mollified by his words, she threatened to throw his slippers out the window, complaining that she did not want to be worshipped but would rather "be necessary to you." She also decried the ease with which he dealt with their separation, and she assumed the stance of a moral philosopher by criticizing men in general, not just Imlay: "When men get immersed in the world, they seem to lose all sensations, excepting those necessary to continue or produce life!"

But her moods shifted quickly; only a week later she pleaded with him: "I intreat you,—Do not turn from me, for indeed I love you fondly, and have been very wretched." She could feel her independence draining from her, writing, "You perceive that sorrow has almost made a child of me" and "My own happiness wholly depends on you." At last, Imlay relented, inviting her to come to stay with him at Le Havre, and Mary jumped at the opportunity. On January 11, she apologized for her doubt in him and rejoiced in the domestic tranquillity he promised would soon be theirs:

> What a picture you have sketched of our fire-side! My love! my fancy was instantly at work, and I found my head on your shoulder, whilst my eyes were fixed on the little creatures that were clinging about your knees. I did not absolutely determine there should be six—if you have not set your heart on this round number.

Mary bade farewell to those friends who were still in Paris. Helen Maria Williams, who had just been released from jail and was planning her own escape from the city, begged Mary to burn the pages she had written on the Revolution before leaving, as she was certain they would land Mary in prison. But Mary considered her new work too important to destroy and swept past the guards at the city's gates with her manuscript in tow, even though she knew her "life would not have been worth much, had it been found." Soon she was in a coach headed west, her heart full of anticipation and her luggage full of unfinished chapters.

The port city of Le Havre was the commercial center of revolutionary France, inhabited by almost twenty-five thousand people. A fifteen-foot seawall separated the town from the harbor, crowding its inhabitants together in a densely packed warren of houses and narrow streets. Le Havre was every bit as radical as Paris, although its residents were dedicated to trade, not politics. Did one have capital to invest? What about a loan? These were the questions people asked here. Not: Do you support Robespierre or the Girondists? Englishmen, revolutionaries, and other indeterminate sorts gathered in the pubs, exchanging get-rich-quick schemes and ways to evade the English embargo. This was the perfect environment for Gilbert. Even though he had sold himself to Mary as an idealist, he was far more pragmatic than he'd initially let on. He had come to France to make his fortune, not to record his thoughts for posterity like Mary and her friends. Mary, on the other hand, felt "quite out of the world." She could not get the Parisian newspapers here. She had left many of her books behind, as well as her friends. And yet she was happy, living at long last with Gilbert. She holed up at her desk, trying to finish her treatise on the Revolution before the baby came.

As ambitious as ever, Mary returned to the great questions of political philosophy she had asked in both of her *Vindications:* What was the origin of society? What are the natural rights of men and women? What role should government play in the life of individuals? Rather than starting her book with the fall of the Bastille, or the National Convention, or for that matter, any time in the eighteenth century, Mary began in ancient Rome. Her goal was to demonstrate how the Revolution fit into the overall arc of human history, and so she traveled briskly through the Middle Ages, Louis XIV, and Louis XV before she arrived at current events. Humankind, she said, had progressed from tribes to nations, from monarchies to republics. The goal of government should be to protect the weak. The American constitution, founded as it was "on the basis of reason and equality," should be an inspiration to other countries. To Mary, "liberty with maternal wing seems to be soaring to regions promising to shelter all mankind." Of course, it was no accident that she would characterize freedom as a mother, not a father.

Across the ocean, John Adams would read *An Historical and Moral View of the French Revolution* twice—once in 1796, when he was vice president, and again more than ten years later. He disagreed with many of Mary's points and yet they sparked his own ideas. He wrote more than ten thousand words in the margins of his copy, which is in the safekeeping of the Boston Public Library and can still be viewed today. Although he scoffed at Mary's naïveté about government and disagreed with her about the natural goodness of the human heart— Mary believed people were good and governments corrupt, while Adams believed the opposite—he shared her underlying hope for a better future. "Amen and Amen! Glorious era come quickly!" wrote Adams in the margin when Mary waxed utopian.

But for Adams, perhaps the book's single most arresting point— maybe because it reminded him of his own wife's ideas—was its discussion of how women's rights and domestic affairs are directly

( 292 )

spected, they began by attacking that of their presumptuous adversaries; and actually surprised the assembly into the unanimous renunciation of all revenues arising from feudal dues, and even into the abolition of tithes. The nobility, also, who saw, that they should gain more by the suppression of tithes, than they should lose by the sacrifice of the obnoxious manorial fees, came into the same system. The steps likewise taken to increase the salaries of the indigent clergy, the most numerous part of the body in the assembly, secured their influence. And by destroying the monopoly of municipal and judicial employments, the support of the cities was obtained.—Thus the national assembly, without a struggle, found itself omnipotent. Their only enemies were individuals, seemingly of importance, it is true, as they had been accustomed to lead the great corporate bodies; but what was their empire, when all their former subjects were withdrawn from their control? of these enemies, the church dignitaries were of the most consequence; but, after the confiscation of ecclesiastical property, it would have been impossible for the court, even supposing a counter-revolution, to provide

*Hear! Read!*

*Hear! Read!*

*i.e. potent enough to destroy itself & the Nation!*

*A page from John Adams's marked-up copy of Wollstonecraft's* An Historical and Moral View of the French Revolution. *Next to Wollstonecraft's account of the formation of the "omnipotent" French National Assembly, Adams wrote, "Hear! Read!" twice, and "i.e. potent enough to destroy itself & the Nation!"*

related to the political and public realms. If men could learn to value "family affections" more than power, money, and land, Mary said, despotism would come to an end. She conflated the tyranny of the king, priest, and husband: What reasonable person, she demanded, believes "that a king can do no wrong?" Or that a priest who cheats a dying man is right just because he is a priest? What misguided person would stand in the way of a woman who leaves an abusive husband? Here Mary brought out all her firepower: Why should the unhappy wife be "treated as an outcast by society . . . because her revolting heart turns from the man, whom, a husband only in name, and by the tyrannical power he has over her person and property, she can neither love or respect, to find comfort in a more congenial or humane bosom?" Years later, her daughter and future son-in-law would read this passage with great interest, applying it to their own situation.

As in both of her *Vindications,* the links that Mary saw between the domestic and public spheres, and between the government and the family, are among her most significant insights and one of the key reasons her work still resonates today. By demonstrating how the denial of the rights of women is linked to other inequities in society, Mary anticipated modern theorists who argue that feminism has never been simply about "women's rights," but is about the societal injustice caused by patriarchy in all its forms. To these writers, modern feminism extends far beyond issues of sexuality, gender, and reproduction to include discussions of class, race, disability, and human rights.

Mary did not analyze Robespierre and the Terror directly, but she lamented the fact that the Revolution had fallen off course. Instead of representing a step forward for human society, the guillotine was a cautionary example of what happened when folly and greed ruled the day. Reason and good judgment were the necessary components of progress, she argued. When leaders were motivated by the lust for power, death would triumph, not liberty.

Mary's *French Revolution* is a more mature articulation of her ideas than the *Rights of Woman;* not only did she discuss her theories of natural liberty and social justice, she emphasized the importance of political science as a discipline and the positive role the political scientist can play in the amelioration of the human condition. And yet, despite the prescience of this groundbreaking work, it is the least well known of all her books, an irony that epitomizes how poorly Wollstonecraft has been treated by history.

FOR THEIR HOME IN LE HAVRE, Gilbert had rented a large house near the water, owned by an English soap merchant. Mary described her new house as "pleasantly situated." From her window, she could see the ships arrive in port, swooping into the bay like gulls. The fishing boats and commercial trading vessels rode close together in the harbor, rising and dipping with the waves and tides. At Gilbert's prompting, she hired a maid to help her with the household chores. Although the rain and wind slashed through the town that winter, Mary took a walk every morning before breakfast and wrote to Ruth that she "was more seriously at work than I have ever been." She also decided to embrace Gilbert's various trading ventures, and with high spirits told him that she would try not to "ruffle" his moods "for a long long time—I am afraid to say never."

When she was not writing, she shopped for groceries and cooked meals. She ordered fabric from Paris to make baby clothes and asked Ruth to send her some material for maternity dresses—dimity, cotton, or calico. When Gilbert was home, he liked to read over Mary's shoulder and see what she was writing. For all his commercial interests, he was still a man of ideas, still the man who had written a novel celebrating liberty. Like a married couple, they took pleasure in domestic details. When Gilbert had to travel for business, Mary wrote a note describing the leg of lamb she had left "smoking on the board" for him to "lard [his] ribs" when he came back home. To Ruth, she described the linens she had found for Gilbert's shirts in Le Havre and proudly noted that she now used "the matrimonial phraseology" of "us," rather than I, having established a domestic partnership "without having clogged my soul by promising obedience &c &c—"

Mary completed *French Revolution* in April. Now she did not care how soon the baby arrived, since "the history is finished and every thing arranged." Finally, on May 14, just two weeks after she turned thirty-five, Mary gave birth to a baby girl, whom she named after her old friend Fanny. She had relied solely on the assistance of a nurse who, Mary told Ruth, "was convinced that I should kill myself and my child" because she had not called a doctor and did not stay in bed for a week after delivery. Though she was tired and sore, she was up the day after giving birth. Labor was a natural process, she declared, not an illness. She trusted in her own physical strength, and although she acknowledged that giving birth "was not smooth work," she and the baby flourished.

Here was yet more evidence for the importance of educating women, Mary felt. She had been able to endure her contractions without terror because she understood the workings of her own body. To Mary, it was essential to tell women about the realities of childbirth, because "this struggle of nature is rendered more cruel by [women's] ignorance and affectation." Delighted by Fanny's vigorous health and her triumphant delivery, Mary gloated to Ruth, "I could almost forget the pain I endured six days ago." Refusing to hire a wet nurse, as was the practice of the day, she breast-fed Fanny and felt "great pleasure at being a mother." Eight days after Fanny's arrival, Mary had resumed her daily walks, and Gilbert's "constant tenderness" made her "regard a fresh tie as a blessing," although she also noticed that he was occasionally "impatient" with "the continual hindrances" that hampered his business ventures. This irritability was a new side to the charming Imlay, but it did not alarm Mary, as most of the time he was loving and affectionate.

As the days lengthened, Mary rejoiced in Fanny's rapid growth, writing to Ruth that the child was "uncommonly healthy, which I rather attribute to my good, that is natural, manner of nursing her, than to any extraordinary strength of faculties. She has not tasted any thing, but my milk, of which I have abundance, since her birth." Fanny soon learned to lift her head and smile at her doting mother, and Mary, ever prouder of her little girl, went everywhere with her—out to dinner, down to the harbor, and to the market. She told Ruth that the baby nursed "so manfully that her father reckons saucily on her writing the second part of the R—ts of Woman."

When the weather grew warmer, the cool ocean air kept mother and daughter comfortable. Mary played with Fanny in the large-windowed rooms of the house, while Gilbert worked long hours on the waterfront, negotiating with captains and sailors and overseeing the black market commodities he was trading. Prices had risen so steeply in France that there was a brisk demand for the basic goods that traders like Gilbert imported illegally from England and America. In addition, Gilbert had recently begun a new, even more dangerous venture. He had capitalized on Robespierre's edict against owning luxury items such as china, silver, art, and glassware, and had purchased thirty-six solid silver platters with the Bourbon crest and glassware for a fraction of their original value. Now he was working on smuggling these goods out of the country to his contacts in Scandinavia. This meant getting past the English blockade of the harbors, as well as the French authorities, but Imlay was clever and persistent, and he could be very persuasive.

The silver was a special case, however. The platters were so precious that to avoid detection, he hired a young Norwegian named Peter Ellefson to captain one of his ships past the English to the port of Gothenburg and his contact there, Elias Backman. The Norwegians were a neutral nation and Norwegian ships were not supposed to be harassed by either British or French authorities, but as a precaution, Ellefson and his first mate were the only ones on board who knew about the silver. Moreover, the ship's papers named Ellefson as the owner. Imlay's tracks were covered. All he could do now was wait for the ship to reach its port safely and hope his gamble would pay off.

Ellefson stayed with them that summer before he sailed for Sweden, and when Mary saw the platters for herself, felt how heavy they were, and saw the royal crest, she realized that their fortune was riding on the young Norwegian. Deeply invested in the success of this scheme, Mary took charge when Gilbert was called away on business, giving Ellefson his final instructions on the day the Norwegian set sail. As the ship tacked out of the harbor, Mary watched it grow smaller and smaller, and prayed that all would go smoothly. If they could get the silver sold for a good price, maybe she, Gilbert, and Fanny could move to America and start their small farm. Maybe she could even bring her sisters with them. Even though Eliza and Everina felt far away, she continued to worry and wrote them letter after letter, despite knowing it was unlikely the girls would ever receive them. The French censors were strict about communication between the two warring nations, and the English, too, were suspicious of mail from France.

Having settled into a routine after the birth of Fanny, Mary and Gilbert had a life that was so quiet they could almost pretend they were not living in the midst of a revolution. But Mary never lost track of what was happening in the capital, following the news from Paris as closely as she could. During July the number of executions skyrocketed from five to more than twenty-five a day until at last

Robespierre was overthrown by the National Convention in a dramatic coup and guillotined on the afternoon of July 28. Suddenly the Terror was over. Mary had still not heard from her sisters, but she wrote to Everina that she hoped "peace [would] take place this winter" and that then they could see one another. Although in some ways this long hiatus from her sisters was a relief—Mary was spared their constant laments and did not have to hear their commentary on her life—the silence made her uneasy. She had written to tell them about Imlay, and then baby Fanny, but she never heard anything back.

For Mary, August was a worrisome month. Now that the Terror had ended, Paris was open again, and Gilbert left to oversee his business concerns there, apprehensive about reports of some "knavery" on the part of one of his underlings. Mary sent him long, loving messages, but she was beginning to suspect he was not as enthusiastic about family life as she was, and on August 17 she wrote him a sardonic letter about his preoccupation with money, saying that "[business] is the idea that most naturally associates with your image." She hoped, she said, that he would aspire to do more with his life than simply "eat and drink, and be stupidly useful to the stupid." The choices he was making, she wrote, were beneath a man of true imagination.

Only two days later, on August 19, she was asserting her self-reliance: If he did not love her as passionately as she loved him and was with her only out of duty, then he should not be with her at all. She could take care of herself and Fanny. "There are qualities in your heart, which demand my affection; but, unless the attachment appears to me clearly mutual, I shall labour only to esteem your character, instead of cherishing a tenderness for your person." But she could not hold on to this brave renunciation for long. In the next paragraph, she confessed the bitterness of her feelings: "I found I could not eat my dinner in the great room—and, when I took up the large knife to carve for myself, tears rushed into my eyes." She ended the letter saying, "you are the friend of my bosom, and the prop of my heart."

The next day, though, Mary reverted to anger, complaining about his "reserve of temper." Too often "you wounded my sensibility, concealing yourself." How she longed for him to be "without disguise." He insisted women were "cunning," but she was always honest, always true. Why did he stay in Paris? Was it his mercantile ambitions? Or was it her? They had been so contented just a week ago. Yes, there were the normal irritations of living with another person, and the baby was demanding, but if he would let go of his desire to make a fortune, they could be happy, she was sure of it. All she wanted, she wrote, was to "be revived and cherished" by his "honest" love. Where was the "epanchement de coeur" she yearned for and felt she deserved? Had he forgotten last summer, their joy in Neuilly, their dreams for the future?

Mary's letter writing campaign was interrupted only when baby Fanny caught smallpox. In the late eighteenth century, this dread disease killed four hundred thousand Europeans a year and left a third of its victims blind. For babies, the odds were even worse; as many as 80 percent of infants in London died from smallpox. But Mary, though frightened, prided herself on possessing up-to-date scientific information. Johnson had recently published John Haygarth's *An Inquiry How to Prevent Small-Pox* (1784), which contained the latest theories on the disease, and so she was well versed in the course of the illness and the best methods of treatment. Instead of bundling the baby up inside an airtight room, as most of her neighbors advised, she bathed Fanny twice a day and opened the windows to keep the child as cool as possible. The residents of Le Havre were appalled at her ministrations, but Mary dismissed their concerns, writing Everina that her neighbors "treat th[e] dreadful disorder very improperly—I however determined to follow the suggestions of my own reason, and saved [Fanny] much pain, probably her life, . . . by putting her twice a day into a warm bath."

A sick baby is always difficult to care for, and Fanny was no exception. She was feverish and miserable. Her body was covered with itchy, painful scabs. She slept only fitfully and nursed incessantly. When the fever was at its height, she lay eerily still. With no one to help her, Mary grew exhausted, pouring what energy she had into saving her daughter. She felt like a "slave," but she loved her baby, writing to Gilbert before the illness struck, "She has got into my heart and imagination, and when I walk out without her, her little figure is dancing before me."

When at last the fever broke and Fanny was on the mend, Mary wanted to join Gilbert in Paris, but he forestalled these plans, announcing that he had to travel to London. He stopped in Le Havre only to make financial arrangements with Mary and to apologize for his absence. He was fond of Fanny and fond of Mary, too, he said reassuringly. But he was adamant that he had to go. The "knavery" he had suspected was all too true. He had lost money, and now that it looked as if England might lift the embargo, he wanted to establish connections with merchants in London. Mary tried not to be suspicious of his intentions, but he seemed remote, lukewarm, even bored. Perhaps he had lost interest in life with her and the baby. Perhaps he meant to desert her.

# MARY SHELLEY:
# ITALY, "THE HAPPY HOURS"

———

[ 1818–1819 ]

*W*HEN THE SHELLEYS ARRIVED IN ITALY ON MARCH 30, 1818, everywhere Mary looked, she saw beauty: "The fruit trees all in blossom and the fields green with the growing corn." Having read Homer to each other on their journey over the Alps to prepare for their first glimpses of classical antiquity, the first thing Mary and Shelley did when they crossed the border was to rush down "a green lane covered with flowers" to see an ancient "triumphal arch that had been erected to the honour of Augustus."

They traveled east through Turin, reaching Milan in mid-April. "In Italy," Mary effused to the Hunts, "we breathe a different air and every thing is pleasant." Shelley's health was steadily improving. The children were thriving. The bread was "the finest and whitest in the world." Even the cows were beautiful, "a delicate dove colour" with liquid eyes that reminded Mary of Homer's descriptions of the goddess Juno's "ox-eyes."

Both Shelley and Mary assumed that Byron would come spend the summer with them, as he had in Geneva. With that in mind, they left Claire in charge of the children and took a coach north to Lake Como to find an elegant villa to rent, one suitable for his lordship, with gardens, a view of the lake, and easy access to boating. They marveled at the lemon and orange orchards, where, Shelley observed, "there is more fruit than leaves." At length, they discovered the Villa

Pliniana, a half-ruined old palace that Mary described as having "two large halls, hung with splendid tapestry, and paved with marble." Like the Villa Diodati at Lake Geneva, it had views of the water and the mountains. There was even a waterfall that came crashing down the nearby rocks into the lake below. One night there was a spectacular thunderstorm, bringing back yet more memories of the summer with Byron. Without Claire and the children, Mary and Shelley were alone for the first time in over a year. For three days, they walked, sunned, wrote, and read to each other, relishing the peace. Shelley did have one of his nightmare visions, but Mary would later recall this time as idyllic. Neither knew it would be one of the last times they would have on their own.

When they returned to Milan, they found a cold letter from Byron informing them that he had no interest in joining their party. He did not want to encourage Claire to think that she had a future with him, nor did he want to correspond with her. All communication would be through Shelley. But his attitude toward Allegra had undergone a dramatic shift; for his own inscrutable reasons, any doubts about her paternity had vanished and he had decided that he wanted them to send the fifteen-month-old to him in Venice, where—though he did not mention this—he continued to attend shockingly bacchanalian parties, drink too much, and have sex with many men and women, all eager to please the rich English lord.

Claire was shattered by the prospect of parting with Alba but knew she had no real choice, nor legal claim. She would have to rely on Byron's goodwill if she wanted to see her daughter again. She had tried to accept that it would be better for Alba to grow up as the daughter of Lord Byron rather than as the illegitimate child of Claire Clairmont. Yet now that reality had struck, she was heartbroken. "I send you my child," she wrote Byron, "because I love her too well to keep her. With you who are powerful and noble and [have] the admiration of the world she will be happy, but I am a miserable and neglected dependant."

When Byron's servant arrived to collect the little girl, however, Claire could not follow through. She declared that Alba was too sick to travel and refused to hand her over. Shelley and Mary knew that it would do no good to anger Byron; they had both seen how ruthless he could be. Perhaps, Mary suggested, if Claire appeased him now, he would allow her to see her little girl for extended visits each year. She also offered to send Elise along to serve as Alba's nurse so that Claire would know her daughter was well looked after. At this, Claire relented, writing his lordship a note (on which it is still possible to see her tear stains):

> I love [Allegra] with a passion that almost destroys my being she goes from me. My dear Lord Byron I most truly love my child. She never checked me—she loves me she stretches out her arms to me & cooes for joy when I take her. . . . I assure you I have wept so much to night that now my eyes seem to drop hot & burning blood.

*Portrait of little Allegra, known as Alba.*

Once again, there was no response from Byron, and so on April 28, Alba and Elise, escorted by Byron's servant, left for Venice. Claire was devastated. The villa on Lake Como now seemed too grand for their little party, but Mary had glimpsed life without Claire and was reluctant to let it go. She wanted to be rid of her sister and spend the summer with Shelley and their two children in one of the little towns on the lake. Nonetheless, Shelley was adamant that they could not abandon Claire.

At length they decided to head southwest to Livorno to meet Wollstonecraft's old friend Maria Reveley, who had taken care of Mary as a baby and had moved to Italy eighteen years earlier with her second husband, John Gisborne. Mary looked forward to reconnecting with Maria but dragged her feet about leaving the north. Years later, she would remember the decision to turn away from Como as an unlucky turning point, the first link in the chain of disasters that would soon befall them.

The party arrived in Livorno on May 9. "A stupid town," Mary reported, unhappy about traveling as a trio once again; even the red-roofed villas, the splendid coast, and the wide stone piazzas did not cheer her up. Her spirits lifted when they called on Maria, who at forty-eight was still beautiful, with "reserved yet . . . easy manners." She was an accomplished painter and musician who shared Mary and Shelley's liberal political views and had been deeply influenced by the ideas of the revolutionary generation, particularly the works of her friends: Godwin's *Political Justice* and Wollstonecraft's *Vindications*. One of the reasons she lived in Italy, she told the travelers, was that she and her husband loathed how conservative Britain had become.

After they arrived, Maria walked along the seawall with Mary, telling her about her mother, how brave she had been, how passionate, and how honest. Mary was deeply moved to be with the woman who had first cradled her and who had been her mother's trusted confidante. She knew that her father had proposed to Maria after Maria's first husband had died and had been refused. If only she had accepted, then Mary would have had the ideal stepmother, cultured and highly literate, someone who knew and celebrated Wollstonecraft, who would have loved her little girls. Fanny might not have succumbed to suicide. Her father might have stayed true to his beliefs. And, best of all, there would have been no Claire.

Maria, a warm and gracious hostess, did not mention the awkward fact that her young visitors had appeared without any warning. Nor did she ask them any difficult questions about why they were in Italy.

Instead, she invited them to stay as long as they needed, advising them against traveling to Florence or Rome, as these cities were notorious for disease in the summer. A woman of the world and a self-proclaimed atheist, like Shelley, Maria had known that Wollstonecraft had an illegitimate daughter and had still befriended her. Still, the Shelleys chose not to fill her in on the details of their ménage. Delighted by Maria's warmth and informality, they did not want to jeopardize their new friendship. Even Maria's enormous dog, Oscar, greeted the travelers with gusty excitement. He took a particular shine to Mary—not a dog enthusiast—drooling on her shoes and nuzzling her when she drank her tea in the Gisbornes' drawing room.

Mr. Gisborne was less immediately charming. He stayed in the background, stepping forward only to declare in a nasal voice that he had discovered a small factual error in Godwin's latest novel, *Mandeville*. Shelley ridiculed him in a caustic letter to Hunt:

> His nose . . . weighs on the imagination to look at it,—it is that sort of nose which transforms all the *g*s its wearer utters into *k*s. It is a nose once seen never to be forgotten and which requires the utmost stretch of Christian charity to forgive. I, you know, have a little turn up nose; Hogg has a large hook one but add them both together, square them, cube them, you would have but a faint idea of the nose to which I refer.

Poor Gisborne. To be preserved this way was an indignity, but he did seem a strange choice for the beautiful and spirited Maria Reveley. Eventually, both Mary and Shelley would acknowledge his erudition and his helpfulness, but he would never be a favorite of theirs.

They stayed for a month with the Gisbornes, and under Maria's watchful eye, Claire slowly regained her spirits and Mary grew less irritable. Mary and Shelley appreciated Maria's "frank affectionate nature" as well as her "most intense love of knowledge." But Maria was also practical and had been running a household in Italy for almost two decades. She told them what vegetables to buy in the markets, and she pointed them toward the strawberries, which had come early that year. She found them a seamstress, a doctor, and a servant named Paolo Foggi, and she advised them to rent a place in the nearby hill country.

After a few weeks of searching, Shelley found a house, the three-story Villa Bertini, perched high in Bagni di Lucca, a fashionable resort a day's ride away from Livorno. Known as the Switzerland of Tuscany for its location in the foothills of the Apennines, the town's hot springs were supposed to cure just about anything: gallstones, sprains, tumors, deafness, headaches, bad teeth, acne, depression, and ugliness. Shelley and Mary were not interested in taking the waters, but they liked the setting of the town, nestled next to the Serchio River.

The Villa Bertini was at the end of a dusty track. A thick hedge of laurels shaded their small patch of lawn and protected them from the possibility of peering eyes; the scent of jasmine filtered in through the windows. The gardens were overgrown and tangled; "I like nothing so much as to be surrounded by the foliage of trees only peeping now and then through the leafy screen on the scene about me," Mary wrote Maria. It was an easy walk down to the town, where there were shops, a drugstore, and an assembly room that hosted dances and concerts for the many tourists whom the Shelleys avoided.

Mary loved their new home. "When I came here," she wrote Maria, "I felt the silence as a return to something very delightful from which I had long been absent." After almost two and a half months of traveling, they settled into their usual schedule—reading, writing, and exploring the countryside. Their new servant, Paolo, helped run errands and negotiate with the locals. A cleaning woman came in every day to do the laundry, scrub the floors, and cook.

Milly, the nursemaid they had brought from England, helped Claire and Mary look after Wilmouse, a busy toddler intent on discovering the world around him. Clara napped and smiled at her admirers. One hot July day, Claire twisted her ankle, giving Mary and Shelley the opportunity to walk alone in the evenings. Later, Mary would remember how they admired the stars, the fireflies, and the pale moon. There was a riding stable in the town and occasionally husband and wife rode, on one memorable occasion visiting *il prato fiorito,* a flowery meadow near the top of one of the tallest mountain peaks. They saw no one else during the steep ascent, hearing only the cicadas, the muffled thud of the horses' hooves, and an occasional cuckoo.

Shelley set up a study inside the house, but was exhilarated by the open skies and the clouds that would glide in from the west, bringing in sudden storms. Before long he found a woodland stream where he felt free to shed the trappings of civilization. In a letter to his friend Peacock, he described his routine:

> My custom is to undress and sit on the rocks, reading Herodotus, until the perspiration has subsided, and then to leap from the edge of the rock into this fountain—a practice in the hot weather exceedingly refreshing. This torrent is composed as it were, of a succession of pools and waterfalls, up which I sometimes amuse myself by climbing when I bathe, and receiving the spray over all my body. . . .

This picture Shelley painted of himself helps explain why those who met him were struck by his mad originality, his playfulness, or, as they called it, his genius. Who else sat on a wet rock, naked, reading ancient Greek? For that matter, who plunged into pools of water without knowing how to swim and then described the whole scene to prim English friends? Only Shelley, who was constantly on the lookout for inspiration, doing whatever he could to invoke the muses.

Bathing naked had never appealed to Mary, as Shelley well remembered from the first time he had invited her to join him. But even if it had, she had a ten-month-old and a two-year-old who came first. In this new home, with the rich drafts of mountain air blowing through the window, the sparkle of the rushing river, and the abundance of fresh vegetables and fruit from the market in the village, she instituted a regime of playtime, frequent baths, and nutritious meals. Wilmouse might consent to play with Aunt Claire or Milly, but he preferred his mother, and she in turn liked to be there to admire his discoveries, answer his questions, or comfort him after a fall; meanwhile little Clara was beginning to get her first teeth and was often so miserable that only her mother could console her.

Mary did not resent these interruptions. After the death of her first baby, she was grateful to have two healthy children. With corn-silk hair, a long elfin face, and huge expressive eyes, Wilmouse was rarely naughty, but quiet like his mother and very attached to her. Although Shelley did not like "squallers," as he called infants, he doted on William, who was now old enough to laugh at his father's games and jokes. Mary had read her mother's books on childrearing and gave Wilmouse far more freedom than was usual for the time. She was planning to allow Clara the same liberties once the little girl could walk. Like Wollstonecraft, she believed in vigorous outdoor exercise for both girls and boys, and this was easy to achieve at the Villa Bertini. Wilmouse could run out onto the lawn and Clara could crawl toward the laurels with no danger from the road. It was an ideal spot for the children. Wilmouse had not had a fever since England. Clara, too, was growing bigger and stronger every day, and when she was not teething, she was growing increasingly independent, giving Mary the time to work.

Alone in her study, she devoted herself to reading Ariosto. This Renaissance poet had once lived in the region, and Mary liked to im-merse herself in the literature of the places where she lived. Shelley had raved about Ariosto's dramatic poem *Orlando Furioso,* which had curious similarities to *Frankenstein.* When Orlando is rejected in love, he goes on a murderous rampage, destroying everything in his path. In addition, there are monsters and several supernatural passages, in-cluding a trip to the moon, as well as many tragic love affairs—exactly the sort of literature the Shelleys enjoyed.

Meanwhile, Shelley had decided his next undertaking would be to translate Plato's *Symposium.* Today this may seem like a staid scholarly choice, but in 1818, the *Symposium* was considered immoral for its frank discussion of homosexual love. In fact, it would take thirty more years for Oxford to include any of Plato's works on the col-lege's list of approved readings. But of course that was precisely what appealed to Shelley. Mary did her best to help him with the transla-tion, studying Greek in the morning, memorizing irregular verbs and learning vocabulary. Like Shelley, she embraced Plato's ideas, writing to Maria:

It is true that in many particulars [*The Symposium*] shocks our present manners, but no one can be a reader of the works of antiquity unless they can transport themselves from these to their times and judge not by our but by their morality.

Mary and Shelley shared a belief in what Shelley called a "civilized love." To Shelley, true love was not mere physical attraction. He and Mary existed on a plane above lust, their souls so in tune with each other that they were like the strings "of two exquisite lyres" that "vibrate" as one. In a commentary on his translation, Shelley asserted Wollstonecraft's point that an imbalance in power between the sexes made men masters and women slaves, and that without equality there could be no true love. This was also Plato's belief, Shelley said, although Plato thought that such an ideal love could exist only between men—a mistake, Shelley argued. Women were not the inferior beings Plato assumed them to be. Wollstonecraft and her daughter were examples of just how brilliant women could be when freed from servitude.

His description of what ancient Greek women were *not* (and why Greek men had to find love with one another) helps explain what he felt he had discovered in Mary:

[Women in ancient Greece] were certainly devoid of that moral and intellectual loveliness with which the acquisition of knowledge and the cultivation of sentiment animates, as with another life of overpowering grace, the lineaments and the gestures of every form which it inhabits. Their eyes could not have been deep and intricate from the workings of the mind, and could have entangled no heart in soul-enwoven labyrinths.

Mary knew that Shelley loved what he called her ability to see "into the truth of things." Again and again, he had told her that it was not her red-gold hair, not her white shoulders, not her smooth forehead or delicate mouth that drew him to her, although all of these helped. It was her spirit and her mind.

During July, Mary copied Shelley's translation in her tidy hand so he could send it to his publisher. As she worked, she felt a quiet satisfaction. She wrote letters to the Hunts and to her father, with whom she and Shelley were in frequent correspondence. Much as she looked forward to hearing from Godwin, his letters were always a mixed blessing. He detailed his financial problems, insisting that it was Shelley's responsibility to pay off his debts. Mary knew that her husband's finances were also in disarray, but she did not like to disappoint her father. In addition, Godwin had resumed his role as Mary's severest critic and urged her to start a new book. He even had a topic he thought she should pursue—a history of the English revolution. But Mary did not feel ready to start a new project. She was happy to steep herself in Shelley's version of Plato. She appreciated his mastery of this beautiful language; reading his translation was like listening to a philosophical discussion between her husband and his scholarly friends.

For seven weeks, they enjoyed their hilltop retreat. Wilmouse thrilled Shelley by saying "Father," and eleven-month-old Clara was on the brink of becoming a toddler. She had begun to eat a little solid food, and although she was not yet walking, she could pull herself up on the furniture and crawl after her big brother on his adventures. She was the right age to point at the birds outside the window, play peek-a-boo, laugh at Wilmouse's antics, and enjoy outings to the village. Mary rejoiced in her little girl, this beautiful second chance at a daughter. She and Claire could teach her the Wollstonecraft legacy of independence and thirst for knowledge. Who knew what this child might accomplish?

But in mid-August, a heat spell crept in over the mountains, and as the days became unbearably humid, everyone suffered. Clara, or little Ca as Shelley called her, developed a high fever, and Mary was desperately worried. Claire's ankle had healed, but she was grumpy after injuring her other leg while riding with Shelley in the woods. Shelley was restless, having lost the attention of both Mary and Claire. Then, on August 14 and 16, two letters arrived in quick succession from Venice. Life with Lord Byron was a disaster, Elise wrote. He had forced her to move out with little Allegra, and if Claire cared about her daughter, she needed to rescue her from his lordship's clutches immediately. Byron was so debauched that he wanted to raise her as his future mistress. Wild though these claims were, Claire took Elise's words at face value. Mary and Shelley did not, but they also realized that something terrible must have happened for Elise to write such an urgent plea. Perhaps Byron had gotten drunk and assaulted Elise. Maybe she was frightened for her own safety.

At Claire's insistence, she and Shelley left immediately for Venice, taking Paolo with them and leaving a disgruntled Mary home with Milly and the two children. Suddenly the silence in Villa Bertini was frightening. When she was living ensconced in her family, the isolation had suited Mary, but now she was too much alone. A two-and-a-half-year-old and an eleven-month-old were a handful in the best of circumstances. The sticky summer heat persisted and Clara's fever spiked—all of her teeth seemed to be coming through at the same time. Milly had no words of advice. Clara was the first baby she had taken care of, and when the baby was this miserable, she refused to leave her mother's lap. Milly tried to entertain the bored and listless Wilmouse, but he, too, clung to his mother. At her wits' end, Mary wrote to the Gisbornes begging for help. Maria, alarmed at the tone of Mary's letter, arrived as fast as she could and found Mary holding a very sick little girl. She did her best to help, but she could not assuage Mary's fears. The death of her first baby haunted the young mother. She could not bear the thought of losing Ca.

Into this misery sailed a letter from Shelley. Mary opened it, hoping he had somehow intuited how awful things were and was coming home. Instead, the letter said he needed her to come to Venice immediately. He had mapped out the trip for her and counted the days it would take her to arrive, allowing one day to pack and four days to travel. She had to come, he said, because he had lied to Byron, telling him that it was Mary who was waiting in the wings to receive Allegra, not Claire; Byron's "horror" of Claire might prevent him from handing the child over, and also, paradoxically, his lordship would disapprove of Shelley's staying alone with Claire. They needed Mary to come if they wanted to save little Alba.

Mary had to make up her mind immediately. Either she started packing or she stayed home, disappointing Shelley and perhaps endangering Allegra. Her old worry that Shelley would abandon her resurfaced. If she did not go, she worried that her husband would never return to her. Perhaps Claire would succeed in stealing him away. She yearned to fly to his side. But she was torn. Clara's fever was worsening and she had begun to suffer from dysentery, one of the most dangerous diseases of the era. Dehydrated, she needed quiet, liquids, and rest. The trip to Venice would be hot, exhausting, and long. The inns were unreliable, as was the food. Finally, though, the thought of letting Shelley down was too much to bear. Mary spent her twenty-first birthday packing up the house while Maria took care of Clara, an uncanny replication of what had happened exactly twenty-one years earlier, although this time around, Maria was tending to Mary's daughter, not Wollstonecraft's motherless girl.

Mary left on August 31. Shelley had sent Paolo to help, but there was little the servant could do to make the trip any easier. It took four days, as Shelley had said it would, and when at last they arrived at the mansion Byron was lending them in Este, a town about a ten-hour journey from Venice, Clara was slipping in and out of consciousness. When she did open her eyes, she did not seem to recognize anyone. Even Wilmouse could not make her smile.

They were greeted by Claire, Allegra, and Shelley, who recited a beautiful little poem he had written for Mary: "As sunset to the sphered moon / As twilight to the western star, / Thou, Beloved, art to me." Despite Clara's worsening condition, Mary's spirits improved after hearing this testimonial to her husband's love. Surely, her daughter would recover here. After all, Shelley was not worried. "Poor little Ca" would get better, he told his wife. Byron's house, Il Cappuccini, was magnificent, as all of his residences were. It was set in the plains of Lombardy; from the garden they could see as far west as the Apennines, and to the east, the horizon "was lost in misty distance." The wide expanse was gratifying after living in the woods in the Villa

Bertini. A stone-flagged path led under a pergola to a summerhouse where Shelley worked each day. The ruins of Este Castle were nearby, just across a ravine, its walls so massive that if William shouted there was a glorious echo. At night owls and bats "flitted forth" and they could watch "the crescent moon s[ink] behind the black and heavy battlements."

But though Clara held on, she did not improve. She turned one on September 2, and as the month drew to an end, she grew steadily weaker. Shelley paid a visit to Byron, who suggested they consult his personal physician in Venice. Mary and Clara left Este at three o'clock in the morning on September 24, leaving William with Claire and Milly. After more than ten hours of travel, the baby started convulsing. Mary was helpless. She kissed the sick child's forehead, smoothed back her hair, sang songs of comfort, tried to get her to sip water, but nothing could slow the terrible process. Clara was slipping away. Alone, exhausted, and overwhelmed, Mary knew that "life and death hung upon our speedy arrival at Venice."

When at last they arrived, Shelley rushed them into the inn, and while Mary waited in the hallway holding the baby, he ran for the doctor. But it was too late. By the time he returned, Ca had stopped breathing. Mary clutched her little girl and would not let go. She refused to speak to Shelley or help make the necessary arrangements. "This is the Journal book of misfortunes," she wrote that night in the notebook that contained her record of the last year, including Fanny and Harriet's deaths. After consulting Byron, Shelley buried Clara on the Lido without erecting any kind of marker, an act that has never been remedied. The Lido is now a crowded beach resort. If one wants to pay tribute to the little girl, one must brave the crowds, the tourists in their swimming suits, the lines outside the pizza joints, and the couples strolling on the sand to imagine one's own memorial for Clara Shelley.

Byron paid the heartbroken Mary a visit and tried to distract her by giving her a task: to copy two of his newest poems for his publisher. Self-centered though it may sound, Byron wanted to help Mary recover, and this was his way of offering her a distraction. Mary politely agreed to transcribe the poems for Byron, but any healing was a long way off. Her spirits did not lift even when she was reunited with Wilmouse in Este. She found it exquisitely painful to watch Claire with Allegra. She believed that her own little girl would still be alive if she had not traveled across Italy to help Claire. Shelley, too, was culpable. He should have been more cautious, less demanding. If William, his favorite, had been the sick one, he would never have allowed them to make the trip.

The reason for their ill-fated journey to Venice—Elise's accusations—no longer mattered to Mary, but Shelley applied himself to finding out whether Allegra was safe with Byron, at last determining that Elise's claims were false. He convinced Claire that Elise had overstated matters, and so once again she surrendered Allegra to Byron, who placed the child in the safekeeping of the British consul in Venice, Richard Hoppner, and his wife. But Elise refused to stay with his lordship, evidence that her terror probably had more to do with her own situation than Allegra's. Shelley took her back as Wilmouse's nurse and sent Milly home to England. Before Clara died, they had decided to spend the winter in Naples, and Shelley kept to the plan, packing up his family and organizing the trip entirely on his own as Mary had retreated into a stony, impervious silence. Saddened by the intensity of her grief and her detachment from him, Shelley recorded his lament in a secret notebook:

> *Wilt thou forget the happy hours*
> *Which we buried in Love's sweet bowers*
> *Heaping over their corpses cold*
> *Blossoms and leaves, instead of mould?*
> *Forget the dead, the past? Oh yet*
> *There are ghosts that may take revenge for it,*
> *Memories that make the heart a tomb,*
> *Regrets which glide through the spirit's gloom,*
> *And with ghastly whispers tell*
> *That joy, once lost, is pain.*

In reality, Shelley did not need to keep this poem hidden from Mary. If she had read these lines, she would likely have nodded in agreement rather than seeing them as an accusation. To her, all joy was indeed gone. And in its place was a terrible, aching nothingness, worse than pain, worse than gloom. She began to wonder if she was being punished for the hurt she had caused others. Maybe this was Harriet's revenge.

# MARY WOLLSTONECRAFT:
# ABANDONED

———

[ 1794–1795 ]

AFTER IMLAY SAILED TO LONDON IN THE LATE SUMMER OF 1794, Mary decided to take Fanny and go to Paris. Le Havre had lost what little charm it had possessed now that Gilbert was gone. Her sense of being alone was intensified, as she had still not received any letters from her sisters. For their part, Eliza and Everina had resorted to writing to Johnson; just as Mary had suspected, they had not received any of her letters, and so it was through him that they learned the news about Mary's "husband" and child. Now they were waiting to hear what impact this would have on their lives. Would Mary invite them to Paris to meet the baby? Would she ask them to live with her and her American? Could they finally quit their jobs? These questions went unresolved for the moment, since the mail remained unreliable.

Having economized by taking a public coach on the trip to Paris, Mary was alarmed when the coach almost tipped over four times. Fanny clung to Mary and cried, refusing to leave her mother's lap. When Mary finally dismounted with her baby in her arms, she went straight to Imlay's old apartment, but once she was there his absence only seemed all the more palpable.

But with each day that passed, Mary adjusted to life back in the capital. It helped that Paris was slowly returning to life. People strolled through the streets, dressed up for parties and the theater, laughing and gossiping without fear of the authorities. There were outdoor concerts and festivals, some of which commemorated the trauma Parisians had experienced in novel ways, such as the famous "Ball of the Victims" at the Hôtel Richelieu. Mary did not go, but everyone was talking about it when she arrived in the city. Only those who had lost someone to the guillotine were invited. Men cut their hair short to emulate the victims, and women painted a thin red line around their necks. There were other equally macabre events. On September 21, Mary took Fanny to the Pantheon to watch the Jacobins exhume the body of Mirabeau—a leader of the early Revolution who had been scorned as too moderate and whom Mary had greatly admired—and bury their hero, the more radical Marat, in Mirabeau's place. Fanny, unaware of what was happening, delighted in the "loud music" and "scarlet waistcoat[s]," Mary wrote Gilbert.

For Mary, some of these changes were more hopeful than others. She was glad to see that it was the rage to avoid any appearance of the "artificiality" that had once been so prized by Lady Kingsborough and Mrs. Dawson, her erstwhile employers. Silk, satin, velvet, brocade, and ribbons had gone the way of the ancien régime; panniers, hoops, and pinched waists stank of aristocratic privilege. Designers looked to ancient Rome and Greece for inspiration. Gowns were meant to reveal the beauties of the natural form, not conceal them.

Although many prim Englishwomen would resist these changes when they crossed the Channel, Mary was delighted to jettison the crippling styles of the past. Without complicated and restrictive undergarments, it was easier to move. Dresses had raised waists, allowing the wearer to breathe and take long strides; skirts were slit, providing even greater freedom of movement. Light-colored cottons, painted gauze, and sheer India muslin had the added benefit of not weighing much—another liberating aspect. Women actually competed over whose dresses weighed the least; in some cases, a costume could weigh as little as eight ounces, including shoes and jewelry.

Although it was true that the gauzy new gowns left little to the imagination, Mary did not think this was such a bad thing. She agreed with Fuseli that the human body was beautiful; her relationship with Gilbert had introduced her to the joys of sensuality. Besides, there was the added benefit that these diaphanous, flowing garments suited her statuesque figure. Count von Schlabrendorf, one of her old admirers, who had also returned to Paris, said that Mary "enthralled" him even more than she had before. He would have liked to pursue a romantic liaison, but Mary remained loyal to Imlay. "She was of an opinion that chastity consisted in fidelity," the count complained. But her refusal did not stop him from paying her frequent visits; she was far more charming than his other acquaintances, and he valued her perceptive observations about Parisian politics.

Mary had not earned any income for more than a year, as Johnson had paid her for *The French Revolution* in advance. Imlay had left instructions with an American friend to provide Mary with funds whenever she needed them, but Mary had refused this offer. She did not want to be Imlay's mistress, and accepting his money seemed perilously close to that sort of arrangement. Now, without anyone to look after her little daughter, even the smallest errands turned into projects. What if Fanny needed to nurse, got sick, or had a tantrum? She had to carry the baby everywhere, to the marketplace, to visit friends, or just to buy the papers. Even though she was exhausted, she was too overwrought to sleep, falling into "reveries and trains of thinking, which agitate and fatigue me." When she did at last manage to close her eyes, she was woken by Fanny, who cried until she was nursed back to sleep.

To conserve what money she had, Mary decided to move to a less expensive apartment, as Imlay had not paid the rent past September. Her new lodgings were with a German family, and when she observed the husband helping his wife take care of their children, she was moved to tears. Again and again she wrote to the absent Gilbert, painting touching domestic scenes, hoping against hope that these vignettes would tempt him back:

> I have been playing and laughing with the little girl so long, that I cannot take up my pen to address you without emotion. Pressing her to my bosom she looked so like you . . . every

nerve seemed to vibrate to the touch, and I began to think there was something in the assertion of man and wife being one—for you seemed to pervade my whole frame, quickening the beat of my heart, and lending me the sympathetic tears you excite. . . . I know that you will love her more and more.

She ended one letter saying, "Take care of yourself, if you wish to be the protector of your child, and the comfort of her mother."

But in fact Fanny had no protector and Mary had no comforter. Gilbert's letters had become infrequent and increasingly careless. Without any help, Mary had no time or energy to work. She could not even read. She received many invitations to parties and salons, but she could not go because she could not leave Fanny alone.

At last, in desperation, she went to Imlay's friend to ask for money. She hated having to do this and picked a fight by belittling Gilbert's moneymaking schemes. The man taunted her for her lover's absence: "He very unmanily exulted over me, on account of your determination to stay," she complained to Imlay.

But the humiliation was worth it, as her new funds enabled her to find a truly exceptional maid, Marguerite, a "vivac[ious]" young woman who was ripe for adventure and who would remain loyal for the rest of Mary's life. For household chores, Mary hired another servant as well, and so she was at last free to work a little and attend soirees and teas. She studied her French and "employed and amused" herself, sallying forth to parties as Mrs. Imlay. Although many of her old friends were dead, or had fled the country—the Barlows were in Germany, Helen Maria Williams and the Christies were in Switzerland, and Thomas Paine still languished in jail, where it was too dangerous for his English friends to visit him—Mary met many new people. These included several male acquaintances, charmed by her liveliness and quick intelligence. "Her manners were interesting, and her conversation spirited," wrote Archibald Rowan, an Irishman exiled from his own country, who often dropped by her lodgings to enjoy "a dish of tea and an hour's rational conversation." In one lighthearted moment, she teased Gilbert that if he did not come back soon, "I shall be half in love with the author of the Marseillaise [Claude-Joseph Rouget de Lisle], who is a handsome man . . . and plays sweetly on the violin."

In fact, Mary attracted so much attention that other women were jealous. The spiteful Madame Schweitzer muttered that Mary neglected her female friends to flirt with men. She told one vicious story about how she had beckoned Mary to come see a sunset— "Come, Mary—come, nature lover,—and enjoy this wonderful spectacle—this transition from colour to colour!"—but Mary ignored her in favor of a male companion "by whom she was at the moment captivated. I must confess that this erotic absorption made such a disagreeable impression on me, that all my pleasure vanished." However, since Madame Schweitzer's husband had recently confessed his attraction to Mary, Madame's motives were likely malicious.

As the days shortened, Mary's money again began to run out. The winter of 1794–95 would be the coldest on record. Bread prices skyrocketed and meat became an unthinkable luxury. Wood grew so expensive that many Parisians resorted to burning their furniture. By the end of December, Mary's letters to Gilbert had become sharply critical. She condemned his mercantile ambitions, using the clear, bold phrases she had employed in her *Vindications*:

> When you first entered into these plans, you bounded your views to the gaining of a thousand pounds. It was sufficient to have procured a farm in America, which would have been an independence. You find now that you did not know yourself, and that a certain situation in life is more necessary to you than you imagined—more necessary than an uncorrupted heart—

Frustrated and abandoned though she felt, Mary had managed to formulate an ethical stance against Gilbert's commercialism, her letters becoming as philosophical as they were personal, elaborating the ideas she had begun to develop the previous summer—the problems of a life devoted to commerce versus a life of the mind:

Believe me, sage sir, you have not sufficient respect for the imagination—I could prove to you in a trice that it is the mother of sentiment, the great distinction of our nature, the only purifier of the passions. . . . The imagination is the true fire, stolen from heaven, to animate this cold creature of clay, producing all those fine sympathies that lead to rapture, fending men social by expanding their hearts, instead of leaving them leisure to calculate how many comforts society affords.

Theirs was a battle between two ways of life, Mary felt, an idea that actually gave her strength as it meant that she was arguing not just for herself but for general principles: human connection over mercantile transactions, art and the imagination over the acquisition of wealth: "I know what I look for to found my happiness on.—It is not money," she declared.

If one reads these letters of Mary's, her philosophical musings can sometimes be overshadowed by the poignancy of her laments. But Mary's theoretical discussions were not, as some critics have said, merely a device to bring Imlay back. Wollstonecraft was an experienced writer, and a distinguished enough public figure to suspect that one day her letters might be published, as indeed they would be. Thus not only was she fighting with Imlay, she was also leaving a written record for the future. Despairing and heartbroken though she was, she was also building the argument that she had begun in her *Vindications* and developed in *French Revolution*. What was important, she said, was not wealth and power, but the bonds between people; what mattered were the ties of domesticity, not material possessions or position in society. To spend one's life trying to gain power over other people was ultimately an empty endeavor, one that would lead to regret and unhappiness.

As a result, when the public did read these letters, they would encounter not just the lovers' drama, but also Mary's ethical position—the personal, the political, and the philosophical woven tightly together—and this would have important consequences for Wollstonecraft's daughter and son-in-law. Wollstonecraft's praise of the imagination sounds eerily like a synopsis of Shelley's *Prometheus Unbound* as well as passages from his *Defense of Poetry*. Her arguments on behalf of the life of the mind would help her daughter survive her own many losses and would inform the writing of her novels. For Mary and Shelley, then, Wollstonecraft's letters were a kind of battle cry, one side of an essential conflict between two warring ideologies.

Worn out by her struggle to get Imlay back, Mary caught a cold that deepened into a lung infection. Worried that she would die and leave Fanny alone in the world, she told Gilbert to let her landlords, the loving German family, raise their daughter. Although Gilbert did not rush to her rescue, her misery did at least goad him into inviting her to London. But the tone of his invitation was distant, and in reality Mary was not sure she wanted to return to England, even if it meant joining him there. Having read how the English press had pilloried Helen Maria Williams and Madame Roland, she knew she would face the same bitter disapprobation. She did not want Fanny to grow up in such a restrictive environment, and she told Imlay that their daughter would be freer if she stayed in France. To compound matters, if anyone found out she was not actually married to Imlay, she would face certain social exile. Besides, how reliable was Gilbert? "Am I only to return to a country, that has not merely lost all charms for me, but for which I feel a repugnance that almost amounts to horror, only to be left there a prey to it!"

At this, Imlay relented, writing the most loving letter he had in months: "Business alone has kept me from you.—Come to any port, and I will fly down to my two dear girls with a heart all their own." These were the words Mary had longed to hear. He did still love her. He did still want to be a father. Maybe his cruel behavior had truly been because of financial preoccupations. Granted, she disapproved of his focus on money, but wrongheadedness was different from infidelity. Far better to chastise the man she loved for thinking too much about business than for falling in love with someone else!

In her rush to rejoin him, Mary entrusted "the good people" of Le Havre to find buyers for their furniture. She spent her final days in France weaning Fanny, since according to common wisdom, nursing mothers were not supposed to have sex with their husbands. This was a sad endeavor, as it meant letting the baby suffer without consolation. She tried to sleep in a separate room from the little girl, but she finally broke down after the third night and scooped her up. She knew too well what it felt like to be abandoned.

On April 9, Mary, Fanny, and Marguerite sailed for London, though Mary still worried about what she would find when she got to England, writing to Gilbert:

> I have indeed been so unhappy this winter, I find it as difficult to acquire fresh hopes, as to regain tranquility.—Enough of this—lie still, foolish heart!—But for the little girl, I could almost wish that it should cease to beat, to be no more alive to the anguish of disappointment.

Marguerite was incapacitated by seasickness, so Fanny held tightly to Mary, who tried to remain calm but failed miserably, dwelling on her memories of the two happy summers she had spent with Imlay. Before long, she had talked herself into believing that Gilbert would share her delight in Fanny's growth, her sparks of humor and intelligence. No more would Mary have to be a proudly struggling single mother. She would be the loving partner of the man she adored. She would have someone to confide in, someone who would help her bear the burdens of parenthood. Together, she and Gilbert would create a cozy domestic life just like that of her German friends in Paris.

But when Mary, Fanny, and Marguerite disembarked in Dover on Saturday, April 11, 1795, there was no Gilbert waiting to greet them. Mary dashed off a note: "Here we are, my love, and mean to set out early in the morning; and, if I can find you, I hope to dine with you tomorrow." She attached a postscript letting him know that she was available to him in every possible way: "I have weaned my [daughter], and she is now eating away at the white bread." She booked passage on a coach to London, and Imlay met them when they arrived. But although she flushed with joy when she saw him, her happiness was short-lived. This polite stranger was not her Gilbert, the eager lover who used to pull her into his arms. He did not look longingly into her eyes. He did not give her a lingering kiss. Instead, he made the sober announcement that he would try to do his duty by her and his daughter. He had rented an elegantly furnished house at 26 Charlotte Street in Soho, a new neighborhood inhabited largely by artists and architects, and he would live with them. But he expected to retain his freedom in all ways.

Mary was caught off guard by this lukewarm greeting, but was certain she could talk him into loving her again. She was a skilled arguer, a philosopher, after all. He used to adore that about her. She would show him where he was wrong and he would be grateful. In the meantime, though, she had to admit that he seemed like a stranger. This new Gilbert had little in common with the man she had been dreaming about, the man she had spent the last eight months talking to in her imagination and in her letters.

Once they were settled into the new house, Mary taught Fanny how to say "Papa," hoping this would touch Gilbert's heart. But though Imlay was kind to his daughter, he was preoccupied with business concerns. He told Mary that the ship that had carried the Bourbon platters was missing. Mary understood the seriousness of this; their financial future had hinged on the sale of the silver. She commiserated with him, and then tried to talk about their future. She still clung to the dream of America. But Imlay refused to discuss their relationship. He was obsessed with how much money he would lose if they could not locate Ellefson and the precious cargo. She wanted him to want her—"to press me very tenderly to your heart"—but he rejected her overtures. At night he disappeared, and when she asked where he had been, he refused to say. She wondered where the man had gone who had told her he loved her and could be counted on to reassure her when she had one of her fits of gloom, but the more she pushed, the more he retreated. After a few weeks, he began to disappear for days at a time.

Mary's desolation grew. She had always experienced what she called her dark moods, but she had managed to fight off the paralysis that often accompanied them. When she had suffered as a child, she had taken care of her siblings and educated herself. When she was cast down by Fuseli's rejection, she had headed straight to revolutionary Paris. She had borne the degradation and loneliness of being a hired worker, first as a lady's companion and then as a governess. After Fanny Blood died, she had almost succumbed, but had instead written her first book. Even when she had faced bitter attacks for the publication of the *Vindications,* she did not break down. She continued to write, publishing reviews and *The French Revolution.* But the misery she felt now was different from any she had experienced before. It overwhelmed her rational faculties. She felt incapable of doing anything but weeping. She tried to fight her way back to life. But instead of fighting for a cause, she fought the man she loved.

She accused him of greed and shallowness. He told her he needed "variety" and amusements. He asked her to stop making scenes. She made more. He begged her not to weep. She wept more. He urged her to stop hounding him for a commitment. She promised "to assume a cheerful face" and "avoid conversations, which only tend to harass your feelings," but a few minutes later she would drive him out of the house with her angry words, then collapse into tears when he was gone.

Gilbert was not a bad man, but he was not a strong man. And it would have taken a very strong man to support the weight of Mary's suffering. The grief that she bore was a lifetime's worth. Not that Gilbert could understand this. To him, she seemed like a woman possessed, as much a stranger as he seemed to her. The independent, resilient woman he had loved in France was gone. Now Mary seemed like one of the heroines in the gothic novels she despised, desperate and pleading for his love.

WHAT NEITHER MARY NOR Gilbert could know was that Mary was in the grip of what would today be called a major episode of depression. It would last another six months, and it carried with it the full force of years of pain. Like so many others who have dared to fight against injustice, she had endured the wrath of her society. Although she had kept going, the sorrow and fear had accumulated. It was not easy to be called a whore and a hyena, to be mocked as insane and immoral. Moreover, there was the added trauma of childbirth, compounded by the challenge of being a single mother. Before Fanny was born, Mary might well have been able to shake off Imlay's rejection and move forward, as she had with Fuseli. But as it was, Mary was exhausted, worried, and lonely, and there was no one to rescue her, the way she had rescued Eliza. She had depended on her own resources for most of her life, what she called "the elasticity" of her nature, and now these resources had run out. Her strength was gone.

In this condition, Mary could not reach out to her old friends. She refused to contact Joseph Johnson. She did write to her sisters that she was back in London, but she told them she could not offer them a place to live, or any money—yet. Ashamed of her situation, she did not mention her difficulties with Gilbert, allowing them to think that they could not be with her because it would be disruptive rather than because she had been abandoned by her lover. "It is my opinion [that] the presence of a third person interrupts or destroys domestic happiness," she wrote. She also told them how much she missed them and how much she would like to have them near, but these sentiments did nothing to mollify the "girls," whose feelings were hurt. Eliza had even quit her job, assuming that Mary would offer her a home, and was now so offended that she maintained a stony, angry silence. Gilbert made things worse by vacillating. He could not love her now, he said, but he was not sure about the future. Maybe someday he would have feelings for her again. She begged him to tell her frankly whether he desired to live with her or part forever. But he continued to waver.

Maybe Imlay truly was unsure, but he may also have worried about what would happen if he broke off their relationship. Mary had been threatening to harm herself for months. And so he went back and forth while Mary existed in a terrible kind of limbo, waiting to hear what he had decided. Finally, in desperation, she knocked on Fuseli's door, hoping that he would understand her heartbreak and console her. But though so much time had passed, he still refused to see her. This was the last straw. Was she so unlovable? She felt that she must be. She worried about little Fanny but felt that the child might be better off without her.

At the end of May, a month after her thirty-sixth birthday, Mary swallowed poison. Later, she described the experience in notes for her unfinished novel, *Maria:*

She swallowed the laudanum; her soul was calm—the tempest had subsided—and nothing remained but an eager longing to forget herself—to fly from the anguish she endured[,] to escape from thought—from this hell of disappointment. . . . her head turned; a stupor ensued; a faintness—"have a little patience," [she] said, holding her swimming head (she thought of her mother), "this cannot last long; and what is a little bodily pain to the pangs I have endured."

# MARY SHELLEY:
# "OUR LITTLE WILL"

———

## [ 1818–1819 ]

*W*HEN MARY, SHELLEY, AND CLAIRE ARRIVED IN NAPLES IN DECEM-ber, they moved into one of the most beautiful houses in the city, No. 250 Riviera di Chiaia, which Shelley had rented with the hope of pleasing Mary. It was rumored that the ruins of Cicero's villa were right under their window. To both Shelleys, the grand old senator stood for the freedom of the Roman republic and was an icon of hope. Nestled below the slopes of Vesuvius, which, as Shelley said, was "a smoke by day and a fire by night," Naples had public gardens and boulevards lined with palm trees. Across the sea, they could see the outline of a mysterious island drifting in and out of the mist. This was the isle of Circe, as local lore had it, the beautiful temptress who lured Odysseus into her bed and kept him there for seven years. Another legend was that Virgil had composed his gentle, pastoral poems here, *The Georgics*. Mary delighted in "looking at almost the same scene that he did—reading about manners little changed since his days." Together, she, Claire, and Shelley explored the famous sites: Pompeii, Herculaneum, Lake Avernus, and the Cumean Sybil's cave.

For once, there was peace between the sisters. Brought together by the loss of their daughters (although Alba was still alive, Claire suffered over their enforced separation), Mary and Claire were kind to each other. The trio climbed Vesuvius and gazed out over the city's steeples and red roofs to the sea. "A poet could not have a more sacred burying place [than] in an olive grove on the shore of a beautiful bay," Mary wrote in her journal that winter, looking out at the pale blue water. Gradually, she was able to take pleasure in the "orange trees in the public gardens next door . . . laden with blossoms. . . . The sky, the shore, all its forms and the sensations it inspires, appear formed and modulated by the Spirit of Good." At least she still had Wilmouse, who was so beautiful their servants tiptoed into his room to watch him sleep.

But the shadow of Clara's death hung between the Shelleys. Mary retreated into her books, avoiding contact with Shelley. She read a history of the Paterins, medieval Italian heretics who believed there was a continual battle between good and evil in the universe, a theme that struck a chord with her: for every joy there was an equal and opposing sorrow. Translated into Mary's terms, this meant that for every baby born, a baby died. For every love, there was the loss of love. So taken was she with this philosophy that she decided to make the Paterins the subject of her next novel, *Valperga,* researching medieval Italian history with true Godwinian meticulousness, plowing through enormous tomes and visiting historical sites.

Shelley did not like how Mary retreated to the past. He wanted her to talk to him and listen to his ideas, to read his poems and discuss them, as she always had. He missed his wife and wanted her grief to end. But for Mary, talking to Shelley was too difficult. She blamed him as well as herself for Clara's death, and she did her best to avoid him, although that was difficult. When they did meet, she was polite, always cordial, but distant. Rarely did she laugh. She rejected Shelley's romantic overtures. She was certain that Clara's death was a punishment of sorts, that their love affair had brought suffering to too many people. Shelley agreed that they were haunted by ghosts, but he did not believe that he was responsible for Clara's death and was mystified by Mary's coldness. Before, when "their two souls had vibrated as one," Mary had seemed to understand everything about him. Now he felt alone, and it was in this spirit that he composed one of his most famous lyrics, *Stanzas Written in Dejection Near Na-*

*ples,* a forty-five-line poem she would discover only after his death, like a lament straight from the grave:

> *I could lie down like a tired child,*
> *And weep away the life of care*
> *Which I have born and yet must bear,*
> *Till death like sleep might steal on me,*
> *And I might feel in the warm air*
> *My cheek grow cold, and hear the sea*
> *Breathe o'er my dying brain its last monotony.*

ON FEBRUARY 27, 1819, the day before they were supposed to leave for Rome, Shelley did something so peculiar that historians are still at a loss to determine what actually happened. With a cheesemonger and a hairdresser as witnesses, he registered a baby at the town hall in the Chiara district. He said the child was his, but to this day no one has been able to identify this baby or her real parents. The information Shelley entered into the official record is fascinating but contradictory. The child's name was Elena Adelaide; she was two months old; she was (he claimed) the legitimate child of his wife, Maria Padurin. He put Maria Padurin's age as twenty-seven when his own Mary was just twenty-one. The interesting part about this detail is that the only person in the Shelley entourage who had reached such an age was Elise.

So, who was this baby? Who were her parents?

Certainly, Elena Adelaide was not Mary's. Mary had no reason to conceal a pregnancy, and even if she had, she would never have consented to leave her new baby in Naples with unfamiliar people, which is what the Shelleys ultimately did. One theory is that Elena was a foster child they had temporarily adopted to cheer Mary up. Shelley had often expressed an interest in adopting children. But then there would have been no reason to cover up the child's parentage. Not only would Mary have been likely to record such an event in her journal, Shelley would have told his friends about it with pride. In fact, when they lived in Marlow and had taken in the little village girl, Polly Rose, they were both proud of their generosity. When they left for Italy, they did not abandon Polly Rose, but sent her to the Hunts', where she worked as a maid.

Shelley's cousin, the notoriously inaccurate biographer Thomas Medwin, declared that Elena was the love child of a mysterious Englishwoman who had followed the Shelleys to Italy and had a brief affair with Shelley, but there is no evidence for such a claim. In fact, the records have been stripped almost bare. Clearly, the Shelleys were good secret keepers when they wanted to be, and their descendants were even better. The paper with little Elena's registration was only discovered in the 1950s. There are no direct references to Elena in Shelley's papers or Mary's journal.

Another rumor, started by the servant Elise to protect her own reputation, claimed that Claire was the mother. In Elise's version of events, told to the Hoppners a few years later, Shelley fathered the child and the guilty couple hid the pregnancy and the birth from Mary, even though the baby was born in their lodgings. Mary defended Shelley against these charges when she got wind of Elise's accusations, writing a long letter, listing the many absurdities of this claim. Certainly it does seem unlikely that Mary would have overlooked her sister's pregnancy, or that she would have missed the labor and delivery. Furthermore, Mary and Shelley drew closer after this incident, an unlikely development if Mary thought that Shelley had fathered a child with Claire. Also, Claire and Mary remained on good terms during this time, a direct contrast to the disastrous spring of 1815, when Claire might well have been pregnant with Shelley's child, and the two sisters fought so bitterly that Claire was forced to retreat to the countryside.

That Elise bothered to fabricate such a tale suggests that she was attempting to conceal something, possibly her own role in Elena's birth. That January, Elise left the Shelleys' service to marry their servant Paolo Foggi at the Shelleys' insistence, according to one of Mary's letters. Mary and Shelley had recently discovered that Paolo had been cheating them out of money and they had planned to fire him. Why, then, would the Shelleys have insisted on a marriage be-

tween their servants, especially as they were fond of Elise and regarded Paolo as a brigand? The best answer seems to be that they had
discovered that Elise was pregnant in the fall of 1818. The Shelleys
liked names that connected babies to their mothers; Elise and Elena
are very similar, and Shelley had said the mother was Elise's age.
Moreover, the heretics Mary had read about and admired were called
the Paterins, or Paderins, which may well have inspired "Maria's" last
name, Padurin. Quite possibly then, Shelley was using a code that
only he and Mary, and maybe Claire, would understand. In fact, the
name Maria Padurin seems far more likely to have been Mary's invention than Shelley's. The Paterins were on *her* mind, not Shelley's. And
in Mary's private lexicon, the name Maria stood for her mother's last
book, *The Wrongs of Woman,* in which Wollstonecraft sought to show
the many abuses women suffered at the hands of men. Jemima, one of
the novel's most important characters, is a working-class woman, like
Elise, who is raped by her employer.

But if Elise was the mother, Paolo could not have been the father,
as Elise had first met him during the ill-fated trip to Venice in late
August or early September, and she would have had to get pregnant
sometime in April to give birth in December. That leaves Shelley,
Byron, or perhaps someone Mary and Shelley did not know, someone whom Elise had met in Venice, as the father.

When all these possibilities are examined, the evidence strongly
suggests Byron. The child did not cause a breakdown in the Shelleys'
marriage, making it probable, as with the Claire story, that Shelley
was not the father. Furthermore, if Byron *was* the father, that would
help explain the urgency of Elise's plea that August: she would have
wanted to rescue herself, not Allegra, from his lordship, especially if
she had realized she was pregnant and that Byron would refuse to
acknowledge the baby as his own. This version is further supported
by the fact that Shelley, who was deeply concerned about Allegra's
welfare, could not find anything amiss in the child's life with Byron,
though he did take Elise back with them to Naples. It is less clear why
the Shelleys chose Paolo to marry Elise. Perhaps he was Elise's choice.
Perhaps he was the only man they could find to marry her for money
and at short notice. Ultimately, it was an unfortunate decision, as

Paolo would become difficult, demanding regular blackmail payments from Shelley long after they had left Naples.

But if Byron was the father and Shelley was not, why would Shelley register Elena as his own? If one factors Mary into the story, then things fall into place. In later years Mary would demonstrate a steadfast commitment to protecting women who had broken society's rules. She would go to enormous lengths to support single mothers with illegitimate children, making them her special cause. If she was concerned about Elise's future, as well as the baby's, she could easily have suggested to Shelley that he give his name to the baby for Elise's sake. She would have reminded Shelley that it was precisely this sort of security that her sister Fanny had lacked.

The idea that Mary played a significant, maybe even a leadership role in the Elena story overturns the arguments of most historians, who have assumed that Shelley was trying to conceal a secret love child. But once one accepts the principle that someone besides Shelley was the father, it is easier to see that Shelley had no reason to hide the child from Mary and that she could easily have helped him plan Elena's future. This theory is reinforced by the fact that in later years Shelley did not conceal Paolo's blackmail attempts from his wife. Far from being the helpless wife of a cheating husband, in this account of events Mary is actually a co-conspirator, helping carry out a plot to save another woman. Granted, there is no way to confirm that the child's legitimization was a joint project, one that Mary may have even masterminded, but it is a hypothesis that must be taken seriously when considering the mystery of Elena.

On February 28, the day after Shelley registered the baby's birth, Mary, Shelley, William, and Claire left for Rome, leaving Elise behind with Paolo. They traveled in slow stages until they reached Gaeta, just south of the great city, on March 3 or 4. Over the previous few months, Mary had slowly warmed toward Shelley enough to smile at him and listen to his ideas and feelings. She still mourned Clara, but she also missed being close to her husband. Delighted by her return, Shelley made a point of shedding Claire to spend the day in Gaeta with Mary, admiring the ruins, walking the beach, and gazing at the Tyrrhenian Sea. They wandered through a lemon orchard, and Shelley remembered looking up "at an emerald sky of leaves starred with innumerable globes of ripening fruit." It was a happy day for the couple, one that seemed to promise a new season of hope. In the evening they played chess on the terrace of their inn, thrilled to be on the site of one of Cicero's summer villas perched high above the town. They spent the night in a romantic room overlooking the water, and it was here that Mary believed their fourth child was conceived.

The next day, the party drove through the deserted landscape of Albano, Shelley marveling at the "arches after arches" of the ancient aqueducts rising "in unending lines" as they approached Rome. When at last they could see the dome of St. Peter's rising up along the Tiber, both Mary and Shelley felt a surge of happiness. Byron's words from *Childe Harold* seemed to fit this glorious moment:

> *Oh Rome! My country! City of the soul!*
> *The orphans of the heart must turn to thee,*
>
> .     .     .     .     .     .
>
> *What are our woes and sufferance? Come and see*
> *The cypress, hear the owl, and plod your way*
> *O'er steps of broken thrones and temples, Ye!*
> *Whose agonies are evils of a day—*
> *A world is at our feet as fragile as our clay.*

Rolling past the medieval castle of Sant'Angelo and across the bridge into the city, to the east they could see the magnificent columns of the Forum and the imposing walls of the Colosseum. Scattered about along the side of the road were piles of ancient rubble, broken pediments and pillars that had fallen over; the past was everywhere, not cordoned off into sightseeing areas. It was a sobering experience to imagine how grand the city had once been. As Byron said, the city's fate made their personal sorrows seem small. To both Mary and Shelley, the air felt heavy with history.

Once they had settled into the rooms Shelley had rented in the Palazzo Verospi on the Corso, the most fashionable street in Rome, they walked the streets in a daze of happiness. "Rome repays for every thing," Mary declared. Even Claire was happy, taking singing lessons, exploring the city, and working on her Italian. Her favorite spot was the Temple of Aesculapius in the Borghese Gardens, where she would sit on the steps and read Wordsworth.

Over the next few months, as the weather grew warmer, Mary and Shelley drew as close as they had been in their early years together. On short expeditions, three-year-old Wilmouse trotted along with them, holding his mother's hand, exclaiming *"O Dio che bella"* at the wonders his parents pointed out. Doting parents, they were proud of how much their son loved Rome, its eccentric mix of ruins and livestock, peasants and cardinals, churches and food stalls: "Our little Will is delighted with the goats and the horses and . . . the ladies' white marble feet," Mary wrote to Maria Gisborne, giving us a glimpse of her lively three-year-old, just tall enough to enjoy the naked toes of the statues his parents exclaimed over. Since he had spent most of his life in Italy, William's Italian was as strong as his English, but although he was a good walker and eager to explore, he was still somewhat delicate, and Mary continued to be anxious about his health. They instituted a regime of cold baths for him, hoping this would ward off illness and keep him strong. No one was allowed to reprimand him too harshly; Mary did not condone spankings, believing that children could be reasoned with. Shelley agreed; the last thing he wanted was for Wilmouse to suffer what he had endured at the hands of Sir Timothy. From all accounts, their system worked; William had grown into a loving, gentle little boy, remarkably unspoiled despite his parents' unstinting adoration.

Although she did not like to be separated from her son, Mary worried about the consequences of exposing him to the notorious Roman sun. Fortunately, Claire enjoyed playing with her nephew, so when Mary and Shelley went on longer expeditions, they left him home with her. One of their favorite spots was the Baths of Caracalla, where they could gaze out over the city. Together they would ascend the "antique winding staircase" and emerge on top of the ruined walls, where they worked and talked and enjoyed a solitude that seemed profound to both young writers. "Never was any desolation more sublime and lovely," Shelley exclaimed. The ruins were huge and stark, silent reminders of the once great empire, another example of the vision Shelley had sketched out in *Ozymandias*. The grass was scattered with violets, anemones, and wallflowers, and the wind smelled of salt and juniper. In April, Mary realized she was pregnant again, and for the first time since Clara had died, she looked forward to the future.

THAT WINTER, SHELLEY HAD begun work on another long poem, *Prometheus Unbound,* which stemmed from the ideas the group had first discussed during the *Frankenstein* summer. Rome seemed the perfect place to finish it, so he devoted himself to writing while Mary sketched, made notes in her journal, and savored the air. "It is a scene of perpetual enchantment to live in this thrice holy city," she reflected. "Rome . . . has such an effect on me that my past life before I saw it appears a blank; and now I begin to live." Lured outside by the beautiful spring evenings, they took a carriage to view the Pantheon by moonlight, where Mary soaked in the "spirit of beauty." "Never before had I so felt the universal graspings of my own mind," she reflected later.

Shelley's status as a baronet enabled them to meet the seventy-seven-year-old pope, who liked to welcome artists and noble foreigners to his city but who made Mary feel "dreadfully tired" because of his own evident weariness; he would die less than four years after their visit. As always, the Shelleys avoided the other English visitors. "The manners of the rich English are wholly unsupportable, and they assume pretensions which they would not venture upon in their own country," Shelley wrote to Peacock. Mary agreed: "The place is full of English, rich, noble—important and foolish. I am sick of it. . . ."

But in early May they were, for once, glad to bump into someone English, an old family friend, the artist Amelia Curran. They at once commissioned her to paint portraits of everyone in the family. A longtime resident of Rome, Amelia took one look at the slender, small-framed William and warned them against Roman fever, advising them to move out of the city immediately now that the summer was coming. But it was difficult to think about leaving when they were all so contented. As a compromise, they moved north to the Via Sestina, just above the Spanish Steps, which, Amelia said, was a healthier location than the Corso.

On May 14, Amelia began to paint William's portrait. Mary did not want him in an artificial pose, so instead of buttoning him into dress clothes, she allowed him to wear his nightshirt. Amelia put a rose in his hand and William let the shirt slide down his shoulder, chattering happily in both Italian and English while Amelia worked at her easel. During the first few days, she made good progress. She captured the little boy's pointed chin and delicate features. A wisp of hair brushes his forehead. His arms are plump and dimpled. He looks past the painter, intent, as though he is listening to someone—his mother, his aunt Claire, or his father, perhaps.

But a few days into the project, the little boy began to feel sick.

*Amelia Curran's*
*portrait of Wilmouse,*
*age three years.*

His stomach hurt. He was tired. This was so unlike her lively Wilmouse that Mary at once called the doctor, who diagnosed worms, assuring her that he should recover; it was a common enough ailment. However, a week later, William was still unwell. "He is so very delicate," Mary wrote to Maria. "We must take the greatest possible care of him this summer."

But there was to be no summer for William. On June 2, Mary called the doctor three times. Two days later, she watched helplessly as Wilmouse fought to stay alive. She recognized the "convulsions of death" that Ca had endured nine months earlier, and her heart froze in terror. Shelley did not move from William's side, spending the next three days sitting on his bed. "The hopes of my life are bound up in him," Mary wrote. But at noon on June 7, William died. Mary's third child was gone. Malaria, or Roman fever, had taken hold while he was weakened from his stomach ailment. Shelley wept. Mary became obsessed with everything they might have done differently. If only they had left the city a month earlier. If only they had never come to Italy. What if they had stayed in England? Was this yet more retribution for their sins of the past? Perhaps Harriet's angry soul, not content with taking Clara, had insisted on taking their boy as well—to match the boy and girl she had had with Shelley.

They did not have a ceremony for their little boy. Shelley arranged to have him buried in the Protestant cemetery, but they did not mark the grave. They talked about erecting a white marble pyramid, but apparently nothing ever came of the idea, since years later, when Mary returned to Rome, she could not find William's grave. "I never know one moment's ease from the wretchedness & despair that possess me," Mary wrote to Marianne Hunt three weeks after her son's death. To Leigh Hunt she wrote, "the world will never be to me again as it was—there was a life & freshness in it that is lost to me. . . ."

Each day, Mary relived the short span of Wilmouse's life, replaying his words, his expressions, his love for her. "William was so good so beautiful so entirely attached to me." It was the closeness of their relationship that hurt her most. William had depended on her to take care of him and to protect him. She had failed him. She had failed Ca. She had failed as a mother. She was a curse, a living curse, or so it seemed during this dark time. Not only had she caused her mother's death, she had allowed her own babies to die.

Shelley, meanwhile, mourned in poetry:

> *My lost William, thou in whom*
> *Some bright spirit lived, and did*
> *That decaying robe consume*
> *Which its luster faintly hid,—*
> *Here its ashes find a tomb,*
> *But beneath this pyramid*
> *Thou art not—if a thing divine*
> *Like thee can die, thy funeral shrine*
> *Is thy mother's grief and mine.*

> *Where are thou, my gentle child?*
> *Let me think thy spirit feeds,*
> *With its life intense and mild,*
> *The love of living leaves and weeds*
> *Among these tombs and ruins wild;—*
> *Let me think that through low seeds*
> *Of sweet flowers and sunny grass*
> *Into their hues and scents may pass*
> *A portion—*

He broke off there, and though he tried again twice more, was never able to finish a poem to commemorate his son.

If Mary had retreated after Ca died, she now vanished completely. Like one of the statues they had admired in Rome, she was silent and impenetrable. "My dearest Mary," Shelley pleaded in a poem he did not show her, "wherefore hast thou gone, / And left me in this dreary world alone? / Thy form is here indeed—a lovely one— / But thou art fled, gone down the dreary road, / That leads to Sorrow's most obscure abode." He hesitated, then finished his thought, but in a much weaker hand: "For thine own sake I cannot follow thee / Do thou return for mine."

Too late, they moved north to a villa just outside Livorno, near the Gisbornes. The wide stone house was cool that summer. At night the fireflies flashed, reminding everyone of the previous year when Wilmouse had chased them across the lawn. It was so quiet that when there was a breeze they could hear the corn rustle in the nearby fields and the calls of the grape pickers working in the vineyards. From the top floor they watched the different moods of the water—flat and calm, white-tipped, dark before a storm—and learned the names of the islands that dotted the sea: Gorgona, Capraja, Elba, Corsica.

Mary shut herself indoors or walked alone in the lanes that led to the fields. She stared at the portrait of William, writing to Amelia to express her despair. "I shall never recover [from] that blow—I feel it more now than at Rome—the thought never leaves me for a single moment—Everything has lost its interest to me." On a nearby hillside, she could see a rose-colored sanctuary called Montenero, built to commemorate a shepherd's vision of the Madonna in the fourteenth century. Its warm pink dome beckoned visitors, especially those, like Mary, who were looking for solace. Hanging inside was a gold-framed painting of the Virgin with her Son, who looked about William's age. Jesus' eyes were dark like William's, his hair a similar golden brown, although it was shorter. Mother and child gazed out at the world with solemnity, even suspicion, as if anticipating the great tragedy to come. It was impossible for Mary to miss the parallels. Two Marys. Two sons. Two deaths. But Wilmouse would never return.

NEITHER CLAIRE NOR SHELLEY gave way to this deep mourning, and both were afraid that Mary might not come back to them. Claire even canceled her trip to visit Allegra, writing to Byron that she could not leave Mary alone; she was too melancholy. For all their conflicts, there was still a tight bond of loyalty between the sisters.

Nonetheless, Mary paid little attention to how Claire and Shelley spent their days. Claire slept until noon, sang for an hour or so, and walked with Shelley in the afternoons. Shelley got up around seven, read in bed for half an hour, ate breakfast by himself, then "ascend[ed]" to a glassed-in balcony on the roof, a common feature of houses in Livorno, where he wrote until two, baking in the sun. Later, Mary would describe this room as "his airy cell," explaining that "the dazzling sunlight and heat made it almost intolerable to every other; but Shelley basked in both, and his health and spirits revived under their influence." Occasionally he took energetic walks to the beach or to the home of the Gisbornes, either alone or with Claire, while Mary stayed behind, wrung out with grief, but also tired from pregnancy. The baby was due in November, but it was impossible now for Mary to look forward to its arrival. In her darkened world, all she could anticipate was loss; soon she would have another child, but for how long?

In the afternoon, she and Shelley came together for a few hours to work on their Italian, translating verses of Dante's *Purgatorio,* a fitting choice given Mary's state of mind. Otherwise she spent her time alone. "I ought to have died on the 7th of June last," she wrote to the Hunts. She listened to the field workers "sing not very melodiously but very loud—Rossini's music *Mi revedrai, ti revedro,*" but what she really wanted was to hear William's voice. If only she could hold him in her lap once again, show him the bright globes of lemons hanging on the trees, brush his hair off his forehead, listen to him prattle about the birds and the flowers, go for walks near the cornfields, laugh at his pranks. She wanted to see him run down the lane. She wanted to hear him call her name. She wanted to feel his hand in hers.

There were times when Mary felt she could not bear to go on living, and the worst part was that no one seemed to understand her sorrow. Her father's reaction was particularly disappointing. When Godwin heard about William, his letter outlined his pecuniary needs first and only then turned to Mary's grief—with love, yes, but Godwinian love, which always contained an element of the Calvinist preacher. She must not indulge herself by grieving too much, he said. Above all, she must guard against the Wollstonecraft tendency to despair. He ended by giving voice to Mary's worst fears:

Though at first your nearest connections may pity you in this state, yet . . . when they see you fixed in selfishness and ill humour, and regardless of the happiness of every one else, they will finally cease to love you, and scarcely learn to endure you.

Godwin was a shrewd judge of human nature—or at least of Shelley's and Mary's. He knew that if his daughter did not return to her loving ways, if she could not focus on Shelley, the quicksilver poet would move on, seeking admiration in other quarters and leaving Mary alone. He warned her of this danger, harsh though it seemed, because he did not know if his daughter could survive such a blow.

# MARY WOLLSTONECRAFT: "SURELY YOU WILL NOT FORGET ME"

———

[ 1795 ]

MARY WAS NOT UNCONSCIOUS FOR VERY LONG BEFORE IMLAY FOUND her. After reading her last despondent note, he had suspected that she might try to kill herself and hurried over on a beautiful May afternoon to find her slumped on her bed, her eyes closed, well on her way to a coma. He sent for a doctor and, as Mary described the experience in her novel *Maria,* "A . . . vision swam before her . . . she tried to listen, to speak, to look!" The doctor induced "violent vomiting" and she was soon out of danger, but her desolation had reached such a pitch that even the insensitive Imlay realized she was desperate enough to try again.

Instead of taking Mary in his arms and consoling her, Imlay came up with a plan to remove her from London. Perhaps he still loved her, but he did not want to give up his freedom, and her suicide attempt had not made him any more willing to bow to her wishes. It also seems likely that he felt guilty or dreaded the embarrassment of having his famous "wife" commit suicide. He gave Mary a few days to recover, then he made a proposition: Would she go to Scandinavia to find out what had happened to the Bourbon silver and his missing ship? This was an astonishing proposal to make to a woman who had just tried to end her life, but Mary, who did not want to give up her belief in Imlay, nor her ideals about the possibilities of a love between equals, saw it as a promising development. He still wanted her in his life as a dear friend and a helper. She would be able to demonstrate her resourcefulness and competence and he would be grateful and impressed, which could easily lead him back to the tenderness he once felt—or so she hoped. Maybe it was true that Gilbert had been neglecting her because of financial worries, and if she could find the missing ship, he would be a rich man, they could move to America, and he could cease the quest for wealth that frustrated her. He also said that he would meet her for a holiday in Basel after her investigation. He did not pretend that he wanted a settled, domestic life with her, and yet Mary allowed herself to hope that he might change his mind.

She took only a few days to pack and organize her affairs. Then she set forth for Scandinavia. In the 1790s, few Englishmen had traveled to northern Europe, and even fewer Englishwomen. Accompanied by Fanny, now just over a year old, and the intrepid Marguerite, who only a few months ago had never been outside of Paris, Mary took a coach north to Hull, the port of departure for Gothenburg. Fanny was fretful during the overnight ride, keeping Mary awake. When at last they arrived at the port, they had to stay in a "tomb-like house" until they could find a ship headed for Sweden. This took a few days, and when Mary did find a vessel, they were forced to wait until the winds were blowing in the right direction. The days rolled slowly by, and one afternoon, Mary made a trip back to Beverley, the town she had once thought so sophisticated. Now it seemed "diminutive," and the people she had once thought cosmopolitan and well-educated seemed closed-minded and parochial. She was struck by the contrast between her own life and theirs: "I could not help wondering how they could thus have vegetated, whilst I was running over a world of sorrow, snatching at pleasure, and throwing off prejudices." Even though she had suffered—or perhaps because she had suffered— she felt herself "greatly improved" by her experiences. These people who had lived in the same place all of their days did not know how strange and curious the world could be. She saw how suspicious they were of outsiders and how fearful of change. How limited their lives seemed!

Exhausted and still enduring the aftershocks of her suicide attempt, each morning Mary was seized by a fit of trembling, as though she had a fever. Fanny had learned her lessons too well, continually calling for "Papa" to "come, come." Sometimes Mary wished she had died, but at other times she felt surprisingly tranquil. What was most difficult was how her moods changed so quickly. One minute, she could not wait for the voyage to begin, the next she dreaded leaving England just as much as she had feared coming back. It occurred to her that Imlay was sending her away so he could be free of her demands. "Surely you will not forget me," she wrote to him plaintively.

On June 16, after almost a week, the little group were finally able to board the ship, but before they could set sail, the wind shifted again and they were stuck for another week in foggy weather, riding the waves, waiting for the right breeze. Marguerite was seasick the moment she set foot on deck, so she stayed below, leaving Mary alone with Fanny. At first Fanny "play[ed] with the cabin boy" and was "gay as a lark," but then she began to teethe and refused to nap, whining and holding tightly to her mother. Mary developed a violent headache but could not lie down since she had to look after both her maid and her toddler. As the boat "tossed about without going forward," Mary did find the energy to write to Gilbert, listing her sufferings and placing the blame at his door. She could not sleep, and when she did she had nightmares about him. She had endured "anguish of mind" and "the sinking of a broken heart." She was hurt that he had not written to her more frequently and with more depth of feeling. Like the ship, she felt flung back and forth on the waves but tethered to the same miserable place.

At last the wind turned and they set sail, arriving in Gothenburg on June 27. The weather there was gloomy; sheets of rain drenched the passengers as they disembarked. When Mary hurried across the slippery rocks to the waiting carriage, she fell and cut her head, frightening the already anxious Marguerite by losing consciousness and lying "in a stupour for a quarter of an hour." She recovered in time to make the twenty-mile journey to town, but the rain poured down without pause, and when they arrived at their inn they could not get a fire or anything warm to eat.

The journey and subsequent events had done little to lift Mary's despair. On her first evening in Sweden, she wrote, "My friend—my friend, I am not well—a deadly weight of sorrow lies heavily on my heart." Gilbert did respond to her laments, but he was not very sympathetic. He told Mary that she was torturing him with her complaints and that she was not being respectful of him or his feelings. Mary wrote back saying she would stop criticizing him, but then she contradicted herself, closing the letter with a meticulous recitation of Gilbert's flaws, dissecting him as though she were reviewing a bad book: he was irresponsible; he was fearful; he was selfish; he was like Hamlet, unable to decide what to do or how to act. Understandably, Imlay did not write back for several days.

Imlay's business associate, Elias Backman, had offered to host her during her stay, and Mary's spirits lifted slightly when she saw the Backmans' clean, comfortable home with crisp white linens and a brood of small children. Having spent most of her life alone with her mother and her nurse, Fanny was at first alarmed by the crowd. But before long, she was playing with the other children in the garden, allowing Mary a few hours to herself each day, a time she used to refine her criticisms of Gilbert. Each day, and sometimes several times a day, she bent over her writing desk, wielding her formidable pen, bombarding him with accusations and questions: Would he *really* meet her in Europe? If she found his ship, would he *really* stop devoting himself to a life of commerce? Was he capable of being a father and a husband? As in Paris, their separation gave Mary the room she needed to develop her ideas. She was intent on proving that she suffered not because of her own weakness or any intrinsic flaw, but because of her capacity to have feelings—*true* feelings—and his inability to have any. "Ah, why do not you love us with more sentiment?" she demanded.

This argument, an extension of her earlier debates with him, represented her embrace of what scholars now call "the culture of sensibility." Having first encountered these ideas in Rousseau, she had long seen "sensibility," or "sentimentality," as a special faculty possessed by only the most enlightened people, such as herself. Now she pitted her refined feelings and elevated mind against Imlay's crass materialism. If only she could teach Gilbert to feel as deeply as she did, then his morals would improve. If only he had her imagination, she told him, he might triumph over "the grossness of [his] senses."

The more she wrote, the more Mary discovered that there was a certain power to being the abandoned one. According to the culture of sentiment, the purity of her heart and spirit meant she stood outside—that is, above—the ordinary run of human beings. It was also true that being abandoned had two meanings: being left behind, but also being wild, or living outside the law. The eighteenth century was fully aware of this paradox, in part because a woman who was alone was not answerable to any man. Paradoxically, then, with each cry of abandonment Mary was also announcing her distinctiveness, her lawlessness, and her independence. Mary Robinson, an actress who was the castoff lover of the Prince Regent and would soon become one of Mary's close friends, expressed this strange condition in a sonnet she wrote after the prince's desertion: the abandoned lover strays "from the tranquil path of wisdom," she says, and is driven into "passion's thorny wild, forlorn to dwell." Abandonment, for Robinson as for Wollstonecraft, becomes a grievous exile from civilization, but at the same time both Marys were declaring something more complicated and compelling than simple sorrow. With the loss of the lover came a certain freedom, a release from all restraint.

The more Mary wrote, the more she saw her suffering as evidence of her superiority to Gilbert. Not only did her grief reveal her freedom from societal mores, it demonstrated her profound sensitivity. To the modern reader, it may seem contradictory—and rather disappointing—that the author of *A Vindication of the Rights of Woman* would exhaust her ex-lover with weeping missives, try to kill herself, and then despair at his rejection, but for Mary each of her laments was an essential building block in the case she was building against Gilbert. She had moved from writing about the abuse of women in general to writing about her own suffering. Having experienced a man's betrayal, she would now bear witness against him, and in the spirit of her *Rights of Women,* she refused to submit to her dismissal gracefully or decorously.

One can almost feel sorry for Gilbert. An intrepid journalist,

Mary knew how to fight with ink. Viewed collectively, her letters to Gilbert are formidable. In the end, not only had Mary composed the equivalent of several treatises that could be called *A Vindication of the Rights of Mary,* as well as a *Treatise on the Wrongs of Gilbert,* she had also written a ferocious condemnation of the sexual double standard and a stirring argument on behalf of "sentiment" and "imagination" when threatened by the forces of the marketplace. Other women might view their pain as unique, pertaining to themselves and no one else, but not Mary. To her, Gilbert's betrayal, his disagreement with her about how to live one's life, represented the ultimate collision of ideologies: he stood for the commercial forces of the Industrial Revolution; she stood for the truth of the mind and the heart. She was having the argument of her life, embarking on what she saw as a clash of the titans; but unfortunately Gilbert, many things though he was, was not a titan. Her battle would turn out to be one-sided, since her opponent did not have nearly her capacity, ability, or vision.

As soon as the stormy weather lightened, the Backmans persuaded Mary to do some sightseeing. Gothenburg was at the time the most prosperous city in Sweden, its ruler-straight canals lined with tidy homes and shops. The streets were wide enough that pedestrians could walk without fear of getting run over by a passing coach. Few cities could have been less like tightly packed London, or Paris. The largest building in Gothenburg was the Swedish East India Company House, a yellowish brick rectangle with a copper roof. Instead of pointing heavenward like Notre Dame or St. Paul's, East India House was squat and wide, stuffed with barrels and crates, baskets and merchandise, an emblem of Gothenburg's flourishing trade with the Far East.

The Swedish devotion to commerce annoyed Mary. All anyone here seemed to think about was making money, a whole city full of Gilberts. But at least there was the countryside. Beeches, lindens, and ashes grew in groves, as though they had been planted by a master gardener, and after the heat of London, a Scandinavian summer was magical. The air, the grasses, the leaves—all fairly hummed with golden light. While Fanny played with the Backman children under Marguerite's watchful eye, Mary clambered over the rocks to the sea, strolled under canopies of enormous pines, ate salmon and anchovies, sipped cordials, and enjoyed bowls of strawberries with cream.

It was a relief to feel this "degree of vivacity." Although she did not like the food—the meat dishes were overly spiced or strangely sweetened, the rye bread was almost impossible to chew because it was baked only twice a year—Mary relished the sheer foreignness of the land. And although she was disturbed by the lack of educated conversation, the poverty of the servants, and the childrearing practices of giving brandy to babies, wrapping them in heavy unwashed flannels even during the summer, and not allowing them to toddle freely outdoors, she enjoyed the adventure of being so far from home. Her compulsion to record Gilbert's failings and analyze the dimensions, origins, and gravity of his sins gradually faded, and in its place she jotted down notes, not only about Sweden and the Swedes, but what it was like to be an Englishwoman recovering from a tragic love affair in the land of the Vikings, where the fields were a blaze of green and the night came creeping in long after midnight. The exercise was therapeutic; she could feel herself slowly returning to health, physically and mentally.

Alone at her desk, she spent hours describing the solace that Nature had to offer:

> I contemplated all nature at rest; the rocks, even grown darker in their appearance, looked as if they partook of the general repose, and reclined more heavily on their foundation.— What, I exclaimed, is this active principle which keeps me still?—Why fly my thoughts abroad when every thing around me appears at home? My child was sleeping with equal calmness—innocent and sweet as the closing flowers.—Some recollections, attached to the idea of home, mingled with reflections respecting the state of society I had been contemplating that evening, made a tear drop on the rosy cheek I had just kissed; and emotions that trembled on the brink of extasy and agony gave a poignancy to my sensations, which made me feel more alive than usual.

Mary had set forth into uncharted territory. Wordsworth had not yet articulated his view of Nature; other late-eighteenth-century writers had celebrated the bucolic beauties of the outdoors, but only Rousseau had treated the landscape as an opportunity for psychological anatomizing, tying thoughts and feelings to lakes, rocks, and trees. And Rousseau had entirely written women out of his universe of sentiment. Recording her thoughts in her notebook at night, the sun still high, celebrating her own capacity for self-examination even as she was smarting from Gilbert's rejections, Mary could not know that her new work would be read by generations of writers to come, particularly Romantic poets such as her future son-in-law who would adopt many of her principles. In Shelley's *Ode to the West Wind,* the poet finds solace in Nature just as Mary did here, moving from despair to wisdom while walking along the Arno.

After a few weeks of research, interviewing people about Imlay's ship to no avail, Mary decided it was time to visit Tonsberg, Norway, where one of Imlay's former employees lived. Perhaps he would know what had happened to the silver. Tonsberg was a day's ferry ride north, and Mary went alone—a difficult choice, as she had never been apart from her baby and relied on Marguerite's cheerfulness to support her when she could not shake off her misery. But she knew it would be more efficient to travel unencumbered and she worried about Marguerite's health, since she was still recovering from the seasickness she had endured on the passage to Scandinavia. Marguerite protested that she did not want to be left behind. She did not trust her volatile mistress to return, and she made Mary promise that she would not try to harm herself while she was gone.

As the ferry drew away from the wharf, Mary stood alone at the rails. Away from Fanny for the first time since she gave birth, she reflected on what it was like to be the mother of a girl:

I feel more than a mother's fondness and anxiety, when I reflect on the dependent and oppressed state of her sex. I dread lest she should be forced to sacrifice her heart to her principles, or principles to her heart. With trembling hand I shall cultivate sensibility, and cherish delicacy of sentiment, lest, whilst I lend fresh blushes to the rose, I sharpen the thorns that will wound the breast I would fain guard—I dread to unfold her mind, lest it should render her unfit for the worlds she is to inhabit— Hapless woman! What a fate is thine!

And yet, much as she missed her child, Mary had not been on her own for over a year and felt free, more liberated than she had for many, many months.


TONSBERG, THE OLDEST SETTLEMENT in Norway, was picturesque, complete with painted wooden houses and a smooth deep-water harbor where its original inhabitants, the Vikings, had once anchored their dragon boats. About sixty miles north of Gothenburg, the town was nestled in a valley. Stands of pine and aspen climbed the hills beyond. Blue-tinted mountains rose in the distance. Farmland rolled along the shore. Seals sunned themselves on the small rocky islands. A fjord cut through the fields outside of the town, the water as clean and clear as any Mary had ever seen. Mayor Wulfsberg, Elias Backman's associate, who had originally investigated the case of Gilbert's missing ship, greeted Mary with genuine warmth, offering assistance to his tired guest. He assured her he would speak to all the interested parties, since she could not understand Norwegian, but she would need to give him time to make his inquiries—at least three weeks. Mary's heart sank at the thought of being away from Fanny for so long, but she liked this kind, intelligent man, and she also liked the lodgings he had found for her. The inn was bright and cheerful, painted barn red with bright yellow trim and a sea blue interior. It was right on the water, so Mary could watch the ships sail in and out of the harbor, just as she had in Le Havre.

An enthusiastic tourist, Mary made it her business to learn about the places she visited. On a sightseeing mission to the Tonsberg church, she stared at a macabre display of embalmed bodies lying in their coffins, arms folded, faces shriveled. Disgusted at these "human petrifications [sic]," she reflected that "nothing is so ugly as the human form when deprived of life and thus dried into stone, merely to preserve the most disgusting image of death. . . . Pugh! My stomach turns." To Mary, this evidence of corporeal decay made the existence of the soul an urgent matter. She did not want to believe that when she died, she would turn into one of these dreadful mummies, or worse, that she would simply disappear. Surely she would live on in some ineffable way. Surely she (and everyone else) had a soul. A few days later, she visited the remains of a thirteenth-century castle, high on a slope overlooking the water. Here was yet another example of the transience of human beings, particularly in contrast to the grandeur and the eternality of Nature.

Often she would "reclin[e] in the mossy down under the shelter of a rock," and so tranquil was the countryside that "the prattling of the sea . . . lulled [her] to sleep." Away from the judgmental eyes of Parisians and Londoners, freed from her responsibilities as a mother, Mary felt as though "my very soul diffused itself in the scene, and seeming to become all senses, glided in the scarcely agitated waves, melted in the freshening breeze." No more would she try "to make my feelings take an orderly course." Instead, she would accept "the extreme affection of my nature" and "the impetuous tide of [my] feelings."

The philosophy she had carved out in her letters was taking hold. Gilbert had urged her to restrain herself, to hold back and be a different person, and although she had fought with him, she had still wanted to please him. But now, here in the Norwegian countryside, she was learning to embrace her most essential qualities: "I must love and admire with warmth, or I sink into sadness." She would trust herself—her instincts, her emotions, her inclinations. She knew who she was. She knew her strengths. Even if he did not.

In the mornings Mary walked to a nearby stream, exulting in the "piney air." In the afternoons she swam and learned to row from a young pregnant woman who took her paddling in shallow waters where starfish "thickened" the water. In the evenings the genial mayor invited her to parties, which she enjoyed despite the fact that communication was largely limited to the waving of arms and the pointing of fingers. Never before had she seen "so much hair with a yellow cast." The young women were pretty, with clear eyes and open faces, and they endeared themselves to Mary by telling her "that it was a pleasure to look at me, I appeared so good natured."

However, Mary noted that the hygiene was poor and the diet un-healthy; the older people's teeth were "uncommonly bad" and the matrons grew plump thanks to an endless round of supper parties, feasts, teas, and picnics. To the abstemious Mary, it seemed that eat-ing was all anyone cared about. She yearned to absent herself from the interminable banquets, but she knew that courtesy demanded she stay. Secretly, she was grateful that she could not understand what people were saying, as she suspected her new friends were guffawing at jokes she would find off color; whenever anyone translated things for her, she was somewhat shocked by the earthy humor of her hosts. However, she did like listening to Norwegians speaking—"the lan-guage is soft, a great proportion of the words ending in vowels"—and ultimately it was a relief not to talk about herself.

As the days passed, Mary slowly returned to the ideas that had interested her before Imlay—the rights of the individual, the re-lationship of the citizen to the state, the course of French politics. After the tumult of the last two and a half years—the affair with Fuseli, the execution of Louis XVI, the Terror, Gilbert's deceptions and rejections—Mary had been disillusioned on almost all fronts. The Revolution had not turned out as she had hoped it would. Gil-bert and Fuseli were not the men she thought they were. She herself had not behaved like the independent, self-sufficient woman she prided herself on being. She questioned what had happened: to her, to Gilbert, to the world. With new insight into the limitations of human nature, freed from the responsibility of looking after Fanny, and after more than a year of deep introspection, she began to make connections between her own experiences and outside events, be-tween herself and her culture. She had always inserted personal re-flections and colloquialisms into her political and historical work, but now she turned her style almost entirely inside out. Instead of writ-ing primarily about politics and history with a few personal asides, she told the story of her love affair with Imlay and of her journey to Scandinavia, integrating philosophical observations and political theories into her own experiences. The result was an original mix of personal narrative and political science, travel writing and philosophical commentary. She described her broken heart even as she discussed her thoughts on the history of human society. She reveled in the beauties of Nature at the same time that she recalled the atrocities of the Terror. She was scarcely aware that she was breaking rules as a writer; what mattered was that the old forms could no longer contain all she wanted to say. Most important, she lost interest in berating Gilbert; he would have to rediscover his love for her on his own, she decided, trusting that when they met in Europe, as he had promised, they would have a joyful reunion.

By the first week of August, Wulfsberg had completed his inquiry, sending Mary to consult with lawyers in Larvik, about twenty miles south of Tonsberg. Once there, she was appalled at the pettiness of the officials and their corruption: "My head turned around[,] my heart grew sick, as I regarded visages deformed by vice," she wrote. Fortunately, she did not have to stay long. The lawyers sent her south to Risor, the last place anyone had seen Imlay's ship. It was here that she would at last get to meet with the captain, Ellefson, whom she had not seen since Le Havre, and who, Judge Wulfsberg believed, had clearly stolen the silver.

She traveled by sea, gazing out at the rocky shoreline and dreaming of a better future, if not for herself, then for humankind, writing in her journal words that young Mary, Claire, and Shelley would find particularly inspiring and that seemed to address them directly: "The view of this wild coast, as we sailed along it, afforded me a continual subject of meditation. I anticipated the future improvement of the world and observed how much man had still to do, to obtain of the earth all it could yield."

When Mary arrived in Risor, she found two hundred dwellings crouched along the U-shaped harbor. The historic white houses and rustic charm did not impress her, however. She could see only desolation: "To be born here was to be bastilled by nature," she complained, using her favorite image for being trapped, the Revolution still on her mind. For many years, what happened next was a mystery, but a recently discovered letter from Mary to the Danish foreign minister,

Count Andreas Peter Bernstorff, details her meeting with the missing ship's captain: "Elefsen [*sic*] waited on me, and, as we were alone, behaved in the humblest manner, wished that the affair had never happened, though he assured me that I never should be able to bring the proofs forward sufficient to convict him. He enlarged on the expense we must run into—appealed to my humanity and assured me that he could not now return the money." Faced with Ellefson's resistance, Mary asked the foreign minister for help in extracting some kind of settlement from Ellefson, but, though everyone was convinced of his guilt, no reparations were ever made.

Not surprisingly, Mary was downcast when she left Risor. She had liked Ellefson when he had stayed with them in Le Havre and felt personally betrayed by his behavior. She also suspected that now that they had final proof of the theft, Imlay would redouble his efforts to earn back the money he had lost and would declare that the dream of a life together in America was impossible. As she prepared to depart, she observed gloomily: "The clouds begin to gather, and summer disappears almost before it has ripened the fruit of autumn."

Discouraged though she was, as she sailed back toward Sweden, Mary allowed herself to hope that Imlay would appreciate her efforts. Maybe their time apart would have given him time to reflect on his behavior and, instead of being disappointed at the loss of the silver, maybe he would at last realize that his commercial enterprises were not worth the effort. After all, despite his exertions (and hers), he had lost his investment. Maybe this would help him remember what was really important in life. Love. Family. Herself. His daughter. She even allowed herself to dream that he would propose beginning again. She could see their future so clearly, as though it had already come true. Together they would enjoy a new life, reveling in their love and rejoicing in Fanny. She had not forgotten the tranquillity she had felt in the Scandinavian countryside, nor the satisfaction she had experienced in filling pages of her journal with her reflections. Nevertheless, though she had made peace with herself, at least temporarily, her feelings for Gilbert came rushing back when she contemplated her reunion with her child and the return home.

Faced with the dispiriting fact that Mary had succumbed once again to Imlay, biographers have variously painted her as pathetic, self-deluded, foolish, and weak. But a century later Freud would explain how the past haunts the present, how unconscious forces shape an individual's interpretation of the world. For Mary, Gilbert's rejection had become wrapped up with the disappointments and suffering of her past. Her mother's neglect, her father's drunkenness, the loss of Fanny Blood, Fuseli's rejection, and the attacks she had sustained for her ideas had all become entangled with his loss. She did not have the tools to understand that her pain was not all caused by Imlay and was instead an understandable response to a lifetime of painful experiences. With admirable courage and resourcefulness, she had already done more than most, effecting a partial self-cure through introspection and writing, but her time in Scandinavia was not enough to heal her entirely. Paradoxically, the strength she had gained had only intensified her resolve to regain Imlay's love. She was a better philosopher than he was. In their battles, her points were accurate and ethically superior. She would make him return to her, she decided. She would win the case against him, and in so doing she would win his love again.

# MARY SHELLEY:
## "THE MIND OF A WOMAN"

———

[ 1819 ]

I N THE LONG, STIFLING DAYS AFTER WILLIAM'S DEATH, MARY SPENT hours alone, gripped by a paralysis that prevented her from picking up her pen or even reading. The distance she and Shelley had bridged five months earlier now gaped like a chasm. The servants, Milly and the woman they had hired to do the heavy cleaning, laughed and chattered as though the world were still intact. Outside, the warblers and orioles chirped until the day's heat grew too intense. At night Mary, Claire, and Shelley sat in the garden, gazing at the stars. One evening there was a little flurry when Milly thought she had discovered a comet; Shelley, amused, said she would "make a stir, like a great astronomer."

But what Mary remembered most about these terrible days was the sameness, the silence. Later, she would regret that she could not see Shelley was mourning in his own way and that he felt abandoned, too. Not only had he lost his son, but in his mind, the woman he loved had disappeared. In her place was a tablet of grief, pale as stone.

In the first weeks after their move from Rome, Shelley poured himself into finishing *Prometheus Unbound*. His Prometheus was a hero who braved the gods to steal fire for humans, giving men the ability to progress, improve, and ultimately transcend their bestial conditions. This was a direct contradiction of Mary's *Frankenstein,* which she had subtitled *The Modern Prometheus*. To Mary, Prometheus

(Frankenstein) was an antihero: his quest for knowledge was disastrous; his ambition led to death.

Pessimism versus optimism; despair versus hope; Mary versus Shelley. They stood on opposite sides of tragedy, their conflict filtering through all aspects of their marriage, shaping not only how they coped with their losses but how they approached each other and their work. If one were unaware of the couple's philosophical fault line, it would be possible to view their books as unrelated rather than as part of a marital debate. Shelley's poem celebrates the powers of human invention; Mary's novel warns against the consequences of unchecked ambition. But when put together, *Prometheus Unbound* emerges as Shelley's response to *The Modern Prometheus,* his side of their argument, through which he holds out for hope against his wife's despair.

Of course, *Prometheus Unbound* is much more than that, but when read in this way it reveals just how distant Mary and Shelley had become. At the time Mary wrote *Frankenstein,* Shelley had not fully agreed with his wife's outlook. Instead, he had found it interesting, even alluring. Now her dark outlook seemed dangerous. To his wife's claim that human beings could not be trusted to manage their own creations, Shelley argued that disease and disaster could be eradicated by human ingenuity. In her novel, Prometheus (Frankenstein) destroys everyone he loves. In his poem, Prometheus saves the world.

By the beginning of July the couple had lost patience with each other. Although Shelley had felt stronger in Naples, his old health complaints were back. Haunted by the fatal diagnosis he had received in England, he remained certain that his time was running out and wrote with a kind of frantic desperation, seeking consolation in the idea that his poetry might live on after his death. Mary, on the other hand, wanted to stop time, or, better yet, turn the clock back. She wanted her children alive and sleeping in their beds. Regret ruled the day. As did second-guessing. Had she traded her children's health for Shelley's? If so, it was too steep a price. Her children had loved her utterly, whereas he was remote, self-absorbed, and inaccessible. If only she could join them on the other side. Her mother's ghost might be there, too, waiting to comfort her grieving daughter.

Much as she wanted to die, Mary was four and a half months

pregnant and would never condemn her unborn child to death. Even if she had not been pregnant, she had been too heavily indoctrinated by Godwin's stern teachings to succumb to suicide. She managed to write a few letters, but only to lament her situation. "May you . . . never know what it is to loose [*sic*] two only & lovely children in one year—to watch their dying moments—& then at last to be left childless & forever miserable," she wrote to Marianne Hunt.

Finally, in August, at Shelley's urging, Mary grudgingly picked up her pen and began to write in her journal. First she quoted an old poem of Shelley's, written after the suicides of Fanny and Harriet:

> *We look on the past, & stare aghast*
> *On the ghosts with aspects strange & wild*
>
> .     .     .     .     .     .     .
>
> *We two yet stand, in a lonely land,*
> *Like tombs to mark the memory*
> *Of joys & griefs that fade & flee*
> *In the light of life's dim morning.*

The lines seemed prescient; she did feel like a "tomb," a marker for the dead. To some extent, she had been raised by Godwin to experience herself this way—she was, after all, the bearer of her dead mother's name—but now these feelings of loss were sharp, unendurable. She was haunted by ghosts she loved. Loath though she was to indulge in what she termed a Clairmont display of feeling, she allowed herself a rare outburst:

> *Wednesday 4th [August 1819]*
>
> *I begin my [third] journal on Shelley's birthday—We have now lived five years together & if all the events of the five years were blotted out I might be happy—but to have won & then cruelly have lost the associations of four years is not an accident to which the human mind can bend without much suffering.*

The act of writing these few words, bitter as they were, helped Mary remember the solace she had always found in her diary. It was the first step in her journey back to life. Each day she returned to writing, little by little, and almost immediately after this entry, a heroine named Matilda arrived in her imagination, fully conceived, trailing a story behind her that in many ways was more frightening than *Frankenstein*.

Mary sketched out the new novel with astonishing rapidity, the gloom of the plot reflecting her desolation. The motherless Matilda discovers that her father harbors an incestuous love for her; he kills himself, then she, too, dies, of self-inflicted consumption, uttering, *"A little patience, and all will be over."* Mary italicized these words, as they are the deathbed words spoken by Wollstonecraft, Wollstonecraft's mother, and the mother in Wollstonecraft's last novel, *Maria*. Matilda's death unites Matilda with her dead father, but Matilda's words also link her to her author and her author's mother.

Incest, as Shelley's poetry had already shown, was a common Romantic theme. Indeed, while Mary was writing about Matilda, Shelley was upstairs working on a tale of father/daughter incest, a play he would call *The Cenci*, based on a historical story he and Mary had discovered together. Beatrice Cenci was a beautiful young girl, famous in Italian history for killing her father after he raped her. The Shelleys had seen her portrait in Rome at the Palazzo Colonna, where Shelley had been struck by her resemblance to Mary. Like Mary, Beatrice was "pale," with a "large and clear" forehead. She seemed "sad and stricken down in spirit. . . . Her eyes, which we are told were remarkable for their vivacity, are swollen with weeping and lusterless, but beautifully tender and serene." Alone, he had made a pilgrimage to the dark, fortresslike Palazzo Cenci in the Piazza delle Cinque Scole, near the Tiber River.

But Mary's take on incest was entirely different from Shelley's. She was intent on exploring the parallels between herself and her fictional creation. Both she and Matilda lose their mothers in childbirth and both lose their fathers; however, Matilda's father kills himself because he loves her too much, whereas Mary's father cut her off because of her love affair with Shelley. For Mary, who had felt rejected by her father when Mary-Jane entered their lives, and again after she ran away with Shelley, the idea of a father loving his daughter too much was undoubtedly a gratifying fantasy. But it was also an apt psychological representation of Mary's own experience. Over the course of their life together, despite no actual sexual relations, Godwin had indeed played the psychic role of the disappointed lover, outraged at being displaced by Shelley.

Ultimately, like the creature in *Frankenstein,* Matilda decides it is she who is monstrous, when in actuality it is her parent who is the true monster. For what, after all, is Matilda's crime, or, for that matter, the creature's? No child can be held accountable for his or her own birth, and so Mary placed the blame squarely on the shoulders of the fathers even as she pointed to the faulty (and tragic) logic of children.

For Shelley, on the other hand, incest was an opportunity to expose the corruption of institutions and the men at their helm. In Count Cenci, Beatrice's father, a cruel historical tyrant, Shelley found the perfect emblem for unchecked paternalistic power. Unlike Mary, he did not explore the psychology of the main characters. He glossed over Beatrice's inner life, using her story to convey his angry defiance of oppression and to articulate his philosophy, derived from Godwin, that the liberty of the individual is a necessary component of a virtuous state. Beatrice is a heroine because she defeats the evil ruler.

To Mary, what mattered most was precisely what Shelley had skipped over: the feelings of the victim, the woman's inner life—the themes her mother had focused on in her books. In *Matilda,* good and evil seep into each other so that all of the characters wander around in a fog of moral gray. Matilda's external world is curiously empty. Not once does she refer to church or state, the evil institutional forces that rule Shelley's *Cenci.* Her tragedy results from her relationship with her father, not from the corruption of power. That Mary was aware of her differences with her husband becomes clear at the end of the novel, when she introduces another character, a young man named Woodville, who bears a striking resemblance to Shelley.

Woodville and Matilda become fast friends, but, strangely, not paramours. Matilda does not want Woodville to fall in love with her; she
wants him to merge with her despair, just as Mary wanted Shelley to
join her in her grief. But Woodville refuses and instead scrutinizes
Matilda from afar, leading her to exclaim:

> I am, I thought, a tragedy; a character that he comes to see me
> act: now and then he gives me my cue that I may make a speech
> more to his purpose; perhaps he is already planning a poem in
> which I am to figure. . . . He takes all the profit and I bear all
> the burthen.

In fictional form, Mary articulated her rage at Shelley's desertion.
Instead of supporting her, Shelley had stepped back and was studying
her, using her as a model for Beatrice. In a retaliatory swipe, Mary has
Matilda beg Woodville to die with her, and when he refuses, because
one day he might be able to do something to improve the world,
Matilda sinks to her death, her words expressing her (and her author's) feeling of betrayal:

> Farewell Woodville, the turf will soon be green on my grave;
> and the violets will bloom on it. There is my hope and expec-
> tation; yours are in this world; may they be fulfilled.

One can almost picture Mary writing these words in the garden
while Shelley was out walking with her stepsister or up on the rooftop
in his glass cell. Although it is understandable that Woodville (Shelley)
would choose life over death, for Matilda (Mary), this choice represented a rejection, a focus on the outside world rather than on the
woman he loved. To Mary, it seemed that Shelley was more interested
in the fictional Beatrice than in her. The other way to see it, which did
not make her feel any better, was that he was making her, his own
wife, into a fictional character. Besides, it was not fair. Neither Mary
nor her fictional alter ego had the same set of choices as Shelley or
Woodville; the world was not open to them as it was to men.

———

AT THE END OF SEPTEMBER the unhappy entourage moved to Florence to be near their favorite physician, Dr. Bell, so he could oversee the birth and watch over Shelley's health. Still, it was difficult to leave Livorno; the Gisbornes had been valiant mainstays that summer, propping them up in their dejection. As the Shelleys rolled down the pitted dirt road, departing from the villa for the last time, the Gisbornes' dog, Oscar, bounded alongside, his tail wagging goodbye. The servant Giuseppe had to "catch him up in his arms to stop his course," Maria later reported in a letter to Shelley. For several days, the dog was inconsolable. He howled "piteously" at dinnertime and "scratch[ed] with all his might at the door of [the Shelleys'] abandoned house."

"Poor Oscar!" Shelley responded. "I feel a kind of remorse to think of the unequal love with which two animated beings regard each other, when I experience no such sensations for him as those which he manifested for us. His importunate regret is however a type of ours as regards you. Our memory—if you will accept so humble a metaphor—is forever scratching at the door of your absence."

They settled into modest lodgings in a rooming house near Santa Maria Novella on the Via Valfonde. The other lodgers were a predictable mix of middlebrow tourists: maiden ladies, widows, and members of the clergy, not unlike the clientele so aptly described a hundred years later by E. M. Forster in his novel *A Room with a View*. Meals were included in the price, but dining at the rooming house's long table was an awkward experience, as the other English visitors regarded the notorious Shelley trio with polite horror.

Mary remained melancholy that fall. She took an immediate dislike to their landlady and did not accompany Shelley on his gallery visits, instead staying at home, resting, reading, and working on *Matilda*. Claire continued her vocal training and began to study French, so Shelley mainly toured the sights alone. One of his favorite walks was outside the city walls, where he spent hours "watching the leaves and the rising and falling of the Arno."

Although he had tried to distance himself from Mary's despair, Shelley had grown increasingly depressed as summer turned to fall. He was preoccupied by an attack on his "personal character" that had appeared in a review of *The Revolt of Islam* in *The Quarterly Review*. The most reputable journal of the era, the *Quarterly* was widely read, and its articles carried considerable weight, which made its criticism even harder to stomach. It had become common knowledge that Shelley had inscribed "Democrat, Philanthropist, and Atheist" in the Chamonix register, and the reviewer spent the bulk of the article on Shelley's immorality, his radical politics, and his stance against religion:

> Mr Shelley would abrogate our laws—this would put an end to felonies and misdemenours [*sic*] at a blow; he would abolish the rights of property, of course there could thenceforward be no violation of them, no heartburnings between the poor and the rich, no disputed wills, no litigated inheritances . . . he would overthrow the constitution, and then we should have no expensive court . . . no army or navy; he would pull down our churches, level our Establishment, and burn our bibles . . . marriage he cannot endure, and there would at once be a stop put to the lamented increase of adulterous connections amongst us, whilst repealing the canon of heaven against incest, he would add to the purity and heighten the ardour of those feelings with which brother and sister now regard each other; finally as the basis of the whole scheme, he would have us renounce our belief in our religion.

Shelley read the article in Delesert's English Library. Most English expatriates recognized the notorious Shelley, and so, unbeknownst to the poet, he was witnessed by a stranger, who later reported that after Shelley had finished reading, "he straightened up suddenly and burst into a convulsive laughter, closed the book with an hysteric laugh, and hastily left the room, his Ha! Ha's! ringing down the stairs."

Although Shelley made light of the review to his friends, calling it "trash," he was profoundly demoralized, a feeling compounded by his growing sense of mortality. One October day, he looked in the mirror and discovered a gray hair. He was no longer a young poet, he told himself. His "passion for reforming the world" was slowly ebbing. The world had rejected him. But worse than that, so had his wife.

# MARY WOLLSTONECRAFT:
# RETURN HOME

———

[ 1795–1796 ]

*W*HEN MARY ARRIVED BACK IN GOTHENBURG IN THE THIRD WEEK of August, Marguerite handed her three letters from Imlay. Mary's heart rose. These would be the letters in which at last Imlay confessed his love, in which he finally realized his loss. But each of Gilbert's letters was worse than the one before. In the first, he announced that he was through vacillating and had decided that he no longer loved Mary and saw her as a burden. In the second, he implored her to see how different they were. In the third, he promised to do his duty by Fanny and said he would try to be kind to Mary, but that was all he could offer. Their affair was over. "Our minds are not congenial," he said flatly, uttering words that were calculated to wound, since he knew that Mary had wanted to believe that their minds were as united as their hearts.

Mary hurled back a response by return post. Yes, she said, she and Gilbert were entirely different, because "I have lived in an ideal world, and fostered sentiments that you do not comprehend or you would not treat me thus." She refused to be "merely an object of compassion" and shrugged off his "protection without his affection." She could earn her own living. He would never hear from her again, she wrote angrily. By all means, if he thought she was a burden, he should forget about her, and Fanny, too, but he should know how much pain he had caused: she was filled with pity for her fatherless child;

her lips shook "from cold," though a "fire" seemed to burn through her veins. Not once did it occur to her that something else might be wrong. Her focus on Gilbert precluded all other explanations. But in hindsight, it seems likely that being a mother was continuing to take a toll on her spirits. Instead of feeling more joyful when she was reunited with Fanny, she had sunk immediately back into her melancholy. Whether or not this was a continuation of the postpartum darkness of the previous year or was more situational—the result of being abandoned to raise her child by herself—is impossible to ascertain. What is striking is that much as she loved her little girl, it had only been when she and Fanny were separated, when she had been deep in the Scandinavian countryside, able to reflect and to write—to be herself again—that she had reestablished any sense of equanimity.

On their way home, Mary, Marguerite, and Fanny traveled through Copenhagen, where Mary vented her feelings by painting a bleak picture in her letters; a recent fire had burned the city almost to the ground. The foolishness of the rulers and the selfishness of the rich, Mary declared, had allowed the flames to get out of hand. She condemned the "indolence" of the population, writing, "If the people of property had taken half as much pains to extinguish the fire, as to reserve their valuables and furniture, it would soon have been got under [control]." The individuals she met struck her as inferior and uncultivated. The men were "domestic tyrants," the women "without accomplishments," and the children were "spoilt."

Though Fanny crowed at the seabirds and Marguerite's chatter helped pass the time, nothing could take Mary's mind off Gilbert's rejection. Perhaps, she thought, it was because she had failed in her commission. She told herself that when Gilbert met them in Hamburg, she would try one more time to persuade him to live with her, but when they arrived in Germany she found that, as usual, he had reneged on his promise. He wrote to inform them that he would not be meeting them in Europe. He was through with Mary's harangues.

Although Mary had promised herself that she would not write to him again, she did, trying her best to convince him he was wrong. Her headaches returned and she began to dream about death once again: "But for this child, I would lay my head on [the rocks], and never open my eyes again!"

They arrived back in England in the first week of October. At last Mary would have the opportunity to convince Imlay in person of his many errors. She sent him several notes from Dover, entreating, then demanding his presence, and waited in port for a few days. The alarmed Marguerite watched Mary fall back into despair and did her best to amuse her mistress and her little charge. "Ah," wrote Mary in yet another letter to Gilbert, she has "a *gaeité du coeur* worth all of my philosophy."

When it became clear that he was not going to materialize, Mary bought seats on the public coach and they made the long journey to London, where Gilbert had rented them a house, hired servants, and left a message that they should let him know if there was anything else they needed. The next day, he paid them a visit and struggled to make peace, but Mary had too much riding on their relationship to let it end quietly. She felt that if she could not have his love, at least she should have his admission that he was a cad. Then she would be the sole occupier of higher ground.

Gilbert refused to admit any wrongdoing, however, and retaliated by staying away for the next week or so. This sort of silence was far more difficult for Mary to bear than arguments and angry letters. She felt the darkness of the previous spring settle in. Now, isolated with her baby, in the shameful situation of being an unwed mother, her philosophy in tatters, she tried to marshal her strength. She began unpacking her boxes, directing the new servants, and organizing her household, and turned her attention to regaining her financial independence. She knew that she needed to start writing again, but she could barely limp through her list of domestic duties. She felt scrutinized and judged by the cook, kitchen maid, and housemaid Gilbert had hired. She and Marguerite were used to managing on their own; now they were living in a fishbowl. She was unfailingly kind to her new staff, but she knew they wondered about her domestic arrangement. Why didn't Mr. Imlay live with his wife? The cook grew suddenly silent whenever Mary entered the room. The maids whispered behind her back. It was clear they were talking about her.

Finally, after a few days of this, Mary did something she was not proud of; she went downstairs to the kitchen and, as she later said, "forced" a "confession" from the cook. This took some prodding, since the poor woman did not want to lose her job and Gilbert paid her salary. But Mary cajoled, urged, reasoned, and reassured until at last the cook broke down and told Mary that Gilbert was living with another woman, a beautiful young actress. To Mary, this was everything she had feared. Gilbert had repeatedly told her that he needed freedom when it came to women. But this was the first time she had evidence of his infidelity. Mary extracted the woman's name and address from the frightened cook and rushed out the door to confront Gilbert.

When she arrived, Gilbert let her in before she could make a public spectacle. Once inside, Mary did not actually upbraid Gilbert for his new love affair. Instead, she announced that she had several ideas about what should happen next: Gilbert should live with her and keep his mistress in a separate establishment. Or, if that would not work, they should all live together. She hoped these proposals would prove to Gilbert (and to herself) how independent she was, and how honorable—his betrayal hurt her on every level, but she would remain true to her beliefs regarding love and relationships. She could do without him as a lover, but she wanted Fanny to have a father, and she wanted his friendship. Unlike Gilbert, she was willing to make sacrifices. She was deeply disappointed that he was so flawed, but she hoped that her selflessness and her rectitude would inspire him to love her again, or at the very least would remind him of his better self. She begged to know if this was a possibility.

Gilbert was used to Mary and her ideas, but what must his young mistress have thought? With wild hair, tears streaming down her cheeks, and passionate declarations, Mary must have seemed like a madwoman. She spoke in a rush, with vehemence, trying to persuade Gilbert to include her in his plans. Loyalty to his new love did not mean he had to cast her and Fanny aside. Why should she have to live alone just because of Gilbert's fickleness and society's rules? Why should a daughter be deprived of a father because Gilbert had fallen in love with someone else? Fanny should grow up in a home with two parents, even if that home had to include her father's mistress. Mary and Gilbert could be companions, loving companions, and he could sleep with his new young woman. Here she turned her attention to her rival. Had she thought about what might happen if Gilbert abandoned her, too? Clearly, he was restless. Soon he would want someone new. Did she have any education or a profession she could fall back on besides prostitution?

At first Gilbert listened, but his mistress, who was in fact far more conventional than either Gilbert or Mary, was having none of it. She refused to live anywhere near this crazy person, she declared, and if Gilbert did not send Mary packing, then she would. Before they could push her out the door, Mary fled home, humiliated and devastated, her face flaming, her head pounding. Back in her room, she paced "in a state of chaos."

Although she tried to envision staying alive for Fanny's sake, Mary could no longer overcome the urge to die. Life was too painful, and Fanny needed a better mother, a real family. It was time to stop fighting; and with this decision she felt suddenly "serene" (just as she had before). She would never have to battle again. Her humiliations were over.

Philosopher that she was, over the last few years Mary had arrived at what she considered sound ethical underpinnings for suicide, and these underpinnings were what she had used to justify her suicide attempt the preceding spring. Choosing death had become a way to assert her integrity and regain some power in the face of her powerlessness. The Revolution had caused her to regard suicide as an honorable form of protest, courageous and highly moral; although most of the brave individuals she had known had not killed themselves of their own accord but had instead been forced to the guillotine, Mary still understood their deaths as noble—they had not recanted their beliefs, but instead had died the sort of principled death that she would like to emulate. Now, having survived her first attempt only to suffer still further, she had come to see death not only as an avenue to peace, but also as a final bid for independence. At last she would be free of all the restrictions she faced as a woman. At last, she could express the purity of her ideals and her condemnation of Gilbert's betrayal. She was strengthened in her resolve by an insight that had struck her upon seeing a waterfall in Norway:

> The impetuous dashing of the rebounding torrent from the dark cavities which mocked the exploring eye, produced an equal activity in my mind: my thoughts darted from earth to heaven, and I asked myself why I was chained to life and its misery? Still the tumultuous emotions this sublime object excited were pleasurable; and viewing it, my soul rose, with renewed dignity, above its cares—grasping at immortality. . . . I stretched out my hand to eternity, bounding over the dark speck of life to come.

Suicide had become more than an escape from suffering; it was a leap into eternal life. Feeling firm in her convictions and holding on to her vision of immortality, she took the night to organize her belongings and her papers. The next morning, October 10, she wrote a final letter to Gilbert, giving him instructions. Fanny should be sent back to France to be raised by Mary's German friends, and Marguerite should be given Mary's clothes. Gilbert must not punish the cook for betraying his location; Mary had compelled the poor woman to tell her the truth. After these details, Mary gave way to her feelings. "I would encounter a thousand deaths, rather than a night like the last. . . . I shall plunge myself into the Thames where there is the least chance of my being snatched from the death I seek." In death she would find peace, she said, since she had behaved with virtue. He, on the other hand, would suffer torturous regret over how he had treated her. Her ghost would haunt him, reminding him of how far he had fallen: "in the midst of business and sensual pleasure, I shall appear before you the victim of your deviation from rectitude." Forever would he be the criminal. Forever would she be the victim. He had chosen money and worldly pursuits over sentiment and imagination. He had allowed himself to be dominated by selfish concerns, whereas she had been too finely wrought and too sensitive for a world ruled by "self interest."

Dressed in her finest clothes, Mary kissed Fanny goodbye and left her with Marguerite. She walked to the Strand in the rain that had just begun to fall and hired a man to row her west to Putney, near where she had lived with Fanny Blood. As they went upriver, the weather worsened, the skies deepened, and by the time they reached their destination, the rain was coming down hard and the landing was deserted. Mary paid the boatman six shillings and climbed out, thanking him, as he remembered later. For the next half hour she walked back and forth along the river, stalling, perhaps, but also waiting for the boat to pull out of sight. By this time it was pouring and she was drenched, but soon she would be in the river and her wet skirts would help her sink.

She climbed the hill to the Putney Bridge, dropped her halfpenny in the tollbox, and headed across. Her hair dripped down the back of her neck. It was cold. But soon she would find comfort; she had to be patient, just as her mother had said on her deathbed. Halfway across the bridge, she climbed the railing and, without pausing, took the sickening plunge. As she went under, the river whirled her around, and Mary strained to stop breathing. She had not realized how difficult it would be to drown; she had pictured slipping into the embrace of death. But in reality it was hard work. Again and again, she had to force her head under and the "bitterness" of the urge to breathe took her by surprise. Finally she floated downriver, drifting into unconsciousness. She had come to the end of her struggles.

Or so she thought.

The Royal Humane Society had recently developed a policy of paying rewards to those who rescued suicides. Although Mary had thought the river was deserted, two canny fishermen were on the lookout for just such a lucrative moment. They hurried after her floating body, catching up with her about two hundred yards downriver, and within a few minutes they had pulled Mary on board, resuscitated her, and dropped her off at the nearest tavern, the Duke's Head, where, presumably, they collected their reward. The tavern keeper's wife helped Mary remove her wet dress and wrapped her in warm blankets. Frozen and stunned, Mary was left in a back room, shivering. On the other side of the door, life went on. She could hear the clink of tankards, raucous shouts, and bursts of laughter. A doc-

*A view of the Putney Bridge, a common place for suicides.*

tor was called, and he pronounced her healthy: her lungs were clear and her heart steady.

Mary expressed no gratitude to her rescuers, or to the doctor. She felt "inhumanely brought back to life and misery"; having won the battle against the physical pain of drowning, she had experienced a brief but glorious respite, had at last felt nothing, and now the living were crowded around her barking questions: Who was she? Why had she done this? Whom should they contact to take her home? This was her second attempt to kill herself, she said with what dignity she could still muster. And she had done it because of her husband's ill treatment.

She knew that by now Gilbert would have received her suicide note and that before long he would track her down. Sure enough, within a few hours a coach rattled up, but instead of Gilbert, in rushed her old friend Rebecca Christie, the wife of Thomas Christie, who, along with Johnson, had hired Mary to write for the *Analytical Review*. Mary had spent many hours with the Christies while they were in Paris and had helped sustain Rebecca through Thomas's public and tempestuous affair with a Frenchwoman. Ultimately, Thomas had come back to Rebecca, and together the Christies had recently returned to London. Fresh from her experience of her husband's infi-

delity, Rebecca was sympathetic and took Mary back to the Christies'
house, sending for Marguerite and Fanny.

At Thomas and Rebecca's comfortable home, Mary recovered
enough to rail against Gilbert. He did not come see her, but he wrote
the next day, wondering "how to extricate ourselves out of the
wretchedness into which we have been plunged." Mary wrote back
angrily, "You are extricated long since." When he offered her money,
she told him he was only trying to protect his reputation. When he
did visit her a few days later, she said it was for the sake of appearances, not to "soothe my distracted mind." Gradually, Mary was beginning to accept that the man she thought she loved was actually of
her own creation, "an imaginary being." The real Imlay was far
weaker; when he was in love with her, Mary's idealism had inspired
him to change, but without her he had reverted to his natural shallow
inclinations.

And yet, curiously, Imlay would not break off the connection.
Maybe he was still attached to Mary. Perhaps he wanted to live up to
her ideals and prove his credentials as a freethinker. Maybe he just
wanted to avoid more dramatic episodes. Or perhaps he simply
wanted to save money: one establishment was cheaper than two. In
any case, a few weeks into her recovery, when Mary again voiced her
idea that they should all live together—Imlay, the mistress, Fanny,
Marguerite, and herself—Gilbert agreed. After all, there would be
some benefits to such an arrangement: Fanny would have a father.
Gilbert would learn to live in a family, which would be good for
him—Mary had said this, and he could see her point—and Mary
would not have to raise a child alone, which would give her the time
to write and earn money.

They rented a house in Finsbury Square near the Christies. The
more Mary regained her strength, the more she managed to feel sorry
for Gilbert's "actress," taking every opportunity to preach the benefits of independence to this young woman, whose name has not come
down through history, but who seems to have had no interest in
being "improved," at least not by Mary. But Mary persisted. If the
actress could be educated, who knew what she could achieve? Perhaps she would even move on from Gilbert. But before Mary had a

chance to teach her anything, the girl put her foot down once again, vetoing the living arrangement for a second time. She could not understand Mary. Instead of seeking to destroy her rival, Mary had tried to be friends. When she fought with Gilbert, she spouted philosophy and quoted foreign writers. She paid no attention to fashion. She did not care what people thought about her. The actress could not see how Gilbert could ever have loved this strange female. She cried and nagged until—in the throes of "passion," as Mary wrote contemptuously—Gilbert bowed to her demands, taking her to Paris toward the end of November. He tried to send Mary money that winter, but she refused his offers, despite the urging of her friends.

Something had finally shifted for Mary. Perhaps it was that at eighteen months, Fanny could say a few words and reach her arms out to her mother, giving Mary a powerful incentive to recover from her despair. Perhaps she had realized that Imlay was not the man she had thought he was. Or perhaps the self-reflection in Scandinavia had taught her more than she realized. She demanded her letters back from Imlay and tried to use them to write a novel about their love affair, but the material was too close to home and so she began developing another idea. She would not fictionalize her experience. Instead, she would edit her letters from Scandinavia and turn her broken heart into a book that would honestly examine her struggle with despair. It would be a travelogue and reflection, an observation and self-examination. When at length she sat down to write, she realized the project had been in the back of her mind all along.

Travel writing was traditionally a male genre, but Mary had reviewed more than twenty travel books for Johnson before she left for Paris, and she felt confident she could write an account of her experience that would be beneficial to her readers and that they would find fascinating. As winter approached, she went through her notes and letters, rediscovering her strength and her resourcefulness. Yes, Imlay had broken her heart, but she had been rescued, brought back to life; she did not know why, but maybe there was a reason, one that she would find if she started writing again.

Mary found her own rooms near Rebecca at 16 Finsbury Place, a quiet neighborhood close to the famous bookstore the Temple of the Muses (owned by Lackington's, the publishing house that would one day publish her daughter's *Frankenstein*), not far from St. Paul's Churchyard and Johnson's house, and there she spent her days cutting and reorganizing the letters, excising self-pity, rage, redundancy, and recrimination and reframing parts of the story. She omitted complaints that made her sound hysterical or irrational. Originally she had written that her spirits were "deranged" when she arrived in Gothenburg, but she revised this so that her arrival was now "peaceful," describing how she "gazed around with rapture." She dropped her stance as "the abandoned woman" and presented herself as a "woman of observation"—a woman in control of her circumstances. To this end, she added descriptions of the habits of the people and the landscapes, as well as hard-won and often humorous self-reflection. Gone were the over-the-top ventings and the emotional indulgences written during the crises, and in their place were artful, carefully designed vignettes.

One of the most poignant captures a farmer and his children heading home from a day in the fields. At first Mary idealizes their rural life, saying she wishes she were the farmer's wife, but then she laughs at herself, reminding the reader of what it is really like to be a farmer's wife: "My eyes followed them to the cottage, and an involuntary sigh whispered to my heart that I envied the mother, much as I dislike cooking, who was preparing their pottage." About small towns, she observes that since no one cares about literature, art, or politics, "a good dinner appears to be the only centre to rally round." She did pursue her feud with Imlay, but only covertly. Instead of attacking him personally, she critiqued business and business interests, mercantilism and the pursuit of wealth.

With each paragraph, she felt her energy returning. Just as it always had, writing was giving Mary a new purchase on life. She began to go out in the evenings with Rebecca Christie, her trusted companion, but more important, she woke up in the morning anticipating the day of work that lay ahead. At times, she even caught herself wondering what the future might now hold for her. By December, she was finished. Joseph Johnson published Mary Wollstonecraft's *Letters Written During a Short Residence in Sweden, Norway, and Denmark* in January 1796.

Readers were instantly captivated by the more personal style Mary had adopted, and the book sold briskly, earning more money than any of her earlier works, and was translated into German, Dutch, Swedish, and Portuguese. Even though some critics carped at the book's unorthodox mixture of sentiment, philosophy, personal revelation, and politics, the inclusion of Mary's reflections and feelings allowed readers to feel connected to her, while at the same time they learned about places they would probably never see. Mary seemed wise, warm, and close enough to touch, so close that one reader—her future husband—would say, "If ever there was a book calculated to make a man in love with its author, this appears to me to be the book." But *Letters* was more than a charming self-portrait, more than the flame that would draw Godwin. The book is a psychological journey, one of the first explicit examinations of an author's inner life, tracing Mary's path from despair to self-acceptance, from desolation to a hard-won tranquillity. As such, *Letters from Sweden* is a reflective, innovative book, an emotional but philosophical announcement of the author's artistic goals, her initiation of an artistic revolution. As one modern critic puts it, Mary's "revolutionary feminism" allowed her to transform the genre of travel writing.

In fact, the avant-garde of her generation viewed *Letters from Sweden* as the most significant and beautiful of all her works, and it would quickly become the touchstone for many of their own poems. Coleridge's meticulous description of psychic pain in *Dejection: An Ode* would echo Mary's record of her suffering: "A grief without a pang, void, dark, and drear, / A stifled, drowsy, unimpassioned grief, / Which finds no natural outlet, no relief, / In word, or sigh, or tear." Many of the lines from *Kubla Khan* were directly inspired by *Letters from Sweden:* "A savage place! As holy and enchanted / As e'er beneath a waning moon was haunted / By woman wailing for her demon-lover," as were passages from *The Rime of the Ancient Mariner* and *Frost at Midnight*. Wordsworth's ideas about Nature and the imagination in *The Prelude* were largely anticipated by Wollstonecraft.

"She has made me in love with a . . . northern moonlight," said the influential poet Robert Southey. And, twenty years later, Shelley derived his thinking about the genius of the poet from *Letters from Sweden,* which he reread many times.

Mary had elevated the exploration of the inner life by integrating self-reflection with political and historical observations. Though Rousseau had done this before her, Mary was among the first English writers to declare that the psychological journey was as important as the external, the self as worthy of exploration as a foreign land. *Letters from Sweden* was more an interior pilgrimage than a travelogue, an account of the author's struggle and her eventual self-acceptance, and as such was the first of its kind. Not only had Mary celebrated the imagination, she had offered a glimpse into her creative inspiration:

> How often do my feelings produce ideas that remind me of the origin of many poetical fictions. In solitude, the imagination bodies forth its conceptions unrestrained, and stops enraptured to adore the beings of its own creation. These are moments of bliss; and the memory recalls them with delight.

That the mind can create actual "beings" and that "feelings" can "produce ideas"; that inspiration comes from inside the self, not outside, from emotions, not logic; that the wanderer can see truths in Nature that the city dweller misses; that in solitary contemplation the artist combines emotion and thought, recollection and observation, to create a new universe, new creatures, a new vision for humankind— these are the principal tenets of Romanticism, and Mary articulated them six years before Wordsworth's famous preface to the *Lyrical Ballads,* traditionally viewed as the first Romantic manifesto in England. In fact, it is *Letters from Sweden* that "vindicated" emotion, subjectivity, and psychological complexity, the book that showed the Romantics a new writing world.

But despite the importance of *Letters from Sweden*'s innovations, Mary's book has only recently been acknowledged for the role it played in literary history. At the time, as with any unorthodox work, *Letters from Sweden* prompted bitter criticism. A French traveler to

Sweden, Bernard de la Tocnaye, called the book "grotesque," "new-fangled," and "modish nonsense." *The Monthly Magazine* and *The American Review* were shocked by Mary's unconventional theology, accusing her of "discard[ing] all faith in Christianity." The writer Anna Seward ridiculed the change Wollstonecraft had undergone from the *Vindications* to *Letters from Sweden*. *The Monthly Mirror* scoffed at the mixture of her personal reflections and political observations, calling her ideas confused and contradictory.

And yet *Letters from Sweden* has had lasting appeal. Fifty years later, it would inspire a generation of British travelers. Among the most famous were two women: Mary Kingsley, who voyaged to Africa and wrote a book exposing the horrors perpetrated by British imperialist policy, and Isabella Bird, who wrote more than fifteen best-selling works about her travels to Hawaii, India, Tibet, Japan, Singapore, Malaysia, China, and Australia. And when *Letters from Sweden* was reissued at the end of the century, Robert Louis Stevenson, the author of *Treasure Island* and a dear friend of Wollstonecraft's grandson, Percy Florence Shelley, took along a dog-eared copy on his voyage to Samoa.

Perhaps most significant of all, though, was the impact the volume had on Mary's own daughter, Mary Shelley, who would one day model her own travel books on *Letters from Sweden*—*History of a Six Weeks' Tour* and *Rambles in Germany and Italy*—works that would bookend her career, the first and the last that she published. Certainly she never forgot her mother's praise of the imagination, immortalizing Wollstonecraft in her famous preface to the revised *Frankenstein* in 1831. Right before she gives her account of the inception of her novel, she describes her own beginnings as an artist: "It was beneath the trees . . . that my true compositions, the airy flights of my imagination, were born and fostered. . . . I could people the hours with creations." What better restatement could there be of her mother's ideas? Mary had found a way to keep her mother's legacy alive.

# MARY SHELLEY:
# "WHEN WINTER COMES"

———

[ 1819–1820 ]

"READ—WORK—WALK—READ—WORK." SUCH IS MARY SHELLEY'S record of her activities in the weeks before her fourth baby was due. Though she rarely used her journal as an emotional outlet, these entries have a strangely flat quality, as though she had nothing else to say. In her letters to the Hunts she wrote that she felt as though she were not quite alive. Caught as she was between death and life, between losing a child and gaining a child, looking forward was as dangerous as looking back. Anything was better than hope. Nothing was worse than memory.

In the evenings, Shelley read aloud—Clarendon's *The History of the Rebellion and Civil Wars in England* and Plato's *Republic*. He had chosen these authors because right before they had arrived in Florence, the Shelleys had heard news from home that shocked them both and provoked Shelley into writing one of his angriest, most political poems, *The Mask of Anarchy*. Although it has since been called "the greatest poem of political protest ever written in English," *The Mask of Anarchy* contained so many radical ideas that publishers refused to print it in Shelley's lifetime.

On August 16, 1819, at St. Peter's Field on the outskirts of Manchester, armed government troops broke up a crowd of sixty thousand working men and women who were staging a public meeting to determine how to achieve reform through "the most legal and effectual means." More than a hundred women and children were seriously injured. The death toll was eleven, including a child who was trampled to death. Liberals everywhere were outraged, and almost immediately the tragic event became known as Peterloo, a notorious example of government brutality.

To Mary, this was yet more fuel for her despair. Yet for Shelley, it was galvanizing—a sign that revolution had to be coming in Britain, for who could tolerate such naked governmental oppression? Surely the people would soon rise up in protest. He spent his time in Florence prowling around the Uffizi gallery, searching for "that ideal beauty of which we have so intense yet so obscure an apprehension." Beauty and justice, like Keats's beauty and truth, had fused in Shelley's mind: the perfect human form achieved by Renaissance sculptors and the perfect government envisioned by Plato, Rousseau, or Locke shared the same source—they sprang from the human imagination. The artist's job was to summon these ideals, to envision and embody them so others could be inspired. Only in this way could the human condition improve. To Shelley, a great work of art could overthrow tyranny just as decisively as an army could. In fact, more decisively, because a painting or a poem could change people's minds and souls, something brute force could never do.

Energized by righteous indignation, Shelley began to prepare for action. He wanted *The Mask of Anarchy* to be the first step in an uprising against oppression. To Shelley it did not matter whether the victim was one person (for example, a wronged artist such as himself) or sixty thousand working men and women, whether the tyrant was one critic or a trained militia sponsored by Parliament. Injustice was injustice. Despotism was despotism. Like the protesters at St. Peter's Field, he, too, had been brutalized, most recently in the *Quarterly*'s review, and it was his obligation to do something about it. "Hope is a duty," he wrote to Maria Gisborne, yet he was finding hope elusive. His mysterious pains were back. His wife was hardly speaking to him. He tried to craft a response to the *Quarterly,* one that spoke for the Peterloo victims as well as himself, but the task became overwhelming, and after a few aborted attempts, he felt so much worse that he gave up, ate lunch, and went for a walk along the river. It was one of those days when a storm was coming—Shelley's favorite kind of weather; the clouds swept across the sky and the wind rattled through the plane trees, at once "tempestuous" and "animating," Shelley said, jotting down his thoughts in the notebook he always carried with him.

His anger at the *Quarterly* dissolved and he stayed outside, roaming along the Arno, until rain began to pelt down. Then he rushed home and poured forth on paper the consolation his walk had offered, how the wind, full of force, had driven his ghosts away, how everything grim and sharp—William's death, his repudiation by the literary world, his wife's sorrow and her reproaches, his aging, his debt, Peterloo, the dual suicides, his father's hatred—had somehow lost its power. Without realizing that these would be among the most famous lines he would ever write, he began with certainty:

> *O wild West wind, thou breath of Autumn's being,*
> *Thou from whose unseen presence the leaves dead*
> *Are driven, like ghosts from an enchanter fleeing.*

He flew through three more stanzas that evening and worked on the poem for the next five days, writing the last lines in another notebook. At first he thought the poem should end with a declaration: "When Winter comes, Spring lags not far behind!" But he decided to change this into a question, darkening the poem and rendering more accurately his own uncertainties: "If winter comes, can spring be far behind?"

Mary could not respond with any kind of reassurance. It is not even clear when she first read this poem. Years later, after Shelley had died, she would have to reconstruct *Western Wind,* divided as it was between two notebooks. To further complicate matters, Shelley had begun drafting a story in Italian in ink over the pencil manuscript of the first three stanzas. Ultimately, piecing together *Western Wind,* as well as Shelley's other poems, would bring Mary to the brink of breakdown. She would berate herself: if only she could have been more compassionate, if only she could have reached out to Shelley and listened to his struggles. At the time, she was too consumed by grief. It was her writing that offered relief, not her husband.

Each day, Mary worked on the final pages of *Matilda,* even though her baby was due any moment. She emphasized the dangers Matilda faced without a mother, an expression of her own loss of Wollstonecraft but also one of her favorite political and literary themes—the indictment of a world without mothers, a world in which women are prevented from occupying leadership roles, either inside the family or out. In *Frankenstein,* without maternal love the creature turns to violence and Frankenstein's ambition is allowed to flourish unchecked; in *Matilda,* the death of her mother exposes Matilda to the predations of her father. In fact, it is the death of the mother that sparks the father's lust, since, to Mary, all problems began with the erasure of maternal influence. For her, the moral was clear: uncontrolled patriarchal power was dangerous for everyone, including men. Women needed to be empowered in order to rein in men's appetites, and, more important, to offer an alternative mode of being, one based on love, education, and cooperation rather than on aggression and ambition.

Mary sent *Matilda* to her father to find a publisher as soon as she had finished, but the novel did not appear in print until nearly a century and a half later, in 1959. Ironically, Mary had her father to thank for this delay. Calling the manuscript "disgusting," he refused to send it to publishers and would not return her copy. Although some biographers have assumed that this was because of the incest theme, Godwin was probably attempting to keep further scandal away from the family. Mary did not contest her father's judgment; she did not want another rupture with him, but this was a significant loss for her career. *Matilda* could easily have been a popular novel, suited as it was to the era's taste for gothic drama.

On November 12, after just two hours of labor, Mary gave birth to little Percy Florence, named after the city where he was born. Nursing her baby helped revive Mary's spirits. Shelley said she looked "a little consoled," and on the day after Percy's birth, she rallied enough to write Mrs. Gisborne:

[He] has a nose that promises to be as large as his grandfather's. . . . His health is good, and he is very lively, and even knowing for his age—although like a little dog I fancy his chief perfection lies in his nose, and that he smells me out, when he becomes quiet the moment I take him.

On a darker note, she told Marianne Hunt:

[Little Percy] is my only one and although he is so healthy and promising that for the life of me I cannot fear yet it is a bitter thought that all should be risked on one yet how much sweeter than to be childless as I was for 5 hateful months—Do not let us talk of those five months; when I think of all I suffered . . . I shudder with horror yet even now a sickening feeling steps in the way of every enjoyment when I think—of what I will not write about.

This "sickening feeling" would stay with Mary the rest of her life, sometimes rising, sometimes in abeyance. She learned to be grateful for those times when it was in the background, almost forgotten.

In the weeks after Percy's birth, the days grew colder and Mary began to worry about his health, asking the Hunts to send flannel to keep him warm and complaining that the Italians made no provisions against winter. Despite her joy over her new son, Mary did not soften toward Shelley. She had lost interest in making love after William died, writing to Marianne that "a woman is not a field to be continually employed in bringing forth or enlarging grain." Shelley, who had hoped the new baby would bring Mary back to him, was disappointed. To both husband and wife, their passion had represented an example of a true union between a man and a woman, as well as a consolation for the sacrifices they had made to be together. But after the losses Mary had sustained, she, who had always been self-contained and even-tempered in domestic life, shied away from his touch and was easily irritated, reproachful, and quarrelsome. Shelley began to dream about taking a long trip to England by himself, and he complained to Maria, "Mary feels no more remorse in torturing me than in torturing her own mind." Claire, meanwhile, warned Mary not to drive her husband away, reflecting, "A bad wife is like Winter in a house."

Claire's metaphor was remarkably apt, as the winter of 1819–20 was the worst Florence had experienced in seventy years. The only way to stay warm was to clutch small warming pots filled with embers. Shelley had found a huge serge cloak with a fur collar that he flung on before leaving the house, but Mary stayed indoors in bed with the baby. Claire entertained her by singing, her voice greatly improved by her many lessons. When he was home, Shelley read to Mary, but these quiet moments became less and less frequent. Sophia Stacey, a pretty young cousin of Shelley's, had arrived in town that December, eager to meet her estranged relative even though he was condemned by the rest of the family.

To Sophia, Shelley's rakishness was part of his appeal. Headstrong and used to getting her own way, Sophia defied the wishes of her elderly traveling companion by knocking on Shelley's door. Before long, he had won over Sophia's guardian, who allowed him to spirit his young cousin off on expeditions, and he had a splendid time showing Sophia the sights. She did not sigh and weep like Mary. Nor did she complain about the cold. Together, they went to parties and visited the galleries. By the end of her stay, Sophia had fallen a little bit in love with her older cousin. In her diary, she carefully recorded how he had held her in his arms when lifting her out of a carriage, and how, when she had a toothache, he had come downstairs and gently applied cotton to the back of her mouth.

The snow fell through most of January. Finally, at the end of the month, there was a thaw, and Shelley seized the opportunity to move the household to Pisa, where the weather was milder. After taking leave of a sorrowful Sophia, who was heartbroken to say goodbye to Shelley, they boarded a boat early in the morning on January 26 and arrived in the late afternoon, repairing immediately to the closest inn, the Albergo delle Tre Donzelle, on the north side of the Arno.

Pisa appealed to Shelley for many reasons. It was affordable, since it was off the beaten tourist track; and as in Florence, the Arno ran through the center of town, so he could take walks along the water's edge and go boating when it was spring. Renaissance palazzi lined the river, their façades faded but their elegance intact. The marble was chipped, the stonework crumbling. Everything seemed old—the mullioned windows, the dark medieval churches, the exotic Byzantine mosaics. Grass grew in the streets. There was an air of Ozymandias here—the decay, the deserted palazzi, the homes of long-gone, nameless princes—all of which suited him, and would, he knew, appeal to his wife.

Margaret King, Mary Wollstonecraft's student from her days in Ireland, was another draw. Now living under the assumed name of Mrs. Mason, after Wollstonecraft's idealized governess in *Original Stories,* she had a home just outside Pisa. At age forty-eight, Margaret was a medical doctor and had grown into exactly the kind of woman Wollstonecraft would have admired. Having been forced by her family to marry a wealthy count (Lord Mountcashell), she had borne eight children. At age twenty-nine, she ran away with a gentle Irishman, George Tighe, who showed his independence of mind by falling for this formidable woman. Margaret was six feet tall with huge muscular arms and no interest in female fripperies. She wore shabby dresses without any stays because she said they hurt the digestion. When she was younger, she had dressed as a man so she could attend medical school in Germany. After she graduated, she and Tighe moved to Italy for the climate and the more relaxed moral atmosphere, and they were raising their two daughters in the Italian countryside.

Both Claire and Mary admired Mrs. Mason's radicalism. Over the years, Margaret had stayed in contact with Godwin, and after Wollstonecraft died, she had paid him several visits in London, meeting young Mary and following her career with interest. Godwin had viewed Margaret's escape from her husband as heroic—yet another reason why his disapproval of the girls' flight to Paris had surprised them.

Mrs. Mason encouraged her young friends to set up housekeeping

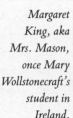

*Margaret King, aka Mrs. Mason, once Mary Wollstonecraft's student in Ireland.*

on the Lung'Arno, the city's most fashionable avenue. Crowded with carriages and pedestrians, this avenue was the heart of Pisa. The grand palaces glittered in the golden light, and although the city would never draw the crowds that flocked to Florence, there were still many tourists who strolled along the long curve of the river admiring the views and enjoying cakes and tea at the outdoor cafés. One visitor said you could hear at least twenty languages on the Lung'Arno. The Shelleys took Mrs. Mason's advice, moving a few times that first year until at last they settled on the spacious top floor of the Casa Frassi, where the winter sunlight streamed in the windows and the view stretched across the farmlands. The apartment had enough rooms for Shelley to have a study all to himself and for Claire and Mary to have separate spaces, vital because the sisters were once again grating on each other. Mary was annoyed by the rekindled camaraderie between Shelley and Claire; Claire was annoyed by Mary's sarcasm and constantly gloomy mood.

Mary, ever the practical one in the family, was relieved that food and other essentials were cheap in Pisa. She wrote to Marianne Hunt that for the first time since she had been with Shelley she was "undisturbed by weekly bills and daily expences." She decorated the front room with potted plants and settled into a routine of taking care of Percy, reading and writing while he napped. However, despite periods of contentment, she remained irritable. She despised the "ragged-haired, shirtless condition" of the men in the street. She ridiculed the Pisan women, who allowed their gowns to drag in the dirt and wore ugly pink hats and white shoes.

They made frequent visits to Mrs. Mason's house, Casa Silva, which was surrounded by the citrus orchards they had come to expect, but also by surprisingly large fields of crops, as though they were back in Ireland. Known as Tatty because of his passion for growing potatoes, George Tighe was widely read in the chemistry of soil compounds and alert to the latest agronomical discoveries, placing his interests in the context of his wife's radicalism. He reasoned that if peasants (particularly Irish ones) could grow crops more effectively and more reliably, they would be less dependent on aristocrats like Margaret's ex-husband, the count.

From potatoes to independence! Shelley loved this idea and, inspired by Tatty's peculiar brand of agrarian republicanism, wrote his famous call to freedom:

> *Men of England, wherefore plough*
> *For the lords who lay ye low?*
> *Wherefore weave with toil and care*
> *The rich robes your tyrants wear?*
> *The seed ye sow, another reaps;*
> *The wealth ye find, another keeps.*

Mary did not participate in Shelley's new enthusiasms. She remained preoccupied with the baby, alternately ignoring her husband or snapping at him, until Shelley broke down and complained about her in letters to his friends, begging them to visit to break the tension. He grew even more despondent when the Gisbornes, who were just back from a trip to England, gave him a new volume of poems by Keats—*Lamia, Isabella, the Eve of St. Agnes, and Other Poems*. Keats, evidently, was enjoying a fertile period while Shelley was not currently working on any important poems, nor did he feel any on the horizon. Instead, he felt exhausted. The previous year, he had written to Ollier, Keats's publisher, that he thought Keats's *Endymion* was full of the "highest and finest gleams of poetry" but was so wordy and lacking in structure that it was impossible to read all the way through—"no person should possibly get to the end of it." Now, as he read Keats's new book, he decided the young poet was just the person he needed to see. Keats's presence would stir him to work again and would also break the stalemate between himself and Mary. It would be like the summer with Byron all over again: there would be a rich exchange of ideas and the pleasure of a new friendship developing; best of all, everyone would write, and so it would be good for Mary, too. At any rate, he and Keats *should* become better friends. The unfinished poem *Hyperion* was the poet's best work, he told Marianne Hunt; it demonstrated that the young man was "destined to become one of the first writers of the age." Shelley was aware that Keats, who suffered from tuberculosis, had been advised to travel to Italy for his health, and so Shelley asked Marianne to extend an invitation to him, since he did not know how to reach the younger man himself:

> I am anxiously expecting him in Italy where I shall take care to bestow every possible attention on him. I consider his a most valuable life, & I am deeply interested in his safety. I intend to be the physician both of his body and his soul, to keep the one warm & to teach the other Greek & Spanish. I am aware indeed in part that I am nourishing a rival who will far surpass me and this is an additional motive & will be an added pleasure.

Shelley could not know that Keats still regarded Shelley with ambivalence after he had ventured to give him publication advice when Hunt introduced them. Keats remained resentful of Shelley's aristocratic background and would not have welcomed Shelley's offer of friendship and hospitality if he had ever heard of it. Certainly, he would have detected Shelley's condescension about his abilities. Keats had also found Mary alarming, regarding her as sharp-tongued and overly precise. After a visit to the Shelleys, Keats had written to Hunt,

"Does Mrs. S cut bread and butter as neatly as ever?" He added sarcastically, "Tell her to procure some fatal scissors and cut the thread of life of all to be disappointed poets."

But even as Shelley was writing to Marianne, inquiring about the young poet's whereabouts, Keats was cooped up on a ship in Naples harbor, unable to disembark until he had waited out the period of quarantine. When at last he was free to go ashore, he did not contact Shelley, and the two men would never see each other again.

Nevertheless, Shelley still hoped for a visit from Keats and waited to hear from him, growing increasingly despondent when there was only silence. With no new company to enliven his days and without a project to work on, Shelley took more long walks—sometimes alone, sometimes with Claire, but never with Mary. However, Claire had her drawbacks, abusing Byron to anyone who would listen. His lordship had forbidden her to be in contact with him directly, leaving Shelley as the go-between—an impossible situation, as Shelley saw it. By early June, around the anniversary of William's death, Claire and Mary had descended into a state of mutual exasperation. As Claire wrote in her journal, "Heigh-ho the Clare & the Mai / Find something to fight about every day." In desperation, Shelley issued an invitation to a childhood friend and distant cousin, Thomas Medwin, to come change the mood in the house. Medwin wrote that he would come but would not arrive for several more weeks.

That summer, news came from Naples that little Elena had died and that their old servant Paolo wanted payment for his role in covering up her identity. Mary urged Shelley to review their finances. She did not want Paolo to ruin them; also, Godwin continued to ask for money, though she had repeatedly told him that they did not have much to spare. With uncharacteristic practicality, her husband agreed, going over his accounts and becoming overwhelmed as he did so. "My affairs are in a state of the most complicated embarrassment," Shelley wrote Godwin, adding that if Godwin petitioned them again, he would not show Mary her father's letters as they "produce an appalling effect on her frame; on one occasion, agitation of mind produced through her a disorder in the child [Percy], similar to that which destroyed our little girl two years ago."

Although Shelley delivered this stern message, it was likely Mary's idea. She was breast-feeding Percy, and her milk supply faltered when she was anxious; when it came to the baby, Godwin's feelings no longer mattered. She was dedicated to Percy's health, determinedly hiking through the countryside, partly because she had heard that exercise stimulated milk production and also, of course, because she had read her mother's books preaching the virtues of maternal vigor.

At the end of the month, Shelley put Paolo off with a token payment and moved his family to a small house in the spa town of Bagni di Pisa, about four miles outside Pisa. Here he wrote *The Witch of Atlas,* a poem that disappointed Mary. This was the first time she had ever been critical of his work. Although she thought it was beautiful, she felt it had no plot and no realistic characters and therefore would not appeal to ordinary readers who lacked Shelley's imaginative powers. Mary longed for Shelley to be a success, not for the wealth it might bring them but for his own sake, for the acclaim she felt he deserved. Still, Shelley was hurt by her lack of enthusiasm and wrote an acerbic little dedication:

To Mary (On Her Objecting to the Following Poem, Upon the Score of Its Containing No Human Interest)

> *How, my dear Mary,—are you critic-bitten*
> *(For vipers kill, though dead) by some review,*
> *That you condemn these verses I have written,*
> *Because they tell no story, false or true?*

Despite this quarrel, life gradually became more tranquil. Mary and Shelley took dips in the baths, explored the countryside, and enjoyed the beauties of the Italian summer. Claire left for a few days to stay with the Masons, giving the two sisters a welcome break from each other. Mrs. Mason, who viewed Claire as an honorary Wollstonecraft, was worried by her reports of the arguments with Mary and began a campaign to persuade Claire to stay in Livorno for the month of September and then move to Florence to prepare herself for suitable employment. When Claire protested, Mrs. Mason asserted her medical expertise, telling her young friend that she needed to leave for the sake of her health. She also worried that if Claire stayed with the Shelleys much longer, she would lose any chance of finding a position as a teacher or lady's companion, not to mention a husband, telling Claire that her continued association with Mary and Shelley was bad for her reputation.

Shelley and Claire did not want to separate, but Mrs. Mason rarely lost a battle, and Shelley, defeated by the ex-countess, delivered Claire to Florence that September, where she set up residence with friends of the Masons. Relieved that Claire was gone, Mary sprang into action, finishing the research for the novel she had begun to dream of in Naples, *Valperga,* and starting to write in earnest, filling her pages with details that Shelley said she had "raked out of fifty old books." And indeed, to the modern reader, *Valperga*'s historical veracity is daunting. The text fairly bristles with Italian phrases; Mary expounds on the ins and outs of thirteenth-century Italian politics, making the novel somewhat slow going for those who are not as interested in this period as Mary was.

What is interesting is the subversive twist Mary gives to the story. She based *Valperga*'s plot on the life of Prince Castruccio Castracani, a historical figure depicted as a hero by Niccolò Machiavelli in his short biography of the man. In Mary's version, though, the prince is a destructive force. His hunger for power destroys the freedom of his people and ultimately leads to the death of the woman he loves, the countess Euthanasia. Mary had to invent this character from scratch, as no such woman could have existed in the thirteenth century. To Mary, in this one case, historical accuracy was less important than creating a female counterforce to Castruccio. In a dramatic departure from Machiavelli, she made Euthanasia a champion of peace and freedom, as well as the leader of the forces who try to stop the prince but fail.

The peculiar names of Mary's hero and heroine point to the themes she wanted to emphasize. The name Castruccio Castracani brings to mind *castrati,* the Italian term for male singers who were castrated to preserve their soprano voice. If only the countess could check or castrate Castruccio, the world would be a happier, more peaceful place, Mary implies. As it is, Euthanasia is fated to die the "good death" that her name suggests; there is no room for her in Castruccio's warlike world.

*Valperga*'s dark message is as much a political diatribe as Shelley's *The Mask of Anarchy.* Mary attacked the values espoused by Machiavelli and adopted by many statesmen ever since. Machiavelli had promoted war, not peace. Falsehood, not truth. Absolute rulers, not freedom. A prince had to commit wicked deeds to secure his power, Machiavelli said—an affront to Mary's idealism. Over the centuries, many other thinkers had condemned Machiavelli's "means to an end" political philosophy, but Mary was the first to write a novel that demonstrated the suffering caused when Machiavelli's advice is put into action. Castruccio betrays those he loves. He fights wars to consolidate his holdings. He is treacherous and cruel, killing opponents without mercy. Like Victor Frankenstein's, his ambition is boundless; he pursues "Honour, fame, dominion," in the face of Euthanasia's protests. As a result, "the people [are] driven from their happy cottages," Euthanasia laments, "often a poor child lost, or haplessly wounded, whose every drop of blood is of more worth than the power of the Caesars. . . ."

Like Shelley, Mary was fighting against injustice, depicting the consequences of tyranny. Under the surface, though, she indicted Shelley himself. The prince causes the death of children. So, Mary thought, had Shelley. And, like Mary, Euthanasia is helpless. She cannot vanquish the prince's army or change his mind, and so she does what Mary sometimes wished for herself: she sails off to die. Her people are left in Castruccio's hands—frightened, poor, and tyrannized.

Mary had made her point, a point that had been made by her mother before her: when men are guided by ambition, not love, and by fame, not family, then women and children pay the price. Castruccio's lust, like Matilda's father's, brings about the destruction of those he loves. Although *Valperga* could not seem more different from Wollstonecraft's *Vindications,* for Mary Shelley—living during a more conservative time than her mother—the best way to call for reform was to use fiction. Besides, she was well aware that one of her mother's original goals as a writer was to explore the minds of women; thus in both *Valperga* and *Matilda* she had tried to achieve this aim, albeit using very different techniques, but always in the service of her mother's philosophy. Mary's estrangement from Shelley, difficult though it was, had the benefit of giving her more independence, aesthetically and politically. Her most influential teacher, as well as her inspiration, was now her dead mother, not her husband.

As Mary put the finishing touches on *Valperga,* news came that the newly crowned King George IV—whom the Shelleys despised—had driven his wife, Queen Caroline, out of England simply because he disliked her. Now the queen, whom they admired as the symbolic leader of the liberal movement in England, was in Italy, a living example of how all women, even queens, were at the mercy of men, and how liberty so often was the victim of tyranny. To Mary, the world had begun to seem a place of eternal contention, a never-ending struggle between evil and good, ambition and love. And, in her experience, evil usually won.

# MARY WOLLSTONECRAFT:
# "A HUMANE AND
# TENDER CONSIDERATION"

---

[ 1796 ]

ELIGHTED BY THE SUCCESS OF *LETTERS FROM SWEDEN,* MARY TOOK
confidence from having persevered in the face of Imlay's rejection.
Only a few months earlier, she had been floating unconscious down
the Thames; now she had achieved new heights, having written her
most popular book to date. In December she had dinner with Mary
Hays, an aspiring writer who had sought out Mary for advice a few
years before. Mary had responded with her usual honesty, telling
Hays not to apologize so much for her work. They had met briefly
once or twice before but had never forged an intimate connection.
Now Mary discovered they had much in common. Both were living
alone. Both were attempting to earn their living by their pen. And
both were nursing a broken heart.

Mary Hays had fallen in love with a revolutionary Unitarian who
enjoyed having long philosophical conversations with her, but did
not want a sexual relationship. Frustrated, she consoled herself with
her work and her close friendships with other men, among them
William Godwin, who had become an international celebrity since
Mary had last met him five years ago. Stiff, short, and awkward
though he was, Godwin had attracted many female followers.

To Mary Hays and her friends, Godwin's tome *An Enquiry Concerning Political Justice, and Its Influence on General Virtue and Happiness,*

published in 1793, was one of the most important protests against the conservative British backlash to the French Revolution. Godwin had witnessed the defeat of the Reform Bills of 1792 and 1793. He had seen the leaders of the reform movement arrested and persecuted by the government. In his eyes, both the monarchy and Parliament were corrupt institutions. He championed natural rights, arguing that all governments, not only unjust ones, impinged on these rights, and that human beings should be allowed to govern themselves. This was less a naïve idealization of the human spirit than an expression of Godwin's disillusionment with both the French revolutionary tribunes and the British constitutional monarchy. In *The Adventures of Caleb Williams,* the novel he wrote the year after *Political Justice* (1794), he declared that his purpose was to demonstrate the various methods "by which man becomes the destroyer of man." He had yet to see a political system that truly promoted equality and justice, he wrote, and so, for all its tightly ordered arguments and dry style, its long lists of philosophical and historical examples, *Political Justice* is an angry book, designed to provoke the authorities and ignite the spirit of reform.

And yet Godwin's call for change was also essentially conservative. He argued for gradual, rational reform, not sudden coups d'état. He was appalled by the bloodshed of the French Revolution, writing that it was reason, and reason alone, that could save human beings from themselves. However, this moderate stance was lost on Godwin's contemporaries. To them, the sheer shock value of *Political Justice* transformed Godwin into an icon of revolution—a misunderstanding of Godwin that persisted after he died, when radicals of all stripes—most notably Peter Kropotkin, one of the first public advocates for anarchism, and Karl Marx and Friedrich Engels—took up Godwin as their hero, citing him as an important influence.

But even though Godwin did not espouse violence, he did believe in liberty. Risking imprisonment, he wrote a formidable defense of twelve radical intellectuals who had proposed legal reforms and were arrested for high treason in 1794. A dangerously on-edge Parliament had cracked down on civil liberties, suspending habeas corpus, arresting as a traitor anyone who disagreed with the king, and outlawing all meetings, pamphlets, and petitions. Godwin published his article in *The Morning Chronicle,* stirring public outrage at their incarceration. All twelve men were released, and Godwin was hailed for his commitment to political freedom. The young William Wordsworth told his friends, "Throw aside your books of chemistry and read Godwin." "Truth, moral truth . . . had taken up its abode [in him]," wrote the essayist William Hazlitt.

For all his newfound fame, *Political Justice* did not earn Godwin much money. The prime minister, William Pitt, laughed at the book's five-hundred-page length as well as its ponderous solemnity. He did not need to censor this enormous volume, he said, because no one would read it, let alone buy it, since, priced at over a pound, it was far too expensive for the ordinary citizen. But Pitt had underestimated the influence of Godwin's words. Throughout the country, reformers swore by *Political Justice,* forming book groups that purchased it for their members to share. Eventually, it sold more than four thousand copies, enough to win Godwin acclaim, but not enough to keep him afloat. He had to stay busy as a writer of novels and political commentary to maintain even the simple life he had chosen. He rented inexpensive rooms far from the center of London, had one servant, an old woman who cleaned his rooms each morning, and allowed himself few luxuries, choosing to write books that pleased his conscience rather than the public.

*Political Justice* was published a few months after Godwin had met Wollstonecraft for the first time at Johnson's dinner party for Thomas Paine, an event he remembered with distaste. As he recalled it, Mary had dominated the conversation, leaving him to twiddle his thumbs at the other end of the table. That everyone else at the party, particularly Paine, had praised her wit and had actually seemed to enjoy her company only made matters worse. Three years later, he still blamed her for his silence that night, characterizing her as loud and intrusive.

Mary, on the other hand, had heard of Godwin's noble achievements from many of her friends when she returned to London, having missed his sudden ascent to fame while she was in France. Still, even his reputation as a staunch defender of reform was not enough to dispel her own unpleasant memories. She, too, remembered their meeting, and she regarded him as rigid and awkward, someone to ridicule, not respect. As she drew closer to Mary Hays, though, Wollstonecraft heard about a different Godwin, a dear friend who had "shown a humane & tender consideration" for Hays when she had confided in him about her wounded heart. Although Mary confessed that she could not picture Godwin as a sensitive listener, she declared that his kindness to Hays had raised Godwin in her esteem. Hays reported Mary's words to Godwin, who was annoyed by the backhanded nature of Wollstonecraft's compliment. She "has frequently amused herself by depreciating me," he muttered, refusing Hays's request that he meet Mary again.

But Hays had decided that her "dear friends" needed to learn to appreciate each other, and she plotted to get the two into the same room so that each could witness the other's "excellent" qualities. She told Godwin that Mary had "a warm and generous heart" and, intriguingly, had almost died of her sufferings despite her strength of mind. Godwin remained unconvinced, and Mary was so focused on her own heartbreak that she was reluctant to meet new men, let alone a man she had found unappealing to begin with. And yet Hays persisted. She insisted that Wollstonecraft and Godwin come to her house for tea. And on January 8, 1796, they did.

When the fateful afternoon finally rolled around, things began badly. Saddled with preconceptions and bad memories, the two principals eyed each other warily. Godwin was condescending and unfriendly, making it painfully obvious that he did not like Mary and was only overlooking what he took to be her many faults because he believed in doing "justice" to his enemies. Mary was no better. She had come to the tea party not to begin a new friendship, she implied, but only to please Mary Hays.

As the afternoon wore on, however, both Godwin and Mary were surprised at the changes time had wrought. Years of social engagements had eased some of Godwin's self-consciousness. Instead of being pedantic, he now seemed eccentric, a genius, a man of importance. Mary, too, had gained in social skills and confidence. She was gentler, more of a listener and far less preoccupied with making her own points; the Revolution and the backlash in England had disillusioned her; political contention no longer seemed so important. Now, as in *Letters from Sweden,* it was affairs of the heart and mind that interested her—emotions, psychology, and the self—essentially, the topics of her battles with Imlay. What role could Nature play in healing an individual's pain? How was civilization harming or helping the human spirit? Could the life of the imagination triumph over a life dedicated to material pleasures? She had not lost interest in politics and current events; it was just that she was now fascinated by the interior life, the reasons and feelings behind people's actions—why they did what they did.

Fortunately, Godwin, too, found these themes engrossing, having explored the psychological effects of tyranny in his novel *Caleb Williams.* And so, as the talk turned literary on this first meeting, it quickly became clear to Mary that Godwin's goal in writing was like hers: to inspire the reading public to take action against political, economic, and social injustice. He, too, had a hatred of arbitrary authority, a faith that writing books could ameliorate the human condition, and a fascination with what lay below the surface of people's motivations: What was the psychology of the oppressor and the oppressed, the tyrant and the victim?

But everything might have stalled there if Mary had not been beautiful. Despite his Calvinist upbringing, Godwin appreciated attractive women, and motherhood had rounded Mary's figure, just as suffering had softened her outlook. Always attractive, at age thirty-six, she was now considered lovely by most who met her. One new acquaintance reported that she was a "very voluptuous looking woman." And though one of her eyes had a slight droop, left over from one of her illnesses, that flaw did not stop the poet Robert Southey from extolling her expressiveness; her face, he told his friends, is "the best, infinitely the best. . . . Her eyes are light brown, and though the lid of one is affected by a little paralysis, they are the most meaning I ever saw." She still called herself Mrs. Imlay, even in these liberal circles where most people knew her story, but her suffering made her seem exotic and original rather than unacceptable, particularly next to Mary Hays, whom even a dear friend described as "old, ugly, and ill-dressed." Godwin's best friend, Thomas Holcroft, a widower, was so smitten with Mary that he penned her a fulsome love letter proposing they embark immediately on a sexual adventure:

> I never touched your lips; yet I have felt them, sleeping and waking, present and absent. I feel them now: and now, starting in disappointment from the beatific trance, ask why I am forbidden to fly and fall on your bosom and there dissolve in bliss such as I have never known, except in reveries like this.

Although she was not attracted to the bespectacled Holcroft, Mary handled his overtures with a diplomacy she had not possessed prior to her own rejections at the hand of Imlay. Her reply to his letter does not survive, but the warm friendship they developed that spring suggests that her words were compassionate and allowed Holcroft to maintain his dignity.

This new Mary was much more to Godwin's liking. For all of his radicalism, he believed that women stood in need of male protection. He valued "the softness of their natures [and] the delicacy of their sentiments." A muted Wollstonecraft better fit his ideas of femininity; she did not interrupt or challenge anyone's opinions, and she looked sadly vulnerable. After their first afternoon, he reflected, "sympathy in her anguish added in my mind to the respect I had always entertained for her talents." When, a week later, they met at another party, he found himself agreeing with his friend Holcroft: Mary was not only an intelligent woman, she was eminently desirable.

Intrigued, Godwin purchased *Letters,* and from the first page he was captivated. In his diary he described his reaction in an unusually long entry:

> [Mary] speaks of her sorrows in a way that fills us with melancholy, and dissolves us in tenderness, at the same time that she displays a genius which commands all our admiration. Afflic-

tion had tempered her heart to a softness almost more than human; and the gentleness of her spirit seems precisely to accord with all the romance of unbounded attachment.

But as impressed as she was with the new Godwin, Mary was still brooding over Imlay. The act of writing *Letters from Sweden* had improved her mood, and she no longer believed that she could truly be happy with Imlay, or even that he was worth loving, but it was still difficult to let go of the idea of him entirely. It was not until mid-February, when Imlay returned to London for business, that she finally accepted her loss. She and Fanny bumped into him at the Christies' and Fanny, immediately recognizing "Papa's" voice, rushed toward him for a hug. Imlay embraced his daughter and spoke gently to Mary, promising to see her the next day, but when he visited, he was his usual noncommittal self. Kind but distant.

Strangely enough, it was this, his matter-of-fact, businesslike reserve, compared to the Sturm und Drang she had provoked from him in their previous confrontations, that finally got through to Mary and she accepted his departure with an equanimity that would have been impossible a year before. She knew that Imlay could never offer her the love or the passion she wanted. And so when she felt the tug of her old despondency, she was wise enough not to let it take hold, packing herself and Fanny into a carriage to visit friends in Berkshire. Here she replenished her energy without any danger of running into Gilbert, and when she returned to London, she wrote to him, "I part with you in peace." Although she had made this declaration many times before, this time Mary meant it. When they met by accident later that spring, she noted that she did not feel particularly cast down.

In fact, her melancholy was receding. Fanny was now almost two years old and was chattering, running, playing with a ball, laughing at jokes, and altogether more independent, giving Mary a sense of renewed freedom. The primroses bloomed, announcing the arrival of spring. The fruit trees flowered, and Canterbury bells, vibernum, iris, stock, sweet peas, and lilacs grew along the paths in the parks. Flush with the glories of Nature, Mary moved to Cumming Street, Pentonville, on the outskirts of London, away from the house in Finsbury Square that she associated with Imlay.

There was a rural feeling to this new part of London. Here she could walk out her front door and see open fields, creeks, and farmland. Cows lowed; sheep grazed. Now and then a stray pig wandered by. Little Fanny was delighted with these country pleasures. She jumped over sticks and marched in place like a soldier. She loved apple pie and wanted to help Marguerite "mix the butter and flour together." She was not allowed to use the big apple-paring knife—little knives for little girls, Mary said—but she was consoled when Mary told her, "When you are as tall as I am, you shall have a knife as large as mine." They adopted a puppy and Mary taught Fanny how to take care of him, recording one of the lessons in the little book she wrote to help Fanny learn to read, "Oh! The poor puppy has tumbled off the stool. Run and stroke him. Put a little milk in a saucer to comfort him." To ensure Fanny's sympathy for the animal, she added, "When the book fell down on your foot, it gave you great pain. The poor dog felt the same pain just now. Take care not to hurt him when you play with him." Mary delighted in these times together as much as Fanny did; after all, she had almost missed watching her daughter grow.

One pleasant spring day, while paying a visit to Rebecca Christie, Mary discovered that Godwin had stopped by, hoping to see her. The spring air, the time with Fanny, and the distance from Imlay had all helped Mary regain her strength, and she was flattered. She waited for Godwin to return, and when he did not appear, she took matters into her own hands. On April 14, she walked to his lodgings on Chalton Street in nearby Somers Town. Although respectable women were not supposed to visit men alone in their rooms, Godwin welcomed her, accepting her unorthodox behavior without any question, and the first of many long conversations began. He invited her for tea the next day and then saw her as frequently as possible, for plays, more teas, walks, and dinner parties.

Usually, they met with the lively circle of friends Godwin had cultivated, including numerous female admirers whom he termed "the fairs." Although he was gratified by their attention, he was not always sure how to negotiate the tricky waters of flirtation. He had many odd habits, including long silences, catnaps at inopportune moments, and startling coughs. When his admirers made romantic overtures, Godwin recoiled, unwilling to reveal his inexperience. One day, about a year before, the unhappily married Maria Reveley had tried to kiss him, but he pulled away in embarrassment—a hesitation he would regret in the years to come.

Maria was beautiful, cultured, and confident enough in her charms to bear Godwin no ill will and she quickly became Mary's favorite of the "fairs." She admired Mary's work and welcomed the opportunity to get to know her. Mary, too, was eager to befriend Maria. She needed new companions, as she had fallen out of touch with Ruth Barlow, and her sisters were cold and distant. Eliza was still not speaking to her, and Everina only occasionally sent a terse note. Mary loved Rebecca Christie and Mary Hays, but Rebecca was not an intellectual and Mary Hays had never lived abroad. Maria, on the other hand, was both a scholar and cosmopolitan. She had been raised in Constantinople and Rome, spoke several different languages, and had a deep interest in political philosophy, literature, and the rights of women. In addition, she had a little boy named Henry who was around the same age as Fanny. The children could play and the women could talk—Mary had never had the opportunity for such a friendship before.

Over the next few weeks, Maria confided in Mary about her neglectful husband, and Mary told Maria about Imlay and her sufferings in France and Sweden. Neither woman could know that they were laying the groundwork for a future in which Mary could play no part—that years later, after her husband died, Maria would marry a man named Gisborne and move to Italy, and there, as though the fates had planned it, befriend the desperately lonely Mary Shelley.

Mary was less keen on Elizabeth Inchbald, a gossipy widow in her early forties, the author of several badly written novels who had the good looks of the girl next door (or, as her contemporaries said, "a milkmaid") and the snobbish manners of a duchess. The poet Coleridge warned Godwin not to trust Inchbald, saying she seemed warm and friendly but underneath was "cold and cunning." He was right. Inchbald was envious of the other women in Godwin's court and did her best to undermine their claims. Amelia Alderson, a beauty with literary aspirations who flirted outrageously with the stiff Godwin, wrote to a friend, "[Mrs. Inchbald] appears to be jealous of G's attention to [me] and makes him believe I prefer [Holcroft] to him." Inchbald already loathed Mary because, long before they met, Mary had panned her literary efforts as naïve, boring, and ridiculous. Now that Godwin was entranced by Wollstonecraft, Inchbald's antipathy only intensified.

But Inchbald was the only "fair" who did not like Mary. The rest of Godwin's admirers immediately warmed to Mary, who felt happier than she had in years. She had stumbled into a group of ready-made female friends and was drawing closer to a man she respected and enjoyed. Nonetheless, she was unsure of Godwin's feelings. A confirmed bachelor, he invited Mary and the others to the opera, or parties, but when it came to any deeper kind of relationship, he kept his distance. In *Political Justice,* he had declared he did not believe in marriage, and so no one thought it surprising that he lived alone. Clearly, he was a pure philosopher who did not need love—or so gossiped those who wondered if he had ever had an affair.

And yet Godwin's time with these graceful, witty women had helped him develop at least some of the elements of playful repartee. He had learned to dress with more flair, according to Amelia, who reported to a friend that Godwin had put aside his fusty old coats and ministerial shirts and now wore "new sharp-toed red morocco slippers [and a] green coat and crimson under waistcoat." He had also cut his unfashionably long hair and stopped powdering it in order to assert his sympathy with the French revolutionaries. Stuffy though he could be, Godwin was a true radical, and even he acknowledged that it was time he looked like one.

Still, despite these sartorial improvements, Godwin could never compete with Imlay's charms. Even the fairs had been unable to help him lose his awkwardness, particularly with women. Atheist that he was, he still had the manners of a clergyman. He disapproved of frivolity, rarely made jokes, frequently looked bored at parties no matter how brilliant the conversation, never complimented anyone, and had no idea how to talk about anything other than literature and political philosophy, and usually his own political philosophy.

Yet for all his irritating ways, for all that she was not sure what he wanted from her or how close he wanted to be, Godwin seemed trustworthy to Mary precisely because he was so adamantly, even defiantly, *not* charming. She saw how loyal he was to his friends, and how he never shied away from speaking his opinions even if he hurt someone's feelings. He was not the sort of man who would run off with a young actress. He would not even want to. Indeed, the stories that circled around Godwin featured his primness, his refusal to embrace even his closest female friends. He was virginal, impregnable, the embodiment of rectitude. Before he met Mary, Godwin had occasionally attempted to embark on a flirtation, but was too shy to succeed. Amelia Alderson was amused at his attempts at gallantry, writing a friend, "It would have entertained you to see [Godwin] bid me farewell. He wished to salute [kiss] me, but his courage failed him. . . ."

After Imlay, Mary liked being with a man who valued the exchange of ideas more than love affairs, and she was unsure whether she desired anything more. Increasingly, she trusted Godwin's stalwart honesty and intellectual rectitude. Yes, he was often silent, coming to life only when he disagreed with someone, believing it his duty to point out holes in other people's arguments; yes, hostesses dreaded his arrival—he was a difficult guest, dozing off when bored, sermonizing when interested—but Mary was not put off. She could see that Godwin admired her and, better yet, was impressed by her moods and sorrows. Imlay had dreaded her displays of feeling, viewing them as burdensome, a demand for something he could not deliver; Godwin regarded Mary's propensity for depression as evidence of her depth, her highly strung nature, her artistic soul.

As the spring turned to summer, both Mary and Godwin began to dream of an unlikely new love, although they hardly confessed these dreams to themselves, let alone to each other. Mary did not want to be hurt again. In retrospect, she realized that she and Imlay had made love with a kind of recklessness that guaranteed disaster. She had not waited to learn about Imlay's character and had allowed herself to be swept along without testing his integrity. Now she kept herself in check. She went for long walks with her staid admirer, who listened with empathy to her complaints, her ideas, and the details of her melancholy reflections, but no kisses were exchanged. They did not even hold hands.

By mid-May, Godwin was eating supper at Mary's house on a regular basis, and early in the summer, Mary took their relationship a step further, allowing Godwin to read the first draft of her latest writing project, a play based on her relationship with Imlay. Even though she never responded well to criticism, Mary listened to his comments, most of which were negative. The story was "crude and imperfect." Her grammar and punctuation were sloppy. Mary did not take offense, however; instead, she asked for guidance. Maybe Godwin, impeccably educated as he was, could teach her the rules of syntax—an unlikely foundation for romance, perhaps, but for Mary, there could be few more intimate exchanges. She wrote to reveal herself to the world; commas, sentences, and paragraphs were the only tools she had. Years earlier, she had begun her passionate friendships with both Fanny Blood and Jane Arden by asking them to correct her grammar.

Godwin found Mary's request exquisitely flattering. Five years earlier, he would never have dreamed that Mary Wollstonecraft would turn to him for advice. Her new deference was gratifying. Besides, their literary discussions gave him an opportunity to sit close to her, almost touching as they pored over her ink-blotted pages.

But even with Godwin's assistance, Mary could not get the play to work. Eventually, she put it aside to start writing a companion piece to *A Vindication of the Rights of Woman,* a novel she called *The Wrongs of Woman.* In this new work, she wanted to dramatize the plight of abused and abandoned females, exposing the falseness of popular novels in which feminine weakness was glorified and the heroine's suffering was a cue for the hero's entrance. In many ways, this was the plot that had almost killed her. She had invested Imlay with all the powers of a hero, giving him the opportunity to rescue her with her first suicide attempt. But he was no hero, and would not become one no matter how long she played the role of the helpless female. To survive, she had been forced to give up hope that he would one day save her, and without the tools of writing and self-reflection, she might have failed. Now she wanted readers to see how dangerous this formula could be. Women needed to be able to stand alone. Men should not be seen as the "rescuers" of women; giving them that kind of power could all too easily make them brutes.

As with *Letters from Sweden,* her old mode of writing, discursive and philosophical, no longer seemed the best way to make her point. Mary wanted readers to have a visceral experience of the suffering of women. At the same time, she was intent on exploring the psychology of her heroines, to show their responses to their harrowing experiences and some of the reasons for their destructive decisions. Her ultimate hope was to help her readers see the necessity for reform. If women continued to be infantilized, society would spiral downward.

That July, she began to map out the plot of her new novel, while Godwin left for a vacation in Norfolk. Having spent so much time together during the previous months, both parties brooded over their relationship while apart. Although by now they recognized that something more than a friendship had begun, both were reluctant to declare themselves: Mary because she did not want to display too much ardor for "fear of outrunning" Godwin; Godwin because he was too well aware of what a poor figure he cut next to Imlay. He had never made love to a woman, and he had been embarrassed when, earlier in the summer, he had sent Mary a stilted love poem and she had scoffed at his efforts, declaring that she did not want an artificial composition, but instead "a bird's eye view of your heart." Do not write me again, she said, "unless you honestly acknowledge yourself bewitched." Godwin, always literal-minded, felt criticized, missing Mary's rather bold invitation to reveal himself. Instead, he could hear only her mocking tone and was too timid to realize that Mary was urging him to declare his love. Inexperienced and afraid, he possessed neither the wisdom nor the experience to know that she was only protecting herself until he declared himself more openly.

Mary must have been more encouraging in person, however, because while he was in Norfolk, Godwin screwed up his courage and tried again, penning a slightly sheepish letter in which he attempted to express his love, albeit in mock-heroic terms, as he could not yet bring himself to risk complete sincerity:

> Now, I take all my Gods to witness . . . that your company in-finitely delights me, that I love your imagination, your delicate epicurism, the malicious leer of your eye, in short every thing that constitutes the bewitching tout ensemble of the celebrated Mary. . . . Shall I write a love letter? May Lucifer fly away with me, if I do! No, when I make love, it shall be with the eloquent tones of my voice, with dying accents, with speaking glances (through the glass of my spectacles), with all the witching of that irresistible, universal passion. Curse on the mechanical icy medium of pen and paper. When I make love, it shall be in a storm, as Jupiter made love to Semele and turned her at once to a cinder. Do not these menaces terrify you?

Mary did not much care for his humor, but she recognized that his facetiousness masked an anxiety that was understandable; after all, she had been in his position only three years earlier. In addition, there was a certain appeal to this reversal: she the confident lover, Godwin the nervous virgin. Yet for all their long walks and conversations, for all the hours spent confiding their fears and dreams to each other, it was still difficult for her to consider being vulnerable again, particu-larly with a famous man who already had a flock of female admirers.

# MARY SHELLEY:
# PISA

———

## [ 1820–1821 ]

THE FALL OF 1820 WAS A QUIETLY PRODUCTIVE TIME FOR MARY Shelley. She wrote during the day, nursed little Percy, went for walks, and bathed in the spa waters of the Bagni di San Giuliano. In the evenings, she and Shelley admired Venus hanging low in the sky, "the softened tints of the olive woods, the purple tinge of the distant mountains . . . the heaven-pointing cypress," the "boat-like moon" casting a "silvery light," the crickets "humming," and the fireflies and glowworms flickering. Looking back, Mary would remember this place as a kind of paradise. But Shelley was restless. A wealthy admirer of his poetry had written to him that summer, inviting him to take an excursion to the Middle East. Shelley did not tell Mary about this offer, knowing it would upset her, but he immediately wrote to Claire proposing that she accompany him and begging her not to tell her sister.

Despite appearances, Shelley was not interested in having an affair with Claire, at least not at this particular juncture—though the events of 1814–15 remain shadowy. Rather, Mary's preoccupation with Percy and her rejection of Shelley after William's death had taken their toll. Shelley felt unimportant, hemmed in by being a husband and a father. Mary was less angry now, but she remained distant sexually and Shelley was frustrated. Lively, enthusiastic Claire worshipped him. He wished she were with them and not in Florence. She understood how cold Mary could be and could always be counted on to commiserate with him over her stepsister's failings.

But in the end, Shelley stayed in Italy, contenting himself with solo ventures into the countryside and hiding his resentment so successfully that Mary was unaware of how he felt. She enjoyed being alone with her husband and child and was disappointed to learn that Shelley had invited Tom Medwin to pay them a visit. When Medwin did arrive that October, he was short on money and happy to have free lodging. Having just returned from seven years in India, where, he said, he had spent his time hunting tigers, riding elephants, and touring Hindu temples, he declared himself eager to renew his friendship with Shelley.

Shelley did not hear the false note in Medwin's stories, but Mary heard the clichés and was less enthralled. Medwin repeated himself, she said; he was puffed up, self-absorbed, and loud; he was always the hero of his own tales and a sponge on their finances. The worst part was that he did not have any particular plans for the future and seemed content to stay with them indefinitely.

But Medwin was not there simply to sponge off the Shelleys. He was genuinely fascinated by his notorious cousin. He had not seen him since they were teenagers and carefully recorded his first impressions:

> His figure was emaciated and somewhat bent; owing to nearsightedness, and his being forced to lean over his books, with his eyes almost touching them; his hair, still profuse, and curling naturally, was partially interspersed with grey . . . but his appearance was youthful, and his countenance, whether grave or animated, strikingly intellectual.

As for Mary, she was not Medwin's type, either in looks or personality, but he thought she was a good match for his cousin, describing how Shelley found respite "in the tenderness of affection and sympathy of her who partook of his genius, and could appreciate his transcendent talents."

At the end of October, they all moved back into Pisa. Shelley had found a new and even more spacious apartment on the Lung'Arno, this time at the Casa Galetti, a villa that stood next to one of the most imposing marble palazzi. They had the entire first floor and two additional rooms on the fourth floor, one for Shelley's study and one for Medwin's bedroom. Shelley had moved from feeling rejected by Mary to rejecting her himself. When he was home, he retreated upstairs. "Congratulate me on my seclusion," he wrote to Claire. Yet Shelley's defection from their living quarters left Medwin largely on Mary's hands, and by mid-November he had gone from being a minor annoyance to a bothersome intrusion, irritating Mary by reading aloud when she was trying to focus on finishing *Valperga*.

Percy turned a year old on November 12. Ruddy-cheeked and independent, he was strong enough for his mother to enjoy parties and receive guests without fussing too much about his health. That winter Mary and Shelley broke from their customary isolation, venturing into society. In part this was because without Claire, Mary could simply be Mrs. Shelley, as opposed to a disreputable member of a ménage à trois, but it was also because neither husband nor wife was sufficient company for the other anymore. Both needed new people and new stimulation.

Early in December, Mary's life was enlivened by a glamorous stranger, a prince, twenty-nine-year-old Alexander Mavrocordato. The black-haired, dark-eyed Greek was in exile and on a mission to raise an army to free his country from the Turks. No cause could have been more appealing to both the Shelleys—freedom for the land of Plato and Homer, the cradle of philosophy and poetry—but Mary was particularly moved. Mavrocordato seemed like a character from a romantic novel, the kind of hero Mary had always longed to meet. Mary herself was unlike any woman Mavrocordato had ever encountered. She was small and very English, but unlike most English people, she was interested in Greece and knew quite a bit about its history. Although she was reserved and rarely smiled, she was attractive—in fact, very attractive. It was almost a year and a half since William had died, and as Mary recovered, she had started to pay more attention to her appearance. She brought out the silk shawls she had bought in Livorno and asked Peacock to send her combs to pin up her hair. The current fashion of high waists and puffed sleeves flattered her wom-

anly figure; at age twenty-three, after four children, she was no longer the slight girl Shelley had fallen in love with. She had a horror of
vulgarity and did not like to call attention to her appearance, wearing
quiet colors, pale pink, light blue, and off-white. Despite the Italian
sun, her skin was still fair and clear. Unlike Shelley, she had not
started to go gray. Her hair shone like copper.

When she told Mavrocordato that she was interested in learning
modern Greek, the prince was delighted to offer his services, visiting
Mary almost every day during the winter of 1821. She usually received him alone, and in a letter to Claire she exclaimed that he was
"much to my taste, gentlemanly—gay learned and full of talent &
enthusiasm for Greece." The contrast between Mavrocordato and her
husband could not have been more pronounced. Shelley was gaunt,
sensitive, and restless; Mavrocordato radiated health and vigor. He
was a soldier, short and stocky, with a thick mustache and a hearty
appetite. However, there was little opportunity for the situation to
become complicated or for feelings to run too deep, as Mavrocordato
was called back to Greece in April to lead an army of ten thousand
men raised by his cousin. He and Mary stayed in touch by letter, but
neither made any attempt to advance the relationship.

The same week Mary met her prince, Shelley was introduced to
the beautiful young Teresa Viviani, the daughter of Pisa's governor,
at a soiree. Tall, with a swanlike neck and a tragic air, the eighteen-
year-old possessed an allure that entranced both Shelleys; she was a
Renaissance virgin with raven locks and alabaster skin, just like the
maiden Shelley had imagined in *The Revolt of Islam*. When she appeared in public, she maintained a melancholy silence and cast down
her eyes when spoken to. Almost immediately, Teresa singled out
Shelley as a man who would sympathize with her, and Shelley was
buoyant at being seen as a hero once again.

It did not take Teresa long to reveal the source of her sorrow. Her
evil stepmother had imprisoned her in a convent, she said in hushed
tones, close to tears. Granted, this convent was the most exclusive
school in Pisa. It was almost next door to her family's palazzo, and it
allowed Teresa to come and go as she pleased, attend parties and concerts, and parade along the Arno with her friends; but both Shelleys

were too enthralled to notice these details. Her story was like Mary's! A lovely, sensitive girl at the mercy of an evil stepmother! Mary went to visit Teresa every day and gave her two caged birds to keep her company.

Shelley decided that Teresa seemed too prosaic a name for such a gorgeous creature and renamed her Emilia. Before long, he began to cherish romantic fantasies about her. Here was another young girl he could rescue. Here was a young woman he could love. He felt alive once more. Not since William's death had he felt so vital, so inspired, and he recorded his feelings in a new poem with the Greek title *Epipsychidion* ("about a little soul"). He dedicated this work to "the noble and unfortunate Lady, Emilia," reiterating his endorsement of free love in lines that would become famous among later generations, but that critics of Shelley's own generation savaged for their "immorality":

> *I never was attached to that great sect,*
> *Whose doctrine is, that each one should select*
> *Out of the crowd a mistress or a friend,*
> *And all the rest, though fair and wise, commend*
> *To cold oblivion . . .*

For Shelley, however, the point of these words was not sex. Nor was it promiscuity. It was freedom, discovery, openness to change, creativity, and vitality. He threw himself into this new relationship with ardor, never consummating it, but dreaming of what it would be like to have "union" with the fair "Emilia," and then writing about it in lush, highly adorned verse. She had brought him back to life; she would be his new muse. He was a poet once again. Not once did he realize that this was a familiar pattern, that this is what had happened before, first with Harriet and then with Mary: He had felt lost, consumed with self-doubt and in despair. Enter a young woman who seemed to embody hope, who, he believed, could guide him back to life, and then, when she could no longer take away his suffering, he became disillusioned, at a loss, ready to meet a new potential savior.

Meanwhile, the maiden launched her own campaign. First she

worked on separating Shelley from Mary, complaining to Shelley that Mary was cold to her. She also sent Mary barbed little notes laced with backhanded compliments; in one, she "confessed" that Shelley had told her Mary's apparent iciness was "only the ash which covers an affectionate heart."

When she was with Shelley, Teresa/Emilia confided her secrets and wept tragic tears, which sent him into a frenzy—if only he could save this beautiful girl, fold her to his heart, and confess his undying affection. By January, Mary understood that Teresa was toying with her husband, but she was herself so deeply involved with the prince that she did not interfere. What did hurt, though, was the finished *Epipsychidion,* in which he described his marriage to Mary as "a death of ice," whereas in a blissful encounter with "Emily," she wraps her arms around him and their two hearts entwine as one.

Only later did Mary confess that she had felt "a good deal of discomfort." At the time, she hid her feelings, worried that if she pressed Shelley, he might think she was sabotaging his freedom and abandon her. She was also wary of complaining in letters, even to close friends, in case the public got wind of yet more scandal. Already people in Pisa were gossiping about how often Shelley and Teresa were seen together. However, that spring, the affair came to an abrupt end when Teresa's family put a stop to Shelley's visits, announcing her engagement to an eminently suitable young man. Poised to take her first steps into adulthood, "Emilia" promptly faded back into Teresa, a proper young Pisan lady. Shelley witnessed her bustling about doing errands in preparation for her wedding, just like any other bourgeois young lady. Disguised, he called her "a cloud instead of a Juno."

For both Shelleys, a different relationship had also begun that winter, one that at first seemed quite ordinary compared to those with the prince and Teresa. Medwin's friends Jane and Edward Williams had arrived in Pisa in January 1821 to visit Medwin, but also to have their second illegitimate child. Theirs was a romantic story. Jane, like Mary, had been a rule breaker. She had run away from the husband she had been forced to marry at age sixteen, and the following year, she fell in love with the already married Edward and eloped with him to Geneva. Here was a couple about their own age who had also braved social conventions. It seemed impossible for them not to like one another. However, at first Mary was disappointed in Jane. For all of her rebellious ways, the twenty-two-year-old beauty was actually quite traditional. She preferred to arrange flowers, sing madrigals, and play with her toddler rather than engage in political debates about Greek freedom or write a novel, which were Mary's chosen activities that spring.

Shelley did not pay much attention to Jane and Edward in the beginning, as he was still obsessed with Emilia and was also dealing with a loss that, to him, felt ominous: twenty-six-year-old John Keats had died in February. Of a broken heart, Shelley thought, mistakenly believing that the young poet had suffered an embolism after hearing that the *Quarterly* had savaged his work. The true cause of the poet's death was tuberculosis. Shelley's misapprehension revealed his feelings toward his own bad reviews—sometimes he felt as though they might kill him—but it also inspired him to put pen to paper.

Gripped by his belief that the younger man was a martyr, a poet who had died for the sake of his art, Shelley, who had never known that Keats distrusted him, mourned by composing a 549-line elegy titled *Adonais,* widely regarded as one of his most accomplished works. Shelley himself thought it was "better, in point of composition than anything I have written." In his prologue, Shelley, thinking perhaps of Wilmouse, describes the Protestant burial ground where Keats was buried as "covered in winter with violet and daisies," and so "sweet a place" that "it might make one half in love with death." To Shelley, the loss of Keats represents the loss of beauty, spirit, and hope. The younger poet has left Shelley behind in a world of "Envy and calumny, and hate and pain." By the end of the poem, Shelley yearns to join Keats in the world of eternal light, declaring, "No more let Life divide what Death can join together." Ironically, for all his romantic words about death, by the time he finished the poem, Shelley felt more alive. True, his new poem contained themes that some might regard as dark, but it was also about art and the importance of the poet, always heartening subjects for Shelley.

That summer, he and Mary retreated to San Giuliano, and the Williamses joined them in a house in nearby Pugnano, about seven miles outside Pisa. Medwin had moved on to Rome and Claire was still in Florence. Released from the spell of Emilia, Shelley warmed to the Williamses, particularly Edward, who, as a naval man, appealed to Shelley. Edward regaled the company with tales of the high seas, presenting himself as an old salt when in fact he had not had much experience as a sailor, having been stationed in India. But Shelley had faith in his new friend's nautical expertise and ignored the early signs of his incompetence. Shelley had purchased a small skiff that April, and on their first boating trip, Williams stood up to adjust the sail, stumbled, and capsized the boat. Fortunately, they were sailing in a narrow canal where the water was quiet and the shore nearby, so Shelley was rescued without too much difficulty. Instead of taking this as a warning, Shelley declared that his "ducking" had only "added fire" to his "nautical ardour," and he spent the rest of the summer sailing up and down the Arno with Williams and by himself. One day, he sailed all the way to the sea and then along the shore to Livorno—a distance of two miles—but he still did not learn to swim.

Jane, too, seemed more appealing than she had in the spring. At first, Shelley had found her a little dull. She was not clever enough for

*Sketch by Edward Williams, probably of Percy Shelley. Williams did not identify his subject, but the time period and similarity to the only other extant portrait of the poet suggest that this is indeed a likeness.*

his taste, and was bored by politics, literature, science, and history. Also, she had been pregnant, which had prevented Shelley from noticing how lovely she was, but having delivered her new baby in March—a little girl named Jane Rosalind—Jane was slender once again. She had dark hair that she wore in ringlets along her pale neck. With enormous eyes, a delicate mouth, and a husky singing voice, Jane had charming manners. If she could not follow a conversation, she contented herself with sitting quietly, arranging herself to best advantage. She was fully aware that men liked her as she was, a little silly, a little deferential—a young woman who needed, and indeed welcomed, instruction and guidance. She hung on the words of Williams and Shelley, praising their wisdom, her husband's bravery, and Shelley's genius. For Shelley, the agreeable Jane was a pleasant relief; she did not fight with her husband, or with anyone for that matter. She was never irritable, melancholy, or regretful, but then, she did not have much to be gloomy about. She had two healthy children. She lived in beautiful and comfortable surroundings with a man who adored her. Life was spread out before her like a feast.

Mary, too, found Jane more likable over time. Although Jane did not enjoy intellectual conversations, she was happy to discuss the difficulties of raising children in Italy—one of Mary's most pressing concerns. For too many years, she had felt alone as a mother, burdened by worries that no one seemed to share, not even Shelley. She had been isolated from other Englishwomen in Italy, as most refused to associate with the scandalous Shelleys. Claire had been too heartbroken over Allegra's absence to join in her sister's domestic concerns. Jane, on the other hand, with a newborn on her hands, had many questions about the care and feeding of an infant during the hot summer months. In addition, her little boy was only a few months younger than Percy, so she and Mary had similar anxieties: How much should a toddler eat? How long should he sleep?

Neither Mary nor Shelley suspected that Jane might not be as lovely or as simple as she seemed. An old friend who had known Jane in Switzerland warned Mary to be careful of her. She was a gossip, he said, and could be cruel. But just as Shelley ignored the warning signs about Williams, Mary chose not to listen to the warnings about Jane. It was lonely living in perpetual exile; Mary needed a friend.

*Portrait of Jane Williams by George Clint (1822).*

Still, there was a drawback to spending time with such a devoted couple. As Shelley watched the Williamses walk hand in hand on the path, or observed Jane gazing adoringly at Edward, Shelley mourned what he and Mary had lost. He told Mary he missed the intensity of their relationship, writing her a sad poem that lamented the distance that had come between them:

> *We are not happy, sweet! our state*
> *Is strange and full of doubt and fear;*
> *More need of words that ills abate;—*
> *Reserve or censure come not near*
> *Our sacred friendship, lest there be*
> *No solace left for thee and me.*

And yet they were still close literary companions, sharing ideas and books and exchanging manuscripts to read. No one understood Shelley's moods better than Mary, and no one supported Mary's writing ambitions more than Shelley. Their seven years together had brought them an intimacy that was as complicated as it was strong. In France, when Mary was a teenager, she had been content to stay in bed all day with Shelley. He, too, had wanted nothing more than to hold Mary in his arms. Now they both had their own pursuits, their own interests. Mary no longer thought of Shelley as a demigod. If she romanticized any man, it was her Greek prince. She spoke sharply to Shelley about their finances and vetoed schemes that she deemed too dangerous for eighteen-month-old Percy. She had become, in fact, a wife. As for Shelley, he felt wounded by what he perceived as her rejections. He had fallen in love with at least one other woman. Their desire for each other had ebbed. Nevertheless, they were still capable of enjoying the long, peaceful evenings, sitting outside, admiring the sky, or reading to each other from the works of Lucan or Homer. Occasionally, Shelley rowed Mary on the nearby river, and later Mary would remember these quiet voyages as among their happiest times, hearing nothing but the splash of the water and the high-pitched cries of the *aziola,* the little downy owls who nested in the stunted pines that grew along the shores. Shelley commemorated these evenings in a poem that records a gentle and loving conversation between husband and wife:

> *"Do you not hear the Aziola cry?*
> *Methinks she must be nigh,"*
> *Said Mary, as we sate*
> *In dusk, ere stars were lit, or candles brought;*
> *And I, who thought*
> *This Aziola was some tedious woman,*
> *Asked "Who is Aziola?"*
>
> .    .    .    .    .
>
> *And Mary saw my soul,*
> *And laughed and said "Disquiet yourself not,*
> *'Tis nothing but a little downy owl."*

—

ONE DAY TOWARD THE end of July, a missive arrived from Ravenna. Byron wanted Shelley to come and visit. Shelley, who was eager for the companionship of the great writer, rushed off to spend ten days with his lordship. While there, he persuaded Byron to spend the winter in Pisa so they could reconvene their literary community from Geneva. They could start a new magazine, one that would publish their work. To Mary, he wrote, "[We must] form for ourselves a society of our own class, as much as possible, in intellect or in feeling." He sent Hunt a letter urging him to come immediately to Italy and be their editor. He, Byron, Medwin, and their other friends would contribute funds, poetry, and essays, ensuring the project's success—welcome words to the increasingly debt-ridden Hunt, whose own literary endeavors had fallen on hard times.

Byron was open to Shelley's suggestion, as he had at last tired of his hectic life in Venice and had decided to share his home with a beautiful Italian contessa, Teresa Guiccioli. He asked Shelley to find him a suitable establishment in Pisa, and so when Shelley returned, he began house hunting. Byron sent Teresa ahead, and she arrived in Pisa the week of Mary's twenty-fourth birthday. Mary immediately paid her a visit and described her as a "nice pretty girl, without pretensions, [with a] good heart and amiable." The twenty-year-old Teresa confessed that she worried Byron might change his mind and not materialize, a fear Mary understood, so she spent many afternoons with Teresa. Claire, who had been vacationing in Livorno and had no idea that Byron was in the offing, wrote to say that she would like to come see them—a plan that worried Mary and Shelley. A few months earlier, Claire had discovered that Byron had sent four-year-old Allegra to a convent in Bagnacavallo, not far from Ravenna. Having heard terrible reports about the school and desperately worried about her daughter, Claire had written Byron a letter so scathing that he now refused to hear her name mentioned. All Claire had left was her pen. She had no legal rights, no power to stop Byron, even though she believed he had endangered their child.

Before I quitted Geneva you promised me—verbally it is true—that my child, whatever its sex, should never be away from its parents. . . . This promise is violated, not only slightly, but in a mode and by a conduct most intolerable to my feeling of love for Allegra. It has been my desire and my practice to interfere with you as little as possible; but were I silent now you would adopt this as an argument against me at some future period. I therefore represent to you that putting Allegra, at her years, into a convent, away from any relation, is to me a serious and deep affliction. . . . Every traveler and writer upon Italy joins in condemning [convents]. . . . This then with every advantage in your power of wealth, of friends, is the education you have chosen for your daughter. This step will procure you an innumerable addition of enemies and blame, for it can be regarded but in one light by the virtuous of whatever sect or denomination. . . . I alone, misled by love to believe you good, trusted to you, and now I reap the fruits. . . . So blind is hatred!

Hearing of the situation, the Williamses offered to put Claire up for a few weeks at their house in the country, an invitation she accepted with eagerness. Once she arrived, Shelley and Mary shuttled back and forth between Pisa and San Giuliano. The time apart had done the sisters good. Claire delighted Mary by playing with Percy. She also helped her pick out furniture for the grand new house in Pisa that Shelley wanted to find for them. Despite Shelley's accumulated debt (over £2,000), he had decided to splurge on a palazzo. He could never keep up with Byron—he had only a tenth of his lordship's income—but he could still try. Together, Mary and Claire chose beds, linens, a looking glass, and high-backed chairs. Claire accompanied Mary and Shelley on a trip to the Gulf of Spezia to spend the last days of summer at a seaside resort; their four days of picnicking, sailing, riding, and sightseeing were so splendid they decided La Spezia should be their summer destination the following year.

During this vacation, Mary could feel the mounting intensity of Shelley's feelings for Claire, but for the first time in their life together she did not protest. If Claire wanted to engage in a passionate relationship with Shelley, then Mary was prepared to accept it. In many ways, Claire was safer than an outsider. Mary knew that Shelley was aware of Claire's limitations: her volatility as well as the lethargy that overcame her at times. She no longer believed that he would desert her for her stepsister. Instead, she appreciated the temporary freedom she gained while Claire was with them. With Shelley happy and busy, Mary could write letters to her Greek prince and focus on Percy. She had written the conclusion of *Valperga*. The only task left was to copy it over. Then she could send it to England and perhaps earn some money, maybe even some fame.

When they returned from La Spezia, Claire began to complain about having to go back to Florence. Why couldn't she live with Mary and Shelley again? Shelley liked the idea, although he remained worried about Byron's reaction. But Mary's newfound enthusiasm for her sister evaporated immediately: a visit from Claire was fine, but living with her was an appalling prospect. She did not mind sharing Shelley for a few days, but she did not relish the idea of having Shelley turn to Claire all winter. Mrs. Mason agreed. The sisters needed to be apart, she said, and she sent such a stern warning to Claire that on the very day Byron arrived in Pisa, Claire was rattling out of town on her way south.

# CHAPTER 30

# MARY WOLLSTONECRAFT:
# IN LOVE AGAIN

———

[ 1796 ]

WHEN GODWIN RETURNED TO LONDON FROM HIS HOLIDAY ON July 24, it was four days later than Mary had expected, and she had worked herself into a prickly state of anxiety. While he was away, she had been certain enough of his feelings to move to 16 Judd Place West, just around the corner from his rooms on Chalton Street. For the first time since she had left for France in 1792, she took her furniture out of storage to set up on a more permanent basis. Now she was wondering if that was a mistake. Perhaps Godwin would turn out to be like Imlay—unreliable, making promises he would not keep. She tried to make light of her worries, writing to him that because he had not returned when he said he would, "I mean to bottle up my kindness, unless something in your countenance, when I do see you, should make the cork fly out."

Godwin came to see her the moment he arrived back in London, but Mary was only partially reassured. He was too anxious to say anything revealing, and for the next few visits, they went back and forth, fencing with each other and only hinting at their feelings. At last, after almost three weeks of this, heartened by the steadiness of Mary's warmth as well as her flirtatious notes—which she sent before and after their meetings—Godwin took courage and confessed his love by kissing her, a momentous occasion for both parties. Later,

Godwin remembered "the sentiment which trembled upon the tongue, burst from the lips."

But still, neither wanted to be the one to take the next step, and so the affair proceeded slowly, with tentative advances and retreats on each side. Sexual intimacy became a kind of chessboard, a test of strategy. For Godwin, whose father "was so puritanical that he considered the fondling of a cat a profanation of the Lord's Day," it seemed shocking to act on his sensual impulses. Mary, on the other hand, felt ready to plunge forward and was disappointed with Godwin's restraint. She began to refer to him as "your sapient Philosophership," partly in jest, but also to provoke him to display his feelings more openly.

Matters were made more difficult by the challenge of finding time alone. At Mary's house, Fanny was underfoot and Marguerite always nearby. At Godwin's, visitors called at all hours. Both knew that the discovery of a love affair between the author of *Political Justice* and the author of the *Vindications* would be a gold mine for the newspapers; they had plenty of enemies who would delight in telling this story, and for all of his radical ideas and writings, Godwin was thin-skinned when it came to scandal. Mary recognized that news of her relationship with Godwin would expose her to dangerous inquiries. Before long, people would guess that Fanny was illegitimate.

The remarkable thing is that they did not let their fears stop them. In the late summer evenings, while both Marguerite and Fanny were asleep, their time together was filled with increasing fervor. Writers that they were, they confessed their feelings in letters, dispatching quick flurries of words after their encounters. Mary told Godwin she could not escape from her "voluptuous sensations." Godwin confessed to Mary, "you set my imagination on fire. . . . For six & thirty hours I could think of nothing else. I longed inexpressibly to have you in my arms." But these rapid missives worked against them, too, making them uneasy when one of them expressed something awkwardly or confessed a moment of anxiety.

After one of their first intimate sessions, Godwin was so humiliated by his inadequacies that he avoided visiting Mary the next day and was cold to her when she stopped by his lodgings. When she sent him a note, trying to win him over by using Fanny's childish lisp—"Won'tee, as Fannikin would say, come and see me to day?"—he did not respond, and when he continued to avoid her, she sent another message asking, "Did you feel very lonely last night?" offering him an opening to express his affections. But the embarrassed Godwin replied grumpily, "I have been very unwell all night. You did not consider me enough in that way yesterday, & therefore unintentionally impressed upon me a mortifying sensation." Mary did not know what this mortifying sensation was and so felt rebuffed.

Godwin, though, had not meant to retreat. Afraid that his inexperience made him appear foolish—he certainly *felt* like a fool—he wanted confirmation of Mary's continued interest. The moment she admitted her despair, he told her he had been yearning for her but had withdrawn because he feared "I might be deceiving myself as to your feelings & that I was feeding my mind with groundless presumptions."

Having declared the seriousness of their intentions and the depth of their feelings, one might suppose the barriers could tumble down and they could fall into each other's arms, but both Godwin and Mary were terrified that the other might withdraw. In addition, as is often the case in love affairs, what one first admires in a partner can quickly become irritating. Godwin, who had at first been impressed with the intensity of Mary's emotions, now found her moods somewhat disturbing and preached the need for greater restraint. "You have the feelings of nature," he wrote Mary. "But do not let them tyrannise over you." Mary, who had admired Godwin's integrity, his reserve, his ability to control his behavior and his impulses, responded by telling him he needed to cultivate his intuition and imagination and act more spontaneously.

Their differences extended to the way they went about their daily lives. Godwin's routine rarely varied, while Mary, through necessity, kept very irregular hours. Fanny got sick. Mary Hays needed to weep over her Unitarian. A tradesman had to be appeased. Maria Reveley and Henry dropped by unannounced. She had also started reviewing for Johnson again, but she was still trying to make headway with *The*

*Wrongs of Woman*. To assume some of the household chores, including the delivery of her notes across the city, she hired a maid, but quiet reflective hours, the bedrock of Godwin's existence, were rare in Mary's life; it was not that she did not want them, but simply that they were hard to come by.

Despite these difficulties, by the end of August Mary and Godwin had consummated their relationship. It took four tries, which Godwin marked in his diary with characteristic understatement: *"chez moi"* (my house), *"chez elle"* (her house) twice, and then finally *"chez elle toute"* (her house—everything). Godwin was no Imlay. An anxious virgin, he needed these three fumbling practice sessions before *toute*. Afterward, he did not effuse. There are no lyrical descriptions of Mary's beauty or of his own rapture. Fortunately, Mary was unaware of Godwin's laconic record keeping, or she might well have seen it as yet more evidence of his coldness.

But Godwin was in fact warming up. His notes to Mary became positively playful as summer turned to fall. By September he was referring to himself as Mary's "boy pupil." In October he added *"bonne"* to his terse *"chez moi."* Mary, too, was learning to trust Godwin. She began to write letters to him that overflowed with feeling: "It is a sublime tranquility I have felt in your arms—Hush! Let not the light see, I was going to say hear it—these confessions should only be uttered—you know where, when the curtains are up and the world shut out." They relied on the birth control system of the time: no sex for three days after menstruation, and then, since everyone believed that frequent intercourse lowered the possibility of conception, a lot of sex for the rest of the month.

Mary still pushed Godwin to be more expressive, though. She wanted "little marks of attention," but Godwin resisted being told what to do, complaining, "You spoil little attentions by anticipating them." Why couldn't she trust that he loved her? Because, Mary wrote, she had found that if she wanted "attention" from him it was "necessary to demand it." She sensed that he was anxious and tackled the problem with characteristic directness. "Can you solve this problem?" she asked. "I was endeavoring to discover last night, in bed, what it is in me of which you are afraid? I was hurt at perceiving that you were—but no more of this—mine is a sick heart." And yet these quarrels were testimony to the intimacy they were developing. Often bewildered by Mary's hurt feelings, Godwin was learning to pay her compliments and reassure her about his commitment. In turn, Mary was learning not to expect too many sentimental tokens from her reserved suitor and to use tact and brevity when expressing disappointment in him, rather than lengthy speeches and sheaves of letters.

Characteristically, neither allowed their affair to slow down their work. Both were deeply involved in literary projects. Godwin was revising *Political Justice* for a second edition while working on a play, the tragedy *Antonio; or, The Soldier's Return* (which was produced in 1799). He brought the manuscript to Mary's house in the evenings and they would go over it together. After a few of these tête-à-têtes, Mary sent an early draft of *The Wrongs of Woman* to Godwin for his advice. His response was not at all what she wanted to hear. There was "a radical defect" in her writing, he said. The grammar was still sloppy despite his tutoring. The ideas incoherent. The story unclear. While Mary had welcomed his comments on her work earlier in the summer, now they felt intrusive and harsh. She was far more invested in *The Wrongs of Woman* than she had been in her play, and she expected more now that they were lovers. He should understand her, she felt, and see the value of her work without her having to argue on its behalf. She sent him a long letter outlining her position:

> What is to be done, I must either disregard your opinion, think it unjust, or throw down my pen in despair; and that would be tantamount to resigning existence. . . . In short, I must reckon on doing some good, and getting the money I want, by my writings, or go to sleep for ever. I shall not be content merely to keep body and soul together. . . . And, for I would wish you to see my heart and mind just as it appears to myself, without drawing any veil of affected humility over it. . . . I am compelled to think that there is something in my writings more valuable than in the productions of some people on whom you bestow warm elogiums—I mean more mind . . . more of the observations of my own senses, more of

the combining of my own imagination—the effusions of my own feelings and passions than the cold workings of the brain on the materials produced by the senses and imagination of other writers.

I am more out of patience with myself than you can form any idea of, when I tell you that I have scarcely written a line to please myself . . . since you saw my M.S.

For all that she respected Godwin, Mary had made it clear that she was not prepared to abandon *The Wrongs of Woman*. The play Godwin had criticized had not been worth continuing, she felt. She had seen that and had put it aside. But *The Wrongs of Woman* was different, its message far more significant. In this book, she would be able to expose the injustices that women faced, the sufferings they endured. Godwin could work on *Political Justice* and his own play as much as he liked, but he must allow her to reveal herself in her writing—to express personal emotions and to describe her visions and nightmares, her fantasies and memories. They had different aims, and hers were as worthy as his.

After receiving her letter, Godwin apologized and said he would continue to help her with her grammar if she wished, which she did, confessing her insecurity: "Yet now you have led me to discover that I write worse, than I thought I did, there is no stopping short—I must improve, or be dissatisfied with myself." Still, his assumption of superiority rankled. Six months later she would rally and write an essay arguing on behalf of her writing ideals. This essay was so well designed that Godwin did not take offense, and indeed may not even have realized that it was directed, at least in part, at him.

As the weather grew cool, they spent many evenings by Mary's fireside, reading, working, talking, and playing with Fanny. Sometimes they went for walks in the nearby fields. Other times they spent afternoons at Godwin's lodgings while Marguerite stayed with Fanny. But these hours felt stolen and brief; both yearned to spend an entire night together, and so they made plans for a secret outing away from London. Mary liked the idea of visiting the country. Godwin liked the idea of uninterrupted privacy. They set a date in September for a weekend outside the city. But their plans were ruined by Fanny, who had become whiny and difficult in the week leading up to their departure and broke out in chicken pox the day before they were supposed to depart. Mary did not want to leave her sick daughter, and so they waited until the spots had almost disappeared before they set forth. In the end, Mary was still so concerned about Fanny that they decided to spend only one night away.

Excited and in love, they took a coach to the village of Ilford, not far from Wollstonecraft's first home in Epping, where they paid a visit to her old house and found it almost unchanged. Since no one was living there, they were free to wander through the fields where Mary had played as a little girl. The past came rushing back to her as they walked: her father's drunken rages, her mother's weakness, the many injustices she had endured—Mary told Godwin everything she remembered, connecting to him the best way she knew how, through stories and memories.

When they returned home, Mary found a very sick little girl. She wrote to tell Godwin this news "with [Fanny] in my arms." The pox had come back; Fanny had refused to sleep without Mary and had itched herself into a scabby fever. Now she dogged her mother's steps, and Mary spent the day trying to amuse her so she would stop scratching her face. Other eighteenth-century mothers might have disciplined their two-year-olds, or tried to, but Mary hoisted her daughter up and lugged her about the house, the little girl clinging like a crab. At night, Fanny still could not sleep and kept Mary up as well; after a few days of this, Mary also became ill.

Godwin, meanwhile, was rolling briskly through his revisions of *Political Justice*. Not once did it occur to him that Mary might need help, and she railed against his self-absorption: "Why could you not say *how do ye do* this morning. It is I who want nursing . . . —are you above the feminine office?" He argued back—it was not his job to take care of her—and promptly withdrew, refusing to respond to her accusations. Mary complained more vigorously, until finally Godwin relented, paying her a bedside visit. Instantly, Mary cheered up. His steadiness more than made up for his selfishness. She saw that he was trying to unbend and give her what she wanted, and in return she tried to demand fewer displays of affection. However, his stiffness continued to irritate her, and when she felt better, she urged him to be more "cheerful, gay, playful; nay, even frolicksome." She was impatient with his literal-mindedness and his stilted conventionality. For his part, Godwin wanted Mary to be more serious, more reasonable. He complained that he could not "distinguish always between your jest and earnest, and know when your satire means too much and when it means nothing. But I will try."

The key, of course, was that he would try. And so, too, would she. Thus, with all its bumps, their relationship solidified, although this solidity gave Mary a new concern. If she and Godwin were really going to have a future together, then Fanny and Godwin needed to love each other.

Mary need not have worried. For all of his rigidity, Godwin had embraced "Fannikin" from the start, and Fanny adored Godwin, demanding to know when "Man" was coming for another visit. When they went on walks, she pulled her mother down Chalton Street, saying, "Go this way Mama, me wants to see Man." By the end of November, Marguerite was dropping Fanny off at Godwin's lodgings, where he plied her with biscuits and puddings while her mother capitalized on her time alone and worked. Mary and Godwin began referring to each other as "mama and papa." Mary enjoyed reporting Fanny's small triumphs to Godwin, one day writing to him that Fanny "came crowing upstairs to tell me that she did not cry when her face was washed." This is what she had dreamed of with Imlay, sharing a daughter.

They continued to keep their affair secret, entertaining guests separately and attending parties alone. Even their best friends remained in the dark. But in December, after a patch of relative tranquillity, Mary began to feel depressed and unwell. On December 6, she felt "an extreme lowness of spirits," and the next day, she saw Godwin at the theater with Mrs. Inchbald, her nemesis, while she sat alone in a cheap seat. "I was a fool not to ask Opie [her friend the portrait painter] to go with me," she said irritably to Godwin, hoping to make him jealous. More small tiffs ensued. By the third week of December the reason for Mary's touchiness had become clear. She was pregnant.

Godwin responded with warmth and excitement to this news; on December 23, Mary wrote to him, "There was a tenderness in your manner, as you seemed to be opening your heart, to a new born affection, that rendered you very dear to me. There are other pleasures in the world, you perceive, beside those know[n] to your philosophy." She, however, was dispirited by her condition. She felt herself descending back into the darkness that had plagued her so many times before. On December 28, "painful recollections" of being pregnant and abandoned came flooding back and she told Godwin that she wished they had never met. She wanted "to cancel all that had passed between us" and have "all the kind things you had written me destroyed." Godwin was hurt and anxious, but he admitted that he did not know how to fix the problems that lay in front of them. The obstacles to their happiness seemed insurmountable: societal disapproval, illegitimate children, and money.

Mary had not earned much from her writing that fall, and her debts were growing. Johnson, who had always taken care of Mary's financial problems, was reluctant to pay her bills because he wanted Mary to force Imlay to contribute to Fanny's upkeep. Mary understood Johnson's reluctance, and finally wrote to Imlay that she would accept his help, but Imlay never responded. Godwin was also of little practical assistance. He had calculated his living expenses down to the last penny, sometimes having to borrow a few pounds to make ends meet. He had never intended to assume the financial responsibility of a family, declaring that such obligations blighted the freedom of the male intellectual. Mary was aware of his principles, but as a pregnant single mother, she was finding it difficult to have much respect for them.

She felt slightly better when Godwin demonstrated his commitment to her by borrowing fifty pounds from a friend to help her get through the winter. Appreciative though she was, however, she did not like that once again, the author of *Rights of Woman* was dependent on a man. She tried to bring in some money by reviewing for Johnson but was too exhausted to accomplish much. It was a difficult winter. The weather was harsh, and, cooped up indoors, Fanny was bored and underfoot. Mary was so tired that running even the smallest errand was onerous. When it snowed, she had to pick her way through the uncleared streets, the hem of her long dress dragging through the drifts, her ankles and feet icy cold. She wrote Godwin, "You have no petticoats to dangle in the snow. Poor women, how they are beset with plagues—within and without." It was galling that she was the one with the daughter, the one who was pregnant, the one who could not work because she did not feel well. She was struggling to get through each day with one child, let alone two, while, as usual, the methodical Godwin wrote from nine to one. He was almost finished with the new edition of *Political Justice*.

Mary did at least manage to keep up her reading, and she and Godwin followed the news and politics. They both finished Mary Hays's novel, *Emma Courtney*. Godwin had her critique his essay on education for *The Enquirer* before he submitted it for publication. Mary advised him to advocate more forcefully for the institution of public day schools, as this would "obviate the evil, of being left with servants, and enable children to converse with children." She said that she did not approve of boarding school (even though she had once run one) because "the exercise of domestic affections" was the "foundation of virtue." She was also still mulling over her novel, *The Wrongs of Woman,* and had decided that her central female character would be an abused wife, imprisoned unjustly in an asylum by her husband. She reread the section of Godwin's *Caleb Williams* in which Caleb is thrown in prison for crimes he did not commit, and then she persuaded Johnson and Godwin to tour Bedlam with her, which they did on February 6.

The asylum was located in Moorfields, near the recently constructed Finsbury Square in what is now northeast London. It was a ramshackle, poverty-stricken part of the city, notorious for beggars and criminals. It was also the center of the secondhand furniture and old clothing trade, and its alleyways were lined with shacks crammed with broken chairs, rickety bedsteads, and yellowed linens. On the same day they went to Bedlam, Mary and Godwin also shopped at an "old clothesmen's" storefront, perhaps to buy clothes for a servant or even for themselves.

Bedlam had once been a magnificent baroque building, but when Mary, Johnson, and Godwin visited, it was over one hundred years old. Its foundations had been laid in the sandy soil of the old London moat, and now its walls were sagging and the whole three-story structure looked as though it might collapse under the weight of its heavy roof and elegant bell towers. Inside, its inmates were starving, naked, and chained to the walls. The barnlike "airing rooms," where those patients who were not deemed dangerous were allowed to roam freely, were open to the viewing public. Indeed, visiting Bedlam was a popular activity in eighteenth-century England. Tourists were charged a penny to come gawk at the poor sufferers. Mary jotted down notes, intent on using the cries she heard and the anguish she saw for her new novel.

Always, however, there was the question of what they should do next as a couple, and they spent the winter debating their options. Since both were famous for their criticisms of marriage, it was difficult to embrace the idea of a wedding, but they also knew that they lived in a world that would shun Mary if she had a child out of wedlock. Only her closest friends knew that she had not actually been married to Imlay, and she was all too aware of the condemnation she would face when the news broke that Imlay was not her husband. Although at first Godwin tried to persuade her to live according to their ideals, he soon realized that philosophy would be little consolation when faced with the wrath of their society. Mary would be severely punished if they did not marry. And yet if they did, he would be ridiculed as a hypocrite. She would be, too, of course, but perhaps this was a lesser evil than the ostracism she would face as an unmarried mother. Godwin tried to fix his own situation by retracting his previous stance against marriage in his new edition of *Political Justice*. Marriage, he wrote, was still a necessary evil in society, but he hoped that someday, in a better world, there would be no need for the institution.

Fanny's situation further complicated matters. Since marriage to Godwin would effectively proclaim her daughter illegitimate, Mary was concerned about society's treatment of her little girl. On the other hand, if she did not legitimize this new relationship, then her second baby would be condemned. Either way, a child was hurt. Either way, her reputation was ruined. Finally, after much debate, she and Godwin decided to get married—an imperfect solution that made neither one happy, yet seemed the best answer to their predicament.

Godwin, meanwhile, was apprehensive about what would happen if they spent too much time together. He did not want to give up his quiet lodgings and subject himself to the confusion of Mary's household, outlining his anxieties in an essay he wrote for *The Enquirer* in which he spoke about the dangers of "cohabitation":

> It seems to be one of the most important of the arts of life, that men should not come too near each other, or touch in too many points. Excessive familiarity is the bane of social happiness.

Like Godwin, Mary dreaded what lay ahead. She kept the plan and her pregnancy secret from her friends, and even from her sister Everina, who paid an uncomfortable visit that winter. This was the first time that Mary had seen one of her sisters since her return from France, but it was far from a joyful reunion. Everina disapproved of Mary's friends. She took an instant dislike to Godwin and refused to speak to him. Although this was the first time that she had met Fanny, she ignored the little girl. She came down with a cold, and Mary and Marguerite had to wait on her. When she did get out of bed, she ran up a bill at the millinery shop that she did not pay. She did nothing to help when there was an emergency: Fanny's cat, Puss, went "wild" and "flew up the chimney." Mary, who loved animals, did not want him destroyed and struggled with what to do about his erratic behavior. At length, she decided that Puss was too dangerous, and with sorrow, she had him drowned, telling Fanny that he was sick and had run away.

Finally, Everina left. Though Mary was relieved that she was gone, she wrote to her sister soon after, promising to send money when she had some, and to Eliza as well, though Eliza still would not speak to Mary. It had been fourteen years since Mary had rescued Eliza from her abusive husband, and yet Mary could not shed her sense that her sister's happiness was her personal responsibility. Everina had told her that Eliza's employer in Wales had practically imprisoned her, preventing her from going outside or taking any breaks from her work. Mary wanted to help, but she felt discouraged. She was older and more pessimistic than when she had written *Rights of Woman;* it now seemed an impossible dream that her sisters, or, for that matter, any ordinary woman, might achieve independence. Like many of the ideals that she and her friends had shared during the last decade—universal human rights, greater equality of rich and poor, the over-turning of the French aristocracy—the dream of improving life for women had come to nothing. Her *Vindications* had not changed the world—another reason she had turned away from essay writing. She herself, who unlike many other women had some means of income at her disposal, could not get out of debt, a situation worsened by her predilection for helping others. In April, she took in her maid's son when he was sick and then paid for him to go to school—a circumstance that prevented her from sending the promised funds to Everina. And so, even if Mary could not fully understand why her sisters seemed perpetually angry, they in turn heard her promises with a jaundiced ear. She had done little to help them for years, and in fact had abandoned them when she returned to London, an abandonment made worse by all that she had said she would do for them but never did.

Mary and Godwin were happy to have their privacy back and enjoyed as many peaceful weeks as they could until the end of March, when Mary's pregnancy would be evident to all. On March 29, she and Godwin walked to St. Pancras, the old country church in Somers Town, and, with Godwin's friend James Marshall as a witness, became husband and wife. Godwin marked the event in his diary with only one syllable—"Panc"—as though he could not bring himself to spell out the whole word, let alone confess that this was his wedding day. And in fact this is precisely the emphasis the couple gave it. They did not have a party or a celebration. What, after all, was there to celebrate? Their wedding was merely a concession to societal prejudice.

Afterward, Godwin went to the theater alone with Mrs. Inchbald, while Mary went home and began to pack up her things. After much discussion, they had decided it was time to move in together, but the fact that this was a difficult decision for them points to just how unconventional they were. It was unheard of for married couples to maintain separate residences at the time, or even express a desire to do so. And so Mary and Godwin devised a set of compromises that would prove to be as revolutionary as their writings: Godwin would rent some cheap rooms down the street from their new home so that he could retreat every day to write. In return, he would not expect Mary to assume full domestic responsibilities for their household—an extraordinary concession. He would respect her right to work; she would respect his. Their partnership, they said, should foster the independence of both man and woman. It should not, at any cost, force either one of them into the sort of domestic imprisonment both dreaded and had fought against for most of their adult lives. They knew of no other couples who had made such an arrangement. As usual, they were trailblazers, so much so that one hundred and thirty years later, Virginia Woolf would look to their marriage for inspiration when she was trying to carve out her own relationship with her husband, Leonard. To Woolf, Mary's marriage would in fact become her most revolutionary act, her "most fruitful experiment."

# MARY SHELLEY:
# "LEAGUE OF INCEST"

———

[ 1821–1822 ]

*T*HE ARRIVAL OF BYRON AND HIS ENTOURAGE WAS ALWAYS A SPEC-tacular event, but especially so in a sleepy little town like Pisa. On November 1, the carts rolled down the Lung'Arno, piled high with supplies, including his enormous bed with the Byron coat of arms carved into the headboard. Then came the Flemish mare, led by a special groom; the goats and donkey trotted along behind; the dogs leapt and barked, straining on their leashes; the geese hissed and shook their feathers; the rest of the menagerie howled in their crates. His lordship arrived last, shuttered inside his Napoleonic carriage, away from the eyes of the curious.

Shelley had found an enormous marble mansion for his lordship, the Palazzo Lanfranchi, the most imposing building on the Arno. Many servants had worked diligently to get the house in running order—polishing, scrubbing, and organizing the "necessities" that were required for such a grand establishment. And yet even its enor-mous rooms could hardly contain the mountain of furniture, linens, and silver Byron had brought with him. For his own family, Shelley had found a house directly across the river, the Tre Palazzi di Chiesa at the end of the Lung'Arno. "We are entirely out of the bustle and disagreeable *puzzi* etc., of the town," Mary noted happily. From their windows they could see the city's formal gardens, its shrubs pruned into cones and cylinders, and beyond the city walls, the open countryside with its patches of olive orchards, dark stands of cypress, and gentle hills rippling all the way to the sea. Shelley and Mary had the top floor, while the Williamses, at Shelley's urging, took the ground floor.

The stage was set. Two poets. Two houses. The Pisans watched in astonishment as Shelley and Byron began to compete against each other in just about everything: Who was the better rider? Who the better shot? Shelley deferred to Byron as "his lordship," although behind his back he declared that most of Byron's faults came from his exaggerated sense of entitlement. Byron bowed to Shelley's aesthetics, declaring that the younger man was the one with the true poetic sensibility, but took smug satisfaction in his own position as the more famous poet.

Never had the town been rocked by so many outlandish escapades. One of Byron's servants stabbed a man. His lordship's house was lit up all night long. The Pisans were up in arms. Did he ever sleep? His wolfish dogs howled. His peacocks shrieked. Occasionally, the monkeys got loose and swung around the city gardens. Every afternoon, he and his friends filed out the city gates armed with their pistols. The Pisan authorities thought revolution was in the air, but when they followed these libertines, they found the Englishmen standing tamely in a row aiming at bull's-eyes. Byron was probably the best shot, although his hand often trembled because he took so long to aim. Shelley was the only one who could challenge him, but his method of shooting was the opposite of his lordship's. He whipped out his pistol and fired instantly, the results either gloriously on target or spectacularly off.

Adding to the chaos were members of the English press, who hurried to the town to report on Byron, labeling the band of friends, as they had before, "the League of Incest and Atheism." The same old rumors spread throughout Europe and England that Byron was sleeping with Mary and that Shelley was promoting anarchy. Even the Tuscan grand duke, usually the center of attention himself, walked up and down outside Byron's house in hopes of catching sight of the famous recluse. But Byron was not in the mood to placate the crowds. Ever since he had been ridiculed as a fat schoolboy, he had been self-

conscious about his girth. Periodically, he would institute fasting regimes in which he would go many days without eating, then feast on
fish and wine. Sometimes all he would eat were potatoes drenched in
vinegar, or hard biscuits and soda water. But over the last year he had
grown quite plump, and he did not want anyone to see how large
he had become. In Pisa, when he did go out, he preferred to drive
through the streets, protected from prying eyes, riding his mare only
when he was safely outside town.

Medwin joined the party that fall, and later he would remember
how Byron asked Shelley to critique a poem he had just written,
*The Deformed Transformed*. Everyone waited to hear Shelley's opinion,
expecting him to shower compliments on his lordship's head. But
when at last Shelley announced his verdict, he startled the group of
Byron fans by saying he "liked it the least of all his works . . . it smelt
too strongly of *Faust*." Byron made a show of destroying the manuscript, tossing it into the fire, though in fact he had another copy carefully stowed away in a desk drawer.

Although Byron often made Shelley feel inadequate, and although
Shelley's eccentricity, paired with his righteous indignation about
nearly everything (from the cruelty of eating animals to the condition of the working classes), irritated Byron, they were still fascinated
by each other. In company, they ignored everyone else, speaking exclusively among themselves, an arrogance that no one protested; instead, conversation ceased so people could listen to the two masters.
The poets exaggerated their conversational styles to make their differences more readily apparent—Byron becoming more Byron-like
and Shelley more Shelley-like. In his diary the worshipful Medwin
tried to capture what it was like to hear them:

> [Byron's] talk was at that time . . . full of persiflage. . . . Both
> professed the same speculative—I might say, skeptical turn of
> mind; the same power of changing the subject from grave to
> gay; the same mastery over the sublime, the pathetic, the
> comic. . . . Shelley frequently lamented that it was almost im-
> possible to keep Byron to any given point. He flew about from

subject to subject like a will-o'-the-wisp. . . . Every word of Shelley's was almost oracular; his reasoning subtle and profound, his opinions, whatever they were, sincere and undisguised; whilst with Byron, such was his love of mystification, it was impossible to know when he was in earnest. . . . He dealt too in the gross and indelicate, of which Shelley had an utter abhorrence, and often left him in ill-disguised disgust.

Byron had the insight to see that Shelley's work, although it had yet to win acclaim or gain a significant following, was extraordinary. Watching Shelley's dangerous exploits with Williams on the wintry Arno from the safety of his balcony, Byron used nautical imagery to capture his sense of Shelley's genius:

[Shelley] alone, in this age of humbug, dares stem the current, as he did today the flooded Arno in his skiff, although I could not observe he made any progress. The attempt is better than being swept along as the rest are, with the filthy garbage scoured from its banks.

On Wednesday nights, the whole group dined at his lordship's; afterward, the two poets stayed up until the early morning talking about ships, poems, and, sometimes, women. To Edward Williams's delight, the poets included him and his newly arrived friend, the dashing Cornish sailor Edward Trelawny, in their inner circle. Mary felt a little shut out from this boys' club. "Our good cavaliers flock together," she wrote Marianne, "and as they do not like fetching a walk with the absurd womankind, Jane . . . and I are off together and talk morality and pluck violets by the way."

Mary had plenty to keep her busy, however. She finished copying *Valperga* that December and sent it to England in January with a stern note from Shelley to their publisher that demanded good financial terms for his wife. While she waited to hear Ollier's response, Byron, who had retained his respect for her talents, asked her to be his copyist, a job she gladly assumed, since she was still an avid admirer of his poetry. For Shelley, Mary's enthusiasm for Byron's work was unnerving, especially since Shelley himself had not written much since his lordship's arrival. Fortunately, there was always the beautiful Jane Williams, who seemed eager to listen to his thoughts and feelings, who did not have writing projects of her own, and who frequently expressed her admiration for his many talents.

One of her most interesting attributes was that she could speak some Hindi. She had spent part of her girlhood in India, where her father had been a merchant, and she sometimes included Indian melodies in the songs she sang—an exoticism that Shelley loved. He listened to her for hours, rapt and inspired. Here at last was his new muse. Emilia had been a disappointment. Mary was too cold. Claire was far away in Florence. Jane's beauty would inspire him to write great poetry—of this he was sure.

For Jane, Shelley's show of interest was a singular triumph over the intellectual Mary. Was it possible, Jane wondered, that Shelley, the genius, preferred her to his brilliant author wife? She trained her dark eyes on the poet, and her worshipful presence—balm to his unadmired soul—led him to compose lyrics of praise, just as he had hoped. He bought her an expensive guitar, inlaid with mother-of-pearl, which he could not afford, and called himself Ariel, the guardian spirit of Miranda (Jane).

It is likely that Jane missed this reference to Shakespeare's *The Tempest,* as she was not well read and had never heard of most of the authors Shelley mentioned. Yet far from minding this, Shelley was reminded of how pleasant it was when a woman did not have her own opinions. He had enjoyed that quality in Emilia, too—an ironic reversal for someone who had once found Mary's education and brilliant abilities so superior to Harriet's ignorance—but his feelings for Jane ran deeper, he decided. Emilia had been a sham. Now it was Jane—her soulful musicality and her worshipful eyes—who represented Shelley's ideal woman. He had always enjoyed playing the teacher, and he began a crash course in literature for this new object of his fascination. By spring, she could be counted on to take Shelley's side on every issue, from history to politics, as well as in any domestic conflicts. In fact, Jane loved nothing more than when he complained about his wife and could always be counted on to contribute her own negative remarks about Mary. According to Jane, the ways in which Mary had failed her husband were positively myriad.

If Mary was aware of Shelley and Jane's duplicity, she hid it remarkably well, finding her own solace in Edward Williams's friend Trelawny. The twenty-nine-year-old seaman had arrived in Pisa in January, right after the Christmas holidays, and at first he seemed to Mary to be everything a real man should be. The younger son of a titled Cornish family, Edward Trelawny said that he had served in the navy—although his biographers cast doubt on this claim—and that he had quit the service at age twenty to roam the world. He did not mention that he lived on only £500 a year and had abandoned a wife and two daughters back in England.

Trelawny was a dashing figure. He had an elegant mustache and long hair that he pushed behind his ears. In her journal, Mary was rhapsodic about his many splendors, noting "his Moorish face . . . his dark hair, his Herculean form." He seemed larger than life, capable of anything. His voice was loud, "His 'Tremendous!' being indeed tremendous," as one friend observed. To Mary, he was like a comet, waking her from "the everyday sleepiness of human intercourse." Brigands, battles, faraway lands, shipwrecks—there was nothing he had not experienced, or so it seemed; listening to his stories was like reading *The Arabian Nights*.

*The dashing Edward Trelawny, Edward Williams's friend.*

At the end of January, Shelley slipped a seven-stanza poem he titled *The Serpent is shut out from Paradise* under the door of the Williamses' apartment. Shelley was fascinated by snakes—their role in mythology, not only as demonic symbols but also as symbols of rebirth and reincarnation. Thus Williams knew that this was meant to be an autobiographical poem, and when he and Jane read it, its meaning was clear. The "Paradise" Shelley was shut out of was the paradise of the Williamses' married life. He was sad and alone; his home with Mary offered him no peace and his feelings for Jane only made him lonelier. He declared that he was going to have to avoid the Williamses—a resolution that he soon broke:

III.

> *Therefore if now I see you seldomer*
> *Dear friends, dear* friend! *Know that I only fly*
> > *Your looks because they stir*
> *Griefs that should sleep, and hopes that cannot die:*
> *The very comfort that they minister*
> > *I scarce can bear; yet I,*
> *So deeply is the arrow gone,*
> *Should quickly perish if it were withdrawn.*

IV.

> *When I return to my cold home, you ask*
> *Why I am not as I have ever been!*
> > *You spoil me for the task*
> *Of acting a forced part on life's dull scene,—*

Shelley had told Edward he could read the poem to Jane, but that "the lines were too dismal for *me* to keep." Williams did read the verses to Jane, who was flattered by Shelley's proclamations of love, but Williams was not unduly concerned, nor was he jealous. In his journal he gave the event no more weight than anything else that happened that day:

Shelley sent us some beautiful but too melancholy lines—
Call'd on Lord B. and accompanied him to the [shooting]
ground—Broke a bottle at 30 paces. Dined with Mary and
Shelley.

Williams did, however, feel sorry for his friend. Mary was not a
person he would ever want to be married to. In his eyes, Mary complained too much, admired Byron too enthusiastically, and fussed too
much over Shelley's sailing adventures. She could be argumentative
and moody. She worried about her son. She nagged about money.
She was not as beautiful as Jane. No wonder Shelley was unhappy.
Her gaiety surfaced only occasionally; to both Jane and Edward, she
seemed a resentful, unpleasant young woman without any real
charms. Entering when they did, they had no way of knowing that
Mary had once idolized her husband, still believed in his poetic genius, and continued to view him as the only person with whom she
could be fully "natural." When he doubted his abilities as a writer, he
could always turn to her. The same held true for Mary; when she was
unsure of herself, she knew that Shelley would say, "Seek to know
your own heart & learning what it best loves—try to enjoy that."
Before he read *Valperga,* for instance, he had written to her, "Be severe in your corrections & expect severity from me, your sincere admirer. I flatter myself you have composed something unequalled in
its kind, & that not content with the honours of your birth & your
hereditary aristocracy, you will add still higher renown to your
name."

Despite Shelley's faith in her work, however, bad news came from
London that spring. Ollier, their publisher, had refused to offer acceptable terms for *Valperga.* Shelley and Mary wanted £500 and had
assumed that £400 would be the lowest they would get; thus, it was
a shock not to sell the book at all. Mary was deeply disappointed. She
had hoped the work would pay their debts and help her father. Secretly, she had expected to receive good reviews; she was proud of
her achievement.

On the heels of Ollier's rejection, Godwin wrote to say that he
was about to be evicted from Skinner Street. Worried, guilty, and

wanting desperately to win her father's approval, Mary instructed Ollier to give Godwin the manuscript as a gift, telling Godwin to use his literary contacts to try to sell the book and to keep the money if he succeeded. But somehow Godwin managed to avert disaster without *Valperga*. He received an infusion of funds and decided to wait until the market improved to try to sell the book. Two more years would pass before he did find a publisher, causing Mary to lament privately to Mrs. Gisborne, "I long to hear some news of it—as with an author's vanity I want to see it in print & hear the praises of my friends."

Unfortunately, when *Valperga* was finally published, although most reviewers praised Mary's graceful style, they missed the complexity of the story entirely, and so Mary never received the accolades she felt were her due. On the title page, she identified herself as the author of *Frankenstein,* asserting her credentials both as a radical and a writer, and yet her powerful homage to her mother was viewed as a tragic love story rather than the highly charged political tale it really was. The one critic who noticed her rebuttal of Machiavelli chastised her for portraying Castruccio as "modern and feminine" rather than "glowing and energetic." He ignored her antiwar philosophy and her condemnation of male ambition—points immediately evident to the modern reader—and instead condemned her for her lack of piety, writing her off as a member of the "Satanic School," the label that poet Robert Southey had bestowed on Shelley and Byron. To the rest of her contemporaries, *Valperga* was merely historical fiction, a novel by a female writer, and as such was not to be taken seriously, either philosophically or politically. For Mary, it was disconcerting to have her ideas ignored, her politics dismissed. She had thought she might be pilloried by conservatives, but she had also assumed that she would become a heroine for liberals. Instead she was to be discounted.

In Pisa, on February 7, Trelawny took Mary to a ball at the home of an elegant Englishwoman, Mrs. Beauclerk, and waltzed with her, something Shelley had never done. Afterward, she gushed about the evening in her journal:

During a long—long evening in mixed society, dancing &
music—how often do ones sensations change—and swift as
the west wind drives the shadows of clouds across the sunny
hill or the waving corn—so swift do sentiments pass.

She was overwhelmed by her feelings. One word from Trelawny
could "excite [her] lagging blood. Laughter dances in the eyes & the
spirits rise proportionably high." Like her Greek prince, he made her
slender will-o'-the-wisp husband seem frail, even effeminate.

Trelawny admired Mary's mix of solemnity and humor that could
sometimes turn giddy, her "calm gray eyes" and her "pedigree of genius." He was also impressed by her "power of expressing her
thoughts in varied and appropriate words, derived from familiarity
with the works of our vigorous old writers."

A few days after the dance, celebrations began for the Pisan Carnival. Unable to resist the excitement, the entire group decided to attend one of the public masked balls. Mary put on a Turkish costume
and Jane wore her "Hindustani dress"—a turban and silk bloomers, a
costume she was proud of as it commemorated her girlhood in India.
They strolled along the Arno, critiquing the other costumes, then
danced until three in the morning.

For the next few weeks, Mary saw Trelawny almost every day.
Mrs. Beauclerk, the hostess of the ball Mary had attended with him
by her side, had taken a liking to Mary, and she urged other English
hostesses to include the Shelleys on their guest lists. Many refused,
not wanting to mix with the "League of Incest," but the possibility
that the notorious Lord Byron might accompany the Shelleys was too
much for some to resist. And so on the strength of Mrs. Beauclerk's
recommendation, as well as their acquaintance with the famous poet,
the Shelleys were invited to soirees and fetes, teas and dances. Shelley
had no interest in such occasions, but Mary took full advantage of
them, bringing Trelawny along as her escort. Now, when Shelley
dined at Byron's and did not come home until the early morning,
Mary did not mind, because she, too, was staying out late. Indeed,
she was discovering there was a certain power to being an attractive

young woman in the world. A Greek count, a friend of her Greek prince, told her that she had "the prettiest little ways, the prettiest little looks, the prettiest little figure . . . the prettiest little movements in the world."

When they were not at parties, she and Trelawny dined together, went for long walks, and discussed their dreams for the future—all with Shelley's tacit permission, since the poet spent most of his time with Byron or the Williamses. As with the mysterious Claire episodes, the key journal pages from this time are missing. The irony, of course, is that these missing pages serve as flags, marking events that either Mary or her descendants did not want others to know. This makes it seem likely that a brief romantic interlude did occur that winter—but also that it did not go much further than a few kisses, as Trelawny almost certainly would have capitalized on such an experience later in life, either in his memoirs or in the letters he would one day write to others about Mary. As for Mary, although she might have been swept up in the excitement of these attentions, she discovered that she was pregnant shortly after the dance, a circumstance that bound her once again to Shelley. Besides, as the weeks passed, she had begun to feel there was something untrustworthy about Trelawny. She could not quite put her finger on it, but although she found him enormously attractive, his tales were so fantastic that she wondered if he was all he appeared to be, writing to Mrs. Gisborne the day after the dance, "for his moral qualities I am yet in the dark[;] he is a strange web which I am endeavoring to unravel." She was dazzled, yet suspicious—not realizing, or not wanting to realize, that danger could lie ahead, that Trelawny might one day do her irreparable harm.

Mary was not the only one being courted by Trelawny over these few months. Eager to attach himself to the rich and the famous, he set himself the task of also winning over Byron and Shelley. This task was made somewhat easier by the fact that both poets admired soldiers as well as nautical men. According to Trelawny, when he apologized for not having read more poetry, Shelley replied, "You have the advantage; you saw the things that we read about; you gained knowledge from the living, and we from the dead." Shelley enlisted the newcomer's help in a scheme he had been dreaming about since December—to build a boat that was sleek, gorgeous, and, most important of all, faster than Byron's magnificent new vessel, the *Bolivar,* named to honor the South American revolutionary who was one of Byron's heroes. Trelawny assured Shelley that he was just the man for the project and set right to work. On January 15, Williams wrote that Trelawny had produced "the model of an American schooner." On the strength of Trelawny's design, they hired an acquaintance of Trelawny's, a Captain Roberts, to build the boat in Genoa. Shelley wanted it finished by spring so they could take it with them to La Spezia, the coastal town they had visited the preceding August, where he wanted to spend the summer.

To trust so completely someone he had just met was entirely in keeping with Shelley's impulsive nature. He treated Trelawny as though they had known each other since childhood and never realized—or worried—that Trelawny was fond of stretching the truth. As one early biographer said, "Trelawny . . . found that a little fiction set off the facts to great advantage." He enjoyed telling stories about himself, and in these stories, "he meets and overcomes all odds; it is truly a glorious Trelawny, the Trelawny of his own imagination."

To Trelawny, Shelley's acceptance of his friendship was the gateway to a glamorous world of art and adventure. He allied himself with the younger poet, taking notes on his activities for a future memoir. Even his flirtation with Mary was a way of drawing closer to Shelley. However, one clue to Trelawny's character is that, unlike the witty Hunt, he did not understand Shelley's humor. When, many years later, Trelawny wrote his portrait of the poet, his Shelley "did not laugh or even smile," although those who were close to Shelley often noted his penchant for practical jokes, as well as his ironic take on the world.

Byron, however, soon grew suspicious of this new member of their group. Like Mary, Byron thought Trelawny's stories seemed far-fetched. Indeed, they sounded uncannily like those of the Corsair, Childe Harold, or Lara—the heroes of Byron's own poems. Although it was foolhardy to try to pass oneself off as a Byronic hero to Byron himself, that seems to have been exactly what Trelawny was trying to do. According to Byron, he even slept with a copy of *The Corsair* under his pillow, so it is no wonder that Byron's enthusiasm waned. What is less clear is why Byron chose to tolerate the Cornishman at all. Perhaps it was because the poet, who had grand sailing plans for the *Bolivar* that summer, saw ways to make use of him just as Shelley had. Trelawny, for his part, never forgave Byron for doubting his stories, and many years later, after Byron was dead, he took revenge in a bitter memoir, describing the poet as "weak" and "ignoble" and comparing him unfavorably with Shelley, who "was totally devoid of selfishness and vanity."

For Mary, the Carnival had been the high point of the season. By the end of February, her pregnancy had taken a toll on her spirits. She felt sick and could not delight in the onset of spring. The almond trees bloomed in drifts of startling pink; delicate anemones and primroses brightened the gardens; but Mary had difficulty sleeping and eating and grew pale with worry and fatigue. She was convinced that there was something wrong with the baby. In March, when fourteen-month-old Percy had a low-grade fever, she sent for the doctor in a panic. Her fears escalated when Claire wrote in April that she was having nightmares that Allegra was dead. Mary associated springtime with evils, remembering William's death and the terrible time in London, right after she had lost her first baby, when she and Claire had fought so bitterly that Claire had had to retreat to the countryside. She had felt this ominous feeling before, and each time it had predicted disaster: Fanny's and Harriet's suicides, Clara's and William's deaths. Over the years, she had come to believe that her dread was an accurate predictor of the future—that she could feel when disaster was going to strike—and this year, the dread was more acute than it had ever been.

As the warm weather set in, everybody but Mary looked forward to their summer plans, dreaming about their holiday on the sea in La Spezia, which lay about fifty miles west of Pisa. Byron almost bowed out of the plan, judging the area too desolate and the water too shallow to accommodate the *Bolivar*. But Shelley persuaded Byron to find a house in nearby Livorno, and once he agreed, the

Spezia plan was all they talked of. They would sail every day! The poets would race their boats!

But to Mary their summer retreat seemed worrisome. Cassandra-like, she tried to suggest that perhaps they should not go, but no one listened. Shelley, Williams, and Trelawny were too excited about their boat-building scheme to heed her warnings. They were impatient for the new vessel to be finished, but there was a delay, as the final design included many more sails than were usual for a boat of this size. Here was a new worry for Mary: perhaps the Gulf of Spezia was not a safe place to sail. She voiced her fears to Jane, but if she had hoped for support, she was to be disappointed. Jane was solely in Shelley's camp now, and she declared she would never dream of doubting either Shelley's or Williams's ability to take care of themselves on the water.

Mary felt alone. Trelawny had spent the end of March closeted with Shelley and Williams, going over nautical charts and sketching out rigging designs. Recently, he had traveled to Rome to visit friends and had expressed no regret when he said goodbye. What Mary could not know was that the Williamses had been filling Trelawny's ears with reports of her coldness and insensitivity. Her low spirits had only served to confirm their reports, and instead of empathizing with her worries, Trelawny joined the Williamses in condemning Mary as a bad wife, not at all suited to the eccentric genius, Shelley.

Once Byron had agreed to stay near Shelley that summer, a slight awkwardness developed between the two poets. The issue of Allegra was always a point of contention, but now, panicked by her nightmares, Claire had written to Shelley, expecting him to persuade Byron to let Allegra leave the convent. If he could not, then she insisted that he and Mary help her kidnap her daughter. Mary and Shelley did their best to dissuade Claire from this plan; privately, they thought it would probably be best for Allegra to stay in her school, away from Byron's profligate lifestyle. They also believed Byron would eventually leave Italy, and then Claire would be free to see her daughter as much as she wanted.

Nonetheless, Shelley, knowing how much Claire was suffering, tried to argue her case with Byron, though the poet still became enraged whenever he heard Claire's name. Her letters were "insolent," Byron said. She had no morals herself. She was "atheistical." Who was she to lecture him on what to do with a little girl? The last thing he wanted was for Allegra to turn out like her mother. His goal was to have her become "a Christian and a married woman if possible." The convent was good for her; her education was advancing. As evidence, he showed Shelley a note she had written to her father: "What is my Dear Papa doing? I am so well, and so happy that I cannot but thank my ever dear Papa who brings me so much happiness and whose blessing I ask for. Your little Allegra sends her loving greetings." Byron did not visit his little girl, but it was his duty, he declared to Shelley, to protect her from her mother's "Bedlam behaviour." It was an irony apparently lost on him that he, one of the world's most notorious rakes, always on the verge of some new outrageous adventure, would condemn either Claire's morality or her sanity.

When Claire arrived from Florence in the middle of April to prepare for their summer trip, Mary was actually glad to see her. And indeed, Claire, alarmed by her sister's low spirits, tried to cheer her, reminding Mary that she was always anxious when she was pregnant, and that the beauties of the Gulf of Spezia would help restore her spirits. On April 23, Claire traveled to the coast to look for houses with the Williamses, leaving Mary behind with Percy and Shelley. Just a few hours after she left, Byron's mistress, Teresa, arrived, distraught and pale; the convent had just sent word that Allegra had died of typhus. She was five years and three months old.

Appalled, Mary wondered if this "evil news" was the catastrophe she had been dreading. Though she was grief-stricken over Allegra's death, her thoughts flew immediately to Percy and whether he would be next. She also worried that Claire would try to take revenge on Byron, especially now that he was living so nearby. The wisest plan, Shelley decided, would be to whisk Claire back to La Spezia when she returned from house hunting and tell her the news once they were far from Pisa.

Accordingly, when Claire and the Williamses came back from their trip, reporting they had found only one acceptable house, the Casa Magni, near the tiny fishing village San Terenzo, they were surprised to hear Shelley say they should head off for the summer immediately and that Mary, instead of resisting, agreed with him. Claire, who was used to Shelley's sudden turns, was not unduly put out, especially since Shelley assured them that they would find another house when they got there, or else they would all live together and that it would be delightful. The blue hills, the rocky coast, the sky, the bay—Claire could sing for them in the evenings surrounded by the beautiful Italian landscape.

On April 26, Mary, Claire, and Percy left for La Spezia, pushed by Shelley, who was "like a torrent, hurrying every thing in its course," Mary wrote Maria Gisborne. He and the Williamses stayed behind to crate their furniture and pack their belongings, giving Shelley the chance to tell the Williamses the sad news and prepare them for the storm ahead.

# MARY WOLLSTONECRAFT:
# "I STILL MEAN TO
# BE INDEPENDENT"

———

## [ 1797 ]

FOR MOST OF THE PAST YEAR, MARY WOLLSTONECRAFT AND GODWIN had kept an eye on the construction of homes in a new neighborhood near Chalton Street called the Polygon. Its open feeling reminded Mary of the villages she had lived in as a girl. Far removed from the filth and noise of the city, it was a bucolic spot. There were hay fields to the north, and each house had a large garden in back. It did not take much discussion for the couple to decide that this was where they wanted to live. They could walk to London if they wanted to see friends, go to the theater, or talk to their publishers. The children would be free to play in the garden, just as Mary had when she was a child.

At the end of March, just before their wedding, they finalized the deal with the landlord and purchased a lease on No. 29. During the first week of April, Mary organized her linens, kitchenware, books, and papers with the help of the maid while Marguerite played with Fanny. On April 6, the couple's boxes and furniture were carted over from their separate lodgings to their new home, and after an exhausting day of unpacking Mary, Godwin, and Fanny spent their first night together as a family. The ceilings were high and the rooms spacious. The windows were large to let in the fresh country air, a marked difference from London apartments, whose windows had to be kept tightly shut against the dirt of the streets. Fanny, who was almost three years old, was delighted with the place and with the fact that "Man" was her new "Papa." She gazed out the windows and declared her determination to go haying.

Mary and Godwin, however, were slightly less cheerful. *The Times* had printed the news: "Mr Godwin, author of a pamphlet against matrimony" has married "the famous Mrs Wollstonecraft, who wrote in support of the Rights of Woman," and so they could no longer put off telling their friends and families. After breakfast, each sat down to write letters—among the most curious wedding announcements in the history of such things. Defiant and apologetic, brash and naïve, anxious and overblown—it was difficult for these two philosophers to strike the right note. For instance, when Mary wrote to one of her favorites among Godwin's fairs, the young Amelia Alderson, not once did she mention happiness, love, or the baby she was expecting; instead she discussed philosophical principles and her intention to remain free of customary domestic obligations:

> It is my wish that Mr. Godwin should visit and dine out as formerly, and I shall do the same; in short I still mean to be independent even to the cultivating sentiments and principles in my children's mind, should I have more—

Amelia laughed when she received this missive, writing to a friend that Mary and Godwin were "extraordinary characters. . . . Heighho! What charming things would sublime theories be, if one could make one's practice keep up with them."

Godwin, too, painted the marriage in unsentimental colors. In almost unbearably stilted prose, he told Mary Hays that the only reason he and Mary had married was so that Mary could change her name from Imlay:

> My fair neighbor desires me to announce to you a piece of news which it is consonant to the regard that she and I entertain for you, you should rather learn from us than from any other quarter. She bids me to remind you of the earnest way in

which you pressed me to prevail upon her to change her name, and she directs me to add, that it has happened to me, like many other disputants, to be entrapped in my own toils; in short we found that there was no way so obvious for her to drop the name of Imlay, as to assume the name of Godwin. Mrs. Godwin—who the devil is that?—will be glad to see you . . . whenever you are inclined to call.

Ironically, after making such a fuss about Mary's name change, when he wrote to his friend Holcroft, he forgot to mention Mary's name at all. Mystified at his friend's oversight, as well as the identity of his bride, Holcroft responded with hurt feelings, saying, "Your secrecy a little pains me." To another friend, Godwin said the marriage was only an obligatory arrangement; he did not believe in it, it contradicted his philosophy, but it was necessary to protect Mary:

Some persons have found an inconsistency between my practice in this instance and my doctrines. But I cannot see it. The doctrine of my "Political Justice" is, that an attachment in some degree permanent, between two persons of opposite sexes is right, but that marriage, as practiced in European countries, is wrong. I still adhere to that opinion. Nothing but a regard for the happiness of the individual, which I had no right to injure, could have induced me to submit to an institution which I wish to see abolished, and which I would recommend to my fellow-men, never to practice, but with the greatest caution. Having done what I thought necessary for the peace and respectability of the individual, I hold myself no otherwise bound than I was before the ceremony took place.

Fuseli scoffed at their union, telling a friend, "The assertrix of female rights has given her hand to the *balancier* of political justice." Maria Reveley cried when she heard the news. Eliza and Everina Wollstonecraft worried about the consequences for their own reputations, and their fears were borne out when, a few weeks after the news hit London, Eliza lost a new and better job because she was

Mary's sister. The writer Anna Barbauld made fun of their unconventional domestic arrangement. "In order to give the connection as little as possible the appearance of such a vulgar and debasing tie as matrimony," she wrote, "the parties have established separate establishments, and the husband only visits his mistress like a lover when each is dressed, rooms in order &c. And this may possibly last till they have a family, then they will probably join quietly in one menage like other folks." Not surprisingly, Mrs. Inchbald wrote Godwin a nasty note canceling a date to go to the theater, a plan made before Mrs. Inchbald knew about the marriage:

> I most sincerely wish you and Mrs. Godwin joy. But, assured that your joyfulness would obliterate from your memory every trifling engagement, I have entreated another person to supply your place. . . . If I have done wrong, when you next marry, I will act differently.

When Mary got wind of this, however, she insisted she and Godwin should both go; she did not want to let Mrs. Inchbald have so much power. But the results were disastrous: Mary and Mrs. Inchbald had a public confrontation and never spoke again.

Other acquaintances also fell away or avoided their company and Godwin struggled with being the butt of ridicule and malicious gossip. After he died, Mary Shelley would write that "the fervour and uncompromising tone assumed by [Godwin] in promulgating his opinions made his followers demand a rigid adherence to them in action, and to comply with the ordinance of marriage was in the eyes of many among them absolute apostacy." Already hated by conservatives for his radical views, Godwin came under fire from many of his old supporters who saw him as a traitor to the cause, the famous opponent to marriage now married himself.

For Mary, it was embarrassing to have presented herself as the victim of a grand passion gone wrong only to set up housekeeping with another man. She defended her actions to Amelia by saying the decision was purely pragmatic and that she still suffered from Imlay's bad treatment:

The wound my unsuspecting heart formerly received is not healed. I found my evenings solitary; and I wished, while fulfilling the duty of a mother, to have some person with similar pursuits, bound to me by affection; and besides, I earnestly desired to resign a name, which seemed to disgrace me.

Fortunately, there were also those who were happy for them. Mary Hays shared Wollstonecraft's impatience with the rules that governed women, and she celebrated her friend's bravery, a stance that allowed Mary to reveal that she remained unshaken in her beliefs despite the criticism she faced:

Those who are bold enough to advance before the age they live in, and to throw off, by the force of their own minds, the prejudices which the maturing reason of the world will in time disavow, must learn to brave censure. We ought not to be too anxious respecting the opinion of others.

Joseph Johnson respected both Godwin and Mary and dined with them the day after their wedding. And Godwin's mother, a pious Methodist widow, was thrilled to hear that her son had given up his stance against marriage. She wrote: "Your broken resolution in regard to matrimony incourages me to hope that you will ere long embrace the Gospel, that sure word of promise to all believers." She sent them some eggs—a simple country gift, but also, perhaps, a present revealing old Mrs. Godwin's hopes for grandchildren, as eggs were a traditional fertility symbol. The eggs would "spoil" if proper care was not taken, she said, and she advised Mary to store them in straw and turn them regularly. She also offered the couple a feather bed— yet another symbol of her hopes that their marriage would be fruitful.

Mary and Godwin had weathered worse controversies, and for all of their protestations to the contrary, both were content with their decision. At age thirty-eight, Mary felt secure, settled, and hopeful for their future. Her feelings for Godwin were different from those she had had for Imlay, less intense, but more durable; she admired Godwin's integrity and intellect; she had lost all respect for Imlay. As for Godwin, although he presented his decision in reluctant terms to the outside world—the philosopher corralled by societal custom—he relished the pleasures of his new life. Many years later, after he had died, his daughter Mary Shelley would write, "all Mr Godwin's inner and more private feelings were contrary to the supposed gist of his doctrines." She had found out the hard way that despite his stated disapproval of marriage, when it came to his daughter, his theories did not hold. Philosopher that he was, he could not always overcome his intrinsic prejudices, fears, and ambitions—or those of the society in which they both lived.

It is also true that by the time Godwin condemned Mary for running away with Shelley, he had changed his mind about marriage, since, right from the start, his union with Mary proved an experience contrary to his "doctrines." His new wife did not try to rope Godwin into doing anything he did not want to do, and, within a few days of the move, he had established a new routine: early each morning he walked the two blocks to his office on Chalton Street, read, ate breakfast, and wrote until one, just as he always had. This arrangement was fine with Mary, who told him, "I wish you, for my soul, to be riveted in my heart; but I do not desire to have you always at my elbow."

Godwin's separate work chambers meant they still needed to rely on notes to communicate during the day, and fortunately, Godwin saved many of Mary's. She tells him the menu for dinner:

> I have ordered some boiled mutton, as the best thing for me, and as the weather will probably prevent you from walking out, you will, perhaps, have no objection to dining at four.

She tells him how to behave with Fanny, and organizes their schedule:

> Fanny is delighted with the thought of dining with you—But I wish you to eat your meat first, and let her come up with the

pudding; but should I not find you, let me now request you not to be too late this evening. (Do not give Fanny butter with her pudding.)

She gets the last word in on arguments:

I am sorry we entered on an altercation this morning, which probably has led us both to justify ourselves at the expence of the other.

And:

To be frank with you . . . I think you wrong—yes, with the most decided conviction I dare to say it, having still in my mind the unswervable principles of justice and humanity.

She makes time for literary assignations:

I have a design on you this evening, to keep you quite to myself (I hope then nobody will call!) and make you read the play—

When Godwin returned home in the afternoon, he joined Mary and Fanny for a meal and then set out for his evening activities, adhering to the couple's policy of seeing friends separately.

By the end of April, Godwin confessed that he loved the feelings he was experiencing and regretted his past, during which he had considered philosophy more important than love. Despite his worries about spending too much time together, he found that he and Mary "were in no danger of satiety":

We seemed to combine, in a considerable degree, the novelty of lively sensation of a visit, with the more delicious and heart-felt pleasures of domestic life.

But even with their unconventional arrangement, Mary still found that the move and the fatigue of pregnancy had set her work back. She spent the rest of April applying herself to her writing and fending off domestic duties. Despite their agreement that she would not become a household drudge, Godwin's escape each morning left the running of the house largely to Mary, and that was precisely what she'd been keen to avoid. Why should she be the one who had to deal with landlords, the plumbing, and "the disagreeable business of settling with tradespeople"? She complained to Godwin:

> I am not well today my spirits have been harassed. Mary [the maid] will tell you about the state of the sink &c do you know you plague me (a little) by not speaking more determinately to the Landlord of whom I have a mean opinion. He tires me by his pitiful way of doing every thing—I like a man who will say yes or no at once.

Theirs was not a usual relationship, she reminded him. He was not the only one in the family who had work to do, nor was he the only one who had the right to private hours of writing:

> my time, appears to me, as valuable as that of other persons accustomed to employ themselves. . . . I feel, to say the truth, as if I was not treated with respect, owing to your desire not to be disturbed—

To the modern ear, this might sound like the ordinary lament of a harried wife. But for the eighteenth century, Mary's claims were unorthodox. In essence, this was applied philosophy; she was asserting the rights she had argued for in *Rights of Woman*. Godwin tried to honor their agreement, saying he would shoulder some of the household responsibilities so that his independent wife could write, but he was never truly able to do so, leaving the bulk of the chores to Mary.

Yet by the end of April, Mary had still managed to dash off an article for a new radical journal, *The Monthly Magazine,* entitled "On Poetry, and Our Relish for the Beauties of Nature." On the surface, this essay seems to be a simple reiteration of some of the Romantic values Mary had first expressed in *Letters from Sweden:* the best writing is inspired by nature; civilization weakens artists, because it distances them from the original source of inspiration. In reality, though, Mary was airing her side of the argument with Godwin that had begun over *The Wrongs of Woman:* What constitutes good writing? How formal should writing be, how personal, how imaginative? These were not dry academic questions. Instead, they raised crucial points about education and gender, class and opportunity. In many ways, Mary's reputation as a writer depended on the answers.

Lacking any formal training in grammar and style as she did, Mary claimed that Godwin's insistence on syntactical accuracy and traditional rhetorical devices had led him to value form over matter—always a mistake, she said. Since truly creative writers derive their force from Nature, their work must always be a little rough, a little raw (like hers). But this rough material has a strength and integrity that renders it superior to magnificently structured philosophical tractates such as *Political Justice.* Mary was advocating for a far more democratic order than Godwin was prepared to accept; she wanted to open the door for more people like herself to join the ranks of writers. An author did not have to be educated at an elite school to properly express his or her ideas, she said. All that was necessary was a good imagination.

To prove her point, she paints a picture of a schoolboy not unlike the young Godwin, who is enamored of the poets of the past and devotes himself to imitating their work, never realizing that he is missing the truth of Nature, unrefined and splendid as "she" is. In fact, such students are actually at a disadvantage, she claims, because

Boys who have received a classical education, load their memory with words, and the correspondent ideas are perhaps never distinctly comprehended. As a proof of this assertion, I must observe, that I have known many young people who could write tolerably smooth verses, and string epithets prettily together, when their prose themes showed the barrenness of their minds, and how superficial the cultivation must have been, which their understanding had received.

Mary's prescription for this problem was for young writers to turn to the outdoors. Shut in a traditional classroom, they could not be inspired by Nature, the true source of all art—a truly democratic premise, since anyone was capable of "genius" if he or she had the right sensibility.

The originality of Mary's stance is that it gave women entry into the hallowed hallways of literature, precisely because they had *not* received a classical education. Women's lack of book learning, far from being a disadvantage, freed them to be closer to Nature. To Mary, a female artist could aspire to bolder innovations than men like Godwin. Mary herself would rather *be* a Greek poet, she implied, than *read* a Greek poet, rather *be* a force of Nature than *describe* one.

This was a brilliant sleight of hand: Mary had taken her lack of formal education and turned it into a strength. Godwin, who had criticized her grammar and her lack of restraint, needed to listen more closely to his heart to attain true greatness. All men did. Spontaneity. Sincerity. These were as important as reason and learned allusions, and were certainly more important than grammatical correctness. She did not disavow philosophy. The rational pursuit of knowledge was still important, as without it, the imagination could be led astray; but she called on those such as Godwin who relied exclusively on logic to open themselves to the "warmth of their feelings."

This argument was not a simpleminded opposition of heart versus intellect, or emotion versus reason. Rather, Mary was declaring her right to be taken seriously as a woman, a wife, an intellectual, and an artist, declaring that what was important in a piece of literature or in a personal debate was the content of what was said and the force with which it was presented, not its erudition, or showy style. Her *Vindications* mattered, therefore, because of the urgency of their message and should not be denigrated because of a few misplaced phrases.

"On Poetry" did not occasion any particular response from readers, even though it was Mary's clearest declaration of the new literary and aesthetic principles of Romanticism. But after she had finished it, she returned to *The Wrongs of Woman,* refreshed and revitalized, taking a break from reviewing for Johnson to give herself more time for the novel. Her aim, she said in her preface, was to show "the misery and oppression, peculiar to women, that arise out of the partial laws and customs of society." She began the story with Maria, the heroine, waking up inside a mental asylum, which Mary was able to render with chilling authenticity after her visit to Bedlam. The cries and wild shrieks of the mad men and women also probably hark back to Mary's teenage years living near Hoxton Asylum. Maria's husband has committed her to the asylum, not because she is crazy, but because he wants her fortune and because she has resisted his efforts to sell her into sexual slavery. Sixty-three years later, Wilkie Collins would use this same plot device in his famous novel *The Woman in White:* the innocent heroine is imprisoned in an asylum so that her villainous husband can claim her money. In Mary's story, Maria has a sympathetic attendant named Jemima who recounts her own story of sexual abuse at the hands of evil masters—a groundbreaking moment for the English novel as Mary allows Jemima, the working-class female, to tell her own dark tale.

There are similar characters in English literature before this, most notably the famous "whore" Moll Flanders, but Moll's story is pure comedy; she is a trickster who triumphs over her enemies and emerges victorious in the end. Jemima has none of Moll's joie de vivre and none of her luck. Mary emphasizes that Jemima has been a *real* prostitute, beaten and abandoned by countless men. This kind of gritty detail pushed Mary into new literary frontiers, since Jemima describes the sexual violence she has experienced in graphic terms, using language that had hitherto been off limits for fiction.

*The Wrongs of Woman* is unfinished and difficult to read, as Mary was still working on it when she died and had not yet decided how it would end. She knew she was entering taboo territory by discussing female sexual exploitation, but since she was intent on exposing the evils that faced women, she never considered watering down her heroines' sufferings. For Mary, the asylum was the central image of the book—its crumbling walls and dark passageways are her metaphor for the plight of eighteenth-century women. This was exactly the fate that Mary had feared for her sister Eliza.

Indeed, by having both Maria and Jemima tell their stories, Mary showed that it did not matter whether a woman was rich or poor—either way, she faced the injustice encoded in the English common law. Jemima could not prosecute her abusers. Her masters had the legal right to rape her and victimize her. The same was true for the upper-class Maria; her husband had the right to tyrannize her despite her wealth and social status. In fact, this is probably one reason why Mary had difficulty developing the plot; female imprisonment is a necessarily static condition.

If Mary had had the time to finish *The Wrongs of Woman,* it might well have been her bestselling book—even more successful than *Letters from Sweden*—as the public was fascinated by stories of spousal abuse. Only eight years earlier, London had been in an uproar over the chilling case of Mary Bowles, the countess of Strathmore, whose husband had kept her locked in a closet, starved her, raped her repeatedly, and tortured her until she almost died. Inconceivably, the English legal system protected the abusive husband, not the countess, since men had an ancient right "to chastise and confine" their wives. Not until 1891 would a husband's right to "detain his wife" finally be overturned. Marital rape would remain legal for another century. The countess's husband spoke for many when he proudly proclaimed himself an "enem[y] of *petticoat government* and the friend of matrimonial subordination." In most people's eyes, "the taming of bad wives" was an honorable undertaking. The countess did manage to obtain a divorce, but her ex-husband retained custody of her children, since they were considered the father's property—a law that infuriated Mary Wollstonecraft. As she had once said to Imlay, "Considering the care and anxiety a woman must have about a child before it comes into the world, it seems to me, by natural right, to belong to her . . . but it is sufficient for man to condescend to get a child, in order to claim it.—A man is a tyrant!"

Toward the end of *The Wrongs of Woman,* Maria pleads her case to a law court: "I exclaim against the laws which . . . force women . . . to sign a [marriage] contract, which renders them dependent on the caprice of the tyrant whom choice or necessity has appointed to reign over them." But the law court ignores Maria's impassioned outcry—a fate that Mary hoped she would not share at the hands of the reading public. She wanted Maria's plea to awaken people, to open their eyes, ears, and hearts to the injustices all women faced.

# MARY SHELLEY:
# "IT'S ALL OVER"

———

[ 1822 ]

When Mary and Claire arrived in San Terenzo, on the Gulf of Spezia, they found a tiny village where the people were desperately poor; the women barefoot, the children large-eyed and hungry. Although it was only a day's ride west of Pisa, San Terenzo seemed cut off from the world. Lerici, the closest town, was about two miles away by boat, and almost impossible to reach by land. A ruined castle hung over the cliffs. There was a little church and some scattered windowless huts for the fishermen. Despite their fluency in Italian, Mary and Claire could not understand what the villagers said, and neither could their Italian servants, as the hamlet had its own dialect and its own customs: "Had we been wrecked on an island of the South Seas, we could scarcely have felt ourselves further from civilization and comfort," Mary wrote.

The only way to get to the Casa Magni was by water, or by stumbling over the rocky beach. There was no path, as the house had originally been a boathouse. The ground floor opened directly onto the bay and could only be used for storing nets, lines, and oars. When the wind was strong, the waves spilled over the low wall that was supposed to mark the border between land and sea. The nearest shop was three miles away on the other side of a river that frequently overflowed. Square and unkempt, the house looked as though it had been

*Casa Magni, the "pale faced tragic villa."*

dropped from the sky, wedged between the shore and a steep hill shrouded with cypress, chestnut, and pine.

Mary valued privacy and quiet retreats, but she hated the house from the moment she saw it. With its dirty whitewashed walls, its five dark arches facing the bay, and its one cavernous main room, it seemed hostile, even threatening. "A sense of misfortune hung over my spirits," Mary recalled. Fifty years later, Henry James would describe the place as the "pale faced tragic villa."

When Shelley arrived with the Williamses and the rest of the servants, everyone helped unload the boats onto the beach. They had to carry the boxes up an outside staircase at the back of the house, the only way to reach their living quarters on the second floor. Three small bedrooms opened off the central room—tight quarters for five adults, three small children, the cook, the maids, and the nurse. And yet Mary and Shelley each took a bedroom, a telling indication of the state of their marriage. Mary's depression that spring had taken a toll on their already strained relationship. In a letter to Mrs. Gisborne, Mary drew a picture of the floor plan: her room was on the south side of the central hall and Shelley's on the north. Not only did they sleep apart, they were in separate areas of the house, as far from one another as possible. The Williamses took the room next to Shelley's. The babies and servants were given cots in the back of the house.

Claire camped out with Mary, or sometimes slept on a couch in the hall.

Before Shelley had even unpacked his things, Mary launched into a litany of complaints: The rooms were inadequate. The house was barbaric. They were cut off from the road. The villagers were "wild & hateful." There was no privacy; the families would have to eat every meal together. The servants were threatening to quit. Shelley could not understand Mary's misery. "The beauty yet strangeness of the scenery" that made Mary "weep and shudder" exhilarated him. He tried to console his miserable wife, but he loved the house. To him, it was as though they were living on a ship, exposed to all the sea's moods, the pounding and shifting of the currents—a setting that matched the high pitch of his excitement that summer.

Claire still did not know about Allegra's death, and keeping this terrible secret put everyone on edge. However, no one wanted to be the one to tell her, and so a week passed and Claire was still in the dark. Finally, on May 2, Mary and Shelley had a meeting with the Williamses to discuss the situation. Claire, wondering where everyone had gone, came looking for them and overheard their discussion from the hallway. She did not have the fit of hysterics everyone had dreaded; nor did she fly into a vengeful rage. Instead, she grieved, intensely and silently, and no one could comfort her, least of all Shelley. He and Mary should have done more, she felt. They should have helped her take back her daughter. Their reluctance had cost Allegra her life.

Shelley did his best to take care of Claire, asking Byron to send her a lock of Allegra's hair and a picture, which Byron immediately did. Byron also told her that she could make all the arrangements for the burial, but Claire did not want to organize a funeral. She wanted Allegra out of the convent and alive. At this point, her rage ignited, and she vented her anger and sorrow at Shelley, who told Byron, "She now seems bewildered; & whether she designs to avail herself further of your permission to regulate the funeral, I know not. In fact, I am so exhausted with the scenes through which I have passed, that I do not dare to ask."

Mary understood the complexity of her sister's loss, how grief and guilt could torture a bereaved mother. Claire had been in the untenable situation of having no rights to Allegra; she had believed her daughter to be in danger but had been unable to do anything to save her. In retrospect, Claire was now certain that her nightmares had been messages from her daughter; Allegra had been crying out for help and her mother had not answered her call. A small girl was dead because the cruelty of her father was backed by the law. This is not the kind of tragedy that one gets over. For the rest of her life, Claire would be haunted by thoughts of her daughter and questions she could not answer. What had the child's final days been like? What had she suffered at the convent?

In 1870, when she was seventy-two years old, long after Byron, Shelley, and Mary were dead, Claire managed to obtain from the convent all the paperwork that pertained to Allegra. There were few new details, but each one was precious: Byron's banker, Signor Pellegrino Chigi, had brought Allegra there on January 22, 1821. She had been wearing a warm ermine coat. At age four, she was too young to be a full-fledged pupil, so she was looked after by a nun, Sister Marianna, along with another little girl, Isabella, the daughter of the Marchese Ghislieri of Bologna. At least Claire now had these facts to add to the ones Shelley had given her after he had paid Allegra a three-hour visit the previous August. He had described her as carefully as he could, since he knew Claire would want every detail:

> She is grown tall and slight for her age, and her face is somewhat altered. The traits have become more delicate, and she is much paler, probably from the effect of improper food. She yet retains the beauty of her deep blue eyes and of her mouth, but she has a contemplative seriousness, which mixed with her excessive vivacity which has not yet deserted her, has a very peculiar effect in a child.

He noted her expensive white muslin dress and black silk apron. Her hair was "beautifully profuse and hangs in large curls on her neck." She seemed "a thing of a finer and a higher order" than the other children. At first she was standoffish, but Shelley had always known how to enchant small children. He gave her "a basket of sweetmeats" and a pretty gold necklace. Before long, "she grew more familiar, and led me all over the garden, and all over the convent, running and skipping so fast that I could hardly keep up with her." She showed him where she slept at night, the chair where she sat for meals, and the garden cart. He observed that she was still as mischievous as before; she rang the convent bell without permission, and the nuns began to file out of their cells to chapel before their prioress could explain that it was only Allegra's prank. Shelley was glad to see that she did not get in trouble for this bit of mischief. However, he was not impressed with her education: "Her intellect is not much cultivated. She knows certain *orazioni* [prayers] by heart, and talks and dreams of Paradiso and angels and all sorts of things."

In Claire's final years, she converted to Catholicism, so perhaps at this stage of life she found it consoling that her daughter had been trained in the Catholic tradition. Maybe that was why she converted in the first place: to share these rituals with her little girl. But in 1822, when Shelley reported Allegra's talk of angels, Claire was appalled that Byron was training her daughter to become the kind of religious young woman who would grow up to condemn her unmarried mother. To her, it was yet more evidence of his master plan to separate her from her daughter, no matter the cost.

Although she could not know it then—she was too grief-stricken, too stunned by pain to know exactly what she thought—for Claire, Allegra's death was a turning point. She and Mary had staked their lives on Shelley's ideals of free love, but when, at the end, she stood back and assessed what she had suffered—indeed what they all had suffered—she decided that she, Mary, little Allegra, Harriet, Jane Williams, and all the other women Byron and Shelley had known and claimed to love had been gravely harmed by the men's deluded ideals. The two great poets had inflicted unspeakable pain, she believed, all in the name of freedom and passion. The loss of Allegra was the case in point. Her daughter was the sacrificial lamb in the Romantic experiment, the little girl who had been worth nothing in the eyes of her father. Near the end of her life, Claire wrote a damning condemnation of both poets. This document was only recently discovered in a sheaf of her papers: "Under the influence of the doctrine and the belief of free love," she declared, "I saw the two first poets of England . . . become monsters of lying, meanness cruelty and treachery—under the influence of free love Lord B became a human tyger slaking his thirst for inflicting pain upon defenceless women who under the influence of free love . . . loved him."

Claire included Shelley in her condemnation because she felt he should have saved Allegra. Indeed, she faulted Shelley in particular; he should have been stronger than Byron, should have been faithful to those who loved him. He had said he adored Claire and her little girl, but he had cruelly neglected both of them, with disastrous consequences. He had said he loved Harriet, but he had abandoned her. And Mary—he had repeatedly betrayed Mary, falling in love with one woman after another, including Claire herself, whenever a new woman represented a fresher dream, a wilder hope, or redemption from his own suffering. The price that she and Mary had paid had been too steep.

In the immediate aftermath of Allegra's death, Byron, who had moved to Livorno for the summer months, took charge of the burial, since Claire refused, arranging for it to take place in the church of his old school, Harrow, never guessing that the priggish vicar would refuse to let the little "bastard" girl be buried inside the church, instead relegating her remains to the church courtyard with no memorial stone.

Allegra's death and funeral preparations again deepened Mary's fears for Percy. She begged Shelley to let them go back to Pisa, but Shelley ignored her pleas, and so Mary reverted to the icy silence that he hated, at times breaking into hysterical tears or raging at him, but mostly punishing him with the "cold neglect [and] averted eyes" that crushed his heart. Later, she would regret this behavior, writing him an anguished apology he would never read:

> *My heart was all thine own—but yet a shell*
> *Closed in its core, which seemed impenetrable,*

> *Till sharp toothed Misery tore the husk in twain*
> *Which gaping lies nor may unite again—*
> *Forgive me!*

But that summer, he was the one who seemed callous, making light of her fears and neglecting her and Percy to spend all of his time with Jane.

To the Williamses, Mary's complaints seemed increasingly outrageous and self-centered. Neither could imagine why she would treat the sweet-tempered Shelley with such unkindness. Why did he stay with her? they wondered. They were enchanted by the house and their holiday. Jane, in particular, was lighthearted. Her children, little Jane (whom they called Dina) and Meddy, were pink-cheeked and strong as soldiers. She basked in the admiration of Shelley and Williams and sunned herself on the terrace that faced the sea, strumming on the guitar Shelley had given her and singing verses he had written for her in her high, light voice. As he watched her one afternoon, Edward felt even sorrier for Shelley. "I am proud," he told Jane, "that *wherever* we may be together you would be cheerful and contented." The comparison was obvious: Mary was neither cheerful nor contented. Instead, she seemed like a shrew—angry, resentful, and weepy.

Shelley had his own way of dealing with Allegra's death. The day after Claire discovered the truth, he had one of his waking visions. A shaken Williams described what happened:

> While walking with Shelley on the terrace and observing the effect of moonshine on the waters, he complained of being unusually nervous, and stopping short he grasped me violently by the arm and stared steadfastly on the white surf that broke upon the beach under our feet. Observing him sensibly affected I demanded of him if he were in pain—but he only answered, saying "There it is again!—there!"

Williams looked but could see nothing. Still, Shelley insisted that he could see a child floating up from the waves, hands clasped. Only great poets could have such visions, Williams told Shelley. He "had felt" the ghost's presence, but only a genius like Shelley could see it.

THIS SPECTRAL CHILD WAS the first of many such hallucinations Shelley had that summer. His moods were becoming increasingly erratic. His Italian doctor had dismissed the long-believed diagnosis of tuberculosis, but Shelley was still having difficulty sleeping. He had been relying on laudanum to ease a rheumatic pain in his side; he did not feel like eating and all too often was flooded by a terrible panic that even the laudanum could not assuage. On his good days, the future seemed exciting and full of promise, but his glorious high spirits made the crushing bouts of depression even harder to bear. On bad days he felt he was a failure; that his poetry would not endure; that he was trapped in his marriage; and that tyranny had ruined the world. After a few weeks of these wild alternations, he stocked up on prussic acid, a lethal form of cyanide, as "a golden key to that perpetual chamber of rest." At night, he had feverish dreams that kept him awake and restless. He was experimenting with a drama that cast Jane as an alluring "Indian enchantress" and writing a dark poem, *The Triumph of Life,* in which he described Life as a relentless procession of masked, demonic figures. The last stanzas he composed are fragmentary and difficult to understand:

> "Then, what is Life?" I said . . . the cripple cast
> His eye upon the car which now had rolled
> Onward, as if that look must be the last
>
> And answered . . . happy those for whom the fold
> Of

Here he stopped, never returning to finish, and covering the back of the sheet with sketches of boats.

With Shelley in this volatile condition, Mary found the business of running a household even more challenging than usual. The children had to be fed, supplies obtained, bills paid, and rooms kept in

*Shelley's sketches of boats. He filled his notebooks with drawings and doodles as well as poems.*

order. The servants were more trouble than help; the Shelleys' servants hated the Williamses' servants and they fought, Mary complained, "like cats and dogs." Eventually, disgusted with their accommodations and the remoteness of the village, both sets made good on their threats to quit, and new help had to be found. "You may imagine," Mary wrote to Mrs. Gisborne in the midst of this chaos, "how ill a large family agrees with my laziness . . . Ma pazienza."

On May 12, the whole party came out onto the terrace to watch Shelley's schooner-rigged ship skim into the bay, heeling sharply and trailed by a dark foamy wake. "She is a most beautiful boat," Shelley exclaimed with delight. However, Mary continued to see the boat as a dangerous new toy. It was all Shelley talked about—her lines, her grace, her perfect slim size; at twenty-four feet long, she was narrow, with two very tall masts, topsails, and more jibs than most vessels her size. Mary could see how intoxicated her husband was, and she feared what stunts he might attempt. An added blow was that he christened her the *Ariel,* in tribute to Jane.

Aside from Mary's chagrin, there were some additional troubles caused by the boat's name. Trelawny had thought they should call the vessel the *Don Juan*. Byron had been much flattered by this and told Trelawny to paint *Don Juan* in huge block letters on the sail before he delivered the ship to Shelley. But since the whole point, in Shelley's mind, was to compete with Byron, not flatter him, Shelley decided to change the name, at which Byron "took fire." Undeterred, Shelley and Williams spent the next three weeks trying to get the paint off. They scrubbed with soap and turpentine and even wine, to no avail. Finally Shelley had the patch of canvas ripped out and resewn, and at last the boat displayed her real name. Shelley had triumphed and was looking forward to flaunting his handiwork at Byron.

When Shelley went off sailing, which he did as frequently as possible, Mary felt completely abandoned, a sea widow. Sometimes he took pity on her, taking her out with him, and she would sit propped against his knees as she had on their first water crossing to Paris when she was sixteen. But she knew he was only trying to be kind to her, that he would much rather have been with Jane. Each morning, he retreated from the household, the crying children, and the new servants to the *Ariel,* using the ship as a floating study, leaning against the mast, reading, writing, and napping, while his frazzled wife attempted to train a cook and a maid, order the dinners, pay the bills, and smooth the feathers of pouting toddlers. If Shelley missed their old intimacy, Mary felt deserted by his airy dismissal of her sorrows and the burdens of running such a complicated household. Jane was no help at all. She ignored the servants and played with her children, untroubled by where their next supplies would come from or what the next meal might be.

In the days leading up to the anniversary of William's death on June 7, a heat wave settled in. Mary wanted Shelley to mourn with her, and when he resisted, she retreated even further than usual, refusing to speak to him, her mood made worse because she was tired and sick. "My nerves were wound up to the utmost irritation," she remembered later. Thunderstorms blew through, which only seemed to make the air thicker, the heat more difficult to bear. The children quarreled; the grownups snapped at each other and, like Coleridge's mariner, began to see things that were not there. In fact, bored and hot, they did their best to outdo one another in visionary capacity. The Williamses were new to this kind of thing, but Jane earned her colors when she saw an apparition of Shelley pass by the window and "trembled exceedingly" from the vision.

On June 8, Mary woke up feeling desperately ill. She did not receive much sympathy from the Williamses, who thought this was yet another ploy to gain Shelley's attention. She bathed in the sea, which gave her some relief, but only temporarily. For Mary, who believed in signs and auguries, it did not seem an accident that this new misery came on the heels of the anniversary of William's death. That afternoon, Trelawny, who had returned from his travels to stay in Livorno with Byron, sailed his lordship's boat into the bay, announcing his arrival by shooting off the war cannon that Byron had insisted be installed on the deck. Shelley and Williams raced out to the terrace to see who had arrived, thinking at first that it was a warship. But when they saw *Bolivar* painted in bold letters on the sails and the contessa's pink flag waving from the mast, they were forced to acknowledge that Byron had outdone Shelley once again. The ship dominated the bay, making the *Ariel* look like a much younger sister, the runt of the litter.

To console himself, Shelley came up with a scheme to lengthen the masts of his already top-heavy boat to make her "sail like a witch." Together, he and Williams designed bigger sails, on the principle that the more canvas, the faster the ship. More experienced sailors would have known the *Ariel* was too light-bottomed a vessel to be able to handle so much sail, but neither Shelley nor Edward realized this, and even if they had, they would probably have continued with their plans anyway. All that mattered was having a faster boat than Byron's.

In better days, Mary could have calmed her husband, convincing him that this was a reckless project, but her mood had worsened. She had passed the three-month mark of her pregnancy at the end of May, usually a turning point for her, but instead of feeling better she grew increasingly weak, and on June 16, she woke up to find blood soaking the sheets. Jane and Claire rushed to her side but had no idea what to do. Mary faded quickly. They sent for the doctor, but he was miles away, and for seven hours Mary bled uncontrollably, believing she was going to die. She did not feel much pain, but she was desperately worried about what would happen to Percy and Shelley. The women tried to keep her conscious by wiping her brow with "brandy, vinegar[,] eau de Cologne etc," but they were losing her. Shelley, who had a smattering of medical knowledge derived in part from his interest in science, but largely from monitoring the vagaries of his own health, had the good sense to send for ice to slow the bleeding, but it took many hours to arrive. At last, when the servants staggered in carrying the melting blocks, Shelley filled a tub with water and ice, lifted the nearly unconscious Mary from the bed, and plunged her in. Aghast at this harsh treatment, Claire and Jane tried to intervene, telling Shelley to wait for the doctor, but fortunately, as Mary said, "Shelley overruled them & by unsparing application of [the ice] I was restored."

Shelley had saved his wife's life, but now she had another loss to grieve. There would be no new baby. Percy was still an only child. His siblings were ghosts. She lay in bed, too weak to get up, while Shelley paced the halls of the Casa Magni, feeling trapped. He wanted to try out the new and "improved" *Ariel,* but Mary pleaded with him to stay with her. The mood in the house was grim. With each passing day, Shelley grew more impatient while Mary wept, growing sadder and clingier. The heat continued to blanket the coast, making them all irritable. Finally, Shelley broke.

About a week after her miscarriage, Mary heard screaming in the middle of the night and then the pounding of feet. Shelley sprang into her room, eyes wide open, still screaming but sound asleep. This pale, monstrous Shelley was like a phantom from her first novel, the white-faced student, Frankenstein. Terrified, Mary leapt out of bed, fell, picked herself up, and ran into the Williamses' room. Shelley, meanwhile, awoke, confused and gasping. He had seen terrible things, he said. He had seen Edward and Jane, not in a dream, but in a vision, in the most horrible condition, their bodies lacerated—their bones starting through their skin, the faces pale yet stained with blood, they could hardly walk, but Edward was the weakest & Jane was supporting him—Edward said—Get up, Shelley, the sea is flooding the house & it is all coming down.

When Shelley looked out the window, he had seen "the sea rushing in." Then the scene changed and he saw himself running down the hallway into Mary's room; he meant to strangle her, he said.

To Mary, this was almost too much to bear. Her husband seemed possessed by a demon, worn down so much by her fears and complaints that he wanted to murder her. During the next week, Mary remained in bed, her spirits desperately low. When news came that Leigh Hunt—who had agreed to come help start the literary journal—had arrived at Byron's house in Livorno with his wife and six children, she was horrified when Shelley said he wanted to sail across the Gulf to see his friends.

Mary implored him to stay, and although at first he listened, the bay continued to beckon; his beautiful, spirited vessel reared and plunged on the waves. He wanted to show her off to his lordship. Finally, on July 1, he and Edward packed the *Ariel* with supplies. He stuffed his copy of Keats's poems in his pocket and put on his favorite nankeen trousers. Mary dragged herself out of bed and again begged Shelley not to abandon her, but he was adamant; he had already put off his trip once because of her and was now determined to go. In despair, Mary jotted a sad little note to Hunt: "I wish I cd write more—I wish I were with you to assist you—I wish I cd break my chains & leave this dungeon—"

On the morning of their departure, Mary watched the *Ariel*'s sails disappear against the horizon with a sense of foreboding. When news came that they had arrived safely, she sent Shelley a plaintive letter begging him to come home soon. He wrote back right away, assuring her they would be back in a week's time, by July 8. But the eighth came and went without any sign. Three more days passed. On Friday, letters arrived from Hunt and Byron, mentioning that Williams and

Shelley had in fact left on Monday as he had promised. When Mary read this, as she later wrote Mrs. Gisborne, "the paper fell from me—I trembled all over—Jane read it—'Then it is all over!' she said. 'No, my dear Jane,' I cried, 'it is not all over, but this suspense is dreadful—come with me, we will go to Leghorn [Livorno] . . . & learn our fate."

They found some locals to row them to Lerici and hired a carriage to drive the twenty miles to Byron's house in Pisa, as he had just returned there from Livorno. They arrived on his doorstop at midnight. Mary, still recovering from her miscarriage, was as pale as death. "A desperate sort of courage seemed to give her energy," Byron said later. "[She] looked more like a ghost than a woman. . . . I have seen nothing in tragedy on the stage so powerful, or so affecting. . . ." But sympathetic though he was, he had no news.

Mary and Jane continued on to Livorno without pausing to rest; here they met Trelawny, who confirmed that the men had indeed sailed on the eighth. The good news was that no accident had been reported. All they could do now was return to Casa Magni. Trelawny came with them, checking for information at every port along the way. When they reached Viareggio, the news was grim. A dinghy had washed ashore along with a water bottle, and the descriptions of both made Mary feel sure they were Shelley's. That is when, as Mary said, "our calamity first began to brake [sic] on us." She did not want to succumb to despair, both for her own sake and for Jane's, and strove to appear hopeful, doing her best not to cry, afraid she would not stop once she started. But when they crossed the Magra River, she almost lost control:

> I felt the water splash about our wheels—I was suffocated—I gasped for breath—I thought I should have gone into convulsions, & I struggled violently that Jane might not perceive it.

When she caught a glimpse of the sea, "a voice from within me seemed to cry aloud," she wrote later, "that this is his grave."

Still, until they knew for certain, the possibility that the men had survived remained. Trelawny left to search for more news, while at Casa Magni a terrible vigil began. "Thrown about by hope & fears,"

Mary stationed herself at Shelley's telescope, training it on each sail that crossed the bay. She took laudanum to sleep but spent most of her time in despair. Unfortunately, the usually silent villagers happened to be celebrating a festival. "They pass the whole night in dancing on the sands close to our door," Mary wrote, "running into the sea then back again & screaming all the time one perpetual air— the most detestable in the world—"

At last, on the evening of July 19, Trelawny arrived. His face, frozen like a death mask, frightened Caterina, the maid. Jane fainted before he could speak. Yet Mary, silent and white, listened to every word. The bodies of Shelley, Williams, and an eighteen-year-old boy named Charles Vivian, whom they had hired as an extra hand, had washed up in different locations along the coast between Massa and Viareggio. The corpses had been partially eaten away and had already begun to decompose. They could identify Edward by his boots. The only things that distinguished Shelley's body from the others were

*This self-portrait of Edward Williams was found in the wreckage*
*of the* Ariel *and suffered extensive water damage.*

his nankeen trousers and the volume of Keats's poems tucked into the pocket of his jacket.

Slowly, the story came together. Shelley and Williams had had a glorious week at Byron's house in Livorno. Shelley had romped with Hunt's children and been so overjoyed to see Hunt that he could not stop saying "how inexpressibly happy" he was. They traveled to Pisa to see the leaning tower and listen to the organ in Pisa's Duomo. "He was looking better than I had ever seen him," Hunt recalled. "We talked of a thousand things—we anticipated a thousand pleasures." Elated, relaxed, and sunburned, Shelley had been in uproarious spirits, laughing so exuberantly at his friends' jokes that at one point he had to lean against a doorway, tears running down his cheeks. He was excited at the prospect of starting his new magazine, *The Liberal*. With Hunt and Byron as his co-conspirators, he began to draw up plans for outraging Parliament and eviscerating the stuffy conservatives back home.

The weather was uncertain on July 8, but Shelley and Williams were determined to sail back to Casa Magni. It would take about seven hours to cover the fifty or so miles between Livorno and La Spezia. They left around two in the afternoon; the sun was high, and under ordinary circumstances, they would have reached the village around nine in the evening. But at five or six o'clock a sudden squall blew in from the southwest. The sky turned black. The rain spattered down and the wind gusted, churning the water into huge waves. The *Ariel* was on the open sea, about ten miles offshore, at least four hours from the protected waters of the Gulf of Spezia and three hours out from Livorno. One or two ships were near enough to see the *Ariel*'s sails, but these vessels, captained by local sailors who understood the seriousness of the storm, headed to shore immediately. One of the captains reported that he had seen the *Ariel* continuing her journey north, braving the wind and the towering waves.

What happened next is less clear. Later in life, Trelawny said he thought that pirates had rammed the side of the boat, sinking it, but this story was one of Trelawny's fabrications, inspired, perhaps, by his guilt over the unseaworthiness of the vessel he had helped design.

Other tales sprang up, too. In these, Shelley was painted as the quintessential Romantic poet, a man who wanted to die because he was disillusioned with life and yearned for freedom from his earthly ties. In one such version, told years after the tragedy, an Italian fisherman had supposedly drawn up beside the *Ariel* and offered to take them on board, but "a shrill voice [Shelley's] . . . was distinctly heard to say 'No.' . . . The waves were running mountains high—a tremendous surf dashed over the boat which to his astonishment was still crowded with sail. 'If you will not come on board for God's sake reef your sails or you are lost,' cried a sailor through the speaking trumpet. One of the gentlemen [Williams] . . . was seen to make an effort to lower the sails—his companion seized him by the arm as in anger."

In fact, just a few weeks shy of his thirtieth birthday, Shelley, for all his moments of despair, was, as both Byron and Hunt had testified, in excellent spirits at the time of the accident. Certainly he had reached his prime as a writer. He was deeply immersed in "The Triumph of Life" and his play about the Indian princess; he was eager to publish political articles in *The Liberal*. He may have been smitten with Jane, but that did not mean he did not love Mary or his little boy. In his last note to Mary, he had written, "How are you my best Mary? Write especially how is your health & how your spirits are, . . . Ever dearest Mary." And so, despite his stock of cyanide, it seems clear that he did not intend to die yet, at least not in the *Ariel*. If anything, he and Williams thought they could outrun the storm, never suspecting that Shelley had made the *Ariel* a death trap in his attempt to make her faster than the *Bolivar*. Not only had he added extra sails to make her faster, he had stored "three tons and a half" of pig iron in her hull to give her more ballast and keep her from capsizing in a heavy wind. The problem was that with all this extra weight she was in danger of sinking if she took on too much water.

As it was, the only hope they would have had of riding out the storm was if the cabin boy, Charles Vivian, had climbed up the mast and taken down the topsails or reefed the mainsails. Otherwise, with her sails up, the already unseaworthy *Ariel* would have been exposed to the full force of the wind. An examination of the vessel after she washed up on shore showed that this probably never happened, as the masts had snapped off the deck. Furthermore, the rudder had ripped from the hull, leaving the men defenseless when the waves poured in. Trapped as they were, they would have had only a few minutes to realize they were going down. Williams was found with his shirt "partly drawn over the head, as if the wearer had been in the act of taking it off." The young cabin boy washed onto shore, as did Shelley and Williams, with his boots still on.

As the maid tried to revive Jane, Trelawny attempted to comfort Mary by praising Shelley: there was no greater poet, he declared, no more ethereal spirit. Later, Mary wrote to her father, "I almost was happy . . . to dwell on the eulogy that his loss thus drew forth from his friend. I have some of his friends about me who worship him—they all agree that he was an elementary being and that death does not apply to him. . . . I am not however so desolate as you might think. He is ever with me, encouraging me to become wise and good, that I may be worthy to join him."

Given Godwin's views of Shelley's morals, it must have been strange to hear his daughter declare that she was going to strive to be as virtuous as her husband, the man who had run away with two of his daughters and, according to Mary-Jane, caused Fanny's suicide.

Mary and Jane, joined by the equally grief-stricken Claire, traveled back to Pisa. Their first task was the problem of the bodies. The officials had thrown lime on the corpses and buried them on the beach where they had washed up, but they could not stay there. To complicate matters, Edward and Shelley had floated ashore miles apart. Two different rites would have to be conducted.

Jane wanted her husband to be buried in England. Mary wanted Shelley next to their son in Rome. The Italian officials chose this moment to become particularly officious. The bodies had to be cremated, they said, and money paid to government offices. Mary was close to collapse, and so Trelawny, who had known Shelley for less than six months, took over. Mary was grateful for his help, little thinking that to Trelawny her surrender was evidence that she did not really care about Shelley, just as the Williamses had said. From here, it was an

The Funeral of Shelley *by Louis Edouard Fournier (1889), a Victorian*
*reimagining of the scene. Pictured from left, Trelawny, Hunt, and Byron,*
*though Hunt stayed in the carriage and Byron left early.*

easy next step to convince himself that he was the person closest to
the poet, in life and in death.

Always dramatic, Trelawny chose precisely the sort of theatrical
rite that Mary would never have selected. Inspired by the fiery funeral pyres he had witnessed in India, he decided that if Shelley had
to be burned, it should be a glorious event. Never having read *Frankenstein,* he did not realize that this plan actually duplicated Mary's
depiction of the monster's wishes for his own funeral: to be burned,
with his ashes "swept into the seas by the winds."

During the next few weeks, Shelley and Williams lay in their temporary graves, while Trelawny wrangled the temperamental Italian
bureaucrats into agreement, and hired a few locals to help him construct the two different pyres, chopping wood, digging peat, and
stacking logs. Finally, on August 15, all was ready. They burned Williams first, and on the sixteenth turned to Shelley. With the Italian
officials looking on, Trelawny and the hired men dug up the poet's
corpse, which had turned "a dark and ghastly indigo colour" from
the lime that had been thrown on it.

Byron and Hunt had driven down from Pisa to pay tribute to their friend, but neither one, according to Trelawny, was very helpful. Before they lit the fire, Byron asked for Shelley's skull, but Trelawny—Shelley's self-appointed protector—refused, explaining later that he had heard a rumor that his lordship had once "used [a skull] as a drinking cup." Hunt stayed in the carriage, unable to bear the smell or the gruesome sight, and when Shelley's body was placed on the flames, even Byron retreated, leaving Trelawny alone to witness the event—yet more "evidence" to Trelawny that he was Shelley's truest friend. He watched the air shiver, the flames uncannily bright. Then "the corpse fell open and the heart was laid bare." This was the perfect memento, far better than a lock of hair or a watercolor; Trelawny reached out, scorching his hand, and snatched it, shriveled and black though it was. Afterward, he and Byron went for a swim in the very same "waves which had overpowered our friends," as he later wrote.

Perhaps if the locals had known how famous the poet would become, they would have turned out for the occasion; as it was, few onlookers were there. A clump of officials gathered at a distance to certify that quarantine regulations were being met. The small group of villagers who had been interested in the antics of the English gentlemen soon left, driven away by the heat. Neither Jane nor Mary was present. No one prevented them from being there, but no one seemed to expect them, either. Mary, though, wanted to know every detail of the proceedings. She carefully recorded Trelawny's account in her journal, even the graphic details about the flames' consumption of the body, and mourned by herself, reliving the summer in an eight-page letter to Maria Gisborne, an honest and heartbreaking account of what had passed:

> The scene of my existence is closed & though there be no pleasure in retracing the scenes that have preceded the event which has crushed my hopes yet there seems to be a necessity in doing so, and I obey the impulse which urges me. . . . All that might have been bright in my life is now despoiled—I shall live to improve myself, to take care of my child, & render myself worthy to join him.

Meanwhile, Trelawny continued to oversee practicalities. He packed Shelley's ashes in a box and sent them to the British consul in Rome. They were stored in the man's wine cellar until the following spring, when Trelawny had dug Shelley's grave in Rome, planted cypress trees, and bought a memorial stone, inscribing it with a quote from *The Tempest*:

> *Nothing of him that doth fade,*
> *But doth suffer a sea-change*
> *Into something rich and strange.*

He saved a burial spot for himself next to Shelley, even digging his own grave so that his body could be placed in it immediately when it was his turn. As an afterthought, he wrote to Mary that there might be room for her as well.

Eight years, almost to the day, had passed since Mary and Claire had run away with Shelley. Mary's twenty-fifth birthday came and went, unmarked. Near breakdown, she strove to maintain a daily routine. Not only did she still have a child to care for, Godwin had taught her to be brave, to hold firm against the Wollstonecraft affliction of despair. Jane, she felt, was weaker than she was, and she wanted to be strong for her grieving friend. Yet this was almost impossible. Already exhausted from her miscarriage, she felt cast adrift, alone. For all of her anger, for all of her disappointments, she had made Shelley the center of her world—husband and friend, father and brother, as well as antagonist and enemy. Now, to cope with her heartbreak, she retreated to the iced-in landscape she had inhabited after each of her children had died.

To their circle of friends, Mary appeared unmoved. Hunt, in particular, was appalled. He had never understood her reserve. Shelley had complained about her lack of feeling on their last visit, and now Hunt could see why. Already a jostling for primacy had begun. Whom had Shelley loved most? Who was most heartbroken that he had died? Hunt put Mary at the bottom of the list and himself at the top. Trelawny agreed, and gave Shelley's heart to Hunt. When Mary asked Hunt if she might have it, he refused, letting her know that he thought she had been unkind to his friend. It was only when Jane, in an unusual act of generosity, asked him to let Mary have it that he relented.

Mary had won that round, but it was only the first in a long series of battles over who would become the keeper of Shelley's flame.

# MARY WOLLSTONECRAFT:
# "A LITTLE PATIENCE"

———

[ 1797 ]

*W*HEN THE WEATHER GREW WARM THAT SPRING, GODWIN DECIDED to take a walking vacation with friends, declaring that he believed he and Mary would enjoy each other even more if they had a little distance. Mary agreed to his plan only reluctantly. She felt slightly anxious letting go of her husband. Before he left, a new female admirer named Miss Pinkerton had cropped up, sending fluttery little notes and dropping by the house frequently—altogether too frequently, Mary thought. Godwin did not set any limits because he felt sorry for her, but also because it was pleasant, after all, to be admired by a pretty young woman.

Mary need not have worried. From almost the moment he set out, Godwin felt pangs of regret, having proposed this trip out of his own predilection for self-denial, not because he wanted to escape Mary's clutches. His Calvinist upbringing made the pleasure he experienced almost too much to bear. He needed to appease his guilt at how happy he was and make sure he could do without Mary, at least for a few weeks.

When his first letter arrived, spelling out his love for her and Fanny, Mary was reassured and wrote him a passionate response, referring to their unborn baby as "Master William" since she and Godwin both assumed she would be giving birth to a boy:

I am well and tranquil, excepting the disturbance produced by Master William's joy, who took it into his head to frisk a little at being informed of your remembrance. I begin to love this little creature and to anticipate his birth as a fresh twist to a knot, which I do not wish to untie. Men are spoilt by frankness, I believe, yet I must tell you that I love you better than I supposed I did, when I promised to love you for ever—and I will add what will gratify your benevolence, if not your heart, that on the whole I may be termed happy.

Godwin's response was even more heartfelt than Mary's:

You cannot imagine how happy your letter made me. No creature expresses, because no creature feels, the tender affections, so perfectly as you do: &, after all one's philosophy, it must be confessed that the knowledge, that there is some one that takes an interest in our happiness . . . is extremely gratifying. We love as it were to multiply our consciousness . . . even at the hazard . . . of opening new avenues for pain and misery to attack us.

Fanny, too, missed Godwin. Mary reported that she had gotten hold of his letter and would not let it go. She asked repeatedly where he had gone, and when Mary told her he had "gone into the country," this became her phrase for anything that was missing; she greatly amused Maria Reveley by saying that a lost toy monkey must have "gone into the country."

Given the complicated natures of both husband and wife, however, a squabble inevitably arose. Godwin postponed his arrival home, citing a desire to go to Coventry Fair and see a young woman reenact Lady Godiva's ride. Lady Godiva! All of Mary's insecurities resurfaced. She was home roasting in the heat, fat, lonely, and cranky while he was admiring a beautiful, scantily clad young woman on horseback. She wrote back, castigating him for his "icy Philosophy" and asking if he thought she was a stick or a stone. Even though this was just one incident, his behavior reminded her of Imlay. All delays and broken promises.

When at last he did arrive home, bearing gifts for Fanny—a mug with an *F* on it and a few other such trinkets—he made matters worse by encouraging Miss Pinkerton's advances, visiting her alone in her chambers and inviting her to come see him at Chalton Street when Mary would not be present. That same week, the weather changed, becoming windy and wet, reminding Mary of the terrible autumn when she had tried to end her life over Imlay's desertion. It was all too much for her, and she wrote an accusatory letter to Godwin that sounds remarkably like the letters she used to write to Imlay:

> I am absurd to look for the affection which I have found only in my own tormented heart; and how can you blame me for tak[ing] refuge in the idea of a God, when I despair of finding sincerity on earth? . . . My old wounds bleed afresh.

But Godwin was not Imlay. He agreed to stop seeing Miss Pinkerton at once, rushing off a note to Mary from his office: "I would on no account willingly do any thing to make you unhappy." That afternoon, Mary drafted a stern note to the young woman, chastising her for her forwardness. Before she sent it, she gave it to Godwin to polish:

> Miss Pinkerton, I forbear to make any comments on your strange behavior; but unless you can determine to behave with propriety, you must excuse me for expressing a wish not to see you at our house.

Godwin amended the note to read "incomprehensible conduct" in place of "strange behavior," and Mary put it in the mail immediately. Miss Pinkerton responded immediately. "I am sensible of the impropriety of my conduct," she wrote Mary. "Tears and communication afford me relief."

This was a new experience for Mary, who, in the past, had always been the third one out. Imlay's actress and Mrs. Fuseli had driven her away. Now, although Miss Pinkerton and Godwin were not actually having an affair, Mary had staked her claim, making it clear that she refused to share her man, and she had won her ground.

Having dealt with Miss Pinkerton, Mary felt calmer and more confident. It helped that others had come forward in the past month to express their admiration and praise the couple for their originality. Thomas Holcroft said, "I think you the most extraordinary married pair in existence." Young poets and intellectuals gathered at the Polygon to pay court to these middle-aged radicals and to admire the partnership that they had forged. The Godwin/Wollstonecraft marriage seemed to unite all the principles they held most dear: freedom, justice, reason, sensibility, and the imagination—in essence, the ideals of the Enlightenment combined with the exciting new tenets of Romanticism.

The nineteen-year-old William Hazlitt, who would one day become one of the great essayists and critics in the English language, admired the egalitarian nature of their arrangement. Mary was neither deferential nor quiet. She actually teased Godwin, laughing at his stiff ways. When Godwin disagreed with her, she refused to back down and instead adopted a "playful, easy air." The young Coleridge praised Mary's creative spirit, finding her far superior to her husband, since in his estimation all "people of the imagination" had "ascendancy" over "those of mere intellect." A few years later, he would change his mind about Godwin, but at the time, he was impressed with the philosopher largely because he had married Wollstonecraft.

Instead of spending the last weeks of her pregnancy napping or doing needlework, the kind of activities recommended for women in her condition, Mary walked vigorously, usually heading out into the fields with Fanny to let her play with her hoop or toy rake. Maria Reveley and her small son, Henry, often accompanied them on these excursions and Mary cherished her last days with Fanny without the distraction of a new baby. Her humor and her ready ability to enter a child's viewpoint are displayed in a note Fanny "dictated" to Henry:

Little Fanny would be very glad to have the promised Rake, in the course of a day or two because she wishes to make Hay in the fields opposite to her house. If Henry will bring it she shall like to have a tumble with him on the Hay. The Pitchfork has been used every day.

Fanny sends her love to Henry, and wishes him to direct his next letter to herself, and she will put it up with her books, in her own closet.

Occasionally, Mary and Godwin walked to the village of Sadler's Wells or downtown to visit Johnson and the other booksellers: she was always happy to hear the latest book gossip. She saw Mary Hays for tea, worked on *The Wrongs of Woman,* and also finished some little stories for Fanny to read once "William" was born. These short passages offer glimpses into Mary and Fanny's daily routines and at the same time show Mary's tenderness and pride in her daughter:

See how much taller you are than William. In four years you have learned to eat, to walk, to talk. Why do you smile? You can do much more, you think: You can wash your hands and face. . . . And you can comb your head with the pretty comb you always put by your own drawer. To be sure, you do all this to be ready to have a walk with me. You would be obliged to stay at home, if you could not comb your own hair. Betty is busy getting the dinner ready, and only brushes William's hair, because he cannot do it himself.

And:

When I caught a cold some time ago, I had such a pain in my head, I could scarcely hold it up. Papa opened the door very softly, because he loves me. You love me, yet you made a noise. You had not the sense to know that it made my head worse, till papa told you.

You say that you do not know how to think. Yes, you do a

little. The other day papa was tired; he had been walking about all the morning. After dinner he fell asleep on the sofa. I did not bid you be quiet, but you thought of what papa said to you, when my head ached. This made you think that you ought not to make a noise, when papa was resting himself. So you came to me, and said to me, very softly, Pray reach me my ball, and I will go and play in the garden, till papa wakes.

You were going out; but thinking again, you came back to me on your tiptoes. Whisper whisper. Pray mamma call me, when papa wakes; for I shall be afraid to open the door to see, lest I should disturb him.

Away you went—Creep, creep—and shut the door as softly as I could have done myself. That was thinking. . . . Another day we will see if you can think about anything else.


THE SECOND WEEK OF August, the famous comet, or, to use Mary Shelley's words, a "strange Star," appeared in the night sky, bewildering all who saw it streak across the heavens. Mary hoped it meant their child would be born soon. She wanted "to regain my activity, and to reduce to some shapeliness the portly shadow, which meets my eye when I take a musing walk."

As the month drew to a close, Mary and Godwin gave up their habit of going out without each other and spent the late summer evenings reading together. The last week of August, they decided to reread a favorite novel, *The Sorrows of Young Werther*. This was a time of "true happiness," Godwin said later. They would "point out unobserved beauties" in this melancholy novel and "were mutually delighted to remark the accord of our feelings, and still more so, as we perceived that accord to be hourly increasing."


ON THE MORNING OF August 30, Mary woke to the first flutters of labor. As in Le Havre, she did not summon a doctor. She believed the odds were in her favor. Fanny's birth had gone briskly without any complications. She was expecting the same for baby William and had found a midwife with a good reputation, a Mrs. Blekinsop, although she did not think there would be much for her to do. She sent Godwin to his office as usual, and after a few hours, the contractions became steady enough for her to write him a note saying, "I have no doubt of seeing the animal today." She also asked him to send over some light reading, a book or newspaper for the long waits between contractions. However, despite her optimistic prognostications, at midday she was still pacing the rooms of the house; the labor was progressing much more slowly than it had with Fanny. At two o'clock, she went up to her bedchamber and summoned the midwife, writing Godwin to tell him the baby would be born soon, and then repeated her mother's dying words: "I must have a little patience."

But the baby did not come soon. Mary had nine more hours of labor to endure. Godwin dined with the Reveleys and did not come home until after dark, only to find Mary still upstairs enduring contractions. The baby was not born until almost midnight on August 30, 1797. The midwife invited Godwin to meet his child—not a boy, after all, but a tiny, weak-looking baby girl. Godwin felt the solemnity of this occasion and would often recall the moment in the years to come, even writing an account of a husband and wife greeting one another after childbirth in his novel *St. Leon:*

> Never shall I forget the interview between us . . . the effusion of soul with which we met each other after all danger seemed to have subsided, the kindness which animated us, increased as it was by ideas of peril and suffering, the sacred sensation . . . the complacency with which we read in each other's eyes a common sentiment of melting tenderness and inviolable attachment!

In awe and overwhelmed by love for his wife, Godwin regarded the new baby as "the joint result of our common affection" and "the shrine in which our sympathies and our life have been poured together, never to be separated. Let other lovers testify their engage-

*Godwin's diary: "Birth of Mary, 20 minutes after 11 at night" (fourth entry down).*

ments by presents and tokens; we record and stamp our attachment in this precious creature."

Mary was too tired to speak, but Godwin stayed by her side, holding their little daughter and rejoicing in her safe delivery, until the midwife shooed him out because Mary still needed to deliver the placenta. After two more hours, however, there was still no afterbirth, leaving Mary at risk of developing an infection. Mrs. Blekinsop alerted Godwin, who leapt into a carriage with "despair . . . in my heart" and raced to the Westminster Hospital to bring back a doctor.

Godwin and a Dr. Poignand arrived back at the Polygon shortly before dawn and Poignand went right to work, ripping out shreds of the placenta without any anesthetic, causing Mary the greatest pain she had ever experienced. She fainted repeatedly and at times wanted to die but "was determined," she whispered, "not to leave [God-win]." At last, after many hours, Dr. Poignand assured them that he had extracted everything. Relieved, Mary finally slept. But the damage had been done. Dr. Poignand had introduced the disease that would kill his patient, never realizing that his efforts to save Mary would cause her death. In 1797, germ theory did not yet exist; the idea that doctors with unwashed hands could spread an infection would have seemed ridiculous.

Once the sun was up, Fanny padded down the hallway to meet her new sister, whom they had decided to name Mary, after her mother. After Fanny had kissed the baby, her weary mother hugged her good-bye. Maria Reveley had offered to take her for a few days so Mary could rest. Godwin sat with his wife that afternoon and Maria came back to visit that evening. All seemed well the following morning, and so Godwin walked to his office to do a little work, called on Mary Hays to give her the news, and did not return until evening. While he was gone, Johnson visited Mary and met the new baby. Godwin also summoned a new doctor, an old friend of Mary's named George Fordyce, who stopped by to check on her, afterward reporting to Godwin that he was optimistic about Mary's recovery. The couple dined together and decided that this would be how they would order their lives for the next few months. Godwin would work. Mary would take care of the infant. They went to sleep that night tranquil, contented with each other and delighted with their new family.

Friday and Saturday were restful, happy days. The baby nursed. Mary napped and began to make plans for the weeks ahead. The first order of business was a nursemaid. Godwin's sister had a friend, Lou-isa Jones, who was interested in the position. On Sunday, she brought her to the Polygon for an interview. But while the two women waited downstairs, a dreadful banging began to shake the walls. Mary had developed a sudden fever and was shivering so acutely that her iron bed bumped across the floorboards, rattling the whole house. An anguished Godwin sent for Dr. Fordyce at once. His sister and Louisa fled, and the household geared to meet the crisis.

It did not take Dr. Fordyce long to diagnose the problem: puerperal or childbed fever. There was still unshed placenta inside Mary and it was decaying; infection had begun and there was nothing anyone could do. To keep Mary calm, Fordyce lied to her, telling her that she would recover and inventing a pretext for why her milk was no longer good for the baby. Since Mary's breasts were stretched painfully taut, they brought in puppies to nurse, an eighteenth-century custom that Mary tried to smile at, but which seemed unbearably cruel when little Mary was in the next room eager to be fed.

Fordyce, meanwhile, had told Godwin the truth. So while Mary clung to the belief that she would live, her husband sank into gloom. The baby was dispatched to the Reveleys to join her sister. Pale and underweight, she was also not expected to live. Godwin moved into Mary's room, sleeping in the chair next to her bed. He "intreated her to recover" and "dwelt with trembling fondness on every favorable circumstance; and, as far as it was possible in so dreadful a situation, she, by her smiles and kind speeches, rewarded my affection." Her friends, led by Mary Hays and Maria Reveley, stationed themselves in the house, and the loyal Marguerite refused to leave Mary's side. Four of Godwin's male friends kept watch downstairs. As Mary Hays said, "The attachment and regret of those who surrounded her appeared to increase every hour." Mary, who was still conscious, touched everyone with her "anxious fondness" for her well-wishers.

Dr. Fordyce paid frequent visits to no avail. To ease her suffering, he told Godwin to ply her with wine. Godwin complied, but felt unsure about how much to give. He did not want to speed her death, but neither did he want her to suffer; he felt as though he had been asked "to play with a life that now seemed all that was dear to me in the universe." It was "too dreadful a task." Mary grew weaker by the hour. Desperate for reassurance, Godwin asked Mary, the servant, what she thought of her mistress's progress and was horrified when Mary said she thought her mistress "was going as fast as possible." Finally, on Friday, September 8, Godwin, suspecting that his wife knew the truth, gave up pretending and had what he called a "solemn communication" with her, trying to discover Mary's wishes for her daughters. But by then Mary did not have the strength to talk, let alone make plans. All she could say was "I know what you are thinking of . . ."

For the next forty-eight hours Mary slipped in and out of consciousness. The shaking fits had stopped and she seemed, as Godwin had thought, to know that she was dying. Her last words were that Godwin was "the kindest, best man in the world." The doctor tried to encourage him by saying it was a miracle that she was still alive and that "it was highly improper to give up all hope." After all, if anyone could survive, it would be Mary. Still, Godwin knew that these were empty words and did his best to prepare for the end.

He slept for a few hours early on Sunday morning, with orders to be woken up if there was any change. At six, the doctor called him to Mary's side and he sat with her until she died, less than two hours later, a little before eight in the morning of September 10. Afterward, Godwin drew three mute lines in his journal. Mary was lost to him forever. It would take him two years to describe what he felt, and when he did, he spoke through a fictional character whose wife had just died in childbirth, conveying far more emotion here than he was able to express in real life:

What is man? And of what are we made? Within that petty frame resided for years all that we worship, for there resided all that we know and can conceive of excellence. That heart is now still. Within the whole extent of that frame there exists no thought, no feeling, no virtue. It remains no longer, but to mock my sense and scoff at my sorrow, to rend my bosom with a woe, complicated, matchless and inexpressible. . . .

Fanny was brought home for dinner that day so she could kiss her mother's body goodbye and then returned to the Reveleys. Since Godwin did not believe in God, he took no comfort in the idea of a reunion in heaven. In his mind, Mary was gone. Utterly gone. He shut himself in his study while Mary's friends cut locks of her hair to remember her by, distributed her possessions, and wrote letters to tell the sad news. The artist John Opie paid a sympathy call and touched Godwin deeply by giving him a portrait of Mary he had painted that summer when she was in the last stages of pregnancy. She looked soft and wistful, as though she knew what was going to happen.

Godwin's friend James Marshall organized the funeral, with Godwin providing the guest list, and on September 15, five days after Mary died, her friends and family gathered in the churchyard of St. Pancras, just a few steps from where she and Godwin had been married five months before.

*The graveyard at old St. Pancras church in London.*

If anyone had hoped to see the widower, however, they were to be disappointed. Godwin was grieving the only way he knew, alone in his study, with a book open and a pen in his hand.

# MARY SHELLEY:
# "THE DEEPEST SOLITUDE"

———

[ 1823–1828 ]

Aꜰᴛᴇʀ Sʜᴇʟʟᴇʏ's ᴅᴇᴀᴛʜ, Mᴀʀʏ ᴡᴀs sᴜʀᴘʀɪsᴇᴅ ᴀɴᴅ sᴀᴅᴅᴇɴᴇᴅ to discover that Hunt now regarded her with suspicion. She thought of him as one of her closest friends, yet he had been cold and aloof ever since he arrived. She did not know that Jane had poisoned Hunt against her, telling him that Mary had made Shelley miserable in his last months, not loving him as he deserved. Nor did Mary know that Shelley had complained about her when he saw Hunt right before he died. Bewildered and hurt, she thought Hunt must still be angry over their quarrel about Shelley's heart.

Shaken, she turned to her journal, speaking to Shelley as though he were still alive: "It is not true that this heart was cold to thee. . . . Did I not in the deepest solitude of thought repeat to myself my good fortune in possessing you?" However, she resisted acting the part of the conventional widow, weeping and sighing like Jane. "No one seems to understand or to sympathize with me," she wrote, crossing out words in her distress. "[They] seem to look on me as one without affections. . . . I feel dejected and cowed before them, feeling as if I might be the ~~unfeeling~~ senseless person they appear to ~~cond~~ consider me. But I am not."

That September, Jane departed for England, but Mary remained behind with the Hunts and Byron. Leaving Italy felt too much like abandoning Shelley, Clara, and William. And so, as she always had, she turned to her studies for support, reading Greek and medieval Italian history. Unlike the loss of William, which had reduced her to silence, Shelley's death unlocked the floodgates. She tried to summon him back with her words, writing long grief-stricken entries in her journal. With the help of Hunt and Byron, she produced the first edition of *The Liberal,* the magazine that Shelley had dreamed up in Pisa and that he had invited Hunt to edit. On October 15, the first issue was published, and it included one of Shelley's recent works, *May-day Night; A Poetical Translation from Goethe's Faust,* which Mary had edited and readied for printing. For the second number, published a month later, she contributed her own work, "A Tale of the Passions; or, The Death of Despina"—a story she had written before Shelley died—and another poem of Shelley's, *Song, Written for an Indian Air.* Hazlitt, one of her father and mother's old admirers, contributed a poignant essay, "My First Acquaintance with Poets," and Byron included his bitter *Vision of Judgment.* Mary's goal was to make a living through her writing. "It is only in books and literary occupations that I shall ever find alleviation," she wrote to Jane that December. Above all, she would not turn to another husband to take care of her. Despite her admiration for her Greek prince and the rush of excitement she had felt with Trelawny, no man could ever live up to Shelley.

Byron had decided to leave Pisa in mid-September and head for Genoa to set up residence in the splendid Casa Saluzzo. She and the Hunts followed suit, moving nearby, renting the forty-room Casa Negroto with a garden and two sweeping staircases—plenty of space to share, Mary thought, especially compared to the Casa Magni. But the Hunts were not in the mood to be pleased. They had come to Italy to start a new magazine, and now one of its principal supporters and contributors had died. As sad as they were, they had their own futures to consider. Marianne was pregnant with her seventh child and homesick for London. Italy was not as romantic as she had thought it would be. Their new accommodations were inadequate, she said: "The number and size of the doors and windows make it look anything but snug."

It was an unseasonably cold autumn. The Casa Negroto had only one central fireplace, and so Mary and Percy were forced to huddle with the Hunts simply to stay warm. The notoriously unruly Hunt children fought, played pranks, overturned furniture, scraped their elbows, and pounded up and down the stairs. Percy was used to the quiet life of an only child and clung to his mother, crying if any of the noisy brood approached him. When the Hunts had stayed with Byron, the children had damaged his house, and Marianne, instead of reprimanding them, had taken umbrage at Byron:

> Can anything be more absurd than a peer of the realm—and a poet—making such a fuss about three or four children disfiguring the walls of a few rooms. The very children would blush for him, fye Lord B.—fye.

Claire had not made the move to Genoa. Back in Pisa, tensions had risen once again between the two sisters. Like Mary, Claire was heartbroken over the loss of Shelley, but she was also still devastated over Allegra and was hurt that Mary was so consumed with her own grief that she could not console her. Then there were money worries. Both Mary and Claire had depended on Shelley financially. It was unclear how they would support themselves and whether they would inherit anything from his estate. Claire had been preparing herself to work as a governess. But she had yet to find a suitable job, and she looked to Mary for assistance. Mary, anxious about her own future with Percy, was not very forthcoming. She gave what money she thought she could spare, but it was not much, so, in a huff, Claire moved to Vienna to be near her brother, hoping to find a position in Austria. She had never let go of the idea of becoming an independent woman in the style of Mary Wollstonecraft and had refused at least one offer of marriage—Henry Reveley, Maria Gisborne's son, had been hopelessly in love with her—to preserve her liberty.

Fortunately for Mary, the most famous member of the Pisan group remained loyal to her. For six years, Byron and Mary had been literary colleagues and friends. He had never lost his respect for her, or his affection, despite his usual sardonic suspicion of women. He saw that she was almost out of money and paid her to copy some of his new work, amending some passages in accordance with her suggestions, asking her advice about publishing his memoirs, and reassuring her that Shelley's father would pay her a generous annuity; after all, she was a widow with a young son.

But Byron was the exception. The English in Genoa refused to acknowledge her, continuing to view Mary as a member of the shocking League of Incest. To Mrs. Gisborne, she confided, "Those about me have no idea of what I suffer; for I talk, aye & smile as usual—& none are sufficiently interested in me to observe that . . . my eyes are blank." Trelawny swept into town with a beautiful new mistress, who was already married to someone else and was trying to keep her adultery a secret. Mary thought that this was hypocritical behavior and said so; if the woman was truly in love, she should sacrifice her reputation to be with Trelawny. That, after all, is what Mary had done for Shelley. Trelawny was furious and cut off relations with her in rage.

By spring, Mary was penniless. Shelley had left behind a complicated tangle of bills, and Sir Timothy had not written to her once, nor had he offered to continue paying her Shelley's monthly income. Mary assumed that this was meant to be a rejection, but Byron assured her that Sir Timothy's silence was undoubtedly due to legal proceedings and sent a letter to Shelley's father on her behalf, informing Sir Timothy of her financial need. Her own father wrote repeatedly, urging her to come home, telling her that he would help her manage Sir Timothy. And so, reluctant though she was to return, she made plans to sail back to England, if only to arrive at an agreement with the Shelleys.

Before Mary left, however, news came that she had been right about Sir Timothy. A letter from his lawyer arrived, announcing that he had no intention of helping the woman who had "estranged my son's mind from his family, and all his first duties in life." He said that he would support Percy, but only if she would agree to part with him. If not, then she could expect nothing. Byron urged her to accept this offer, but Mary refused. "I should not live ten days separate from [Percy]," she declared. Though the situation seemed bleak, Mary decided to go through with the trip home, hoping that Shelley's father would soften once he met his grandson.

A few weeks before her departure, Mary and Hunt had a rapprochement. Hunt had witnessed her quiet misery all winter long, as well as the depth of her pride. He remembered Mary's reserve from their summer in Marlow and knew that she was not capable of falsehood. At last he came to the conclusion that Jane had been spreading lies and wrote Jane an angry letter, but Jane never acknowledged any wrongdoing and continued to tell her malicious stories.

Relieved to be back on good terms with Hunt, Mary invested her last thirty pounds in the trip home, beginning with a hot, dusty eighteen-day odyssey to Paris. Without Shelley, there were no private coaches or elegant inns. She bumped north in the public stagecoach, pressed against other sweaty, ill-tempered passengers, with Percy on her lap. She had read Wollstonecraft's *Letters from Sweden* so many times that it was easy to imagine herself in her mother's shoes, traveling alone with a small child, abandoned by the man she loved, and from this she took comfort. In addition, Percy was remarkably even-tempered, displaying a mildness that was both a comfort and a heartbreaking surprise to his mother, who every day searched his countenance for evidence of his volatile father.

When at last they arrived in London it was August 25, five days before Mary's twenty-sixth birthday. Godwin met her at the wharf with William, the twenty-year-old half brother she had not seen since he was fifteen. She had been gone for five years, but London had changed so much in her absence that without her father to guide her, Mary would have been completely lost. "I think I could find my way better on foot to the Coliseum at Rome than hence to Grosvenor Square," she said somewhat wistfully.

The most startling development was the newly dug Regent's Canal, which ran in a straight line through the city, reaching north into the villages of Mary's childhood, cutting off streets and reshaping neighborhoods. But there were other significant changes as well.

Huge factories had sprung up near Paddington, St. Pancras, and Camden Town, coughing smoke into the already polluted London air. Gaslights bloomed on every street corner, transforming night-time London from a dusty, dark rabbit warren to a brightly illuminated hive, a change that Dickens would later lament in *Sketches by Boz*. The shops on the newly designed Regent Street lured people away from Mayfair to gawk at the novelties produced by factories: cheap china dishes and ready-made cloaks, mass-produced fans and powdered cinnamon.

But even if Mary no longer knew London, London had not forgotten her. In the first week of August, the Lyceum Theater had mounted a production called *Presumption; or, The Fate of Frankenstein*. Protesters marched outside the theater, bearing placards condemning "the monstrous Drama founded on the improper work called 'Frankenstein.'" Appalled though she was by this hostility to her book, Mary still enjoyed going to the theater to see the play. She could feel a "breathless eagerness in the audience." She also felt Godwin's pride. "Lo & behold," she wrote to Hunt, "I found myself famous."

Unfortunately, Mary earned no money from this production, nor from any of the others based on her book. In nineteenth-century England, playwrights were allowed to borrow freely from novels without crediting the original author. They were also under no obligation to adhere to the original story. Stage versions of *Frankenstein* focused on simplifying the intricacies of the novel, making it easier for audiences to digest. In the hands of these adaptors, Mary's multifaceted creature became one-dimensional, a pure villain, rather than the complex mix of victim and murderer Mary had written. Another odd development was that over time Mary's hubristic Dr. Frankenstein almost entirely disappeared from public awareness; by the 1840s, the word "Frankenstein" had become synonymous with "monster"; in one early instance, a *Punch* cartoonist pointed out the dangers of relaxing English rule in Ireland by drawing a monster in the act of destroying a town, labeling it "The Irish Frankenstein." To the public, Mary's name became inextricably entwined with that of a murderous fiend. As her fame grew, the many layers and multiple perspectives of the novel were gradually forgotten.

During the first few weeks of the autumn of 1823, Mary and her father visited old friends, went to exhibitions, and took a boat ride down to Richmond. Her younger brother proved to be an amusing companion, delighting Mary by referring to the sixty-seven-year-old Godwin as "the old gentleman"—an irreverence she had never allowed herself. To her surprise, Mary-Jane left her largely alone. If anything, her stepmother seemed a pitiful figure these days, overwrought, histrionic, and bitter.

When at length they met Sir Timothy's lawyer, William Whitton, he emphasized Sir Timothy's animosity, underlining the fact that Shelley's father wanted nothing to do with his son's widow or with young Percy. He refused to meet them, but did offer some financial support, granting Mary a scant £200 a year—£100 for her and £100 for Percy. In modern equivalencies, this gave them less than $20,000 or about £12,000 a year to live on. Furthermore, he made the money contingent on her continued residence in England, and, worse, on a kind of gag rule. She was not to publish any of Shelley's works or write anything about him. If she disregarded either of these stipulations, she would be cut off without a penny. Finally, if Sir Timothy discovered that Mary was in debt and could not support herself and her son, then he would seize Percy—Mary's greatest fear.

This was crushing news. Mary had sustained herself with visions of writing her husband's biography, extolling his genius and defending him against the claims of immorality still clinging to his name. She had not been dissuaded by the fact that defending Shelley was a dangerous undertaking—John Chalk Claris ("Arthur Brooke"), a poet who had dared to write an elegy for Shelley, was castigated by no fewer than five different journals, and Hunt's sister-in-law, Bess Kent, was reviled simply for quoting one of Shelley's poems in her botanical treatise on houseplants.

Nevertheless, she needed Sir Timothy's money, and thus would have to wait before she could give Shelley his due. To augment her income, Mary turned her hand to writing for magazines. Her father introduced her to his literary contacts, but otherwise he made no move to help, maintaining his position that it was Mary's job to support him financially, dead husband or no. Dutiful daughter that she was, when she published a story in *The London Magazine,* she gave her father what funds she could spare. Later that fall, on the strength of her earnings, she moved into her own quarters with Percy, staving off her loneliness by spending most of the time she was not writing with her father and brother. On rare occasions she visited Jane Williams, who, as an unmarried woman with two illegitimate children, was suffering in enforced isolation outside London in Kentish Town.

Unaware as she was of Jane's malicious gossiping, Mary began to contemplate a move out of the city to be nearer her old friend. Sometimes she even dreamed of earning enough money to take Jane and her children back with her to Italy. And with Shelley's death, her notion that she did not belong among the living had resurfaced. Not only her dead husband, but her children, her sister Fanny, and her own mother waited for her on the other side. Sometimes, they felt close enough to touch. Only Percy, and sometimes her father and brother, could break through her melancholy shell.

Sir Timothy's order notwithstanding, Mary decided to produce a volume of Shelley's work anonymously. However, this project was bigger than it initially seemed. Shelley had never been a tidy person, and his papers were in greater disarray than Mary had expected. He had written when inspired, on whatever was available, and had jammed scraps and notebooks into his writing desk, scribbled on the backs of envelopes, and stuck pieces of paper into whatever book he happened to be reading. Many poems had been composed on different sheets, making it difficult to tell where new poems began and old ones ended. Those poems that were written on one piece of paper were often lodged between doodles of trees and sailboats.

For Mary, daunting though the project was, sifting through Shelley's papers helped her resurrect her husband's presence, giving her the sense that they were still in communication, that he was still speaking to her. She made the additions and deletions he seemed to indicate, choosing final versions and piecing together lines written in different locations. Fortunately, she was not working with entirely foreign material. She and Shelley had talked about some of the drafts; the collaborative spirit between husband and wife that had begun in the joint journal in Paris, when Mary was sixteen and Shelley twenty-one, held even after his death.

But there were also plenty of poems that they had not discussed and that Mary was reading for the first time. Many of these had been written during the tragedies of the last years and lamented his loneliness, or praised Jane or Emilia at her expense. As difficult as these were to read, Mary knew that if she wanted the public to see his best work, she would have to push herself to piece together these verses as well. This was a painful enterprise, but she did not hesitate, as she believed that her personal feelings did not matter when it came to art. Great literature was great literature, even if it caused her pain. Accordingly, she set herself the task of sewing stanzas together, reordering and deleting, ultimately creating one of her greatest and most unsung achievements: a coherent collection of Shelley's work.

Interestingly, despite the significant role Mary played in bringing his work into public view, no one has ever accused Shelley of not writing his own poems, although Mary's contributions are at least as substantial as his edits were to *Frankenstein*. This is because, unlike Shelley, Mary covered her tracks. Although she wrote an anonymous preface to the edition, not once did she refer to her own editorial role. On the one hand, she had to hide her identity from Sir Timothy, but she also wanted to present Shelley as a great artist who needed no editing. In addition, she was aware that, as a woman, she would face criticism for daring to tamper with her husband's work, no matter how much everyone disapproved of Shelley in the first place.

Within six months, *Posthumous Poems* was ready for publication. It went on sale in June of 1824 and sold briskly until Sir Timothy got wind of it. Although he could not prove it, he knew that this was Mary's doing. Furious at his daughter-in-law, he stopped sales, forcing the publisher to recall all unsold copies, but he was too late to stop Mary's vision of Shelley from taking hold. Those lucky enough to own a copy passed *Posthumous Poems* along to their friends, while those who did not have the book contented themselves with copying poems from others and sharing them. The unsigned preface declared that Shelley had been an ethereal spirit, a gentle artist removed from politics and controversy. Mary did not mention his radicalism—his calls for reform, his atheism, his declarations on behalf of free love. Her intention was to free his name from scandal, not to inflame the public.

In 1824, though, it was impossible for Mary to know how well she had succeeded at establishing a new reputation for Shelley, and, deprived of the right to publish his work, or even mention his name in print, she turned back to her own writing. Gradually her imagination reasserted itself and a story gathered shape that would result in a new novel, *The Last Man,* as cheerless as its title suggests. Mary set the story in the twenty-first century, when a mysterious plague wipes out all of humanity except for one survivor who cries, "I am a tree rent by lightning . . . I am alone in the world . . . ," sentiments that perfectly reflected Mary's own feelings.

That May, while she drafted the early pages of *The Last Man,* more bad news arrived. It was beginning to seem to Mary like a "law of nature" that those she loved would die. This time it was Byron. He had succumbed to a fever while fighting for Greece's independence from Turkey. Those who were left—the Hunts, Thomas Hogg, Jane Williams, Edward Trelawny, and Claire—could never measure up to Shelley and Byron, or "the Elect," as she called them. In her diary, she reflected that her new novel now seemed an even more apt description of her real experiences: "The Last Man! Yes, I may well describe that solitary being's feeling, feeling myself as the last relic of a beloved race, my companions extinct before me."

When summer came, Mary acted on her desire to be near Jane and moved to Kentish Town, a sleepy country hamlet sheltered by the wooded high country of Hampstead and connected to the city by only one road, a dirt track that ran right past Mary's new lodgings. The railroad would soon invade this peaceful village, not far from Somers Town, but in the 1820s, farmhouses and gentlemen's retreats dotted the countryside. Percy was delighted to see Jane's children, his Italian playfellows, and Mary was happy to live near the fields of her childhood. In the afternoons she watched Percy play outside, disappearing from view in the hay, flying his kite, far from the smog and grime of the city.

The reality of her most recent loss was brought home when Byron's funeral procession marched by her house, winding its way north to his lordship's ancestral estates in Newstead. Mary watched from the window, her heart aching. She saw herself as a victim of fate, spared for reasons she could not know or understand, and she poured these feelings into her novel: in the book's climactic scene, the last man steps on board a ship, bound for nowhere, adrift and alone.

To ease her sorrow, she devoted herself to Jane and stayed on in Kentish Town when the fall came. In the afternoons, the two women walked for miles in the countryside. Percy went to a small day school down the street, allowing Mary to work without distraction in the morning. What she did not know, and, indeed had never known, was that Jane continued to be duplicitous. Her latest secret was that she was conducting an affair, her evenings enlivened by a visitor she did not mention to Mary.

Thomas Hogg, in keeping with his pattern of falling in love with Shelley's wives and paramours, had become smitten with Jane when she returned to London. Jane had intrigued him when she whispered that she and not Mary had been Shelley's last and truest love. Although Jane was not particularly attracted to the prosaic and awkward Hogg, it had been difficult to return to London as an unwed mother; she had been snubbed, attacked, and ridiculed. It was refreshing to be admired and so she allowed the affair to begin, although she insisted they keep it hidden from their friends and family. That summer she had made a partial confession to Mary, telling her about Hogg's advances but also implying she had rejected him. Mary could understand spurning Hogg, not only because she had once done so, but because she, too, had to discourage potential suitors. The American playwright John Howard Payne had proposed to Mary after meeting her at her father's house. Other men, whose names she did not bother to record in her journal, also stepped forward, fascinated by the idea of her being Shelley's widow and attracted by her brilliance and her gentle manners. As she lamented to Byron's grieving mistress, Teresa, "if you knew the men that dare to aspire to be the successors of Shelley and Williams—My God—we are reduced to this."

This situation could not last long, and by the end of January, disaster struck. One night Hogg arrived for a visit while Mary and Percy were still at Jane's expecting their customary evening of games and conversation by the fire, but Jane wanted time alone with Hogg and told Mary to leave, so abruptly and so unkindly that the reverberations are still audible in Mary's journal: "I know now why I am outcast—So be it! . . . I make not her happiness—she is happy now—has been so all day—while I in ~~gr~~ disgrace—'with fortune and men's eyes / I all alone beweep my outcast state,'" Mary raged. Too late she understood the true nature of Jane's relationship with Hogg. "O miserable fool—grieve but be not mad—" she scrawled, and then the rest of the page is ripped out. Clearly someone, perhaps Mary, though more likely her Victorian descendants, deemed her words too scandalous for posterity. Perhaps Mary was overly explicit in her condemnation of Jane's sexual relationship with Hogg. Intriguingly, however, it may have been that Mary was overly explicit in her own feelings, raising the question of the exact nature of her relationship with Jane.

Mary knew plenty of women who had female lovers. The famous ladies of Llangolen, who had fled their disapproving families to live together in Wales in 1780, were celebrities of the era and counted Godwin as one of their friends. Shelley had visited them when he and Harriet lived in Wales. Byron, too, had made a pilgrimage to their cottage. To the poets and their friends, the ladies offered a real-life example of how they might follow the dictates of the heart rather than the rules of society. Mary herself had a new acquaintance, Mary Diana Dods (Doddy), the illegitimate daughter of a Scottish earl, who was notorious for her love affairs with women. She had been introduced to Doddy at a party Jane had urged her to attend and been impressed by her "charm and fascination" and "the extraordinary talent which her conversation . . . displayed." It did not hurt that Doddy fell immediately in love with Mary, deluging her with letters describing the anguish she felt on the days they did not meet.

Still, with Doddy, at least, Mary was interested only in pursuing a friendship. Her feelings for Jane at this point are less clear. Certainly, Mary regarded Hogg as a competitor, but whether this was the jealousy of a lover or a dear friend is uncertain. What is certain is that she instantly began a counterattack, lecturing her weaker friend that Hogg was not a worthy successor to Williams. She assured Jane that she would meet a more deserving man in the future, and in the meantime urged her to rely instead on their friendship. Promising Jane that she would take care of her, Mary reminded her that one day Percy would inherit the Shelley fortune and then they could all breathe a sigh of relief. Jane relented, sending Hogg away. Perhaps if he went to Rome and soaked in some art, he might achieve a more poetic outlook, Mary suggested politely. Jane relayed this message, and Hogg, seeking to please Jane, set forth on an extended European tour.

Jane had never liked being on her own, and with Hogg gone, she turned the full force of her charm on Mary, telling Mary that she loved her and needed her more than anyone else. These were the words that Mary had longed to hear ever since Shelley had died—not from suitors, as they could never live up to her image of her husband, but Jane was another story. Shelley had cared about Jane—Mary did not yet know how much—and Jane had been part of the company of "the Elect." With Jane, Mary could retain her connection to the past, since Jane remembered her as she had once been—the wife of a baronet, living a life dedicated to art and literature.

Delighted by Jane's professions of loyalty, Mary renewed her vows of undying allegiance. She poured out all of the love that otherwise would have been spent on Shelley, and from here the relationship deepened quickly. By that summer, Mary's letters to Jane certainly appear to be love letters, suggestive, flirty, and full of praise. "I am not sure that male eyes will not trace these lines, so I will endeavor to be as demure as an old maid," she teased. Jane was her "bright lily," her "Fairy girl." She mentions their sexual parts—"our pretty N— the word is too wrong I must not write it"—worried about Jane's health, and told Hunt "the hope & consolation of my life is the society of [Jane]. To her, for better or worse, I am wedded."

By the winter, their relationship was so close that Mary turned to Jane for solace when *The Last Man* was published in January 1826 and received scathing reviews. One critic was shocked by its "sickening repetition of horrors"; another muttered that Mary's imagination was "diseased" and that her writing was "perverted" and "morbid." In an era that celebrated conquest and the growth of empire, when bestselling novels such as James Fenimore Cooper's *The Last of the Mohicans* glorified the dream of Manifest Destiny, *The Last Man* stands out as a single voice of protest against war and conquest. There is no such thing as progress, Mary says. A man setting sail is not a glorious symbol of expansion. Rather, exploration is yet another meaningless action, a futile gesture in a world where all empires decay and die.

As with *Frankenstein,* Mary's largely male audience wondered what kind of *woman* would dream up such a nightmare vision. Books by female novelists were supposed to celebrate beauty; their tone should be gentle, their themes soft and tender. But Mary did not want to write books she considered "weak." Like her mother, she aspired to the "masculine" virtues of strength and vigor, boldness and prophecy. Although she was encouraged by the few positive responses—the artist John Martin painted a series of works inspired by the novel, "An Ideal Design of the Last Man," and the book was translated into French—her only real comfort during this bleak time remained her relationship with Jane. "She is in truth my all, my sole delight," she wrote to Leigh Hunt.

Unfortunately, though, Jane's nature had not changed. For one thing, Jane, like Claire, had never stopped being jealous of Mary. She still said cutting things behind her back, repeating her old story that Mary had been cruel to Shelley and that she was the one Shelley had really loved, not Mary. In addition, Jane had never stopped missing the protection of a man, even a man as graceless as Hogg.

That spring, Hogg returned from his European adventures, able to pontificate about the joys of Mediterranean culture but otherwise unchanged. His insistence that he loved her was too much for Jane to resist, and by December 1826 she had secretly renewed their relationship. The truth finally came out when she discovered that she was pregnant. In February, she confessed her news to Mary, adding that she and Hogg planned to live together with their new baby. Outraged and deeply disappointed though she was, Mary tried to support Jane's decision, but in her journal worried that Jane would not be happy—and then, always honest with herself, worried that she did not *want* Jane to be happy.

With a healthy sense of self-preservation, Mary gave up her home in Kentish Town that May and vacationed away from the pregnant Jane, choosing a new friend for her escort, a young woman named Isabel Robinson, whom she had met at a party given by a friend of the Hunts that spring. Nineteen-year-old Isabel had dark eyes, a brooding disposition, and short, curling black hair. She delighted everyone she encountered, men and women alike. Doddy, having realized that Mary would never return her feelings, was secretly and hopelessly in love with her. Seductive and flirtatious, Isabel had already sustained one love affair with an American journalist and had fled to France to give birth to their baby. When Mary met her, she was thin, melancholy, and desperate for a confidante. Mary, the tragic widow of Shelley, seemed like the perfect candidate, and so Isabel drew Mary into a corner and poured out her sorrows: Adeline, her baby, was living with a wet nurse nearby. If Isabel's father discovered that she had a child, he would cast her out; she did not want to be exiled, but she was pining for her daughter. In tears, she declared she was going to run away with her baby and brave the future alone.

This sad story moved Mary to take action. She was an expert on the miseries of having illegitimate children. Doddy, too, was eager to proffer assistance, as Isabel's curls and slender figure were difficult to resist. At length, after many discussions, Mary and Doddy concocted a plan. Doddy knew that many people thought she looked masculine. She felt masculine. Why not capitalize on people's misapprehensions, live the life she had always wanted, and save the gorgeous Isabel at the same time? She would disguise herself as a man and set off for France with Isabel, where they would pretend to be man and wife. After a few years, Doddy would fade away and Isabel could come back home to England, a respectable widow with a child. It was an absurd plan, crazy even. But Mary was her mother's daughter. She knew that Mrs. Mason had successfully disguised herself as a man at medical school; she believed in Isabel's cause; and so she assumed the role of mastermind. There were many dangers—if anyone caught on, all three women would be in permanent disgrace—but at the end of the summer, with Mary's assistance, the strange couple moved to France, and a few years later, Isabel returned to England with her daughter. No one was ever the wiser.

Before they left for Paris, however, Isabel took Mary aside. Over the course of her friendship with Mary, she had met Jane, who, true to form, had whispered terrible things about her to the young woman. Thinking her savior should know that Jane was not to be trusted, Isabel told Mary everything Jane had said, including the rumor that Shelley had never loved his wife. And now there was a new twist. According to Isabel, Jane implied that Shelley had been so unhappy in his marriage that he had hoped he would die when he sailed for home that fatal day. Mary was devastated. "My friend has proved false & treacherous," she scrawled in her journal. "Have I not been a fool."

Mary did not confront Jane immediately, as in November, Jane's baby died a few days after being born. Putting her feelings aside, Mary rushed to her old friend, full of empathy for her loss, and waited until February to confront her about her duplicity. Jane denied that she had done anything wrong, but Isabel's words seemed irrefutable. They helped explain Hunt's coldness back in Italy, and they also brought home a truth that Mary could no longer deny: Jane had been her competitor in Italy and remained her competitor, even though Mary had chosen not to see it.

Mary did not sever her ties with Jane. Cruel though Jane had been, she meant too much for Mary to give her up entirely. Instead, Mary maintained a careful distance that would remain for the rest of their lives. Jane begged for forgiveness, but their friendship was now entirely on Mary's terms. When, periodically, Jane tried to explain away her treachery, Mary put a stop to it, telling her that the harm could not be undone.

In the summer of 1828, Trelawny arrived back in England. It had been six years since those terrible months after Shelley's drowning when he and Mary had clashed over her criticism of his mistress. She had not seen him since, but over the years they had exchanged letters. Trelawny had gone with Byron to fight for Greek independence, thus earning Mary's respect, and when Jane betrayed her, Mary had written him long, confiding letters, expressing her passionate friendship and her longing to see him. Overcome by memories of his kindness toward her, memories that eclipsed their arguments, Mary wrote to Jane "how ardently I desire to see him." She did not reveal her secret hope; but she had not forgotten the thrill she had felt dancing in his arms all those years ago at the ball in Pisa.

Trelawny, however, did not appear to remember any particular tie between them, displaying none of the fervor of a suitor, or, for that matter, any of the warmth of a good friend. Mary had moved to London the previous fall, enrolling Percy in a grammar school, but instead of rushing to her front door to see her when he arrived in the city, Trelawny put her off time and again. When at last he did pay a visit, he immediately launched into an angry critique of how Mary was handling Shelley's literary legacy. She should continue to publish Shelley's poems, he said, and not obey his father. Shelley would have wanted her to rebel.

Having just left behind his own daughter (whom he would never bother to see again), Trelawny had no understanding of how Mary was haunted by Sir Timothy's threat that she would be separated from Percy if she broke his rules or could not stay out of debt. Such concerns seemed trivial to Trelawny, dedicated as he was to living life as a Byronic hero. Where was Mary's lust for battle? Why did she keep compromising instead of fighting? For Trelawny, Shelley's name was working wonders; his friendship with the dead poet enhanced his reputation as a dashing Romantic, a swashbuckler, and was almost as useful as his connection to Byron when it came to attracting the attention of London society. People came to parties expressly to hear his tales, even though they still refused to talk to Shelley's widow.

A few months after Trelawny's return, Claire, too, came back to England. After Vienna, she had spent five years as a governess in Russia, leaving only when her employers somehow learned of her liaison with Byron and fired her. Exposed as a woman of ill repute, she was left without a job or a place to stay, as no one would hire her. Now she was home for an extended visit, but if Mary had hoped for support from her stepsister, she was to be disappointed. Claire agreed with Trelawny that her stepsister was being weak, complaining that Mary had given up everything for "a share in the corruptions of society." She implied that she, Claire, would never have been so lacking in principle, and she did not let Mary forget that she had spent the years they had been apart living in accordance with Wollstonecraft's philosophy of independence, teaching these ideals to her students while Mary had let her mother's standard fall. Mary, however, refused to be drawn into battle. She needed to keep a low profile. Sir Timothy had been horrified by *The Last Man,* withholding her allowance in an attempt to stop her from writing, and had only recently relented. The Godwins, and Claire herself, depended on Mary's capacity to earn a living.

The irony is that even as she criticized Mary, Claire made herself at home in Mary's guest room, eating Mary's food and enjoying the

This idealized portrait of Mary Shelley is meant to represent her appearance as a young widow. Painted posthumously, it was based on recollections of her son and daughter-in-law, as well as on a death mask.

comforts of her lodgings on Tarrant Street, not far from the Godwins. Mary, meanwhile, shut herself away each morning, writing stories to pay the rent. Her resistance to injustice would always have to be underground, but it would not be any the less formidable. She continued to have her work published, and although her stories were for ladies' annuals, they contained many of her beliefs—disguised and softened, but still in evidence. There was much to be said for quiet, steady behind-the-scenes work. "A solitary woman is the world's victim," she reflected, "and there is heroism in her consecration."

# MARY WOLLSTONECRAFT: THE MEMOIR

---

[ 1797–1801 ]

WILLIAM GODWIN HAD NEVER BEEN GIVEN TO PERSONAL SPECU-lation, but in the first few weeks after he lost his wife, he allowed himself to wonder what might have happened if he had met Mary Wollstonecraft at the Hoxton haberdashery all those years ago. He had been nineteen and attending Hoxton Academy, and she sixteen, living only a half mile away. He liked to think that had he made po-lite inquiries, found out where she lived, and asked her feckless father for her hand in marriage, their lives would have been entirely differ-ent. They would have had twenty-two years together, writing, read-ing, and loving each other.

Nevertheless, Godwin did not fool himself into thinking he could have changed her. He was diffident, she was passionate. He was logi-cal, she was imaginative. He had learned more from her than from all of his books. With Mary, he had felt a delicious, "voluptuary" plea-sure that was a revelation.

Her friends helped him pay for a plain monument to mark her grave. Godwin had it inscribed simply, with no mention of reli-gion:

MARY WOLLSTONECRAFT

GODWIN

AUTHOR OF

A VINDICATION

OF THE RIGHTS OF WOMAN

BORN 27TH APRIL, 1759

DIED 10TH SEPTEMBER, 1797

Still, this was not enough of a memorial, he felt. This extraordinary woman's life could not be over just like that. But there were many others who felt the same way, and, as a result, a contest over who had been closest to Mary and who had the rights to her story began only days after she died. Although it was not as dramatic as the competition over Shelley's heart, the repercussions would be just as telling.

Godwin had left Henry Fuseli off the guest list for the funeral, and Johnson took Godwin to task, telling him that even though Fuseli and Mary were no longer close, Fuseli had been "the first of her friends"; Fuseli had met Mary long before she knew Godwin, and so had Johnson, but Godwin did not relent; he knew how hurt Mary had been by Fuseli's rejection before her first suicide attempt. And so, like the thirteenth fairy, the resentful Fuseli took revenge, spreading poisonous rumors about Mary. She was so desperate for his love, he said, that she bombarded him with letters—none of which he read. She pursued him so relentlessly for sex that even he was embarrassed for her sake.

Godwin also dismissed Mary's relationships with her female friends and her sisters. During Mary's final days, Godwin had picked a fight with Mary Hays, telling her there were too many people in the house and she should go home. When Hays protested, saying she was "not altogether insignificant" and she felt she was offering comfort to her dying friend, Godwin snapped at her, saying Hays was not respecting his grief and was poisoning their friendship. Hays never forgave Godwin, but unlike Fuseli, she remained loyal to Mary's memory.

Godwin was even crueler when it came to Everina and Eliza. He did not write to either of his wife's sisters after Mary died. Instead, he told Mary's friend Eliza Fenwick to write to Everina, though not to Eliza, who had refused to speak to Mary after her return to London. He did tell Mrs. Fenwick to include a message for Eliza that Mary had a "sincere and earnest affection" for her, and Mrs. Fenwick obeyed, telling Everina: "No woman was ever more happy in marriage than Mrs. Godwin. Who ever endured more anguish than Mr Godwin endures?"

Godwin can perhaps be forgiven after the shock of his loss, but Eliza Fenwick should have known better. Godwin was not the only person in pain. The sisters could easily have felt as much anguish as the heartbroken widower. They had been angry with Mary, but that did not destroy their bond with her. She had been a far better protector to them than their own mother. Even at the end, when they were estranged, she had felt so concerned about their future that she had been looking for money to send them in the weeks before her death. Now she would never be able to build a bridge between them, and neither would they. The conflict was left permanently unresolved, "the girls" in a painful state of limbo, and Godwin was doing nothing to help.

In fact, Godwin was actively distancing himself from those who had once been close to his wife. Like Fuseli, many of Mary's friends were put off by his pronouncements that he was the only one who had *truly* understood her, with dangerous repercussions, since, as writers, they were capable of penning their own versions of her life. And a few of them would do just that—solely to spite Godwin.

Wollstonecraft, after all, was a notable figure, a famous woman. People were curious about her. They wanted to know the real story behind her public face. Already, glowing death notices and obituaries were appearing in *The Monthly Magazine* and *The Annual Necrology*.

Godwin's competitive ire was raised. Those who ventured forth with opinions about Mary needed to be put in their place. Before a week was up, he had begun to write her story. This would allow him to stake his claim while raising money to take care of their daughters. He had no doubt such a book would sell.

On September 24, nine days after the funeral he did not attend,

Godwin recorded in his diary that he had finished the first two pages of *A Memoir of the Author of the Vindication,* the book that would ruin Mary's reputation for almost two hundred years. The first words he wrote—"It has always appeared to me, that to give to the public some account of the life of a person of eminent merit deceased, is a duty incumbent on survivors"—sound strangely distant for a man who had just lost his wife, but Godwin was being as emotional as it was possible for him to be. To call Mary "a person of eminent merit" was high praise for this stiff philosopher. He had never met a person like Mary, he said; she had been so candid, so actively searching for answers, so brave, so determined.

Disciplined though Godwin was, it was not easy to work at the Polygon in the weeks after Mary's death, and not just because of his own grief. The household was in an uproar. The cook did not know what to make for dinner. There were no clean linens for three-year-old Fanny. Baby Mary never seemed to stop crying. No one remembered how Godwin liked his tea. The kitchen ran out of eggs. Without Mary, the staff was bereft as well as bewildered. Not only had Wollstonecraft provided them with their directions, she had asked them about their lives and sympathized with their problems. They had loved her. Her grief-stricken friends compounded matters, dropping in at all hours to weep in the front parlor. Never one for niceties, Godwin was sharp with visitors and annoyed by the servants.

If Mary had been watching her husband struggle to work in this chaos, she might well have felt a little sorry for him, but she might have also been amused. To save money and restore order, Godwin had given up his Chalton Street office and moved into his wife's study. Here, he hung the portrait John Opie had given him above the fireplace and put her books on his shelves. Yet now that he was in her position, he was discovering the truth of her words about the many interruptions of domesticity. Just as he settled down to write, Fanny would try to talk to him. The maid and cook had quandaries that it seemed only he could solve. Merchants sent messengers to dun him for payment. Workmen came to repair the window sashes.

Finally, at his wits' end, Godwin instituted a new rule: the staff could not bother him during his writing hours, and neither could his stepdaughter. This meant that Fanny, who had always had the run of her mother's office, had to endure yet another loss. She was not allowed to knock on the study door, let alone open it and whisper to him; he was out of bounds until he dined at one o'clock, a rule from which he never wavered, even when he heard the baby's cries floating downstairs from the nursery.

Having established this system, Godwin could now square up to the challenges of writing *A Memoir*. He had known Mary for only the last eighteen months of her life, but he dismissed that as a trivial detail. She had told him stories about her childhood; he understood her inner spirit. Any facts he did not know, he could easily discover for himself. What mattered—he was sure—was the deep love that had bound them together, the special insight that he and he alone had into her character.

He spent hours sifting through Mary's unpublished manuscripts, and to the horror of future scholars, he burned the play she had worked on during their first summer together, deeming it unworthy of Mary's talents. He read the old letters that she had copied with an eye toward posterity, and wrote to friends for any others they might have in their possession. He interviewed Margaret Kingsborough (the future Mrs. Mason), Mary's charge from her days as a governess. Yet he did not take the most obvious step of all. He never contacted Mary's sisters. Instead, he wrote a letter to someone who hardly knew her: Hugh Skeys, Fanny Blood's widower, asking the basic questions Eliza and Everina were best equipped to answer. Mary had not been in touch with Hugh for many years and had little respect for him, but that did not stop Godwin: "I should be glad to be informed," he wrote to Skeys, sounding like a solicitor rather than a bereaved husband, "respecting the schools she was sent to & any other anecdotes of her girlish years. I wish to obtain the maiden name of her mother, & any circumstances respecting her father's or her mother's families." As an afterthought, he added, "Her sisters probably could tell some things that would be useful to me respecting the period when they lived together at Newington Green."

One can understand why he did not reach out to Mary's brothers, as they had long been out of touch. No one knew where Henry was.

Charles had gone to America. James had been in France, but he had been accused of being a British spy and his whereabouts were unknown. Edward had never been worth talking to as far as Mary was concerned. But it is difficult to know why Godwin did not write to the Wollstonecraft sisters at this stage of the project. Perhaps he was worried about upsetting them, or about what they would think of him publishing a "life" so swiftly. But if he had wanted to offend "the girls," he could not have chosen a more effective strategy; Everina and Eliza were outraged when they realized he was not consulting them. Skeys had sent them Godwin's questions, but Godwin was moving forward with *A Memoir* so quickly that they would not have time to send him their input. Once she understood what was happening, Everina wrote to Godwin with her concerns:

> When Eliza and I first learnt your intention of publishing immediately my sister Mary's life, we concluded, that you only meant a sketch to prevent your design concerning her memoirs from being anticipated. . . . At a future date we would willingly have given whatever information was necessary and even now we would not have shrunk from the task, however anxious we may be to avoid reviving the recollections it would raise, or loath to fall into the pain of thoughts it must lead to, did we suppose it possible to accomplish the work you have undertaken in the time you specify. . . . I think it is impossible for you to be even tolerably accurate.

Although Godwin would paint Mary's sisters as jealous women who had never appreciated their famous sister, this letter suggests that the sisters were clearly suffering from the shock of Mary's death. For their sister's sake, Everina says, they would have endured the pain of going back and remembering times long past, if only they had been asked.

Everina wrote with the same verve and righteousness as Mary often had. Above all, she knew how much research was entailed in writing a good biography, and like her sister, she was not afraid to tell Godwin his mistakes—in this case, that his "life" was "premature."

He did not even know their mother's maiden name! She did not bother to ask the most pressing question: Why had he not written to them directly? The answer seemed obvious. He did not care what they had to say. Unfortunately, Godwin, famous though he was for his logic and philosophical bent, ignored Everina's cautions. Everina wanted him to draw back and wait until his feelings had cooled; Godwin wanted to write while white-hot with grief. This was a mistake. His neglect of Eliza and Everina's storehouse of information hurt his *Memoir* at the same time that it sealed his estrangement from the women who had grown up with Mary and who were the blood relations of little Fanny, the very people most likely to take an active interest in her.

The modern biographer can only mourn this loss. Few people could have told him more about the first part of Mary's life than her sisters. They could have given Godwin a glimpse of what it was like to live with Mary, confide in Mary, and be taken care of by Mary when they were small children. They could have explained why they were angry with Mary and what it felt like to hate her—and to love her. They admired her enough, after all, to live according to her philosophy of self-reliance. Granted, their choices were limited. But neither had surrendered to a loveless marriage; nor had they resorted to life with their brother, Ned. Both were determined to maintain themselves. Indeed, this sense that they *could* be independent was the greatest lesson their sister had taught them, and it is one that Godwin overlooked completely. That is because the bold Mary, the adventurer, the girl who had taken care of her sisters, found them jobs, started a school, fought against their father and eldest brother, and taught them to be free at all costs—the woman who said she did not need a man to live a good life and neither did they—this Mary was not Godwin's favorite version of his wife. He had been repelled by Mary's brashness when he met her at Johnson's house with Tom Paine. She was too assertive for him then, too confident and too pushy. For all of Godwin's lofty ideas, he was still a man of his time. Once, as a reprimand to Mary Hays, he told her that she was not being feminine enough. "To speak frankly," he said, "I think you have forgotten a little of that simplicity & unpresuming mildness which so well becomes a woman."

For Godwin, then, Mary's sisters were not only beside the point, they had things to say that he did not want to hear. He had fallen in love with a wounded Mary. She had tried to kill herself just a few months before they met, and to him, strangely enough, this made her seem more appealing. She was like a female Werther—the hero of the novel they had read the night before she went into labor; Werther, too, had been driven mad by love. Werther, too, had tried to die because of his broken heart. Sublime passion, the ability to be consumed by love—that is what he admired about Mary; that is what he wanted to show the world. She was soft and yielding, a woman whose tender heart had been trodden upon, a "fair" who needed to be saved, a heroine of high romance. She was not—he was emphatic about this—the virago that many, including himself, had thought her to be after she published *Rights of Woman*.

With these priorities in mind, he felt no need of the petty domestic details her sisters could provide. Even Mary's literary achievements were secondary in his mind. What really mattered were the grand events of her life, and these were her love affairs. A bestselling novelist, Godwin knew how to craft a story. He dwelt on Mary's painful childhood to show the reader the hardship she overcame, but only briefly mentioned her positions as a lady's companion and governess; he skimmed over her experience as a professional journalist, but focused undue attention on her relationships with Fuseli, Imlay, and himself. In his hands, then, Mary becomes a tragic heroine; a woman defined in relation to men, not an independent individual, making her own choices and way in the world.

As a result, the book reads like a page-turning gothic drama, not an analytic study. Mary suffers at the hand of her despotic father, falls in love with Fuseli, and flees to France to escape his rejection. She stays in France during the Terror because of her grand passion for Imlay, has a child out of wedlock, and tries to kill herself twice. Only at the end of her life does she find happiness. And this happiness was, of course, with Godwin.

When it came to Mary's intellectual achievements, Godwin criticized or discounted any elements that disrupted his "plot." *A Vindication of the Rights of Woman,* he wrote, was flawed by "sentiments . . . of a rather masculine description" and was "amazonian"—an insult—with too many "passages of a stern and rugged feature." She was "too contemptuous" of Burke. These were only momentary lapses, Godwin assured his reader—"incompatible with the writer's essential character" and her "trembling delicacy of sentiment"—but they were also the reasons why her most famous work was not a masterpiece: "When tried by the long established laws of literary composition, [*Rights of Woman*] can scarcely maintain its claim to be placed in the first class of human productions." Emotional and passionate as she was, Godwin argued, Mary was incapable of following the rules of logic and rhetoric: *Rights of Woman* was "an unequal performance and eminently deficient in method and arrangement." He had consented to its inscription on her gravestone because it was her most famous work, but he worried that its readers would judge her as "rude, pedantic [and] dictatorial." To him, it was essential that the public understand that Mary was "a woman, lovely in her person, and . . . feminine in her manner."

In the course of this exegesis, not only did he neglect her philosophical influences, he ignored the final essay Mary wrote, "On Poetry, and Our Relish for the Beauties of Nature," her clearest articulation of her goals as a writer. Thus, readers of *A Memoir* never learn that Mary believed that authors should strive for the power and honesty that comes from Nature rather than an artificial correctness of structure and style. They never read that she wanted to reach readers' emotions and passions, not just their intellect as Godwin had in *Political Justice.* To Godwin, his wife's goals did not seem worth mentioning, as he deemed them incoherent and incomprehensible. He disliked the repetition, colloquial language, and autobiographical asides she employed, viewing these elements as evidence of an untrained mind, rather than rhetorical tools or innovations. Even worse, in his view, were her use of humor and her sudden shifts between formal and informal language; these marred the polish of her books and revealed her lack of discipline. Poor Mary, Godwin said, no one had ever helped her. She had not had the education she deserved; she was not (unlike himself) trained as a scholar, and her books suffered accordingly. For him, her tangents and self-revelations ruined the coherence of her arguments and revealed her weakness as a thinker rather than her originality. He did not mention her book on the French Revolution, even though others, including John Adams, would continue to reread it long after she died, and he completely failed to acknowledge her stylistic innovations in *Letters from Sweden*.

Regrettably, Godwin's assessment of Mary's work shaped the thinking of subsequent generations of readers, who condemned her for venturing into "masculine" territory. To most nineteenth-century critics, her books were too many things at once: personal and fictional, historical and autobiographical, formal and informal—a mélange that no longer seems odd to modern readers but that at the time seemed indecorous, raw, untaught, and inchoate. Even in the twentieth century, with a few notable exceptions, including Virginia Woolf's essay on Wollstonecraft in 1929 and Ralph Wardles's *Mary Wollstonecraft: A Critical Biography* in 1951, most readers criticized Wollstonecraft for her inclusion of personal reflection and informal language in philosophical, political, and historical works. Not until the 1970s, in the wake of a new interest in women's literature, did critics begin to reexamine Wollstonecraft's contributions to history. Now most scholars view Mary's mixture of writing styles as sophisticated rather than sloppy, innovative rather than naïve.

At last, Mary began to be seen as a seasoned professional, acutely aware of what she wanted to achieve as a writer, rather than as the overly emotional, ill-trained amateur depicted by her husband. Only those writers with "less vigorous" minds create works of "elegance and uniformity," she declared, whereas those who "speak the language of truth and nature" will by necessity produce work with "inequalities" and "roughness." By implication, she knew which category she was in. Impatient with restrictions, she *wanted* to break rules, stylistically and thematically. In the same way that she lived a headlong life, overturning traditions and following her own path, she wrote works that shattered convention and destroyed stultifying customs. She could not do otherwise. She had never been able to submit to authority. In her writing, her voice rings out, unpolished, inelegant, and filled with the force of truth.

It took Godwin less than eight weeks to finish *A Memoir*. On November 15, two months after Mary's funeral, he had completed the first draft. He revised it in four days, and on November 19 he handed it to Johnson for publication. The result was a disaster. The speed with which Godwin had written had indeed harmed his story, just as Everina had predicted. The facts had not been sifted and checked; much was missing. Godwin's own prejudices colored his assessment of Mary's contributions to political philosophy, and, worst of all, his frankness about her sexual experiences and his characterization of her as the heroine of many love affairs seemed calculated to alienate his audience. However, if Johnson had reservations about publishing the book, he did not mention them; he knew how much Godwin needed the money, and he believed that the reading audience should be offered the details of Mary's life, controversial though these had been. But perhaps it was he who suggested that the book be called a memoir, not a biography—an important change, since it reminds the reader that the book is meant to be a personal remembrance rather than a balanced accounting.

When *A Memoir* appeared in the bookstalls in January 1798, the elegies from the weekly magazines and newspapers came to an abrupt halt. No longer was Mary depicted as a beacon of Enlightenment values. Her ideas were now "scripture . . . for propagating w[hore]s," said *The Anti-Jacobin Review*. Even her admirers were shocked, less by her escapades—they had already known about these—than by the fact that Godwin had exposed them. According to one of her keenest fans, the poet Robert Southey, Godwin was guilty of "stripping his dead wife naked." Little Fanny became the most notorious bastard of her generation. Wollstonecraft's ideas were now completely overshadowed by her notoriety as a "fallen woman."

The government, which secretly funded *The Anti-Jacobin Review*, seized this opportunity to discredit the author of *Political Justice,* encouraging the publication of articles and reviews that lambasted Godwin, Wollstonecraft, and liberal social values in general. Even three years later, the campaign was still going strong. One of the most notorious attacks was a ribald verse that satirized Godwin's exposure of Wollstonecraft's personal history:

> *William hath penn'd a wagon-load of stuff,*
> *And Mary's life at last he needs must write,*
> *Thinking her whoredoms were not known enough,*
> *Till fairly printed off in black and white.*
> *With wondrous glee and pride, this simple wight*
> *Her brothel feats of wantonness sets down,*
> *Being her spouse, he tells, with huge delight,*
> *How oft she cuckolded the silly clown*
> *And lent, O lovely piece! herself to half the town.*

Many popular novels appeared that ridiculed Wollstonecraft's feminist principles, turning back the tide on any advances inspired by her ideas. Overnight, it seemed, the character of the female philosopher became a stock character, a villain or a figure of fun. In Elizabeth Hamilton's novel *Memoirs of Modern Philosophers* (1800), the heroine, Julia Demond, espouses the ideas of Godwin and Wollstonecraft, which ultimately lead to her ruin; she falls in love with a libertine because she thinks he is a philosopher, but he turns out to be a cad, abandoning her when she is pregnant. *The Anti-Jacobin Review* applauded Hamilton's stance against the "voluptuous dogmas of Mary Godwin." In Maria Edgeworth's *Belinda,* Harriet Freke is a female philosopher whose foolish "antics" land herself and her friends in scrapes that are both absurd and dangerous. Elinor Joddrel in Fanny Burney's *The Wanderer* (1814) is painted as a pathetic young woman who, though she lives through the Terror and advocates for the rights of woman, tries to kill herself when she is rejected by the man she loves. Interestingly, both Elinor and Harriet dress as men in several key scenes, demonstrating the common belief that female philosophers were "unsex'd," having lost their feminine identity when they attempted to cross over to the "masculine" world of reason and logic. Even Amelia Alderson, one of "the fairs," poked fun at both Godwin and Wollstonecraft in her novel *Adeline Mowbray,* in which the central characters are geniuses whose absurd ideals are impracticable and end up causing them heartbreak.

Although *A Memoir* provoked an uproar, it did not sell well. The same conservatives who were writing scurrilous articles told people not to endorse the sinful behavior of Godwin and his paramour by buying the book. For that matter, they declared, the purchase of any volume by Godwin or Wollstonecraft would contribute to the moral turpitude of English society. Even some liberal admirers distanced themselves. Godwin, who had been famous ever since the publication of *Political Justice,* plummeted in the eyes of the public. Having once stood for the Enlightenment values of reason and freedom, his name was now synonymous with immorality and decadence. His status as a well-respected spokesperson for the Reform movement had been shattered. A decade or so later, the establishment's assault would work in his favor, as young men like Shelley would view Godwin as a martyr, but at the time it was difficult for Godwin to sustain this blow to his reputation.

Only a few of Godwin's contemporaries recognized the real damage the book had done. The *Analytical Review,* one of the magazines Mary had written for, argued that Godwin's emphasis on her passions rather than her intellect did not do her justice: *A Memoir* gives "no correct history of the formation of Mrs G's mind. We are neither informed of her favorite books, her hours of study, nor her attainments in languages and philosophy."

Nevertheless, buoyed by a strong sense of his own rectitude, Godwin believed he was honoring his wife. He must have known that people would condemn both Mary and Fanny, but he wanted to make it clear that he was not ashamed of how she had lived her life. He was unaware that his motivations might have been murky, that some part of him might have wanted to destroy the woman who had abandoned him, and to represent himself as her savior. All he was certain of was that he had lost the woman he loved. Even her daughters, he said, had not lost as much as he. With *A Memoir,* he staked a final claim on her life, shaping her story according to his own conscious and unconscious dictates, attempting to demonstrate that he was the man who had known her best, the one who had won her from all other contestants. No one, least of all the heartbroken Godwin, could have foreseen the harm his book would do.

# MARY SHELLEY:
# A WRITING LIFE

———

[ 1832–1836 ]

*I*N THE SPRING OF 1832, AT AGE THIRTY-FOUR, MARY ATTRACTED THE attention of a handsome and intelligent man, thirty-one-year-old Aubrey Beauclerk. It had been ten years since Shelley died and she had assumed that she would never fall in love again, but Aubrey stood out from the other men she had met. Like Shelley, he was idealistic, gentle, and aristocratic. In addition, he seemed to admire her for precisely those things that scandalized most people: her writing, her politics, and even her decision to run away with Shelley. The son of the Mrs. Beauclerk who had hosted the ball in Pisa where Mary had danced with Trelawny, Aubrey had been raised almost entirely by his enterprising mother. Thanks to her and to his many energetic, lively sisters, Aubrey was comfortable with women and was a veteran of many love affairs by the time he was introduced to Mary. He had fathered two illegitimate children by different mothers. Although he did not marry either woman, unlike many men of his class he had given the children his name and large financial settlements.

Long before they encountered each other, Aubrey had heard glowing reports about Mary from his mother, who was far more open to unusual domestic arrangements than most people of her social background. Emily Beauclerk was the only daughter of the notorious Duchess of Leinster and her second husband, William Ogilvie.

After her first husband, the duke, died, the duchess had outraged her family and friends by marrying Ogilvie, her children's tutor. By all reports, the duchess and her second husband remained in love throughout the course of their long marriage. Having witnessed her parents' happiness firsthand, Emily taught her children to step outside the prejudices of their class in their own quest for love. She herself had flagrantly broken her marriage vows, having found her husband so uncongenial that she had taken a lover (Lord Dudley) with whom she reputedly had several children. As a result, when she took her brood of seven daughters to Italy to find them husbands, she had had no qualms about leaving her own spouse behind, circumstances that no doubt made her more open to welcoming Mary at her balls than she might otherwise have been.

In the winter of 1831, Aubrey and Mary saw each other frequently. Aubrey's sister Gee had become one of Mary's closest friends when Gee moved to London with her husband, John Paul. Eight years Mary's junior, Gee had admired Mary ever since they first met in Pisa. To her, Mary and Shelley's self-imposed exile seemed glamorous. They were the quintessential Romantic hero and heroine, as they had given up everything for love. Mary, in turn, was grateful to Gee for her warmth. Though she had made many literary and artistic contacts in the years after Shelley's death, most "proper" Londoners still refused to acknowledge her.

Gee had given enthusiastic reports of Mary's virtues to her older brother, and he made efforts to draw Mary out when they met at the Pauls'. But this was not always easy. Although she could be giddy when surrounded by her friends, Mary tended to be quiet in the company of strangers. Those who encountered her for the first time were often surprised to find that the notorious poet's wife was neither a hoyden nor a seductress. Indeed, Mary was just the opposite: reserved and dignified. One new friend described her as strikingly "gentle, feminine, lady-like." Another acquaintance confessed that although he thought the author of *Frankenstein* would be "rather indiscreet, and even extravagant," he found her "cool, quiet, feminine," revealing how difficult it was for Mary's contemporaries to square the boldness of her work with its creator. Instead of being loud or "masculine," she appeared to embody their ideas of what "proper" womanhood should be.

Still, Aubrey did not give up. The more time they spent together, the more captivated he became. Mary's hair was still the distinctive red gold of her youth; her eyes were soft and understanding. She had never lost her habit of wearing light-colored dresses unless she was going to the theater; then she wore low-cut black gowns that revealed her white shoulders and the curve of her breasts. She also had a highly developed spirit of fun. She earned the adulation of her friends' children by treating the teenagers as though they were adults, and she amused the younger ones by displaying her double-jointed wrists, bending her long tapering fingers back at an impossible angle.

Yet nothing might have come of their relationship if a crisis with Gee had not occurred. In November 1831, Gee was driven out of her house by her husband when he discovered that she was having an affair. Mary instantly leapt to the rescue. "My first impulse," she said, "is to befriend a woman." She stood by Gee during the scandal that ensued and consoled her as she prepared to move away from London to live with a cousin in Ireland. The Beauclerks were grateful to Mary for her support of Gee, Aubrey in particular. He and Gee were so close that she had named her first (and only) child after him.

Drawn together by Gee's problems, Aubrey and Mary began to take strolls in the country, sometimes heading north toward Mary's childhood home in St. Pancras. They went to the theater and concerts, met at dinner parties, and after a few months enjoyed moments of what Mary called "ineffable bliss" in each other's arms. A newly elected MP for East Surrey, Aubrey held the same political views as Mary and her father. He fought for the abolition of slavery, supported the Irish cause, and was one of the most energetic advocates for the Reform Bill being debated in Parliament that spring. "Liberty must and will raise her head o'er the grave of bigotry and ignorance," he had declared in the House of Commons in 1828.

As an up-and-coming politician, Aubrey needed a wife who would help him advance his career. Beleaguered by debt and scandal,

Mary Shelley was hardly the obvious choice, even if she was the daughter of one of his heroes, William Godwin. But Aubrey could not resist spending time with his new love. He found talking to Mary exhilarating. From Godwin, Shelley, and Byron, Mary had learned how to discuss politics, a topic that was usually off limits for women. She knew how to ask helpful questions and suggest new points and ideas. She also had her own opinions. Political strategy sessions and literary discussions were her forte. For the aristocratic Aubrey, who was not used to dining with intellectuals and radicals, Mary's erudition and liberal credentials were somewhat intimidating, and yet, like the other men in Mary's past, he found her fascinating. She was a beautiful woman who was smarter and better educated than most of the men he knew, including himself.

To Mary, Aubrey was a tamer version of Shelley, a dreamer who was also reliable, a reformer who was also respectable. Dedicated to the cause of social justice, he had chosen to work from within the system rather than from the rocky promontory of exile. Neither reckless nor wild, he plotted his moves with caution and forethought. He seemed trustworthy, a man she could love with safety, a man worthy of her affections. When the Reform Bill that he had helped sponsor passed, they both regarded this triumph as an endorsement of his political career. "I hope things will turn out well—I trust they will," she wrote Jane, having sworn to tell her if she ever fell in love again.

After almost a year of happiness, Mary was so sure of Aubrey's affections that she made the decisive move of introducing him to her father, inviting both men to a dinner party at her home in April 1833. Godwin approved, and Mary allowed herself to envision a future with Aubrey, albeit tentatively, writing in her journal that May, "the aspect of my life is changed—I enjoy myself much yet nothing is certain."

That summer, while Mary was in the country on vacation, she fell ill with influenza, and during the many weeks it took for her to recover, Aubrey did not visit or even write. When she returned to health in early August, she found out why: he had proposed marriage to another woman, a rich baronetess named Ida Goring, who at nineteen was fifteen years younger than Mary. Ida was unremarkable, but she was well connected and an advantageous match.

In Mary's eyes, Aubrey had made a heartless decision, choosing convention and propriety over love. "Dark night shadows the world," she scrawled in her journal. She wrote to Claire saying she hoped this would be her final year on earth. Alarmed, Claire wrote back, urging her to remember her son, her father, and her work. Still, for all her desolate words, Mary knew how to combat despair.

To avoid seeing Aubrey, she moved out of London, renting a house in the village of Harrow, where Percy had started school the previous year. Living with her son would help assuage her loneliness, and it would also help her economize, as the school's fees for room and board were a drain on her finances. Unlike many teenagers, the fourteen-year-old Percy welcomed the arrival of his mother. Though Mary sometimes found him disappointing—he had a stoop; he refused to speak in public; he was pudgy, short, and not at all interested in poetry—she was devoted to him, and he to her. Their interests did not dovetail—he liked hunting and, even worse, sailing, and he did not want to be the philosopher she had hoped he would be—but she never lost sight of his loyalty, his loving nature, his innocence, and his desire to protect her. Most of all, he was alive, a survivor just as she was.

Safely out of London, Mary did what she had always done in times of disaster: she immersed herself in work, launching herself into the world of another novel, *Lodore,* a direct response not only to Aubrey but to Godwin and Shelley, the men in her life who had broken her heart time and again. In the world of *Lodore* there are no heroes. The male characters are so weak that the women must save one another from harm and find happiness on their own. Although there is a young bride who at first glance seems to be the heroine, the only idealized figure in the story is the intellectual Fanny Derham, an independent woman who reads philosophy, dedicating herself to cultivating her own "genius" and that of others. It is no accident that Mary named her heroine Fanny: Fanny lives the life she wished her sister could have had. Self-sufficient, untrammeled by men, and supported by her female friends, Fanny Derham, unlike Fanny Godwin, does not commit suicide. Instead, she educates herself, helps and advises her friends, and works toward reforming society, embodying the Wollstonecraft axiom: provide women with freedom and the world will be a better place for everyone.

Writing *Lodore* was a cathartic exercise. Mary took a stand against those who had tried to discredit her mother's ideas at the same time that she asserted the benefits of independence for all women. By the time Mary was finished, she had healed from Aubrey's betrayal and drawn strength from her own and her mother's ideas. When *Lodore* was published in 1835, the reviews were more positive than those for her other books and it sold briskly.

The solace she gained from this experience helped solidify Mary's goals. She needed to fulfill her destiny as a writer, she decided. She did not need a man. The years before Aubrey's rejection had been full of authorial achievements. In 1830, the *Athenaeum* had listed her as the most distinguished literary woman of her time. The following year, she had published her fourth novel, *Perkin Warbeck,* based on a medieval pretender to the English throne. Although it did not sell well, it received positive reviews and raised her stature as a writer. Most important, Bentley's Standard Novel series offered Mary a place on its list for *Frankenstein* if she revised it so that Bentley could own the copyright.

Mary was happy for the opportunity to rethink her first novel. Far from becoming more conventional after Shelley died, as Trelawny and Claire had claimed, she had grown increasingly disillusioned with the hypocrisy she witnessed in daily life. When she sat down at her writing desk, she applied herself to painting an even bleaker picture than in the original, making changes that emphasized her darkened outlook. In her first version, Victor Frankenstein has the freedom to choose whether to pursue his ambition to create a man. When he makes the wrong choice, it is his own action that brings about his downfall; like a character in a Sophoclean drama, his actions determine his future. But in the 1831 version, Mary strips him of any agency. Victor is a puppet in the hands of inexorable forces, both inner and outer, a man who *must* obey his impulses and is helpless in the hands of the fates. She lengthens Walton's letters to his sister, having Frankenstein redouble his warnings against ambition: "Unhappy man! Do you share my madness?" Frankenstein says to Walton, "Have you drunk also of the intoxicating draught? Hear me,—let me reveal my tale, and you will dash the cup from your lips!" Elizabeth, Frankenstein's bride, who was no paragon of strength in the first edition, is now even more powerless, silent and weak, reflecting Mary's pessimism about women's chances for happiness when they are dependent on men.

By the time she had finished, Mary had written a new *Frankenstein* that was far more critical of society than the first. The 1831 edition depicts the harm caused by human (male) ambition and the lust for power. The female characters may lack the ability to save themselves or others, but they are entirely innocent. They suffer solely because they are connected to Frankenstein. For those naysayers who believed that Percy Shelley was responsible for the writing of the first version, and for those, such as Trelawny and Claire, who accused Mary of being a timid compromiser, the 1831 *Frankenstein* stands as a supremely original accomplishment, a dystopian vision created entirely by its author, Mary Shelley. Without Shelley by her side, Mary had been forced to become increasingly independent, and, in becoming so, she was now able to write a more complex and powerful book than when she was nineteen years old and her beloved was still alive.

Critical response was largely negative, since, as in *The Last Man,* the novel's bitterness undercut the ideal that most nineteenth-century readers held dear, and that Shelley himself had endorsed—that science would ensure the rosy future of Western civilization. But Mary had no patience with these clichés. She knew she was going against the tide, but she was driven by her need to expose class hatred, racism, and unabated prejudice.

Unpopular though her ideas were, the reissuing of *Frankenstein* confirmed Mary's fame. The stage versions continued to grow in popularity and keep Mary's name in the public eye, although they also continued to stray from the original story. And yet, despite the acclaim, she was still poor. In the ten years since Shelley had died, Sir Timothy had never raised her allowance. The ladies' magazine paid her comparatively well, but barely enough to cover the expense of Harrow, let alone fund those who continued to cling to her for financial support. Fortunately, while she was in the midst of finishing *Lodore,* Dionysus Lardner, a friend of her father, invited her to compose biographical essays for *The Cabinet Cyclopedia,* the first encyclopedia. This was a signal honor, since Lardner had his pick of contributors and intended to reach a wide audience. Also, he paid well. The assignment he gave Mary was to write essays on the literary men of Italy, Spain, Portugal, and France. She was one of the few writers he knew who had the requisite language skills, erudition, and talent to take on this challenge. Pleased to be recognized for her abilities, Mary gladly accepted Lardner's offer, making her the only female contributor in a literary stable that included luminaries such as Sir Walter Scott.

Excited to start a new literary challenge, she began work on the essays in November 1833, three months after Aubrey's betrayal. For the next four and a half years, she researched and wrote more than fifty portraits of the "Most Eminent Literary and Scientific Men of Italy, Spain, and Portugal and France," finishing in May 1838. For many years, scholars underestimated how many of these articles Mary had written, as Lardner did not always identify the authors. Now there is consensus that Mary wrote at least three quarters of the 1,757-page project. She relied largely on her own translations, and the results are among her best literary efforts. Her writing is uncluttered, clear, and forceful. She chose compelling details to illuminate the characters. Her scholarship was impeccable. The tragedy is that the essays are difficult for the modern reader to find.

"My life & reason have been saved by these 'Lives,'" she wrote. The partial anonymity of the articles—not all were signed, and then usually just with initials—allowed her to express her views without fear of repercussions, just as her mother had in her early days as a reviewer. In addition, these "Lives," focused and informative as they were, released Mary from the limitations of writing fiction. Instead of having to advance a plot, she could include her own meditations, even parts of her own story, albeit refracted through the biographies of great men.

To this end, she spent hours excavating the lives of the mothers, wives, daughters, and sisters of her subjects. Loyal female friends, mistresses, and widows crowd the pages. In fact, after the initial stages of research, she became so interested in these women's lives that she proposed a volume on historical female figures to Lardner. When he refused, she returned to her undercover strategy, embedding the lives of women in her biographies and sometimes allowing the women to overtake the men.

Not only did Mary's work on these biographies help her forget Aubrey, they released her from the bitter isolation of parochial Harrow. The long empty evenings had filled her with crippling dread before she began the project, but her immersion in her subjects' lives helped her endure the loneliness of the small town. The local minister was the notoriously pompous prude who had refused to bury Allegra inside the chapel. In 1832, the year before she began writing for the *Cyclopedia,* her cherished brother William had died during a cholera epidemic. Her father was increasingly frail and refused to travel the twelve miles from London to visit; her friends were also loath to make the trip. To Mary's envy, in early 1836, Jane had a new baby daughter she named Prudentia—an ironic name for the child of a woman who had lived such a dashingly imprudent life, but perhaps Jane hoped her baby would make more considered choices. Jane herself was unhappy. Her relationship with Hogg had deteriorated. Bored and lonely, she had attempted to start a new flirtation, but Hogg had caught her. Now they were trapped together, quarreling, irritable, and suspicious.

Claire was also out of reach, having moved to Pisa to be a governess during the day and to sow the seeds for a women's community of like-minded souls by night. This left only Percy, and for two years Mary devoted herself to her work and to her son, but finally she could no longer bear the isolation. "You must consider me as one buried alive," she wrote to Maria Gisborne in the summer of 1835. At times she resented Percy, saying, "I have bartered my existence for his good," but that was rare; for the most part, she was grateful to him. When his friends teased him for living at home, she reached out to them, inviting them over for tea. She borrowed money to buy him a tailcoat. He yearned for a horse, which they could not afford, but she let him have a terrier.

Although Mary was concerned by Percy's poor academic performance—he scraped by, still evincing no interest in his studies—she was proud of how ruddy and strong he was becoming. He devoted himself largely to sports and terrified his mother in the grand tradition of his father by taking up rowing and sailing, although, unlike Shelley, he was always cautious.

In the winter of 1836, during Percy's last year at Harrow, they received the sad news that Mr. Gisborne, the husband of Mary's beloved Maria Reveley, had died. A few months later, Maria was also dead. Mary's closest connection to her mother was gone. Harrow was suddenly intolerable. With an urgency born of panic, she removed Percy from school, reasoning (rightly) that he was not getting much out of his classes, and they moved to London near Regent's Park. She had not given up on Percy attending university, hiring him a tutor that winter, but she knew that she could not stand any more time immured in the country. She needed to be close to her father and her London friends.

That spring the eighty-year-old Godwin contracted a bad cough and fever. By the first week of April, he was seriously ill. Mary and Mary-Jane took turns by his bedside as he expressed "great horror of being left to servants." Occasionally, he roused himself to speak, but, as Mary wrote to her mother's old friend Mary Hays, "his thoughts wandered a good deal." They did not give up hope; Godwin himself thought he would recover; but on the evening of April 7, 1836, Mary reported that "a slight rattle called us to his side." Then, after a few hours of struggle, he stopped breathing. His heart had stopped.

Mary consoled herself that Godwin had died without suffering, but her own pain was immense. "What I then went through— watching alone his dying hours!" Mary wrote in her journal, discounting Mary-Jane's presence, as she always had.

The funeral was a macabre affair. With no consideration for the feelings of the living, Godwin had written in his will that he wanted to be buried "as near" his first wife "as possible." And so Mary, Percy, and Mary-Jane watched as the gravediggers shoveled the dirt out of Mary Wollstonecraft's grave. "Her coffin was found uninjured," wrote Mary, and everyone stared down into the hole where they could see "the cloth still over it—& the plate tarnished but legible." It was the closest Mary had come to her mother since she was a few days old. And now her father was gone, too.

Since Claire and Charles lived outside the country, the care of her widowed stepmother fell squarely on Mary's shoulders. She worked diligently to get her old enemy a pension from the state, supplementing it with her own earnings. She also visited Mary-Jane regularly, a chore she resented but discharged for the sake of her father. Although these demands hampered her work, they were far less onerous than those Godwin still required of her. Before he died, he had appointed Mary as his literary executor, making it clear that he expected her to cement his place in the pantheon of English literature by writing his biography and editing his unfinished works for publication. In true Godwinian fashion, he had given little thought to the impact this might have on his daughter's life. Mary knew her father would not be content with a brief memoir like the one he had written of her mother. Only a comprehensive exegesis of his life and philosophical contributions would do.

She began dutifully enough, but soon became bogged down in the piles of papers that littered Godwin's desk. Convinced as he was of his own place in history, Godwin had kept a copy of almost every document he had ever composed, as well as most of the letters he had received, which made sorting through his accounting books, correspondence, journals, drafts, and articles a dusty, tedious, and painful business. And yet, despite his conviction of their future significance, he had left his affairs in a mess. Furthermore, he was elliptical, mysterious, and obfuscatory, referring to friends only by initials and to his ideas and important events in shorthand—slashes, dashes, parentheses—a code that was almost impossible to decipher.

Mary knew that he would not consider his difficult habits an excuse for not completing the job; he himself would have worked briskly and diligently to bring the task to a close, as he had for her mother. But the memoir he had composed for Wollstonecraft had dire results. Mary had never articulated her feelings about her father's exposure of her mother's private life, but she was only too well aware of what would happen if she revisited the tragedies and the old scandals. If she told the story of Fanny's suicide, her own elopement, her mother's affairs, and Godwin's assault on governmental authority, she and Percy would be ostracized forever. She might never be offered work again. And yet, despite her misgivings, out of loyalty to her contradictory, unyielding father, she began the project, and she worked on it steadily for almost four years before stopping.

When at last she gave up, she tortured herself, feeling that once again she was falling short, once again disappointing her father. Yet the more time she had spent with the material, the more she was certain that Percy would be ruined by the publication of such a book. At one point, as a compromise, she decided to have the memoir end right before her father met her mother. In another version, she included her mother but falsified the date of their marriage. But Mary was not a liar. She could not publish a book that was untrue. Neither could she write one that would harm her son.

Godwin had also wanted her to arrange for the publication of his final manuscript, a weighty diatribe against Christianity. With his customary rigor and systematic logic, her father criticized the Catholic Church, the Church of England, and the Reformed churches, building the kind of comprehensive argument he believed was essential and relying on his formidable knowledge of history to back up his points.

Mary was familiar with his ideas, having heard them before, both from Godwin and from Shelley, and though she did not disagree with them, she, like her mother, found occasional solace in the liturgy of the Church of England. However, as with the biography, she decided the public was not ready for such a book and never submitted it to a publisher. She had learned from Shelley's career what the public thought of atheists. Besides, her experience in the literary marketplace had taught her that publishing such a long, scholarly book was a doomed enterprise; no one would buy it or read it, so there seemed little point in putting the family through the kind of suffering that would result from revealing Godwin's hostility to religion. Nevertheless, her decision gave fuel to her enemies. When Trelawny got wind of it, he renewed his attacks against her, accusing her of being shallow, of repressing important philosophical truths, and of being overly concerned with the opinions of others. But Mary stood firm, and in doing so she was far braver than Trelawny could ever understand: she was breaking the rules that governed nineteenth-century daughters, placing her own concerns and those of Percy ahead of her father's wishes.

Although Godwin's projects consumed much of Mary's time, she did not stop her own literary endeavors. A year after he died, when she was forty, she finished a new novel, *Falkner.* Interestingly, she thought this book her best, an opinion difficult for modern readers to share given the obtrusive plot contrivances, wooden characters, and stilted dialogue. However, Mary did not judge her books by their ability to capture the realities of daily life, or the actual rhythms of conversation. She cared about ideas, assessing her books—and all books, for that matter—on their philosophy. If one follows these criteria, then Mary is right; in *Falkner,* she gives full voice, at last, to many of the ideas she had only hinted at before.

The heroine of *Falkner* shares the same name as Frankenstein's bride, but she is far stronger than the first Elizabeth. Whereas in *Frankenstein* Elizabeth is killed by the monster and is a symbol of helpless innocence, in *Falkner* the new Elizabeth vanquishes her foes and saves the men in her life. A heroine protecting the men she loves would have been unimaginable in Mary's earlier novels. The Countess Euthanasia is defeated by the warrior prince, Valperga; all the women die in *The Last Man;* and even in the more optimistic *Lodore,* the daughter cannot save her father. But in *Falkner,* Elizabeth persuades both her father and lover to lead a quiet domestic life rather than chasing after their dreams of glory. Her values triumph over theirs and they are all happier for it.

Mary's work had come full circle. In *Frankenstein,* the hero's ambition destroys everyone he loved. Homes are burned down; family ties; annihilated. Margaret Saville, the sister of Robert Walton, does help rescue her brother, but this point is overshadowed by Frankenstein's downfall and his helplessness in the face of his desire for knowledge, fame, and power. In *Falkner,* on the other hand, Mary emphasizes the power of the heroine to save the male characters from their ambitions, preserving their lives and bringing them into the warmth of the family. Although the revolutionary implications of this might be lost on today's audience, to contemporary readers the novel's subversive conclusion is unmistakable. Acting not as a warrior, but as an advocate for peace, Elizabeth creates a utopia based on the "feminine" values of compassion, love, and family. Without the follies caused by male ambition, Mary implies, there would be no more war, no more children lost.

Most critics disliked this overturning of values. Men were supposed to save women; women were not supposed to save men. And, besides, war was glorious. Only cowards backed away from battle. Yet *Falkner* did receive a few compliments for its imaginative reach and philosophical reflections. The *Athenaeum* thought it one of Mary's finest novels. *The Age* also admired it, but *The Examiner* complained about the novel's lack of morality and other reviewers found it just too depressing. Sales were sluggish and Mary, who was in the midst of the Spanish and Portuguese "Lives," which she finished that summer, decided that *Falkner* would be her last novel. There was too great an emotional cost in writing a book and then watching as people abused it.

# MARY WOLLSTONECRAFT:
# THE WRONGS

———

## [ 1797–1798 ]

*I*N GOING THROUGH MARY'S PAPERS WHILE WRITING *A MEMOIR,* GODWIN had discovered the unfinished novel, *The Wrongs of Woman,* as well as the passages she had cut from her letters to Imlay—the long strings of insults, the repetitive catalogues of suffering, her rage at his abandonment. By removing these sections from the final version of *Letters from Sweden,* Mary had demonstrated literary judgment of the highest order, but Godwin did not heed his wife's decisions. He pieced the excised passages back together again and published them as a section of a new book he entitled *The Posthumous Works of the Author of a Vindication of the Rights of Woman.*

As with *A Memoir,* this publication would gravely harm his wife's stature as a writer, but Godwin was not consciously trying to hurt her legacy. He had different standards for letters than for works such as the *Vindications.* Mary's passionate missives did not have to prove a point or have a logical structure, he believed; rather, their depth of "feeling" was a positive feature, revealing her to be tender and womanly instead of "amazonian." He hoped they would help win the sympathy of readers and redeem her literary reputation. On the other hand, he did edit several of Mary's other works, most notably her essay "On Poetry," diluting her ideas to make them less radical and reshaping the essay to conform to his own notions about what constituted good writing.

Many of these revisions were Godwin's misguided attempt to make his wife seem more acceptable to the public and to help the book sell. Desperate to raise enough money to settle Mary's bills and his own, he signed over the copyright to Johnson, who agreed to pay off Mary's creditors in return. This was an act of charity on Johnson's part, since he knew he would never make money from a book that the public, still horrified by Godwin's account of Wollstonecraft's life, would refuse to buy. However, Johnson was a man of principle. He wanted to help his old friend, and he believed that Mary's unpublished works were worthy of publication, even if unfinished or flawed.

If there had been a book to salvage Mary's literary reputation, *Posthumous Works* was not it. Readers overlooked the single most important essay, "On Poetry," taken aback by the furious tone and obsessive quality of Mary's unedited letters to Imlay. To them, her bold professions of love, her demands, the pleading and the rage—all of which Godwin had seen as evidence of his wife's romantic nature—confirmed her as a dissolute and hysterical woman, obsessed with love and sex. She became notorious for being exactly what her published *Letters from Sweden* had proved she was not: undisciplined, histrionic, and self-absorbed.

After *Posthumous Works* went on sale in the spring of 1798, any standing that Wollstonecraft had retained after Godwin's *Memoir* was almost entirely eradicated. Gone were the professional author, the political correspondent, the hard-edged philosopher, the educational innovator, and the bold businesswoman who single-handedly supported her family and friends. Gone, too, were the loving mother, the sensible partner, and the empathic lover. In her place was a crazed, self-destructive, sex-starved radical. If one looks up "Prostitution" in the index of *The Anti-Jacobin Review,* the entry reads, "*see* Mary Wollstonecraft." Experts warned parents against letting their daughters read Wollstonecraft's books, claiming her words could promote suicide, foster licentiousness, and destroy the very fabric of decent society.

Mary had always been a controversial figure. Her enemies had routinely hurled epithets at her morality as well as her politics, but now Godwin had provided the ammunition they needed to bury her for good. Not only were her ideas incendiary, they claimed, but she herself was disgraceful, her life a series of disasters. In article after article, they dismantled her status as a leading intellectual and made her name a watchword, a warning of the dangers that would ensue if women were allowed too much leeway.

The atmosphere in London was already tense when *Posthumous Works* appeared. The Irish had risen in revolt and London workers, angry at bread prices, pelted the king's carriage with rocks, staging protests in the streets. The newspapers blamed Godwin, Wollstonecraft, and other radicals for bringing anarchy to the kingdom, suggesting that they were French agents. To a nation on edge, the ideas of these reformers appeared as dangerous as the army that Napoleon was building across the Channel.

Matters were further exacerbated by a scandal that occurred around the same time as the publication of *A Memoir* and *Posthumous Works*. Mary's former charge, sixteen-year-old Mary, the youngest daughter of Lord and Lady Kingsborough, ran away with a married cousin twice her age. In a fit of vengeful fury, her brother killed the cousin and was tried for murder. The court proceedings were widely publicized, and before long, a savvy journalist made the connection: Wollstonecraft had been Mary's governess. The promiscuous author of *Rights of Woman* was to blame for "the misconduct of one of [her] pupils, who has lately brought disgrace on herself, death on her paramour, risk to the lives of her brother and father, and misery to all her relatives. . . ." Ten years had passed since Wollstonecraft had taught Mary, but this did nothing to slow the avalanche of criticism. If other women followed Wollstonecraft's example, one critic spluttered, there would be "the most pernicious consequences to society." Mary's influence could lead to the disintegration of the family and the kingdom as a whole.

Of her many friends, only Mary Hays was willing to publish a defense of Wollstonecraft. The others remained silent. Godwin had gone too far and the times were too dangerous. Besides, it was difficult to defend Wollstonecraft, since in many ways her detractors were right: her work was indeed a sustained call to arms, a battle cry for the natural rights of both men and women. She *did* want the status quo overturned; she *was* on the side of revolutions; she loathed what she called "the good old rules of conduct." There were exceptions to the generalized condemnation—Blake, Coleridge, and the other Romantics still supported her ideas and held firm to their belief in her genius—but they were not particularly helpful. Having themselves been pilloried by the critics, they had learned to dismiss their enemies. It would not have occurred to them that Mary Wollstonecraft needed them to defend her.

But unfortunately, she did. As a woman writer, her case was different from theirs. In the years after Wollstonecraft's death, it became increasingly risky for women to venture into the "male" territory of philosophy and politics. Anyone following in Wollstonecraft's footsteps risked being called a whore, her reputation ruined. In England, in the century after her death, few philosophical works would dare to address "the woman question," with the exception of John Stuart Mill's *The Subjection of Women,* which declared his belief in the equality of the sexes. But even Mill, who had read and admired Wollstonecraft's work, did not mention her once. Later generations of women's rights advocates continued to distance themselves from Wollstonecraft, believing her notoriety would hurt their cause. In 1877, the Victorian reformer Harriet Martineau disparaged Wollstonecraft as "a poor victim of passion," arguing that the "best friends" of the women's movement "are women who . . . must be clearly seen to speak from conviction of the truth, and not from personal unhappiness." Robert Browning cemented her image as a "desperate" spinster in his poem *Wollstonecraft and Fuseli* despite an urgent letter from Godwin's biographer, C. Kegan Paul, who told Browning that Godwin had been deceived by Fuseli in *A Memoir,* and that he actually knew very little about his wife's early life. In 1885, when Karl Pearson, the leader of a socialist group, proposed naming the organization after Wollstonecraft, the female members threatened to resign. Few people wanted to be associated with the pathetic figure that she had become in the popular imagination.

And yet Godwin's ill-advised attempts to celebrate his wife's memory did not entirely fail. *Posthumous Works* preserved and compiled many of her drafts, unedited letters, and unfinished works, offering future scholars insight into her process as a writer as well as evidence of her artistry. In addition, he used *Posthumous Works* to continue his exploration of the question that he had introduced in *A Memoir,* the question Mary herself had asked over and over again: What was it that set her apart? Was it her character, her life experience, or some mysterious personal quality? Mary had tried to answer this in all of her books, declaring that she was "the hero of each tale" she composed. In both *Mary* and *Maria,* she had been intent on "tracing the outline of the first period of her own existence." "A person has a right . . . to talk of himself," she had announced in an "advertisement" to *Letters from Sweden.* But the grammatically correct male pronoun betrays the difficulties she faced when she wanted to talk about *her*self. As Mary knew only too well, women were not supposed to place their experience at the center of any narrative, fictional or otherwise.

Mostly, her deeply held beliefs sustained her. On the one hand, she was unique, the first of a new genus, but like all women she had endured prejudice and hate; her sufferings, though specific to her, exemplified the injustices that others also had to suffer; and it was the general experience that she wanted to expose. If she could show her readers what it felt like to be powerless, what it was like to be a woman without legal recourse, poor, abused, and at the mercy of others, if she could reveal the root causes of human suffering and misogyny, then perhaps she could galvanize her readers and save others from the same miseries.

Fortunately, Wollstonecraft had already built a loyal audience before she died, and this select group kept her ideas alive despite the campaign to obliterate her name. For them, it was her most controversial books that were the most important. The Utopian socialist Robert Owen, only twenty-six years old when Wollstonecraft died, was so inspired by her call for justice that he included a quotation from one or the other of the *Vindications* in almost all of his tracts and pamphlets. In 1881, when Elizabeth Cady Stanton and Susan B. Anthony published the first volume of their monumental *History of Suffrage,* they put Wollstonecraft at the top of their list of heroic women "[w]hose earnest lives and fearless words, in demanding political rights for women have been, in the preparation of these pages, a constant inspiration." Carrie Chapman Catt, the president of the International Woman Suffrage Alliance, declared that all women owed gratitude to Wollstonecraft for sacrificing herself for the sake of the human race. Catt even set the first annual meeting of the Alliance on the 150th anniversary of Wollstonecraft's birth—April 27, 1909.

Women writers were also inspired by her bravery. She became a secret lifeline between generations, or, as Elizabeth Barrett Browning put it, a literary "grandmother." Despite her husband's negative portrait of Wollstonecraft in his poetry, Wollstonecraft and her daughter Mary were important role models for Elizabeth. Reading Wollstonecraft at age twelve gave her the courage to flee her repressive father. She saw herself as another Mary Shelley and eloped with Browning to Italy, where she devoted herself to the cause of women's advancement, creating an independent literary heroine named Aurora Leigh who turned down offers of marriage for the sake of art, poetry, and freedom.

In the mid-1850s the Victorian author Mary Ann Evans, writing under the name of George Eliot, penned an essay praising Wollstonecraft for her "loftiness of moral tone," seeking to free her from the cloud of shame that still clung to her name. For Eliot, who lived with a married man and wrote books that criticized the hypocrisy of Victorian society, Wollstonecraft's fate was a disturbing example of what could happen to a female intellectual if she broke the rules of sexual conduct. To counter the "prejudice against the *Rights of Woman* as in some way or other a reprehensible book," she declared that readers would be "surprised to find it eminently serious, severely moral, and withal rather heavy—the true reason, perhaps, that no edition has been published since 1796, and that it is now rather scarce."

Almost a century later, Virginia Woolf laid claim to Wollstonecraft, publishing an essay in 1935 in which she declared:

> Many millions have died and been forgotten in the . . . years that have passed since [Wollstonecraft] was buried; and yet as we read her letters and listen to her arguments and consider her

experiments, and realize the high handed and hot blooded manner in which she cut her way to the quick of life, one form of immortality is hers undoubtedly: she is alive and active, she argues and experiments, we hear her voice and trace her influence even now among the living.

In place of Eliot's grave Victorian philosopher, Woolf depicts a lively young woman, the perfect emblem for the modern woman, brimming with passion for politics, dedicated to reform and social justice, and with no patience for dishonesty or stupidity. In Woolf's hands, Wollstonecraft suddenly seems alive, fun, even, unharmed by the bitter calumny that has been heaped on her head, a brave impetuous woman whose ideas are worthy of emulation.

And yet, despite the efforts of these writers, Wollstonecraft still remained largely unread, regarded as a curiosity rather than an essential figure until the advent of the women's movement in the 1970s. Over the last four decades, innumerable biographies and critical studies have redeemed her work and placed her ideas and her life in historical and cultural context. She is now a fixture in anthologies of philosophy, British literature, and women's literature and is a staple in courses on intellectual history, the history of women, and feminist theory. Nevertheless, though this might seem like a triumph, the tale of Wollstonecraft's legacy is a cautionary one. She was almost lost to history, her name nearly obliterated. Her critics used sexual scandal to try to silence her words, and they nearly succeeded. Wollstonecraft was almost forgotten, *A Vindication of the Rights of Woman* unread, and her call for justice unheard.

# MARY SHELLEY:
# RAMBLINGS

———

## [ 1837–1848 ]

*I*N THE SUMMER OF 1838, JUST BEFORE MARY TURNED FORTY-ONE, Edward Moxon, Tennyson's publisher, offered her £500 to edit a four-volume set of Shelley's collected works. He also wanted her to provide biographical material for those readers who had already encountered Shelley's poems and were eager to know more about him. Here it was at last: the opportunity Mary had dreamed of for more than a decade, but would Sir Timothy allow the project to move forward? Mary wanted to complete it quickly because several pirated copies of Shelley's poems, marred by mistakes and misprints, had sprung into print since his death. There were now five unauthorized collections in circulation.

In the intervening years, Sir Timothy's lawyer had died and he had hired a new representative named John Gregson, who was sympathetic to Mary's cause. An admirer of Shelley's poetry, Gregson had talked Sir Timothy into paying Percy's tuition at Cambridge, and as a result Percy had just completed his first year at Trinity College. Now Gregson persuaded Sir Timothy to allow Mary to publish Shelley's work by telling him he should be proud of his son's poetry and reminding him that the Shelley name no longer spelled scandal. Sir Timothy drew the line at a biography, however. He did not want the old stories retold. It had taken sixteen years, but at last Shelley's reputation as a poet had begun to displace his reputation as a philanderer and atheist. Mary's preface to *Posthumous Poems* had helped, as had the passage of time. Many of the scandalmongers of the previous generation had died.

Mary was pleased to have the chance to put Shelley's work before the public, though she remained frustrated that Sir Timothy would not allow her to write an authoritative account of Shelley's life. Having anticipated his refusal, however, she had devised a strategy that would allow her to publish her version of Shelley's biography while escaping Sir Timothy's attention. She would write extensive notes on each poem, far more comprehensive than the notes in the 1824 edition, setting the works in context and revealing those parts of Shelley's experience she felt the public should hear, but all under the guise of an "editor," not a biographer.

She began immediately, once again opening up the diaries and organizing the papers she had not looked at for more than a decade. The task was monumental and far more painful than sifting through her father's notes. Back came Shelley, little Clara, William, Allegra, Fanny, and Byron. So, too, her younger self: cold, angry, and resentful. There was also a host of happier memories—Geneva, Marlow, the early years in Italy—but these were, if anything, even more difficult to bear. Most exhausting of all, though, was confronting Harriet's ghost. "Poor Harriet to whose sad fate I attribute so many of my own heavy sorrows as the atonement claimed by fate for her death," she wrote.

She had found all his secrets during her first round of editing and had brooded over what to do with these painful details for many years. Should she offer them to the reader, risking her husband's reputation? No, she decided. Not because of her dignity, but because of his literary legacy. If they knew too much about his private life, most people would refuse to read his work, just as they refused to read her mother's books after Godwin wrote his tell-all memoir. She was not going to do to Shelley what her father had done to Wollstonecraft.

The most honorable thing, she decided, would be to leave out the biographical details her audience would find shocking, but tell them

she was doing so. That way, readers would know that there were secrets *and* that she was not going to reveal them. "This is not the time
to relate the truth," she wrote in the preface, "and I should reject any
colouring of the truth." Thus she makes no mention of the other
women in Shelley's life, nor does she discuss her own elopement. Instead, she uses silence like a censor's pen, at once marking and covering the deleted passages, a gesture toward a greater truth, the stories
she could not tell.

As compensation, she included fascinating tidbits about the circumstances in which Shelley composed his poems, painting vignettes
of her husband wandering through the shady park at Marlow and
gazing at the sea from the glass room on top of the house near Pisa.
She describes him propped against the mast of his boat reading and
writing, marveling at the fireflies in Bagni di Lucca, and spotting the
bird that would inspire *To a Skylark*. Throughout her notes she emphasized Shelley's lyrical voice and his spiritual qualities—how pure
he was, how little he sought worldly fame, how passionately he loved
his art. Having been the target of criticism for so many years, Mary
knew that if she wanted people to accept and love Shelley the poet,
she must skirt the issue of his politics, his eccentric ideas about morality, and his lack of religious faith.

It took months of effort, during which time she became ill and
depleted. By February 1839, Mary was worn out; "I am torn to pieces
by Memory," she wrote in her journal. Even her new cottage in Putney along the Thames, with its view of gardens on the nearby hillside, did little to cheer her up. In March, she was filled with a "sort of
unspeakable sensation of wildness & irritation." She had to take periodic rests, but when Moxon suggested she slow down publication of
the next volume, she refused. She finished in May, and in her introduction apologized for the illness that she felt had weakened her
work.

When the reviews came for the first volume, the critics praised
Shelley but complained about Mary. *The Examiner* disagreed with her
interpretations of her husband's work, and *The Spectator* and the *Athenaeum* criticized her editing. They felt she had left too much out—an

opinion seconded by Shelley's old friends, led of course by the bitter Trelawny. She was the worst possible editor for Shelley's work, he claimed. In response to these criticisms, Mary and Moxon published a new edition of the first volume that included more of the controversial material, particularly Shelley's political verses and the poems that explicitly undercut the accepted morals of the day. Just as Mary had predicted, conservative readers took umbrage, resulting in a suit for blasphemy against Moxon, the last case of the kind in England. The book remained in print, but the legal battle that ensued was a costly reminder of all that Mary had feared.

She spent the summer and fall preparing the prose volumes, wrestling with what to include and what to leave out. She did not want "to mutilate" Shelley's work and yet she knew that some of his ideas were too shocking for the public to handle. She did not include many of his letters to her father, even though Godwin had kept most of them, as they revealed too much about their private lives; she also did not include passages that were atheistic. Nevertheless, she was prepared to take some risks. For example, when Leigh Hunt suggested that she tone down the homosexual references in Shelley's translation of the *Symposium,* she refused, saying it was important to retain "as many of Shelley's own words as possible." Weighted down by her sense of responsibility to the future and to the poet, she labored to make the decisions she felt he would have wanted. When at last she was finished in 1840, she felt as though she could never write another word.

For all of Mary's apologies, her four-volume edition of Shelley's complete works crowned the campaign she had begun with *Posthumous Poems.* In painting her portrait of Shelley, she went even further than she had in 1824, no longer simply hinting at his angelic status, but telling her readers that he had left this world to dwell in a higher sphere:

His spirit gathers peace in its new state from the sense that . . . his exertions were not made in vain, and in the progress of the liberty he so fondly loved. . . . It is our best consolation to know that such a pure-minded and exalted being was once among us, and now exists where we hope one day to join him. . . .

Skillful fiction writer that she was, Mary had turned her atheistic, free-love, antigovernment, radical husband into a Victorian martyr. The only liberty she had taken, she believed, was to leave out what was personal, what the public could not understand, and what was not, at any rate, their business. Thus, to the modern eye Mary's portrait of Shelley seems incomplete, but Mary believed she had captured the *essence* of Shelley on paper. Indeed, if she had not played the editorial role for which she has been castigated ever since, nineteenth-century readers might never have encountered her husband's work and it might have been lost forever. Unlike her mother and her father (or Shelley, for that matter), she chose not to confront her audience head-on, tempering her notes to suit their tastes. A sellout, some might say, but Mary was a veteran of the literary marketplace; she knew what readers would like and what they would not.

And she was right. New readers, unaware of Shelley's radical ideas and the scandals attached to his name, bowed to Shelley's genius and ushered him into the halls of the great English poets. Looking back, it may seem odd that no one wondered how Shelley had gone from being a famous atheist to "Christian hearted," from being an unknown poet to a literary star. But Mary had done her job so well that no one asked any troubling questions. He was praised in most quarters, even those where he would have been spurned had he still been alive. The priggish chaplain at Eton College dedicated a fulsome elegy to his memory, exclaiming over his spiritual virtue and artistic genius.

The finishing touch was Mary's invisibility. Just as in *Posthumous Poems,* not once does she mention her role as editor. For all anyone knew, Shelley had left behind an orderly pile of finished poems and essays that were ready for publication. Mary did not reveal the effort she had poured into his work, declaring that she was simply an apostle to a great man whose lessons of love and purity could not be understood by just anyone, let alone herself. And so it was that she created her greatest fiction of all: "Mary Shelley," the humble Victorian wife, an individual who bears as little resemblance to the actual Mary as "Shelley the poet" does to the real Shelley.

At the same time, Mary's own fame was steadily growing. In the winter of 1839, her friend Richard Rothwell painted her portrait to display at the Royal Academy. For the sitting, she chose to wear a black dress that looks as though it might slide off her snowy shoulders. Her hair is combed tightly back. She looks pale, sorrowful, and

*Portrait of Mary Shelley by Richard Rothwell,*
*displayed at the Royal Academy in 1839.*

worn down, as indeed she was—too tired to smile or to hide her sadness from the artist. "Time . . . adds only to the keenness & vividness with which I view the past," she told Hunt, "for when tragedies & most bitter dramas were in the course of acting I did not feel their meaning & their consequences as poignantly as I now do."

For all her melancholy, at age forty-two Mary was coming into her own. She had many new friends, an impressive array of political and creative thinkers including Benjamin Disraeli, Samuel Rogers, Walter Savage Landor, and the Carlyles. She had remained friendly with Aubrey's sisters and had forgiven him enough to meet his wife, Ida, and their children. Even better, she had shed those who had betrayed her or been cruel to her. She rarely saw Jane. And her relationship with Trelawny, always on shaky ground, had come to a bitter end in 1838. Trelawny had eloped with one of Mary's married friends, Augusta Goring, the sister of Aubrey's wife. Rejected by London society, he and Augusta lived in virtual exile, not far from Putney. Mary could usually be counted on to be sympathetic in such situations, but when Trelawny asked her to reach out to Augusta, Mary refused. He had denounced her in public one time too many. Later, Trelawny would cite this as further evidence of her shallowness, but if anything, it was proof of Mary's hard-earned wisdom. She had a long record of helping those who chose to live outside the rules of society, but in the case of Trelawny and Augusta, she did not see why she should risk her own social standing (or, more important, Percy's) to further the cause of a man who had done nothing to help her and had in fact intentionally hurt her with his criticisms, no matter how blameless Augusta might be. As a result they never spoke again, and Trelawny escalated his campaign against her, writing to Claire, "She lives on hogs wash—what utter failures most people are!"

Then, one day late in 1839, Mary received the news that Aubrey's wife, Ida, had drowned in an accident on the family's country estate. Almost instantly, Aubrey was at her side again, turning to her for comfort. With four small children to manage, he felt overwhelmed and lonely, confessing his struggles to Mary. As they had in the days before his marriage, they spent many hours alone, strolling through the London parks and drinking tea in her drawing room. Mary hoped that this time they might marry, but by the summer, she was still uncertain about how he felt. "Another hope—Can I have another hope?" she wrote in her journal.

Aubrey could not remarry until the requisite period of mourning was at an end, and since he had not yet declared himself, Mary decided to go forward with a plan she had been dreaming of for almost two decades—a return to Europe. After years of scrimping, she had finally saved enough money, and she, Percy, and one of his friends from Cambridge set forth for Italy in June 1840. Mary's spirits soared the moment they were on the road; "I feel a good deal of the gipsy coming upon me," she wrote.

They traveled along the Rhine to Frankfurt and Zurich, and when at last they crossed the Alps into Lombardy, Mary reflected that she had returned "to my own land." Her fluency in Italian came flooding back; she delighted in the sun, the yellow hills, the vineyards, and the fresh lemons and strawberries. But she was also stunned by the sorrow she felt, "amounting almost to agony"; the pines, the glimmer of Lake Como, the fishermen calling to one another—all seemed unchanged: Shelley at her side; Wilmouse reaching for her hand. At times, her head ached so much that she was forced to lie down. Other times, she was gripped by violent tremors. She attributed these ills to the sorrows she had endured, the pain of remembering those she had loved and lost, and although that may well have been true, there was also a biological basis for Mary's physical ailments, one she never suspected. The headaches and the fatigue were the first signs of the brain disease meningioma that would eventually end her life.

While the boys sailed and explored, Mary wrote long letters and visited with other guests at the hotels. She tried not to fix her hopes on a future with Aubrey, but it was difficult to control her dreams. Earlier that year, she had written in her journal:

A friendship secure helpful—enduring—a union with a generous heart—& yet a suffering one whom I may comfort & bless—if it be so I am happy indeed. . . . I can indeed confide in A's inalterable gentleness & affection . . . but will not events place us asunder—& prevent me from being comfort to him—he from being the prop on which I may lean—We shall see—If I can impart any permanent pleasure to his now blighted existence, & revivify it through the force of sincere & disinterested attachment—I shall be happy.

But as had happened before, the weeks passed and no letters arrived from Aubrey. Mary's forebodings grew. At the end of September, she sent the boys back to England to return to the university while she made her way north to Paris, where Aubrey's brother, Charles, had offered her his apartment on the Rue de la Paix. Here she entertained friends, receiving visits from admirers of her work and of Shelley's, including the poet Alphonse de Lamartine and the writer Charles Sainte-Beuve. Then bad news came. Claire, who had moved back to London to take care of the elderly Mary-Jane, wrote that Aubrey had become engaged to Rosa Robinson, a friend of Mary's and the younger sister of Isabel, the young woman Mary had helped rescue thirteen years earlier. Rosa was young and respectable. She offered the hope of more children and would make a good wife for a politician. They were to be married in December.

Rejected and humiliated, Mary remained in Paris through January of 1841. When at last she did return to her empty cottage, it was a difficult homecoming, "unhappy, betrayed, alone!" she wrote in her journal. The only brightness in her life was that Percy, having earned his degree from Cambridge, would turn twenty-one in November and his grandfather had promised to give him an allowance of £400 a year. Combining his income with hers, they would have more than enough to live on. When the big day came, they celebrated by buying some furniture and moving to Half Moon Street, a fashionable Mayfair neighborhood.

Yet the freedom from debt also gave Mary more time to brood. "I gave all the treasure of my heart; all was accepted readily—& more & more asked—& when more I could not give—behold me betrayed, deserted; fearfully betrayed so that I wd rather die than any of them more—" She did not finish the sentence. In fact, she never wrote another word in her journal. The emotional cost had become too much to bear.

That June, the end of an era came. Mary-Jane Godwin died, having expressed a wish to be buried in St. Pancras churchyard next to Godwin. Claire, who had loathed her time in London, joined Mary at the graveyard for the funeral and then, after requesting another loan from Mary, sailed to Paris. The distance between the two sisters had become an established fact—neither wanted more of a connection, but neither did they want to sever all ties. Each needed her independence, but each acknowledged the other's importance, writing on a regular basis and always making plans for visits. They had shared too much to lose each other.

Mary felt no particular sadness at the death of her stepmother, but neither did she feel the relief she had once imagined she would. Instead, she felt as though one of the last links to her childhood was gone. She and the Clairmont children, Claire and Charles, were the only ones left from their strangely mingled family. Charles had married and had children, but he lived in Europe.

Alone in London, Mary found herself increasingly dependent on Percy. But Percy was beginning to pull away, enjoying flirtations with various young women, and Mary worried that he would choose the wrong person. The blood of Godwin, Wollstonecraft, and Shelley ran in Percy's veins, making him a sort of crown prince in Mary's eyes, a royal son of literature. The woman he chose to marry was of the utmost importance. There was also the added worry that the wrong wife would resent Mary's presence and try to separate her from her son. For Mary, this would have been disastrous, since Percy remained at the center of her life, and she feared that he would leave her behind now that he had come of age. However, Percy showed no sign of discontent and never considered living apart from his mother. He allowed Mary to submit the young women he met to a sharp-eyed scrutiny and remained perfectly tranquil when his mother whisked him back to Europe in the summer of 1842 to remove him from a relationship she deemed unsuitable.

For Mary, however, this new trip seemed ill-fated. The heat in Dresden drained their energy, the friends they had invited to travel with them were difficult and moody, and everything was too expensive. However, when they arrived in Italy, Mary revived. Venice,

Florence, and Rome, particularly Rome, delighted her, although, as before, her joy was tinged by sorrow. This time she tried to find the graves of Clara and William, but they were unmarked, and she was unable to locate them. Only Shelley lay in stately repose in the Protestant cemetery in Rome. Trelawny had planted cypresses around his tombstone, a startlingly large white rectangular slab set in the ground like an enormous paving stone. The quote from *The Tempest* was engraved in an elegant cursive script, and above it in large block letters was the Latin phrase that Hunt had suggested: *cor cordium,* heart of hearts.

*Shelley's grave.*

Twenty-three-year-old Percy, on the other hand, missed home and dragged his feet when she suggested they visit a gallery or historical site. Unlike his scholarly mother, he did not like spending hours reading and writing. He missed the English countryside, disliked the heat, and had little interest in art. He would much rather have been sailing on the Thames than gazing contemplatively at the hills of Tuscany.

Finally, in August 1843, after a year of being abroad, Percy had had enough and said so. Mary was disappointed, but she listened. She had done her best to shape him into a poet or a philosopher, a Godwin, a Shelley, or a Wollstonecraft, but he had steadfastly remained his country squire self. Fortunately, she realized that it was time to accept her son for who he was—loving, loyal, and sturdy—and encouraged him to return to England while she spent a month in Paris with Claire.

When fall came, she joined Percy in London and they decided to return to Putney. Percy wanted to live close to the river, and Mary was happy to move out of the center of the city. Their cottage was small, but it was quiet and had a pretty garden. Here Mary organized the notes she had taken on their trip, and by January 1844 she had finished the first volume of what would be her last work, a travel book she called *Rambles in Germany and Italy*, a final tribute to her mother. Consciously imitating Wollstonecraft's *Letters from Sweden,* she described how she felt uplifted by the landscape, blessed by "the immeasurable goodness of our Maker." Like her mother, she preached the healing powers of solitude and Nature, and, in true Wollstonecraft/Godwin/Shelley fashion, she also delved into politics, arguing against Austria's occupation of Italy. She devoted many pages to the art she had encountered, revealing her own analytic brilliance while drawing on ideas from *The Symposium*. Artists should not be censored for depicting scenes of homosexual love, she declared—a bold stance that was anathema to most Victorians.

However, when the book came to press, no one noted her erudition or her observations on art, many of which would be echoed by Ruskin less than fifty years later, earning him the respect denied

Mary. Instead, most reviewers confined themselves to applauding her anti-Austrian stance, as it dovetailed with popular foreign policy of the time, although of course a few were unhappy that a woman would dare write about politics at all. Mary was not unduly cast down; for her, there was nothing new about being misread and overlooked. In addition, she had received some news that had been a long time coming.

On April 24, 1844, Sir Timothy finally died. Percy was now Sir Percy, the proud owner of Field Place, the Shelley ancestral home in Sussex. Mary was relieved that he had come into his inheritance, but also worried that Sir Timothy might have found some underhanded way to deprive her son of the estate. Perhaps there was no money left. Maybe the surviving Shelleys would make it impossible for Percy to claim his rightful share.

Her fears were well founded. Lady Shelley had stripped Field Place of every bit of furniture except the fire grates. Shelley had promised bequests to Claire, Hunt, Peacock, and Hogg. He had also promised £6,000 for Ianthe, his daughter by Harriet. The total came to £22,500, which left Mary and Percy in desperate straits, unable to pay off their creditors or honor Shelley's intentions. Ordinarily, they could have relied on the Shelley holdings, which brought in an annual income of £5,000 or more, to help them get back on their feet. But the summer of 1845 brought terrible weather; the crops died, and the farmers could not pay their rents. Luckily, Mary, a veteran of dire fiscal problems, knew how to manage. She sold off parts of the estate, cut their expenses, negotiated with creditors, and made a plan to slowly pay off their debts while gradually honoring Shelley's bequests. However, the legatees were suspicious about why they had not received their money. Claire was the worst offender. She wrote frequent furious letters: Where was her inheritance? Were Percy and Mary trying to deprive her of what was rightfully hers? Only when she came home to England for four months and saw that Mary and Percy were doing their best to manage a difficult situation did she soften. When she returned to Paris, she wrote a peacemaking letter, saying that it had done her good to be with them:

Near you and Percy it is impossible to be unhappy, for your unity is so charming and there is so much calm and happiness in you it imparts a most beneficial influence . . . and then your conversation so nice and so universal draws one out of the narrow cares of self.

Mary wrote back that her only goals were "To do a little good—to watch over those dear—to enjoy quiet—& if one can be a little amused voila tout?"

It was impossible to live at the crumbling Field Place, and so Mary and Percy continued to stay in Putney, where old friends often came to visit, including Leigh Hunt and, surprisingly, Aubrey and his wife, Rosa, as Mary had come to accept Aubrey's second betrayal with remarkable dignity. Over the next few years, she devoted herself to turning the few resources she and Percy had into a solid foundation. After a few good harvests and careful economy, Mary had settled their debts, leaving them with enough income to buy a home in London, a four-story town house at 24 Chester Square in Pimlico. There was even enough left over for Percy to purchase a yacht. Mary tried not to worry, as she knew that Percy was far more sensible than his father, and his new vessel was sturdy and well equipped for all weather. Besides, he knew how to swim.

But for all their newfound security, Mary felt increasingly ill. The headaches she had endured six years ago in Italy had continued intermittently, and now they returned in full force. The doctor she consulted said it was "neuralgia of the heart"—a misdiagnosis. Her back hurt, the nerves felt tingly, "alive," and at times she thought her "spine would altogether give up the ghost." She was troubled by a tremor that made it difficult to write, eat, walk, or take care of her daily needs. The doctors were at a loss, and finally, as they often did with gentlewomen of Mary's class and background, they diagnosed a nervous complaint, just as they had with the poet Elizabeth Barrett, who had been confined to her bed before she ran off to Italy with Browning, inspired by Mary's own elopement with Shelley.

However, Mary was not yet ready to retire to her bedchamber.

She sought cures in Baden-Baden and Brighton and consulted different physicians. And yet, though she had periods when her back pain subsided, the headaches never really went away. She read light novels and followed politics but could not do any work that was too taxing. She consoled herself by entertaining friends when she felt up to it and keeping watch for a suitable bride for Percy. At last, in March 1848, the right young woman appeared at the home of friends in Bayswater.

Small and plump, Jane Gibson St. John had already been married; her husband had died, leaving her a widow at age twenty-four, the same age Mary had been when Shelley died. She was neither beautiful nor artistic, but her merits were just what Mary had been looking for. She was sensible, loyal, and loving toward Percy. In addition, she was deeply reverential toward Mary. Years later, when she recalled meeting her husband for the first time, it would be her mother-in-law she would describe, not Percy: Mary was "tall and slim," with "the most beautiful deep set eyes I have ever seen." She wore dresses of a "long soft grey material, simply and beautifully made." No one else had ever described Mary as tall, but then Jane was short and plump.

Here at last was a daughter, Mary felt. It did not take much to persuade Percy that Jane was the right woman. He felt appreciated, even admired, by Jane. Although he and his mother had come to an understanding after the last European expedition, Mary still had a way of making him feel inadequate. She pushed him to read more, to follow politics, and to go to the theater and galleries. He knew she worried about his passion for his yacht. Jane, on the other hand, seemed to like him as he was. She did not ask him what he was reading or wonder what his thoughts were on Italian unification. She encouraged him to go sailing. Best of all, she had never met his brilliant father, so she could never compare them and find him wanting.

Their courtship was rapid, even though Percy was not much of a suitor, largely because the women had already decided the matter. Percy proposed in March and married Jane on June 22, 1848, a wedding that resulted in a long and loving partnership, although they had no children. Jane was happy to let Percy putter around on the river.

She oversaw his wardrobe and meals, and spent most of her time with her mother-in-law, reading quietly, chatting, and listening to stories about the past.

The family's finances were in far better shape now, thanks to Mary's management of their affairs, and so the young couple renovated Field Place and moved there with Mary in the fall of 1848. Mary took Shelley's old bedroom for herself; from there, she could look out over the grounds to a grove of cedar trees and watch the sun set in a splash of lavender and orange. Shelley had told her stories about the "Great Old Snake" who lived in the garden and the "Great Tortoise" who used to trundle across the lawn to visit him. But the snake had been accidentally killed by the gardener and no one but Shelley had ever reported seeing the tortoise.

The house had once been a simple farm dwelling that Shelley's grandfather had turned into a stately gentleman's manor with a Georgian façade and two wings that enclosed a wide green lawn. Shelley had once terrorized his little sisters with stories about an alchemist who lived behind a locked door in one of the garrets under the rafters. There was a huge kitchen with an old stone floor, and an enormous oak staircase. In the long, graceful drawing room where Shelley's parents had entertained the local gentry, the young Percy had pleased his father by reciting Latin poetry after tea, waving his arms in a theatrical way, which made his little sisters laugh. He also liked to perform his mother's favorite, Gray's poem "Ode on the Death of a Favorite Cat, Drowned in a Tub of Gold Fishes." There were stables in the back, an orchard, and, on the other side of the south meadow, a large lake called Warnham Pond where Shelley's father had kept a rowboat for his son to paddle about and explore the surrounding rivers and creeks. One cannot help but wonder why the Shelleys did not teach young Percy to swim.

Beautiful though it was, Field Place was low-lying and wet, dangerously placed for the health of both ladies. "The whole place is a swamp—Nothing can be so bad for me," Mary wrote to Claire, blaming the house for her suffering since the true source of her ailments had still not been diagnosed. Confused and now frightened by periodic bouts of paralysis, Mary found even short walks exhausting.

She could hardly ride in a carriage. It was too difficult to write much anymore, even letters. The doctors continued to attribute her complaints to nervousness, prescribing cod liver oil and rest. In February 1849 she updated Claire, "I walk very well—but must not use my head—or strange feelings come on—"

Jane was a devoted nurse. She fussed over Mary, plumping her pillows, making tea, and reading to her. She also assumed more responsibility for running the estate. Although Percy had nicknamed her Wren, this was a misleading moniker, as Jane was more like a hawk when it came to those she loved. For instance, when Claire came to visit in the spring of 1849, it was Jane who protected Mary and Percy from a terrible outbreak of Claire's wrath.

Claire's niece, Charles's daughter Clari, had arrived at Field Place a few weeks before her aunt, met John Knox, a friend of Percy's, and promptly fallen in love. The young couple had become engaged, but unfortunately no one had thought to write Claire and apprise her of this. When she arrived, Claire, caught unaware by her niece's plans, jumped to the conclusion that Clari's engagement was the result of a secret plot concocted by her sister. She raged at Mary, at Clari, and at Percy until Jane swept in and took charge. She shooed Mary upstairs to her bedroom, threatened Claire until she left the house swearing never to return, and then sat right down with Clari to plan her wedding. A month later, under Jane's watchful eye, Clari married John Knox, and the Shelleys held a ball to celebrate the occasion. Claire was not invited and never forgave Jane, or Percy, for that matter. In fact, she issued an ultimatum to her relations: there could be no communication with any of the Shelleys:

> Until they have made reparation for their insolence to us, it stamps with dishonour any member of our family, who holds any intercourse but a hostile one with them, and my resolution is taken and I will part from any of my relations who do.

For Mary, the whole matter raised her estimation of Jane even higher. If Jane could subdue Claire, she could handle anything, and so it was without any regrets that Mary gave up the reins of the household to her forceful daughter-in-law. To Jane, however, this surrender was yet another symptom of her mother-in-law's failing health. She and Percy took Mary to the south of France that fall, hoping the mild weather would renew her strength, and, at first, the plan worked. Mary felt well enough to sip wine and tour the coastland on the back of a donkey. When they returned to England the following summer, she felt much improved. She could sit outside in the gardens watching Percy's dogs run freely about the grounds and listening to the doves cooing in their dovecote. But as the weather worsened that fall, her headaches grew more intense and she felt a constant numbness on her right side. To Jane, it was clear that her mother-in-law needed to be near the best doctors, and so the trio settled in Chester Square, where at last, on December 17, 1850, Dr. Richard Bright (discoverer of Bright's disease) diagnosed Mary with a brain tumor.

Percy was not in the room when Mary heard this news, and she and Jane held a whispered conference, deciding to keep the diagnosis secret, as it would only worry him. For the rest of the month the two women kept him in the dark. Mary managed to sit up a little every day, and Percy and Jane took turns by her bedside. But by the beginning of January, there could be no more secrets. Mary's left leg was entirely paralyzed, and it was almost impossible for her to speak. When they told him about the tumor, Percy grew pale and silent. He had lived with his mother for almost all of his life. They had rarely spent more than a few months apart. He stayed by her bedside, praying for her to recover, but to no avail.

On January 23, Mary suffered a series of violent convulsions and was never conscious again. She lay in a coma for eight days, dying on the evening of February 1, 1851. She was fifty-three years old. Percy and Jane were with her when "her sweet gentle spirit passed away without even a sigh," as Jane later recalled. Percy was inconsolable. A world without Mary was unthinkable.

# CHAPTER 40

# MARY AND MARY:
# HEROIC EXERTIONS

——

AFTER MARY SHELLEY DIED, HER REPUTATION UNDERWENT A SLOW and invidious transformation. Her obituaries focused on her roles as a wife and daughter and minimized her work as a writer and editor. "It is not . . . as the authoress even of *Frankenstein* . . . that she derives her most enduring and endearing title to our affection," read the column in *The Literary Gazette,* "but as the faithful and devoted wife of Percy Bysshe Shelley." Even the liberal *Leader* identified her first as the daughter of Wollstonecraft and Godwin, then as the wife of the "most Christian hearted" Percy, and only as an afterthought as the author of *Frankenstein.* The one obituary that did focus on her literary achievement ran in the *Athenaeum,* but though it praised *Frankenstein,* it dismissed most of her other writing. There was only a brief mention of her biographical essays and travel books, a lukewarm assessment of *The Last Man,* and no discussion of her other novels. Not one reviewer noted her role in promoting and editing her husband's work. Mary had almost painted herself out of the picture.

The view of Mary as a secondary light, the wife of the great poet and not much more, was so durable that it lasted almost a century. Critics ignored or misunderstood Mary's novels, writing them off as trivial or "romances"; her encyclopedia articles went unread, and her actions to promote the welfare of women remained hidden, buried in archives and unseen letters. It was not until 1951, in Muriel Spark's groundbreaking biography, that readers were introduced to Mary's sophistication as a writer and her decidedly non-Victorian ideas. The character known as "Mrs. Shelley" was finally challenged as the fiction it had always been.

In the 1970s, Mary's standing, like her mother's, benefited from the women's movement, but rebuilding her reputation was still a slow process. The scholar Betty T. Bennett noted that when she published the first volume of Mary Shelley's letters in 1980 one reviewer "suggested that Mary Shelley's letters were not worth publishing." Undeterred by such criticisms, over the last thirty years, many distinguished literary scholars have devoted their careers to analyzing Mary Shelley's work, shedding light on her innovations, brilliance, and stratagems. Combing through archives in America, England, and Italy, biographers have restored the complexity of her relationship with Shelley, refuting the claims of previous writers who, following Trelawny's lead, had deemed her unworthy of her genius husband. As a result, Mary's self-discipline as a professional writer, her originality as a novelist, and her seriousness as a political thinker have finally emerged from the fog that threatened to obscure her name forever.

But until recently most readers did not fully understand the impact of her mother on Mary Shelley. Radicals criticized her for straying from her mother's ideals. She was accused of being a coward, even though throughout her life she had remained a staunch disciple of her mother. Her body of work is notable for her commitment to the rights of women and her condemnation of unchecked male ambition. She had devoted her life to upholding her mother's philosophy, and one of her greatest fears was that she would fall short of Wollstonecraft's brilliance. In 1827, she wrote a friend:

> The memory of my Mother has always been the pride and delight of my life & the admiration of others for her, has been the cause of most of the happiness . . . I have enjoyed. Her greatness of soul [has] perpetually reminded me that I ought to degenerate as little as I could from those from whom I derived my being.

After her father died, when she was struggling to write his biography, she allowed herself to pause and write an extended section praising her mother:

Mary Wollstonecraft was one of those beings who appear once perhaps in a generation, to gild humanity with a ray which no difference of opinion nor chance of circumstances can cloud. Her genius was undeniable. She had been bred in the hard school of adversity, and having experienced the sorrows entailed on the poor and the oppressed, an earnest desire was kindled within her to diminish these sorrows. Her sound understanding, her intrepidity, her sensibility and eager sympathy, stamped all her writings with force and truth, and endowed them with a tender charm that enchants while it enlightens. She was one whom all loved who had ever seen her. Many years are passed since that beating heart has been laid in the cold still grave, but no one who has ever seen her speaks of her without enthusiastic veneration.

In 1831, in a preface Mary wrote for a new edition of Godwin's *Caleb Williams,* she publicly linked herself to her mother's radical tradition, expressing unqualified admiration for Wollstonecraft:

The writings of this celebrated woman are monuments of her moral and intellectual superiority. Her lofty spirit, her eager assertion of the claims of her sex, animate the "Vindication of the Rights of Woman"; while the sweetness and taste displayed in her "Letters from Norway" depict the softer qualities of her admirable character. Even now, those who have survived her so many years, never speak of her without uncontrollable enthusiasm. Her unwearied exertions for the benefit of others, her rectitude, her independence, joined to a warm affectionate heart and the most refined softness of manners, made her the idol of all who knew her.

The laudatory tone of these passages makes it tempting to wonder what would have happened if Mary Shelley had directed her talents to the rehabilitation of her mother's reputation, writing an analysis of Wollstonecraft's ideas and innovations. Perhaps if her own life had not been interrupted by her husband's death and then by her brain tumor, she might have embarked on this project. At the end of her writing life, after all, she had turned exclusively to the writing of biography and nonfiction.

However, Mary's allegiance to her mother has been invisible to some because, unlike Wollstonecraft, Mary did not embrace the political arena, nor did she write political philosophy. She was far more suspicious of the legislative process than her mother, father, or husband, having seen how little was gained by their public stands and how much was lost. But that did not mean that she wanted to distance herself from her mother's radicalism. For Mary, change could come about only through art, through the actions of individuals and the integrity of one's relationships. She announced her allegiance to Wollstonecraft in her five novels and two travel books, as well as in her essays on prominent writers for the *Cyclopedia* and in the more than two dozen stories, essays, translations, reviews, and poems she published in her lifetime. In all of her work, she emphasized the importance of the independence and education of women and critiqued the traditionally male values of conquest and self-promotion.

Mary Shelley also left behind an enormous cache of papers for historians, so that a biographer who lived in more open-minded times could use them to tell the stories she could not. Painfully aware that a true biography of her husband had not yet been published, she never concealed the history of her relationship with Shelley, and she protested vigorously when one writer attempted to whitewash their liaison, leaving out any mention of Harriet in the story of their courtship. On a more personal level, she risked her reputation for the sake of other women, supporting Aubrey's sister Gee when she separated from her husband and masterminding Isabel Robinson's escape with Doddy.

Indeed, her last public act demonstrates that she remained true to her mother's principles right to the end. A few months before Mary died, her old friend Isabella Booth wrote to ask if she would petition the Royal Literary Fund for assistance on her behalf. Having nursed her much older husband through a long illness, Isabella was penniless and weary. She and Mary had not seen each other since Mary's years in Scotland, and yet Mary, near death, hardly able to pen a legible word, wrote the Fund, putting her reputation on the line for the wife of a man who not only was notorious for his irreverent and reformist views but had also refused to let Isabella visit Mary because of her elopement with Shelley. Just as Wollstonecraft would have done, Mary connected Isabella's plight to the sufferings of all women. "[Her husband's] malady demanded a care & courage in nursing," she wrote, "which for a woman to undertake & go through with alone demanded heroic exertion."

Mary's words about Isabella's "heroic exertion" have a larger resonance, perhaps because they are the last she ever wrote, but also because they could be said of her path through life. Like Isabella's, her challenges had been daunting. True, there had been moments of joy. In the last year of her life, on Lake Como with Jane and Percy, she had written Isabella, "with the sun shining the blue lake at my feet & the Mountains in all their Majesty & beauty around & my beloved children happy & well, I must mark this as a peaceful & happy hour." But mostly, Mary had felt alone, forced to support herself and those who depended on her in a world that condemned her for the choices she had made as a sixteen-year-old girl.

The Fund shared none of Mary's concern for indigent gentlewomen, rejecting her request. But Mary did not abandon Isabella, asking Percy to send her an allowance of £50 each year for the rest of Isabella's life. In her novels, essays, and stories, and in her quiet behind-the-scenes actions, Mary Shelley had made the plight of women the driving force of her life, just as her mother had.

DURING HER FINAL YEARS, Mary had put her literary affairs in careful order. She remembered all too well what it was like to deal with Shelley's disorganized papers, and those of her father, and so she arranged her diaries and letters and Shelley's notebooks for the generations to come. She believed that her daughter-in-law, Jane, would guide scholars to the papers she could not publish, the notes she had kept hidden. One of her most important treasures was a lock of her mother's hair, to which she attached a note, "Jane and Percy to respect." Many years later Jane would make the thick reddish locks into a necklace that is still held at the Bodleian Library in Oxford.

Mary also talked to Jane about final arrangements, asking Jane to bury her in St. Pancras next to her mother and father. Despite her devotion to Shelley, despite the years of mourning and the love they had shared, Mary wanted her final resting place to be with her parents and not her husband. She may have felt unable to assert the views and ideals she shared with her mother in Wollstonecraft-like "vindications," but she could make it clear that she considered herself, first and foremost, the daughter of the most famous radical female of the previous generation, as well as the daughter of the author of *Political Justice*.

Jane was not averse to burying her mother-in-law separately from Shelley, but she was appalled at the thought of burying her in St. Pancras churchyard. "It would have broken my heart to let her loveliness wither in such a dreadful place," she said. Over the last few decades, the church had become derelict; the new railroad had come to the north of London, splintering Mary's old neighborhood and destroying the farmland. The graveyard had become a notorious site of "fishing," or grave robbing, a macabre activity made famous in Dickens's *A Tale of Two Cities*.

A new location would have to be found, Jane decided, one suitable for her beloved mother-in-law, and it would have to be found soon, as the government had decreed that many of the St. Pancras graves were to be exhumed to make way for the railroad. Oddly enough, the young Thomas Hardy, the future novelist, was to oversee this project. Appointed by the Bishop of London, Hardy had the job of keeping track of which coffins went with which gravestones. When one visits St. Pancras today, the gravestones are stacked neatly around the twisted roots of an ash tree, a reminder of how many graves this churchyard once housed.

After months of searching, Jane found a secluded churchyard at St. Peter's in Bournemouth, where she and Percy had moved for the mild weather and sea air. She was pleased that it was near their new home, Boscombe Manor, as then they could pay tribute to Mary as often as they wished. The only obstacle was that the vicar did not want famous radicals buried in his graveyard. Jane, who was used to getting her own way, ignored his protests, hiring some sturdy men to dig up the coffins of Wollstonecraft and Godwin. Once they were safely loaded in her private carriage, she drove to the gates of the Bournemouth church, where she waited with her skeletal companions until the vicar, reluctant to have a scene, let her in. His last plaintive caveat was that the burial take place late at night.

Godwin and Wollstonecraft were reunited with their daughter in a large grave on the hill behind the church. For Mary's epitaph, Jane and Percy memorialized her identity as a daughter, wife, and mother: "Mary Wollstonecraft Shelley, Daughter of William and Mary Wollstonecraft Godwin, and Widow of the Late Percy Bysshe Shelley." They left out any mention of *Frankenstein,* even though for Wollstonecraft and Godwin's commemoration they cited *Political Justice* and *A Vindication of the Rights of Woman.* They also made no mention of Mary-Jane in the plaque they put up to memorialize the family. When Claire heard this, she was furious. Her mother had been buried next to Godwin in St. Pancras churchyard, but Jane had left her behind, the eternal third wheel. She also left behind Wollstonecraft's original gravestone—the one that Mary Godwin used to trace her letters on when she was a girl—which still stands in St. Pancras today.

Jane did not care if Claire was offended. Just like *Frankenstein,* Mary-Jane was not part of the legacy she was trying to create. She wanted her mother-in-law to be seen as a noble, grieving widow and a loving daughter and mother, not as a rebellious stepdaughter or the author of a disgraceful novel. Most of all, she did not want her to be seen as following the promiscuous example of Wollstonecraft. In a red-draped corner of the drawing room at Boscombe Manor, she built a shrine, painting the ceiling blue with little yellow dots for stars. She hung the Rothwell portrait of Mary on the wall behind a row of glass-covered cases swathed in orange satin to keep the sunlight out. Devotees were ushered in to peek at the relics displayed on the shelves: Mary Shelley's hand mirror and Mary Wollstonecraft's amethyst ring, hair bracelets, manuscripts, and love letters, and an urn containing the remains of Shelley's heart, discovered by Percy a year after Mary died. He had been reluctant to unlock his mother's writing desk, but when at last he did, he found her journal, a copy of Shelley's *Adonais,* and, wrapped inside, the dusty remains of his father.

For Jane, Mary's journal contained many unwelcome surprises, as did her letters. Shocked by what she found, Jane destroyed anything that might harm the Shelley name. The Naples incident—baby Elena and her questionable history—went up in smoke, as did many of Shelley's letters to other women. Jane was neither as respectful nor as dedicated to the truth as her mother-in-law; in fact, she was far more conventional than Mary had ever dreamed—so much so that her actions are one of the central reasons that Mary's political and literary ideals were misrepresented for so many years.

Perhaps the most striking example of Jane's revision of history is her version of Mary and Shelley's courtship in a book she entitled *Shelley Memorials.* Published in 1859, this antiseptic little volume was designed and edited by Jane in order to clear the family of all scandals. Declaring she had gleaned the story of their love affair straight from Mary's lips, Jane wrote that Shelley and Mary first confessed their feelings only after Harriet had died, and that Shelley had spouted a selfless anthem of love to reveal the depths of his passion for Mary:

> [Shelley], in burning words, poured forth the tale of his wild past—how he had suffered, how he had been misled, and how, if supported by her love, he hoped in future years to enroll his name with the wise and good who had done battle for their fellow-men, and been true through all adverse storms to the cause of humanity.

In one sweep, she erased the irrational Shelley, the confused, terrified, and at times selfish young man who made love to one young woman while married to another. Vanished, also, was the rebellious red-haired beauty, the outrageous daughter of Wollstonecraft, the passionate teenager who ran away with a married man. In her place was a selfless wife and daughter, obedient and pliant, the embodiment of nineteenth-century womanhood, a Victorian ideal. Whether she knew it or not, Jane had acted in the spirit of Dr. Frankenstein, stitching together a new creature, one who bore little resemblance to her actual mother-in-law.

Victorian society read Jane's words and embraced Mary Shelley as a paragon of virtue—modest and unassuming—prompting those brave souls who still revered Wollstonecraft to dismiss her daughter as a hypocrite. The vindictive Trelawny capitalized on these criticisms in his account of Shelley's life, *Records of Shelley, Byron, and the Author* (1878), painting Shelley's marriage to Mary as "the utmost malice of fortune," and Mary herself as a conventional, small-minded prig.

Mary Shelley's jealousy must have sorely vexed Shelley— indeed she was not a suitable companion for the poet—his first wife Harriett [*sic*] must have been more suitable—Mary was the most conventionable slave I ever met—she even affected the pious dodge, such was her yearning for society—she was devoid of imagination and Poetry.

Trelawny even twisted the story of Shelley's heart. In his version, Mary had been repulsed when he handed it to her after the pyre and had quickly given it to Leigh Hunt without a second thought.

Of course, Claire, the final survivor of the Shelley circle, had also recorded her thoughts on their shared history, but since her bitter words about free love were uncovered only a few years ago, Mary's hagiography of Shelley remained in place for over a century. The poet as an otherworldly "blithe spirit" dominated the imagination of nineteenth-century readers, as did Jane's portrait of Mary as his ideal companion. Readers adored Mary's Shelley—pure, fey, and brilliantly imaginative—and Jane's Mary—pure, innocent, and eminently respectable. It was partly the times: Keats, too, became a saint. Even Byron went through a Victorian whitewashing, transformed from the leader of the League of Incest to a heroic poet who died for the sake of freedom.

It is a sobering tale, the rise and fall of both Marys, since it so clearly points to how difficult it is to know the past and how mutable the historical record can be. For almost two hundred years, Wollstonecraft was written off, first as a whore and then as a hysteric, an irrational female hardly worth reading—slander that proved so effective in undercutting the ideals of *A Vindication of the Rights of Woman* that it persists today in the rhetoric of those who oppose feminist principles. Mary Shelley, on the other hand, would be condemned for compromising the revolutionary values of her genius husband and her pioneering mother. Viewed as a woman who cared more about her place in society than about political ideas or artistic integrity, she was discounted as an intellectual lightweight, her only important work done with the help of her husband. They were attacks from opposite grounds, but both were equally and terrifyingly successful.

At the end of her life, Mary Shelley could never have suspected that she and her mother would be treated so differently by history. She had spent her entire life following her mother's lead. As a small child, staring at the words on the gravestone, "Mary Wollstonecraft Godwin, Author of *A Vindication of the Rights of Woman,*" she had believed that it was here, near her mother, that she could be most herself. And that, after all, was what she wanted most, a desire mother and daughter shared. To be themselves. The hurdles, the critics, the enemies, the insults, the ostracism, the betrayals, the neglect, even the heartbreaks—none of this had stopped them.

Today, in their portraits, with their long skirts and solemn faces, both mother and daughter seem staid and venerable, as though they had lived their lives at their desks plotting out their essays and novels. The scandals are forgotten. The hubbub has died down. In the anthologies of English literature, their names are listed in the table of contents, before Dickens and after Milton, their entries as significant and weighty as those for the men of their generation.

But the paradox of their success is that most modern readers are unaware of the overwhelming obstacles both women had to overcome. Without knowing the history of the era, the difficulties Wollstonecraft and Shelley faced are largely invisible, their bravery incomprehensible. Both women were what Wollstonecraft termed "outlaws." Not only did they write world-changing books, they

*Mary Wollstonecraft's tombstone can still be found in the graveyard
of old St. Pancras church, though her remains were moved to Bournemouth
so they could be with those of her daughter, Mary Shelley.*

broke from the strictures that governed women's conduct, not once but time and again, profoundly challenging the moral code of the day. Their refusal to bow down, to subside and surrender, to be quiet and subservient, to apologize and hide, makes their lives as memorable as the words they left behind. They asserted their right to determine their own destinies, starting a revolution that has yet to end.

# ACKNOWLEDGMENTS

———

I would like to thank:

My incomparable agent, Brettne Bloom, who believed in this book from the very beginning and gave me the courage to tell the story of these remarkable women.

The team at Random House, especially Barbara Bachman, Jenn Backe, Steve Messina, Emily DeHuff, Chris Jerome, Karen Mugler, Joe Perez, and my editors—the brilliant Susanna Porter, whose vision, expertise, wisdom, and clarity were indispensable during the long years of writing this book and whose delight in the Marys buoyed me during the inevitable difficulties of such an enormous project; and the talented Priyanka Krishnan, whose patience, humor, clearheadedness, and organizational skills helped me shape the first draft into a coherent final version.

The team at Random House UK, especially Sarah Rigby, whose comments and editorial suggestions helped tighten and clarify the narrative, and whose good cheer gave me strength in the final stretches.

The outstanding literary biographers whose groundbreaking research and insightful analysis of Wollstonecraft and the Shelleys made it possible for me to write this dual biography: Lyndall Gordon (*Vindication: A Life of Mary Wollstonecraft*), Richard Holmes (*Shelley: The Pursuit*), Miranda Seymour (*Mary Shelley*), Janet Todd (*Mary Wollstonecraft: A Revolutionary Life*), and Claire Tomalin (*The Life and Death of Mary Wollstonecraft*).

The editors who made the letters and journals of Mary Shelley, Claire Clairmont, and Mary Wollstonecraft available to the public: Betty T. Bennett, Marion Kingston Stocking, and Janet Todd.

The Pforzheimer Collection's Shelley and His Circle volumes, edited by Kenneth Neill Cameron, Donald Reiman, Doucet Fischer, and others.

The staff and librarians at the New York Public Library, the Bodleian Library, the British Library, and the Honnold/Mudd Library at the Claremont Colleges, particularly Elizabeth Denlinger, Bruce Barker-Benfield, and Carrie Marsh.

My research assistant, Eva Schlitz, for reviewing the manuscript and formatting and organizing the notes and bibliography; Allie Graham and Helen Gordon for invaluable help with technology, images, and copyrights; and Todd Wemmer for the photographs.

My early readers: Nola Anderson, Laura Harrington, and Gabrielle Watling.

Endicott College, especially President Richard Wylie and Vice President and Dean of the Undergraduate College Laura Rossi-Le, and the Endicott Library staff, especially Betty Roland and Brian Courtemanche, for providing me with the support I needed to write this book. Thanks also to Mark Herlihy, Gene Wong, and my many colleagues and friends at the college.

My loyal friends: Heather Atwood, Carolyn Cooke, Paul Fisher, Laila Goodman, Jo Kreilick, Vicki Lincoln, Phoebe Potts, Ruth Rich, Chris Stodolski, Gabrielle Watling, and Jim Watras.

My siblings: Richard, Liz, Jacques, and Helen.

Brooks, who has lived with the Marys for as long as I have. And Mark, who has supported us through all stages of the writing process, from cooking dinner and taking care of the family to reading the opening and closing lines of this book more times than I can count.

And finally, my mother, who has been my inspiration, always.

# NOTES

———

| | |
|---|---|
| *Matilda* | Mary Shelley, *Matilda* |
| *Memoirs* | William Godwin, ed., *Memoirs of the Author of a Vindication of the Rights of Woman* |
| *MS* | Miranda Seymour, *Mary Shelley* |
| *MS:R&R* | Emily Sunstein, *Mary Shelley: Romance and Reality* |
| *MW:ARL* | Janet Todd, *Mary Wollstonecraft: A Revolutionary Life* |
| *Political Justice* | William Godwin, *An Enquiry Concerning Political Justice* |
| *Recollections* | Edward Trelawny, *Recollections of the Last Days of Shelley and Byron* |
| *Shelley's Friends* | Frederick Jones, ed., *Maria Gisborne and Edward E. Williams, Shelley's Friends: Their Journals and Letters* |
| "Supplement" | W. Clark Durant, "Supplement" in *Memoirs of the Author of a Vindication of the Rights of Woman,* ed. William Godwin |
| *TCC* | Marion Kingston Stocking, ed., *The Clairmont Correspondence* |
| *VAL* | Lyndall Gordon, *Vindication: A Life of Mary Wollstonecraft* |
| *Vindication of Woman* | Mary Wollstonecraft, *A Vindication of the Rights of Woman* |

## CHAPTER ONE: A DEATH AND A BIRTH (1797–1801)

3  **William Godwin did not think** Emily W. Sunstein, *Mary Shelley: Romance and Reality* (Baltimore: Johns Hopkins University Press, 1989), 26.

3  **"greater and wiser"** This passage, from "The Elder Son," is Mary Shelley's description of the feelings of one of her fictional father-raised characters. Charles E. Robinson, ed., *Mary Shelley: Collected Tales and Stories* (Baltimore: Johns Hopkins University Press, 1976), 256. In her later fiction, Mary represented the love between fathers and daughters as a sacred bond, drawing a direct link between herself and her fictional daughters, writing, "When a father is all that a father may be . . . the love of a daughter is one of the deepest and strongest, as it is the purest passion of which our natures are capable." C. Kegan Paul, *William Godwin: His Friends and Contemporaries* (Boston: Roberts Brothers, 1876), vol. 1, 276.

4  **"The mouth was too much"** Paul, *Friends,* 1:290.

5  **"outleap" of London** William Hone, *The Year Book of Daily Recreation and Information* (London: 1838), 317.

5  **A muffin seller** Miranda Seymour, *Mary Shelley* (New York: Grove, 2000), 42. This passage is based on Seymour's description of the Polygon as well as Edward Walford's in "Somers Town and Euston Square," *Old and New London* (1878), 5:340–55. Also available online at http://www.british-history.ac.uk/report.aspx?compid=45241.

6  **Godwin worked until one** Sunstein, *MS:R&R,* 25.

6  **Together they enjoyed** Ibid., 26.

6  **"When you were hungry"** Camilla Jebb, *Mary Wollstonecraft* (Chicago: F. G. Browne & Co., 1913), 281.

6  **In the late afternoons** Sunstein, *MS:R&R,* 21.

7   "quick," "pretty" Paul, *Friends,* 2:214.

8   "knew me instantly" Una Taylor, *Guests and Memories: Annals of a Seaside Villa* (London: Oxford University Press, 1924), 28.

9   Coleridge was a spellbinding One listener described letting the poet's voice "flow" over him like "a stream of rich distilled perfumes." James Gillman, *The Life of Samuel Taylor Coleridge* (London: William Pickering, 1838), 1:112.

9   "[My father] never caressed me" "The Elder Son," Robinson, ed., *Mary Shelley: Collected Tales and Stories,* 256.

9   "using the air" Ernest Hartley Coleridge, ed., *Letters of Samuel Taylor Coleridge,* 2 vols. (Boston: Houghton Mifflin, 1895), 1:359.

9   "gave the philosopher" Ibid., 321.

9   "I pun, conundrumize" Samuel T. Coleridge to John Thewall, 1797, in Coleridge, ed., *Letters of Samuel Taylor Coleridge,* 1: 220.

9   "fly like stags" Ernest Hartley Coleridge, ed., *The Poetical Works of Samuel Taylor Coleridge* (London: Oxford University Press, 1912), 30. I am indebted to Michael Dineen for pointing out this poem.

CHAPTER TWO: MARY WOLLSTONECRAFT:
THE EARLY YEARS (1759–1774)

11  "[A mother's] parental" Mary Wollstonecraft, *"A Vindication of the Rights of Woman" and "The Wrongs of Woman; or, Maria,"* ed. Anne Mellor, Longman Cultural Editions (Pearson, 2007), 185.

13  Spitalfields silk weavers As the nineteenth-century historian Edward Walford remarked, "Riots among the Spitalfields weavers, for many a century were of frequent occurrence." See "Spitalfields," in *Old and New London* (London: 1878), 2:149–52. Also available online at http://www.british-history.ac.uk/report .aspx?compid=45086.

13  Although Edward Senior Roy Porter, *English Society in the Eighteenth Century* (London: Penguin Books, 1982; reprint, 1990), 87. Porter discusses the discrepancies between rich and poor in the eighteenth century, citing the voices of contemporaries to demonstrate the anger of the lower and middle classes, individuals whose socioeconomic status closely resembled that of the Wollstonecrafts.

14  "an old mansion" Elizabeth Ogborne, *The History of Essex: From the Earliest Period to the Present Time* (London: Longman, Hurst, Rees, Orme and Brown, 1814), 161.

14  "despised dolls" William Godwin, *Memoirs of the Author of a Vindication of the Rights of Woman,* 2nd ed. (London: J. Johnson, St. Pauls Church Yard, 1798), 13.

14  "deputy tyrant" Mary Wollstonecraft, *Maria* (1798). In *Mary Wollstonecraft: Mary and Maria; Mary Shelley: Matilda.* Edited by Janet Todd, 55–148. London: Penguin Classics, 1992, 95.

14  "quick and impetuous" Godwin, *Memoirs,* 7.

15  the "agony" of her childhood Ibid., 11.

15  peopling the countryside Mary Wollstonecraft, *Mary* (1788). In *Mary Wollstonecraft: Mary and Maria; Mary Shelley: Matilda.* Edited by Janet Todd, 1–54. London: Penguin Classics, 1992, 8.

15  "gaze on the moon" Ibid.

16  "without daring to utter a word" Godwin, *Memoirs,* 8.

16  little secrets Wollstonecraft, *Mary,* 9.

16  "the whole house" Wollstonecraft, *Maria,* 95.

16  It was a shock Godwin, *Memoirs,* 15.

17  There were stores Porter, *English Society in the Eighteenth Century,* 215.

17  handsome doors Ibid.

17  **Inside, when the sun shone** Beverley Minster, "History and Building," http://
beverleyminster.org.uk/visit-us/history-and-building. Janet Todd also provides
a description of the Minster in *Mary Wollstonecraft: A Revolutionary Life* (London:
Weidenfeld and Nicolson, 2000), 10.

18  **With indignation** Wollstonecraft, *Vindication of Woman*, 159.

18  **Local dialect** Yorkshire Dialect Society, "Word Recognition," http://www
.yorkshiredialectsociety.org.uk/word-recognition/ (accessed August 23, 2014).
See also "A Fact Sheet on Yorkshire Dialect," West Winds, http://www.west
windsinyorkshire.co.uk/attachments/AnAncientTongueWestWinds.pdf (accessed August 23, 2014).

18  **"If you happen to have any learning"** John Gregory, *A Father's Legacy to His
Daughters* (London: 1774), quoted in Wollstonecraft, *Vindication of Woman*, 124.

18  **"with as much solicitude"** Arthur Ropes, ed. *Lady Mary Wortley Montagu: Select
Passages from Her Letters* (London: 1892), 237.

18  **Jane Arden** This overview of the friendship is taken from the letters of Wollstonecraft to Jane Arden. Janet Todd, ed., *The Collected Letters of Mary Wollstonecraft* (New York: Columbia University Press, 2003), 1–18.

19  **"If I did not love you"** MW to Jane Arden, c. mid–late 1773–11/16/1774, ibid., 13.

19  **"Love and jealousy"** Ibid., 14.

19  **"I spent part of the night in tears"** Ibid., 15.

19  **electricity, gravitation** Lyndall Gordon, *Vindication: A Life of Mary Wollstonecraft*
(New York: Harper Perennial, 2006), 12.

19  **It had become fashionable** "Knowledge is become a fashionable thing," Benjamin
Martin, an itinerant lecturer, observed, "and philosophy is the science a la mode."
Porter, *English Society in the Eighteenth Century,* 240.

20  **including her in the lessons** Todd, *MW:ARL,* 14–15.

20  **when the Ardens suggested** Gordon, *VAL,* 13.

20  **"The oddest mortal"** MW to Jane Arden, mid–late 1773, *Letters MW,* 9. Both
Jane's and Mary's words come from the same letter, as Mary quoted a passage of
Jane's that particularly delighted her and responded to it.

21  **"did not scruple"** MW to Jane Arden, ?early 1780, ibid., 23.

21  **London's lunatics** The Hoxton Trust, "Real Hoxton: The Lunatic Asylums,"
http://www.realhoxton.co.uk/history.htm#lunatic-asylums.

21  **"the most terrific of ruins"** Wollstonecraft, *Maria,* 67.

21  **"Melancholy and imbecility"** Ibid.

CHAPTER THREE: MARY GODWIN: CHILDHOOD AND
A NEW FAMILY (1801–1812)

23  **"Is it possible"** Paul, *Friends,* 2:58.

24  **Mary-Jane clasped her hands** Maud Rolleston, *Talks with Lady Shelley* (London:
Norwood Editions, 1897; reprint, 1978), 35.

25  **Mary Wollstonecraft's perfections** Godwin's *Memoirs of the Author of a Vindication of
the Rights of Woman,* published only ten months after Wollstonecraft's death, was
a complicated book, but it did publicize his adoration of his dead wife: he calls
her "a person of eminent merit" and one of the "illustrious dead" and asserts,
"There are not many individuals with whose character the public welfare and
improvement are more intimately connected, than with the author of the *Vindication of the Rights of Woman*" (1–3). The women he courted would have found it
difficult to escape Wollstonecraft's shadow.

25  **"Meet Mrs. Clairmont"** May 5, 1801, Victoria Myers, David O'Shaughnessy, and

Mark Philip, eds., *The Diary of William Godwin* (Oxford: Oxford Digital Library, http://godwindiary.bodleian.ox.ac.uk, 2010).

25  **lines drawn horizontally** September 10, 1797, ibid.

25  **a four-letter abbreviation ("Panc")** March 29, 1797, ibid.

25  **a series of dots, dashes** For a complete account of Godwin's code when referring to his sexual relationship with Wollstonecraft, see St. Clair, *The Godwins and the Shelleys,* 497–503.

25  **In the second week of July** July 13, 1801, Myers, O'Shaughnessy, and Philip, eds., *Diary of William Godwin.*

26  **"Manage and economize"** Paul, *Friends,* 2:75.

26  **"soured and spoiled"** Ibid., 77.

26  **"possession of a woman"** William Godwin, *An Enquiry Concerning Political Justice,* 3rd ed., 2 vols. (London: Robinson, 1798), 2:508.

26  **"Do not . . . get rid of all your faults"** Paul, *Friends,* 2:77.

26  **Her first love** Mary-Jane's real background has only recently been uncovered. For a comprehensive account of the current state of research on Mary-Jane's history, see Seymour, *MS,* 46–47.

27  **"second mamma"** Sunstein, *MS:R&R,* 32. See also Seymour, *MS,* 46.

27  **"excessive and romantic"** MWS to Maria Gisborne, October 30–November 17, 1824, Betty Bennett, ed., *The Letters of Mary Wollstonecraft Shelley,* 3 vols. (Baltimore: Johns Hopkins University Press, 1980–88).

28  **Mary-Jane's own daughter** One friend of the family recalled that Jane was "rather unmanageable." Florence Marshall, *The Life and Letters of Mary Wollstonecraft Shelley* (London: Bentley, 1889), 1:33–34.

28  **Poor Jane** For a detailed description of the Clairmont/Godwin conflicts, see Seymour, *MS,* 49–50.

28  **Mary would use "Clairmont"** Sunstein, *MS:R&R,* 35.

29  **It was not that Mary-Jane was always cruel** For a description of the complicated relationship between Mary-Jane and the Godwin girls, see Paul, *Friends,* 2:108; Seymour, *MS,* 47–50; Anne K. Mellor, *Mary Shelley: Her Life, Her Fiction, Her Monsters* (New York: Routledge, 1989), 12–13.

30  **On the evening of Coleridge's visit** Paul, *Friends,* 2:58.

30  **"Ah! Well a-day!"** Coleridge, ed. *Poetical Works of Samuel Taylor Coleridge,* 191.

31  **what he termed "deliquium"** This is Godwin's word, which begins to appear frequently in his diaries around this time. July 17, 1803, Myers, O'Shaughnessy, and Philip, eds., *Diary of William Godwin.*

31·  **a diagnosis of mental stress** Seymour, *MS,* 52.

32  **41 Skinner Street** Much of this description is based on Seymour's account, ibid., 57.

34  **Mary delivered her opinions** Sunstein, *MS:R&R,* 59. Sunstein describes how Mary enjoyed "disputations" with her peers and family.

34  **"les goddesses"** Aaron Burr, *The Private Journal of Aaron Burr, During His Residence of Four Years in Europe,* vol. 2, ed. Mathew L. Davis (New York: Harper & Brothers, 1838), 318.

34  **"The Influence of government"** Ibid., 307.

CHAPTER FOUR: MARY WOLLSTONECRAFT: HOXTON AND BATH (1774–1782)

36  **"My philosophy"** MW to Jane Arden, ?April 1781, *Letters MW,* 28.

36  **"began to consider"** Wollstonecraft, *Mary,* 8.

36 **Mary tried to confide** Wollstonecraft's heroine, Mary, attempts to tell her mother secrets, but her mother "laughs at" her. Ibid., 9.

38 **He introduced Mary to the ideas of John Locke** Godwin, *Memoirs*, 16–18. Later, Mary remembered how the Clares "took some pains to cultivate my understanding . . . they not only recommended proper books to me, but made me read them." *Letters MW*, MW to Jane Arden, early 1780, 24.

38 **"creatures of the same species and rank"** John Locke, *The Second Treatise of Government and a Letter Concerning Toleration,* ed. Paul Negri (Dover Thrift Editions reprint, 2002), 2.

38 **"no more power"** Ibid., 37.

38 **"sanctuary of liberty"** Edmund Burke, *The Works of the Right Honourable Edmund Burke,* 3 vols. (London: Rivington, 1801), 3:124.

39 **busily employed** Godwin, *Memoirs,* 21.

39 **By the time the visit was over** "Before the interview was concluded," Godwin would later write, "[Mary] had taken, in her heart, the vows of an eternal friendship." Ibid., 22.

39 **William Curtis** Gordon, *VAL,* 16. See Gordon for a more detailed description of Curtis's work.

39 **"masculine," Mary said** MW to Jane Arden, ?early 1780, *Letters MW,* 25.

39 **"I could dwell for ever"** MW to Jane Arden, ?early 1780, ibid. Mary's relationship with Fanny was "so fervent, as for years to have constituted the ruling passion of her mind." Godwin, *Memoirs,* 20.

40 **"I know this resolution"** MW to Jane Arden, ?early 1780, *Letters MW,* 25.

40 **"decent personal reserve"** Wollstonecraft, *Vindication of Woman,* 157–58.

40 **"the most rational"** MW to Jane Arden, ?early 1780, *Letters MW,* 25.

41 **the ill-tempered and arrogant Sarah Dawson** Godwin described Mrs. Dawson as having a "great peculiarity of temper." He was struck by Mary's ability to persevere despite her unpleasant employer. "Mary was not discouraged," Godwin wrote; she applied herself to "making her situation tolerable." *Memoirs,* 26.

41 **"Pain and disappointment"** MW to Jane Arden, ?early 1780, *Letters MW,* 22.

41 **"the unmeaning civilities"** MW to Jane Arden, ?April 1781, ibid., 28.

42 **Society ladies** For a discussion of women's fashion during the era, see Gordon, *VAL,* 24.

43 **"teaze" it** Ibid.

44 **"I wish to retire"** MW to Jane Arden, ?April 1781, ibid.

44 **Men were drawn to her** Todd, *MW:ARL,* 34.

45 **worried about the poor** These details are from Mary's description of her fictional character "Mary," which she explicitly based on her own life. See Wollstonecraft, *Mary,* 11.

45 **"I am just going to sup"** MW to Jane Arden, late summer ?1781, *Letters MW,* 35.

45 **"I think it murder"** MW to Jane Arden, ?late summer 1781, ibid., 34.

45 **enough "regard" for her family** MW to Eliza Wollstonecraft, 8/17/?1781, ibid., 32. Mary complains, "of late [my mother] has not even desired to be remembered to me.—Some time or the other, in this world or a better she may be convinced of my regard—and then may think I deserve not to be thought harshly of—."

45 **The letters they exchanged were angry** Ibid., 31–32. For example, see MW to Eliza Wollstonecraft, 8/17/?1781. MW wrote, "there is an air of irony through your whole epistle that hurts me exceedingly."

46 **Mary termed it dropsy** MW to Jane Arden, c. mid–late 1782, ibid., 36.

47 **"A little patience"** Godwin, *Memoirs,* 28.

47 **"Alas my daughter"** Wollstonecraft, *Mary,* 15.

47 **she was "fatigued"** MW to Jane Arden, c. mid–late 1782, *Letters MW,* 36.

48   **Eliza and Everina, on the other hand** Wollstonecraft, *Vindication of Woman*, 88. Wollstonecraft reflects on this situation, saying that when sisters live with brothers, it may go smoothly, until he marries, whereupon the sister "is viewed with averted looks as an intruder, an unnecessary burden."

48   **"done well, and married a worthy man"** MW to Jane Arden, c. late 1782, *Letters MW*, 38.

## CHAPTER FIVE: MARY GODWIN: SCOTLAND, AN "EYRY OF FREEDOM" (1810–1814)

50   **Mary-Jane had scraped together** Anne K. Mellor, *Mary Shelley*, 13.

50   **"torpor" that she could not** Quoted in Gordon, *VAL*, 418.

50   **depression as "indolence"** Paul, *Friends*, 2:214.

50   **"bold" ways** Ibid.

50   **"imperious"** Ibid.

50   **"Godwin . . . extended"** Paul, *Friends*, 1:36–38.

50   **Even Godwin admitted** Too often, Godwin wrote, he would "proclaim his wishes and commands in a way somewhat sententious and authoritative, and occasionally . . . utter his censures with seriousness and emphasis." Mrs. Julian Marshall, *The Life and Letters of Mary Wollstonecraft Shelley*, 2 vols. (London: Richard Bentley & Son, 1889), 28.

51   **"I believe she has nothing"** Ibid., 29.

51   **"a thousand anxieties"** Ibid.

52   **The streams in Scotland** Dorothy Wordsworth makes repeated references to the children's bare feet, comparing their "freedom" to the restrictions endured by English children. "[The Scottish children] were all without shoes and stockings, which, making them fearless of hurting or being hurt, gave a freedom to the action of their limbs which I never saw in England children." *Recollections of a Tour Made in Scotland, 1803*, ed. Carol Kyros Walker (New Haven: Yale University Press, 1997), 127.

52   **"Scotland is the country"** Ibid, 55.

53   **"blank and dreary"** Mary Shelley, introduction to *Frankenstein* (New York: Collier, 1978), 7–8.

53   **her quiet manner** Godwin wrote a long letter to William Baxter to explain his daughter's faults. He found her incomprehensible, he admitted, because she was often so silent. Godwin to W. Baxter, August 6, 1812, Marshall, *The Life and Letters of Mary Wollstonecraft Shelley*, 1:27–29.

54   **She revered Charlotte Corday** Seymour, *MS*, 74.

54   **"the devil"** Ibid., 76.

55   **Isabella even dreamed** See Seymour for a more detailed description of David Booth and Isabella Baxter, Booth's house, and Broughty Ferry. Ibid., 77.

55   **her wobbly** Ibid., 76.

57   **post-death payments** For a more thorough explanation of this financial practice, see ibid., 88, and Richard Holmes, *Shelley: The Pursuit* (1974; New York: New York Review of Books, 1994), 219, 223–25. Citations are to the New York Review of Books edition.

58   **"Marriage, as now understood"** Godwin, *Political Justice*, 2:507.

58   **But everything changed** For a more complete description of Shelley's relationship with Harriet, see Holmes, *Shelley*, 222–29.

58   **"a rash and heartless union"** PBS to Thomas Hogg, October 1814, *The Letters of Percy Bysshe Shelley*, ed. Frederick Jones (Oxford: Clarendon Press, 1964), 1:402.

59  **a hawk, an eclipse** PBS to Hogg, October, 1814, ibid. This account is based on Shelley's version of events in which he was awaiting a "change."

59  **As her mother had observed** Wollstonecraft discusses this issue in the chapter entitled "Unfortunate Situation of Females, Fashionably Educated, and Left Without a Fortune" in *Thoughts on the Education of Daughters* (London: 1788), 69–78.

**CHAPTER SIX: MARY WOLLSTONECRAFT: INDEPENDENCE (1783–1785)**

60  **"fits of phrensy"** MW to Everina, c. late 1783, *Letters MW*, 39.

61  **"Her ideas"** Ibid.

61  **"lion or a spannial"** Ibid., 41.

61  **"I don't know"** Ibid., 40.

62  **"a wife being as much a man's property"** Wollstonecraft, *Maria*, 118.

62  **she had been "ill-used"** MW to Everina, [January 5, 1784], *Letters MW*, 43.

63  **"I can't help"** MW to Everina, c. late 1783, ibid., 41.

63  **"even tho' the contrary is clear"** Ibid.

63  **reassuring herself** Mary wrote Everina, "The poor brat it had got hold of my affections, some time or other I hope we shall get it." MW to Everina, [January 11, 18, or 25, 1784], ibid., 45.

63  **"Those who would save Bess"** MW to Everina, c. late 1783, ibid., 41.

64  **gnawing her wedding ring** MW to Everina, c. January 1784, ibid., 43.

64  **"I hope Bishop will not discover us"** MW to Everina, [c. January 1784], ibid., 43–44.

64  **"endeavor to make Mrs. B. happy"** MW to Everina, Tuesday night [c. January, 1784], ibid., 49.

65  **interring them in asylums** Gordon cites the historian Lawrence Stone, who writes, "One of the most terrible fates that could be inflicted on a wife by a husband was to be confined . . . in a private madhouse . . . where she might linger for . . . years." *VAL*, 33–34.

65  **"the shameful incendiary"** MW to Everina, [c. January 1784], *Letters MW*, 47.

65  **food and wine** Mrs. Claire brought "pye and a bottle." MW to Everina, [c. January 1784], ibid., 50.

65  **"Let not some small difficulties"** MW to Jane Arden, ?April 1781, ibid., 29–30.

66  **Hannah Burgh offered Mary** Gordon calls Mrs. Burgh a "fairy godmother." *VAL*, 40.

67  **a shady green** See Gordon's description, Ibid., 42.

68  **to think for themselves** Wollstonecraft first outlines her educational philosophy in *Daughters*, 22.

68  **"I am sick"** Ibid., 52.

68  **"a different mode of treatment"** Mary Wollstonecraft, *Original Stories* (London: 1906), xviii.

69  **a tragedy for all humankind** Price argued, "The American Revolution may prove the most important step in the progressive course of human improvement." Richard Price, *Observations on the Importance of the American Revolution* (Bedford, MA: Applewood Books; reprint, 2009), 50–52, 6.

69  **healthy eating habits** Wollstonecraft wrote, "A moderate quantity of proper food recruits our exhausted spirits." *Original Stories from Real Life* (London: 1796), 39.

69  **Instead of shaming** According to Godwin, "It was kindness and sympathy alone" that guided her teaching. He said, "She never was concerned in the education of one child, who was not personally attached to her, and earnestly concerned not to incur her displeasure." Godwin, *Memoirs*, 35, 45.

69   **compose their own stories** Wollstonecraft, *Daughters,* 34. Wollstonecraft despised what she termed "exterior accomplishments." *Daughters,* 29.

69   **"Let there be no disguise"** Ibid., 45–46.

69   **"the beaten track"** Ibid., 25.

69   **trifling mistakes** Wollstonecraft wrote, "Accidents or giddy mistakes are too frequently punished." Ibid., 15.

69   **Eliza and Everina disliked the long days** MW to George Blood, July 20 [1785], *Letters MW,* 56.

70   **They did not like being left** This summary is based on Todd's description of the sisters in *MW:ARL,* 62.

71   **smoothing feathers** For a more complete explanation of Fanny's role in the school and the Wollstonecraft sisters' behavior, see Gordon, *VAL,* 61.

71   **"He is much fatter"** quoted in Todd, *MW:ARL,* 62.

72   **"I could as soon"** MW to George Blood, July 20 [1785], *Letters MW,* 55.

72   **Londoners sneered** Abigail Adams to Cotton Tufts, August 18, 1785, *The Adams Family Correspondence,* ed. Lyman H. Butterfield, Marc Friedlaender, and Richard Alan Ryerson, 6 vols. (Boston: Massachusetts Historical Society, 1993), 6:283.

72   **"the whole scope"** Quoted in David McCullough, *John Adams* (New York: Simon & Schuster, 2001), 417.

72   **"in the new code"** Abigail Adams to John Adams, March 31, 1776, *The Letters of John and Abigail Adams,* ed. Frank Shuffleton (New York: Penguin, 2003), 91.

73   **"disciple of Wollstonecraft"** John Adams to Abigail Adams, January 22, 1794, *Adams Family Correspondence,* 6:254.

73   **"I thank you, Miss W."** John Adams, notations on Mary Wollstonecraft, *An Historical and Moral View of the Origin and Progress of the French Revolution,* in the Boston Public Library Rare Books Department, available online at https://archive .org/details/historicalmoralvoowoll.

73   **Four hours after Mary walked in the door** This account is based on a longer version in Todd, *MW:ARL,* 68.

73   **"life seems a burden"** MW to George Blood, February 4, 1786, *Letters MW,* 65.

## CHAPTER SEVEN: MARY GODWIN: "THE SUBLIME AND RAPTUROUS MOMENT" (1814)

74   **he had seen "manifestations"** Shelley wrote, "Manifestations of my approaching change tinged my waking thoughts. . . . A train of visionary events arranged themselves in my imagination. . . ." PBS to Thomas Hogg, October 3, 1814, *Letters PBS,* 1:402.

74   **a flirtatious sidelong glance** Sunstein, *MS:R&R,* 58.

75   **"wild, intellectual, unearthly"** Holmes, *Pursuit,* 172.

75   **"thoughtful" greenish-gray eyes** Percy Shelley, dedication to "The Revolt of Islam," *The Poetical Works of Coleridge, Shelley, and Keats* (Philadelphia: Thomas, Cowperthwait & Co., 1844), 252–53.

76   **"of sunny and burnished"** *The Journals of Claire Clairmont,* ed. Marion Kingston Stocking (Cambridge, MA: Harvard University Press, 1968), 431.

76   **"very much like her mother"** Harriet Shelley to Catherine Nugent, ?October 1814, quoted in Seymour, *MS,* 79.

76   **"They say that thou wert lovely"** Percy Shelley, dedication to "The Revolt of Islam," *Poetical Works of Coleridge, Shelley, and Keats,* 253.

77   **"A lamp"** Ibid.

77   **Godwin nodded** According to Shelley's friend Hogg, Godwin flattered Shelley and sought to win his favor before the poet ran away with Mary. Holmes, *Pursuit,* 227.

78  **"while the fair young lady"** Rosalie Glynn Grylls, *Claire Clairmont, Mother of Byron's Allegra* (London: John Murray, 1939), appendix D, 277.

78  **"the door was partially and softly opened"** T. J. Hogg, *The Life of Percy Bysshe Shelley* (London: 1858), 2:538.

78  **their favorite place** Paul, *Friends*, 2:215.

78  **Here, they read aloud** Holmes speculates about their conversations in *Pursuit*, 230.

78  **"pale ghost"** Mary Shelley frequently used this phrase in her fiction to denote a child's mourning for a dead parent. See *Lodore* (London: 1835), 127; *Falkner* (London: 1837; Google Books, 2009), 99; http://books.google.com/books?id=cZk _AAAAYAAJ&dq=Falkner&source=gbs_navlinks.

79  **"in genuine elevation"** PBS to Hogg, October 3–4, 1814, *Letters PBS*, 1:401–3.

80  **In mid-June** Holmes, *Pursuit*, 231. The dates were June 19–29.

80  **"by a spirit"** PBS to Hogg, October 4, 1814, *Letters PBS*, 1:403.

80  **"full ardour"** MWS, "Life of Shelley" (1823), Bodleian, facsimile and transcript ed. A. M. Weinberg, Bodleian Shelley Manuscripts, 22 pt 2 (1997), 266–67. Seymour, *MS*, 92.

81  **"How beautiful and calm"** *Poetical Works of Coleridge, Shelley, and Keats*, 252.

81  **"But our church"** Ibid., 403.

82  **Shelley claimed** For more on Shelley's fabrications, see Seymour, *MS*, 92.

82  **Certainly, Shelley *felt*** As Seymour writes, Shelley liked to "let his imagination loose on the past." Ibid.

82  **"Mary was determined"** Harriet Shelley to Catherine Nugent, November 20, 1814, *Letters PBS*, 1:421. Harriet's letters are provided in chronological notes to Shelley's letters. For a more comprehensive explanation of the different accounts of Mary and Shelley's love affair, see Seymour, *MS*, 93.

83  **In the last week of July** This account is based on Mrs. Godwin's letter to Lady Mountcashell (Margaret King), August 20, 1814, in Edward Dowden, *The Life of Percy Bysshe Shelley* (London, 1886), 2:544. Also in Holmes, *Pursuit*, 233.

83  **Shelley left** From Mrs. Godwin's account. See also Seymour, *MS*, 97–98.

84  **"after the decay"** *Poetical Works of Coleridge, Shelley, and Keats*, 374.

84  **"Love is free"** Ibid.

84  **"This book is sacred to me"** St. Clair, *Godwins and the Shelleys*, 366.

85  **"I remember your words"** Ibid., 358.

85  **chopped down his father's precious fir trees** Holmes, *Pursuit*, 23.

85  **poked holes** Ibid., 3.

85  **used gunpowder to blow up** Ibid., 13, 24.

85  **set the butler** Ibid., 3.

85  **"collect" his little sisters** Hellen Shelley to Jane [Williams] Hogg in Hogg, *Life of Percy Bysshe Shelley*, 9.

85  **he ignited his parents' baronial estate** Holmes, *Pursuit*, 18.

86  **solar microscope** Ibid., 17.

86  **One night, he sneaked into a church** Ibid., 24–25.

CHAPTER EIGHT: MARY WOLLSTONECRAFT: *ON THE EDUCATION OF DAUGHTERS (1785–1787)*

87  **"I can scarcely find"** MW to George Blood, June 18, [1786], *Letters MW*, 72.

87  **"My hopes of happiness"** MW to George Blood, May 1, [1786], ibid., 68.

87  **like "furies"** Ibid., 69.

87  **One night she had a dream** Ibid., 72.

88  **"the diligent improvement"** John Hewlett, *Sermons on Various Subjects*, 4th ed., 2 vols. (London: Johnson, 1798), 1:22.

88    **this is what God was** Ibid., 10.

89    **"Few are the modes"** Wollstonecraft, *Daughters*, 70–71.

89    **For the time** As Kirstin Hanley argues, "Wollstonecraft appropriates and revises the work of eighteenth-century writers on the subject of women's education such as Jean-Jacques Rousseau and Dr. John Gregory, epitomizing a feminist didactic approach later (re)deployed by Jane Austen and Charlotte Brontë." *Redefining Didactic Traditions: Mary Wollstonecraft and Feminist Discourses of Appropriation, 1749–1847* (unpublished doctoral dissertation, University of Pittsburgh, 2007). However, some scholars have declared there is little of interest to be found in *Thoughts on the Education of Daughters*. "There is really little originality in its contents or striking merit in the method of treating them," says Elizabeth Robins Pennell, Wollstonecraft's first biographer, setting the tone for future critics. *Mary Wollstonecraft* (1884; Fairford, UK: Echo Library, 2008), 68.

89    **girls too "delicate"** William McCarthy and Elizabeth Kraft, eds., *The Poems of Anna Letitia Barbauld* (Athens: University of Georgia Press, 1994), 77.

89    **"bold, independent"** Hannah More, *The Complete Works of Hannah More*, 2 vols. (New York: 1856), 2:568.

90    **the flowery style** Wollstonecraft, *Vindication of Woman*, 26.

92    **Mary felt she had entered a prison** To Everina, she wrote that she was "going into the Bastille." October 30 [1786], *Letters MW*, 84.

92    **This was precisely the kind of excess** She wrote Everina that Mitchelstown "had a solemn kind of stupidity." Ibid.

93    **the rape of Proserpina** Gordon discusses the implications of this painting in *VAL*, 84.

93    **Mary had heard whispers** Ibid., 93.

93    **"a host of females"** MW to Everina, October 30, 1786, *Letters MW*, 84–85.

94    **"Wild," she thought** Ibid.

94    **"no softness in her manners"** MW to Everina, October 30, [1786], ibid., 86.

94    **in baby talk** MW wrote Everina that Lady Kingsborough "us[ed] infantine expression" when speaking to her dogs, October 30, [1786], ibid., 85.

94    **Mary, appalled at her ladyship's cold heart** She wrote Everina, "Her ladyship visited [the girls] in a formal way—though their situation called forth my tenderness—and I endeavored to amuse them." November 17, [1786], ibid., 91.

94    **"very much afraid"** MW to Eliza Bishop, November 5, [1786], ibid., 88.

94    **Margaret was intelligent** MW wrote Eliza that the girl had a "wonderful capacity." Ibid.

94    **"heap of rubbish"** MW to Eliza Bishop, November 5, [1786], *Letters MW*, 88.

95    **"haughti[ness]" and "condescension"** MW to Everina, March 3, [1787], ibid., 108.

95    **"betwixt and between"** MW to Eliza Bishop, November 5, [1786], ibid., 88.

95    **"between forty and fifty"** MW to Everina, March 25, [1787], ibid., 116.

96    **"disgust to the follies of dress"** Margaret King's unpublished autobiography, quoted in ibid., 124 n286.

96    **"I fell into . . . a violent fit"** MW to Everina, February 12, [1787], ibid., 104.

96    **"Rousseau declares that a woman should never"** Wollstonecraft, *Vindication of Woman*, 43.

96    **"the mind of a woman"** "Advertisement" in Wollstonecraft, *Mary*, 3.

97    **her heroine would not be a "Sophie"** Ibid.

97    **"that world where"** Ibid., 53.

97    **"She had two"** Ibid., 6.

98    **"freed her mind"** Margaret's unpublished autobiography, quoted in Janet Todd, *MW:ARL*, 116.

CHAPTER NINE: MARY GODWIN: THE BREAK (1814)

100    **who held her tightly** Mary and Shelley kept a joint journal until Shelley's death. In Shelley's account of their elopement, he wrote, "she was in my arms." PBS, July 28, 1814. Paula Feldman and Diana Scott-Kilvert, eds., *The Journals of Mary Wollstonecraft Shelley 1814–1844* (Baltimore: Johns Hopkins University Press, 1987; reprint, 1995), 6.

101    **"Mary, look"** July 28, 1814, *Journals MWS,* 7.

101    **"a fat lady"** July 29, 1814, ibid.

101    **freedom from slavery** PBS, July 29, 1814, ibid., 8.

101    **Mary-Jane was a dangerous** For an example of one such letter, see Mary-Jane Godwin to Lady Mountcashell, November 15, 1814, in Dowden, *Life of Shelley,* appendix, 2:546–48.

102    **Harriet, also launched** Seymour, *MS,* 100.

102    **He had won** This is Seymour's point. She argues that Shelley believed "Tyranny had been vanquished." Ibid., 99.

103    **Buttoned up to the chin** Seymour writes, "the primly dressed and bonneted English girls felt embarrassed and out of place among the revealing, clinging gowns of Parisian ladies." *MS,* 105.

103    **"too happy"** August 2, 1814, *Journals MWS,* 9.

103    **their "bridal night"** "The Revolt of Islam." In this, Shelley's second long poem after "Queen Mab," Shelley's description of the romantic union of Laon and Cyntha is based on his relationship with Mary. The passages used to describe Mary and Shelley's first night together are from Laon and Cyntha's first night of passion: "eager lips," stanza xxxiii; "her white arms," stanza xxix; "I felt the blood," stanza xxxiv; "speechless swoon," stanza xxxiv. Thomas Hutchinson, ed. *The Complete Poetical Works of Percy Bysshe Shelley,* 2 vols., vol. 1 (Oxford: Oxford University Press, 1914).

104    **Mary told Shelley** In their joint journal, Shelley wrote, "[Mary] feels as if our love would alone suffice to resist the invasions of calamity. She rested on my bosom & seemed even indifferent to take sufficient food for the sustenance of life." August 7, 1814, *Journals MWS,* 11.

104    **"delightful" to walk** August 7, 1814, ibid.

105    **"filth, misery, and famine"** PBS to HS, August 13, 1814, *Letters PBS,* 1:392.

105    **rats ran across Jane's face** August 12, 1814, *Journals MWS,* 13.

106    **"the glorious founders"** William Godwin, *Fleetwood* (London: 1853), 74.

106    **"firm and constant"** PBS to HS, August 13, 1814, *Letters PBS,* 1:392.

106    **"Their immensity"** August 19, 1814, *Journals MWS,* 17.

107    **Mary had lied** August 20, 1814, Marion Kingston Stocking, ed., *The Journals of Claire Clairmont* (Cambridge, MA: Harvard University Press, 1968). Jane, who changed her name to Claire, added this story when she revised her original journal in 1820. The original diary is in the British Library (Ashley 394).

107    **ridiculously puritanical** Ibid.

107    **the Swiss "are rich"** August 25, 1814, ibid.

108    **"conjectur[ing] the astonishment"** August 26, 1814, *Journals MWS,* 20.

108    **forests of beech** Godwin, *Fleetwood,* 73.

108    **they had to wait** August 26, 1814, *Journals MWS,* 20.

108    **"Our only wish"** August 28, 1814, ibid.

109    **There was a disturbing legend** For a more complete retelling of the legend, see Seymour, *MS,* 11.

CHAPTER TEN: MARY WOLLSTONECRAFT: LONDON (1786–1787)

112 **"philosophical sloven"** John Knowles, *The Life and Writings of Henry Fuseli* (London: 1831), 164.

114 **"despair and vexations"** This is a phrase that Mary used later that fall to describe her situation. MW to Everina, November 7, [1787], *Letters MW,* 139.

115 **Between 1750 and 1801** Roy Porter, *London: A Social History* (Cambridge, MA: Harvard University Press, 2001), 131.

115 **"Here you have the Advantage of solitude"** Henry Fielding, *The Works of Henry Fielding, with Memoir of the Author,* ed. Thomas Roscoe (Oxford: Oxford University Press, 1845), 121. Also available on Google Books, http://books.google.com /books?id=JGYOAAAAQAAJ&printsec=frontcover&source=gbs_ge_summary _r&cad=0#v=onepage&q&f=false.

115 **"the clouds of Stinking Breathes"** Quoted in Porter, *London: A Social History,* 162.

115 **"a common and most noisome sewer"** Quoted in ibid.

115 **the average age** Porter, *English Society in the Eighteenth Century,* 13.

116 **"whoever is sick"** Quoted in Porter, *London: A Social History,* 165.

116 **the river "was almost hidden"** Ibid., 138.

116 **"a long wintry forest"** Quoted in ibid., 136.

118 **"I am then going to be the first of a new genus"** MW to Everina, November 7, [1787], *Letters MW,* 139.

118 **But Mary was the first female writer** "Wollstonecraft differed from previous literary women," writes the scholar Mary Waters, because "her connection with Johnson was not simply that of an author to the bookseller who purchased her finished manuscripts for publication. . . . Rather, Wollstonecraft had engaged with Johnson as a staff writer who would accept the work assigned to her and in return could count on a steady supply of literary work coming her way." *British Women Writers and the Profession of Literary Criticism 1789–1832* (New York: Palgrave Macmillan, 2004), 86.

118 **"I have determined on one thing"** MW to George Blood, May 16, [1788], *Letters MW,* 154.

119 **"disasters and difficulties"** MW to George Blood, March 3, [1788], ibid., 148.

119 **"If I have ever any money"** MW to Everina, March 22, [1788], ibid., 152.

121 **Mary made many dramatic departures** My discussion of Wollstonecraft's translation is based on Todd's exegesis in *MW:ARL,* 135–36.

121 **like "fetters"** Christian Salzmann, *Elements of Morality, for the Use of Children,* 3 vols. (London: 1792), 2:106.

121 **"[He] put her hair in papers"** Ibid., 106–7.

122 **"Why do you wish to go"** Ibid., 114–17.


CHAPTER ELEVEN: MARY GODWIN: LONDON AND
            BISHOPSGATE (1814–1815)

124 **"was sick as death"** September 11, 1814, *Journals CC.*

125 **One afternoon, Mary-Jane** Holmes, *Pursuit,* 251.

125 **Furious at the pain** Sunstein, *MS:R&R,* 88–89. Shelley wrote Mary, "I have been shocked and staggered by Godwin's cold injustice." October 24, 1814, *Letters PBS,* 1:420.

126 **he would have to be everything** Mary wrote to Shelley, "hug your own Mary to your heart perhaps she will one day have a father till then be everything to me love," October 28, 1814, Bennett, ed., *Letters MWS,* 1:3.

126  "the witching hour" October 7, 1814, *Journals MWS*, 32.

126  "Just as the dawn" Ibid., 33.

128  he "sheltered himself" Mary Shelley, *Notes to the Complete Poetical Works of Percy Bysshe Shelley* (1839; Project Gutenberg, 2002, http://www.gutenberg.org /files/4695/4695.txt).

128  she also decided to change her name For a discussion of why Jane changed her name to Claire, see Deirdre Coleman, "Claire Clairmont and Mary Shelley: Identification and Rivalry Within the 'Tribe of the Otaheite Philosophers,'" *Women's Writing* 6, no. 3 (1999), 309–28, http://www.tandfonline.com/doi/abs/10.1080 /09699089900200075?journalCode=rwow20#preview (accessed September 18, 2013).

129  "I made one dark, the other fair" Jean-Jacques Rousseau, *The Confessions of Jean-Jacques Rousseau* (New York: Modern Library, 1945), 444.

130  "community of women" Marion Kingston Stocking, the editor of Claire's journals, suggests that Claire's idea of a "community of women" may have come from reading Ludvig Holberg's book *A Journey to the World Under-Ground*, which describes an underground society in which women are superior. October 7, 1814, *Journals MWS*, 32 n1.

130  She dreamed of writing a novel *Journals CC*, 40.

130  "Let every female" James Lawrence, introduction to *The Empire of the Nairs; or, The Rights of Women: An Utopian Romance, in Twelve Books*, 4 vols. (London: T. Hookham, 1811), I, xvii.

131  "ought to be ushered" December 6, 1814, *Journals MWS*, 50.

132  "love of Wisdom" November 29, 1814, ibid., 48.

132  weak and confused Ibid. For more complaints about Hogg, see November 20, 1814, ibid.

132  "I . . . love him" MWS to Hogg, January 24, 1815, *Letters MWS*, 1:9.

133  Mary backpedaled See Seymour's account of the complicated relationship of Shelley, Hogg, and Mary in *MS*, 125–30.

133  "My baby is dead" MWS to Hogg, [March 6, 1815], *Letters MWS*, 1:11.

133  "Dream that my little baby" March 19, 1815, *Journals MWS*, 70.

134  witty little notes Referring to herself as "the Dormouse," Mary wrote, "The Dormouse is going to take a long ramble today among green fields & solitary lanes as happy as any little Animal could be in finding herself in her native nests again," MWS to Hogg, April 25, 1815, *Letters MWS*, 1:14.

134  Shelley's "friend" May 12, 1815, *Journals MWS*, 78.

135  "so much discontent" CC to FG, May 5, 1815, *Letters CC*.

135  her "regeneration" May [date?], 1815, *Journals MWS*, 79.

136  "Mary, have I dined?" quoted in Sunstein, *MS:R&R*, 104.

136  According to Hogg *Life of Shelley*, 2:320–22.

137  "hereditary aristocracy" quoted in Sunstein, *MS:R&R*, 105.

137  "I never before felt the integrity" PBS to Hogg, October 4, 1814, *Letters PBS*, 1:403.

137  "You alone reconcile me" PBS to MWS, November 4, 1814, ibid., 1:419.

138  "elfin Knight" May 1815, *Journals MWS*, 80.

139  "a poet's heart" Mary Shelley, "Notes on Alastor, by Mrs. Shelley" in Percy Bysshe Shelley, *The Works of Percy Bysshe Shelley*, ed. Roger Ingpen and Walter E. Peck (1816; London: Scribner's, 1926–30), 10 vols., 1:198.

139  the issue that most gripped her Seymour provides a comprehensive account of Mary's reading on slavery. *MS*, 138–39.

139  "My astonishment" PBS to Godwin, March 1816, *Letters PBS*, 1:460.

140   **the annual income of skilled** Brian Mitchell, *British Historical Statistics* (Cambridge: Cambridge University Press, 1988), 153.

## CHAPTER TWELVE: MARY WOLLSTONECRAFT: THE FIRST VINDICATION (1787–1791)

142   **"the HISTORIANS of the Republic"** Stuart Andrews, *The British Periodical Press and the French Revolution, 1789–99* (New York: Palgrave, 2000), 157.

142   **"add to the stock"** Gerald Tyson, *Joseph Johnson: A Liberal Publisher* (Iowa City: University of Iowa Press, 1979), 99.

143   **were "trash"** MW to Joseph Johnson, [c. July 1788], *Letters MW,* 156.

143   **"unnatural characters"** *Analytical Review* 2/1789, in Janet Todd and Marilyn Butler, eds., *The Works of Mary Wollstonecraft* (New York: New York University Press, 1989), 7:82–83.

143   **"scribbling women"** Mitzi Myers, "Mary Wollstonecraft's Literary Reviews," in *The Cambridge Companion to Mary Wollstonecraft,* ed. Claudia Johnson (Cambridge: Cambridge University Press, 2002), 85.

143   **"poison the minds"** quoted in ibid.

143   **"Why is virtue to be always rewarded"** *Analytical Review,* in Todd and Butler, ed., *Works of Mary Wollstonecraft,* 7:228.

143   **This does not mean that Mary was against sentiment** See Myers, "Mary Wollstonecraft's Literary Reviews," in *Cambridge Companion to Mary Wollstonecraft,* 84.

144   **"indiscriminately from tea cups"** Knowles, *The Life and Writings of Henry Fuseli* (London: 1831), 165.

145   **"timid, mean"** quoted in Todd, *MW:ARL,* 138.

145   **"an heterogeneous"** *Analytical Review* in Todd and Butler, ed., *Works of Mary Wollstonecraft,* 7:19.

145   **"Ye dungeons"** "The Task" in William Cowper and James Thomson, *The Works of Cowper and Thomson* (Philadelphia: 1832), 88.

145   **"Advice is received from Paris"** St. Clair, *Godwins and the Shelleys,* 41.

146   **"I have seen, within a year"** Quoted in Kirstin Olsen, *Daily Life in Eighteenth-Century England* (Westport, CT: Greenwood, 1999), 10.

146   **"hailed the dawn"** *The French Revolution,* 213. Wollstonecraft wrote these words a few years later, when she had come to view the taking of the Bastille as a far more complicated event than she had at first hoped. Ultimately, she would argue that the taking of the prison unleashed the violence that would result in the Terror. But she always acknowledged its fall as an important event in the history of the Revolution and remembered how she too had believed that it would result in greater freedom for the French and for all humankind. Diane Jacobs provides a thorough analysis of Wollstonecraft's graduated endorsement of the Revolution. She also connects Wollstonecraft's "melting" over the Bastille with her new relationship with Henry Fuseli. *Her Own Woman: The Life of Mary Wollstonecraft* (New York: Simon & Schuster, 2001), 88.

146   **his liaisons with men and women** Todd, *MW:ARL,* 153.

147   **"phallic coiffures"** Simon Schama, *A History of Britain,* vol. 3, *The Fate of Empire, 1776–2000* (New York: Miramax Books, Hyperion, 2002), 76.

147   **Recent scholars have even suggested** Lyndall Gordon writes, "Is it possible that Mary stumbled on love at the heart of the lifelong intimacy of Johnson and Fuseli? Same sex love could explain Mary's silence on the subject of Fuseli. . . ." *VAL,* 386–87.

148    **"masculine" style** Wollstonecraft, *Vindication of Woman,* 26–27.

148    **ready to embrace the new ideals** Although many scholars agree with this depiction of Wollstonecraft as a pioneering figure in the Romantic movement, there are some notable exceptions. Barbara Taylor argues, "Not much is to be gained, in my view, from classifying Wollstonecraft as a romantic or pre-romantic writer. Her debt to earlier eighteenth-century sources for her 'romantic' themes is readily traced . . . and treating her ideas as anticipations of later romantic motifs is less illuminating to my mind than understanding them in their own terms." *Mary Wollstonecraft and the Feminist Imagination* (Cambridge: Cambridge University Press, 2003), 282 n208.

148    **"artless energy"** *Analytic Review* 7 (May 1790). Jacobs provides a comprehensive discussion of the change in Wollstonecraft's outlook during this period; see *HOW,* 89.

149    **to make Fuseli's wife uneasy** "an uneasy mind," Todd, *MW:ARL,* 154.

149    **"My die is cast!"** MW to Everina, September 4, [1790], *Letters MW,* 178.

150    **"precedent, authority, and example"** Edmund Burke, *Reflections on the Revolution in France, and on the Proceedings in Certain Societies in London* (London: J. Dodsley, 1790), 45.

151    **"turgid bombast"** Mary Wollstonecraft, *A Vindication of the Rights of Men in a Letter to the Right Honourable Edmund Burke* (London: J. Johnson, 1790), 62.

151    **"flowers of rhetoric"** Ibid., 6. Wollstonecraft would also use this argument against the "flowers of rhetoric" in *A Vindication of the Rights of Woman.* As Laura Runge writes, "Wollstonecraft employs her strongest rhetoric to counteract the persuasiveness of gallantry, 'those pretty feminine phrases, which the men condescendingly use to soften our slavish dependence.' . . . She exposes the illusion of female mastery that is ambiguously encoded in the language of gallantry by emphasizing how the seductive forms of language actually infantilize women and circumscribe their agency." *Gender and Language in British Literary Criticism* (Cambridge: Cambridge University Press, 2005), 24.

151    **"[The poor] must respect"** Ibid., 135–36.

151    **"Charity is not"** Ibid., 11.

151    **"champion of property"** Ibid., 19.

152    **"piqued her pride"** Godwin, *Memoirs,* 78.

152    **"hyena in petticoats"** Horace Walpole to Hannah More, January 24, 1795. Helen Toynbee and Paget Toynbee, ed., *The Letters of Horace Walpole: Fourth Earl of Oxford,* vol. 15 (Oxford: Clarendon, 1905), 337.

152    **"The *rights of men* asserted by a fair lady!"** *The Gentleman's Magazine* 1791, 151, http://books.google.com/books?id=1K5JAAAAYAAJ&pg=PA151&lpg=PA151&dq=The+rights+of+men+asserted+by+a+fair+lady!+.

153    **"happy in having such an advocate"** Dr. Price to MW, January 17, 1790, Carl H. Pforzheimer Collection of Shelley and His Circle (New York: New York Public Library, Astor, Lenox, and Tilden Foundations, 1822).

CHAPTER THIRTEEN: MARY GODWIN: "MAD, BAD AND DANGEROUS TO KNOW" (1816)

155    **"mad, bad and dangerous to know"** Quoted in Paul Douglas, *The Life of Lady Caroline Lamb* (New York: Palgrave Macmillan, 2004), 104.

156    **"I can never resist"** Claire's remarks about marriage come directly after she has quoted Dante's "inscription over the gate of Hell 'Lasciate ogni speranza, voi ch'entrate' [Abandon hope, all who enter here]. I think it is a most admirable description of marriage. The subject makes me prolix." CC to Byron, [March or

April 1816], Marion Kingston Stocking, ed., *The Clairmont Correspondence: Letters of Claire Clairmont, Charles Clairmont, and Fanny Imlay Godwin* (Baltimore: Johns Hopkins University Press, 1995), 31.

158 **"There be none of Beauty's daughters"** "Stanzas for Music," Lord Byron, *The Works of Lord Byron,* ed. Ernest Hartley Coleridge (1900; Project Gutenberg, 2007, http://www.gutenberg.org/files/21811/21811.txt).

158 **But his enthusiasm soon ebbed** For a summary of their relationship with excerpts from their letters, see Mayne, *Byron,* 62–65.

158 **Mary did love Byron's poetry** See Seymour on Mary, Shelley, and Claire's admiration of Byron, *MS,* 148–49.

158 **"But I am exclusively thine"** Mary Shelley's inscription in "Queen Mab," quoted in St. Clair, *Godwins and the Shelleys,* 366.

159 **"The glance"** Byron, "To Thyrza" in *The Works of Lord Byron,* ed. Coleridge.

159 **"I have pledged"** Mary Shelley's inscription in "Queen Mab," quoted in St. Clair, *Godwins and the Shelleys,* 366.

159 **She had some trepidation** In a letter to Byron, preparing him for the meeting with Mary, Claire urged him to be on time: "On Thursday Evening I waited nearly a quarter of an hour in your hall, which though I may overlook the disagreeableness—she, who is not in love would not. . . . She is very curious to see you." CC to Byron, April 21, 1816, *TCC,* 39.

160 **"Mary is delighted"** CC to Byron, April 21, 1816, ibid.

161 **"desert my native country"** PBS to Godwin, February 21, 1816, *Letters PBS,* 1:453.

161 **"morbidly sensitive"** PBS to Godwin, December 1816, *Letters PBS,* 1:460.

161 **"You will I dare say"** CC to Byron, May 6, 1816, *TCC,* 43.

162 **"the year without a summer"** For an overview of the worldwide effects of the eruption, see Henry Stommel and Elizabeth Stommel, *Volcano Weather: The Story of the Year Without a Summer* (Los Angeles: Seven Seas Press, 1983).

162 **"Never was a scene"** MWS to Fanny, May 17, 1816, *Letters MWS,* 1:13.

163 **"blue as the heavens"** Ibid.

163 **Elise Duvillard** For a more complete portrait of Elise, see Seymour, *MS,* 152.

164 **"We do not enter"** MWS to Fanny, May 17, 1816, *Letters MWS,* 1:13.

164 **"the delightful scent"** Ibid.

164 **"Look . . . at the innumerable fish"** Mary Shelley, *Frankenstein,* 164.

165 **He and the emperor had "soar[ed]"** "Ode to Napoleon," in Byron, *The Works of Lord Byron* (1828), 513. For more on Byron's adulation of Napoleon, see John Clubbe, "Between Emperor and Exile: Byron and Napoleon 1814–1816," *Napoleonic Scholarship: The Journal of the International Napoleonic Society* 1 (April 1997), http://www.napoleonicsociety.com/english/scholarship97/c_byron.html.

165 **"Childe Harolded"** J. G. Lockhart, *Memoirs of Sir Walter Scott,* vol. 5 (Edinburgh: Adam and Charles Black, 1882), 140.

165 **"Farewell to the Land"** George Gordon, Lord Byron, *The Works of Lord Byron* (London: 1828), 537.

165 **"eight enormous dogs"** PBS to Peacock, August [10], 1821, Ingpen, ed., *The Letters of Percy Bysshe Shelley,* 2 vols. (London: Sir Isaac Pitman & Sons, 1912), 2:897. This letter was written six years after the Geneva summer, but according to contemporaries, Byron's collection of animals never underwent any significant change.

166 **"I have been in this weary hotel"** Grylls, *Claire Clairmont: Mother of Byron's Allegra,* 65; CC to Byron, May 27, 1816, *TCC,* 47.

166 **"bashful, shy, consumptive"** May 27, 1815. William Rossetti, ed., *The Diary of Dr. John William Polidori* (London: Elkin Mathews, 1911).

166 **to recite Coleridge's** *A War Eclogue,* June 1–5, 1816, ibid., 113.

166  **"Read Italian"** May 31, 1816, ibid.

167  **"Our late great Arrival"** "J.S." to "Stuart," June 6, 1816. Quoted in Seymour, *MS,* 153.

167  **"league of incest"** Byron to John Cam Hobhouse, November 11, 1818, John Murray, ed. *Lord Byron's Correspondence,* 2 vols. (New York: Charles Scribner's Sons, 1922), 2:89.

168  **"There was no story"** Thomas Medwin, *Conversations of Lord Byron: Noted During a Residence with His Lordship* (London: Henry Colburn, 1824), 14.

168  **the white drapes** Byron recalled, "I was watched by glasses on the opposite side of the lake, and by glasses, too, that must have had very distorted optics." Ibid. Seymour writes, "Monsieur Dejean promptly installed a telescope for the use of visitors to his hotel. Spying across the lake, the hotel guests argued about whether it was Mrs. Shelley's or her sister's nightdress they could see. . . ." *MS,* 153.

## CHAPTER FOURTEEN: MARY WOLLSTONECRAFT: "A REVOLUTION IN FEMALE MANNERS" (1791–1792)

170  **"I myself"** MW to William Roscoe, October 6, 1791. *Letters MW.*

170  **"the glowing colours"** Ibid.

171  **"as a philosopher"** Wollstonecraft, *Vindication of Woman,* 53.

171  **the present state** Ibid., 28.

171  **"strength of mind"** Ibid.

171  **"What nonsense"** Ibid., 45.

172  **"The education"** Ibid., 105–6.

173  **"to be the toy"** Ibid., 52.

173  **"Love, in [women's] bosoms"** Ibid., 56.

173  **"A revolution in female manners"** Ibid., 65.

173  **"I here throw down my gauntlet"** Ibid., 71.

174  **Some write** Mary wrote, "Rousseau exerts himself to prove that all *was* right originally: a crowd of authors that all *is* now right: and I, that all will *be* right." Ibid., 31.

174  ***Rights of Brutes*** This work appeared anonymously, but the copy in the British Museum asserts that Taylor was indeed the author. Thomas Taylor, *A Vindication of the Rights of Brutes* (London: 1792).

174  **decency and propriety** Review of Mary Wollstonecraft's *A Vindication of the Rights of Woman* in *Critical Review,* second series, vol. 5 (1792), 141.

174  **"the absurdity"** Review of Mary Wollstonecraft's *A Vindication of the Rights of Woman* in *Critical Review,* second series, vol. 4 (1792), 389–90.

175  **"We shall leave"** *Critical Review,* second series, vol. 5 (1792), 141.

176  **"mist of words"** Wollstonecraft, *Vindication of Woman,* 29.

176  **"the most melancholy"** Ibid., 23.

176  **"Another argument"** Godwin, *Political Justice,* vi.

177  **"These are the times"** Thomas Paine, *The American Crisis* (Rockville, MD: Wildside Press, 2010, 1776), 7.

178  **"I can scarcely begin"** Paul, *Friends,* 1:360.

178  **"I have a singular"** Ibid.

178  **"could do no credit"** Godwin, *Memoirs,* 57.

179  **"It is wandering"** Wollstonecraft, *Vindication of Woman,* 41.

179  **the "gloomy side"** Godwin, *Memoirs,* 57.

179  **"the delicate frame"** William Godwin, *Things as They Are; or, The Adventures of Caleb Williams* (1794; London: Penguin, 1988), 50.

180  **"Had I allowed"** MW to William Roscoe, January 3, 1792, *Letters MW*, 194.

180  **In May, after Paine** From the safety of Paris, Paine lashed back at King George, "If, to expose the fraud and imposition of monarchy . . . to promote universal peace, civilization, and commerce, and to break the chains of political superstition, and raise degraded man to his proper rank; if these things be libellous . . . let the name of libeller be engraved on my tomb." "Letter Addressed to the Addressers on the Late Proclamation," in *The Thomas Paine Reader*, ed. Michael Foot and Isaac Kramnick (London: Penguin Classics, 1987), 374.

181  **"If I thought"** MW to Henry Fuseli, ?late 1792, *Letters MW*, 204–5. This letter is actually a reconstruction of the different fragments recorded by Fuseli's biographer, John Knowles, 204 n471.

181  **"was in an agony"** MW to Joseph Johnson, ?October, 1792, *Letters MW*, 205.

181  **"I find that I cannot live"** John Knowles, *The Life and Writings of Henry Fuseli* (London, 1831), 167. This is Fuseli's version of events, recorded by his devoted amanuensis, Knowles. Mary did not leave behind her version of the story. Thus, despite the frequency with which the details of this scene are cited by Wollstonecraft's biographers, in reality it is difficult to ascertain the exact details of her relationship with Fuseli. In later years, Fuseli enjoyed bragging about his conquest of the author of *Vindication of the Rights of Woman*. His biographer, Knowles, does not question Fuseli's assertions about his relationship with Mary, and Mary herself did not leave behind much evidence about her feelings, except for a few allusions in her letters.

182  **But in 1883, Godwin's biographer** Paul wrote, "I utterly disbelieve that there was anything whatever in the relations of Mary and Fuseli, than those of a young woman to an elderly *fatherly* married friend, with whose wife she was on most affectionate terms. Godwin in part adopted [this story], but he really had known next to nothing of his wife's early life. He is even demonstrably wrong in much that he says which he might have known. . . . The letters [between Fuseli and Mary] which exist are of the most common place character, and I have read them all. . . ." Beineke Rare Book and Manuscript Library, Yale University, quoted in Gordon, *VAL*, 387–88. Gordon further complicates matters by suggesting that Mary did have romantic feelings for Fuseli but discovered that Fuseli and Johnson were having a secret affair and that that is why she felt rejected. *VAL*, 386–87. This is a compelling argument, but it must remain speculative, as there is no scholarly consensus about the exact nature of the Fuseli/Wollstonecraft relationship. It does seem clear that Mary had deep feelings for Fuseli. Also, it seems true that she felt rejected by him. But the details of this rejection, as well as the true nature of her desire, have never been confirmed by her papers.

182  **"I intend no longer"** MW to William Roscoe, November 12, 1792, *Letters MW*, 206.

183  **"her breasts"** Todd, *MW:ARL*, 199.

183  **"I shall not now"** MW to William Roscoe, November 12, 1792, *Letters MW*, 208.

## CHAPTER FIFTEEN: MARY GODWIN: FITS OF FANTASY (1816)

184  **Byron amused himself** Thomas Moore, *The Life of Lord Byron: With His Letters and Journals* (London: John Murray, 1851), 319. Mary Shelley was Moore's source for the account of the Geneva summer with the Shelleys.

184  **a little brother** June 18, 1816. Rossetti, ed., *Diary of Dr. John William Polidori*, 127.

185  **"worth nothing"** June 15, 1816, ibid., 123.

186  **"super-added"** quoted in Richard Holmes, *The Age of Wonder* (New York: Vintage, 2010), 317.

186  **"[W]hat is it"** *Quarterly Review,* 1819, quoted in ibid., 318.

186  **He did not go as far** Moore's comparison of Byron and Shelley is useful here. He writes that Byron was more of a pragmatist than Shelley: Byron was "a believer in the existence of Matter and Evil, while Shelley so far refined upon the theory of Berkeley . . . to add . . . Love and Beauty." *Life of Lord Byron,* 317.

186  **"the experiments"** Mary Shelley, introduction to *Frankenstein,* 10.

186  **"a piece of vermicelli"** Ibid.

187  **everyone should write a ghost story** Moore, *Life of Lord Byron,* 394.

187  **"I saw—with shut eyes"** Mary Shelley, introduction to *Frankenstein,* 10.

188  **"agreed to write each a story"** Percy Shelley, "Preface to the 1818 Edition," in *The Original Frankenstein,* ed. Charles E. Robinson (New York: Vintage, 2009), 432.

188  **Polidori's diary** I am indebted to Miranda Seymour for this insight. She writes, "[Mary's] assertion is undone by Polidori's diary in which, writing at the time as Mary was not, he stated that they all, with the exception of himself, began writing at once. It is unlikely that he would have neglected to mention the consoling fact, had it been a fact, that his admired Mary was also short of an idea." *MS,* 157.

189  **"When I placed my head"** Mary Shelley, *Frankenstein,* 10.

189  ***Kubla Khan*** Coleridge described the experience of composing this poem as a waking dream, referring to himself in the third person. It was as if "all the images rose up before him as things . . . without any sensation or consciousness of effort. On awaking, he appeared to himself to have a distinct recollection of the whole, and taking his pen, ink, and paper, instantly and eagerly wrote down the lines that are here preserved." M. H. Abrams, ed., *The Norton Anthology of English Literature,* 4th ed., 2 vols. (New York: W. W. Norton, 1979), 2:353.

189  **Dreams were unbidden** Mary Shelley, introduction to *Frankenstein,* "My imagination, unbidden, possessed and guided me," 10.

189  **Edgar Allan Poe** Poe's description of how he composed *The Raven,* treating the act of composition as a logical puzzle to be solved, and, interestingly, stating his debt to William Godwin, can be found in "The Philosophy of Composition." Nina Baym, ed., *The Norton Anthology of American Literature,* 5th ed., 2 vols. (New York: W. W. Norton, 1998), 1:1573–80.

189  **more drawn to Shelley** Fiona MacCarthy writes, "Meeting Shelley at this juncture was more important to Byron than he ever admitted. . . . The younger man's purity of attitude, his radical idealism, sustained a solemn belief in the intrinsic value of poetry and in Byron's responsibility to himself and to others as one of poetry's supreme practitioners." *Byron: Life and Legend* (London: John Murray, 2002), 291.

189  **His earliest love affairs** "Thyrza" was actually John Edleston, a Trinity College chorister. Byron met and fell in love with Edleston in 1805. Definitive evidence of this attachment emerged in 1974, when a new "Thyrza" poem was discovered in the archives of John Murray, Byron's publisher, with the words "Edleston, Edleston, Edleston" inscribed on top. MacCarthy, *Byron: Life and Legend,* 145–46.

190  **For Shelley, the relationship was more** Holmes writes, "Shelley was unusually subdued in the elder poet's presence." He also suggests that Byron "inhibit[ed]" Shelley. *Pursuit,* 334–36.

190  **"really began"** June 18, 1816. Rossetti, ed., *Diary of Dr. John William Polidori,* 128.

190  **"Beneath the lamp"** ll. 245–54, Abrams, ed., *Norton Anthology of English Literature,* 362.

191  **"shrieking and putting"** June 18, 1816. Rossetti, ed., *Diary of Dr. John William Polidori,* 128.

191   **This strange image** For further explanation of the origins of Shelley's vision, see Sunstein's account, *MS:R&R*, 112. See also Holmes, *Pursuit*, 328–29.

191   **"fit of fantasy"** Moore, *Life of Byron*, 394.

191   **No one thought** Richard Holmes writes that imaginative endeavors and scientific experiments were not seen as opposite activities during this era, but were directly related; Romantic science and Romantic poetry were linked by "the notion of wonder." *Age of Wonder*, xv–xxi.

192   **"so possessed"** Mary Shelley, introduction to *Frankenstein*, 11.

192   **"It was on a dreary night"** Mary Shelley, *Original Frankenstein*, ed. Robinson, 80.

192   **she could hear** In her introduction to the revised *Frankenstein* (1831), Mary Shelley re-creates the setting for her dream: "I see them still; the very room, the dark parquet, the closed shutters, with the moonlight struggling through, and the sense I had that the glassy lake and white high Alps were beyond." *Frankenstein*, 11.

192   **he and Byron had barely survived** PBS to Thomas Love Peacock, July 12, 1816, *Letters PBS*, 483.

195   **"pretty babe"** July 26, 1816, *Journals MWS*, 121.

195   **"fervid with ghostly"** Quoted in Holmes, *Pursuit*, 343.

195   **"Democrat, Philanthropist, Atheist"** Holmes, *Pursuit*, 342. See Gavin de Beer, "The Atheist: An Incident at Chamonix," in Edmund Blunden, Gavin de Beer, and Sylva Norman, *On Shelley* (Oxford: Oxford University Press, 1938), 43–54.

196   **"[The view]"** Mary Shelley, *Frankenstein*, 82.

196   **his sentence sounding** The comparison has been drawn by many scholars. My attention was drawn to it by Seymour, *MS*, 159.

## CHAPTER SIXTEEN: MARY WOLLSTONECRAFT: PARIS (1792–1793)

199   **Both of Mary's sisters** For an analysis of the situations of both sisters, see Todd, *MW:ARL*, 174.

200   **"You will easily"** MW to Everina, December 24, 1792, *Letters MW*, 214.

200   **"Not the distant"** MW to Johnson, December 26, 1792, ibid., 217.

200   **"I apply"** MW to Everina, December 24, 1792, ibid., 214.

200   **"an old pair"** Richard Twiss, *A Trip to Paris in July and August, 1792* (London: 1792), 105.

201   **"very difficult"** Ibid., 89.

201   **Walking was unpleasant** For a detailed description of the streets of eighteenth-century Paris, see Jacobs, *HOW*, 118.

201   **She hated the dirty** MW to Everina, December 24, 1792, *Letters MW*, 215.

201   **"the striking contrast"** Mary Wollstonecraft, *Posthumous Works of the Author of a Vindication of the Rights of Woman*, edited by William Godwin, 4 vols. (1798), 3:39–42.

202   **"a few strokes"** MW to Johnson, December 26, 1792, *Letters MW*, 216.

203   **"The inhabitants flocked"** Ibid.

203   **"Europe observes"** Joseph Trapp, ed., *Proceedings of the French National Convention on the Trial of Louis XVI, Late King of France and Navarre, from the Paper of the World* (London: 1793), 53–58.

204   **"I am grieved"** Wollstonecraft, *Posthumous Works*, 44.

205   **For Camus** For a study of the legacy of the regicide, see Susan Dunn, *The Deaths of Louis XVI: Regicide and the French Political Imagination* (Princeton: Princeton University Press, 1994).

205   **one gentleman** MW to Ruth Barlow, February 1–14, 1793, *Letters MW*, 220.

206   **"Women should have"** Charles Seymour and Donald Paige Frary, *How the World*

*Votes: The Story of Democratic Development in Elections* (New York: C. A. Nichols, 1918), 12.

206    **"Bliss was it"** William Wordsworth, *The Prelude,* in *The Collected Poems of William Wordsworth* (London: Wordsworth Editions, 1994), 245.

206    **"She wept"** Ibid., 735.

206    **"the simple goodness"** MW to Everina, December 24, 1792, *Letters MW,* 215.

207    **Mary's embrace** Not all biographers agree with this depiction of Mary's initial attitude toward sexuality. For example, Janet Todd argues, "the *Rights of Woman* had revealed a puritanical attitude toward pleasure, consonant with [Wollstonecraft's] experience and upbringing. Although procreative sex was proper, recreative sex was in the main distasteful and unwise." *MW:ARL,* 235. In 1986, Cora Kaplan famously argued that Wollstonecraft failed to embrace female sexuality because she remained in thrall to Rousseau's depiction of female sexuality as uncontrollable and dangerous. Kaplan writes, "She accepts Rousseau's ascription of female inferiority and locates it even more firmly than he does in an excess of sensibility." See "Wild Nights: Pleasure/Sexuality/Feminism" in *Sea Changes: Essays in Culture and Feminism* (London: Verso, 1986), 38–39, 45–46. However, *Rights of Woman* is meant to be a critique of the power imbalance between men and women, and the inherent dangers for women of living inside such a system. It was not written as a critique of female sexuality, but as a critique of the system that allowed and, indeed, encouraged the abuse and rape of women.

208    **"charming grace"** Emma Rauschenbusch-Clough, *A Study of Mary Wollstonecraft and the Rights of Woman* (London: Longmans, Green & Co., 1898), 201–2.

208    **"Woman is born free"** Olympe de Gouges, *The Rights of Woman,* trans. Nupur Chaudhuri, in *Women, the Family and Freedom: The Debate in Documents,* vol. 1, *1750–1880,* ed. Susan Groag Bell and Karen Offen (1791; Stanford: Stanford University Press, 1983), 104.

208    **"mothers, daughters"** Olympe de Gouges, *Oeuvres,* ed. Benoîte Groult (Paris: Mercure de France, 1986), 105.

208    **"legal sexual equality"** Megan Conway, "Olympe de Gouges: Revolutionary in Search of an Audience," in *Orthodoxy and Heresy in Eighteenth-Century Society: Essays from the Debartolo Conference,* ed. Regina Hewitt and Pat Rogers (Lewisburg, PA: Bucknell University Press, 2002), 253.

208    **"a woman has the right to mount the scaffold"** de Gouges, *The Rights of Woman,* 104–9.

209    **The marquis de Condorcet** Todd, *MW:ARL,* 211. Todd argues that Wollstonecraft found de Gouges's ideas too extreme, but although Wollstonecraft's *Rights of Woman* never goes as far as de Gouges's call to arms, this is due in large part to context. Paris in the 1790s was far more radical than London in the 1780s, allowing de Gouges to take positions that were more revolutionary than Wollstonecraft could have dared to articulate in conservative England.

209    **Even more notorious** Lucy Moore, *Liberty: The Lives and Times of Six Women in Revolutionary France* (London: Harper Perennial, 2011), 48–51.

209    **"play the role"** Ibid., 49.

209    **"Let us raise ourselves"** Ibid., 118. See also Linda Kelly, *Women of the French Revolution* (London: Hamish Hamilton, 1989), 49.

210    **he had known many** Gordon, *VAL,* 211, 250–51, 275, 281–82. Later, Wollstonecraft would frequently accuse Imlay of being unable to control his appetite for women. For example, see MW to Imlay, February 10 1795, *Letters MW,* 283.

## CHAPTER SEVENTEEN: MARY SHELLEY:
### RETRIBUTION (1816–1817)

211   **"I shall love"** CC to Byron, August ?29, 1816, *TCC*, 70.

211   **the gloomy weather** October 7, 1816. Edward A. Bloom and Lillian D. Bloom, eds., *The Piozzi Letters: 1811–1816* (Plainsboro, NJ: Associated University Presses, 1999), 521.

211   **"Mary is reading"** PBS to Byron, September 29, 1816, *Letters PBS*, 1:508.

212   **"Seek happiness from tranquillity"** Mary Shelley, *Frankenstein*, 185.

212   **Margaret's cautionary words** Walton's sister was named Margaret Walton Saville. Anne Mellor points out that these initials, M.W.S., "are those Mary Wollstonecraft Godwin coveted and gained when she married the widowed Percy Shelley." Although we never meet this sister, Mellor points out that it is interesting to note that Walton often mentions his sister's tempering influence, helping him resist the pull of his ambition. Anne Mellor, "Making a 'Monster': An Introduction to *Frankenstein*," in *The Cambridge Companion to Mary Shelley*, ed. Esther Schor (Cambridge: Cambridge University Press, 2003), 12.

213   **Mary should push Shelley** Fanny to MWS, October 3, 1816, *TCC*, 81. Fanny's actual words were "Is it not your and Shelley's duty to consider these things?"

214   **"stupid letter"** October 4, 1816, *Journals MWS*, 138.

214   **"Her voice did quiver"** "On Fanny Godwin," Hutchinson, ed., *Complete Poetical Works of Percy Bysshe Shelley*, 2:45.

214   **"very alarming"** October 9, 1816, *Journals MWS*, 139.

214   **"depart immediately"** Godwin to MWS, October 13, 1816, Dowden, *Life of Percy Bysshe Shelley*, 58.

214   **"the worst"** October 11, 1816, *Journals MWS*, 141.

214   **The *Cambrian*** quoted in Ibid., 139–40 n2.

214   **wearing stays** Sunstein, *MS:R&R*, 127.

215   **"of a being"** Dowden, *Life of Percy Bysshe Shelley*, 57. See also *Journals MWS*, 139–40 n2.

215   **Her use of the word** Wollstonecraft inscribed her reading primer for Fanny: "The first book of a series which I intended to have written for my unfortunate girl." Jebb, *Mary Wollstonecraft*, 289.

215   **"Go not to Swansea"** Godwin to MWS, October 13, 1816. Dowden, *Life of Percy Bysshe Shelley*, 58; see also *Journals MWS*, 139–40 n2.

215   **the Godwins said** Godwin to MWS, October 13, 1816, Dowden, *Life of Percy Bysshe Shelley*, 58.

216   **"much agitated"** MWS to PBS, December 18, 1816, *Letters MWS*, 1:24.

216   **Shelley made comments** Charles Robinson writes, "Collaboration seems to have been the hallmark of the Shelleys' literary relationship. . . . The manuscript evidence actually enables us to imagine the ways in which the Shelleys passed the notebooks back and forth between August/September 1816 and mid-April 1817." Introduction to Mary Shelley, *Original Frankenstein*, 25.

216   **"peculiarly interesting"** For a brief survey of Shelley's changes to the manuscript, see ibid., 26–28.

216   **four thousand original words** Ibid., 25.

216   ***The Waste Land* and *The Great Gatsby*** The editor Max Perkins pushed F. Scott Fitzgerald to develop a "vague" character into the famous Jay Gatsby, even supplying Fitzgerald with ideas for what Gatsby should say and do. Perkins said that Fitzgerald's vagueness about Gatsby "may be somewhat of an artistic intention, but I think it is mistaken. Couldn't he be physically described as distinctly as the others, and couldn't you add one or two characteristics like the use of that phrase

'old sport'—not verbal, but physical ones, perhaps." Max Perkins to Scott Fitzgerald, November 20, 1924, in Gerald Gross, *Editors on Editing* (New York: Harper and Row, 1985), 281. In addition, Perkins cut ninety thousand words from the original draft of Thomas Wolfe's *Look Homeward, Angel*. In one of the other most famous examples of collaboration, T. S. Eliot's friend the poet Ezra Pound deleted almost six hundred lines from the thousand-line first draft of *The Waste Land* while Eliot was hospitalized for mental illness, removing both the original rhyme scheme and the meter and leaving only 434 lines of free verse intact. In fact, most scholars agree that *The Waste Land* is a coauthored work. Jack Stillinger writes: "The majority view is that the 434 lines of *The Waste Land* were lying hidden from the beginning in the 1,000 lines of draft, rather in the manner of one of Michelangelo's slumbering figures waiting to be rescued from the block of marble. But Michelangelo, in this analogy, was both artist and reviser simultaneously. In the case of *The Waste Land,* it took one poetic genius to create those 434 lines in the first place, and another to get rid of the several hundred inferior lines surrounding and obscuring them." *Multiple Authorship and the Myth of Solitary Genius* (New York: Oxford University Press, 1991).

217    **sometimes his suggestions** Robinson writes, "not all of Percy Shelley's changes to Mary Shelley's text in the Draft are for the better." Introduction to *Original Frankenstein,* 26.

217    **Moreover, both Mary and Shelley** See Daisy Hay for a full discussion of the importance of sociability and collaboration, not just for Mary and Shelley but for their group of friends as well. She writes, "*Frankenstein,* like Shelley's *Alastor,* is a critique of selfish, isolated creativity. . . . Frankenstein brings about his own downfall through an act of self-aggrandizing creation which is characterized by his failure to consider the social ramifications of his actions. He rejects the communal, institutional context of the University of Ingolstadt to lurk in charnel houses and his attic room in pursuit of personal glory. *Frankenstein* . . . is Mary's manifest for the idealized community of enlightened individuals she and Shelley attempted to assemble." Daisy Hay, *Young Romantics: The Tangled Lives of English Poetry's Greatest Generation* (New York: Farrar, Straus and Giroux, 2010), 86–87.

217    **more bad news** T. Hookham to PBS, quoted in Dowden, *Life of Percy Bysshe Shelley,* 67.

217    **"far advanced"** December 12, 1816, *The Times,* quoted in Seymour, *MS,* 175.

217    **she wept over** Mary wrote, "Poor Harriet to whose sad fate I attribute so many of my own heavy sorrows as the atonement claimed by fate for her death." February 12, 1839, *Journals MWS,* 560.

217    **"Ah! My best love"** MWS to PBS, December 17, 1816, *Letters MWS,* 1:24.

218    **"I need not"** PBS to Byron, January 17, 1817, *Letters PBS,* 1:539–40.

218    **"Dearest Claire"** PBS to CC, December 30, 1816, ibid., 1:524–25.

219    **"Mrs G. and G."** Ibid.

219    **"good marriage"** PBS describes "the magical effects" of the wedding on the Godwins, ibid.

220    **"Those darling treasures"** MWS to PBS, December 17, 1816. *Letters MWS,* 1:24.

220    **Shelley's thoughtlessness** MWS to Marianne Hunt, January 13, 1817, ibid., 1:27.

221    **Leigh Hunt was a glamorous figure** For a more complete portrait of Hunt, see Hay, *Young Romantics,* 54–57.

222    **"unintelligible," "tiresome"** John Wilson Croker, "Keats, *Endymion:* A Poetic Romance," *Quarterly Review* (1818): 204.

223    **"Cockney," background** John Gibson Lockhart, "On the Cockney School of Poetry," *Blackwood's Edinburgh Magazine* (1818): 519.

223   **"had been moved"** Roger Ingpen, ed., *The Autobiography of Leigh Hunt: With Reminiscences of Friends and Contemporaries, and with Thornton Hunt's Introduction and Postscript,* vol. 2 (London: 1903), 37.

224   **"frightful creatures"** Ibid.

224   **Elizabeth Kent** For more on Hunt and Elizabeth Kent, see Hay, *Young Romantics,* 7, 15–18, 55, 60, 70, 72–75, 96–97, 115–18, 226, 262.

CHAPTER EIGHTEEN: MARY WOLLSTONECRAFT: IN LOVE (1792)

228   **"freedom is enthroned"** Gilbert Imlay, *A Topographical Description of the Western Territory of North America* (London: 1792), 159.

228   **"state of degradation"** Gilbert Imlay, *The Emigrants,* ed. W. Verhoeven and Amanda Gilroy (New York: Penguin, 1998), 101.

228   **"fairy scene"** Mary Wollstonecraft, *An Historical and Moral View of the Origin and Progress of the French Revolution* (London: 1794), 476.

229   **"Between you and me"** Joel to Ruth Barlow, April 19, 1793, quoted in Eleanor Flexner, *Mary Wollstonecraft: A Biography* (New York: Coward, McCann and Geoghegan, 1972), 181.

229   **"glistened with sympathy"** MW to Imlay, December [date?], 1793, *Letters MW,* 234.

230   **"Tant pis"** W. Clark Durant, "Supplement," in *Memoirs of the Author of a Vindication of the Rights of Woman,* ed. William Godwin (London: Constable and Co., 1927), 237.

230   **rosy glow** MW to Imlay, December [date?], 1793, *Letters MW,* 234.

231   **The "air is chill"** Wollstonecraft, *The French Revolution,* 162.

231   **The "gigantic" portraits** Ibid., 161.

231   **"I weep"** Ibid., 163.

231   **"dear girl"** MW to Imlay, August [date?], 1793, *Letters MW,* 228.

232   **"cheerful poultry"** Wollstonecraft, *A Vindication of the Rights of Men* (London: J. Johnson, 1790), 141.

232   **captivating places** Imlay, *Emigrants,* 54.

232   **"You can scarcely imagine"** MW to Imlay, August [date?], 1793, *Letters MW,* 228.

233   **"revolution in the minds"** Wollstonecraft, *The French Revolution,* 396.

233   **the best plan** Todd, *MW:ARL,* 240.

235   **"inclined to faint"** MW to Imlay, November [date?], 1793, *Letters MW,* 232.

236   **"for the wings"** Helen Maria Williams, *Letters Containing a Sketch of the Politics of France, from the 31st of May 1793, Till the 28th of July 1794, and of the Scenes Which Have Passed in the Prisons of Paris* (1795; University of Oxford Text Archive), 37, http://ota.ox.ac.uk/text/4517.html.

236   **"If this young lady"** *The British Critic,* vol. 2 (1793; Google Books, 2008), 252, http://books.google.com/books?id=EP8vAAAAYAAJ&dq.

236   **"politics are a study"** quoted in Deborah Kennedy, *Helen Maria and the Age of Revolution* (Plainsboro, NJ: Associated University Presses, 2002), 106.

236   **"Madame Roland"** Quoted in ibid., 115.

236   **"uterine furies"** Lynn Avery Hunt, *The Family Romance of the French Revolution* (Berkeley: University of California Press, 1993), 121.

237   **"each sex"** Quoted in ibid., 122.

237   **"In general"** Quoted in ibid., 119.

237   **"My sentiments"** Quoted in Linda Kelly, *Women of the French Revolution* (London: Hamish Hamilton, 1989), 123.

238   **"Recall that virago"** Quoted in M. J. Diamond, *Women and Revolution: Global Expressions* (New York: Springer, 1998), 14.

238  "O liberty!" quoted in Gary Kelly, *Women, Writing and Revolution, 1790–1827* (Oxford: Clarendon Press, 1993), 55–56.

238  "I have felt" MW to Imlay, November [date?], 1793. *Letters MW*, 232–33.

## CHAPTER NINETEEN: MARY SHELLEY: MARLOW AND LONDON (1817–1818)

240  "descended the steps" PBS to MWS, December 16, 1816, *Letters PBS*, 1:521.

241  "yon nymph" Leigh Hunt to MWS, November 16, 1821, *The Correspondence of Leigh Hunt*, ed. Thornton Hunt, 2 vols. (London: Smith, Elder and Co., 1862), 1:106.

242  "a sedate-faced" Leigh Hunt to MWS, July 25–27, 1819, St. Clair, *Godwins and the Shelleys*, 6:846.

242  "jumps about like" MWS to PBS, January 17, 1817, *Catalogue of the Library of the Late Charles W. Frederickson: A Carefully Selected and Valuable Collection of English Literature, Comprising a Large Number of First and Other Rare Editions, Especially of Byron, Gray, Keats, Lamb, Shakspeare, Scott, and an Unrivalled Collection of the Works of Shelley and Shelleyanna; Also Autograph Letters and Manuscripts of the Greatest Intrinsic Interest and Value* (Cambridge, MA: D. Taylor & Company, 1897), 231, quoted in Seymour, *MS*, 180. This passage is from earlier in the year but is one of Mary's most vivid expressions of delight in little William.

242  "of the dead" MWS to Leigh Hunt, May 3, 1817, *Letters MWS*, 1:32.

242  "offspring" or "progeny" Mary Shelley, introduction to *Frankenstein*, 11.

242  as a "dilat[ion]" Ibid., 7.

242  **Although Mary did not provide** Anne Mellor provides an analysis of these dates in "Making a 'Monster': An Introduction to *Frankenstein*," 12, and *Mary Shelley: Her Life, Her Fiction, Her Monsters* (New York: Routledge, 1989), 54–55.

243  it is as though Anne Mellor writes, "the novel is written by the author to an audience of one, herself." For a more thorough discussion of this idea, see *Mary Shelley*, 54–55.

243  **No matter how hard** Mellor writes, "Victor's quest is precisely to usurp from nature the female power of biological reproduction. Making a 'Monster,'" 19.

243  bread and raisins Dowden, *Life of Percy Bysshe Shelley*, 123.

243  "his face upwards" Elizabeth Kent, *Flora Domestica* (London: 1823), xix.

243  "fair and very young" Dowden, *Life of Percy Bysshe Shelley*, 123.

243  **The villagers** Ibid., 120–22.

246  "many complements" Jeanne Moskal, "Introductory note" in Mary Shelley, *The Novels and Selected Works of Mary Shelley* (London: William Pickering, 1996), 8:4.

246  "the perusal" Benjamin Colbert, "Contemporary Notice of the Shelleys' *History of a Six Weeks' Tour*: Two New Early Reviews," *Keats-Shelley Journal* 48 (1999).

246  "the master theme" PBS to Byron, September 8, 1816, *Letters PBS*, 1:504.

246  "to startle" *The Complete Poetry of Percy Bysshe Shelley*, ed. Donald H. Reiman, Neil Fraistat, and Nora Crook (Baltimore: Johns Hopkins University Press, 2012), 3:120.

247  "Can man be free" Ibid., 3:167.

247  *The Revolt of Islam* For a comprehensive analysis of the poem, see Holmes, *Pursuit*, 390–402.

247  "So now my summer" *Complete Poetry of Shelley*, ed. Reiman, Fraistat, and Crook, 123.

248  **The competition** Mary wrote, "Clare [*sic*] is forever wearying with her idle & childish complaints." MWS to PBS, October 18, 1817, *Letters MWS*, 1:57.

248  "Mary has presented" PBS to Byron, September 24, 1817, *Letters PBS*, 1:557.

248  **She wrote Shelley many letters** "Come back as soon as you may," MWS to PBS, September 26, 1817, *Letters MWS,* 1:52. See also September 24 and 28, October 2, 16, and 18. She complains about Alba, Claire, and the Hunts, but the most consistent theme is Shelley's absence.

249  **"Mourn then"** David Clark, ed., *Shelley's Prose: or, The Trumpet of a Prophecy* (Albuquerque: University of New Mexico Press, 1966), 168.

249  **Godwin had read** Many years later, after Shelley's death, Godwin would tell Mary, "[*Frankenstein*] is the most wonderful book to have been written at twenty years of age that I ever heard of." Paul, *Friends,* 2:282.

249  **received immediate and angry reviews** Seymour provides a summary of the response to *Frankenstein* in *MS,* 196.

249  **"respect to those persons"** MWS to Sir Walter Scott, June 14, 1818, *Letters MWS,* 1:34.

250  **a few grudging reviews** For an overview of the critical response, see Holmes, *Pursuit,* 403–4.

251  **a lump or two of bread** Hogg frequently refers to Shelley as so pure or "sensitive" that he did not need food. *Life of Shelley,* 2:114, 2:187, 2:305, 2:517.

251  **"affectionate and mild"** PBS to Byron, December 17, 1817, *Letters PBS,* 1:557.

251  **"pure air"** MWS to PBS, September 26, 1817, *Letters MWS,* 1:27.

252  **"I met a traveler"** *Complete Poetry of Shelley,* ed. Reiman, Fraistat, and Crook, 3:4–5.

CHAPTER TWENTY: MARY WOLLSTONECRAFT:
"MOTHERHOOD" (1793–1794)

254  **"I told them"** MW to Imlay, January 1, 1794, *Letters MW,* 238.

254  **"chat as long"** MW to Ruth Barlow, [c. mid-1793], ibid., 229.

254  **increasingly melancholy** MW to Imlay, September [date?], 1793, ibid., 231.

255  **"I have been"** Ibid.

255  **"money-getting face"** MW to Imlay, December [date?], 1793, ibid., 234.

255  **"My head aches"** MW to Imlay, January 1, 1794, ibid., 238.

255  **"loved [her] like"** Ibid.

255  **"I intreat you"** MW to Imlay, January 8, 1794, ibid., 241.

256  **"What a picture"** MW to Imlay, January 11, 1794, ibid., 243.

256  **"life would not"** MW to Everina, March 10, 1794, ibid., 248.

256  **"quite out of the world"** MW to Ruth Barlow, February 3, 1794, ibid., 247.

257  **the origin of society** Wollstonecraft, *The French Revolution,* 7.

257  **"on the basis"** Ibid., 13.

257  **"liberty with maternal"** Ibid., 19.

257  **"Amen and Amen"** John Adams, notations on Mary Wollstonecraft, *An Historical and Moral View of the Origin and Progress of the French Revolution,* in the Boston Public Library Rare Books Department, available online at https://archive.org/details/historicalmoralvoowoll. Daniel O'Neill writes that Adams's notes on Wollstonecraft's texts constitute a "dialogue" between Adams and Wollstonecraft on "the theoretical basis for their very different evaluations of the French Revolution's significance." He adds that the lack of scholarly work on this "dialogue" is as much a "gap in the literature on Wollstonecraft as in that on Adams." "John Adams versus Mary Wollstonecraft on the French Revolution and Democracy," *Journal of the History of Ideas* 68, no. 3 (July 2007), 453. For another analysis of the Adams/Wollstonecraft debate, see Gordon, *VAL,* 374, 461, 475.

258  **"family affections"** Wollstonecraft, *The French Revolution,* 254.

259  **"pleasantly situated"** MW to Ruth Barlow, February 3, 1794, *Letters MW,* 247.

260  **"ruffle" his moods** MW to Imlay, January 15, 1794, ibid., 246.

260 **"smoking on the board"** MW to Imlay, March [date?], 1794, ibid., 250.

260 **"matrimonial phraseology"** MW to Ruth Barlow, April 27, 1794, ibid., 251.

260 **"the history is finished"** Ibid., 252.

260 **"was convinced"** MW to Ruth Barlow, May 20, 1794, ibid., 253.

261 **"this struggle"** Ibid., 252.

261 **"uncommonly healthy"** MW to Ruth Barlow, July 8, 1794, ibid., 254.

261 **"so manfully"** MW to Ruth Barlow, May 20, 1794, ibid.

262 **giving Ellefson** According to a recently discovered letter (2005) that Mary wrote to the Danish foreign minister in 1796, she was actually the last English person to see the silver and had been the one to give Ellefson his parting instructions, as Imlay was away on business when Ellefson set sail: "I, Sir, gave Elefsen [*sic*] his last orders," she declared. See Lyndall Gordon and Gunnar Molder, "The Treasure Seeker," *The Guardian*, January 7, 2005.

263 **"peace [would] take place"** MW to Everina, September 20, 1794, *Letters MW*, 262.

263 **some "knavery"** MW to Imlay, August 20, 1794, ibid., 259.

263 **"[business] is the idea"** MW to Imlay, August 17, 1794, ibid., 257.

263 **"There are qualities"** MW to Imlay, August 19, 1794, ibid., 258.

263 **"reserve of temper"** MW to Imlay, August 20, 1794. ibid., 259.

264 **four hundred thousand Europeans** Stefan Riedel, "Edward Jenner and the History of Smallpox and Vaccination," *Baylor University Medical Center Proceedings* 18, no. 1 (2005), http://www.ncbi.nlm.nih.gov/pmc/articles/PMC1200696/.

264 **"treat th[e] dreadful"** MW to Everina, September 20, 1794, *Letters MW*, 262.

264 **like a "slave"** MW to Imlay, September 28, 1794, ibid., 267.

264 **"She has got"** MW to Imlay, August 19, 1794, ibid., 258.

## CHAPTER TWENTY-ONE: MARY SHELLEY: ITALY, "THE HAPPY HOURS" (1818–1819)

266 **"The fruit trees"** MWS to the Hunts, April [6], 1818, *Letters MWS*, 1:63.

266 **"there is more fruit"** PBS to Peacock, April 20, 1818, Percy Shelley, *Essays, Letters from Abroad, Translations and Fragments,* ed. Mary Shelley (London: Moxon, 1845), 106.

267 **"two large halls"** Mary's description of a fictional villa in *The Last Man* was based on the Villa Pliniana. Mary Shelley, *The Last Man* (1826; Rockville, MD: Wildside Press, 2007), 373.

267 **shockingly bachanalian** Fiona MacCarthy argues that Byron had sex with many women in order to repress and master his homosexual impulses. *Byron*, 163, 173.

267 **"I send you my child"** CC to Byron, April 27, 1818, *TCC*, 1:115.

268 **"I love [Allegra]"** CC to Byron, ibid.

269 **"a stupid town"** *Journals MWS*, 209.

270 **Maria's enormous dog, Oscar** Maria Gisborne to MWS, *Maria Gisborne and Edward E. Williams, Shelley's Friends: Their Journals and Letters,* ed. Frederick Jones (Norman: University of Oklahoma Press, 1951), 53. Later, Mrs. Gisborne wrote the Shelleys that Oscar suffered terribly when they left, *Letters from Abroad*, 186.

270 **"His nose"** PBS to Peacock, August [22], 1819, *Letters PBS*, 2:114.

270 **"frank affectionate"** Mary Shelley, preface in *Letters from Abroad*, 1:xix.

271 **"I like nothing"** MWS to Mrs. Gisborne, June 15, 1818, *Letters MWS*, 1:72.

271 **"When I came here"** Ibid.

272 ***il prato fiorito*** MWS to Maria Gisborne, July 2, 1818, ibid., 1:74.

272 **"My custom"** PBS to Peacock, July 25, 1818, *Letters PBS*, 2:96.

274 **"It is true"** MWS to Maria Gisborne, August 17, 1818, *Letters MWS*, 1:77.

274 **"of two"** Richard Holmes, ed., *Shelley on Love* (Berkeley: University of California Press, 1980), 72.

274　"[Women in ancient Greece] were" Richard Shepherd, ed., *The Prose Works of Percy Bysshe Shelley*, 2 vols. (London: 1897), 2:45.

274　"into the truth" PBS to Hogg, April 10, 1814, *Letters PBS*, 1:389.

276　Byron's "horror" PBS to MWS, August 23, 1818, *Letters PBS*, 2:37–38.

277　Mary had to make up her Her father's daughter, Mary summed this debate up in her journal with one word: "consultation." August 28, 1818, *Journals MWS*, 225.

277　"As sunset" "To Mary," in Hutchinson, ed., *Complete Poetical Works of Percy Bysshe Shelley*, 549.

277　"Poor little Ca" PBS to MWS, September 22, 1818, *Letters PBS*, 39–40.

277　"was lost in misty distance" Mary Shelley, "Editor's note" in *Poetical Works of Percy Bysshe Shelley*, ed. Mary Shelley (London, 1839), 160–61.

278　"life and death" "Letter VI," Mary Shelley, *Rambles in Germany and Italy, in 1840, 1842, and 1843* (London, 1844), 79.

278　"This is the Journal" September 24, 1818, *Journals MWS*, 226.

279　"Wilt thou forget" "The Past" in Hutchinson, ed., *Complete Poetical Works of Percy Bysshe Shelley*, 549.

## CHAPTER TWENTY-TWO: MARY WOLLSTONECRAFT: ABANDONED (1794–1795)

282　"loud music" MW to Imlay, September 22, 1794, *Letters MW*, 263.

283　"enthralled him" Durant, "Supplement," 251–52.

283　"reveries and trains" MW to Imlay, September 23, 1794, *Letters MW*, 266.

283　"I have been playing" Ibid.

284　"Take care of yourself" MW to Imlay, September 28, 1794, ibid., 267.

284　"He very unmanily" MW to Imlay, February 10, 1795, ibid., 282.

284　"vivac[ious]," young woman MW to Imlay, October 1, 1794, ibid., 269.

284　"employed and amused" MW to Imlay, October 26, 1794, ibid., 270.

284　"Her manners" William Drummond, ed., *The Autobiography of Archibald Hamilton Rowan* (Shannon: Irish University Press, 1972), 253–54, 56, 49.

285　"I shall be half in love" MW to Imlay, October 26, 1794, *Letters MW*, 270.

285　"Come, Mary—come" Durant, "Supplement," 247.

285　"When you first" MW to Imlay, February 10, 1795, *Letters MW*, 282.

286　"Believe me" MW to Imlay, September 22, 1794, ibid., 264.

286　"I know what I look for" MW to Imlay, February 9, 1795, ibid., 281.

286　What was important Lyndall Gordon also argues that the struggle between Imlay and Mary was philosophical as well as personal. *VAL*, 242–52.

287　their daughter would be freer MW to Imlay, February 19, 1795, ibid., 284.

287　"Am I only to return" Ibid.

287　"Business alone" Imlay to MW, quoted in ibid., 285 n643.

287　"the good people" MW to Archibald Hamilton Rowan, April [date?], 1795, ibid., 288.

288　"I have indeed been so unhappy" MW to Imlay, April 7, 1795, ibid., 286.

288　"Here we are" MW to Imlay, April 11, 1795, ibid., 289.

289　"to press me" MW to Imlay, September 28, 1794, ibid., 267.

290　he needed "variety" MW to Imlay, June 12, 1795, ibid., 297.

290　"to assume" MW to Imlay, May 22, 1795, ibid., 293.

291　the "elasticity" "How am I altered by disappointment!" Mary wrote. "When going to [Lisbon], ten years ago, the elasticity of my mind was sufficient to ward off weariness." MW to Imlay, June 20, 1795, ibid., 304.

291　"It is my opinion" MW to Eliza, April 23, 1795, ibid., 290.

292　"She swallowed the laudanum" Wollstonecraft, *Maria*, 147.

CHAPTER TWENTY-THREE: MARY SHELLEY:
"OUR LITTLE WILL" (1818–1819)

293  "a smoke" PBS to Peacock, December 22, 1818, *Letters from Abroad,* 140.

293  "looking at almost the same scene" MWS to Maria Gisborne, January 22, 1819, *Letters MWS,* 1:85.

294  "A poet could not have a more sacred" November 30, 1818, *Journals MWS,* 241.

294  "orange trees" MWS to Sophia Stacey, March 7, 1820. Betty Bennett, "Newly Uncovered Letters and Poems by Mary Wollstonecraft Shelley," *Keats-Shelley Memorial Bulletin* 46 (July 1997).

294  their servants tiptoed Sunstein, *MS:R&R,* 159.

295  "I could lie down" Hutchinson, ed. *Complete Poetical Works of Percy Bysshe Shelley,* 567.

295  So, who was this baby? Many theories have been put forward. For an overview, see Seymour, *MS,* 221–28. See also Holmes's earlier summary, *Pursuit,* 481–84. As usual, the Shelleys, or their descendants, did a superb job of covering their tracks. Unfortunately, at least one crucial letter is missing. We know that many months later Mary wrote to the Gisbornes explaining why they would have to return to Naples for six months in the summer of 1819, as the Gisbornes mention receiving such a letter, but the letter was either destroyed or lost, leaving us in the dark.

296  Claire was the mother The only evidence for this claim is Mary's notation that Claire was "unwell" on December 27, 1818, *Journals MWS,* 246.

296  Mary defended Shelley MWS to Isabella Hoppner, August 10, 1821, *Letters MWS,* 1:207.

299  "at an emerald sky" PBS to Peacock, March 23, 1819, *Letters PBS,* 2:84.

299  "arches after arches" Ibid.

299  "Oh Rome!" Byron, "Childe Harold," Canto IV, LXXVIII, *Lord Byron: Selected Poems,* ed. Susan Wolfson and Peter Manning (New York: Penguin Classics, 2006), 537.

300  "Rome repays" MWS to Marianne Hunt, March 12, 1819, *Letters MWS,* 1:88.

300  Even Claire was happy Holmes, *Pursuit,* 221.

300  "O Dio che bella" MWS to Marianne Hunt, March 12, 1819, *Letters MWS,* 1:88–89.

300  "Our little Will" MWS to Maria Gisborne, April 9, 1819, ibid., 1:93.

300  "antique winding staircase" PBS to Peacock, March 23, 1819, *Letters PBS,* 2:84–85.

301  "It is a scene of perpetual enchantment" MWS to Marianne Hunt, March 12, 1819, *Letters MWS,* 1:89.

301  "spirit of beauty" Mary Shelley, *Valperga* (Oxford: Oxford University Press, 2000), 96.

301  "dreadfully tired" MWS to Marianne Hunt, March 12, 1819, *Letters MWS,* 1:88.

301  "The manners of the rich" PBS to Peacock, March 23, 1819, *Letters PBS,* 2:85.

301  "The place is full of English" MWS to Maria Gisborne, April 9, 1819, *Letters MWS,* 1:93.

301  Amelia Curran For a more complete portrait of Curran, see Holmes, *Pursuit,* 513–14.

303  "He is so very delicate" MWS to Maria Gisborne, May 30, 1819, *Letters MWS,* 1:98.

303  "convulsions of death" MWS to Mrs. Gisborne, June 5, 1819, ibid., 1:99.

303  "I never know one moment's ease" MWS to Marianne Hunt, June 29, 1819, ibid., 1:101.

303  "The world" MWS to Leigh Hunt, September 24, 1819, ibid., 1:108.

303  "William was so good" MWS to Marianne Hunt, June 29, 1819, ibid., 1:102.

304    "My lost William" Hutchinson, ed. *Complete Poetical Works of Percy Bysshe Shelley*, 576.

304    "My dearest Mary" Ibid., 577.

305    "I shall never recover" MWS to Amelia Curran, June 27, 1819, *Letters MWS*, 1:100.

305    then "ascend[ed]" PBS to Peacock, August 22, 1819, *Letters PBS*, 2:114.

306    "his airy cell" Mary Shelley, "Preface" to *The Cenci*, in Hutchinson, ed., *Complete Poetical Works of Percy Bysshe Shelley*, 336.

306    "I ought to have died" MWS to Leigh Hunt, September 24, 1819, *Letters MWS*, 1:108.

306    "sing not very" MWS to Marianne Hunt, August 28, 1819, ibid., 1:102.

306    "Though at first" Godwin to MWS, September 9, 1819, Paul, *Friends*, 2:270.

CHAPTER TWENTY-FOUR: MARY WOLLSTONECRAFT:
"SURELY YOU WILL NOT FORGET ME" (1795)

308    "A . . . vision" Wollstonecraft, *Maria*, 147.

308    Imlay came up with a plan For an overview of what Imlay's motives may have been, see Todd, *MW:ARL*, 303–5.

309    "tomb-like house" MW to Imlay, June 10, 1795, *Letters MW*, 295.

309    seemed "diminutive" MW to Imlay, June 14, 1795, ibid., 300.

310    "Papa" to "come" MW to Imlay, June 12, 1795, ibid., 299.

310    "Surely, you" MW to Imlay, June 16, 1795, ibid., 301.

310    "play[ed] with the cabin boy" MW to Imlay, June 17, 1795, ibid., 303.

310    "anguish of mind" MW to Imlay, June 18, 1795, ibid., 303.

310    "in a stupour" MW to Imlay, June 27, 1795, ibid., 306.

311    "My friend" MW to Imlay, June 29, 1795, ibid., 307.

311    torturing him When Imlay complained that her letters were upsetting him, Mary wrote, "Believe me (and my eyes fill with tears of tenderness as I assure you) there is nothing I would not endure in the way of privation, rather than disturb your tranquility." MW to Imlay, July 3, 1795, ibid., 309.

311    "Ah, why do you" MW to Imlay, July 4, 1795, ibid., 311.

311    "the culture of sensibility" Originally known as "the cult of sensibility." G. J. Barker-Benfield introduces this term in his groundbreaking study *The Culture of Sensibility: Sex and Society in Eighteenth-Century Britain* (Chicago: University of Chicago Press, 1992).

312    "the grossness" MW to Imlay, July 4, 1795, ibid., 311.

312    being abandoned had two meanings For an analysis of the double meaning of "abandonment," see Lawrence Lipking, *Abandoned Women and Poetic Tradition* (Chicago: University of Chicago Press, 1988), 82.

312    "from the tranquil" Mary Robinson, Sonnet V, *Sappho and Phaon* (1796; Whitefish, MT: Kessinger Publishing, reprint, 2004), 14.

314    "degree of vivacity" MW to Imlay, July 4, 1795, *Letters MW*, 311.

314    "I contemplated all nature at rest" Mary Wollstonecraft, *Letters Written During a Short Residence in Sweden, Norway, and Denmark* (London: J. Johnson, 1796), 14.

315    "I feel more than a mother's fondness" Ibid., 66.

316    "human petrifications" Ibid., 91.

317    "reclin[e] in the mossy" Ibid., 93–95.

317    "I must love" Ibid.

317    "piney air" Ibid.

317    "thickened" the water Ibid., 97.

317    "so much hair with a yellow" Ibid., 100.

318    **"uncommonly bad"** Ibid., 102.

318    **"the language is soft"** Ibid., 104.

319    **"My head turned"** Ibid., 119.

319    **"The view"** Ibid., 132.

319    **"To be born"** Ibid., 133.

319    **A recently discovered** Gunnar Molden is the Norwegian historian who found the missing letter. For a full account of his discovery, see Lyndall Gordon and Gunnar Molden, "The Treasure Seeker," *The Guardian,* January 7, 2005. Also *VAL,* 260–62.

320    **"The clouds"** Ibid., 167.

321    **For Mary, Gilbert's rejection** Eleanor Ty argues that Wollstonecraft's sense of loss had far deeper roots than Imlay's rejections. She writes, "In both Freud's and Lacan's psychoanalytic theories, desire and sexuality are linked to an original object that is lost. . . . Thus, Wollstonecraft's desire is not solely for Gilbert Imlay, or for another lover." Ty goes on to argue that even if Imlay had committed himself to Wollstonecraft, his love would have never fulfilled her desire, as "he is merely an object that stands for something else." "'The History of My Own Heart': Inscribing Self, Inscribing Desire in Wollstonecraft's Letters from Norway," in *Mary Shelley and Mary Wollstonecraft: Writing Lives,* ed. Helen M. Buss, D. L. Macdonald, and Anne McWhir (Waterloo, Ontario: Wilfrid Laurier University Press, 2001), 71.

CHAPTER TWENTY-FIVE: MARY SHELLEY: "THE MIND OF
A WOMAN" (1819)

322    **"make a stir"** PBS to Peacock, July 6, 1819, Ingpen, ed., *Letters PBS,* 696.

323    **Pessimism versus optimism** Mary Shelley's pessimism is so emphatic, writes Barbara Jane O'Sullivan, that she can be said to have a "Cassandra" complex: "Mary Shelley develops an alternative to the Promethean optimism of Romanticism. Percy Shelley heralded his triumphant poetic vision with the embodiment of a Prometheus Unbound—a hero-god at the center of a metaphysical tale of the renewal and release of creative energy. Mary Shelley, on the other hand, portrays a tragic and all-too-human heroine, who is reminiscent of the ancient prophetess Cassandra. A close study of Mary Shelley's works reveals that the Cassandra figure is a pervasive image, and that Mary Shelley felt a strong personal identification with Cassandra at certain times in her life." "Beatrice in Valperga: A New Cassandra," in *The Other Mary Shelley: Beyond Frankenstein,* ed. Audrey A. Fisch, Anne K. Mellor, and Esther H. Schor (New York: Oxford University Press, 1993), 140.

324    **"May you . . . never"** MWS to Marianne Hunt, June 29, 1819, *Letters MWS,* 1:101.

324    **"We look on the past"** August 4, 1819, *Journals MWS,* 293.

324    **"Wednesday 4th"** Ibid.

325    ***"A little patience"*** Mary Shelley, *Matilda,* in *Mary Wollstonecraft: Mary and Maria; Mary Shelley: Matilda,* ed. Janet Todd (London: Penguin Classics, 1992), 201.

325    **Incest, as Shelley's poetry had already shown** Later, Shelley would write: "Incest is, like many other incorrect things, a very poetical circumstance. It may be the defiance of everything for the sake of another, which clothes itself in the glory of the highest heroism; or it may be that cynical rage which confounding the good and the bad in existing opinions, breaks through them for the purpose of rioting in selfishness and antipathy." PBS to Mrs. Gisborne, November 16, 1819, Ingpen, ed., *Letters PBS,* 749.

325    **Like Mary, Beatrice was "pale"** Although Shelley's biographer Richard Holmes

believes that Shelley's description of Beatrice bears an uncanny resemblance to Shelley himself, Shelley's adjectives are ones he often used for Mary—"pale" and "clear." And Mary's eyes were certainly swollen with weeping. See Holmes, *Pursuit*, 516–17.

325  **Mary's take on incest** Janet Todd points out an interesting parallel between Mary Shelley and the French psychoanalyst Marie Bonaparte, one of Freud's most famous patients, whose own mother had died giving birth to her. Bonaparte wrote about the phenomenon of the daughter who longs to be both her father's wife (her own mother) and her father's child. "To be dead for me was to be identified with the mother, was to be in the place of the wife of my father, was like my mother to die." *Revue française de psychanalyse* 2.3 (1928), quoted in Janet Todd, introduction to *Mary Wollstonecraft: Mary and Maria; Mary Shelley: Matilda* (London: Penguin Classics, 1992), xx.

327  **"I am, I thought, a tragedy"** Mary Shelley, *Matilda*, 199.

327  **In a retaliatory swipe** Claire Raymond writes that although Mary Shelley does not explicitly cite *The Cenci*, yet *Matilda* "implicitly responds to Percy Shelley's text, arguing with his vision of what constitutes bravery. *Matilda* contradicts the image of the courageous Beatrice Cenci in Percy Shelley's play by presenting in her stead the slow methodical self mortification of a defeated daughter who has suffered but not committed sin. Matilda gets her revenge through text, however, a lasting response to betrayal." Claire Raymond, *The Posthumous Voice in Women's Writing, from Mary Shelley to Sylvia Plath* (Burlington, VT: Ashgate Publishing, 2006), 86.

327  **"Farewell Woodville, the turf will soon be green"** Ibid., 210.

328  **The servant Giuseppe** Mrs. Gisborne to PBS, October [date?], 1819, Mary Shelley, ed., *Works of Percy Bysshe Shelley* (Oxford: Oxford University Press, 1847), 133.

328  **"Poor Oscar!"** PBS to Mrs. Gisborne, October 13 or 14, 1819, Ingpen, ed., *Letters PBS*, 723.

328  **E. M. Forster in his novel** Seymour takes note of this similarity in *MS*, 238.

328  **She took an immediate dislike** Mary complained to Mrs. Gisborne, writing, "Madame M. might go on exceedingly well & gain if she had the brains of a goose but her head is a sive [*sic*] and her temper worse than wildfire." December 28, 1819, *Letters MWS*, 1:122.

328  **"watching the leaves"** PBS to the Gisbornes, November 6, 1819, *Letters PBS*, 2:150.

329  **"personal character"** PBS to Ollier, October 15, 1819, *Letters PBS*, 2:128.

329  **"Mr Shelley would abrogate"** Newman Ivey White, *The Unextinguished Hearth* (London: Octagon Books, 1966), 141. For further discussion of this review, see Holmes, *Pursuit*, 545.

329  **"he straightened up suddenly"** Thomas Medwin, *The Life of Percy Bysshe Shelley* (Oxford: Oxford University Press, 1913), 226.

330  **calling it "trash"** PBS to Ollier, October 15, 1819, *Letters PBS*, 2:128. See Holmes's detailed account of this period in Shelley's life, *Pursuit*, 545.

330  **discovered a gray hair** Holmes, *Pursuit*, 546.

330  **"passion for reforming"** Ibid.

CHAPTER TWENTY-SIX: MARY WOLLSTONECRAFT:
RETURN HOME (1795–1796)

331  **"Our minds are not congenial"** We do not have Imlay's letters, but Mary quotes him in her responses. MW to Imlay, August 26, 1795, *Letters MW*, 319.

331  **"I have lived"** Ibid.

332    **Not once did it occur** Eleanor Ty uses the theories of both Freud and Lacan to analyze Wollstonecraft's letters, arguing that Wollstonecraft's stated yearning for her lover was actually a far deeper desire, one that was linked to all her experiences of loss. She writes, "At the time that she was travelling, Wollstonecraft expressed the wish to be united with her lover. However, in Lacanian terms this articulated demand . . . is always addressed to an Other, and falls short of what one needs." "'The History of My Own Heart,'" in *Mary Wollstonecraft and Mary Shelley: Writing Lives,* ed. Buss, Macdonald, and McWhir, 71. Also see the final note to chapter 24.

332    **the "indolence"** Wollstonecraft, *Letters from Sweden,* 201–2.

333    **"But for this child"** MW to Imlay, September 6, 1795, ibid., 320.

333    **"Ah," wrote Mary** Wollstonecraft, *Letters from Sweden,* 235.

334    **"forced" a "confession"** MW to Imlay, October 10, 1795, *Letters MW,* 326.

335    **"state of chaos"** MW to Imlay, ibid.

335    **The Revolution had caused** Todd writes, "Wollstonecraft had encountered many 'rational' suicides among politicians during the French Revolution." *Letters MW,* 327 n694. See also *MW:ARL,* 354.

336    **"The impetuous dashing"** Wollstonecraft, *Letters from Sweden,* 174.

336    **"I would encounter"** MW to Imlay, October 10, 1795, *Letters MW,* 326.

336    **"self interest"** MW to Imlay, September 27, 1795, *Letters MW,* 322.

337    **the "bitterness"** MW to Imlay, Sunday morning, [c. October 1795], *Letters MW,* 327.

337    **The Royal Humane Society** Todd, *MW:ARL,* 356.

338    **"inhumanely brought"** MW to Imlay, Sunday morning [c. October 1795], *Letters MW,* 327.

339    **"how to extricate ourselves"** Ibid.

339    **"an imaginary being"** MW to Imlay, December 8, 1795, ibid., 334.

340    **of "passion"** MW to Imlay, November 27, 1795, ibid., 332.

341    **She omitted complaints** Mary Favret supplies the examples I cite as well as a brilliant analysis of Wollstonecraft's strategies in organizing and composing *Letters from Sweden.* Favret, *Romantic Correspondence: Women, Politics, and the Fiction of Letters* (Cambridge: Cambridge University Press, 2005), 102–3. Favret argues that Wollstonecraft's published letters "deliberately rewrite and replace the love letters, transforming Wollstonecraft's emotional dependence and personal grief into a public confrontation with social corruption," 101.

341    **"My eyes"** Wollstonecraft, *Letters from Sweden,* 187.

341    **"a good dinner"** Ibid., 20.

342    **"If ever there was a book"** Godwin, *Memoirs,* 133.

342    **"revolutionary feminism"** Gary Kelly, *Revolutionary Feminism: The Mind and Career of Mary Wollstonecraft* (New York: St. Martin's Press, 1992), 178–79.

342    **"A grief without a pang"** Samuel Taylor Coleridge, *Dejection: An Ode,* in *The Poetical Works of Coleridge, Shelley, and Keats* (Philadelphia: Thomas Cowperthwait & Co., 1844), 48–49.

342    **"A savage place!"** These examples from Coleridge, Wordsworth, and Southey are quoted in Richard Holmes, introduction to *A Short Residence in Sweden, Norway, and Denmark and Memoirs of the Author of a Vindication of the Rights of Woman* (New York: Penguin, 1987), 17.

343    **"How often"** Wollstonecraft, *Letters from Sweden,* 110.

343    **A French traveler** quoted in Todd, *MW:ARL,* 369 n6.

344    **"discard[ing] all faith"** quoted in Mary Poovey, *The Proper Lady and the Woman Writer: Ideology as Style in the Works of Mary Wollstonecraft, Mary Shelley, and Jane Austen* (Chicago: University of Chicago Press, 1984), 256 n8.

344   **Anna Seward** Seward wrote, "We should at least have expected her to conceal the weakness, whose disclosure evinced the incompetence of all her maxims." Quoted in Todd, *MW:ARL*, 369 n5.

344   *The Monthly Mirror* Ibid., 369 n6.

344   **a generation of British travelers** Richard Holmes, introduction to *Letters from Sweden*, 41. The connection to Bird and Kingsley is first established by Holmes.

344   **"It was beneath the trees"** Mary Shelley, introduction to *Frankenstein*, 7–8.

CHAPTER TWENTY-SEVEN: MARY SHELLEY:
"WHEN WINTER COMES" (1819–1820)

345   **"Read—Work"** See entries in September, October, and November 1819, *Journals MWS*, 294–301.

345   **"the greatest poem"** Holmes, *Pursuit*, 532.

345   **"the most legal and effectual means"** quoted in ibid., 530.

346   **"that ideal beauty"** PBS to Mrs. Gisborne, October 13 or 14, 1819, *Letters PBS*, 2:126.

346   **"Hope is a duty"** Ibid.

347   **"tempestuous" and "animating"** Shelley's account of the composition of "Ode to the West Wind" in Hutchinson, ed., *Complete Poetical Works of Percy Bysshe Shelley*, 577.

347   **His anger** For a comprehensive account of the composition of "Ode to the West Wind," see Holmes, *Pursuit*, 547.

347   **"O wild West Wind"** Hutchinson, ed., *Complete Poetical Works of Percy Bysshe Shelley*, 573.

347   **At first he thought** Neville Rogers, *Shelley at Work: A Critical Inquiry* (Oxford: Clarendon Press, 1956), 228.

348   **Calling the manuscript "disgusting"** Jones, ed., *Shelley's Friends*, 44.

349   **"a little consoled"** PBS to Leigh Hunt, November 13, 1819, *Letters PBS*, 2:151.

349   **"[He] has a nose"** MWS to Mrs. Gisborne, November 13, 1819, *Letters MWS*, 1:112.

349   **"[Little Percy] is my only"** MWS to Marianne Hunt, November 24, 1819, ibid., 1:114.

349   **"a woman is not"** MWS to Marianne Hunt, March 24, 1820, ibid., 1:136.

350   **"Mary feels no remorse"** March 11, 1820, quoted in Seymour, *MS*, 240.

350   **"A bad wife"** February 8, 1820, *Journal CC*, 123.

350   **Sophia Stacey, a pretty young cousin** For excerpts from Stacey's diary, see Helena Rossetti Angeli, *Shelley and His Friends in Italy* (London: 1911). See also Holmes, *Pursuit*, 564–68, 579, 632.

352   **"undisturbed by weekly bills"** February 24 [error for March 24], 1820, *Letters MWS*, 1:136.

353   **"ragged-haired"** Ibid.

353   **"Men of England"** Hutchinson, ed., *Complete Poetical Works of Percy Bysshe Shelley*, 568.

354   **"highest and finest"** PBS to Ollier, September 1819, *Letters PBS*, 2:17. For more on Shelley's opinion about Keats's poetry, see Holmes, *Pursuit*, 613–14.

354   **"destined to become"** PBS to Marianne Hunt, October 29, 1820, *Letters PBS*, 1:239–40.

354   **"I am anxiously expecting him in Italy"** Ibid.

355   **"Does Mrs. S"** John Keats to Leigh Hunt, May 10, 1817, *The Correspondence of Leigh Hunt*, ed. Thornton Hunt (London: Smith, Elder and Co., 1862), 1:106.

355   **"Heigh-ho the Clare"** July 4, 1820, *Journals CC*, 154.

355   **"My affairs are in a state"** PBS to Godwin, August 7, 1820, ibid., 2:229.

356    **"To Mary"** Hutchinson, ed., *Complete Poetical Works of Percy Bysshe Shelley,* 366.

357    **"raked out of"** PBS to Peacock, November 8, 1820, *Letters PBS,* 2:245.

357    **In Mary's version** For an analysis of Mary Shelley's radical politics in *Valperga,* see Stuart Curran, "Valperga," in *Cambridge Companion to Mary Shelley,* 111–15.

357    **a female counterforce** Stuart Curran writes that the novel "offers a democratic and feminist alternative to the politics of the era." Ibid., 110.

358    **"Honour, fame, dominion"** Mary Shelley, *Valperga,* 205–6.

## CHAPTER TWENTY-EIGHT: MARY WOLLSTONECRAFT: "A HUMANE AND TENDER CONSIDERATION" (1796)

361    **"by which man"** William Godwin, *Caleb Williams,* ed. Maurice Hindle (New York: Penguin, 1988), 3.

362    **"Throw aside"** quoted in William Hazlitt, *The Spirit of the Age* (1825; reprint, New York: E. P. Dutton, 1955), 182.

363    **"shown a humane & tender"** Mary Hays to Godwin, January 11, 1796, in "Appendix A: Selections from the Mary Hays and William Godwin Correspondence," *Memoirs of Emma Courtney,* ed. Marilyn L. Brooks (Peterborough, Ontario: Broadview Press, 2000), 236.

363    **She "has frequently"** Godwin to Mary Hays, January [date?], 1796, in Durant, "Supplement," 311.

363    **"excellent" qualities** Mary Hays to Godwin, January 11, 1796, in "Appendix A: Selections from the Mary Hays and William Godwin Correspondence," *Memoirs of Emma Courtney,* ed. Brooks, 236.

364    **"very voluptuous"** Amelia Alderson to MW, August 28, 1796, Abinger MSS, Dep. b. 210/6, quoted in Todd, *MW:ARL,* 377.

364    **"the best"** Robert Southey to Joseph Cottle, March 13, 1787, *Life and Correspondence of Robert Southey,* ed. C. C. Southey (London, 1849).

365    **"old, ugly"** Amelia Alderson, August 28, 1796, Abinger MSS, Dep. b. 210/6, quoted in Todd, *MW:ARL,* 377.

365    **"I never touched your lips"** St. Clair, *Godwins and the Shelleys,* 162. Although most scholars are fairly certain that Holcroft wrote this letter, Holcroft's identity must remain speculative as the letter was sent anonymously. However, Todd argues that Holcroft is the likely author based on the language of the letter as well as the ideas expressed. See Todd, *MW:ARL,* 377–78 n20.

365    **Mary handled his overtures** Todd writes, "if she knew the anonymous writer to be Holcroft, she handled the situation with unusual tact." *MW:ARL,* 378.

365    **"the softness"** This passage is from a letter Godwin wrote to Maria Reveley after Mary Wollstonecraft had died to try to persuade Maria to marry him. Despite his relationship with Wollstonecraft, it is clear that he still held to his society's view of women: "the two sexes . . . are different in our structure; we are perhaps still more different in our education. Woman stands in need of the courage of man to defend her, of his constancy to inspire her with firmness, and, at present at least, of his science and information to furnish to her resources of amusement, and materials for studying. Women richly repay us for all that we can bring into the common stock, by the softness of their natures, the delicacy of their sentiments, and that peculiar and instantaneous sensibility by which they are qualified to guide our tastes and to correct our scepticism. For my part I am incapable of conceiving how domestic happiness could be so well generated without this disparity of character. I would not, if I could[,] marry a man in female form, though that form were the form of a Venus." September [date?], 1799, Paul, *Friends,* 336. Also, Pforzheimer Collection, reel 6.

365  "sympathy in her anguish" Godwin, *Memoirs,* 154.

365  "[Mary] speaks of her sorrows" Ibid., 133.

366  "I part with you in peace" MW to Imlay, March [date?], 1796, *Letters MW,* 339.

367  "mix the butter and flour together" Jebb, *Mary Wollstonecraft,* 291–92.

368  a milkmaid Paul, *Friends,* 74.

368  "cold and cunning" Coleridge did not mince words. "Mrs. Inchbald I do not like at all; every time I recollect her I like her less. That segment of a look at the corner of her eye—O God in heaven! It is so cold and cunning. Through worlds of wildernesses I would run away from the look, that heart-picking look!" Coleridge to Godwin, May 21, 1800, in *The Living Age* (Boston: 1864), vol. 81, 276. Also Pforzheimer Collection, reel 6.

369  "[Mrs. Inchbald]" Cecilia L. Brightwell, ed., *Memorials of the Life of Amelia Opie* (London: Longman, Brown, 1854), 57.

369  "new sharp-toed red morocco slippers" Amelia Alderson to Mrs. Taylor, in *The Living Age,* vol. 198 (Boston, 1893), 709.

370  "It would have entertained you" Ibid.

371  "crude and imperfect" Godwin, *Memoirs,* 152.

372  "fear of outrunning" Wollstonecraft, *Maria,* 78.

372  "a bird's eye view" MW to Godwin, July 1, 1796, *Letters MW,* 342.

373  "Now, I take" Ralph Wardle, *Godwin and Mary* (Lincoln: University of Nebraska Press, 1977), 8.

CHAPTER TWENTY-NINE: MARY SHELLEY: PISA (1820–1821)

374  "the softened tints" Mary Shelley, *Valperga,* 207.

374  He wished she were with them For more on Claire and Shelley at this stage of their relationship, see Holmes, *Pursuit,* 618, and Seymour, *MS,* 255, 57.

375  Having just returned For more on Medwin's character and appearance, see Seymour, *MS,* 255–56.

375  "His figure was emaciated" Thomas Medwin, *The Life of Percy Bysshe Shelley,* 2 vols. (London: 1847), 2:2.

375  "in the tenderness" Thomas Medwin, *Memoir of Percy Bysshe Shelley* (London: Whittaker, Treacher, & Co., 1833), 57.

376  "Congratulate me" October 29, 1820, *Letters PBS,* 2:241.

376  she had started to pay more attention This overview of Mary's appearance is from Seymour, *MS,* 260.

377  "much to my taste" MWS to CC, January 21, 1821, *Letters MWS,* 1:182.

377  the source of her sorrow MWS to Marianne Hunt, December 3, 1820, ibid., 1:165, 167. According to Mary, Emilia was "very beautiful, very talented," and "most unhappy. Her mother is a very bad woman; and, as she is jealous of the talents and beauty of her daughter, she shuts her up in a convent. . . ."

378  "the noble and unfortunate Lady" Hutchinson, ed., *Complete Poetical Works of Percy Bysshe Shelley,* 420–21.

379  "only the ash" Emilia Viviani to MWS, December 24, 1820. The Italian originals can be found in Enrica Viviani della Robbia, *Vita di una donna* (Florence: G. C. Sansoni, 1936), quoted in Betty Bennett, ed., *Selected Letters of Mary Wollstonecraft Shelley* (Baltimore: Johns Hopkins University Press, 1995), 120 n5.

379  "a death of ice" Hutchinson, ed., *Complete Poetical Works of Percy Bysshe Shelley,* 413.

379  "a good deal" MWS to Maria Gisborne, March 7, 1822, *Letters MWS,* 1:222.

379  people in Pisa PBS to Byron, September 14, 1821, *Letters PBS,* 2:347.

379  "a cloud" PBS to Mr. Gisborne, June 18, 1822, ibid., 2:434.

380  Of a broken heart Shelley wrote Byron that "Young Keats, whose 'Hyperion'

showed so great a promise, died lately at Rome from the consequences of breaking a blood-vessel, in paroxysms of despair at the contemptuous attack on his
book in the *Quarterly Review*." April 16, 1821, *Letters PBS*, 2:284. Byron did
not subscribe to Shelley's explanation of Keats's death: "I am very sorry to hear
what you say of Keats—is it *actually* true? I did not think criticism had been so
killing. . . . I read the review of 'Endymion' in the Quarterly. It was severe,—but
surely not so severe as many reviews in that and other journals upon others."
Byron to PBS, April 26, 1821, ed. Thomas Moore, *Letters and Journals of Lord
Byron: Complete in One Volume* (London: 1830), 479.

380  **"better, in point"** PBS to the Gisbornes, June 5, 1821, *Letters from Abroad*, 148.

380  **"Envy and calumny, and hate"** "Adonais" in Hutchinson, ed., *Complete Poetical
Works of Percy Bysshe Shelley*, 435.

381  **Shelley warmed** He wrote John Gisborne, "I like Jane more and more, and I find
Williams the most amiable of companions." June 18, 1822, Dowden, *Life of Shelley*, 2:512.

381  **Shelley had purchased** For more on this new vessel, see Holmes, *Pursuit*, 646–47.

381  **his "ducking"** PBS to Henry Reveley, April 17, 1821, *Letters PBS*, 2:285.

382  **An old friend** Seymour cites Sir John St. Aubyn's warning to Mary: "There are
subjects I entertain few people with, and whatever regard I may have for Mrs.
Williams, she is not of the number I should choose." *MS*, 271n.

383  **"We are not happy"** Hutchinson, ed., *Complete Poetical Works of Percy Bysshe Shelley*, 519.

384  **"Do you not hear the Aziola"** Ibid., 636.

385  **"[We must] form for ourselves"** PBS to MWS, August 15, 1821, *Letters PBS*, 2:339.

385  **He sent Hunt** PBS to Leigh Hunt, August 26, 1821, ibid., 2:344.

385  **"nice pretty"** MWS to Mrs. Gisborne, November 30, 1821, *Letters MWS*, 1:209.

386  **"Before I quitted"** CC to Byron, May [date?], 1821, Isabel Constance Clarke, *Shelley and Byron: A Tragic Friendship* (1934; reprint, New York: Ardent Media), 163.

386  **(over £2,000)** Sunstein, *MS:R&R*, 203.

386  **Mary and Claire chose** Ibid.

## CHAPTER THIRTY: MARY WOLLSTONECRAFT: IN LOVE AGAIN (1796)

388  **"I mean to bottle up my kindness"** MW to Godwin, July 21, 1796, *Letters MW*,
343–44.

389  **"the sentiment which trembled"** Godwin, *Memoirs*, 159.

389  **"was so puritanical"** Elizabeth Pennell, *Life of Mary Wollstonecraft* (Boston: Roberts Brothers, 1884), 290.

389  **"your sapient Philosophership"** MW to Godwin, August 11, 1796, *Letters MW*,
347.

389  **"voluptuous sensations"** MW to Godwin, September 13, 1796, ibid., 363.

389  **"you set"** Godwin to MW, August [date?], 1796, ibid., 349 n733.

390  **"Won't'ee, as Fannikin"** MW to Godwin, August 11, 1796, ibid., 347.

390  **"Did you"** MW to Godwin, August 16, 1796, ibid., 348.

390  **"I have been"** Godwin to MW, August 16, 1796, Wardle, *Godwin and Mary*, 14.

390  **and so felt rebuffed** MW to Godwin, August 17, 1796, *Letters MW*, 348.

390  **"I might be"** Godwin to MW, August 17, 1796, Wardle, *Godwin and Mary*, 16.

390  **"You have the feelings"** Ibid., 17.

391  *"chez moi"* For a brief explanation of Godwin's notation system, see Todd, *Letters
MW*, 348 n730. For a more complete description, see "William Godwin's Diary,"
Bodleian Library, http://godwindiary.bodleian.ox.ac.uk.

391   **"boy pupil"** Godwin to Mary, undated, 1796, Wardle, *Godwin and Mary,* 44.

391   **he added *"bonne"*** "William Godwin's Diary," October 9, 1796, http://godwin diary.bodleian.ox.ac.uk.

391   **"It is a sublime"** MW to Godwin, October 4, 1796, *Letters MW,* 371.

391   **"little marks"** MW to Godwin, November 18, 1796, ibid., 376.

391   **"You spoil little attentions"** Godwin to MW, undated, 1796, Wardle, *Godwin and Mary,* 49.

391   **"attention" from him** MW to Godwin, November 28, 1796, *Letters MW,* 381.

391   **"Can you solve this problem?"** MW to Godwin, October 7, 1796, ibid., 372.

392   **"a radical defect"** MW quoted Godwin in her letter, responding to his criticisms, September 4, 1796, ibid., 357–58.

392   **"What is to be done"** Ibid.

393   **"Yet now"** MW to Godwin, September 15, 1796, ibid., 365.

394   **"with [Fanny]"** MW to Godwin, September 17, 1796, ibid., 366.

394   **"Why could"** MW to Godwin, September 19, 1796, ibid.

395   **"cheerful, gay"** MW to Godwin, November 19, 1796, ibid., 377.

395   **"distinguish always between your jest and earnest"** Godwin to MW, undated, Wardle, *Godwin and Mary,* 50.

395   **"Go this way"** MW to Godwin, September 10, 1796, ibid., 359.

395   **"came crowing"** MW to Godwin, November 19, 1796, ibid., 377.

395   **"an extreme lowness"** MW to Godwin, December 6, 1796, ibid., 382.

395   **"I was a fool not to ask Opie"** MW to Godwin, December 7, 1796, ibid.

396   **"There was a tenderness"** MW to Godwin, December 23, 1796, ibid., 386.

396   **"painful recollections"** MW to Godwin, December 28, 1796, ibid., 387.

397   **"You have no petticoats"** MW to Godwin, January 12, 1797, ibid., 391.

397   **"obviate the evil"** MW to Godwin, December 31, 1796, ibid., 388.

397   **on February 6** For a comprehensive discussion of the sources that influenced Mary's depiction of madness in *The Wrongs of Woman,* see chapter 36, particularly notes 23–28, in Todd, *MW:ARL.*

397   **The asylum was located** For a comprehensive history of Bedlam during this period, see Catherine Arnold, *Bedlam* (London: Simon & Schuster, 2008), 172–80.

397   **shopped at an "old clothesmen's" storefront** "William Godwin's Diary," http:// godwindiary.bodleian.ox.ac.uk. On February 6, 1797, Godwin wrote, "old Clothes-man and Bedlam with Johnson and Wollstonecraft." Todd suggests that maybe they saw an "old Clothes-man" in Bedlam. *MW:ARL,* 492 n23.

399   **"It seems"** William Godwin, *The Enquirer: Reflections on Education, Manners, and Literature* (London: G. G. and J. Robinson, 1797), 86.

399   **Puss went "wild"** MW to Godwin, early 1797, ibid., 400.

401   **"most fruitful experiment"** Virginia Woolf, *The Second Common Reader* (1932; reprint, New York: Harcourt, Brace and World, 1960), 148.

**CHAPTER THIRTY-ONE: MARY SHELLEY:**
   **"LEAGUE OF INCEST" (1821–1822)**

402   **"We are entirely"** MWS to Mrs. Gisborne, November 30, 1821, *Letters MWS,* 1:209.

403   **Byron was probably** Medwin, *Life of Shelley,* 329.

403   **"the League of Incest"** According to Byron, this story had its origins in a rumor spread by the poet Robert Southey. In 1818, Byron wrote his friend John Cam Hobhouse that Southey had said that Byron and Shelley "had formed a League of Incest" while they were in Switzerland. Marchand, ed., *Byron's Letters and Journals,* 10.

403   **fat schoolboy** There are many different accounts of Byron's odd eating habits. But Andrew Stott points out that for Byron, his weight was not simply an aesthetic issue. Although he preferred the way he looked when he was slender, he also worried about how vigorous he felt when he was heavier. On the one hand, he enjoyed this vigor, but he also worried that it gave rise to his sexual binges and infamous rages, and so he dedicated himself to "starv[ing] the devil out." See "The Diets of the Romantic Poets," *Lapham's Quarterly,* http://www.laphams quarterly.org/roundtable/roundtable/the-diets-of-the-romantic-poets.php, accessed 9/23/13.

404   **"liked it the least"** Medwin, *Life of Shelley,* 335.

404   **"[Byron's] talk was"** Ibid., 330–31.

405   **"[Shelley] alone"** Edward Trelawny, *Recollections of the Last Days of Shelley and Byron* (London: Edward Moxon, 1858), 39.

405   **"Our good cavaliers"** MWS to Marianne Hunt, March 5, 1822, *Letters MWS,* 1:221.

406   **and called himself Ariel** Hutchinson, ed., *Complete Poetical Works of Percy Bysshe Shelley,* 665. Shelley's Ariel pose originated in a poem he entitled "With a Guitar: To Jane":

> *Ariel to Miranda: Take*
> *This slave of Music, for the sake*
> *Of him who is the slave of thee,*
> *And teach it all the harmony*
> *In which thou canst, and only thou.*

To John Gisborne, Shelley wrote, "[Jane] has a taste for music, and an elegance of form and motions that compensate in some degree for the lack of literary refinement. You know my gross ideas of music and will forgive me when I say that I listen the whole evening on our terrace to the simple melodies with excessive delight." June 18, 1822. He told Jane that she was his only "source of . . . consolation." July 4, 1822, *Letters PBS.*

407   **his biographers** The earliest skepticism about Trelawny's life story comes in Edward Garnett's introduction to Trelawny's memoir, *Adventures of a Younger Son* (London: 1890), 8.

407   **"his Moorish face"** January 19, 1822, *Journals MWS,* 391.

407   **"His 'Tremendous!' being indeed tremendous"** Garnett, introduction to *Adventures,* 17.

407   **"the everyday sleepiness"** January 19, 1822, *Journals MWS,* 391.

408   **"The Serpent is shut"** Hutchinson, ed., *Complete Poetical Works of Percy Bysshe Shelley,* 637.

408   **"the lines were too dismal"** PBS to Edward Williams, January [date?], 1822, *Letters PBS,* 2:384–86.

409   **"Shelley sent us some beautiful"** Jones, ed., *Shelley's Friends,* 125.

409   **fully "natural"** October 2, 1822, *Journals MWS,* 429.

409   **"Seek to know"** October 2, 1822, ibid., 430.

409   **"Be severe"** PBS to MWS, August 8, 1821, *Letters from Abroad,* 253.

409   **Shelley and Mary wanted £500** PBS to Ollier, September 25, 1821, *Letters PBS,* 2:353.

410   **"I long"** MWS to Mrs. Gisborne, February 9, 1822, *Letters MWS,* 1:218.

410   **Unfortunately, when *Valperga*** For an overview of the novel's reception, see Stuart Curran, "Valperga," in *Cambridge Companion to Mary Shelley,* 110–11.

410   **On the title page** Stuart Curran argues that when Mary declares herself as the

author of *Frankenstein* she is advertising her radical credentials for her audience. He writes, "subscribing herself on the title page as 'the Author of "Frankenstein" ' she makes clear that she will do so on her own terms, conspicuously refusing to accept the implicit gender limits that barred women from focusing upon public issues in their writing." Ibid., 114.

410 **The one critic** John Gibson Lockhart reviewed *Valperga* in *Blackwood's Edinburgh Magazine,* March 1823, quoted in ibid., 111. See also Michael Rossington, "Introduction" to *Valperga* (Oxford: Oxford University Press, 2000), xii–xix.

411 **"During a long—long evening"** February 8, 1822, *Journals MWS,* 396.

411 **"calm gray eyes"** Trelawny, *Recollections,* 28–29.

411 **"Hindustani dress"** Jones, ed., *Shelley's Friends,* 131.

412 **"the prettiest"** "Portrait de Mme. Shelley par le Comte de Metaxa," in Sunstein, *MS:R&R,* 208.

412 **"for his moral"** February 9, 1822, *Letters MWS,* 1:218.

412 **"You have"** Trelawny, *Recollections,* xv.

413 **"the model of an American"** Jones, ed., *Shelley's Friends,* 125.

413 **"Trelawny . . . found"** Garnett, introduction to *Adventures,* 8.

413 **Shelley "did not laugh"** Edward Trelawny, *Records of Shelley, Byron, and the Author* (London: 1878), xvi.

414 *The Corsair* Byron wrote Teresa, "I have met today the personification of my Corsair. He sleeps with the poem under his pillow, and all his past adventures and present manners aim at this personification." "La Vie de Lord Byron" by Teresa Guiccioli, quoted in *Journals MWS,* 392 n1.

414 **"weak" and "ignoble"** Trelawny, *Adventures of a Younger Son,* 20.

414 **Mary associated springtime** "Spring is our unlucky season," MWS to CC, March 20, 1822, *Letters MWS,* 1:226.

414 **the "Spezia plan"** This is Holmes's term. *Pursuit,* 696.

415 **declared that she would never dream** There are different versions of Jane's attitude toward the sailing plan. In general, most biographers agree that Jane expressed no uneasiness over the plan. But according to one report, "Mary said to Jane, 'I hate this boat, though I say nothing.' Said Jane, 'So do I, but speaking would be useless, and only spoil their pleasure.' " Dowden, *Life of Percy Bysshe Shelley,* 2:465.

415 **Claire had written** The letters that Claire wrote to PBS are lost, but her anxiety and her dream of kidnapping Allegra were well known to the whole circle. See *Journals CC,* 279–84.

416 **"insolent," Byron said** Quoted in Clarke, *Shelley and Byron: A Tragic Friendship,* 163.

416 **What is my Dear Papa doing?** Bodleian Library, University of Oxford, Shelfmark: MS. Abinger c 69, fol. 1r. Also available online, "Shelley's Ghost: Letter from Allegra to her father Lord Byron," http://shelleysghost.bodleian.ox.ac.uk /letter-from-allegra-to-her-father-lord-byron.

416 **"Bedlam behaviour"** Quoted in Clarke, *Shelley and Byron: A Tragic Friendship,* 163.

416 **"evil news"** April 23, 1822, *Journals MWS,* 408.

416 **The wisest plan** MWS to Mrs. Gisborne, June 2, 1822, *Letters MWS,* 1:236.

417 **"like a torrent"** June 2, 1822, ibid.

CHAPTER THIRTY-TWO: MARY WOLLSTONECRAFT: "I STILL MEAN TO BE INDEPENDENT" (1797)

419 **declared her determination** MW to Maria Reveley, Wednesday morning [c. spring/ summer 1797], *Letters MW,* 425.

419    *The Times* Quoted in Richard Holmes, *Sidetracks: Explorations of a Romantic Biographer* (New York: Random House, 2001), 208.

419    "It is my wish" MW to Amelia Alderson, April 11, 1797, *Letters MW,* 408–9.

419    "extraordinary characters" Brightwell, ed., *Memorials of Amelia Opie,* 63.

419    "My fair neighbor" Godwin to Mary Hays, April 10, 1797, C. Kegan Paul, "Prefatory Memoir" in *Letters to Imlay* by Mary Wollstonecraft, lv.

420    "Your secrecy" Thomas Holcroft to Godwin, April 6, 1797, in Paul, *Friends,* 1:240.

420    "Some persons" Godwin to Tom Wedgewood, April 1796, ibid.

420    "The assertrix" Knowles, *Fuseli,* 170.

421    "In order to" Durant, "Supplement," 313–14.

421    "I most sincerely" Paul, *Friends,* 1:240.

421    "the fervour" Ibid., 1:238.

422    "The wound" MW to Amelia Alderson, April 11, 1797, ibid., 409.

422    "Those who are bold" MW to Mary Hays, April [date?], 1797, *Letters MW,* 410.

422    "Your broken resolution" Paul, *Friends,* 1:238.

423    "all Mr Godwin's" Ibid.

423    "I wish you" MW to Godwin, June 6, 1797, *Letters MW,* 418.

423    "I have ordered" MW to Godwin, July 3, 1797, ibid., 427.

423    "Fanny is delighted" MW to Godwin, April 20, 1797, ibid., 410.

424    "I am sorry" MW to Godwin, May 21, 1797, ibid., 414.

424    "To be frank" MW to Godwin, July 4, 1797, ibid., 428.

424    "I have a design" MW to Godwin, July 3, 1797, ibid., 426.

424    "were in no danger" Godwin, *Memoirs,* 174.

425    "the disagreeable business" MW to Godwin, April 11, 1797, *Letters MW,* 407.

425    "my time, appears to me" Ibid.

426    **Mary claimed that Godwin's insistence** Todd writes, "In reiterating her belief in truth from observation and the necessity of independent thinking and self-expression, [Wollstonecraft's] essay, ostensibly a meditation on art, nature and the artist, formed another answer to Godwin and his incomprehension of her personal method of writing." *MW:ARL,* 425.

426    **All that was necessary** Harriet Jump Devine argues that "On Poetry" is Wollstonecraft's definitive defense of the imagination as a central tenet of Romantic aesthetics. See "'A Kind of Witchcraft': Mary Wollstonecraft and the Poetic Imagination," *Women's Writing* 4, no. 2 (1997): 235–45.

426    **"Boys who have received a classical education"** Mary Wollstonecraft, "On Poetry, and Our Relish for the Beauties of Nature," in *Posthumous Works of the Author of a Vindication of the Rights of Woman,* 4 vols., ed. William Godwin (1798), 3:169–70.

427    "warmth of their feelings" Ibid.

428    "the misery and oppression" Wollstonecraft, *Maria,* 59.

429    "to chastise and confine" Wendy Moore, *Wedlock: The True Story of the Disastrous Marriage and Remarkable Divorce of Mary Eleanor Bowes, Countess of Strathmore* (New York: Crown, 2009), 288.

429    "enem[y] of petticoat government" Ibid., 287.

429    "Considering the care" MW to Imlay, January 1, 1794, *Letters MW,* 238.

429    "I exclaim" Wollstonecraft, *Maria,* 142–43.

CHAPTER THIRTY-THREE: MARY SHELLEY: "IT'S ALL OVER" (1822)

431    "Had we been wrecked" MWS, "Notes on Poems of 1822," in Hutchinson, ed., *Complete Poetical Works of Percy Bysshe Shelley,* 670.

432 **"A sense of misfortune"** MWS to Mrs. Gisborne, August 15, 1822, *Letters MWS,* 1:244.

432 **"pale faced tragic villa"** "Italy Revisited," in Henry James, *Collected Travel Writings* (Library of America, 1877; reprint, 1993), 399.

433 **"wild & hateful"** MWS to Mrs. Gisborne, August 15, 1822, *Letters MWS,* 1:244.

433 **"The beauty yet strangeness"** Ibid.

433 **on May 2** Dowden, *Life of Shelley,* 547. Mary Shelley gives a slightly different account in a letter to Maria Gisborne, writing that Claire had decided to return to Florence a few days after they arrived at the Casa Magni and so Shelley was forced to tell her. June 2, 1822, *Letters MWS,* 1:238.

433 **"She now seems"** PBS to Byron, May 8, 1822, *Letters PBS,* 2:416.

434 **Byron's banker** Clarke, *Shelley and Byron: A Tragic Friendship,* 163.

434 **"She is grown tall and slight"** PBS to MWS, August 15, 1821, in Dowden, *Life of Shelley,* 435.

436 **"Under the influence of the doctrine"** Pforzheimer Collection, uncataloged manuscript, filed in Claire Clairmont to Lady Mountcashell, September 24, 1822. Published for the first time in Hay, *Young Romantics: The Tangled Lives of English Poetry's Greatest Generation,* 307–9.

436 **"cold neglect"** "The Choice," in *Journals MWS,* 491.

436 **"My heart was all thine own"** Ibid.

437 **"I am proud"** Jones, ed., *Shelley's Friends,* 162.

437 **"While walking"** Ibid., 147.

438 **"a golden key"** PBS to Trelawny, June 18, 1822, *Letters PBS,* 2:433.

438 **"Then, what is life?"** Holmes, *The Pursuit,* 724. See also Donald H. Reiman, *Shelley's "The Triumph of Life": A Critical Study* (Champaign: University of Illinois Press, 1965).

439 **"like cats"** MWS to Mrs. Gisborne, June 2, 1822, *Letters MWS,* 1:236.

439 **"You may imagine"** Ibid.

439 **"She is a most beautiful boat"** PBS to Captain Roberts, May 12, 1822, *Letters PBS,* 2:419.

440 **"took fire"** MWS to Mrs. Gisborne, August 15, 1822, *Letters MWS,* 1:236. As a result, many biographers still refer to Shelley's boat as the *Don Juan.*

440 **"My nerves"** August 15, 1822, MWS to Mrs. Gisborne, *Letters MWS,* 1:236.

441 **"trembled exceedingly"** MWS to Mrs. Gisborne, August 15, 1822, *Letters MWS,* 1:245.

441 **"sail like a witch"** May 15, 1822, Jones, ed., *Shelley's Friends,* 149.

442 **"brandy, vinegar"** MWS to Mrs. Gisborne, August 15, 1822, *Letters MWS,* 1:244.

442 **"Shelley overruled them"** Ibid.

442 **Mary heard** Ibid.

443 **"in the most horrible"** Ibid.

443 **"I wish I cd write more"** MWS to Leigh Hunt, June 30, 1822, ibid., 1:238.

444 **"the paper fell from me"** MWS to Mrs. Gisborne, August 15, 1822, ibid., 1:247.

444 **"A desperate sort of courage"** Ernest J. Lovell, ed., *Lady Blessington's Conversations with Lord Byron* (Princeton: Princeton University Press, 1969), 53.

444 **"[She] looked"** MWS to Mrs. Gisborne, August 15, 1822, *Letters MWS,* 3:247.

444 **"our calamity"** Ibid.

444 **"I felt the water"** Ibid.

444 **"Thrown about"** Ibid.

445 **Caterina, the maid** Trelawny, *Recollections,* 126.

446 **"how inexpressibly happy"** Thornton Hunt, quoted in Dowden, *Life of Shelley,* 564.

446 **They traveled to Pisa** Ibid., 566.

446    **"He was looking better"** Leigh Hunt, quoted in ibid.

446    **laughing so exuberantly** Holmes, *Pursuit,* 728.

446    **Trelawny said he thought** Trelawny, *Records of Shelley, Byron, and the Author,* 196.

447    **"a shrill voice"** *The Journal of Clarissa Trant* (London, 1826; reprint, 1925), 198–99. For an overview of the different accounts of the accident, see Dowden, *Life of Shelley,* 2:534–36, and Holmes, *Pursuit,* 729 n56.

447    **"How are you my best Mary?"** PBS to MWS, July 4, 1822, *Letters PBS,* 2:720.

447    **"three tons and a half"** Trelawny, *Records of Shelley, Byron, and the Author,* 200.

448    **"partly drawn over the head"** Trelawny, *Recollections,* 123.

448    **"I almost"** MWS to Godwin, July 19, 1822. St. Clair, *Godwins and the Shelleys,* 555.

448    **to Trelawny her surrender was evidence** Trelawny recorded his efforts in both of his memoirs, *Records of Shelley, Byron, and the Author* and *Recollections of the Last Days of Byron and Shelley,* the latter of which is an embellished version of his first account of the death of the poets. In both memoirs, Trelawny stresses his own importance in the poets' lives, stretching the facts and fabricating stories to serve his purpose. However, some sections of his memoirs appear to be reliable, particularly details which are not self-serving, such as his description of the *Ariel*'s unseaworthiness. When he took over the funeral arrangements, however, he began a process of reinvention that would be harmful to Mary. As Seymour writes, "This was the moment at which Trelawny converted himself into a keeper of the shrine, an earnest defender of the man he had known for less than six months but towards whom he now felt a veneration which would in time rival and threaten Mary's own dedicated love." *MS,* 304–5. For more on the legacy of Shelley's death, the myths that arose, and the contest among varying accounts, see Richard Holmes, "Death and Destiny," *Guardian,* January 24, 2004, http://www.theguardian.com /books/2004/jan/24/featuresreviews.guardianreview1.

449    **"swept into the seas"** Mary Shelley, *Frankenstein,* 190.

449    **"a dark and ghastly indigo color"** Trelawny, *Recollections,* 133.

450    **"used [a skull] as a drinking cup"** Ibid.

450    **He watched the air shiver** Ibid., 134.

450    **"waves which had overpowered"** *Journals MWS,* 423.

450    **"The scene of my existence"** MWS to Mrs. Gisborne, August 15, 1822, *Letters MWS,* 1:244–52.

451    **As an afterthought, he wrote to Mary** Trelawny to MWS, April [date?], 1823: "I . . . removed his ashes to [the tomb], placed a stone over it, am now planting it, and have ordered a granite to be prepared for myself, which I shall place in this beautiful recess . . . for when I am dead." Henry Buxton Forman, ed., *Letters of Edward John Trelawny* (London: Henry Frowde, Oxford University Press, 1910).

451    **Mary appeared unmoved** *Journals MWS,* 440.

451    **When Mary asked** The story of Shelley's heart is famous. For an early summary of the story, see Dowden, *Life of Shelley,* 2:534.

CHAPTER THIRTY-FOUR: MARY WOLLSTONECRAFT:
"A LITTLE PATIENCE" (1797)

453    **"Master William"** MW to Godwin, June 6, 1797, *Letters MW,* 416–17.

454    **"You cannot imagine"** Godwin to MW, June [date?], 1797, Wardle, *Godwin and Mary,* 89.

454    **"gone into the country"** MW to Godwin, June 10, 1797, *Letters MW,* 420.

454    **"icy Philosophy"** MW to Godwin, June 19, 1797, ibid., 421.

455    **"I am absurd"** MW to Godwin, July 4, 1797, ibid., 428.

455    **"I would on no account"** Godwin to MW, July 4, 1797, 115.

455  "Miss Pinkerton" MW to Miss Pinkerton, August 9, 1797, *Letters MW,* 434.

455  "incomprehensible conduct" Ibid., 434 n951.

455  "I am sensible" Miss Pinkerton to MW, [date?], 1797, ibid., 434 n952.

456  "I think you" Thomas Holcroft to Godwin and MW, April 6, 1797, Paul, *Friends,* 1:334.

456  "playful, easy air" William Hazlitt, "My First Acquaintance with Poets," *Selected Essays,* ed. George Sampson (1823; reprint, Cambridge: Cambridge University Press, 1958), 7.

456  "people of the imagination" Coleridge, quoted in ibid.

457  "Little Fanny" MW to Maria Reveley, spring/summer, 1797, *Letters MW,* 425.

457  "See how" Jebb, *Mary Wollstonecraft,* 291.

458  "strange Star" "The Choice," in *Journals MWS,* 491.

458  "to regain" MW to James Marshall, August 21, 1797, *Letters MW,* 435.

458  "true happiness" Godwin based his depiction of a widower's grief on his own experience of losing Mary Wollstonecraft in the novel *St. Leon: A Tale of the Sixteenth Century,* ed. William Dean Brewer (Peterborough, Ontario: Broadview Press, 2006), 87.

459  "I have" MW to Godwin, August 30, 1797, *Letters MW,* 436.

459  "Never shall I" Godwin, *St. Leon,* 89.

460  "despair . . . in" Godwin, *Memoirs,* 187.

461  "was determined" Ibid., 182.

462  "intreated her" Ibid., 189.

462  "The attachment" Paul, *Friends,* 1:282.

462  "to play with" Godwin, *Memoirs,* 189–90.

462  "I know" Paul, *Friends,* 1:197.

463  "the kindest" Ibid., 1:283.

463  "it was highly improper" Godwin, *Memoirs,* 199.

463  "What is man" Godwin, *St. Leon,* 297.

CHAPTER THIRTY-FIVE: MARY SHELLEY:
"THE DEEPEST SOLITUDE" (1823–1828)

465  "It is not true" October 2, 1822, *Journals MWS,* 429–30.

465  "No one seems" October 21, 1822, ibid., 440–41.

466  "It is only" MWS to Jane Williams, December 5, 1822, *Letters MWS,* 265.

466  "The number" Marianne Hunt, October 7, 1822, "Unpublished Diary of Mrs. Leigh Hunt," *Bulletin and Review of the Keats-Shelley Memorial,* Issues 1–2 (New York: Macmillan, 1910), 68.

467  "Can anything be more absurd" Marianne Hunt, September 23, 1822, "Unpublished Diary," 73.

468  "Those about me have no idea" MWS to Mrs. Gisborne, September 17, 1822, *Letters MWS,* 1:261.

468  Mary thought that this was hypocritical behavior She wrote Jane, "I hate & despise the intrigues of married women, nor in my opinion can the chains which custom throws upon them justify . . . deceit." December 5, 1822, ibid., 1:264.

468  "estranged my son's mind" Sir Timothy Shelley to Byron, February 6, 1823, in Doris Langley Moore, *Accounts Rendered* (London: John Murray, 1974), 404–5.

469  "I should not live" MWS to Byron, February 25, 1823, *Letters MWS,* 1:315.

469  "I think I could find my way better" MWS to Louisa Holcroft, October 2, 1823, ibid., 3:388.

469  significant changes For a more comprehensive overview of the "new" London, see Porter, *London,* 200.

470    **"the monstrous Drama"** *Theatrical Observer,* August 9, 1823. Miranda Seymour suggests that these "protesters" were hired by the theater to promote the play. *MS,* 334.

470    **"breathless eagerness"** MWS to Leigh Hunt, September 9–11, 1823, *Letters MWS,* 1:378.

470    **Unfortunately, Mary earned no money** Seymour writes, "playwrights were under no obligation to hand over money for their use of a book." *MS,* 335.

470    **a *Punch* cartoonist** November 4, 1843, *Mr. Punch's Victorian Era: An Illustrated Chronicle of the Reign of Her Majesty the Queen,* vol. 1 (London: Bradbury, Agnew & Co., 1887), 23.

471    **"the old gentleman"** For more on William Godwin, see Seymour, *MS,* 333.

471    **John Chalk Claris** *The Literary Gazette* declared: "This wretched composition on the lamentable and appalling death of Shelley . . . is corrupt; its sentiments vapid, unintelligible or wicked; and its poetical demerits of the most obnoxious character." September 21, 1822, no. 296, 591. For a complete listing of references to Shelley in the 1820s, see Karsten Klejs Engelberg, *The Making of the Shelley Myth: An Annotated Bibliography of Criticism of Percy Bysshe Shelley, 1822–60* (London: Mansell, 1988).

471    **Bess Kent** *Monthly Magazine,* August 1, 1823, vol. 56, no. 385.

472    **However, this project was bigger** For a comprehensive exegesis of Mary as editor, see Susan Wolfson, "Mary Shelley, Editor," in *The Cambridge Companion to Mary Shelley,* ed. Esther Schor (Cambridge: Cambridge University Press, 2003), 193–210.

472    **She made the additions** For a perceptive and careful analysis of Mary's contributions to shaping Shelley's work and literary legacy, see ibid., 191–210.

473    **Mary covered her tracks** Wolfson points out that Mary inserted her authorial presence through her notes and her biographical additions, but to her contemporary audience, she posed as a humble wife, a helpful disciple. See ibid., 191–210. Wolfson writes, "By fragments and wholes, Mary Shelley produced 'Percy Bysshe Shelley.'" Ibid., 197.

474    **"I am a tree"** Mary Shelley, *Last Man,* 391.

474    **"law of nature"** MWS to Teresa Guiccioli, May 16, 1824, *Letters MWS,* 1:422.

474    **"The Last Man!"** May 14, 1824, *Journals MWS,* 476.

475    **"if you knew"** MWS to Teresa Guiccioli, December 30, 1824, *Letters MWS,* 1:460.

476    **"I know now"** January 30, 1825, *Journals MWS,* 489.

476    **"charm and fascination"** Eliza Rennie, *Traits of Character; Being Twenty-Five Years of Literary and Personal Recollections,* 2 vols. (London: 1860), 2:207–8.

476    **deluging her with letters** Doddy addresses Mary as "my Pretty" and "Meine Liebling." She adds that five days apart cause her anguish. "Counting on my fingers last night in thy company like a child looking forward to its promised holiday, I felt something approaching to pain. . . ." Maria Diana Dods to MWS, n.d. (Oxford, Bodleian Library, Abinger Dep. c. 516/11).

477    **"I am not sure that male eyes"** MWS to Jane Williams, July 28, 1826, *Letters MWS,* 1:556.

477    **"our pretty N——"** MWS to Jane Williams, summer, 1826, ibid., 1:573. Later in life, Mary would reflect on this relationship to Trelawny, using a curious term, "tousy-mousy," that does seem to suggest a sexual relationship: "Ten years ago I was so ready to give myself away—& being afraid of men, I was apt to get *tousy-mousy* for women" (October 12, 1835, *Letters MWS,* 2:256). Betty Bennett, the editor of Mary Shelley's letters and the scholar who discovered Doddy's trans-

vestite identity, writes a thorough explanation of the term "tousy-mousy" in the nineteenth century: "According to contemporary polite usage, 'to touse and mouse' meant 'to pull around roughly.' See *Dictionary of Obsolete and Provincial English*, ed. Thomas Wright (London: Henry G. Bohn, 1851). A variant, 'towsy-mousy,' was also slang for the female pudendum. See *Slang and Its Analogues*, eds. J. S. Farmer and W. E. Henley (1st ed., 1890–1904; reprint, New York: Arno Press, 1970)," in *Mary Diana Dods: A Gentleman and a Scholar* (Baltimore: Johns Hopkins Press, 1994), 286 n18. The *OED* defines "tousy" or "towsy" as "disheveled, unkempt, tousled; shaggy, rough" and notes that it also occurs in combinations. However, despite these contemporary understandings of the term, Bennett rejects the idea that Mary Shelley was ever sexually attracted to women. I disagree. My interpretation of these letters is that Mary and Jane shared an important and close relationship that was at times sexual in nature.

477 **"the hope & consolation of my life"** MWS to Leigh Hunt, June 27, 1825, *Letters MWS*, 1:491.

477 **"sickening repetition of horrors"** Review of *The Last Man*, *Literary Gazette*, vol. 10 (London: Henry Colburn, 1826), 103; Google Books. For a comprehensive account of the reception and publication history of *The Last Man*, see Morton D. Paley, "*The Last Man*: Apocalypse Without Millennium," in *The Other Mary Shelley: Beyond Frankenstein*, ed. Audrey A. Fisch, Anne K. Mellor, and Esther H. Schor (New York: Oxford University Press, 1993), 107–22.

478 **imagination was "diseased"** This unsigned review in *The Monthly Review* linked Mary to Shelley, Godwin, and Wollstonecraft: "Mrs Shelley, true to the genius of her family, has found this breathing world and the operations and scenes which enliven it, so little worthy of her soaring fancy, that she once more ventures to create a world of her own, to people it with beings modelled by her own hand, and to govern it by laws drawn from the visionary theories which she has been so long taught to admire as the perfection of wisdom. . . . Her imagination appears to delight in inventions which have no foundation in ordinary occurrences, and no charm for the common sympathies of mankind. . . . The whole course of her ambiton has been to pourtray [sic] monsters which could have existed only in her own conceptions, and to involve them in scenes and events which are wholly unparalleled by any thing that the world has yet witnessed. . . . The whole appears to us to be the offspring of a diseased imagination, and of a most polluted taste." *Monthly Review, from January to April Inclusive*, vol. 1, 1826 (London: R Griffiths, 1826), Google Books, 335.

478 **James Fenimore Cooper's** Morton Paley addresses the contrast between Mary's work and that of her contemporaries. See "*The Last Man*: Apocalypse Without Millennium," in *The Other Mary Shelley: Beyond Frankenstein*, ed. Audrey A. Fisch, Anne K. Mellor, and Esther H. Schor (New York: Oxford University Press, 1993), 107–22.

478 **"She is in truth"** MWS to Leigh Hunt, August 12, 1826, *Letters MWS*, 1:528.

479 **Doddy knew that many people thought** For more on the problematic issue of writing about transvestism and lesbian identity as a literary biographer, with a particular focus on the issues of Doddy's gender identity, see Geraldine Friedman, "Pseudonymity, Passing, and Queer Biography: The Case of Mary Diana Dods," *Romanticism on the Net 23(2001)*, Michael Eberle-Sinatra, ed., Richard Sha, guest ed., doi: 10:7202/005985ar. Betty Bennett is the first to have discovered Doddy's identity as a transvestite. She tells the story of her discovery and the evidence she found in *Mary Diana Dods*.

480    **"My friend"** July 13, 1827, *Journals MW,* 502–3.

480    **Mary put a stop to it** "Do not I earnestly pray you, allude to the past, or the changes which cannot be unchanged—" MWS to Jane Williams Hogg, June 5, 1828, *Selected Letters MWS,* 205.

481    **"how ardently I desire to see him"** MWS to Jane Williams Hogg, June 5, 1828, *Letters MWS,* 2:42.

481    **an angry critique** Mary would defend herself against Trelawny's criticisms, writing him a long letter: "you are angry with me, you speak of evasions—What do you ask, what do I refuse? Let me write to you as to my own heart and do not show this letter to any one—You talk of writing Shelley's life and ask me for materials—Shelley's life as far as the public had to do with it consisted of very few events and these are publicly known—The private events were sad and tragical." December 15, 1829, ibid., 2:94.

482    **"a share"** CC to Trelawny, dated by Stocking to after 1828 because Claire refers to her time in Dresden earlier in the passage. Apparently, Claire had not yet condemned Shelley for his stance on free love, as she was still championing him as an ideal of virtue. Later in this same letter, she declares, "Would to God she [Mary] could perish without note or remembrance, so the brightness of his [Shelley's] name might not be darkened by the corruptions she sheds upon it. What low ambition is that, that seeks for tinsil [sic] and gaudiness when the reality of all that is noble and worthy has passed away." *Journals CC,* 432.

483    **She continued to have her work** Mary Shelley wrote twenty-one stories for magazines and annuals between 1823 and 1839. Her heroines suffer at the hands of their enemies, and often die rather than conform to the demands of society. In many ways, these stories serve as Mary's protest against the strictures of marriage and what Charlotte Sussman calls "the commodification" of women. Sussman writes: "Shelley's critiques of the way women's economic value is controlled by the marriage market arrive in a medium that helped construct another form of value within the domestic sphere: a medium that construed women not merely as marriageable bodies, but as readers and writers. If the images in the annuals offer a piece of femininity preserved in amber, the stories and poems within them undermine both that ideal of femininity, and that structure of economic value." "Stories for the Keepsake," in *Cambridge Companion to Mary Shelley,* 178.

483    **"A solitary woman"** Mary Shelley, "Review, 'The Loves of the Poets,'" *Westminster Review* 11, October 2, 1829 (London: 1829), 476.

## CHAPTER THIRTY-SIX: MARY WOLLSTONECRAFT: THE MEMOIR (1797–1801)

485    **"the first of her friends"** Johnson to Godwin, September 12, 1797, Gerald P. Tyson, *Joseph Johnson: A Liberal Publisher* (Iowa City: University of Iowa Press, 1979), 150–51.

485    **"not altogether"** Mary Hays to Godwin, October 1797, Abinger: Dep. b. 227/8.

486    **"sincere and earnest"** Paul, *Friends,* 1:283.

486    **Already, glowing death notices** Mary Hays had written a laudatory obituary in *The Monthly Magazine,* as well as a fifty-page biographical tribute in *The Annual Necrology,* in which she declared: "[Wollstonecraft's] conceptions were bold and original, her freedom of thinking, and courage in stemming popular opinions, worthy of admiration. An obscure individual, unknown and unsupported, she raised herself by her own exertions to an eminence that excited, in an extraordinary degree, public attention, and afforded her a celebrity extending beyond the limits of the country which gave her birth. [She possessed] a feminine sensibility

and tenderness united with masculine strength and fortitude, a combination as admirable as rare. . . . Her own sex has lost, in the premature fate of this extraordinary woman, an able champion; yet she has not labored in vain: the spirit of reform is silently pursuing its course. Who can mark its limits?" Mary Hays, *The Annual Necrology for 1797–98; Including, also, Various Articles of Neglected Biography,* vol. 1 (1798), 426.

487    **"It has always"** Godwin, *Memoirs,* 1.

488    **"I should be glad"** Godwin to Skeys, October [date?], 1797: Abinger: Dep. b. 227/8. See also a second note, Dep. b. 229/1(a) October 17, 1797.

489    **"When Eliza and I first learnt"** Everina to Godwin, November 24, 1797. Abinger: Dep. c. 523.

490    **"To speak frankly"** For the argument between Hays and Godwin, see their letters: October 5, 10, 22, and 27, 1797, Abinger: Dep. b. 227/8.

492    **flawed by "sentiments"** Godwin, *Memoirs,* 81–83.

492    **"too contemptuous" of Burke** Ibid., 76.

492    **"incompatible with the writer's essential character"** Ibid., 81–83.

493    **Not until the 1970s** The first full-scale biography to celebrate Wollstonecraft's achievements was Claire Tomalin's *The Life and Death of Mary Wollstonecraft* (London: Penguin, 1974).

493    **"less vigorous" minds** Mary Wollstonecraft, *Posthumous Works of the Author of a Vindication of the Rights of Woman,* 4 vols. (London: 1798), 164.

494    **"scripture . . . for propagating whores"** *Anti-Jacobin Review and Magazine, or Monthly Political and Literary Censor* 5 (1800), 25.

494    **"stripping his dead wife naked"** Robert Southey to William Taylor, July 1, 1804, no. 958, in *A Memoir of the Life and Writings of the Late William Taylor of Norwich,* 2 vols. (London: 1843), 1:506. Also available online: *The Collected Letters of Robert Southey,* Part 3: *1804–1809,* ed. Carol Bolton and Tim Fulford: A Romantic Circles Electronic Edition, February 17, 2014, http://romantic.arhu.umd.edu /editions/southey_letters/Part_Three/HTML/letterEEd.26.958.html.

495    **"William hath penn'd"** *Anti-Jacobin Review* 5 (1800), 25.

495    **"voluptuous dogmas of Mary Godwin"** *Anti-Jacobin Review* 7 (1801), 374 (Google Books). For an overview of Elizabeth Hamilton's philosophy and work, see Claire Grogan, introduction to *Memoirs of Modern Philosophers* by Elizabeth Hamilton (Peterborough, Ontario: Broadview Press, 2000).

495    **In Maria Edgeworth's *Belinda*** Deborah Weiss suggests that Edgeworth's portrait of Harriet Freke is not meant to be a caricature of Wollstonecraft, but in fact extends and develops Wollstonecraft's theories about sexuality, as, like Wollstonecraft, Edgeworth rejected "the period's essentialist understanding of gender." "The Extraordinary Ordinary Belinda: Maria Edgeworth's Female Philosopher," *Eighteenth Century Fiction* 19, no. 4, article 5 (2007). http://digitalcommons .mcmaster.ca/ecf/vol19/iss4/5.

496    **"no correct history"** *Analytical Review* 27 (1798), 238.

## CHAPTER THIRTY-SEVEN: MARY SHELLEY: A WRITING LIFE (1832–1836)

499    **"gentle, feminine"** For a full account, see Eliza Rennie, "An Evening at Dr Kitchiner's," in *Friendship's Offering* (London: 1842), 2:243–49.

499    **"rather indiscreet"** Viscount Dillon to MWS, March 18, 1829, Marshall, *The Life and Letters of Mary Wollstonecraft Shelley,* 2:197.

500    **"My first impulse"** November 18, 1831, *Journals MWS,* 524.

500    **"ineffable bliss"** October 5, 1839, ibid., 563.

500    **"Liberty must and will raise her head"** Peter Beauclerk Dewar and Donald Adamson, *The House of Nell Gwynn: The Fortunes of the Beauclerk Family* (London: William Kimber, 1974), quoted in Sunstein, *MS:R&R,* 316.

501    **a tamer version** The comparison between Aubrey Beauclerk and Percy Shelley is based on Sunstein, *MS:R&R,* 316–17.

501    **"I hope"** MWS to Jane Hogg, May 5, 1833, *Letters MWS,* 2:189.

501    **"the aspect"** April or May, 1833, *Journals MWS,* 529.

502    **"Dark night"** August [date?], 1833, ibid., 530.

503    **Victor is a puppet** Anne Mellor argues this case slightly differently. She points out the difference in Mary Shelley's depiction of fate and Nature in the two versions, but argues that although her vision of fate is darker in the 1831 *Frankenstein,* her view of human nature, of Frankenstein himself, is slightly more positive. Mellor writes, "In 1818 Victor Frankenstein possessed free will or the capacity for meaningful moral choice—he could have abandoned his quest for the 'principle of life,' he could have cared for his creature, he could have protected Elizabeth. In 1831, such choice is denied to him. He is the pawn of forces beyond his knowledge or control." *Mary Shelley: Her Life, Her Fiction, Her Monsters* (1988; reprint, New York: Routledge, 1989), 171. Thus, according to Mellor, in 1831, Mary's fatalistic vision excuses Frankenstein from some of his crimes since he is helpless. Mellor also makes the important point that Mary presents herself in the same role as Frankenstein, helpless in the hands of fate; Mary Shelley "disclaimed responsibility for her hideous progeny and insisted that she had remained passive before it, 'leaving the core and substance of it untouched.' . . . Like Victor Frankenstein, she has become the unwilling 'author of unalterable evils.' " *Mary Shelley: Her Life,* 176. For another discussion of the role of fate in the two different versions of *Frankenstein,* see Mary Poovey, *The Proper Lady and the Woman Writer: Ideology as Style in the Works of Mary Wollstonecraft, Mary Shelley, and Jane Austen* (Chicago: University of Chicago Press, 1884), 133–41. See also John R. Reed, "Will and Fate in *Frankenstein,*" *Bulletin of Research in the Humanities* 83 (1980): 319–38.

504    **"Unhappy man! Do you share?"** Mary Shelley, *Frankenstein,* 24.

505    **there is consensus** For a comprehensive discussion of Mary's work as a biographer, see Greg Kucich, "Biographer," in *The Cambridge Companion to Mary Shelley,* ed. Esther Schor (Cambridge: Cambridge University Press, 2003), 226–41.

505    **"My life & reason"** December 2, 1834, *Journals MWS,* 543.

506    **she spent hours excavating** For example, in her portrait of Montaigne, his youthful admirer, Marie de Gournay le Jars, steals the spotlight from the great male writer; Marie, like Mary, promoted the work of the man she loves: "It was she who edited and published his essays, writing a preface in which she ably defended the work from the attacks made against it." Indeed, in Mary's hands, Marie sounds a good deal like Mary herself: "[Marie was] a young person of great merit, and afterwards esteemed one of the most learned and excellent ladies of the day; and honored by the abuse of pedants, who attacked her personal appearance and her age, in revenge for her transcending even their sex in accomplishments and understanding: while, on the other hand, she was regarded with respect and friendship by the first men of her time." Mary Shelley, *Lives of the Most Eminent French Writers* (Philadelphia: Lea and Blanchard, 1840), 44.

506    **"You must consider me"** MWS to Mrs. Gisborne, June 11, 1835, *Letters MWS,* 2:245.

506    **"I have bartered my existence"** December 2, 1834, *Journals MWS,* 542.

507    **"great horror"** MWS to Mary Hays, April 20, 1836, *Letters MWS,* 2:270.

507    **"What I then went through"** June 7, 1836, *Journals MWS,* 549.

507    **"as near"** MWS to Mary Hays, April 20, 1836, *Letters MWS,* 2:271.

510    **But Mary stood firm** To Trelawny's accusations, Mary replied, "Could you not trust that I thought anxiously—decided carefully—& from disinterested motives—not to save myself but my child from evil—" MWS to Trelawny, January 26, 1837, *Letters MWS,* 2:282.

510    **The heroine of *Falkner*** For an insightful comparison of the two Elizabeths, see Kate Ferguson Ellis, "*Falkner* and Other Fictions," in *Cambridge Companion to Mary Shelley,* 151–62.

511    **the novel's subversive conclusion** Until fairly recently, Shelley's work was viewed as growing increasingly conservative over time. As Kate Ferguson Ellis writes, "[Mary] Shelley's later fiction is not usually considered particularly feminist." "*Falkner* and Other Fictions," in *Cambridge Companion to Mary Shelley,* 161. In 1984, Mary Poovey argued that *Falkner* is a far less innovative and political novel than *Frankenstein,* as Shelley had retreated from political topics to a celebration of the domestic sphere. *The Proper Lady and the Woman Writer,* 164–65. But as Ellis points out, basing her argument on the ideas of Anne Mellor in *Mary Shelley: Her Life, Her Fiction, Her Monsters,* in *Falkner* Shelley takes the radical step of attempting to depict what Mellor calls "the egalitarian bourgeois family." "*Falkner* and Other Fictions," 161. For further insight into Shelley's radical politics in *Falkner,* see Melissa Sites, "Utopian Domesticity as Social Reform in Mary Shelley's *Falkner,*" *Keats-Shelley Journal* 54 (2005): 148–72.

511    **Most critics disliked** For an overview of the novel's critical reception, see Seymour, *MS,* 445–46.

511    ***The Age*** *The Age,* April 2, 1837, 106.

## CHAPTER THIRTY-EIGHT: MARY WOLLSTONECRAFT: THE WRONGS (1797–1798)

512    **he did edit several of Mary's** Harriet Devine Jump analyzes the ways in which Godwin changed Wollstonecraft's "On Poetry" to make it more conservative and more in keeping with Enlightenment values, rather than the new Romantic aesthetics. She writes that he "removed or amended no less than four references to the imagination." "'A Kind of Witchcraft': Mary Wollstonecraft and the Poetic Imagination," *Women's Writing* 4, no. 2 (1997): 242–43. Tilomatta Rajan suggests that Godwin included "On Poetry" in Wollstonecraft's *Posthumous Works* to paint a picture of Wollstonecraft as a "private and ruminative" writer instead of a "public" author. See "Framing the Corpus: Godwin's 'Editing' of Wollstonecraft in 1798," *Studies in Romanticism* 39 (2005): 511–31, 515.

512    **diluting her ideas** Having never agreed with Mary's arguments that the best writing should come straight from the heart and the imagination, that it was better to have an unpolished essay that was honest and powerful than an overly refined one that contained little of merit, he cut four of her references to the imagination. But this was a profound misrepresentation of her ideas, since, for Wollstonecraft, the imagination represented a democratic opportunity. Anyone could have an imagination. Not everyone could have an education. In addition, her "poetic reveries" allowed her to break down gender stereotypes and ideological boundaries. As Lawrence R. Kennard writes, "[Wollstonecraft's] poetics of sensibility and her poetical reveries represent attempts to reconstruct both self and reality. . . . Wollstonecraft's reveries . . . offer a critique, not simply of generic conventions but also of ideological binarism and the stereotyped subject." "Rev-

eries of Reality," in *Mary Wollstonecraft and Mary Shelley: Writing Lives,* eds. Buss, Macdonald, and McWhir, 66.

513    **If one looks up "Prostitution"** *European Magazine,* April 1798 (33: 246–51), in Durant, "Supplement," 340. For an excellent overview of the critical response to Wollstonecraft, see Claudia Johnson, "Introduction," and Cora Kaplan, "Mary Wollstonecraft's Reception and Legacies," in *The Cambridge Companion to Mary Wollstonecraft,* ed. Claudia Johnson (Cambridge: Cambridge University Press, 2002), 1–6, 246–70.

513    **foster licentiousness** Durant, "Supplement," 344.

514    **"the misconduct of one of [her]"** Ibid., 340.

514    **"the most pernicious consequences"** Ibid.

515    **"the good old rules"** Wollstonecraft, *Wrongs of Woman,* ed. Mellor, 354.

515    **"a poor victim"** Quoted in Miriam Wallraven, *Writing Halfway Between Theory and Fiction: Mediating Feminism from the Seventeenth to the Twentieth Century* (Würzburg, Ger.: Königshausen & Neumann, 2007), 93.

515    **Robert Browning cemented** Robert Browning, "Wollstonecraft and Fuseli," in *Jocoseria* (London: Smith, Elder, & Co., 1883), 48.

515    **In 1885, when Karl Pearson** Gordon, *VAL,* 389.

516    **"the hero of each tale"** Wollstonecraft, advertisement for *Letters from Sweden.*

516    **"tracing the outline"** Godwin, *Memoirs,* 8.

517    **"[w]hose earnest lives"** *History of Woman Suffrage,* ed. Elizabeth Cady Stanton, Susan B. Anthony, and Matilda Joslyn Gage, vol. 1 (1881; Project Gutenberg, 2007), 831, http://www.gutenberg.org/files/28020/28020-h/28020-h.htm #CHAPTER_I.

517    **Carrie Chapman Catt** On June 9, 1936, in a commencement speech at Sweet Briar College, Catt declared, "Just when the woman movement began, no one knows. I like to think that the definite woman movement was lifted out of the disconnected and far scattered agitation by Mary Wollstonecraft's book, 'A Vindication of the Rights of Woman.'" www.loc.gov/rr/mss/text/catt.html#speech.

517    **a literary "grandmother"** This is Browning's famous complaint about the lack of female literary forebears: "I look everywhere for grandmothers and see none." Elizabeth Barrett Browning to Henry Chorley, January 7, 1845, in *The Letters of Elizabeth Barrett Browning,* ed. Frederic G. Kenyon, vol. 1 (London: Smith, Elder, & Co., 1898), 232.

517    **Reading Wollstonecraft at age twelve** "I read Mary Wolstonecraft [*sic*] when I was thirteen—no, twelve! . . . and, through the whole course of my childhood, I had a steady indignation against nature who made me a woman, & a determinate resolution to dress up in men's clothes as soon as ever I was free of the nursery, & go into the world 'to seek my fortune.'" Elizabeth Barrett Browning to Mary Russell Mitford, July 22, 1842, ibid. For further discussion of the importance of Wollstonecraft to the young Elizabeth Barrett, see Susan Wolfson, *Borderlines: The Shiftings of Gender in British Romanticism* (Redwood City, CA: Stanford University Press, 2006), 87.

517    **"loftiness of moral"** George Eliot, "Margaret Fuller and Mary Wollstonecraft," *Leader* 6 (October 13, 1855), 988. Reprinted in *Essays of George Eliot,* ed. Thomas Pinney (London: Routledge, 1968).

517    **"Many millions have died"** Virginia Woolf, *The Second Common Reader* (1932, repr. London: Harcourt, Brace & World, 1960), 148.

CHAPTER THIRTY-NINE: MARY SHELLEY: RAMBLINGS
(1837–1848)

520    **"Poor Harriet"** February 12, 1839, *Journals MWS,* 560.

521    **"This is not the time"** "Preface" in Hutchinson, ed., *Complete Poetical Works of Percy Bysshe Shelley,* 1:x.

521    **"I am torn"** February 12, 1839, *Journals MWS,* 559.

521    **"sort of unspeakable"** MWS to Leigh Hunt, July 20, 1839, *Letters MWS,* 2:318.

521    *The Examiner* For the negative response to Mary's work as an editor, see *Letters MWS,* 2:282 n1.

522    **"to mutilate"** MWS to Leigh Hunt, December 14, 1839, ibid., 2:326.

522    **"as many of Shelley's own words"** MWS to Leigh Hunt, October 10, 1839, ibid., 2:327.

522    **"His spirit"** Hutchinson, ed., *Complete Poetical Works of Percy Bysshe Shelley,* 1:xii–xiii.

523    **"Christian hearted"** George Lewes and Thornton Hunt, obituary in *The Leader,* 1851, quoted in *MS:R&R,* 384.

525    **"Time . . . adds only to the keenness"** MWS to Leigh Hunt, December 23, 1839, *Letters MWS,* 2:335.

525    **"She lives on hogs wash"** Trelawny to CC, August 17, 1838, Forman, ed., *Letters of Edward Trelawny,* 209.

526    **"Another hope"** November 27, 1839, *Journals MWS,* 563–64.

526    **"I feel a good deal of the gipsy"** Mary Shelley, *Rambles in Germany and Italy in 1840, 1842, and 1843* (London: Moxon, 1844), 1:9.

526    **"to my own land"** MWS to Abraham Hayward, October 26, 1840, *Letters MWS,* 3:5.

526    **"amounting almost to agony"** Shelley, *Rambles,* 1:61.

526    **"A friendship secure"** November 27, 1839, *Journals MWS,* 563.

527    **"unhappy, betrayed, alone"** Mary wrote this in Italian on January 12, 1841, ibid., 570–71. "Pare che le mie calde preghiere sono udite esaudite—Pare—dio volesse che sara—ed io—se veramente tutto va bene—felice me! partire di questo paese fra poco."

527    **"I gave all"** February 26, 1841, ibid., 573.

530    **"the immeasurable goodness"** Mary Shelley, *Rambles,* 1:12.

530    **arguing against Austria's occupation** For an analysis of Mary Shelley's politics in *Rambles,* see Jeanne Moskal, "Travel Writing," in *Cambridge Companion to Mary Shelley,* ed. Esther Schor (Cambridge: Cambridge University Press, 2003), 247–50. For Mary Shelley's art criticism, see Moskal, "Speaking the Unspeakable: Art Criticism as Life Writing in Mary Shelley's *Rambles in Germany and Italy,*" in *Mary Wollstonecraft and Mary Shelley: Writing Lives,* ed. Helen Buss, D. L. Macdonald, and Anne McWhir (Waterloo, Ontario: Wilfrid Laurier University Press, 2001), 189–216.

530    **no one noted** Overall, however, the book was received enthusiastically. One reviewer praised *Rambles,* declaring that Mary Shelley had proven herself to be "a woman who thinks for herself on all subjects, and who dares to say what she thinks." Quoted in Elizabeth Nitchie, "Mary Shelley, Traveller," *Keats-Shelley Journal* 10 (1961): 22–42, 34. A review in the *Atlas* lauded her "rich fancy, her intense love of nature and her sensitive apprehension of all that is good, and beautiful and free." Quoted in Jeanne Moskal, introductory note to *Rambles* in *The Novels and Selected Works of Mary Shelley,* vol. 8, ed. Jeanne Moskal (London: Pickering and Chatto, 1996), 52. Yet there were some naysayers; one reviewer in

*The Observer* complained, "With her, as with all women, politics is a matter of the heart, and not as the more robust nature of man, of the head. . . . It is an idle and unprofitable theme for a woman." Quoted in Moskal, "Travel Writing," 250.

532 **"Near you"** CC to MWS, May 7, 1845, *TCC,* 428.

532 **"To do a little good"** MWS to CC, June 6, 1845, *Letters MWS,* 3:185.

532 **"neuralgia of the heart"** For a comprehensive discussion of Mary's illness, see Sunstein, *MS:R&R,* 373.

532 **tingly, "alive"** Quoted in ibid.

532 **Elizabeth Barrett** For this connection, see ibid.

533 **"tall and slim"** Rolleston, *Talks with Lady Shelley,* 25–28.

534 **the "Great Old Snake"** The snake and tortoise legends come from a letter written by Shelley's sister Hellen in Hogg, *Life of Shelley,* 1:7.

534 **his mother's favorite** Hellen Shelley wrote, "I have heard that Bysshe's memory was singularly retentive. Even as a little child, Gray's lines on the Cat and the Gold Fish were repeated, word for word, after once reading; a fact I have frequently heard from my mother." Ibid., 9.

534 **"The whole place"** MWS to CC, August 28, 1848, *Letters MWS,* 3:346.

535 **"I walk"** MWS to CC, February 5, 1849, ibid., 3:356.

535 **"Until they have"** CC to Antonia Clairmont, August 1, 1850, *TCC,* 533.

536 **"her sweet"** Jane Shelley to Alexander Berry, March 7, 1851, *Letters MWS,* 3:394.

## CHAPTER FORTY: MARY AND MARY: HEROIC EXERTIONS

537 **Her obituaries focused** Sunstein, *MS:R&R,* 384.

537 **Muriel Spark's** Spark was determined to bring Mary Shelley back into the forefront of literary history. She argued that Shelley was one of the first writers of science fiction and that it was time for a reassessment of Shelley's work. See Spark's biography, *Child of Light: A Reassessment of Mary Wollstonecraft Shelley* (Essex, UK: Tower Bridge, 1951). Spark revised her biography in 1988, after the publication of Betty T. Bennett's edition of Shelley's letters was published. An expanded edition was later published as *Mary Shelley* (London: Carcanet, 2013).

538 **"suggested that Mary Shelley's letters"** Betty T. Bennett, "Finding Mary Shelley in Her Letters," *Romantic Revisions,* ed. Robert Brinkley and Keith Hanley (Cambridge: Cambridge University Press, 1992), 291.

538 **Her body of work** The radical viewpoints embedded in Mary Shelley's novels were routinely overlooked until fairly recently. As Betty T. Bennett wrote about *The Last Man,* "the political significance of the novel received little notice, no doubt because women were not expected to deal with politics. One of the major barriers Mary Shelley encountered in her audiences then—and often now—was a failure to see how all of her major works are structured around politics, both civil and domestic." "Radical Imagining: Mary Shelley's *The Last Man,*" *The Wordsworth Circle* 26, no. 3 (Summer 1995), 147–52. *Romantic Circles,* http://www.rc.umd.edu/editions/mws/lastman/bennett.htm.

538 **"The memory of my Mother"** MWS to Frances Wright, *Letters MWS,* 2:3–4.

539 **"Mary Wollstonecraft was one of those"** Paul, *Friends,* 1:231.

539 **"The writings of this celebrated woman"** Mary Shelley, preface to William Godwin, *The Adventures of Caleb Williams* (London: Harper & Brothers, 1870), 11.

539 **tempting to wonder** Charles Robinson introduces this question, speculating about what would have happened if Mary Shelley had "turned her hand to redeeming her mother rather than her husband by her editorial and biographical work." Robinson, "A Mother's Daughter: An Intersection of Mary Shelley's

*Frankenstein* and Mary Wollstonecraft's *A Vindication of the Rights of Woman,*" in *Writing Lives,* ed. Buss, Macdonald, and McWhir, 130.

541  **"[Her husband's] malady demanded"** MWS to Octavian Blewitt, November 15, 1850, *Letters MWS,* 3:387.

541  **"with the sun shining"** MWS to Isabella Booth, May 26, 1850, ibid., 3:376.

542  **Mary also talked to Jane** Rolleston, *Talks with Lady Shelley,* 90.

543  **In a red-draped corner** This description of the shrine is from Seymour, *MS,* 542.

544  **"[Shelley], in burning words"** *Shelley Memorials,* ed. Lady Jane Gibson Shelley (London: Henry S. King & Co., 1859), 77.

545  **"the utmost malice"** Trelawny, *Records of Shelley, Byron, and the Author,* 230.

545  **"Mary Shelley's jealousy"** Trelawny to CC, April 3, 1870, Forman, ed., *Letters of Edward John Trelawny.*

546  **For almost two hundred years** As a result of the scandals that surrounded Wollstonecraft's name, Cora Kaplan argues that Mary Wollstonecraft's life has been analyzed far more closely than her work. "Wollstonecraft's Reception," in *The Cambridge Companion to Mary Wollstonecraft,* ed. Claudia Johnson, 247.

546  **What Wollstonecraft termed "outlaws"** Wollstonecraft, *Maria,* 318.

# BIBLIOGRAPHIC NOTE: PERCY BYSSHE SHELLEY'S LETTERS

---

"There are no neutral facts or neutral editors," Betty Bennett, the editor of Mary Shelley's letters, warned readers when she was in the midst of editing Mary Shelley's voluminous and problematic correspondence. "There are only theoretical and interpretative editorial processes that, like 'the awful shadow of some unseen Power,' should not float unrecognized among us."[1] This is particularly true of Percy Shelley's letters. Even though Percy died almost two hundred years ago, there is still no authoritative edition of Shelley's letters. Warring factions continue to contest their opponents' right to publish Shelley's correspondence.

Mary Shelley appointed her daughter-in-law, Jane Shelley, as the literary executor of the Shelley papers. But Jane sought to control what biographers published about her beloved mother-in-law by curtailing the access of researchers to the original sources. Ultimately, Jane printed her own book, *Shelley and Mary,* in which she presented her own edited versions of Shelley's and Mary's letters.

In 1909, ten years after Jane Shelley died in 1899, Roger Ingpen published the first comprehensive edition of Shelley's correspondence. For the next fifty or so years, Ingpen's volume was the standard text. But in 1964, Frederick Jones published a two-volume edition of Shelley's letters, instigating a conflict with the editors of Shelley and His Circle (1961), who argued that Jones had overstepped

---

1.  Betty Bennett, "The Editor of Letters as Critic: A Denial of Blameless Neutrality," in *Text: Transactions of the Society for Textual Scholarship* 6 (1994), 222.

his rights by publishing letters owned by the Pforzheimer Collection. This dispute has never been fully resolved, and so today there are two separate editions of Shelley's letters, both of which purport to be the standard texts. However, these editions differ markedly. The Shelley and His Circle edition retains much of the spontaneous feeling of the original letters, as the editors have meticulously transcribed and annotated each letter, providing the reader with a far more accurate sense of the letters as physical objects, complete with spots from sealing wax and postmarks. The Jones edition, on the other hand, is far more polished, but, as the scholar Daisy Hay notes, it lacks "the impetuous, idiosyncratic immediacy of the originals."[2] The differences between the editions are a necessary warning to readers that letters are, as Hay says, "always editorially constructed, and that the published epistle has a separate existence to the autograph scrawl."[3] For this book, I consulted all the available sources, the Shelley and His Circle edition as well as the Ingpen and Jones editions. I have also used the letters that Mary Shelley published after Percy died in an edition she entitled *Essays, Letters from Abroad, Translations and Fragments*. For each letter, I have supplied the citation source I used. The Jones and Ingpen editions were particularly useful in terms of supplying biographical context, while the Shelley and His Circle edition helped me understand the circumstances under which Shelley was actually composing each letter.

2.   Daisy Hay, "Shelley's Letters," in *The Oxford Handbook of Percy Bysshe Shelley,* ed. Michael O'Neill and Anthony Howe (Oxford: Oxford University Press, 2013), 210.

3.   Ibid., 211.

# SELECTED BIBLIOGRAPHY

Abrams, M. H., ed. *The Norton Anthology of English Literature*. 4th ed. 2 vols. New York: W. W. Norton, 1979.

*The Age*. April 2, 1837, 106.

Andrews, Stuart. *The British Periodical Press and the French Revolution, 1789–99*. New York: Palgrave, 2000.

Angeli, Helen Rossetti. *Shelley and His Friends in Italy*. London, 1911.

Arnold, Catherine. *Bedlam*. London: Simon & Schuster, 2008.

Barker-Benfield, G. J. *The Culture of Sensibility: Sex and Society in Eighteenth-Century Britain*. Chicago: University of Chicago Press, 1992.

Baym, Nina, ed. *The Norton Anthology of American Literature*. 5th ed. 2 vols. New York: W. W. Norton, 1998.

Bennett, Betty T. "Biographical Imaginings and Mary Shelley's (Extant and Missing) Correspondence." In *Mary Wollstonecraft and Mary Shelley: Writing Lives*. Edited by Helen M. Buss, D. L. Macdonald, and Anne McWhir, 217–32. Waterloo, Ontario: Wilfrid Laurier University Press, 2001.

———. "The Editor of Letters as Critic: A Denial of Blameless Neutrality." *Text: Transactions of the Society for Textual Scholarship* 6 (1994): 213–23.

———. "Finding Mary Shelley in Her Letters." In *Romantic Revisions*. Edited by Robert Brinkley and Keith Hanley. Cambridge: Cambridge University Press, 1992.

———, ed. *The Letters of Mary Wollstonecraft Shelley*. 3 vols. Baltimore: Johns Hopkins University Press, 1980–88.

———. *Mary Diana Dods: A Gentleman and a Scholar*. Baltimore: Johns Hopkins University Press, 1994.

———. *Mary Wollstonecraft Shelley: An Introduction*. Baltimore: Johns Hopkins University Press, 1998.

———. "Newly Uncovered Letters and Poems by Mary Wollstonecraft Shelley." *Keats-Shelley Memorial Bulletin* 46 (July 1997).

———. "Radical Imagining: Mary Shelley's *The Last Man*," *The Wordsworth Circle*, 26.3 Summer 1995, 147–52. *Romantic Circles*. http://www.rc.umd.edu/editions /mws/lastman/bennett.htm.

———. *Selected Letters of Mary Wollstonecraft Shelley*. Baltimore: Johns Hopkins University Press, 1995.

Beverley Minster. "Beverley Minster, History and Building." http://beverleyminster .org.uk/visit-us/history-and-building/.

Bloom, Edward A., and Lillian D. Bloom, eds. *The Piozzi Letters: 1811–1816*. London: Associated University Presses, 1999.

Blunden, Edmund, Gavin de Beer, and Sylva Norman. *On Shelley*. Oxford: Oxford University Press, 1938.

Bolton, Carol, and Tim Fulford, eds. *The Collected Letters of Robert Southey*, part 3: *1804–1809*. A Romantic Circles Electronic Edition. Accessed February 17, 2014.

Boswell, James. *Life of Johnson*. 3rd ed. London: 1799.

Braithwaite, Helen. *Romanticism, Publishing and Dissent: Joseph Johnson and the Cause of Liberty*. New York: Palgrave Macmillan, 2003.

Brant, Clara. *Eighteenth-Century Letters and British Culture*. Basingstoke: Palgrave Macmillan, 2006.

Brewer, William D. "Mary Shelley's *Valperga:* The Triumph of Euthanasia's Mind." *European Romantic Review* 5 (1995): 133–48.

Brightwell, C. L., ed. *Memorials of the Life of Amelia Opie*. London: Longman, Brown, 1854.

Brinkley, Robert, and Keith Hanley, eds. *Romantic Revisions*. Cambridge: Cambridge University Press, 1992.

*The British Critic*. Vol. 2. 1793. Via Google Books, 2008. http://books.google.com /books?id=EP8vAAAAYAAJ&dq.

Browning, Robert. *Jocoseria*. London: Smith, Elder, & Co., 1883.

Burke, Edmund. *Reflections on the Revolution in France, and on the Proceedings in Certain Societies in London*. 2nd ed. London: J. Dodsley, 1790.

———. *The Works of the Right Honourable Edmund Burke*. 3 vols. London: Rivington, 1801.

Burr, Aaron. *The Private Journal of Aaron Burr, During His Residence of Four Years in Europe*, vol. 2. Edited by Mathew L. Davis. New York: Harper & Brothers, 1838.

Buss, Helen M. "Memoirs Discourse and William Godwin's *Memoirs of the Author of a Vindication of the Rights of Woman*." In *Mary Wollstonecraft and Mary Shelley: Writing Lives*. Edited by Helen M. Buss, D. L. Macdonald, and Anne McWhir, 113–26. Waterloo, Ontario: Wilfrid Laurier University Press, 2001.

———, D. L. Macdonald, and Anne McWhir, eds. *Mary Wollstonecraft and Mary Shelley: Writing Lives*. Waterloo, Ontario: Wilfrid Laurier University Press, 2001.

Butler, Marilyn. *Burke, Paine, Godwin, and the Revolution Controversy*. Cambridge: Cambridge University Press, 1984.

———. "Culture's Medium: The Role of the Review." In *The Cambridge Companion to British Romanticism*. Edited by Stuart Curran. Cambridge: Cambridge University Press, 1993.

———. *Romantics, Rebels and Reactionaries: English Literature and Its Background, 1760–1830*. Oxford: Oxford University Press, 1998.

Butterfield, Lyman H., Marc Friedlaender, and Richard Alan Ryerson, eds. *The Adams Family Correspondence*, 6 vols. Boston: Massachusetts Historical Society, 1993.

Byron, Allegra, letter to Lord Byron, [1822]. The Bodleian Library, University of Oxford, Shelfmark: MS. Abinger c 69, fol. 1r, Bodleian Library, Oxford University.

Byron, George Gordon, Lord. *The Works of Lord Byron*. Paris: Galignani, 1828.

———. *The Works of Lord Byron*, ed. Ernest Hartley Coleridge. 1900; Project Gutenberg, 2007. http://www.gutenberg.org/files/21811/21811.txt.

The Carl H. Pforzheimer Collection of Shelley and His Circle. New York: New York Public Library, Astor, Lenox, and Tilden Foundations, 1822.

Catt, Carrie Chapman. "A Message to Sweet Briar College." June 9, 1936. www.loc .gov/rr/mss/text/catt.html#speech.

"CK." *Anti-Jacobin Review and Magazine, or Monthly Political and Literary Censor*. April–August 1801, 515–20.

Clairmont, Claire. "Claire Clairmont to Lady Mountcashell, 24/09/1822." In Carl H. Pforzheimer Collection of Shelley and His Circle. New York: New York Public Library, Astor, Lenox, and Tilden Foundations, 1822.

Clark, David, ed. *Shelley's Prose; or, The Trumpet of a Prophecy*. Albuquerque: University of New Mexico Press, 1966.

Clarke, Isabel Constance. *Shelley and Byron: A Tragic Friendship*. London: Hutchinson & Co., 1934; reprint, New York: Ardent Media, 1971.

Clemit, Pamela. "Holding Proteus: William Godwin in His Letters." In *Repossessing the Romantic Past*. Edited by Heather Glen and Paul Hamilton. Cambridge: Cambridge University Press, 2006.

———. "*Valperga:* 'A Book of Promise.' " In *The Godwinian Novel: The Rational Fictions of Godwin, Brockden Brown, and Mary Shelley*. Oxford: Oxford University Press, 1993, 175–83.

Clubbe, John. "Between Emperor and Exile: Byron and Napoleon 1814–1816." *Napoleonic Scholarship: The Journal of the International Napoleonic Society* (April 1997), http://www.napoleonicsociety.com/english/scholarship97/c_byron.html.

Colbert, Benjamin. "Contemporary Notice of the Shelleys' *History of a Six Weeks' Tour:* Two New Early Reviews." *Keats-Shelley Journal* 48, 1999.

———. *Shelley's Eye: Travel Writing and Aesthetic Vision*. Aldershot, UK: Ashgate Publishing, 2005.

Coleman, Deirdre. "Claire Clairmont and Mary Shelley: Identification and Rivalry Within the 'Tribe of the Otaheite Philosophers.' " *Women's Writing*, no. 3 (1999), http://www.tandfonline.com/doi/abs/10.1080/09699089900200075?journalCode=rwow20#preview.

Coleridge, Ernest Hartley, ed. *The Poetical Works of Samuel Taylor Coleridge*. London: Oxford University Press, 1912.

———, ed. *Letters of Samuel Taylor Coleridge*. 2 vols. Boston: Houghton Mifflin, 1895.

Coleridge, Samuel Taylor. *Biographia Literaria: Biographical Sketches of My Literary Life and Opinions*. 2 vols. London: William Pickering, 1847.

———, Percy Bysshe Shelley, and John Keats. *The Poetical Works of Coleridge, Shelley, and Keats*. Philadelphia: Thomas Cowperthwait & Co., 1844.

Conger, Syndy M., Frederick S. Frank, and Gregory O'Dea, eds. *Iconoclastic Departures: Mary Shelley After Frankenstein*. Madison: University of Wisconsin Press, 1997.

Conway, Megan. "Olympe de Gouges: Revolutionary in Search of an Audience." In *Orthodoxy and Heresy in Eighteenth-Century Society: Essays from the Debartolo Conference*. Edited by Regina Hewitt and Pat Rogers, 247–65. Lewisburg, PA: Bucknell University Press, 2002.

Cowden Clarke, Charles and Mary. *Recollections of Writers*. Sussex, UK: Centaur Press, 1969; first published 1878.

Cowden Clarke, Mary. *My Long Life*. London: T. Fisher Unwin, 1896.

Cowper, William, and James Thomson. *The Works of Cowper and Thomson*. Philadelphia: 1832.

Croker, John Wilson. "Keats, *Endymion*: A Poetic Romance." *Quarterly Review*, 1818, 204–8.

Curran, Stuart. "Valperga." In *The Cambridge Companion to Mary Shelley*. Edited by Esther Schor, 103–15. Cambridge: Cambridge University Press, 2003.

de Beer, Gavin. "The Atheist: An Incident at Chamonix." In Edmund Blunden, Gavin de Beer, and Sylva Norman, *On Shelley*. Oxford: Oxford University Press, 1938.

de Gouges, Olympe. *Oeuvres*. Edited by Benoîte Groult. Paris: Mercure de France, 1986.

————. *The Rights of Woman*. Translated by Nupur Chaudhuri. In *Women, the Family and Freedom: The Debate in Documents,* vol. 1, *1750–1880*. Edited by Susan Groag Bell and Karen Offen. Stanford: Stanford University Press, 1983.

Dewar, Peter Beauclerk, and Donald Adamson. *The House of Nell Gwynn: The Fortunes of the Beauclerk Family*. London: William Kimber, 1974.

Diamond, M. J. *Women and Revolution*. Dordrecht, Neth.: Kluewer Academic Publishers, 1998; reprint, New York: Springer, 1998.

Dods, Maria Diana, letter to Mary Shelley, n.d. Oxford, Bodleian Library, Abinger Dep. c. 516/11.

Douglas, Paul. *The Life of Lady Caroline Lamb*. New York: Palgrave Macmillan, 2004.

Dowden, Edward. *The Life of Percy Bysshe Shelley*. 2 vols. London: 1886.

Drummond, William, ed. *The Autobiography of Archibald Hamilton Rowan*. Shannon: Irish University Press, 1972.

Dunn, Susan. *The Deaths of Louis XVI: Regicide and the French Political Imagination*. Princeton: Princeton University Press, 1994.

Durant, W. Clark. "Supplement." In *Memoirs of the Author of a Vindication of the Rights of Woman*. Edited by William Godwin. London: Constable and Co., 1927.

Eberle-Sinatra, Michael, ed. *Mary Shelley's Fictions: From Frankenstein to Falkner*. New York: St. Martin's Press, 2000.

Eliot, George. "Margaret Fuller and Mary Wollstonecraft." *The Leader,* October 13, 1855, 988–89. Reprinted in *Essays of George Eliot*. Edited by Thomas Pinney. London: Routledge, 1968.

Ellis, Kate Ferguson. "*Falkner* and Other Fictions." In *The Cambridge Companion to Mary Shelley*. Edited by Esther Schor. Cambridge: Cambridge University Press, 2003.

Engelberg, Karsten Klejs. *The Making of the Shelley Myth: An Annotated Bibliography of Criticism of Percy Bysshe Shelley, 1822–60*. London: Mansell, 1988.

Enno, Ruge. "Is the Entire Correspondence a Fiction? Shelley's Letters and the Eighteenth-Century Epistolary Novel." In *Alternative Romanticisms, Proceedings of the Grimma Conference 2001*. Edited by Werner Huber and Marie-Luise Egbert, 111–21, 2003.

Falco, Maria J., ed. *Feminist Interpretations of Mary Wollstonecraft*. University Park: Pennsylvania State University Press, 1996.

Farmer, J. S., and W. E. Henley, eds. *Slang and Its Analogues*. 1st ed., 1890–1904; reprint, New York: Arno Press, 1970.

Favret, Mary. *Romantic Correspondence: Women, Politics, and the Fiction of Letters*. Cambridge: Cambridge University Press, 2005.

Feldman, Paula R., and Diana Scott-Kilvert, eds. *The Journals of Mary Shelley, 1814–1844*. Baltimore: Johns Hopkins University Press, 1987.

Fielding, Henry. *The Works of Henry Fielding, with a Memoir of the Author*. Edited by Thomas Roscoe. Oxford: Oxford University Press, 1845.

Fisch, Audrey A., Anne K. Mellor, and Esther H. Schor, eds. *The Other Mary Shelley: Beyond Frankenstein*. New York: Oxford University Press, 1993.

Flexner, Eleanor. *Mary Wollstonecraft: A Biography*. New York: Coward, McCann and Geoghegan, 1972.

Foot, Michael, and Isaac Kramnick, eds. *The Thomas Paine Reader*. London: Penguin Classics, 1987.

Forman, Henry Buxton, ed. *Letters of Edward John Trelawny*. London: Henry Frowde, Oxford University Press, 1910.

Friedman, Geraldine. "Pseudonymity, Passing, and Queer Biography: The Case of Mary Diana Dods." Edited by Michael Eberle-Sinatra, Richard Sha, guest ed. *Romanticism on the Net* (2001). doi: 10:7202/005985ar.

Garnett, Edward. "Introduction" to *Adventures of a Younger Son* by Edward Trelawny. London: 1890.

Gay, Peter. *The Enlightenment: The Science of Freedom.* New York: W. W. Norton, 1996.

Gelpi, Barbara. *Shelley's Goddess: Maternity, Language, Subjectivity.* Oxford: Oxford University Press, 1992.

*The Gentleman's Magazine.* 1791, http://books.google.com/books?id=1K5JAAAAYAAJ &pg=PA151&lpg=PA151&dq=The+rights+of+men+asserted+by+a+fair+lady!+.

Gillman, James. *The Life of Samuel Taylor Coleridge.* Vol. 1. London: William Pickering, 1838.

Godwin, William. *An Enquiry Concerning Political Justice and Its Influence on Morals.* 2 vols. London: Robinson, 1798.

———. *The Enquirer: Reflections on Education, Manners, and Literature.* London: G. G. and J. Robinson, 1797.

———. *Fleetwood.* London, 1853.

———, ed. *Memoirs of the Author of a Vindication of the Rights of Woman.* 2nd ed. London: J. Johnson, St. Pauls Church Yard, 1798.

———. *St. Leon: A Tale of the Sixteenth Century.* Edited by William Dean Brewer. Peterborough, Ontario: Broadview Press, 2006.

———. *Things as They Are; or, The Adventures of Caleb Williams.* Edited by Maurice Hindle: Penguin, 1988.

———. *Thoughts Occasioned by the Perusal of Dr. Parr's Spital Sermon, Preached at Christ Church, April 15, 1800.* London: Taylor and Wilks, 1801.

Gordon, Lyndall. *Vindication: A Life of Mary Wollstonecraft.* New York: Harper Perennial, 2006.

Greer, Germaine. "Yes, *Frankenstein* Really Was Written by Mary Shelley. It's Obvious—Because the Book Is So Bad." *The Guardian* (2007), http://www .guardian.co.uk/world/2007/apr/09/gender.books.

Grogan, Claire. "Introduction," in *Memoirs of Modern Philosophers* by Elizabeth Hamilton. Peterborough, Ontario: Broadview Press, 2000.

Gross, Gerald. *Editors on Editing.* New York: Harper and Row, 1985.

Grylls, Rosalie Glynn. *Claire Clairmont, Mother of Byron's Allegra.* London: J. Murray, 1939.

Hanley, Kirstin. "Redefining Didactic Traditions: Mary Wollstonecraft and Feminist Discourses of Appropriation, 1749–1847." Unpublished doctoral dissertation, University of Pittsburgh, 2007.

Harper, Henry H., ed. *Letters of Mary W. Shelley (Mostly Unpublished).* Cornell University Library Digital Collections, 1918.

Hawtrey, E. C. *Sermons and Letters Delivered to Eton College Chapel, 1848–49.* Eton: 1849.

Hay, Daisy. "Shelley's Letters." In *The Oxford Handbook of Percy Bysshe Shelley.* Edited by Michael O'Neill and Anthony Howe, 208–24. Oxford: Oxford University Press, 2013.

———. *Young Romantics: The Tangled Lives of English Poetry's Greatest Generation.* New York: Farrar, Straus and Giroux, 2010.

Hays, Mary. *The Annual Necrology for 1797–98; Including, also, Various Articles of Neglected Biography.* Vol. 1 (1798): 426.

————. *Memoirs of Emma Courtney*. Edited by Marilyn L. Brooks. Peterborough, Ontario: Broadview Press, 2000.

Hazlitt, William. "My First Acquaintance with Poets." In *Selected Essays*. Edited by George Sampson. Cambridge: Cambridge University Press, 1958.

————. *The Spirit of the Age*. New York: E. P. Dutton, 1955.

Hewlett, John. *Sermons on Various Subjects*. 4th ed. 2 vols. London: Johnson, 1798.

Hill-Miller, Katherine C. *"My Hideous Progeny": Mary Shelley, William Godwin, and the Father-Daughter Relationship*. Newark: University of Delaware Press, 1995.

Hogg, Thomas Jefferson. *The Life of Percy Bysshe Shelley*. London: 1858.

Holbert, Ludvig. *A Journey to the World Under-Ground*. Trans. John Gierlow. Boston: Saxton, Pierce & Co., 1845. http://www.gutenberg.org/files/27884/27884-h /27884-h.htm.

Holmes, Richard. *The Age of Wonder*. New York: Vintage, 2010.

————. "Introduction." In *A Short Residence in Sweden, Norway, and Denmark and Memoirs of the Author of a Vindication of the Rights of Woman*. New York: Penguin, 1987.

————, ed. *Shelley on Love*. Berkeley: University of California Press, 1980.

————. *Shelley: The Pursuit*. New York: New York Review Books, 1994.

————. *Sidetracks: Explorations of a Romantic Biographer*. New York: Random House, 2001.

Hone, William. *The Year Book of Daily Recreation and Information*. London: 1838.

The Hoxton Trust. "Real Hoxton: The Lunatic Asylums," http://www.realhoxton.co .uk/history.htm#lunatic-asylums.

Hudson, Jane. *Language and Revolution in Burke, Wollstonecraft, Paine, and Godwin*. London: Ashgate, 2007.

Hunt, Leigh. *The Autobiography of Leigh Hunt with Reminiscences of Friends and Contemporaries*. 2 vols. London: Harper & Brothers, 1850.

————. *The Correspondence of Leigh Hunt*. Edited by Thornton Hunt. 2 vols. London: Smith, Elder and Co., 1862.

Hunt, Lynn Avery. *The Family Romance of the French Revolution*. Berkeley: University of California Press, 1993.

Hunt, Marianne. "The Unpublished Diary of Mrs. Leigh Hunt." *Bulletin and Review of the Keats-Shelley Memorial*. Issues 1–2. New York: Macmillan, 1910.

Hutchinson, Thomas, ed. *The Complete Poetical Works of Percy Bysshe Shelley*. 2 vols. Oxford: Oxford University Press, 1914.

Imlay, Gilbert. *The Emigrants*. Edited by W. Verhoeven and Amanda Gilroy. 1793; New York: Penguin, 1998.

————. *A Topographical Description of the Western Territory of North America*. London, 1792; reprint, New York: Penguin, 1998.

Ingpen, Roger, ed. *The Autobiography of Leigh Hunt: With Reminiscences of Friends and Contemporaries, and with Thornton Hunt's Introduction and Postscript*. Vol. 2. London, 1903.

————, ed. *The Letters of Percy Bysshe Shelley*. 2 vols. London: Sir Isaac Pitman and Sons, Ltd., 1912.

Jacob, Margaret C. *The Enlightenment: A Brief History with Documents*. Edited by Ernest R. May, Natalie Zemon Davis, and David W. Blight, Bedford Series in History and Culture. Boston: Bedford / St. Martin's, 2001.

Jacobs, Diane. *Her Own Woman: The Life of Mary Wollstonecraft*. New York: Simon & Schuster, 2001.

James, Henry. "Italy Revisited." In *Collected Travel Writings*. Library of America, 1877. Reprint, 1993.

Jebb, Camilla. *Mary Wollstonecraft*. Chicago: F. G. Browne & Co., 1913.

Johnson, Barbara. "The Last Man." In *The Other Mary Shelley: Beyond Frankenstein*. Edited by Audrey A. Fisch, Anne K. Mellor, and Esther H. Schor. New York: Oxford University Press, 1993.

———. *A World of Difference*. Baltimore: Johns Hopkins University Press, 1987.

Johnson, Claudia. *Equivocal Beings: Politics, Gender, and Sentimentality in the 1790s*. Chicago: University of Chicago Press, 1995.

———. "Introduction." In *The Cambridge Companion to Mary Wollstonecraft*. Edited by Claudia Johnson. Cambridge: Cambridge University Press, 2002.

Johnson, Joseph. "Letters." In *Johnson's Letters*. In Carl H. Pforzheimer Collection of Shelley and His Circle. New York: New York Public Library, Astor, Lenox, and Tilden Foundations, 1822.

Jones, Chris. "Mary Wollstonecraft's Vindications and Their Political Tradition." In *The Cambridge Companion to Mary Wollstonecraft*. Edited by Claudia Johnson. Cambridge: Cambridge University Press, 2002.

Jones, Frederick L., ed. *The Letters of Mary W. Shelley*. Norman: University of Oklahoma Press, 1944.

———, ed. *The Letters of Percy Bysshe Shelley*. 2 vols. Oxford: Clarendon Press, 1964.

———, ed. *Maria Gisborne and Edward E. Williams, Shelley's Friends: Their Journals and Letters*. Norman: University of Oklahoma Press, 1951.

Jones, Vivien. "Women Writing Revolution: Narratives of History and Sexuality in Wollstonecraft and Williams." In *Beyond Romanticisim: New Approaches to Texts and Contexts, 1789–1832*. Edited by Stephen Copley and John Whale. London: Routledge, 1992.

Jump, Harriet Devine. "'A Kind of Witchcraft': Mary Wollstonecraft and the Poetic Imagination." In *Women's Writing* 4, no. 2 (1997): 235–45.

———. *Mary Wollstonecraft and the Critics, 1788–2001*. 2 vols. New York: Routledge, 2003.

———. *Mary Wollstonecraft: Writer*. London: Harvester Wheatsheaf, 1994.

Kaplan, Cora. "Mary Wollstonecraft's Reception and Legacies." In *The Cambridge Companion to Mary Wollstonecraft*. Edited by Claudia Johnson, 246–70. Cambridge: Cambridge University Press, 2002.

———. "Pandora's Box: Subjectivity, Class and Sexuality in Socialist-Feminist Criticism." In *Making a Difference: Feminist Literary Criticism*. Edited by Gayle Greene and Coppelia Kahn, 146–76. London: Methuen, 1985.

———. "Wild Nights: Pleasure/Sexuality/Feminism," in *Sea Changes*. London: Verso, 1986, 31–56.

Keats-Shelley Memorial, Rome. *Bulletin and Review of the Keats-Shelley Memorial*. Issues 1 and 2. New York: Macmillan, 1910.

Kelly, Gary. "The Politics of Autobiography in Mary Wollstonecraft and Mary Shelley." In *Mary Wollstonecraft and Mary Shelley: Writing Lives*. Edited by Helen M. Buss, D. L. Macdonald, and Anne McWhir, 19–30. Waterloo, Ontario: Wilfrid Laurier University Press, 2001.

———. *Revolutionary Feminism: The Mind and Career of Mary Wollstonecraft*. New York: St. Martin's Press, 1992.

———. *Women, Writing and Revolution, 1790–1827*. Oxford: Clarendon Press, 1993.

Kelly, Linda. *Women of the French Revolution*. London: Hamish Hamilton, 1989.

Kennard, Lawrence. "Reveries of Reality: Mary Wollstonecraft's Poetics of Sensibility." In *Mary Wollstonecraft and Mary Shelley: Writing Lives*. Edited by Helen M. Buss, D. L. Macdonald, and Anne McWhir, 55–68. Waterloo, Ontario: Wilfrid Laurier University Press, 2001.

Kennedy, Deborah. *Helen Maria and the Age of Revolution*. Cranbury, NJ: Associated University Presses, 2002.

Kent, Elizabeth. *Flora Domestica*. London: 1823.

Kenyon, Frederic G., ed. *The Letters of Elizabeth Barrett Browning*. London: Smith, Elder, and Co., 1898.

Kilgour, Maggie. " 'One Immortality': The Shaping of the Shelleys in *The Last Man*." *European Romantic Review*, 2005, 563–88.

Knott, Sarah, and Barbara Taylor, eds. *Women, Gender and Enlightenment*. London: Palgrave Macmillan, 2005.

Knowles, John, ed. *The Life and Writings of Henry Fuseli*. London: 1831.

Kucich, Greg. "Biographer." In *The Cambridge Companion to Mary Shelley*. Edited by Esther Schor, 226–41. Cambridge: Cambridge University Press, 2003.

Lawrence, James. Introduction to *The Empire of the Nairs; or, The Rights of Women: An Utopian Romance, in Twelve Books*. 4 vols. London: T. Hookham, 1811.

Lew, Joseph W. "God's Sister: History and Ideology in *Valperga*." In *The Other Mary Shelley: Beyond Frankenstein*. Edited by Audrey A. Fisch, Anne K. Mellor, and Esther H. Schor, 159–84. New York: Oxford University Press, 1993.

Lipking, Lawrence. *Abandoned Women and Poetic Tradition*. Chicago: University of Chicago Press, 1988.

*Literary Gazette*. September 21, 1822, no. 296.

*Literary Gazette*. "Review of *The Last Man*." Vol. 10. London: Henry Colburn, 1826.

Locke, John. *The Second Treatise of Government and a Letter Concerning Toleration*. Edited by Paul Negri. Mineola, NY: Dover Thrift Editions, 2002.

Lockhart, J. G. *Memoirs of Sir Walter Scott*. Vol. 5. Edinburgh: Adam and Charles Black, 1882.

————. "On the Cockney School of Poetry." *Blackwood's Edinburgh Magazine*, 1818, 519–24.

Lovell, Ernest J., ed. *Lady Blessington's Conversations with Lord Byron*. Princeton: Princeton University Press, 1969.

Lynch, Deidre. "Historical Novelist." In *The Cambridge Companion to Mary Shelley*. Edited by Esther Schor, 135–50. Cambridge: Cambridge University Press, 2003.

Lyster, Gertrude, ed. *A Family Chronicle Derived from Notes and Letters Selected by Barbarina, the Honorable Lady Grey*. London, 1908.

MacCarthy, Fiona. *Byron: Life and Legend*. New York: Farrar, Straus and Giroux, 2002.

Marchand, Leslie, ed. *Byron's Letters and Journals*. Cambridge, MA: Harvard University Press, 1973.

Marshall, Mrs. Julian. *The Life and Letters of Mary Wollstonecraft Shelley*. 2 vols. London: Richard Bently and Son, 1889.

Marshall, Peter. *William Godwin*. New Haven: Yale University Press, 1984.

Mayne, Ethel. *Byron*. 2 vols. New York: Scribner's, 1912.

McCarthy, William, and Elizabeth Kraft, eds. *The Poems of Anna Letitia Barbauld*. Athens: University of Georgia Press, 1994.

McCullough, *John Adams*. New York: Simon & Schuster, 2001.

McWhir, Anne. " 'Unconceiving Marble': Anatomy and Animation in *Frankenstein* and *The Last Man*." In *Mary Wollstonecraft and Mary Shelley: Writing Lives*. Edited by

Helen M. Buss, D. L. Macdonald, and Anne McWhir, 159–76. Waterloo, Ontario: Wilfrid Laurier University Press, 2001.

Medwin, Thomas. *Conversations of Lord Byron: Noted During a Residence with His Lordship*. London: Henry Colburn, 1824.

———. *The Life of Percy Bysshe Shelley*. London: Oxford University Press, 1913.

———. *Memoir of Percy Bysshe Shelley*. London: Whittaker, Treacher, and Co., 1833.

Mellor, Anne K. "Making a 'Monster': An Introduction to *Frankenstein*." In *The Cambridge Companion to Mary Shelley*. Edited by Esther Schor, 9–25. Cambridge: Cambridge University Press, 2003.

———. *Mary Shelley: Her Life, Her Fiction, Her Monsters*. New York: Routledge, 1989.

———. "Reflections on Writing Mary Shelley's Life." In *Mary Wollstonecraft and Mary Shelley: Writing Lives*. Edited by Helen M. Buss, D. L. Macdonald, and Anne McWhir, 233–42. Waterloo, Ontario: Wilfrid Laurier University Press, 2001.

Middeke, Martin, and Werner Huber, eds. *Biofictions: The Rewriting of Romantic Lives in Contemporary Fiction and Drama*. Rochester, NY. Camden House, 1999.

Mitchell, Brian R. *British Historical Statistics*. Cambridge: Cambridge University Press, 1988.

*Monthly Magazine,* August 1, 1823, vol. 56, no. 385.

*Monthly Review, from January to April inclusive,* vol. 1, *1826*. London: R. Griffiths, 1826. Google Books, 335.

Moore, Doris Langley. *Accounts Rendered*. London: John Murray, 1974.

Moore, Jane. "Plagiarism with a Difference: Subjectivity in *Kubla Khan* and *Letters Written During a Short Residence in Sweden, Norway, and Denmark*." In *Beyond Romanticism*. Edited by Stephen Copley and John Whale. London: Routledge, 1992.

Moore, Lucy. *Liberty: The Lives and Times of Six Women in Revolutionary France*. London: Harper Perennial, 2011.

Moore, Thomas, ed. *Letters and Journals of Lord Byron: Complete in One Volume*. London, 1830.

———. *The Life of Lord Byron: With His Letters and Journals*. London: John Murray, 1851.

Moore, Wendy. *Wedlock: The True Story of the Disastrous Marriage and Remarkable Divorce of Mary Eleanor Bowes, Countess of Strathmore*. New York: Crown, 2009.

More, Hannah. *The Complete Works of Hannah More*. 2 vols. New York: 1856.

Moskal, Jeanne. "Introductory Note." In *The Novels and Selected Works of Mary Shelley*, by Mary Shelley. London: William Pickering, 1996.

———. "Speaking the Unspeakable: Art Criticism as Life Writing in Mary Shelley's *Rambles in Germany and Italy*." In *Mary Wollstonecraft and Mary Shelley: Writing Lives*. Edited by Helen M. Buss, D. L. Macdonald, and Anne McWhir, 189–216. Waterloo, Ontario: Wilfrid Laurier University Press, 2001.

———. "Travel Writing." In *The Cambridge Companion to Mary Shelley*. Edited by Esther Schor. Cambridge: Cambridge University Press, 2003.

*Mr. Punch's Victorian Era: An Illustrated Chronicle of the Reign of Her Majesty the Queen*. Vol. 1. London: Bradbury, Agnew and Co., 1887.

Murray, John, ed. *Lord Byron's Correspondence*. 2 vols. New York: Charles Scribner's Sons, 1922.

Myers, Mitzi. "Mary Wollstonecraft's Literary Reviews." In *The Cambridge Companion to Mary Wollstonecraft*. Edited by Claudia Johnson. Cambridge: Cambridge University Press, 2002.

———. "Sensibility and the 'Walk of Reason': Mary Wollstonecraft's Literary Reviews as Cultural Critique." In *Sensibility in Transformation: Creative Resistance to*

*Sentiment from the Augustans to the Romantics.* Edited by Syndy Conger. Rutherford, NJ: Fairleigh Dickinson University Press, 1990.

Myers, Victoria, David O'Shaughnessy, and Mark Philip, eds. *The Diary of William Godwin.* Oxford: Oxford Digital Library. http://godwindiary.bodleian.ox.ac .uk, 2010.

Nitchie, Elizabeth. "Mary Shelley, Traveller." *Keats-Shelley Journal* 10 (1961).

Norman, Sylva, ed. *After Shelley: The Letters of Thomas Jefferson Hogg to Jane Williams.* Oxford: Oxford University Press, 1934.

Ogborne, Elizabeth. *The History of Essex: From the Earliest Period to the Present Time.* London: Longman, Hurst, Rees, Orme and Brown, 1814.

Olsen, Kirsten. *Daily Life in Eighteenth-Century England.* Westport, CT: Greenwood, 1999.

O'Neill, Daniel. *The Burke-Wollstonecraft Debate: Savagery, Civilization, and Democracy.* University Park: Pennsylvania State University Press, 2007.

———. "John Adams Versus Mary Wollstonecraft on the French Revolution and Democracy." *Journal of the History of Ideas,* no. 3 (2007).

Opie, Amelia. *Adeline Mowbray.* Edited by Shelley King and John Pierce. Oxford University Press, 2000.

O'Sullivan, Barbara Jane. "Beatrice in *Valperga:* A New Cassandra." In *The Other Mary Shelley: Beyond Frankenstein.* Edited by Audrey A. Fisch, Anne K. Mellor, and Esther H. Schor, 140–59. New York: Oxford University Press, 1993.

Overy, Richard, ed. *The Enlightenment: Studies in European History.* 2nd ed. New York: Palgrave, 2001.

Paine, Thomas. *The American Crisis: 16 Revolutionary War Pamphlets.* Rockville, MD: Wildside Press, 2010.

———. "Letter Addressed to the Addressers on the Late Proclamation." In *The Thomas Paine Reader.* Edited by Michael Foot and Isaac Kramnick. London: Penguin Classics, 1987.

Paley, Morton D. *"The Last Man:* Apocalypse Without Millennium." In *The Other Mary Shelley: Beyond Frankenstein.* Edited by Audrey A. Fisch, Anne K. Mellor, and Esther H. Schor. New York: Oxford University Press, 1993.

Paul, Charles Kegan. *William Godwin: His Friends and Contemporaries.* 2 vols. Boston: Roberts Brothers, 1876.

Pennell, Elizabeth. *Life of Mary Wollstonecraft.* Boston: Roberts Brothers, 1884.

Pennell, Elizabeth Robins. *Mary Wollstonecraft.* Fairford, UK: Echo Library, 2008.

Poovey, Mary. *The Proper Lady and the Woman Writer: Ideology as Style in the Works of Mary Wollstonecraft, Mary Shelley, and Jane Austen.* Chicago: University of Chicago Press, 1984.

Porter, Roy. *English Society in the Eighteenth Century.* London: Penguin Books, 1982. Reprint, 1990.

———. *London: A Social History.* 4th printing. Cambridge, MA: Harvard University Press, 2001.

Price, Richard. *Observations on the Importance of the American Revolution.* Bedford, MA: Applewood Books, 2009.

Rajan, Tilomatta. "Framing the Corpus: Godwin's 'Editing' of Wollstonecraft in 1798." *Studies in Romanticism* 39 (2005): 511–31.

Rauschenbusch-Clough, Emma. *A Study of Mary Wollstonecraft and the Rights of Woman.* Longmans, Green & Co., 1898.

Raymond, Claire. *The Posthumous Voice in Women's Writing, from Mary Shelley to Sylvia Plath*. Burlington, VT: Ashgate Publishing, 2006.

Reed, John R. "Will and Fate in *Frankenstein*." *Bulletin of Research in the Humanities* 83 (1980): 319–38.

Reiman, Donald H. *Shelley's "The Triumph of Life": A Critical Study*. Champaign: University of Illinois Press, 1965.

———, and Doucet Devin Fischer, eds. *Shelley and His Circle*. Cambridge, MA: Harvard University Press, 1961.

———, Neil Fraistat, and Nora Crook, eds. *The Complete Poetry of Percy Bysshe Shelley*. Vol. 3. Baltimore: Johns Hopkins University Press, 2012.

Rennie, Eliza. "An Evening at Dr Kitchiner's." In *Friendship's Offering*, 243–49. London: 1842.

———. *Traits of Character: Being Twenty-Five Years of Literary and Personal Recollections*. 2 vols. London: 1860.

Richardson, Alan. "Mary Wollstonecraft on Education." In *The Cambridge Companion to Mary Wollstonecraft*. Edited by Claudia Johnson. Cambridge: Cambridge University Press, 2002.

Riedel, Stefan. "Edward Jenner and the History of Smallpox and Vaccination." *Baylor University Medical Center Proceedings*, no. 1 (2005), http://www.ncbi.nlm.nih.gov/pmc/articles/PMC1200696/.

Robinson, Charles E., ed. *The Frankenstein Notebooks: A Facsimile Edition of Mary Shelley's Manuscript Novel, 1816–17*. 2 vols. New York: Routledge, 1996.

———, ed. *Mary Shelley: Collected Tales and Stories*. Baltimore: Johns Hopkins University Press, 1976.

———. "A Mother's Daughter: An Intersection of Mary Shelley's *Frankenstein* and Mary Wollstonecraft's *A Vindication of the Rights of Woman*." In *Mary Wollstonecraft and Mary Shelley: Writing Lives*. Edited by Helen M. Buss, D. L. Macdonald, and Anne McWhir, 127–38. Waterloo, Ontario: Wilfrid Laurier University Press, 2001.

———. *Shelley and Byron: The Snake and Eagle Wreathed in Fight*. Baltimore: Johns Hopkins University Press, 1976.

Robinson, Mary. *Sappho and Phaon*. London: S. Gosnell, 1796; reprint, Whitefish, MT: Kessinger Publishing, 2004.

Rogers, Neville. *Shelley at Work: A Critical Inquiry*. Oxford: Clarendon Press, 1956.

Rolleston, Maud. *Talks with Lady Shelley*. London: Norwood Editions, 1897. Reprint, 1978.

Ropes, Arthur, ed. *Lady Mary Wortley Montagu: Select Passages from Her Letters*. London, 1892.

Rossetti, William, ed. *The Diary of Dr. John William Polidori*. London: Elkin Mathews, 1911.

Rousseau, Jean-Jacques. *The Confessions of Jean-Jacques Rousseau*. New York: Modern Library, 1945.

———. *Émile; or, On Education*. Translated by Allan Bloom. New York: Basic Books, 1979.

Runge, Laura. *Gender and Language in British Literary Criticism, 1660–1790*. Cambridge: Cambridge University Press, 2005.

Sacks, Peter. *The English Elegy: Studies in the Genre from Spenser to Yeats*. Baltimore: Johns Hopkins University Press, 1985.

Salzmann, Christian. *Elements of Morality, for the Use of Children*. 3 vols. London: 1792.

Sapiro, Virginia. *A Vindication of Political Virtue: The Political Theory of Mary Wollstonecraft*. Chicago: University of Chicago Press, 1992.

Schama, Simon. *A History of Britain,* vol. 3: *The Fate of Empire, 1776–2000*. New York: Miramax Books, Hyperion, 2002.

Seymour, Charles, and Donald Paige Frary. *How the World Votes: The Story of Democratic Development in Elections*. New York: C. A. Nichols, 1918.

Seymour, Miranda. *Mary Shelley*. New York: Grove, 2000.

Shelley, Lady, ed. *Shelley Memorials: From Authentic Sources*. Boston, 1859.

Shelley, Mary, ed. *Essays, Letters from Abroad*. 2 vols. London, 1852.

———. *Falkner*. London, 1837; Google Books, 2009.

———. *Frankenstein*. 1831; New York: Collier Books, 1978.

———. *The Last Man*. 1826; Rockville, MD: Wildside Press, 2007.

———. "Life of Shelley" (1823?) Bodleian, facsimile and transcript ed. A. M. Weinberg, The Bodleian Shelley Manuscripts, 22 pt 2 (1997).

———. *Lives of the Most Eminent French Writers*. 2 vols. Philadelphia: Lea and Blanchard, 1840.

———. *Lives of the Most Eminent Literary and Scientific Men of Italy, Spain, and Portugal*. 2 vols. London: 1835.

———. *Lodore*. 3 vols. London: 1835.

———. *Matilda*. In *Mary Wollstonecraft: Mary and Maria; Mary Shelley: Matilda*. Edited by Janet Todd, 148–210. London: Penguin Classics, 1992.

———. "Notes on *Alastor*, by Mrs. Shelley." In *The Works of Percy Bysshe Shelley*. Edited by Roger Ingpen and Walter E. Peck. 10 vols. London: Scribner's, 1926–30.

———. *The Novels and Selected Works of Mary Shelley*. Edited by Jeanne Moskal. London: William Pickering, 1996.

——— (with Percy Shelley). *The Original Frankenstein*. Edited by Charles E. Robinson. New York: Vintage, 2009.

———, ed. *The Poetical Works of Percy Bysshe Shelley*. 2 vols. London, 1839.

———. "Preface." In *Things as They Are; or, The Adventures of Caleb Williams,* by William Godwin. London: Harper and Brothers, 1870.

———. *Rambles in Germany and Italy, in 1840, 1842, and 1843*. 2 vols. London: Moxon, 1844.

———. "Review, 'The Loves of the Poets.'" *Westminster Review,* October 2, 1829, 472–77.

———. *Valperga*. Oxford: Oxford University Press, 2000.

Shelley, Percy. "Preface to the 1818 Edition." In *The Original Frankenstein*. Edited by Charles E. Robinson. New York: Vintage, 2009.

Shepherd, Richard, ed. *The Prose Works of Percy Bysshe Shelley*. 2 vols. London: 1897.

Shuffleton, Frank, ed. *The Letters of John and Abigail Adams*. New York: Penguin, 2003.

Sites, Melissa. "Utopian Domesticity as Social Reform in Mary Shelley's *Falkner*." *Keats-Shelley Journal* 54 (2005): 148–72.

Smith, Johanna M. "'Hideous Progenies': Texts of *Frankenstein*." In *Texts and Textuality: Textual Instability, Theory and Interpretation*. Edited by Philip Cohen. New York: Garland Publishing, 1997, 121–40.

Smollett, Tobias. *The Critical Review, or Annals of Literature*. Second series. Vols. 4–5. 1792.

Southey, C. C., ed. *Life and Correspondence of Robert Southey*. London, 1849.

Spark, Muriel. *Child of Light: A Reassessment of Mary Wollstonecraft Shelley*. Essex, UK:

Tower Bridge, 1951. Expanded edition published as *Mary Shelley*. London: Carcanet, 2013.

Stanton, Elizabeth Cady, Susan Anthony, Matilda Gage, and Ida Harper, eds. *History of Woman Suffrage: 1876–1885*. Vol. 3. Princeton: Gowler and Wells, 1886.

St. Clair, William. *The Godwins and the Shelleys*. London: Faber, 1989.

Stewart, Sally. "Mary Wollstonecraft's Contributions to the *Analytical Review*." *Essays in Literature* 11, no. 2 (1984): 187–99.

Stillinger, Jack. *Multiple Authorships and the Myth of Solitary Genius*. New York: Oxford University Press, 1991.

Stocking, Marion Kingston, ed. *The Clairmont Correspondence: Letters of Claire Clairmont, Charles Clairmont, and Fanny Imlay Godwin*. 2 vols. Baltimore: Johns Hopkins University Press, 1995.

———, ed. *The Journals of Claire Clairmont*. Cambridge, MA: Harvard University Press, 1968.

Stommel, Henry, and Elizabeth Stommel. *Volcano Weather: The Story of the Year Without a Summer*. Newport, RI: Seven Seas Press, 1983.

Stott, Andrew. "The Diets of the Romantic Poets." *Lapham's Quarterly* (2013), http://www.laphamsquarterly.org/roundtable/roundtable/the-diets-of-the-romantic-poets.php.

Sunstein, Emily W. *Mary Shelley: Romance and Reality*. Baltimore: Johns Hopkins University Press, 1989.

Sussman, Charlotte. "Stories for the Keepsake." In *The Cambridge Companion to Mary Shelley*. Edited by Esther Schor. Cambridge: Cambridge University Press, 2003.

Taylor, Thomas. "A Vindication of the Rights of Brutes." London: 1792.

Taylor, Una. *Guest and Memories: Annals of a Seaside Villa*. London: Oxford University Press, 1924.

Taylor, William. *A Memoir of the Life and Writings of the Late William Taylor of Norwich*. 2 vols. London: 1843.

Teich, Nathaniel. "The Analytical Review." *British Literary Magazines: The Augustan Age and the Age of Johnson, 1698–1788*. Edited by Alvin Sullivan. Westport, CT: Greenwood Press, 1983.

*Theatrical Observer*. August 9, 1823.

Todd, Janet, ed. *The Collected Letters of Mary Wollstonecraft*. New York: Columbia University Press, 2003.

———. *Daughters of Ireland: The Rebellious Kingsborough Sisters and the Making of a Modern Nation*. New York: Ballantine Books, 2003.

———. *Death and the Maidens: Fanny Wollstonecraft and the Shelley Circle*. London: Profile, 2007.

———. *Mary Wollstonecraft: A Revolutionary Life*. New York: Columbia University Press, 2000.

———, ed. *Mary Wollstonecraft: Mary and Maria; Mary Shelley: Matilda*. London: Penguin Classics, 1992.

Tomalin, Claire. *The Life and Death of Mary Wollstonecraft*. London: Penguin, 1974.

Toynbee, Helen, and Paget Toynbee, eds. *The Letters of Horace Walpole: Fourth Earl of Oxford*. Vols. 15 and 16. Oxford: Clarendon, 1905.

Trant, Clarissa. *The Journal of Clarissa Trant*. London, 1826. Reprint, 1925.

Trapp, Joseph, ed. *Proceedings of the French National Convention on the Trial of Louis XVI. Late King of France and Navarre from the Paper of the World*. London: 1793.

Trelawny, Edward. *Adventures of a Younger Son*. London: 1890.

———. *Recollections of the Last Days of Shelley and Byron*. London: Edward Moxon, 1858.

———. *Records of Shelley, Byron, and the Author*. London: 1878.

Twiss, Richard. *A Trip to Paris in July and August, 1792*. London: 1792.

Ty, Eleanor. "'The History of My Own Heart': Inscribing Self, Inscribing Desire in Wollstonecraft's *Letters from Norway*." In *Mary Wollstonecraft and Mary Shelley: Writing Lives*. Edited by Helen M. Buss, D. L. Macdonald, and Anne McWhir, 69–84. Waterloo, Ontario: Wilfrid Laurier University Press, 2001.

Tyson, Gerald P. *Joseph Johnson: A Liberal Publisher*. Iowa City: University of Iowa Press, 1979.

Vargo, Lisa. "Further Thoughts on the Education of Daughters: *Lodore* as an Imagined Conversation with Mary Wollstonecraft." In *Mary Wollstonecraft and Mary Shelley: Writing Lives*. Edited by Helen M. Buss, D. L. Macdonald, and Anne McWhir, 177–88. Waterloo, Ontario: Wilfrid Laurier University Press, 2001.

Walford, Edward. "Somers Town and Euston Square," *Old and New London* (1878), 5:340–55. http://www.british-history.ac.uk/report.aspx?compid=45241.

———. "Spitalfields." *Old and New London* (1878), 2:149–52. http://www.british -history.ac.uk/report.aspx?compid=45086.

Walker, Gina Luria, ed. *The Idea of Being Free: A Mary Hays Reader*. Peterborough, Ontario: Broadview Press, 2005.

Wallraven, Miriam. *A Writing Halfway between Theory and Fiction: Mediating Feminism from the Seventeenth to the Twentieth Century*. Würzburg, Ger.: Königshausen & Neumann, 2007.

Wardle, Ralph. *Godwin and Mary*. Lincoln: University of Nebraska Press, 1977.

———. *Mary Wollstonecraft: A Critical Biography*. Lincoln: University of Nebraska Press, 1951.

Waters, Mary. *British Women Writers and the Profession of Literary Criticism, 1789–1832*. New York: Palgrave Macmillan, 2004.

Weiss, Deborah. "The Extraordinary Ordinary Belinda: Maria Edgeworth's Female Philosopher." *Eighteenth-Century Fiction*, no. 4 (2007). http://digitalcommons .mcmaster.ca/ecf/vol19/iss4/5.

Wheelock, John Hall, ed. *Editor to Author: The Letters of Maxwell E. Perkins*. New York: Charles Scribner's Sons. Reprint, 1979.

White, Newman Ivey. *The Unextinguished Hearth*. London: Octagon Books, 1966.

Williams, Helen Maria. *Letters Containing a Sketch of the Politics of France, from the 31st of May 1793, Till the 28th of July 1794, and of the Scenes Which Have Passed in the Prisons of Paris*. London: 1795. University of Oxford Text Archive. http://ota.ox.ac.uk /text/4517.html.

Wilson, Ben. *The Making of Victorian Values: Decency and Dissent in Britain, 1789–1837*. New York: Penguin Press, 2007.

Wolfson, Susan. *Borderlines: The Shiftings of Gender in British Romanticism*. Redwood City, CA: Stanford University Press, 2006.

———. "Mary Shelley, Editor." In *The Cambridge Companion to Mary Shelley*. Edited by Esther Schor, 193–210. Cambridge: Cambridge University Press, 2003.

———, and Peter Manning, eds. *Lord Byron: Selected Poems*. New York: Penguin Classics, 2006.

Wollstonecraft, Mary. *Analytical Review* 2/1789. In *The Works of Mary Wollstonecraft*. Edited by Janet Todd and Marilyn Butler. New York: New York University Press, 1989.

———. *An Historical and Moral View of the Origin and Progress of the French Revolution*. London: 1794.

————. *Letters to Imlay with Prefatory Memoir by C. Kegan Paul*. London: 1879.

————. *Letters Written During a Short Residence in Sweden, Norway, and Denmark*. London: J. Johnson, 1796.

————. *Maria*. In *Mary Wollstonecraft: Mary and Maria; Mary Shelley: Matilda*. Edited by Janet Todd, 55–148. London: Penguin Classics, 1992.

————. *Mary*. In *Mary Wollstonecraft: Mary and Maria; Mary Shelley: Matilda*. Edited by Janet Todd, 1–54. London: Penguin Classics, 1992.

————. *Original Stories*. London: 1906.

————. *Original Stories from Real Life*. London: 1796.

————. *Posthumous Works of the Author of a Vindication of the Rights of Woman*. Edited by William Godwin. 4 vols. 1798.

————. *Thoughts on the Education of Daughters, with Reflections on Female Conduct*. London: J. Johnson, 1788.

————. *A Vindication of the Rights of Men in a Letter to the Right Honourable Edmund Burke*. London: J. Johnson, 1790.

————. *"A Vindication of the Rights of Woman" and "The Wrongs of Woman; or, Maria."* Edited by Anne Mellor and Noelle Chao. Longman Cultural Editions: Pearson, 2007.

Woodford, Adrian. "Brenta Canal River Cruise: At Home in a Watery Hinterland." *The Telegraph* (2009), http://www.telegraph.co.uk/travel/cruises/riversandcanals/5612695/Brenta-Canal-river-cruise-At-home-in-a-watery-hinterland.html.

Woolf, Virginia. *The Common Reader: Second Series*. 3 vols. London: Hogarth Press, 1953.

Wordsworth, Dorothy. *Recollections of a Tour Made in Scotland, 1803*. Edited by Carol Kyros Walker. New Haven: Yale University Press, 1997.

Wordsworth, William. *The Collected Poems of William Wordsworth*. London: Wordsworth Editions, 1994.

Wright, Thomas, ed. *Dictionary of Obsolete and Provincial English*. London: Henry G. Bohn, 1851.

# IMAGE CREDITS

———

464    Old St. Pancras church, London (engraving), by George Cooke (1793–1849). Private collection/© Look and Learn/Peter Jackson Collection/Bridgeman Images.

482    Mary Shelley (watercolor on ivory laid on card), by Reginald Easton, sometime between 1851 and 1893. Bodleian Library, University of Oxford, Shelley relics (d).

524    Portrait of Mary Shelley by Richard Rothwell. National Portrait Gallery, London, photo © Tarker/Bridgeman Images.

529    Shelley's grave. Courtesy of Brooks Richon.

547    Mary Wollstonecraft's grave. Courtesy of Brooks Richon.

# INDEX

Page numbers in *italics* refer to illustrations.

PHOTO: © JASON GROW

CHARLOTTE GORDON is the author of *Mistress Bradstreet: The Untold Life of America's First Poet* and *The Woman Who Named God: Abraham's Dilemma and the Birth of Three Faiths*. She has also published two books of poetry, *When the Grateful Dead Came to St. Louis* and *Two Girls on a Raft*. She is an associate professor of English at Endicott College and lives in Gloucester, Massachusetts.

charlottegordonbooks.com

@Chargordbooks